FOR LIBRARY USE ONLY

DAVID O. MCKAY LIBRARY

P9-DUH-269

THE COMPLETE GUIDE TO HUMAN RESOURCES AND THE LAW

2003 Edition

Dana S

DATE DUE

I^LL SEP 1 2 2003		
ILL JUN 0 8 2004		

Demco

WITHDRAWN

SEP 1 2 2022

DAVID O. McKAY LIBRARY
BYU-IDAHO

ct

JAN 28 2003

PUBLISHERS

1185 Avenue of the Americas, New York, NY 10036
www.aspenpublishers.com

PROPERTY OF:
DAVID O. McKAY LIBRARY
BYU-IDAHO
REXBURG ID 83460-0405

This publication is designed to provide accurate and authoritative information in regard to the subject matter covered. It is sold with the understanding that the publisher is not engaged in rendering legal, accounting, or other professional services. If legal advice or other professional assistance is required, the services of a competent professional person should be sought.

— From a *Declaration of Principles* jointly adopted by
a Committee of the American Bar Association and a
Committee of Publishers and Associations

Copyright © 2003 by Aspen Publishers, Inc.
A Wolters Kluwer Company
www.aspenpublishers.com

All rights reserved. No part of this publication may be reproduced or transmitted in any form or by any means, electronic or mechanical, including photocopy, recording, or any information storage and retrieval system, without permission in writing from the publisher. Requests for permission to make copies of any part of this publication should be mailed to:

Permissions
Aspen Publishers
1185 Avenue of the Americas
New York, NY 10036

Printed in the United States of America

ISBN 0-7355-3650-3

1 2 3 4 5 6 7 8 9 0

About Aspen Publishers

Aspen Publishers is a leading publisher of authoritative and timely treatises, practice manuals, information services, and journals written by specialists to assist attorneys, financial and tax advisors, and other business professionals. Our mission is to provide practical solution-based how-to information keyed to the latest legislative, judicial, and regulatory developments.

We offer publications in the areas of compensation and benefits, pensions, payroll, employment, civil rights, taxation, estate planning, financial planning, and elder law.

Other Aspen products treating human resources issues include:

401(k) Answer Book
Defined Benefit Answer Book
Employee Benefits Answer Book
Employee Stock Ownership Plan Answer Book
Employer's Guide to Managing Personnel Costs
Employment Law Answer Book
ERISA Law Answer Book
Flexible Benefits Answer Book
Handbook of ERISA Litigation
Mandated Benefits Compliance Guide
Pension Answer Book
Practical Guide to Employment Law
Preventing Workplace Harassment
Quick Reference to COBRA Compliance
Quick Reference to HIPAA Compliance
Quick Reference to IRCA
Solving On-the-Job People Problems
State by State Guide to Human Resources Law
The Complete Do-It-Yourself Human Resources Department
U.S. Employer's Guide

Subscription & Electronic Products
  HR Briefing Newsletter
  Spencer's Reports on Employee Benefits
  HR Manager's Library on CD-ROM

ASPEN PUBLISHERS
www.aspenpublishers.com

SUBSCRIPTION NOTICE

This Aspen product is updated on a periodic basis with supplements to reflect important changes in the subject matter. If you purchased this product directly from Aspen, we have already recorded your subscription for the update service.

If, however, you purchased this product from a bookstore and wish to receive future updates and revised or related volumes billed separately with a 30-day examination review, please contact our Customer Service Department at 1-800-234-1660, or send your name, company name (if applicable), address, and the title of the product to:

ASPEN PUBLISHERS
7201 McKinney Circle
Frederick, MD 21704

SUMMARY OF CONTENTS

Contents

Preface

CONTENTS

*A complete table of contents for each chapter
is included in the beginning of the chapter.*

Chapter 5
DEFINED BENEFIT PLANS

Chapter 6
DEFINED CONTRIBUTION AND 401(k) PLANS

Chapter 7
CASH BALANCE PLANS

Chapter 8
NONQUALIFIED PLANS

Chapter 9
EARLY RETIREMENT AND RETIREE HEALTH BENEFITS

Part III: PENSION PLAN ADMINISTRATION

Chapter 10
ADOPTING AND ADMINISTERING A PLAN

Chapter 11
COMMUNICATIONS WITH EMPLOYEES AND REGULATORS

Chapter 12
PLAN DISTRIBUTIONS

CONTENTS

Chapter 43
INSURANCE COVERAGE FOR CLAIMS AGAINST THE EMPLOYER

Index

PREFACE

The first edition of this book was published in 1998, in a different and in some ways better and more optimistic climate. The 2003 Edition, incorporating and updating three cumulative supplements and developments up through January 1, 2002 (with a few major developments between the beginning of that year and press time), reflects a nation at war, a recession, and a rugged stock market.

This book is directed at the HR professional who is not an attorney but who needs to place legal principles and developments in the context of the practical problems he or she faces every day. "The law" is not one single, simple thing. It is an ever-growing, ever-changing body of information that involves not just court cases but also statutes and the regulations of administrative agencies such as the Department of Labor and the Equal Employment Opportunity Commission.

The 2003 Edition not only updates the book for changes in law and business but also adds more practical tips and checklists. There's been an extensive reorganization, with more and shorter chapters, to make the book easier to use. The organization of the book has been completely rethought to group topics together in a more natural and useful way.

The 2003 Edition is divided into 43 chapters, in eight parts:

- Part I: Pay Planning, including compensation planning, bonuses, severance pay, and tax issues.
- Part II: Pension Law, comprising basic pension concepts, defined benefit plans, and the transition from the predominance of defined benefit plans to the rise of defined contribution and 401(k) plans; cash balance plans; nonqualified plans; and plans for early retirement and retiree health benefits.
- Part III: Pension Plan Administration, going from the adoption of a plan to disclosures to plan participants, handling claims and appeals, amending the plan, complying with ERISA and tax rules, handling plans in the context of corporate transitions such as mergers and acquisitions, and terminating a plan.
- Part IV: Benefit Plans, such as health plans, continuation coverage and portability requirements for health insurance, plans that provide insurance coverage, and disability plans.
- Part V: The HR Function, including hiring and recruitment, HR computing, recordkeeping, corporate communications, employee privacy rights, diversity issues, and work-family issues.
- Part VI: Employee Relations, not only the major topic of labor law but also occupational safety and health, unemployment insurance, and worker's compensation.

- Part VII: Substantive Laws Against Discrimination, focusing on Title VII (and sexual harassment, which is considered a form of sex discrimination), age discrimination, disability discrimination, the Family and Medical Leave Act, and wrongful termination suits.
- Part VIII: Procedure for Handling Discrimination Charges, not only in the context of lawsuits brought by the EEOC, by state regulators, or by private individuals, but by using arbitration and other alternative dispute resolution methods to resolve problems without going to court.

NOTE ON WEB SOURCES: American Lawyer Media's excellent Web site, <http://www.law.com>, uses very long URLs that are hard to cite. Therefore, for convenience, citations to cases and articles appearing there are simply cited to law.com; do a search for the name of the article if you'd like to retrieve it.

Unfortunately, items on the Web, and Web sites themselves, can "go out of print." In some instances, by the time the current edition of this book was ready for print, items that I had read or downloaded in the past and mentioned in the text are no longer available online or are not available to the general public. In those cases, the item is cited as "Posted to [name of cite] on [date]."

PART I

PAY PLANNING

CHAPTER 1

PAY PLANNING

§1.01 INTRODUCTION

When the first edition of this book was published in 1998, many employers—especially those in industries involving media or e-commerce—found themselves in a seller's market. Dot-coms were absorbing many workers, often at salaries and benefit packages so lavish that other employers found it difficult to compete.

Since then, the collapse of the dot-coms, serious stock market declines, the September 11 attack, and an overall economic downturn have changed the picture. Employers have the luxury of getting many excellent resumes for every job opening—and of holding the line on compensation and benefits instead of having to "pump up the volume" to attract and retain good employees. Until mid-2000, it was often assumed that stock prices follow one inevitable trend: upward. This was not, of course, a rational assumption. Many businesses experienced "underwater" stock options (the price at which the employee can purchase shares is actually higher than the market price of the shares).

In many businesses (especially service businesses), payroll is one of the largest—or even *the* largest—corporate expense. So increasing the payroll will have tremendous bottom-line impact.

Although salary is an important element of compensation, it must be considered not only in the context of an entire compensation package, but in the context of noncompensation considerations such as work-family issues or whether the company is a good place to build a career.

§1.02 DECISION FACTORS IN SETTING COMPENSATION

A business's compensation policies reflect many factors:

- What the business can afford to pay;
- Competitive factors (other local companies competing for workers, prevailing wages, unemployment rates);
- Impact on cash flow (until recently, cash-poor companies with bright prospects often relied heavily on stock options and/or the potential for an IPO as elements of compensation);
- Effect on future financing (venture capitalists who expect one-third of the shares in a new business, or a business receiving later rounds of funding, will not want too many of the shares to be assigned to employees);
- The compensation package favored by the kind of workers the employer wants to attract. If the objective is to minimize turnover, for instance, workers with families will place a high value on health benefits, whereas more mobile younger workers will tend to favor higher cash compensation and pension portability;
- Tax factors for both employer and employee; the objective is for the employer to get the highest permissible deduction, and for the employee to retain as much as possible after taxes.

§ 1.03   BENEFITS AS AN ELEMENT OF COMPENSATION

The accepted rule of thumb is that the cost of benefits adds about one-third to the employee's stated salary. This may be too low: the Society of Human Relations Management's 1997 survey, for instance, showed benefits as costing approximately 40% of salary.

The size of the benefit package is often directly related to the size of the company. Generally, for any particular benefit, the percentage of companies offering that benefit increases with the size of the workforce, and it is also often true that larger companies offer a more generous benefit package.

For private industry, BLS statistics show that, during the three-month period ending September 2001, total compensation increased by 0.9%. However, benefits costs increased 1.4% during this time period, twice as much as the 0.7% increase in wages and salaries. [*See* Table 1, "Seasonally Adjusted Employment Cost Index for Total Compensation," <http://www.bls.gov/ncs/ect/sp/ecisfl.txt>]

§ 1.04   AVOIDING DISCRIMINATION

The Equal Employment Opportunity Commission (EEOC) Compliance Manual contains a section dealing with compensation issues in the context of various antidiscrimination statutes. The EEOC's position is that antidiscrimination laws apply to all aspects of compensation, including salary, overtime, bonuses, options, profit sharing, fringe benefits, and expense accounts. The agency says that employers are never justified in taking race, color, sex, national origin, religion, age, or disability into account in setting compensation.

The EEOC says that equal severance benefits are required for all similarly situated employees, regardless of age. Employers may not deny severance because the employee is eligible for a pension, although sometimes pension benefits can be offset against the severance pay. Denying recall rights to older workers operates as involuntary retirement. Because the cost of providing severance pay does not rise with the employees' ages, employers are not allowed to assert an equal cost defense.

However, retiree health benefits can legitimately be offset against severance if the retiree is eligible for an immediate pension; if he actually receives health benefit coverage; and the retiree benefits are at least comparable to Medicare in type and value. If the retiree is over 65, benefits must be at least comparable to one-fourth the value of Medicare benefits. The offset itself must be reduced by any percentage by which the pension is reduced for retirement before normal retirement age, and by any percentage of the premium that the retiree has to pay for retiree health coverage.

The Compliance Manual says that "if the employer provides additional pension benefits that are enough, or are higher than those necessary to bring an employee up to the level of an unreduced pension, the employer can offset the full amount of those benefits. On the other hand, if the employer offers benefits that are insufficient to raise the employee to an unreduced pension, the employer cannot claim any offset at all."

§ 1.05 VARIABLE PAY

A variable pay system makes part of the compensation dependent on meeting goals or targets. Almost three-quarters of U.S. companies have at least some variable pay elements in their compensation system. In 1990, only 4.2% of the total corporate payroll was variable pay; for 1999, the corresponding figure was 7.8%. [*See Variable Compensation Plans Increasing and Improving, But Still Delivering Mixed Results*, <http://www.hewitt.com/news/pressrel/1998/10-07-98.htm> (posted to www.hewitt.com on Oct. 7, 1998) and *Variable Compensation Plans Often Miss the Mark*, RIA Compensation & Benefits Update, March 25, 1998 at p. 6]

Because these plans are supposed to create incentives for better work, communication is key. Formal annual review explaining how the award was calculated is useful to pinpoint areas in which employees succeeded and those in which more work is necessary. The most effective plans had "moderate stretch" (i.e., they asked employees to achieve targets that were not impossible, but were not comfortably in view either).

§ 1.06 WAGE AND HOUR ISSUES

The HR department's many and varied responsibilities probably include handling (or outsourcing and supervising) payroll matters, including paying employees subject to the appropriate deductions.

The Fair Labor Standards Act (FLSA) [29 U.S.C. §§ 201–219 and 251–262] regulates wages and hour matters. The FLSA forbids sex discrimination in compensation, sets a minimum wage, requires extra pay when a "non-exempt" worker puts in overtime hours, and sets standards for record keeping and record retention. The Department of Labor's Wage and Hour Division is responsible for administering the FLSA.

State laws that do not conflict with the FLSA, and that provide additional protection for employees, are not preempted by the federal law. Therefore, you should check your state law to see if it covers employees who are not covered by the FLSA, or if the law imposes additional compliance burdens.

Employees have a private right of action (that is, they can sue their employers) for unpaid minimum wages and/or overtime, plus liquidated damages, attorneys' fees, and court costs. Courts have the power to order legal and equitable relief against employers who fire employees, or otherwise discriminate or retaliate against them for making an FLSA complaint or participating in a Wage and Hour Division proceeding. [29 U.S.C. § 216] An employee who has a good-faith belief that the employer committed wage-hour violations can sue the employer for retaliation—even if, in fact, the employer was exempt from the FLSA because its gross sales were lower than the FLSA's jurisdictional minimum. [*Sapperstein v. Hager*, 188 F.3d 852 (7th Cir. 1999)]

Not only can employees sue their employers, the Secretary of Labor has the power to sue for unpaid minimum wages and overtime. The funds go directly to the employees who should have received them, not to the Department of Labor (DOL). The court can enjoin the employer against committing any further violations. Willful violations of the FLSA are criminal rather than civil in nature, so prosecution by the federal Attorney General's office is possible, in addition to DOL actions or civil suits by the employees.

Tip: Employees can waive their rights by inaction. After 30 years of not objecting to not being paid for time changing into and out of uniforms, corrections officers could not raise FLSA claims. The time was not compensable time because the practice was a result of a custom or practice under a bona fide collective bargaining agreement (even though it had never become a formal subject of negotiation). [*Turner v. Philadelphia*, 262 F.3d 222 (3d Cir. 2001)]

The FLSA allows the pay of hourly (but not salaried) workers to be docked for absenteeism. DOL Opinion Letter No. 89 [discussed in Employment Alert, March 5, 1998 at p. 11] says that a deduction to reflect unpaid leave under the Family and Medical Leave Act (FMLA) does not convert an otherwise exempt person into a nonexempt hourly worker. However, this relief provision is limited to FMLA leave, where both the worker and the employer company come under the FMLA's provisions.

Courts differ as to whether FLSA punitive damages are available. The Seventh Circuit and Eastern District of Pennsylvania said yes, because it is a form of relief provided in egregious cases; the Eleventh said no, because the FLSA statute doesn't specifically allow punitive damages. [*See* Shannon P. Duffy, *Punitive Damages Available Under FLSA, Federal Judge Rules*, The Legal Intelligencer (Oct. 15, 2001) (law.com); *Travis v. Gary Community Mental Health Center,* 921 F.2d 108 (7th Cir. 1990); *Snapp v. Unlimited Concepts Inc.,* 208 F.3d 928 (11th Cir. 2000)]

The FLSA is a growing litigation area. The number of federal suits went up by almost 25% between 1998 and 2000 (from 1,562 to 1,935 a year), and many state cases were brought, especially because some states allow class actions. FLSA class actions are not allowed, and it is often economically impractical to bring a suit for just one person's claims. [*See* David Hechler, *Workers' Suits Over Wages on the Rise*, National Law Journal (Nov. 29, 2001) (law.com)]

§ 1.07   MINIMUM WAGE

The minimum wage is $5.15 per hour. One Eighth Circuit case allowed payment of less than minimum wage under the facts of the case.

"On-call" time, when employees had to be able to report to the hospital within 20 minutes, had to be reachable by telephone, cell phone, or pager, and had to abstain from drugs and alcohol, was not "work" time because of the limited re-strictions on employees' activities. Therefore, it was acceptable to pay less than the minimum wage for this time. [*Reimer v. Champion Healthcare Corp.*, 258 F.3d 720 (8th Cir. 2001)]

The Department of Labor permits unpaid internships for trainees, so the trainees can acquire usable job skills. The criteria for an acceptable internship pro-gram include the following conditions:

- Even though the employer's facilities are used, the training is similar to the cur-riculum of a vocational school;
- The real benefit of the training goes to the trainee, not the employer (in fact, the employer's operations may even be slowed down by the actions of the novices);
- Trainees are closely supervised, but do not replace regular employees;
- The trainee explicitly agrees to work without pay;
- There is no guarantee that the trainee will be hired for a paid job.

Boeing required new hires to go through an unpaid orientation period. A class action in Washington State court accepted the plaintiffs' contention that the orientation period was really work. The lower court required payment at the mini-mum wage for the orientation period—and then the Washington Court of Appeals required pay at the normal contract rate for the job. [*Seattle Professional Eng'g Employees Ass'n v. Boeing*, 963 P.2d 204 (Wash. App. 1998)]

§ 1.08   DETERMINING WHO IS AN "EMPLOYEE"

There are many reasons why it becomes necessary to determine if a particu-lar person who performs services is an independent contractor or an employee of the company for which the services are performed. For example, employment sta-tus is involved in determining who is allowed to participate in pension and benefit plans; who is entitled to overtime; who is entitled to unemployment benefits and Worker's Compensation; and who can sue under antidiscrimination laws. Al-though similar factors are used in analyses for different purposes, it is possible that someone will be considered an employee for some purposes but not for others.

If the individual is an employee, the employer will be responsible for paying FUTA taxes and its own share of FICA, and will have to withhold income taxes. In contrast, independent contractors are responsible for their own tax compliance.

Clearly, the company saves money if it can characterize workers as inde-pendent contractors, because it saves on taxes and benefits (even if the cash com-pensation is the same). To prevent abuses, this is an area where the IRS and other regulators are active in determining whether the so-called independent contractor is really an employee.

The Internal Revenue Code specifically identifies some groups as statutory employees, and others as statutory non-employees. [IRC §§ 3121, 3401, 3306, 3508] The categories of statutory employees are:

- Agents or commission drivers who deliver food products, laundry, or dry cleaning;
- Full-time traveling salespersons who solicit orders for merchandise to be delivered later;
- Full-time life insurance salespersons;
- Corporate officers;
- People who work in their own homes, but under the supervision of someone who supplies the materials to be used in work (e.g., assembling clothing components).

However, a licensed real estate agent who is not paid on the basis of hours worked, and who has a written contract identifying him or her as an independent contractor, will not be considered an employee. Neither will a "direct seller" who sells consumer products outside of a permanent resale establishment, who is paid on the basis of output, and who has a written contract as an independent contractor.

Under I.R.C. § 414(n), a long-term leased employee may have to be counted in testing pension and benefit plans for discrimination. A safe harbor is permitted when a company gets less than 20% of its non-highly-compensated employees through leasing services, and if those services provide adequate pension coverage for their employees.

Bronk v. Mountain States Telephone & Telegraph Inc. [140 F.3d 1335 (10th Cir. 1998)] holds that, although the Employment Retirement Income Security Act (ERISA) [29 U.S.C. § 1001 *et seq.*] forbids excluding employees from the plan once they have satisfied minimum age and service requirements, it is permissible to draft the plan to deny participation to leased employees, even if they are common-law employees of the sponsor company. The Tenth Circuit position is that I.R.C. § 414(n)(1)(A) merely requires that leased employees be treated as employees; it doesn't require them to be offered plan participation.

The Ninth Circuit held that people who had worked at the defendant company (for 12 years!) through a temporary agency were not leased employees. [*Burrey v. Pacific Gas & Electricity*, 159 P.3d 388 (9th Cir. 1998)]

An IRS determination that someone who did recruitment and management work for a company, pursuant to a contract, was an employee is not determinative with respect to the FLSA or minimum wage law, because there was no evidence that the IRS actually litigated the question of employee status. [*Morrison v. Int'l Programs Consortium Inc.*, 253 F.3d 5 (D.C. Cir. 2001)]

§ 1.09 STAFFING ARRANGEMENTS

The U.S. workforce can no longer be divided simply into full-time and part-time workers, or permanent workers and "temps." Many other arrangements have evolved, although, as noted above, the employer's characterization of the arrangement is not always accepted for tax and other legal purposes. Some of the possibilities are:

- Workers who are actually employed by a temporary agency that recruits, trains, and sends workers to companies that are clients of the agency;
- Long-term temporary assignments—where the temporary worker stays at one location for weeks or months, instead of being hired on a daily basis;
- Payrolling—a company wants to hire a specific person, and therefore arranges for a temporary agency to hire that person and be responsible for payment, taxes, and other employment-related matters;
- Part-time workers;
- Independent contractors—who are genuinely self-directed; have clients rather than employers who control their work; and are responsible for their own tax compliance;
- Contract workers—an arrangement usually made with technical workers who are formally employed by a technical services firm. This arrangement is often used for long-range projects, including those that require the contract worker to relocate to the employer's site;
- Leased employees—who are paid by the leasing company, which also handles administrative tasks like tax and Worker's Compensation compliance;
- Outsourcing—delegating a function such as payroll processing, guarding a worksite, or operating an employee cafeteria to a company that specializes in that function.

An article by Frederick D. Baron, Carrie Battilega, and Mitch Danzig [*Workforce 2000: Alternative Staffing Arrangements*, <http://www.lawnews network.com>] gives some practical suggestions for trouble-free use of temporary workers:

- Have a written contract with the temp agency, clarifying the status of the workers;
- Don't train the temporary workers at your site—have the temp agency provide whatever training is required;
- Check to make sure that the agency maintains the appropriate Worker's Compensation coverage for its staff;
- If you ask your own employees to sign confidentiality agreements, you can impose the same requirement on temps—but use a separate form that refers to their temporary status;
- If you decide to offer a permanent job to a temp, make it clear that the start date is the date he or she became a permanent employee (unless you have advice of counsel that an earlier start date is required).

§ 1.10   SIZE OF THE CONTINGENT WORKFORCE

Clearly, many ways to work have evolved. The Bureau of Labor Statistics' (BLS) news release [*Contingent and Alternative Employment Arrangements, February 2001* <http://www.bls.gov/news.release/conemp.nr0.htm>] shows that, after remaining essentially stable between February 1997 and February 1999, the percentage of contingent workers declined slightly between February 1999 and February 2001. (The BLS does surveys in every other year, not annually.)

The BLS uses more than one definition for "contingent workers," the broadest of which is 5.4 million workers "who do not expect their current job to last." In February 2001, depending on the definition used, anywhere from 1.7% to 4.0% of the U.S. workforce consisted of contingent workers (versus 1.9–4.3% in February 2001).

The BLS also collects information about "alternative" work arrangements (employment can be both contingent and alternative at the same time), finding that in February 2001, there were 8.6 million independent contractors (6.4% of all workers), 2.1 million people working on an on-call basis (1.6%), 1.2 million working for temporary agencies (0.9% of the workforce and about 600,000 people (0.5% of all workers) working for contract companies. [*Contingent and Alternative Employment Arrangements, February 2001* <http://www.bls.gov/news.release/conemp.nr0.htm>]

The American Staffing Association and the BLS estimate that in 1999, the percentage of temporary workers had stabilized at about 2.2% of the nonfarm work force (about twice as high as the 1990 level).

The question is how to interpret these trends. One argument is that workers like and benefit by greater flexibility (especially if they have to combine work and family obligations). The contrary point of view is that career-level full-time jobs with benefits are eroding, and many people are forced to work shorter hours or for less money and fewer benefits with less security than they would prefer.

According to the Pension Research Council, "direct-hire temporaries" (who are hired for a project or seasonal work) account for more than 3% of the workforce. About one-eighth of the workforce consists of independent contractors, agency temps, on-call workers, contract company workers, and direct-hire temps. The report [Susan N. Houseman, *The Benefits Implication of Recent Trends in Flexible Staffing Arrangements*, PRC WP 2001-19 (Pension Research Council) (Sept. 2001) <http://prc.wharton.upenn.edu/prc/PRC/WP/wp2001-19.pdf> (no www)] notes that agency temporary workers are far less likely to be eligible for health insurance than regular full-time workers. Furthermore, temporary workers are often ineligible for unemployment compensation. For instance, their unemployment might be deemed voluntary because they deliberately accepted a job with a known ending date, or if they refuse another assignment when one assignment ends.

§ 1.11   CO-EMPLOYERS

It's not always possible to say that one company is the employer and the other has no responsibility. Sometimes two companies (such as a leasing company and the company where the individual actually performs services) will be jointly liable—e.g., if the individual is injured at the workplace or harms someone else.

In August 2000, the NLRB reversed its earlier decision. The agency now allows temporary workers to be included in the same collective bargaining unit as permanent employees, as long as the characteristics of the jobs are similar. This is true even if the agency supplying the workers, the company where the services are performed, or both, oppose including the temporary workers in the bargaining unit. [*M.B. Sturgis Inc.*, 331 N.L.R. No. 173 (Aug. 25, 2000)]

For FLSA purposes, the First Circuit ruled that a staffing company and its client companies do not become co-employers. The staffing company is the FLSA employer, because it hires and controls the workers, assigns them to job sites, and controls their schedules. [*Baystate Alternative Staffing Inc. v. Herman*, 163 F.3d 668 (1st Cir. 1998)]

In contrast, the Occupational Safety and Health Review Commission (OSHRC) decided that an employee-leasing company was not subject to the Occupational Safety and Health Act, because the workers were not their employees. In this reading, employees work in the employer's "business," and here the leased workers were assigned to a factory where the leasing company did not exercise significant control over them. [*Sec'y of Labor v. Team Am. Corp.*, 1998 WL 733708 (OSHRC 1998)]

According to the EEOC's Compliance Manual, both employment agencies and companies where services are rendered are generally liable for civil rights violations committed in the placement of contingent workers. If both the staffing firm and its client have control over the worker, then both are joint employers. The staffing agency has the burden of taking immediate and appropriate action (such as refusing to supply any more workers) if it finds that a client company has discriminated against a temporary worker. [*See* <http://www.eeoc.gov/press/12-8-97.html>]

§ 1.12   APPLICABLE TESTS

[A]   The 20-Factor Test

Determining employee status is not a simple matter. The internal IRS documents used to train tax auditors set out 20 factors to be used to determine if income tax withholding is required:

1. If the employer gives instructions that the employee has to follow;
2. If the employer trains the employee;

> **Tip:** Don't assign independent contractors to take training sessions with employees!

3. If the person renders services that are specific to him or her and can't be delegated to someone else;
4. If the employer provides whatever assistants are needed for the work

(someone who provides his own assistants is more likely to be an independent contractor);

5. Whether the services are integrated into the employer's ordinary work, or are separate;
6. If the work relationship continues over time;

> **Tip:** Independent contractors should not be asked to be on call.

7. If the worker is subject to a shift system or other established, structured work hours or work schedule;
8. If the employer demands the worker's full-time commitment;
9. If the worker works for other companies at the same time (if the answer is "yes," it tends to imply independent contractor status, although part-time common-law employees may hold more than one job);
10. If work is done on the employer's premises;
11. If the employer determines the order or sequence of tasks to be done to accomplish the overall task;
12. If the worker has to submit regular oral or written reports;
13. If payment is by time (hour, week, or month) rather than project;
14. If the employer supplies tools and materials;
15. If the worker has to make a significant financial investment to accomplish the tasks;
16. If the employer pays business and travel expenses;
17. If the worker has a profit-and-loss interest in the underlying business of the employer;
18. If the worker gets paid by the employer's customers;
19. The employer's right to fire the worker (as distinct from carrying out the termination provisions of a contract, or refusing to renew the contract) tends to imply employee status;
20. The possibility of the worker's becoming liable to the employer if he or she quits suggests independent contractor status, because this is consistent with remedies for breach of contract.

At a minimum, if the IRS examines records and determines that common-law employees were incorrectly treated as independent contractors, the employer will have to make up the employment taxes that should have been paid but were not. Additional penalties may also be imposed. If the employer filed the required information returns (W-2s and 1099s) and did not intentionally misclassify the worker, then the penalty will be limited to 1.5% of the employee's wages, plus 20% of the FICA taxes that went unpaid because of the incorrect classification.

Those penalties are doubled if the information returns were not filed (unless there was no willful neglect, and there was reasonable cause for failure to file). Even heavier penalties are assessed if the employer not merely was mistaken about filing responsibilities, but deliberately attempted to avoid taxation.

[B] Safe Harbor Treatment

In 1979, Congress passed a safe harbor provision, Section 530 of the Revenue Act of 1978. Under this provision, if an employer treats someone as an independent contractor, the IRS will not be able to reclassify that person as an employee (and will not be able to assess back taxes and penalties) as long as the employer made the characterization reasonably and in good faith. Employers can also apply for a refund of penalties that they believe were improperly assessed.

There are three safe harbor tests for reasonableness:

1. The court system or the IRS has created published authority (e.g., decisions, IRS rulings, or IRS Technical Advice Memorandums) that justifies independent contractor treatment in similar situations;
2. The IRS has already audited the employer, and the audit did not uncover any problems of worker characterization;
3. There is an established practice, within a significant segment of the employer's industry, of treating people who do similar work as independent contractors.

To use the safe harbor, the employer must have treated the person consistently as an independent contractor, including filing Form 1099 as necessary. If the person was treated as a common-law employee at any time after December 31, 1977, the safe harbor will not be available.

[C] Other Tests of Employee Status

The fundamental test is ability to control work behavior, both as to methods and as to results. This is the test used to determine employee status for ERISA purposes.

State unemployment insurance coverage typically depends either on the common-law right of control, or supplying a worker with a workplace, tools, and materials in addition to control. Most states use an "ABC test": someone who performs services is an employee, and the employer must pay unemployment insurance premiums for that person, unless:

*   the person is customarily engaged in an independent trade, business, profession, or occupation;
*   no direction or control is given in performing the services;
*   the services are not performed in the usual course of the employer's business, or are not performed within any regular business location of the employer.

The employer must pay unemployment insurance plus penalties and interest for misclassified workers.

The FLSA test is based on economic reality. In other words, someone who is not economically dependent on a company, and is not an integral part of its operations, would not be an employee. Factors in the decision include:

- The worker's investment in facilities or equipment;
- Presence or absence of opportunity to earn profits or suffer losses due to managerial or special skills;
- Degree of control others have over the person's work;
- Permanence of the work relationship;
- Skill required to perform the services.

In this case, misclassification can lead to a duty to pay any unpaid minimum wages and overtime, plus liquidated damages, attorneys' fees, and court costs.

§ 1.13   BENEFITS FOR CONTINGENT WORKERS

This issue came to prominence in connection with Microsoft "perma-temps" who were characterized by the company as freelancers and independent contractors, paid through invoices submitted to the accounts payable department rather than through the payroll process. The IRS ruled that these people were really common-law employees. They sued to be held eligible to participate in Microsoft's savings and employee stock ownership plans.

The Ninth Circuit ruled that eligibility for participation depends on being a common-law employee; the form in which payment is rendered is not relevant. The court also rejected the agreement signed by the workers, characterizing them as ineligible for plan participation, on the grounds that an agreement of this type cannot alter employee status. [*Vizcaino v. Microsoft Corp.*, 97 F.3d 1187 (9th Cir. 1996), *aff'd*, 120 F.3d 1006 (9th Cir. 1997), *cert. denied*, 118 S. Ct. 899]

The case was sent back to the district court to sort out the rights of individual plaintiffs. The district court narrowed down the plaintiff class to certain employees of temporary agencies and workers who were reclassified as common-law employees by the IRS.

The Ninth Circuit ruled on the case again in May 1999 [1998 WL 122084], holding that temporary agency workers who also satisfy the common-law control test can be considered Microsoft employees entitled to participate in the stock plan. The case went back to the district court yet again [142 F. Supp. 2d 1299 (W.D. Wash. 2001)], and on January 9, 2000, the Supreme Court again refused to hear an appeal of the decision. [*cert. denied*, 522 U.S. 109 (2000)]

In December 2000, Microsoft agreed to pay $96.9 million to settle the *Vizcaino* case and another pending case. However, two of the class members appealed the settlement in May 2001. More than 2,500 members of the class filed claims against the fund, but damages and attorneys' fees cannot be paid out until the appeal of the settlement is resolved. [The settlement agreement can be found at <http://www.bs-s.com>. *See also Center for a Changing Workforce News* (December 2001) <http://www.cfcw.org>]

This litigation reminds us that there are special rules for computer professionals. FLSA § 13(a) exempts computer systems analysts, programmers, and software engineers earning $27.63 or more per hour (this peculiar figure comes from 29 C.F.R. § 541.303(c), which pegs it to six and a half times the minimum wage). The exemption does not apply to entry-level workers or repair and maintenance technicians. [*See* Victoria Roberts, *Employers Must be Vigilant in Classifying Work of Computer Professionals Under FLSA*, 69 L.W. 2355 (Dec. 19, 2000)]

§ 1.14   WORK SCHEDULING

[A]   Overview

To an ever-increasing extent, new (and usually longer) schedules are replacing the conventional nine-to-five or eight-to-four workday. Sometimes, the operation has to be open around the clock to accommodate emergencies. Many retail and service businesses add longer hours to accommodate customers who work long hours themselves and need to do business on weekends, evenings, and holidays. Demand for a factory's products might be so high that the only way to cope is to schedule two or even three shifts a day. Demand might be high but unpredictable, or predictably seasonal, so that the plant runs at full steam for several months, then layoffs and terminations are required on the off season.

For all these reasons, some employees will have to work overtime and weekend hours occasionally. Some will have to work unconventional hours as a long-range or permanent condition of employment. As business becomes more international, it becomes necessary to be able to deal with customers during their work week—which may occur on a very different schedule from the traditions of the U.S. workplace.

The 40-hour work week is only conventional, not sacred. The five-day week is also a fairly recent innovation: the six-day schedule prevailed for part of the twentieth century. In some environments, a 40-hour week over just four days works well, because employees like having the extra day off, and are sometimes more productive in the longer day than in more, shorter work days.

"Flextime" is a schedule under which employees commit to working at least a certain number of hours per day, week, or month, and also agree to be present at certain agreed-upon times (e.g., for the weekly staff meeting or when customer demand is highest). Otherwise, they can work any schedule that suits their needs and allows them to complete their work tasks. Flextime can work for employees who have work-family problems (e.g., caring for children or elderly relatives). Flextime can be an Americans With Disabilities Act (ADA) "reasonable accommodation" and can also be used by employees taking FMLA leave.

In November 2000, Hewitt Associates surveyed a thousand employers; 57% said they offered flexible work schedules. Bureau of Labor Statistics economist Thomas M. Beers said that 25% of workers have access to a flexible work schedule, but usually by informal arrangement. Only 6% of employers had a formal flextime plan. Women are more likely to have flextime schedules than men, and white workers more likely than minority workers. Flextime is more common in executive, administrative, managerial, and sales positions than in shift-based jobs such as manufacturing, nursing, teaching, police work, and firefighting. [Carol Kleinman, *Many Flex Schedules Are Informal Arrangements*, Chicago Tribune (Nov. 1, 2000)]

There is a basic division between hourly workers, who get more pay if they put in longer hours, and salaried workers, whose compensation does not vary with the number of hours worked. A time clock or other system must be used to track the hours of hourly workers. Salaried workers may have to keep track of time if their time is billed out to clients, or if management wants to analyze task and time performance.

It is customary, although not legally required, for hourly employees to clock out when they leave the workplace (e.g., for lunch breaks or to do personal errands). They are not normally paid for this nonwork time. Salaried employees are usually not charged for such nonwork time, although personal time is sometimes charged against their sick leave. In a unionized workplace, the Collective Bargaining Agreement (CBA) determines issues like scheduling of meal breaks and when employees have to punch in and punch out.

The Second Circuit says that, if the employer requires employees to stay on the job site during their lunch breaks (in this case, for security purposes at an outdoor site), then the employees are working and must be compensated for this time. [*Reich v. Southern New England Telecommunications Corp.*, 121 F.3d 58 (2d Cir. 1997)]

[B] Telecommuting

To an increasing extent, employees are working from home or from other remote locations by "telecommuting," working on a computer and dealing with other employees and clients or customers by telephone or e-mail. The International Telework Association and Council says that nearly 29 million Americans— about one-fifth of all workers—telecommute at least occasionally. [Telework in the United States: Telework America Survey 2001 (10/01) <http://www. telecommute.org/twa/index.htm>] However, the role of telecommuting seems to be declining, rather than increasing, over time, because it can be hard to participate fully in the business. Nor have broadband connections spread as fast as they were projected. Telecommuting also creates security problems for the company's data.

The percentage of companies allowing telework varies greatly by industry, from 58% in information services; 41% in financial, insurance, and real estate companies; 33% in utilities, construction, and transportation; and only 19% in wholesale and retail trade. [*See* Kemba J. Dunham, *Telecommuters' Lament*, Wall Street Journal, Oct. 31, 2000, at p. B1; PR Newswire, *Number of Teleworkers Increases by 17 Percent* (Oct. 23, 2001) <http://www.ifebp.org/2001/10/23/pr/ 0000-22457-dc-itac-telework-incr.asp> (posted to www.ifebp.org on October 2001); Dylan Loeb McClain, *Want to Join the Telecommuting Crowd? Most Bosses Just*

Say No, New York Times, Nov. 28, 2001, at p. G1; Sue Shellenbarger, *"Telework" Is on the Rise, But It Isn't Just Done From Home Anymore*, Wall Street Journal, Jan. 23, 2002, at p. B1; Susan J. Wells, *Making Telecommuting Work*, HR Magazine, October 2001, at p. 35] However, telecommuting has clearly not achieved the status predicted for it; pundits expected 55 million teleworkers by the early 2000s.

Telecommuting can be useful for employees who are recovering from an injury or illness; those who have family responsibilities; part-timers and project workers; and those who would otherwise have to relocate or face a long commute each day. Telecommuting also reduces the size of the office that the employer has to maintain.

However, telecommuting is not a panacea. Some people find it very hard to be productive in light of the greater distractions available outside the workplace. It can be difficult to maintain lines of communication or to coordinate the efforts of workers at different locations.

In many organizations, the limiting factor is management's unwillingness to adopt or expand telework programs. Some supervisors demand to see their employees working; some managers don't understand the business case for telecommuting; and others are more interested in increasing their power base by increasing the number of visible employees in the office reporting to them.

There are many practical steps that a company can take to make the arrangement smoother and more productive. The "teleworkers" should sign written agreements clarifying whether they are independent contractors or common-law employees; who they will report to; whether the telework assignment is expected to be temporary or permanent; how often they will be expected to go to the office; how many hours they will work; their work schedule; and promotion possibilities.

A project that is suitable for telecommuting is one that can be handled by one person, with limited input from others, with input that has to be effective via telephone or computer, rather than in person. The project should be clearly defined and easily measured, so the supervisor will be able to assess if milestones are being met and the teleworker's performance is adequate.

Personality characteristics of successful telecommuters include being comfortable working essentially alone, without office social contacts; being able to schedule tasks and hold to a schedule; being able to get the job done despite distractions and family needs; and having the discipline to perform away from the supervisor's eyes.

Telecommuting relies heavily on electronics, so it's important to safeguard hardware and data. If possible, the telecommuter should have back-up equipment (perhaps a laptop that can be used while traveling or when the desktop computer is out of order). Telecommuters should be required to back up their data frequently, to have a high-quality uninterruptable power source to give them time to save work before the computer goes down, and they should be required to keep back-up disks and other media in a safe location (such as a fireproof safe or a safe deposit box)— preferably somewhere outside the home. It's also possible to "deliver" data to an Internet storage site.

Make sure the telecommuter has homeowner's insurance (if necessary, in the form of a rider or a separate policy) that covers the computer equipment against theft and damage. This is especially important if the employer supplies the equipment. A "consequential damages" provision that covers lost data and business opportunities is hard to find, but a valuable addition to the policy. [*See* the Department of Labor's study, *Telework and the New Workplace of the 21st Century,* <http://www.dol.gov/asp/telework/execsum.htm>] Part I of the study deals with the evolution and economics of telework. Part II relates telework to organizational behavior; and Part III examines the cultural and social implications of working from remote locations with electronic tools]

§ 1.15   OVERTIME AND OVERTIME PLANNING

[A]   Generally

One of the major functions of the FLSA is to require "time and a half for overtime" to be paid to all nonexempt hourly employees who work more than 40 hours in a work week. They must receive 150% of their normal pay rate for the additional hours.

> **Tip:** The Workers Economic Opportunity Act [Pub. L. No. 106-202 (May 18, 2000)] amends the FLSA to make it clear that stock options are not part of the "regular rate of pay" for FLSA purposes. The statute explains the wage-and-hour consequences of stock option and stock appreciation rights plans. Although the FLSA does not require it, many companies offer "comp time"—additional time off—if an hourly employee puts in more than his or her normal schedule, but less than 40 hours, during a workweek.

Certain categories of employees are exempt from the FLSA's minimum wage and overtime provisions. [29 U.S.C. § 213(a)(1)] The major exempt categories are executives, administrators, professionals, and outside salespersons. Whether a person is exempt depends on the actual duties of the job, not the job title. Exemption is based on "primary duties"—what the person does for 50% or more of the work time. The calculation is based on the standard work week for the employer's nonexempt employees. Exempt employees must also satisfy minimum compensation standards [*see* 29 C.F.R. Part 541], but the dollar amounts are very low: $155 a week, or $250 a week if the "short test" is used to calculate the exemption.

In 1998, about one-quarter of the U.S. workforce, about 19–26 million workers, was exempt from overtime because the workers fell within one of the exempt categories. The proportion of exempt workers continues to rise for many reasons. The service sector is growing, and many service workers are exempt. As the proportion of female workers in the work force increases (33% in 1983, 42% in 1998), so does the number of white-collar workers. [*See* "Fair Labor Standards Act: White-Collar Exemptions in the Modern Work Place," GAO/HEHS-99-164]

Exempt workers do not have to be paid for weeks in which they do not work at all, but otherwise 29 C.F.R. § 541.118(a) provides that their salary cannot be reduced based on the number of hours worked or the number of hours of absences. The employer cannot reduce the wages of exempt employees for absences that were caused by the employer or the operating requirements of its business. Nor can the employer take deductions to penalize an exempt worker for work place infractions, other than violations of major safety rules.

Specifically, docking a worker's pay for "variations in quantity or quality of work" is appropriate for hourly workers who are entitled to overtime, but not for exempt workers. The real test, however, is whether reductions are ever taken. In 1997, the Supreme Court ruled that police officers were exempt salaried employees, even though the employee manual said that pay could be docked for various disciplinary infractions: the mere possibility didn't make them non-exempt. [*Auer v. Robbins*, 159 U.S. 452 (1997)]

> **Tip:** If an exempt employee is absent for less than one day for sickness, disability, or personal reasons, the employer is not permitted to reduce the employee's paycheck, although some court cases say that it's permissible for the employer to reduce the amount of leave available to the employee.

[B]   Categories of Exempt Employees

The FLSA defines executives, professionals, and other categories of workers, based on their main responsibilities. For instance, an executive manages a whole enterprise, or a recognized department or subdivision of an enterprise, and regularly directs the work of the equivalent of two or more full-time employees.

An administrator uses discretion and independent judgment to perform office or nonmanual work. A professional's primary duties are the practice of a learned, artistic, or educational profession. The work is primarily intellectual and varied in character, calling for constant exercise of judgment and discretion. Output cannot be standardized according to time.

An outside salesperson is one who operates outside the employer's place of business, securing sales or orders for sales. The person has received special sales training, and commissions are a significant part of his or her compensation. [29 C.F.R. § 779.415(b) provides detailed information about the FLSA implication of various commission arrangements] The outside salesperson works with little direct supervision and has a written contract designating him or her as exempt.

The FLSA definition also limits the amount of time that can be spent on tasks outside the primary role—generally, no more than 20%.

Retail and service establishments do not have to pay overtime to employees who are paid partly or entirely on a commission basis (commissions represent 50% or more of compensation for a representative period of at least one month). To qualify for this exemption, the employer must pay a regular rate of at least 150% of the minimum wage.

[C]   Payment of Overtime

Nonexempt hourly employees must be paid time-and-a-half (150% of their normal pay rate, including commissions) when they work more than 40 hours in any work week. Work time is all the time when the employer controls the employee's actions, including times the employee is required to be on duty or at a prescribed place. However, bona fide meal periods are not considered work time. Ordinary commuting to work is not work time, Work-related travel, such as an assignment to deliver something or go to a meeting at a client's office, is work time.

These are some items that may require compensation or overtime:

- Rest breaks under 20 minutes;
- Down time or on-call time that prevents the employee from carrying out personal business;
- Preparation before shift or clean-up after shift;
- Mandatory classes, meetings, or conventions;
- Travel time other than normal commuting.

As long as the entire workweek is under 40 hours, 29 C.F.R. § 778.602(a) does not require the employer to pay overtime if a particular work day exceeds eight hours, or if weekend work is required. (However, in a unionized workplace, the CBA often requires extra payment in these situations.)

The general rule is that overtime must be paid in cash, on the regular payday for the pay period in which the overtime is worked. Allowing 1½ hours off for every overtime hour worked is permissible, as long as the comp time is given in the same period and is not carried over.

The work week doesn't have to be Monday–Friday, 9–5: it can be defined as any 168 consecutive hours, starting any time. It doesn't have to be the same as the payroll period. Different work groups or individuals can have different work weeks. Usually, once an employer sets a work week, it has to abide by it—but a permanent change that is not a subterfuge to evade the FLSA's overtime requirements is permitted. [See 29 C.F.R. § 778.104, averaging a long and a short week to see if overtime is payable is not allowed]

If the premium rate (such as differentials for Sunday or holiday work) is at least 150% of the nonpremium rate, the premium rate is not included in the calculation of the regular rate. A "clock pattern" premium (which is required by many CBAs) for working past basic hours is not included in the basic rate if it meets the 150% test. However, a shift differential, such as additional payment for working the night shift, is included in determining the rate to which overtime is applied.

[D]   Case Law on Overtime

Several recent cases stress that it is the actual duties of the job, not the title, that determine whether overtime is payable. Class actions were brought in California, involving major corporations, and some were settled based on claims that ordinary hourly workers were given meaningless "assistant manager" titles to avoid the obligation to pay overtime. There have been major settlements, e.g., the $10 million Pizza Hut agreed to pay in May 2001, and the $80 million judgment (under appeal) against Farmers Insurance Exchange. [*See* Shannon Lafferty, *Meaningless Titles Ploy to Avoid Overtime, Say California Workers*, The Recorder (Feb. 15, 2001) (law.com); Eve Tahmincioglu, *Overtime Becomes Class-Action Fodder*, New York Times, Dec. 12, 2001, at p. G1]

An auto dealer's office manager was held not to be an exempt "executive", although she could be deemed an exempt "administrator" because she did office work and supervised four other people. [*Lott v. Howard Wilson Chrysler-Plymouth*, 203 F.3d 326 (5th Cir. 2000)]

Because their compensation was reduced for lack of work when business in the individual store was slow, Wal-Mart pharmacists were hourly rather than salaried employees, and thus qualified for overtime when business picked up and they had to work long hours. [*Presley v. Wal-Mart Stores Inc.*, 1999 WL 591994 (D. Colo. 1999)]

A refrigerator repairman had to report to his first scheduled job of the day by 8:00 A.M., and to cover repair sites in a three-state area. He was paid an hourly wage for the 8:00–4:30 P.M. shift. He could not get overtime for his extensive driving time (often, seven to eight hours a day) because driving to the first job site, and home from the last job site, however time-consuming, still fell within the definition of "normal travel" between home and work that is not compensable and therefore not subject to overtime. [*Kavanagh v. Grand Union Co.*, 192 F.3d 269 (2d Cir. 1999)]

The plaintiff in *Valerio v. Putnam Associates Inc.* [1999 WL 188284 (1st Cir. 1999)] was hired as a receptionist/administrative assistant, and was told that the job was exempt. Later, the District Court determined that the job was actually nonexempt. She asked for more research and administrative tasks, but was told that she was just a receptionist. She sent a letter to the employer, saying that she should receive overtime pay. She was fired, and her final check included overtime pay.

She sued under the FLSA for additional overtime payments, and for damages for retaliation for exercising her FLSA rights. The First Circuit (like the Sixth, Eighth, Tenth, and Eleventh, but unlike the Second, Fourth, and Ninth) takes the position that a letter within an organization can constitute protected activity, so retaliation on the basis of such a letter is illegal. The Second, Fourth, and Ninth Circuits only allow retaliation claims if the employee brought a suit or made a formal agency complaint. [*See, e.g., Ball v. Memphis Bar-B-Q Co.*, 228 F.3d 360 (4th Cir. 2000)] According to the Eleventh Circuit, punitive damages are not available for violation of the antiretaliation provision. [*Snapp v. Unlimited Concepts, Inc.*, 208 F.3d 928 (11th Cir. 2000)]

[E]   Scheduling Workers for Overtime

Sometimes, the employer will have to provide additional incentives, such as meal vouchers or free meals in the employee cafeteria or transportation home, for overtime work. But it is more common for employees to compete to be able to put in extra hours at the higher overtime rate. It is legitimate to assign overtime in order of seniority: to let employees bid for overtime work, with priority to the most senior.

In a unionized workplace, the CBA determines how much notice the company must give when overtime will be required; the extent to which overtime is assigned and when it is voluntary; who gets to bid on it; maximum overtime hours; and meal and rest breaks during overtime. If the employer assigns overtime, the disciplinary procedure should be drafted to specify that refusal to work mandatory overtime is a legitimate subject for discipline.

The FLSA allows employers to maintain a policy under which overtime work must be authorized. (Otherwise, employees would have an incentive to goof off during the day and catch up during better-paid overtime hours). But overtime pay is required if the employer permits or even is aware that nonexempt employees are working more than 40 hours a week.

Tip: The amount of overtime can be reduced by

- Planning further in advance;
- Being more realistic about deadlines;
- Coordinating tasks better, so materials and intermediate products are available when the production cycle requires them;
- Coordinating vacation and leave schedules so there will be enough employees available and it won't be necessary for a few workers to put in extra hours to cover for those who are absent.

---

§ 1.16   VACATIONS AND VACATION PAY

Some degree of paid vacation time, including major holidays and two to four weeks of vacation time, is almost universal in U.S. corporations. (European entitlement to vacation time is both greater and more formal—it's usually a matter of labor law, not left up to the employer's discretion.)

The needs of employees have gotten more complex. An employee might prefer to take a day or two at a time to relax or spend more time with family, instead of taking a long vacation. But brief absences could be harder for the company to work around than a solid block of time when projects can be postponed or delegated to a co-worker.

> **Tip:** Audit requirements may actually require employees with access to the firm's cash and books to take at least two consecutive weeks of vacation. An employee who never uses his or her full allotment of vacation time could be a conscientious person who wants to cope with a backlog, a workaholic who really needs to "get a life" outside the office, a sub-par employee who needs extra time to make up for incompetence, or an embezzler who has to hang around to prevent crooked schemes from unraveling!

A report by Hewitt Associates [*Managing Time Off 2000/2001*, <http://was.hewitt.com/hewitt/resource/rptspubs/subrptspubs/managing_time_off.htm> (no www)] says that over 96% of the respondents to a survey covering vacation days, sick days, managed disability, paid time-off banks, sabbaticals, and vacation bonus programs agree that time off is effective in attracting and retaining desirable employees. About two-thirds of the respondents (63–64%) allow employees to carry over unused vacation days. Fifteen percent allow redemption in cash of unused days, and 10% allow buying and/or selling vacation days among employees.

The California Division of Labor Standards Enforcement's position is that it is unlawful for a company to try to save money by forcing salaried employees to take time off without pay—or to make them take vacation days when they don't want to. In this view, an exempt worker is entitled to receive a set wage that can't be reduced, even if the employer is in economic difficulties. However, even the California regulators admit that this is stricter than federal law, which does permit the employer to order exempt employees to take vacation, and does not require payment for time there was no work for the employee. [Mike McKee, *California Workers Can't Be Forced To Take Vacation*, The Recorder (June 7, 2001) (law.com)]

A paid time-off (PTO) bank, combining sick and vacation days, perhaps in addition to personal days, holidays, and days to cope with family illnesses, is a fast-growing perk. Only 6% of respondents to the 1997 survey offered it, versus 18% in the 2000-2001 survey. [For more information about PTO banks, *see* Jeff Olson, *Curing Sick Leave Ills* (December 2001) <http://accounting.smartpros.com/x31835.xml> (no www). He suggests starting the PTO bank with a new fiscal year, so employees won't think that they're losing entitlements (although the net result is that people usually end up taking off less total time if they are entitled to a certain number of days off per year than if they feel they might as well take off when they have unused sick days).] Employees usually prefer to be able to take time off without concocting an excuse, and the PTO bank saves paperwork for tracking.

However, the downside is that employees who should take a sick day (and avoid passing germs around the workplace) may come in to work if they want to accrue days off for later use. Some states also require the employer to pay for accrued PTO days when the employee quits or is fired or laid off. In those states, it makes more sense to define the PTO as accruing on a monthly or weekly basis instead of being awarded at the beginning of the year; that way, the terminated employee will only be entitled to pay for accrued but unused PTO.

> **Tip:** Get legal advice about how to run a PTO bank that complies with the FMLA. If the vacation plan is part of a cafeteria plan, remember the I.R.C. § 125 ban on carryovers. Cafeteria plan vacation time must be on a "use it or lose it" basis.

IRS Private Letter Ruling 9635002 allows the employer to add the value of any unused vacation days to an employee's 401(k) plan account. Payroll taxes do not have to be paid or withheld on such amounts, and income tax on the value of the vacation days is deferred until the 401(k) account is accessed. The value of the vacation days does not reduce the amount of cash compensation that the employee can defer.

In the wake of the September 11 attack, the IRS issued interim guidance on leave-based donation programs, under which employees agree to trade vacation days, sick days, or personal leave if the employer contributes to charitable organizations that respond to the attack and its victims. [*See* Notice 2001-69, 2001-46 I.R.B. 491]

Similarly, the "group emergency pool" technique can be used to maintain the paycheck of a sick employee who would not otherwise be entitled to pay. It works especially well in smaller companies that cannot afford a short-term disability plan. Employees donate unused vacation days, and the donor's salary for those days is contributed to the sick employee. The company can allow pooling of vacation time only, sick leave only, or both. Usually, the maximum donation is 80 hours, so that donor employees can take at least some vacation. The donation can be accounted for on an hour-for-hour basis, or a dollar-for-dollar basis if participants have widely varying salaries. [*See* Carla Joinson, *Time Share*, HR Magazine, December 1998 at p. 104]

In *Mange v. Petrolite Corp.* [135 F.3d 570 (8th Cir. 1998)], the plaintiff employees took voluntary retirement or voluntary separation as part of a RIF. The company's vacation policy treated vacation benefits as vesting at the end of the fiscal year. The plaintiffs claimed that their vacation vested on the last day of employment, entitling them to be paid for unused vacation days. They lost in court, because the RIF program didn't cover pay for unused vacation days. The employees waived their claims under the regular plan by accepting the RIF incentives.

§ 1.17   GARNISHMENTS AND DEDUCTIONS FOR SUPPORT ORDERS

[A]   Assignments versus Garnishments

There may be instances in which the HR department is asked to apply some of an employee's wages to a debt, such as consumer debts, student loan debt, and the obligation to support children, and/or an ex-spouse.

An "assignment" is an action undertaken by an individual to direct some of his or her future compensation to creditors. A "garnishment" is a deduction from wages made pursuant to a court order. Federal law doesn't say anything about wage assignments, although many states limit the amount or percentage of each paycheck that can be assigned, permit assignments only for certain classes of debts, or require the spouse's consent to the assignment.

Pensions cannot be assigned before they are received (except through a Qualified Domestic Relations Order (QDRO). *See* § 12.08). Once a pension payment is made, the recipient can do whatever he or she wants with it, but the "anti-alienation" rules of ERISA prevent advance assignment.

The federal Consumer Credit Protection Act (CCPA) [15 U.S.C. § 1671 et seq.] puts limits on garnishment. Generally, the maximum permitted garnishment will be 25% of the employee's "disposable" earnings, with stricter limits on garnishments for very low-income workers. "Disposable earnings" is defined as approximately equal to gross income minus Social Security taxes and withheld income taxes. Health insurance premiums and spousal and child support are not deducted, even if the support is ordered by a court. Thus, serious problems can occur if the same individual is subject to garnishment both for consumer debt and support payments.

Garnishment for support rather than consumer debt can be higher [15 U.S.C. § 1673]:

- 50%, if the employee is supporting a spouse or child other than the subject of the order, and the garnishment order covers less than 12 weeks' worth of arrears;
- 55%, if conditions are the same but more than 12 weeks of arrears are involved;
- 60%, if the employee does not have a new family to support, and arrears are 12 weeks or less;
- 65%, if there is no second family and arrears exceed 12 weeks.

There is no limit on garnishments that respond to an order issued by a Chapter 11 or Chapter 13 bankruptcy court, or on a debt due for any state or federal tax. The general rule against alienation of plan benefits doesn't prevent the IRS from garnishing a taxpayer's (or rather, nontaxpayer's) vested interest in qualified benefits when the agency has a judgment for unpaid taxes.

The CCPA says that, if state law limits garnishment more than the federal law does, employees are entitled to the protection of the stricter state-law limits. In other words, the garnishment is limited to what is permitted by state law. Under the CCPA, it's illegal to fire an employee for having one garnishment, but it's lawful to fire if additional garnishments are imposed. [16 U.S.C. § 1674] Willful violation of this provision can be punished by a $1,000 fine and/or one year's imprisonment.

Under Maryland and Colorado law, cash tips received from customers are considered "remuneration" that has to be included in the garnishment calculations.

[*United Guaranteed Res. Ins. Co. v. Demmick*, 916 P.2d 638 (Colo. App. 1996); *Shanks v. Lowe*, 774 A.2d 411 (Md. 2001)]

The federal Fair Debt Collection Practices Act (FDCPA) [28 U.S.C. § 3001] lets the federal government collect its judgments by garnishing property held by a third party on the basis of the debtor's "substantial non-exempt interest" in the property. According to the Sixth Circuit, tax levies do not violate ERISA's anti-alienation provisions. [*U.S. v. Sawaf*, 74 F.3d 119 (6th Cir. 1996)]

[B] Student Loan Garnishments

There are separate federal rules at 20 U.S.C. § 1095a with respect to garnishment to repay student loans. Up to 10% of disposable earnings can be garnished to repay those loans. The employee can sign a document agreeing to a higher garnishment level. Before the garnishment order is submitted to the employer, the employee has the right to contest the garnishment and suggest a voluntary repayment schedule. If a person is fired or laid off from a job, and is rehired (by the original employer or someone else) within 12 months after termination, student loan garnishment is deferred until the person has been back in the workforce for 12 months.

The federal provisions do not require employers to change or depart from their normal payment mechanisms to comply with student loan garnishment orders, but if they fail to comply with the order entirely, employers can be penalized by the amount that should have been withheld to satisfy the garnishment, plus costs, fees, and punitive damages.

Federal law forbids an employer to discharge, refuse to hire, or discipline a person because he or she is subject to a student loan garnishment. Employers that violate this rule can be ordered to reinstate the affected employee with back pay, and can also be ordered to pay punitive damages and attorneys' fees.

[C] Child Support Collection

State governments are heavily involved in child support enforcement, to prevent children from becoming welfare recipients because their parents do not support them. The federal government also requires state governments to take this enforcement role. Under a federal statute, the Child Support Enforcement Amendments of 1984 [A.L. 98-378], states can lose federal funding if they do not enact laws requiring wage withholding for support arrears. States must also have a procedure for Qualified Medical Child Support Orders (QMCSOs) under which parents who are covered by an Employee Group Health Plan (EGHP) are required to take steps to enroll their children under the plan.

Federal law also requires state-court child support orders to contain a withholding provision, so a withholding order can be issued as soon as a parent falls behind on support, with no need for separate court proceedings. The state child support enforcement agency notifies the employer that a particular employee has child support arrears. The employer is obligated to impose withholding as of the first pay period after 14 days of the date the agency mailed its notice. Once with-holding begins, the employer has an obligation to notify the child support agency promptly if the employee quits or gets fired. The notice should give the termina-tion date, the employee's last known address, and the address of the new employer (if known).

The CCPA percentage limits discussed above apply to child support orders. Depending on circumstances, up to 65% of disposable income may be subject to withholding for support. The Child Support Enforcement Amendments allow states to impose a late payment fee of 3–6% of the overdue support. Support with-holding takes priority over other legal processes (e.g., for consumer debts or stu-dent loans) applying to the same income.

Employers must also submit data about newly hired employees to the state unemployment insurance agency within 20 days of hiring. The information is ag-gregated into a National Directory of New Hires that is used to track down "dead-beat parents" who fail to pay child support.

The basic federal report (which can be made by mail or magnetic tape; state support enforcement agencies can accept telephoned, faxed, and e-mailed reports) consists of:

- Employer's name, address, and Taxpayer Identification Number;
- Employee's name;
- Employee's address;
- Employee's Social Security number.

States may impose additional requirements, such as telephone numbers, driver's license number, and information about the group health plan (to be used in con-junction with a QMCSO). The employer also has to make a quarterly report of wages paid, for use in instituting withholding orders. Failure to make a required report can be penalized by $25 per employee, or $500 for conspiracy with an em-ployee to avoid the requirement.

CHAPTER 2
TAX ASPECTS OF PAY PLANNING

§ 2.01 INTRODUCTION

One reason why corporations adopt pension and benefit plans is that, under appropriate circumstances, the employer will get a tax deduction, and the employee will receive valuable benefits—but the employee will not have immediately taxable income as a result of the benefits (or only part of the benefit will generate taxable income).

Therefore, an important part of pay planning is determining what portion of each employee's compensation is taxable, and performing tax withholding, depositing taxes, issuing information returns, and maintaining tax records.

> **Tip:** IRS Publication 15, available in hard copy or online, is an important guide to employment tax compliance. Each year, Publication 509 is revised to give the latest version of the tax compliance calendar.

The basic tax rule is that everything received is taxable income, unless there is a specific exclusion. Therefore, the tax definition of "wages" includes vacation pay, commissions, bonuses, and some fringe benefits, not just straight salary. Severance pay is considered taxable wages, but payments for cancellation of an employment contract are not wages.

These items have been granted exclusions from taxable income:

- Worker's Compensation benefits;
- The employer's contributions to qualified pension plans (but the employee's pretax deferrals placed into 401(k) plans are FUTA and FICA wages);
- Up to $50,000 in § 79 group-term life insurance coverage. Additional coverage is taxable income that must be reported on the W-2 form, but income tax withholding is not required. The excess coverage is not subject to FUTA, but is subject to both the employer and employee share of FICA;
- Certain fringe benefits, e.g., employee discounts, working condition and de minimis fringes, qualified transportation fringes, qualified dependent care assistance within limits, etc.

When a new employee is hired the employer must use Form I-9 to verify immigration status and that the person can lawfully work within the United States. [*See* § 23.11 for more information about immigration issues in hiring]

§ 2.02 THE COMPENSATION DEDUCTION

Internal Revenue Code § 162 allows a corporation to deduct its ordinary and necessary business expenses, including reasonable salaries in exchange for personal services rendered to the corporation. Salaries are only reasonable if the person hired is qualified to perform the services, and actually performs them. If vacation pay is treated as deferred compensation, it is not deductible until the year it is actually paid. [*See* I.R.C. § 404(a)(5)]

When the Tax Court decided the case of *Exacto Spring Corp. v. C.I.R.* [196 F.3d 833 (7th Cir. 1999)] it used a seven-factor test to determine the reasonableness of executive compensation, using factors such as the difficulty of finding qualified employees, the employee's contribution to the business, his or her qualifications and earnings history, and what comparable executives earned in other companies.

When the case was appealed, the Seventh Circuit held that the seven-factor test was not valid. It didn't explain how to weight the various factors; some of the factors were vague; and some of them didn't relate to I.R.C. § 162's objective of preventing corporations from disguising dividends paid to stockholders (which are not deductible by the corporation) as compensation to employees. Although the Seventh Circuit considered the compensation at issue here ($1.1 million in one year, $1.3 million in another) to be somewhat higher than reasonable, most of it was deductible because it rewarded the CEO for his unusually great success in increasing stockholders' return on their investment.

The Second Circuit said that the test of reasonableness is whether a hypothetical independent investor in the company would be willing to approve that level of compensation. Consideration should also be given to whether comparable companies paid extra to CEOs who also acted as CFO and treasurer. [*Doxsil Corp.*, T.C. Memo 1999-155] The Sixth Circuit treated $4.4 million paid to a company's president and sole shareholder as all reasonable and deductible. Much of the company's profits were directly attributable to him, and it was fair to compensate him highly when the company had funds to make up for underpayment in earlier years. [*Alpha Medical Inc.*, 83 A.F.T.R.2d ¶99-697 (6th Cir. April 19, 1999)]

Internal Revenue Code § 162(m) provides that a public corporation (i.e., one whose stock is traded on public markets, unlike closely-held private companies) is not allowed to deduct any portion of any employee's compensation that exceed $1 million. In this context, compensation means salary plus benefits, but does not include qualified retirement plans. Furthermore, compensation over $1 million can be deducted if:

- It represents commissions paid on sales;
- It is paid under a contract that was already in effect on February 17, 1993 (the effective date of § 162(m)), and has not been materially modified after that date and before the compensation was paid;
- The compensation is based on performance measured by objective goals set by a Board of Directors compensation committee. The performance-based arrangement must be disclosed to the stockholders, and must be ratified by a majority vote. The money can't be paid until the compensation committee certifies that the performance goals have been met.

§ 2.03   INCOME TAX WITHHOLDING

[A]   Calculation

At the time of hiring, the employer must also have the employee submit Form W-4 (Employee's Withholding Allowance Certificate) to indicate the filing status (married filing a joint return, married filing a separate return, single, head of household) and the number of withholding allowances that he or she claims. The more withholding allowances, the less that will be withheld from the employee's paycheck.

Tip: If the employer doesn't have a W-4 for a particular employee, the deductions can be calculated as if the employee were single with zero withholding exemptions (i.e., the method least favorable to the employee) who can correct this simply by submitting the W-4.

Although there are other methods, the amount of income tax to be withheld is usually calculated under either the percentage method or the wage bracket method. (The calculations will be done by the payroll preparation contractor, if the employer outsources this function.)

Under the percentage method, the IRS tables in Publication 15 are used. The number of allowances claimed is multiplied by the amount from the allowance table; the result is subtracted from the employee's wages. The wage rate table gives the actual dollar amount to be withheld.

Under the wage bracket method, tables are used to compute withholding per weekly, semiweekly, or other pay period, based on wage level, marital status, and number of claimed exemptions.

For income tax purposes, "supplemental wages" means compensation other than, or in addition to, ordinary cash compensation. Bonuses, commissions, overtime pay, severance pay, back pay, taxable fringe benefits, and payments for accumulated sick leave are all supplemental wages.

If the supplemental wages are combined with ordinary compensation in a paycheck, with no allocation between the two, withholding should be done as if the supplemental wages were ordinary compensation. However, if the supplemental amount is paid in a separate check, or as part of the regular paycheck but with an explicit allocation, then either the supplemental and regular wages can be treated and withheld as a single payment (with a credit for amounts already withheld) or a 28% flat rate can be applied to the supplemental wages.

The withholding system must distinguish between compensation paid to the employee and reimbursement of legitimate business expenses that the employee incurred on the employer's behalf (reimbursement is not taxable income). For tax purposes, expense accounts are either "accountable" or "non-accountable" plans. Amounts paid under an accountable plan are not wages for the employee, and therefore are not subject to FICA or FUTA. Withholding is not required. Employees must meet two tests under an accountable plan:

- They paid or incurred deductible expenses in the course of employment;
- They are required to provide adequate accounts of the expenses within a reasonable time of incurring them.

If they receive any amount over and above the expenses, they have an obligation to return it within a reasonable time. The general tax rule is that it is reasonable for employees to be reimbursed within 30 days of spending money; to provide an expense account within 60 days of spending the money; and to return excess amounts within 120 days of the initial advance.

Accounting for a per diem or a fixed allowance (e.g., X cents per mile for business travel) is considered adequate as long as the payment is no higher than the government per diem rates for meals and lodging [*see* IRS Publication 1542] and the standard mileage rate for travel. [IRS Publication 553]

If these tests are not met, the money is treated as if it were paid under a nonaccountable plan (one which does not require documentation of expenses). Expenses reimbursed under a nonaccountable plan are considered wages, included in income and subject to withholding in the first payroll period after there has been an reasonable time to return any excess funds.

All of the employee's taxable income is subject to income tax withholding, except to the degree that a withholding exemption is available. FICA (Social Security) taxes are imposed on the employee's taxable income, up to a certain amount (for 2002, the amount is $84,900; each year's wage base must be published in the Federal Register no later than November 1 of the preceding year). The employer and employee are each taxed at a rate of 6.2% on income up to the limit. Therefore, the maximum FICA tax is $5,263.80 each from employer and employee.

According to the Eighth Circuit, payments made under an early retirement incentive program, to tenured faculty members, were not wages for FICA purposes, because tenure is a property right and not just an employment right. Therefore, the faculty members were being paid for giving up a property right, not for the work they did for the university. [*North Dakota State Univ. v. United States*, CCH Unempl. Ins. Rep. ¶16,568 (8th Cir. June 18, 2001)] But severance payments to retiring employees that reflect past work are subject to FICA. [*Abrahamsen*, CCH UI Reporter ¶16,429B (Fed. Cir. 2000)]

In addition, all of the employee's taxable income is subject to Medicare tax, paid at the rate of 1.45% each by employer and employee. Income tax, Social Security, and Medicare taxes are reported by the employer on Form 941 (Employer's Quarterly Federal Tax Return).

[B] Withholding on Pensions

The general rule is that income tax withholding is required when a plan makes payments to retired employees. There are circumstances under which the retirees can elect to waive withholding, but there are other circumstances in which withholding is mandatory.

For ordinary pension payments in annuity form, the plan can use its regular withholding procedures, based on the number of withholding exemptions on the retiree's Form W-4P. If no W-4P is submitted, the plan should withhold as if the retiree were married and claimed three withholding allowances.

However, if the distribution is a lump sum or other nonperiodic payment and not an annuity, the question is whether it is an "eligible rollover distribution." If it is not, the basic requirement is to withhold at a 10% rate, although the person receiving the lump sum can use the W-4P to claim exemption from withholding. If the recipient of the lump sum expects to be in a high tax bracket, the person can ask for withholding at a rate higher than 10%.

An eligible rollover distribution is an amount that could be placed in the retiree's IRA, Roth IRA, or transferred to another qualified plan. Any such amount that is not rolled over is subject to withholding at a rate of at least 20%. The recipient of the distribution can increase the withholding rate, but cannot lower it below 20% or claim a withholding exemption. *See* the instructions for Form 1099-R.

One effect of the Economic Growth and Tax Relief Reconciliation Act of 2001 (EGTRRA) [P.L. 107-16] is to broaden the category of amounts that can be rolled over, and therefore that may be subject to withholding on this basis—although EGTRRA also lowers income tax rates, so 20% may in fact be higher than the retiree's actual tax rate.

Withholding from lump-sum pension distributions is not reported on Form 941. Instead, Form 945 (Annual Return of Withheld Federal Income Tax) is used. The pension withholding amounts should be combined with the other Form 945 amounts, but for nonpayroll withholding only, not payroll taxes. [*See* Form 945 instructions] The recipient of the distribution receives a Form 1099-R (Distributions from Pensions, Annuities, Retirement or Profit-Sharing Plans). [*See* Chapter 12 for further information on distributions from qualified plans]

§ 2.04 FUTA TAX

FUTA (federal unemployment) taxes are paid entirely by the employer, on the first $7,000 of the employee's wages that are subject to FUTA. The short-form FUTA return is the Form 940-EZ; the long form is Form 940. The net tax rate is 0.8%. The states have their own taxable wage bases, ranging from $7,000 in several states to $28,400 (Hawaii).

IRS Final Regulations issued January 29, 1999, affecting I.R.C. § 3121 deal with the status of nonqualified deferred compensation for FICA and FUTA purposes. Wages are subject to FUTA (and FICA) when they are paid, or considered constructively paid. Welfare plan benefits and severance pay are not considered deferred compensation. Window benefits (early retirement incentives that are available only for a limited time) are not deferred compensation if paid after January 1, 2000. Nonqualified deferred compensation counts for FICA and FUTA either when the work giving rise to the compensation is done or when the right to collect the deferred amounts is no longer subject to a substantial risk of forfeiture—whichever comes later. The Code has "nonduplication" rules to make sure the same amount is not subject to FICA and FUTA both when the work is done and when the funds are paid out. [*See* Rev. Proc. 2001-9, 2001-3 I.R.B. 328 for the specifications for e-filing Form 940 or filing it online (TeleFile is not available). Nor can late or amended forms be filed electronically. There is a telephone eFile Help Line: (512) 460-8900]

Before filing electronically, the employer must apply to the IRS, which has 45 days to either accept or reject the application. Once accepted, the employer will have to send a successful test transmittal before the IRS finalizes permission to file electronically. Due dates for electronic filing are the same as for paper forms: the first day of the first calendar month after the year for which the return is made; or, if tax deposits have been made as they come due, the tenth day of the second calendar month after the end of the year.

The Supreme Court seldom tackles employment tax issues, but see its 2001 decision in *United States v. Cleveland Indians Baseball Co.* [532 U.S. 200 (2001)] If an employee settles an employment case and receives back pay, for FICA and FUTA purposes the money is taxed in the year in which the wages were actually paid and not the year in which they were earned—whether the tax rates in the year of payment were higher or lower than the rates for the year in which the money was earned.

§ 2.05   TRUST FUND TAX COMPLIANCE AND THE 100% PENALTY

The FICA tax withheld from employees' salary (both the OASDI and the Medicare components) is called a "trust fund tax." (Although the employer must pay its FICA share, and must pay FUTA, these are not trust fund taxes).

Frequently, the employer will collect employee FICA tax from each payroll, but will not have to deposit the tax until the end of the quarter. A cash-strapped company's temptation to "borrow" that money for its own immediate needs is strong. To reduce the temptation, I.R.C. § 6672 imposes a 100% penalty that cannot be discharged in bankruptcy on "responsible persons" who willfully fail to submit the withheld trust fund taxes to the government. The 100% penalty means that the penalty is as large as the amount of taxes that were not properly paid. Furthermore, all of the personal assets of the responsible party can be attached to satisfy the debt.

Tax law creates a very large class of responsible persons, including the corporation's officers, shareholders, and directors, based on their level of responsibility within the corporation. The factors include authority to hire and fire; to decide which creditors will be paid and in what order, control over payroll, and power to deposit federal tax amounts. Top managers will probably be liable because of their degree of control over corporate financial managers. Lower-level managers probably will not be liable unless their duties include actually writing checks (and thus actual knowledge of amounts disbursed or not disbursed). Even parties outside the corporation, such as its bankers and its accountants, can be liable if they have the real control over corporate funds.

When a penalty is due, the government can either collect all of it from one responsible person or divide it among several. To avoid liability, an individual has to prove that he or she was incorrectly characterized as a responsible person, or that the failure to pay over the money was not willful. In this context, "willfulness" only means knowledge that the taxes were not submitted, and a failure to correct the situation. If a responsible person finds out that a payment was missed in one quarter, that creates a duty to investigate to find out if other payments were missed as well.

The responsible person's duty is to use all of the corporations "unencumbered funds" to pay trust fund taxes. Unencumbered funds are those not already assigned to a debt that existed before the tax liability arose.

> **Tip:** To protect yourself, get your corporate board of directors to adopt a policy that allocates funds to the trust taxes first. In fact, if the company owes money to the IRS under several tax provisions, make sure that the tax payments are allocated first to the trust fund taxes, because the other penalties are lower than 100%. Without clear instructions from the taxpayer, the IRS will apply the taxes that yields the highest penalties, not the lowest. Furthermore, employees can indicate the allocation when they make voluntary payments—but once the IRS starts collection activities, it won't take instructions about how to apportion the funds.

Thanks to the Taxpayer Bill of Rights 2 [P.L. No. 104-168] a responsible person is entitled to notice before the IRS imposes the 100% penalty. The notice must also give the names of other responsible persons, the IRS' collection efforts against them, and the success of those efforts. (The other responsible parties who actually pay the IRS can sue other responsible parties to make them pay their fair share.) The recipient of the notice can pay the penalty and sue for a refund, or contest the penalty in federal court. Collection efforts will be suspended until the case is resolved.

Larson v. United States [84 A.F.T.R.2d ¶99-5696 (D. Wash. 1999)] upholds the imposition of the 100% penalty on an attorney who was the majority shareholder in a closely held corporation, even though he was not an officer or director and was not involved in daily operations. Personal liability was deemed appropriate because he had the power to sign checks, control operations, and incur debt on behalf of the corporation. In fact, he took out a personal loan to pay taxes for the corporation.

Underpaying taxes creates an obligation to catch up on the payments, plus interest. Penalties may also be assessed for, e.g., failure to file, late filing, or serious understatement of the amount of tax. Furthermore, criminal liability can be imposed in five situations:

- Willful failure to collect or pay over federal tax (the penalty is up to $10,000 and/or five years in prison, plus the costs of prosecution);

- Willful failure to pay tax, make a return, keep records, or provide mandated information to the IRS is a misdemeanor (not a felony); the penalty is up to a year in jail and/or a $25,000 fine for an individual, or a $100,000 fine (corporation), plus prosecution costs;
- Willful furnishing of a false or fraudulent tax statement, or willful refusal to furnish a required statement, carries a penalty of up to $1,000 and/or one year's imprisonment per violation;
- Willful tax evasion can be punished by up to five years in prison and/or $100,000 (for an individual) or $500,000 (for a corporation);
- It is perjury to willfully sign a return or other tax document that the signer knows to be false or inaccurate. The penalty can be up to three years' imprisonment and/or $100,000 (individual) or $500,000 (corporation).

Although these penalties are heavy, in practice the IRS often attempts to collect civil penalties instead of criminal ones, because it's easy to prove that taxes were not paid as required, but hard to prove the state of mind of the person or organization who was supposed to make the payment.

§ 2.06   W-2 FORMS

The W-2 form, used to report employee compensation, is a multipart form. Forms are sent to the IRS and to state tax authorities (and city authorities, in cities that impose their own income tax). The employer must also furnish the employee with copies that the employees can use to prepare their tax returns. Of course, the fact that the employer submits the same information to the taxing authorities makes it harder for employees to omit employment income from their tax returns.

EGTRRA, the 2001 tax bill, made many dramatic changes, some of which are reflected on the W-2 form. [*See* Announcement 2001-93, 2001-44 I.R.B. 416, for an explanation of how to report I.R.C. § 414(v) catch-up contributions made by plan participants over age 50] For 2002, employers are instructed to report the elective deferrals on the Form W-2 in box 12, using Codes D-H and S. Although the IRS does not expect major changes in Forms 1099-R and 5498 as a result of EGTRRA, the Instructions for 2002 will reflect EGTRRA requirements.

§ 2.07   TAX DEPOSITS

Employment taxes (withheld income taxes, FICA) are usually remitted by the employer either once a month or every other week. The schedule for reporting depends on the size of the employer's tax obligation for the previous year; the IRS notifies employers every November which category they will fall into for the next year. [*See* Treas. Reg. § 31.6302-1]

If the employer had a total of $50,000 or less in employment taxes during the previous year, then the employer will probably have to make a deposit once a month, no later than the fifteenth of the month following the month that the taxes relate to.

Employers who had a larger employment tax roll for the previous year usually have to make semiweekly deposits, on the Wednesday after payday (if payday is Wednesday, Thursday, or Friday; on the Friday after payday if payday is Saturday, Sunday, Monday, or Tuesday). The purpose of these schedules is to give employers at least three business days after payday to deposit the funds.

There is also a "one-day rule" under I.R.C. § 6302(g): if the tax liability for a period reaches $100,000, the tax money must be deposited on the first banking day after the $100,000 level is reached.

At the other end of the scale, a very small amount (less than $2,500 a quarter or year) does not have to be deposited, as long as a timely return for the period is accompanied by the full amount of the liability. [T.D. 8946, 2001-24 I.R.B. 1332, Treas. Reg. § 31.6302-1(f), effective for periods beginning on or after January 1, 2001]

The basic reporting form is the quarterly Form 941, but income tax and backup withholding on nonpayroll amounts are reported once a year on Form 945—Annual Return of Withheld Federal Income Tax.

§ 2.08   TRANSITION TO ELECTRONIC FILING

There were employment taxes long before there were computers, so originally the system was set up on the basis of paper forms that were filled out and mailed to the IRS. Soon, all filing will occur electronically. The IRS is gradually implementing this transition, so that now, in a minority of cases, employers can continue to file paper forms. Under appropriate circumstances, they are encouraged to file electronically, over the Internet. There are also transitional methods involving magnetic media such as magnetic tapes and diskettes. Forms 5500, 940, and 941 can be filed via magnetic media.

Form 941 can be filed online, through Electronic Data Interchange (EDI). This can be done by payroll processing companies, reporting agents that file in bulk, and companies that buy, license, or develop their own EDI software. Since early 1998, it has also been possible to TeleFile Form 941—i.e., to use a TouchTone telephone to input the necessary information.

The traditional method of paying taxes is to make quarterly or annual deposits, accompanied by a paper deposit coupon [Form 8109, Federal Tax Deposit Coupon] at a Federal Reserve bank. However, as of December 31, 2000, the last remaining Federal Reserve Bank that handled this task ceased to do so. Any paper documents that are still used can be mailed to the Financial Agent, Federal Tax Deposit Processing, PO Box 970030, St. Louis, MO 63197.

The IRS is phasing in mandatory electronic deposit under the Electronic Federal Tax Payment System (EFTPS).

> **Tip:** EFTPS replaces the old TAXLINK system which was in operation from 1994 to part of 1997. Any business can use EFTPS to satisfy its employment tax responsibilities; more and more taxpayers are required to use it.

EFTPS payments can be made either direct (funds are transferred from the corporation's bank account to the IRS) or through a financial institution, which makes electronic funds transfers to the IRS based on the client's instructions. Direct payments can be handled by phone, using software for PCs, or over the Internet.

I.R.C. § 6302 covers circumstances under which "depository taxes" over and above a minimum amount will have to be paid through Electronic Funds Transfer (EFT) to the IRS. "Depository taxes" means withheld income taxes (whether or not withheld from payroll), FICA, FUTA, and corporate estimated and income taxes.

> **Tip:** If a taxpayer ever becomes subject to the electronic payment requirement, it will not be allowed to go back to remitting tax payments by check.

The threshold amount was $50,000 for taxes to be deposited with respect to calendar years 1995–1997, and is $200,000 for later years. [Reg. 531.6302-1(h)(3)(ii)] The IRS has the power to exempt a taxpayer (e.g., a small business that can't afford the necessary computer power) from making electronic deposits.

CHAPTER 3
BONUSES AND SEVERANCE PAY

§ 3.01   INTRODUCTION

Although regular compensation and benefits are the main focus of compensation planning, there are two important types of nonrecurring compensation that also play an important role: bonuses and severance pay. In a booming economy, bonuses often seem more significant, as a means of recruiting and retention in a competitive environment, and as a means of "sharing the wealth" within the enterprise. However, in an economic downturn, it often becomes necessary to reduce the headcount, and severance benefits become extremely important.

§ 3.02   BONUSES

According to ECS/Watson Wyatt Data Services, in 1998 about two-thirds of top managers surveyed received at least some of their compensation in the form of bonus awards. The typical bonus was about one-third of base pay. About four-fifths of executives whose bonus depended on meeting a target did achieve the target and received a bonus. [*Bonuses, Deferred Compensation Typify Pay Plans for Top Management,* Compensation & Benefits Update, Aug. 12, 1998, at p. 5]

The Pay for Performance Report [September 1999 issue: <http://www.ioma.com>] says that, despite attention to alternative pay techniques, annual bonuses are still the most popular and effective motivators. Other effective techniques are one-time awards for outstanding performance; individual incentives; and long-term incentives for executives.

Only about a third of large U.S. companies currently offer Christmas or other bonuses; in fact, more than half never offered such bonuses, and one-eighth used to but discontinued the practice. Performance-based bonuses are much more effective, because of the greater incentive they provide. [*Holiday Bonuses Alive But Fading*, <http://www.hewitt.com/news/pressrel/1999/12-22-99.htm> (posted to www.hewitt.com on Dec. 22, 1999)]

It seems likely that, after 2001, bonuses will become less significant in executive compensation. For example, in February 2002 the Investor Responsibility Research Center looked at 81 companies whose fiscal year ended before December 31, 2001. More than half (44%) cut the salary and bonuses paid to their CEOs. [Lynn Cowan and Gaston F. Ceron, *Companies Pare Executive Compensation*, Wall Street Journal, Feb. 13, 2002, at p. B9D] Computer Associates International Inc., for example, did not issue a bonus or stock options to its CEO, Sanjay Kumar, after a year marked by an intense proxy battle. In 2000, however, Mr. Kumar got a $3.16 million bonus, stock options for 750,000 shares, and $4.7 million in restricted stock. However, the Investor Responsibility Research Center found that many companies provided larger option awards when they reduced bonuses and other cash compensation for the CEO.

New York State's highest court, the Court of Appeals, decided in October 2000 that discretionary bonuses used by investment banks and law firms are not "wages" that are protected by state labor law. The bonus is not considered a wage, even if part of it is based on the firm's performance. [*Truelove v. Northeast Capital & Advisory Inc.,* 95 N.Y.2d 220 (2000)]

§ 3.03   SEVERANCE PAY

[A]   Generally

There is no federal law requiring that employees receive severance pay, but nevertheless it is very common for employers to provide this type of compensation (unless the employee was fired for misconduct). Severance pay is often defined as a certain number of days or weeks of pay for every year of service with the employer.

The most important characteristic of severance pay is that it is over and above the normal salary or wages earned for past services. Severance payments are by and large discretionary, unlike payment for past services, which must be made when employment terminates. If the employer enters into an express or implied contract to provide severance benefits, that contract can be enforced. However, employers typically retain the right to alter their severance pay plans, and this is sometimes done just before a major layoff. Employers may also provide benefits to only certain persons affected by a mass layoff, claiming that the others were terminated for poor performance. [*See* Carol Hymowitz, *Firms That Get Stingy With Layoff Packages May Pay a High Price*, Wall Street Journal, Oct. 30, 2001, at p. B1]

In mid-2001, Unifi Network (a subsidiary of Pricewaterhousecoopers) surveyed about 120 employers throughout the United States. About half of the companies had downsized during the preceding 18 months, and 50% of those planned even more cuts within the next two years. Nearly all (88%) of the employers had a formal severance policy, usually covering all the positions in the organization. Three-quarters of those with formal policies imposed a length-of-service requirement to qualify for severance. The most usual requirement was 12 months' service; the second-most usual requirement was six months' service. Senior managers were usually exempt from the service requirements. [*See* <http://www.unifi networksurveys.com> discussed in Bill Leonard, *HR Update*, HR Magazine, August 2001, at p. 28]

Manchester, Inc., a Florida outplacement firm, found that even before the September 11 attack, middle managers received 15% less severance than those who were terminated in 1997, and senior executives got 12% less severance pay. For 2001, the average maximum severance pay available to middle managers was 28 weeks (down from 33 weeks in 1997, and a full year's pay in 1992). Senior executives averaged 37 weeks' pay in 2001, 42 weeks in 1997, and two years for 1992). In both 2000 and 2001, the median time for a terminated middle manager to find a new job was 13 weeks, but the median was 16 weeks for persons over 40, and 22 weeks for those earning over $100,000. About three-quarters of the firms surveyed allowed terminated executives to keep the full amount of severance even if they found a new job quickly. [Kelly Gates, *Severance Pay Declines Amid Still-Healthy Market* <http://www.careerjournal.com/salaries/industries/seniorexec/20010808-gates.html> (posted to www.careerjournal.com on August 2001); Kris Frieswick, *Softer Landings: Severance Packages are Growing More Generous as Companies*

Position Themselves for a Recovery, CFO.com, (October 16, 2001); Watson Wyatt Insider, *Workforce Reductions: Strategies in Today's Market*, <http://www.watson wyatt.com/us/pubs/insider/showarticle.asp?ArticleID=8982&Component= The+Insider>]

The Bureau of Labor Statistics also detected a decline in severance benefits. In 1999, 31% of employees in companies with 100 or more employees were potentially eligible for severance pay—down from 50% in 1988, 41% in 1991, 42% in 1993, and 36% in 1997. Like many other benefits, this was far more common in large than in small firms: in 1999, only 13% of workers in companies with 100 or fewer employees had access to severance pay. [Carlos Tejada, *Work Week*, Wall Street Journal, Jan. 8, 2002, at p. A1]

It can be good business to use severance packages to reduce the impact of layoffs, because when the economy recovers, your company may need to recruit. There is also a trend toward emphasizing noncash benefits, such as continuing health insurance outside of COBRA.

Tip: It may also be necessary to offer a lump-sum bonus for employees who stay on until a project or division is wound up in an orderly fashion instead of leaving as soon as they know their job is endangered.

Corporate Counsel magazine suggests some tactics for handling layoffs properly:

- Apply criteria for selecting employees to be laid off consistently—don't use the layoff as a method of getting rid of trouble-makers;
- Be sympathetic and sensitive to terminated employees;
- Communicate as much about the company's plans as possible, as soon as possible;
- Provide as much notice as you can;
- Use early retirement programs and other incentives to get voluntary resignations, thus limiting the number of layoffs you have to make;
- Get releases from everyone who gets severance pay;
- Consider offering tuition assistance so terminated employees can be retrained;
- Work with a reputable outplacement firm;
- Inform your ex-employees if you have new job openings;
- Make a policy of encouraging re-employment wherever appropriate;
- Forward voicemail and e-mail to ex-employees for at least a month after termination.

[*Do the Right Thing*, Corporate Counsel, Nov. 21, 2001 (law.com)]

Tip: If the employees being outplaced are over 40, make sure that their severance agreement conforms to the Older Workers Benefit Protection Act. [*See* Darryl Van Duch, *EEOC Takes a Close Look at No-Sue Severance Agreements*, Corporate Counsel, May 22, 2001 (law.com)]

[B] Severance Arrangements as ERISA "Plans"

ERISA is not involved in an employer's one-time decision to grant or enhance severance benefits. Nor is there an ERISA component to an employer's payroll practices or payments of extra money for active workers' overtime or holiday work. However, ERISA does come into play if severance payments are made in connection with a "plan," and even an unwritten or informal arrangement might constitute a plan.

Once the severance payment comes within the ambit of ERISA, the degree and nature of regulation depend on whether the plan is characterized as a pension plan or a welfare benefit plan. The arrangement will not be a pension plan (and therefore will not be subject to the stringent rules imposed on pension plans) if:

- Payments are not contingent on the recipient's retirement—i.e., the recipient can retain the payments even if he or she gets another job;
- The total payments do not exceed twice the recipient's compensation for the year just before the termination;
- The payments are completed within 24 months of the termination. If the termination is part of a "limited program of terminations" then payments can be completed within 24 months of the time the recipient reaches normal retirement age, if that is later.

[*See* DOL Reg. § 2510.3-2(b) and 29 C.F.R. § 2510.3-1(a)]

In *Welles v. Brach & Brock Confections Inc.* [2001 U.S. App. LEXIS 16205 (7th Cir. 2001)] the plaintiff was hired under a letter that summarized salary and benefits. The letter specified 12 months' severance pay on termination, but also said that benefits could be modified at any time. About a year after he was hired, the plan was amended to reduce severance to 32 weeks. The employee was notified of the reduction, and terminated eight days later. The plaintiff sued for the full 52 weeks' severance. The case was dismissed. His claim under state law was preempted by ERISA because the claim related to a severance plan. The Seventh Circuit did not accept his argument that the letter created a separate ERISA plan.

A voluntary termination program that offered a one-time lump sum at severance, based either on compensation or years of service, was offered during a "window" period that could be extended at the discretion of the employer. The plaintiffs in *Rodowicz v. Mass. Mutual Life Ins. Co.* [1999 WL 701724 (1st Cir. 1999)] alleged that they were told the benefit program would not change. In fact, after they retired, a better package was offered.

The First Circuit ruled that the severance arrangement was not an ERISA plan: there was only a single lump sum requiring limited administration, not an ongoing arrangement. Because there was no ERISA plan, the case was governed by state laws about estoppel and misrepresentation. Under Massachusetts law, the test was not whether the revised plan was under "serious consideration," but whether it was more likely than not that a reasonable employee would have relied on the misrepresentation and retired on that basis.

A Chief Financial Officer's contract called for monthly payments of $75,000 a year for ten years, starting 60 days after his retirement or termination of employment. The employer also promised to pay the premiums on life insurance payable to the beneficiaries selected by the CFO, and the CFO entered into a covenant not to compete. After the CFO's retirement, the company alleged that he violated the covenant not to compete, and refused to make the payments. When he sued in federal court, the employer's argument was that there was no "plan" and therefore no jurisdiction.

The Western District of Pennsylvania held that the existence of a plan depends on reasonably ascertainable terms for benefits, a stable source of financing, an ongoing administrative scheme, and a determination of who receives benefits and how. [*Nelson v. Jones & Brown Inc.*, Civ. No. 01-481 (W.D. Pa. 2001)] The court refused to grant the employer's motion to dismiss, because there were clearly terms for payment of funds. The court also opined that monitoring compliance with the noncompete provisions suggested ongoing administration.

The employer in *Crews v. General American Life Ins. Co.* [2001 U.S. App. LEXIS 26776 (8th Cir. Dec. 17, 2001)] had an ERISA severance plan, under which terminated employees could get a week of severance pay for each year of service. The award was at the employer's discretion. The company lost a major contract and allegedly promised employees who stayed until a certain date eight weeks of severance plus one week per year of service—but without reference to the ERISA plan. A group of employees sued in state court, claiming that they did not receive the promised stay-on bonus. The employer removed the case to federal court. The federal District Court dismissed the state claims for breach of contract and misrepresentation on the grounds that they were preempted by ERISA.

However, the Eighth Circuit held that the claims were not preempted, and remanded the case to state court. In this analysis, the promise of the stay-on bonus was separate from the original ERISA severance plan. The stay-on bonus was not discretionary, so preemption arguments involving the ERISA plan were not applicable. The stay-on bonus was a single lump-sum payment, with no ongoing obligations, and determining benefit eligibility was simple and mechanical—so it was really a matter for state contract law, not ERISA, to determine.[*See also* Nixon Peabody LLP Benefits Briefs (January 2002), <http://www.nixonpeabody.com/publications_new_fulltext.asp?ID=1389&BACK=publications_new.asp%3FCategory%3DPublications>, for a discussion of this case.]

In *Hamilton Sundstrand Corp. v. Healey* [2001 U.S. Dist. LEXIS 16415 (N.D. Ill. Oct. 12, 2001)] terminated employees complained to the state Department of Labor that their former employer had not made the severance payment promised when they were terminated as a result of the employer's outsourcing certain functions. The employees were hired by the outsourcing firm so, although nominally their employer changed, they did not have a period of unemployment. The employer didn't make the severance payments because, before the terminations, the plan documents had been amended to eliminate severance pay when outsourcing occurred. The employer was able to get a federal declaratory judgment that the employees' claims were preempted by ERISA, leaving the state DOL no jurisdiction to investigate. The District Court accepted the argument that the severance plan was an ERISA plan because it involved ongoing administration.

In another case involving a change of control, the plaintiff left his job when his employer company was acquired. He sued for severance benefits under the company's plan, which covered employees suffering a loss of employment within a year after a change in control. He said he was entitled to benefits even though he quit, because the plan covered resignations due to cuts in authority, duties, responsibilities, or status. The court agreed with him on this point, but disagreed with his contention that the plan was not subject to ERISA (because the plan involved discretion as to coverage plus ongoing administration). So he received severance benefits, but not a supplemental bonus. He was also entitled to an award of attorneys' fees, because the terms of the plan called for fee awards to eligible employees seeking to enforce benefits under the plan. [*Bowles v. Quantum Chem. Co.*, 266 F.3d 622 (7th Cir. 2001)]

[C]   Case Law on Other Severance Pay Issues

Yochum v. Barnett Banks [234 F.3d 541 (11th Cir. 2000)] involves an employee who worked for a bank that was sold to NationsBank. The first employer's severance plan denied severance benefits to anyone who rejected a written offer of comparable employment. The plaintiff was offered a job that would result in forfeiture of his stock options, and would reduce the duration of his salary guarantee from two years to one year. He did not accept the job; he went to work for a competitor. Based on his rejection of a "comparable" job, the plan's administrative committee denied severance benefits. The Eleventh Circuit did not require de novo review (because the plan had reserved discretion). But, because the committee had a conflict of interest and made its decision based on "false and incomplete" information, a heightened arbitrary and capricious standard of review was applied. The committee failed to examine the employment contract, and did not realize that the salary guarantee had been reduced. [*See Denial of Severance Benefits Was Reversed*, <http://www.ebia.com/weekly/articles/2000/ERISA001207Yochum.html>]

Section 7001 of the IRS Restructuring and Reform Act of 1998 [Pub. L. No. 105-206] provides that, when deciding whether money constitutes "deferred compensation" under I.R.C. § 404(a), the money is not considered to be paid or received until it is actually received by the employee. Although the statute has its greatest applicability in the context of nonqualified deferred compensation plans for executives, the statute was passed to overturn *Schmidt Baking Co.* [107 T.C. 271 (1996)], a case involving a company's accrued liabilities for severance and vacation pay.

According to the Eighth Circuit, a settlement award to a laid-off employee, reflecting his age, years of service, and earnings impairment, constitute "wages" for income and FICA tax purposes. [*Mayberry v. U.S.*, 151 F.3d 855 (8th Cir. 1998)] The court did not accept the employee's contention that the money was a nontaxable personal injury award. The funds replaced wages and did not come from settling tort claims, so they should be taxed as wages.

In *Bock v. Computer Associates International* [257 F.3d 700 (7th Cir. 2001)], the plaintiff was covered by a severance pay program that provided severance pay equal to the "bonus amount" plus twice the highest base salary plus 12 months' worth of "incentive compensation." The plaintiff was terminated and received severance of twice his base salary. (He was a sales executive who received large commissions but did not get an annual bonus.)

The suit arose because he said his $675,000 in commission income should have been included in the calculation. The question is whether commissions or only annual bonuses are considered "incentive compensation." The Seventh Circuit remanded the case to see whether the plaintiff knew or had reason to know how the employer defined "incentive compensation." If he knew that commissions were not counted, the ex-employer might be able to avoid using them in calculating his severance. Otherwise, the plain meaning of the term "incentive" does include commissions. The plaintiff couldn't raise an estoppel argument, because he didn't rely on the employer's representations to his detriment.

The firm of Thomas & Betts bought a New Jersey company, then announced relocation of core functions to Memphis. The company's president announced that engineers who refused the reassignment to Memphis had voluntarily resigned and therefore were not entitled to severance pay. The engineers sued, and won at the District Court level. However, the Third Circuit viewed the characterization of engineers as essential to the relocated company as a valid business decision. Therefore, it was legitimate to deny severance benefits. [*Noorily v. Thomas & Betts Corp.*, 188 F.3d 153 (3d Cir. 1999)]

Abramowicz v. Rohm and Haas Co. [2001 U.S. Dist. LEXIS 17693 (E.D. Pa. Oct. 30, 2001)] is yet another change-of-control case. Rohm and Haas made a job offer to the plaintiff to induce him to go to work for a joint venture in which Rohm and Haas was participating. The plaintiff took the job. When ownership of the joint venture changed, he refused to work for either the original employer or the new owner of the joint venture.

His job offer said that he would be entitled to severance if the joint venture discontinued operations within two years and the employee could not return to his present position. However, the severance plan was amended in the interim, eliminating his entitlement. The court applied *Sprague v. General Motors* [133 F.3d 388 (6th Cir. 1998)], which says that in the absence of fraud, an informal, nonplan document cannot amend a plan. Therefore, the job offer did not amend the severance plan, and the plaintiff was not entitled to severance benefits.

The case of *Kosakow v. New Rochelle Radiology Associates* [274 F.3d 706 (2d Cir. 2001)] has been before the courts many times, especially in connection with Family and Medical Leave issues. The Second Circuit December 2001 decision interprets the policy manual language (that terminated employees will "receive appropriate severance where applicable") to mean that the plan administrator did not have discretion. Therefore, the court had to review the case de novo. It determined that severance pay was applicable except in two situations, and because the plaintiff was not in these categories, she was entitled to severance pay.

[D] Parachute Payments

A specialized form of severance, the "parachute" payment comes into play in the course of a hostile takeover or takeover attempt. The best-known form is the "golden parachute" for executives—the counterpart of the "golden handcuff" compensation packages that are supposed to keep top managers from leaving companies that depend on their services. A golden parachute arrangement is supposed to deter unwanted takeover attempts, because so much cash severance (and other benefits, such as stock, enhanced pension benefits, and insurance) is owed to the top managers that the acquisition becomes even more expensive—perhaps prohibitively so. A few states mandate the payment of "tin parachutes" to rank-and-file employees when they lose their jobs during a corporate transition.

A "single-trigger" golden parachute agreement gives the executive the right to additional compensation whenever the employer company merges or is acquired. A "double-trigger" agreement doesn't become effective until there has not only been a corporate transition, but the executive has been demoted or terminated and therefore has a real economic injury.

Internal Revenue Code §§ 280G(b) and 4999 impose a 20% excise tax on excess parachute payments—and, furthermore, the payor corporation cannot deduct whatever portion of the payment is not reasonable and therefore does not constitute an ordinary and necessary business expense. (Payments from a qualified pension plan are not considered parachute payments, so they do not affect the excess calculation.)

An excess parachute payment is an amount that:

- Is not reasonable compensation for work done either before the change in ownership and control, or is scheduled to be done after the change; and
- Exceeds three times the "base amount."

A parachute payment is a payment contingent on change in the corporation's ownership or control, or the ownership or control of a significant portion of the corporation's assets. If the executive and corporation entered into a compensation agreement within the year before a change in ownership or control, the payments are presumed to be parachute payments unless there is clear and convincing evidence of a different motivation for the payments.

The base amount is the executive's average annual compensation for the five years just before the change in ownership or control. Bonuses, fringe benefits, pensions, and severance pay as well as cash compensation are used in the calculation.

PART II

PENSION LAW

CHAPTER 4

BASIC PENSION CONCEPTS

§ 4.01   INTRODUCTION

This chapter provides a summary and overview of the major ERISA and tax issues that help shape plan design. Many of these subjects are taken up in greater detail in the other chapters in this Part of the volume.

The conventional wisdom is that, although saving for retirement is a good thing, few people would have the resources or the wisdom or self-discipline to save enough on their own to provide for comfortable retirement. Therefore, the federal government collects FICA (Social Security) taxes from employers and employees, and dispenses Social Security benefits to retired and disabled workers and their families. In the private sector, employers make part of the employee's compensation available immediately in cash.

The employee's total compensation package also includes benefits such as health insurance and fringe benefits, plus deferred compensation that will eventually provide a lump sum or income at the time of the employee's normal, disability, or early or late retirement.

The subject of pensions and benefits is an important one. Because of the high risk of improprieties or mistakes in handling the funds that the employees rely on for future security, pension plans are administered by fiduciaries. A fiduciary is an individual or institution that takes care of the property of others, and therefore must be held to the highest standards of ethics and prudence. [See Chapter 15 for further discussion of the obligations of plan fiduciaries, and penalties that can be imposed for misconduct or failure]

In 1974, Congress, concerned about potential abuses of pension plans, passed the Employee Retirement Income Security Act (ERISA). ERISA provides very detailed rules for how pension plans must be administered; how they must accumulate funds for later benefit payments; who qualifies for various kinds of benefits; how those benefits are to be distributed; and how the plan must keep records and communicate with its participants and beneficiaries. ERISA governs not only how ongoing plans operate, but how they can be created and how they can change form by merging with other plans or undergoing termination.

Furthermore, ERISA establishes pensions and benefits as an entirely and inherently federal area of jurisdiction. States are forbidden to legislate in this area, so the question of whether "ERISA preemption" has occurred is an important one.

The bulk of ERISA deals with pension plans, although the statute has less extensive provisions dealing with other types of plan, including profit-sharing plans, stock bonus plans, and welfare benefit plans such as health plans, vacation plans, and cafeteria plans.

The legal definition of a pension plan describes it as a plan established and maintained primarily to pay definitely determinable benefits to participants—usually monthly for the rest of the retiree's life, although lump sum payouts and annuities for a term of years are also permissible. Unlike profit-sharing plans, pension plans normally make distributions only on the basis of retirement, death, disability, or term of employment; hardship distributions are usually not available.

The management of a pension plan is complex, time-consuming, and expensive. On one level, employers have an incentive to do this because it makes it easier to recruit and retain quality employees in a competitive market. On another level, employers are motivated to maintain a plan that satisfies Internal Revenue Code requirements because the employer will be entitled to get a tax deduction for its contributions to, and administrative costs of running, a plan that satisfies the Code's numerous requirements for "qualified" plans.

As a general rule, the employer's tax deduction is taken on a cash basis—for the year in which money was contributed to a qualified plan. Employers that maintain nonqualified plans instead of, or in addition to, qualified plans do not get a deduction until the employee receives benefits from the nonqualified plan and includes them in income.

One of the most important criteria for plan qualification is that the plan must not discriminate in favor of highly compensated employees (HCEs). For 2001, HCEs are those who earn $85,000 a year or more; for 2002, the HCE figure is $90,000 or more. Yet many companies identify a need for additional benefits to stay competitive in the executive recruiting stakes. It is legal to maintain nonqualified plans limited to, or offering superior benefits for, HCEs [*see* Chapter 8 for more discussion], but the expenses associated with these plans will not be federally tax deductible.

Tip: Pension law was dramatically affected by the 2001 tax bill, the Economic Growth and Tax Relief Reconciliation Act (EGTRRA) [P.L. No. 107-16], and less dramatically so by the 2002 economic stimulus package, the Job Creation and Worker Assistance Act of 2002 (JCWAA) [P.L. No. 107-147], so make sure that before you take any action with regard to a qualified plan, you have complied with EGTRRA and JCWAA.

---

§ 4.02   EXTENT OF COVERAGE

In a September 2001 report to Congress, the GAO stated that tax preferences for qualified pensions plans (in both public and private sectors) cost the federal Treasury $85 billion a year—more than the revenue losses on account of health benefits or home mortgages.

According to the 1998 Survey of Consumer Finances (a study sponsored by the Federal Reserve System every three years), 47% of all full- and part-time workers participated in a pension plan. About one-third (36%) of all workers participated in a defined contribution plan. Over half (57%) of all participants earned $40,000 a year or less, so it can be argued that pensions do a lot to provide retirement security for low- and moderate-income employees.

As a counter-argument, however, participation was much higher (70%) for people earning between $40,000 and $75,000 a year than for those earning less than $40,000 (38%). [*Private Pensions: Issues of Coverage and Increasing Contribution Limits for Defined Contribution Plans*, GAO-01-846 (September 2001).

See also Private Pensions: Improving Worker Coverage and Benefit, GAO-02-225 (April 2002)]

The Economic Policy Institute, a think tank in Washington, says that three-quarters of the workers in the top fifth of the income distribution have pensions, but this is true of only 17% of those in the lowest-paid fifth. [David Wessel, *Enron and a Bigger Ill: Americans Don't Save,* Wall Street Journal, March 1, 2002, at p. A1] The highest-paid workers also get larger Social Security benefits, and are much more likely to have private savings, than those who earn the least.

According to the GAO, increases in the statutory level of employer contributions, like those enacted by EGTRRA, are likely to benefit about 8% of defined contribution plan participants—about 3.1 million people. The GAO's estimate was that about 11% of those eligible to make catch-up contributions would do so—about 721,000 participants in defined contribution plans would therefore benefit from this statutory change.

Tip: Hewitt Associates found that 80% of employers would allow catch-up contributions, and a further 16% were considering permitting catch-up contributions. Only 10% immediately decided to match the catch-up contributions; 14% were considering doing that. Two-thirds of survey respondents planned to increase contribution limits in their 401(k) plans because of EGTRRA's increase in the defined contribution annual limit. [*Employer Reaction to EGTRRA Legislation 2001 Survey Findings,* <http://was.hewitt.com/hewitt/resource/rptspubs/subrptspubs/er_egtrra.htm> (no www)]

Department of Labor figures for 1999 show that 48% of employees in private industry were covered by pension plans: 21% by defined benefit plans, 36% by defined contribution plans—9% had both types of plans. Over half (56%) of full-time employees had retirement benefits, versus only 21% of part-timers. The percentage of companies offering retirement plans increased greatly with the size of the firm. [*Employee Benefits in Private Industry,* USDL 01-473, <http://www.bls.gov/news.release/ebs2.nr0.htm>]

According to the William H. Mercer firm, companies with traditional defined benefit plans tend to offer better defined contribution plans (including 401(k) plans) than companies that have only defined contribution plans. In this context, "better" refers to more liberal eligibility requirements and faster vesting. For example, 45% of companies that offer both defined benefit and defined contribution plans offer immediate vesting as soon as employees are eligible for employer matching contributions, as compared with 27% of organizations with defined contribution plans only. [Dow Jones Newswires, *Companies With Defined-Benefit Pensions Offer Better 401(k) Plans, Study Finds,* (Oct. 22, 2001) <http://www.cfo.com/Article?article=5494>]

In 1998, there were approximately $9.4 trillion of assets in all types of retirement plans:

- Defined contribution plans: $2.2 trillion (23% of all plan assets);
- IRAs: $2.0 trillion (21%);
- Private trusteed defined benefit plans: $2.0 trillion (21%);
- State and local government plans: $1.7 trillion (18%);
- Private life insurance: $0.9 trillion (9%);
- Federal government plans: $0.7 trillion (7%).

[Carolyn Hirschman, *The Taxman Giveth*, HR Magazine, October 2001 at p. 70; the figures add up to less than 100% because of rounding.]

§ 4.03   EFFECT OF DEMOGRAPHICS ON PLANS

The Baby Boom, people born after World War II, are the largest age cohort in U.S. history. The oldest boomers are already 55 years old—and perhaps eligible for early retirement. [Segal Special Report, *The Aging of Aquarius: The Baby Boom Generation Matures* (February 2001) <http://www.segalco.com/publications/segalspecialreports/feb01aquarius.pdf>. *See also Census 2000: Geographic Breakdowns of Demographic Data*, (December 2001) <http://www.segalco.com/publications/indepths/dec01census.pdf>] The next generation, sometimes called Generation X, is much smaller.

That means that soon, employers will not only face the challenge of paying pensions to a very large group of retirees—they will have a smaller group of active workers to generate corporate income and profits. Furthermore, retirees may take priceless and irreplaceable skills and work ethics with them when they leave the workforce.

The population is aging. In 2001, senior citizens made up 12.4% of the population. The fastest-growing demographic group was the "oldest old": people over 85. Senior citizens consume more health services than younger people, so retiree health benefits [*see* Chapter 9] and the Medicare system will be severely strained.

It may be necessary to amend ERISA and the Internal Revenue Code to facilitate phased retirement; many companies may find it desirable to keep older employees on the payroll at least part-time, while making limited pension payments to them.

In February 2001, 54.8% of workers aged 21–64 worked for a company that had a pension plan—somewhat higher than the 51% figure for February 1995. At that time, pensions provided 19.1% of the total income of the elderly population. (The rest came from Social Security benefits—41.3%; earned income 19.7%; and income from investments 17.8%.) [*EBRI Notes Executive Summary* (December 2001) <http://www.ebri.org/notesx/1201note.htm>]

§ 4.04   INVESTMENT FACTORS

For many years, the strong investment climate allowed plans to reduce or even suspend their contributions to defined benefit plans, because the plans were ample to satisfy the obligation to make future payments.

Then, in 2000 and 2001, plans suffered multiple blows. The collapse of the dot-com bubble gravely damaged the stock market. The September 11 attack and the Enron scandal subjected the market—and therefore plan investments—to additional stresses.

According to consulting firm Towers, Perrin, for instance, a typical 60% equity-40% fixed income plan investment portfolio showed a decline of 3.9% in the period 2000–2001. The only other two-year period of decline in the past three decades was 1973–1974. Furthermore, plans were battered further by declining interest rates (suppressing returns on the fixed income portion of the portfolio). [The Benchmark Companies, *The Shape of Things to Come* (December 2001) <http://www.benchmarkalert.com/library/alerts/1201.html>; IFEBP Business Wire, *Unique Combination of Capital Market Conditions and Events in 2000 and 2001 Has Major Impact on Pension Plans*, (Feb. 19, 2002) <http://www.ifebp.org/2002/02/19/bw/0000-0732-ny-towers-perrin.asp> (posted to www.ifebp.com on February 2002)]

§ 4.05   DEFINED BENEFIT/DEFINED CONTRIBUTION

The traditional kind of pension plan, the one usually in effect when ERISA was passed, is the defined benefit plan. In a plan of this type, the employer agrees to provide benefits according to a formula. A typical formula would set the pension level as x% times the number of years the employee worked before retirement times the employee's average pay for his or her last five years working for the employer—or perhaps the average of the three years in which he or she earned the most.

The employer's contributions for all employees go into a single account or trust for the entire plan. However, there must be a separate account balance for each participant who makes voluntary contributions. [I.R.C. § 411(b)(2)(A)]

In some ways, this arrangement is problematic both from the employer's and the employee's point of view. When employees retire, they receive a fixed pension that will probably not be inflation-indexed and will not offer cost of living adjustments. In a highly inflationary environment, they will find that their pension buys less and less over time. Nor will their pension increase if the investment climate is favorable.

From the employer's point of view, defined benefit plans carry heavy burdens, including uncertainty. The employer's commitment is to contribute enough to the plan each year to ensure that the participants will receive the promised level of benefits. Not only does this require elaborate (and expensive) actuarial calculations, it places the investment risk on the employer, who will have to make larger contributions in years in which the value of the plan's securities portfolio declines.

Tip: The qualified plan rules do not allow the employer to have discretion over the actuarial assumptions used by a defined benefit plan.

Defined benefit plans are required to maintain liquid assets of at least three times the amount paid out in the previous 12 months. Failure to maintain this amount is called "liquidity shortfall," and plans in this category are required to make quarterly payments to increase the assets and eliminate the shortfall. There is a 10% excise tax for failure to make the payment—and a 100% excise tax if the shortfall continues for five consecutive quarters. However, for plan years in and after 1994, the IRS can waive part or all of the excise tax if the employer had reasonable cause for the shortfall, there was no willful neglect, and the employer is taking reasonable measures to eliminate the shortfall. [I.R.C. § 4971(f)(4)]

Defined benefit plans are also subject to full funding limitations. [*See* § 5.05[E]]

A defined contribution plan is a different, and much simpler, structure. The employer establishes a separate account for each employee who has satisfied the criteria for plan participation. If the plan requires or accepts employee contributions, there will usually be separate subaccounts for employer and employee contributions, but this is not a legal requirement.

The employer's commitment is to contribute the amount required by the plan formula—generally a simple percentage of compensation. ERISA § 404(c) permits the plan to give control over the assets to the participant. If this is done, the plan's fiduciaries will not be liable for losses that result from the control exercised by the participants.

There is no limit on the number of plans a particular employer can maintain, and it is not uncommon for an employer to maintain both defined benefit and defined contribution plans. Under prior law, § 415(e) imposed a limit on benefits from a combination of defined benefit and defined contribution plans, but that limitation was repealed for limitation years beginning on or after January 1, 2000. [*See* IRS Notice 99-44, 1999-35 IRB 326 for implications of repeal]

ERISA § 404(c) requires the plan to give participants adequate information about the investment options they have for their accounts. The plan must offer at least three diversified investment types, with materially different characteristics with respect to risk and return.

In a sense, the Social Security system is a kind of pension plan. Both employers and employees pay FICA taxes to fund retirement benefits. Although all earned income is subject to Medicare taxes, the FICA tax phases out at a figure that changes every year. (For 2002, only the first $89,400 of earned income is subject to FICA tax.) The employer makes FICA contributions on all or nearly all of rank-and-file workers' pay, but only on a smaller proportion of the compensation of top earners.

The Internal Revenue Code contains "permitted disparity" rules for "integrating" a qualified plan with Social Security (disparities are not permitted in 401(k) plans). Within limits, the employer can reduce its plan contributions on behalf of rank-and-file employees to compensate for the employer's FICA contributions. As long as the permitted disparity rules are satisfied, the plan will remain qualified, and will not be considered discriminatory—even though the practical effect is to cut down on contributions and lower the pension the rank-and-file employees will eventually receive.

§ 4.06 OTHER TYPES OF PLAN

[A] Money Purchase Plan

A money purchase plan provides definitely determinable benefits, funded by fixed employer contributions made in accordance with a single allocation formula for all participants. Money purchase plans are subject to the I.R.C. § 412 minimum funding standard. The plan must offer QJSAs and QPSAs. [*See* §§ 12.05, 12.06] Money purchase plans can accept employee contributions and make plan loans to participants.

[B] Profit-Sharing Plan

A profit-sharing plan must have a definite formula, set in advance, for allocating the employer's total contribution among the various plan participants, and for distributing the account money to participants. Distributions can be made after the funds have been in the account for a certain length of time (ERISA requires this to be at least two years), attainment of a stated age (which does not have to be retirement age) or an event such as retirement, termination, illness, or disability. Profit-sharing plans have to have formulas for allocating and distributing employer contributions, but the corporation's Board of Directors can legitimately be given discretion to set the level of contributions each year. Since 1986, it has not been necessary for the contributions to be made from corporate profits, or only in a year in which there are profits. The maximum contribution that the employer can deduct is 15% of the participant's contribution for the year. Profit-sharing plans are allowed to make plan loans.

[C] Target-Benefit Plan

A target-benefit plan is a money purchase plan (and therefore subject to the defined contribution rules), but contributions are calculated to fund a specified level of retirement benefits at normal retirement age. The participant receives the aggregate of all contributions plus their earnings, although the actual benefit may be either higher or lower than the target, depending on investment results.

[D] Floor-Offset Plan

A floor-offset plan is a hybrid plan, where the defined benefit portion of the plan guarantees a minimum level of benefits, offset by the annuity the retiree could purchase at retirement with the balance in the defined contribution portion of the plan. *Lunn v. Montgomery Ward & Co. Retirement Security Plan* [166 F.3d 880 (7th Cir. 1999)] holds that an employee who retired four years after normal retirement age was not entitled to additional retirement benefits to make up for the reduced duration of benefits. The court upheld the idea of floor-offset plans, finding that this type of plan does not violate ERISA benefit accrual requirements or antiforfeiture provisions.

[E]   New Comparability Plan

A new comparability plan is a special type of defined contribution plan (or combination of defined contribution and defined benefit plan) that can increase the allocation for HCEs without violating the antidiscrimination rules.

[F]   SEP

A SEP (Simplified Employer Pension) is an IRA sponsored by the employer, under a written plan whose contribution formula does not discriminate in favor of HCEs.

[G]   SIMPLE

A Savings Incentive Match Plan for Employees (SIMPLE) plan, available only to companies with 100 or fewer employees, involves employer contributions to employees' own IRAs.

§ 4.07   IRA/QUALIFIED PLAN INTERFACE

As the name suggests, an Individual Retirement Arrangement (IRA) is maintained by an individual on his or her own behalf, not by a corporation. However, the two types of plan interact when an IRA is used as a "conduit" for a transfer of funds between two qualified plans, or when distributions from a qualified plan are sheltered from immediate taxation by being rolled over to an IRA.

Employers can maintain a program under which employees authorize payroll deductions to be invested in either regular or Roth IRAs. Such arrangements do not constitute ERISA plans (and therefore do not subject the employer to regulation or potential supervision) if:

- The employer doesn't make any contributions;
- Employee participation in the arrangement is completely voluntary;
- The employer's sole involvement is letting employees participate (without endorsing participation), making the payroll deductions, and forwarding the amounts to the IRA sponsor.

The employer can collect reasonable reimbursement for its services in connection with the employees' IRAs, but no other compensation. The employer can provide educational materials about IRAs and the value of saving for retirement, but must make it clear that the employer's role is purely administrative and does not involve contributions to the plan. It's also permissible for the employer to distribute literature prepared by the IRA sponsor, and even to display its own logo on the materials.

Either the employer can choose a single IRA sponsor or inform employees of criteria for choosing a sponsor. However, it is not permitted for the employer to negotiate special terms for its own employees that are not available to everyone who buys IRAs through that sponsor. The employer should inform employees that there are other ways to fund IRAs; that IRAs are not a suitable investment for everybody; and that IRAs work the same way whether the employee authorizes a payroll deduction or submits the contribution directly to the IRA sponsor. [*See* IRS Announcement 99-2, 1999-2 IRB 44, 29 C.F.R. § 2510.3-2(d), and DOL Interpretive Bulletin 99-1, 66 FR 32999-33003 (June 18, 1999)]

EGTRRA increases the maximum amount that can be contributed to an IRA (especially by persons over 50) and institutes a tax credit for low-income IRA investors, so IRA options will be more attractive than ever before.

EGTRRA also creates another option, the "deemed IRA," for plan years beginning after December 31, 2002. A qualified plan can permit employees to contribute to a separate account within a qualified plan. If the separate account meets the criteria for being either a conventional or a Roth IRA, it is treated as an IRA and not a qualified plan—and the employer's qualified plan won't lose its qualified status just because of the IRA subaccounts. The difference between a deemed IRA and the payroll deduction plan described above is that the employer, not the employee, sets up the account, although deemed IRAs can take payroll deductions.

§ 4.08   INCIDENTAL BENEFITS

A qualified plan is permitted to offer incidental benefits such as disability, Social Security supplements for early retirees, lump-sum death benefits, incidental death benefits, or 401(h) retiree health benefits. Life insurance can be provided as an incidental benefit as long as the death benefit does not exceed 100 times the estimated monthly retirement benefit under the qualified plan it supplements. However, offering other benefits, such as other medical benefits or layoff benefits, is forbidden, and can lead to loss of plan qualification.

§ 4.09   STRUCTURE OF ERISA

ERISA is not an easy statute to understand. A vast variety of plan provisions can legally be embodied in qualified plans, and many of these provisions depend on complex mathematical formulas. Furthermore, ERISA is both a labor law and a comprehensive and difficult piece of tax legislation.

Title I of ERISA, also referred to as the labor title, covers issues such as plan structure, fiduciary conduct, and prohibited transactions. Title II is the tax title, covering the requirements for plan qualification and tax deductions. The Title II provisions are duplicated in the Internal Revenue Code. There is some overlap between the two titles. For instance, prohibited transactions are defined in Title I, but the excise tax penalty is imposed under Title II.

Many of the provisions that are most significant for plan administration are found in Title I, Subtitle B. This subtitle is divided into six parts:

- Part 1: Reporting and disclosure;
- Part 2: Participation and vesting standards;
- Part 3: Funding standards;
- Part 4: Fiduciary responsibility;
- Part 5: Administration and enforcement;
- Part 6: Continuation coverage for health insurance.

Although there are some exceptions, the safest way to operate is just to assume that all benefit plans will be subject to at least some ERISA requirements. For example, a welfare plan (one that provides nonpension benefits such as health insurance or severance pay) is subject to most of the rules on reporting and disclosure, and the fiduciary, administration, and enforcement rules of Parts 4 and 5, but does not have to satisfy the participation, vesting, or funding standards.

§ 4.10   REQUIRED PROVISIONS FOR ALL QUALIFIED PLANS

Although within these confines a tremendous number of variations can be created, ERISA and the I.R.C. impose certain obligations on all qualified pension plans:

- The plan must be in writing [ERISA § 402(a)(1)];
- The employer must intend the plan to be permanent (although mergers and terminations are permitted under appropriate circumstances) [Reg. § 1.401-1(b)(2). Annuity, profit-sharing, and stock bonus plans are also subject to this requirement];
- The plan must provide a procedure for amendments and must indicate who has the authority to amend the plan [ERISA § 402(a)(1)];
- Plan funds must be managed through use of a trust [ERISA § 403(a), I.R.C. § 401(a)], unless they are held in a custodial account that is invested and managed by someone other than the account custodian. Defined contribution plans can allow participants to direct the investment of the assets allocated to their accounts, but the participants cannot actually hold the assets [Rev. Rul. 89-52, 1989-1 CB 110];
- The plan must be operated for the exclusive benefit of its participants and their beneficiaries. [I.R.C. § 401(a)(2)] If the employer attempts to violate this rule by obtaining reversions of plan assets, an excise tax will be imposed under I.R.C. § 4980 unless an exception to the general rule applies. Even on termination, defined contribution plans generally cannot return any assets to the employer. Independent contractors must not be allowed to participate, because they are not considered employees;
- The plan must have a published funding policy [ERISA § 402(b)(1)];
- Contributions made to the plan, or benefits received under the plan, are subject to the limitations of the I.R.C.;
- Benefits must not be decreased when Social Security benefits increase;

- Employees must be permitted to participate in the plan as soon as they satisfy the plan's minimum participation standards [I.R.C. §§ 401(a)(3), 410];
- The plan must satisfy minimum coverage requirements, and defined benefit plans must satisfy a minimum participation rule;
- Employee contributions and salary deferrals intended for 401(k) plans must be deposited into the plan as soon as possible, always within 90 days [DOL Reg. § 2510.3-102];
- The plan must not discriminate in favor of highly compensated employees (HCEs);
- The plan's vesting schedule must satisfy federal standards—and if the plan is top-heavy (concentrates its benefits on the highest-paid group) it must vest even faster than the basic rule [I.R.C. §§ 401(a)(7), 404(a)(2), 411(b)] EGTRRA, the 2001 tax law, also increased the speed with which employer matching contributions must vest;
- Benefits must be distributed only to participants and their beneficiaries (including "alternate payees" under Qualified Domestic Relations Orders). This is known as the "anti-alienation" rule. In particular, creditors cannot reach pension benefits before they have been distributed;
- Pension benefits must start within 60 days of the end of the plan year in which the individual reaches the plan's normal retirement age (NRA), reaches age 65, terminates service or has 10 years of service—whichever occurs last;
- The plan must furnish Summary Plan Descriptions (SPDs), Summaries of Material Modifications (SMMs) and other disclosure documents [*see* Chapter 11];
- The plan must designate at least one fiduciary who is responsible for management. Named fiduciaries are allowed to delegate certain plan responsibilities to other people, such as investment managers—but only if the plan specifically permits such delegation;
- The plan must have a procedure for making claims and appealing denials of applications. The claims procedure must be disclosed in the Summary Plan Description [*see* §§ 10.05, 11.02] but need not be included in the plan document itself;
- Defined benefit plans must pay premiums to the Pension Benefits Guaranty Corporation (PBGC);
- Transfers of assets between plans, and mergers and terminations of plans, are also regulated. [*See* I.R.C. § 411(d)(3)]

§ 4.11   NORMAL RETIREMENT AGE

Many ERISA and tax rules depend on the concept of drawing a pension at, before, or after the plan's Normal Retirement Age (NRA). The standard NRA remains 65, although perhaps this will change not only as life expectancies increase, but as the Social Security system phases in a higher age for receiving unreduced benefits. (The basic Social Security retirement age is gradually being increased from 65 to 67.)

However, a plan can set the NRA either higher or lower than 65. The plan can choose an NRA lower than 65 if this is customary for the company or for its industry—as long as this choice is not a device to accelerate funding. If the NRA is very low—below 55—I.R.C. § 415(b) requires that maximum pension payable under the plan be reduced, in light of the large number of payments that will be made. However, a profit-sharing plan is allowed to have an NRA lower than 55, even if this is below the industry average.

> **Tip:** If the plan does not specify an NRA, the NRA will be deemed to be the age at which accrued benefits no longer increase solely on account of age or service.

If the plan sets the NRA above 65, or if there is no definition in the plan, then each participant will have an individual NRA. It will be either his or her 65th birthday or the fifth anniversary of plan participation, whichever comes later.

§ 4.12 NORMAL RETIREMENT BENEFIT

The NRB, or Normal Retirement Benefit, is a related concept. It is either the benefit commencing at the NRA or the early retirement benefit (if the plan provides one)—whichever is greater. The early retirement benefit is not adjusted actuarially for this purpose, even though it will be paid for more years than if benefits had commenced at the NRA. Early retirement subsidies are not counted if they continue only until the retiree becomes eligible for Social Security, and if they do not exceed the Social Security benefit.

Not everyone retires on the anniversary of plan participation. If benefits depend on average compensation for, e.g., three or five years, then Treas. Reg. § 1.411(a)-7(c)(5) mandates treatment of the last partial year of service as a full year.

> **Tip:** If an employee retires and benefits begin and then the employee is rehired by the same employer, the benefit payments can be suspended until the employee retires once again. However, current tax law creates some difficulties for individuals who want a "phased retirement" (combining a reduced work schedule and reduced salary with at least some pension benefits) rather than an abrupt cessation of employment followed by total retirement.

§ 4.13 PARTICIPATION AND COVERAGE

Both defined benefit and defined contribution plans are subject to "minimum coverage" rules under I.R.C. § 410(b). Remember, one of the main motives in passing ERISA was to prevent plans from concentrating unduly on providing benefits to stockholders and managers. However, it can be difficult to satisfy the various tests in a small company [see § 4.14[A] for top-heavy plan rules] or in a company where there is a great disparity between managers' pay and rank-and-file pay, or where there is a stable group of HCEs but heavy turnover in rank-and-file employees.

To satisfy the minimum coverage rules, the plan must either cover a percentage of the rank and file that is at least 70% of the percentage of highly compensated employees covered by the plan; or the plan must cover a reasonable classification of employees that is not discriminatory. Furthermore, the contributions made on behalf of, or the benefits provided to, the rank-and-file must equal at least 70% of those made or provided to the highly compensated.

Defined benefit plans are subject to a minimum participation rule. On each day of the plan year, the plan must benefit either 40% of all the company's work force, or 50 people, whichever is less. However, plans that are not top-heavy and do not benefit any highly compensated employee or former employee are exempt from the minimum participation rule.

The I.R.C. does not require qualified plans to cover all employees from the time of hiring. It is permissible for a plan to require employees to be at least 21 years old and to have completed one year of service before being eligible for participation. Part-time employees must be covered if they can work 1,000 hours within a 12-month period. If plan benefits become 100% vested after only two years, a qualified plan (other than a 401(k) plan) can require two years of service for participation.

§ 4.14 VESTING

[A] Generally

Participation in a plan is only the first step toward eventually receiving a pension. Vesting is the process of the benefits becoming nonforfeitable. ERISA includes detailed vesting rules to prevent earlier abuses, under which plans were often drafted so that so many years of service were required to achieve a pension that many rank-and-file employees would end up forfeiting their pensions (with the forfeitures going to swell the accounts of highly compensated executives and stockholders).

The normal benefit must always be nonforfeitable at the normal retirement age. It is not required that employees immediately gain 100% ownership of their defined contribution accounts, or the amounts contributed on their behalf to a defined benefit plan. Vesting is the process of moving toward 100% ownership. The Code prescribes minimum funding schedules; employers are always permitted to give employees faster vesting.

There are only two basic vesting schedules allowed by I.R.C. § 411(a):

- Five-year cliff vesting: participants are not vested at all for the first five years of service, but then they are immediately 100% vested as to employer contributions;

- Three-to-seven graded vesting: no vesting at all for three years, but full vesting by seven years of service, increasing proportionately in years 4, 5, and 6.

Top-heavy plans must provide even faster vesting—three-year cliff or six-year graded—but plans with a lot of participants usually are not top-heavy.

For example, if a participant leaves employment at a time when he or she is 60% vested, then a participant in a defined contribution plan will be entitled to $60 of every $100 in his or her individual account. A participant in a defined benefit plan will be entitled to an annuity of $60/month for every $100/month that would have been payable if he or she had remained at work until becoming 100% vested.

EGTRRA, the 2001 tax legislation, provides even faster vesting for employer matching contributions (as distinct from the employer's own contributions). Vesting for matching contributions must be either three-year cliff vesting or graded vesting over two to six years (20% in the second year of service, 40% in the third year, etc.).

[B] Vesting on Termination

All qualified plans must provide that, if the plan is completely or partially terminated, all affected participants immediately become 100% vested. [I.R.C. § 411(d)(3)] For plans that are not subject to the minimum funding standard of I.R.C. § 412 (for instance, profit-sharing and stock bonus plans), 100% vesting must also occur when the employer completely ceases to make contributions to the plan. A profit-sharing or stock bonus plan is deemed terminated on the day when the plan administrator notifies the IRS of the cessation of contributions.

[C] Vesting and Service

For vesting purposes, a year of service is a period of 12 consecutive months during which the employee performs at least 1,000 hours of service. Plans are not required to provide fractional years of service credit—i.e., if someone works only 500 hours, the employer does not have to credit half a year of service.

> **Tip:** For the purposes of vesting or participation for accrual purposes, a year of service can be any period of 12 consecutive months that the employer designates. But a year of service for plan eligibility purposes must start on the first day of employment. A plan can have more than one vesting year. If the plan selects a single vesting year for convenience, it doesn't have to be the same as the plan year.

§ 4.15 BREAK-IN-SERVICE RULES

For some pension-related purposes, it makes a big difference whether the individual has been continuously employed by the employer sponsoring the plan, or whether employment has been interrupted: whether the person has been laid off and then recalled, for instance. Interruption of continuous employment is called a "break in service"—a concept that has many implications.

A one-year break in service has occurred when a person renders 501 or fewer hours of service for the employer in a particular year. If someone works more than 501 but less than 1000 hours for the employer in a given year the employer does not have to credit a year of service, but cannot penalize the employee for the break in service.

After someone has had a one-year break, the employer can disregard service before the break for vesting purposes until the employee has come back to work and completed a year of service. After there have been five consecutive one-year breaks in service, a defined contribution plan, or some insured defined benefit plans, can treat the vested benefits as forfeited, and allocate them to other participants.

If the participant was 0% vested before the break in service, the "Rule of Parity" requires the plan to add up the number of years of service before the break. If the number of consecutive one-year breaks is at least five, or is greater than or equal to the aggregate number of pre-break years of service (whichever is greater), the rule allows the pre-break years to be disregarded for vesting purposes, even if the participant is later rehired.

However, under the Retirement Equity Act of 1984 [P.L. No. 98-397], a break in service that is caused by parenting leave probably cannot be counted against the employee.

§ 4.16   PLAN LIMITS

One of the basic purposes of ERISA is to prevent plans from unduly favoring executives, managers, and other highly paid employees. One of the ways ERISA furthers this objective is by placing limits on the amount that can be contributed each year to a defined contribution plan, deferred in a 401(k) plan, or provided as a benefit under a defined benefit plan.

The underlying principle is that plan limits are adjusted annually. The adjustment reflects changes in the Consumer Price Index. Starting in 2003, the changes will be rounded down in $5,000 increments; until then, changes are adjusted in $10,000 increments.

Before 2000, I.R.C. § 415(e) imposed a combined limitation on the allocations to defined contribution plans plus accrued benefits from defined benefit plans. However, as of 2000, plans are permitted to—but not obligated to—impose a combined limitation with respect to employees who participate in both types of plans. Defined benefit plans are allowed to increase benefits (for retirees as well as active employees) to reflect repeal of the combined limitation.

These are the limits for the 2001 and 2002 tax years (the first figure is for 2001, the second for 2002), as provided by Notice 2000-66, 2000-52 I.R.B. 600 and by EGTRRA as set out in IRS News Release IR-2001-115:

- I.R.C. § 415(b)(1)(A) defined benefit plan annual benefit: $140,000/$160,000, reduced for benefits beginning before age 62, increased for benefits beginning after age 65. (*But see* the Job Creation and Worker Assistance Act of 2002 for a relief provision that spares employers from EGTRRA-related automatic increases in plan limits, if this is not what they want;)

- I.R.C. § 415(c)(1)(A) maximum contribution to a defined contribution plan: $35,000 (and 25% of compensation)/$40,000 (and 100% of compensation)—but the limit remains $35,000 for defined contribution plans whose non-calendar limitation year begins before January 1, 2002, and ends after December 31, 2001;
- I.R.C. § 414(q)(1)(B) definition of a highly compensated employee: $85,000 a year/$90,000 a year
- I.R.C. §§ 401(a)(17), 404(l) limit on annual compensation to be included in making calculations: $170,000/$200,000
- Maximum 401(k) deferral: $10,500/$11,000 for 2002, $12,000 for 2003, $13,000 for 2004, $14,000 for 2005, $15,000 for 2006, indexed for 2007-2010, plus catch-up contributions.

§ 4.17   EMPLOYEE CONTRIBUTIONS

Although 401(k) plans get their basic funding from employees' deferred salary (and may get matching contributions from the employer), pension plans work the other way around. They get their basic funding from the employer, but some plans require and other plans permit employees to make additional contributions to the plan. Internal Revenue Code § 411(c)(2) characterizes employee contributions as mandatory if making the contribution is a precondition of the employer match.

Employee contributions are also important in determining whether or not a plan discriminates in favor of highly compensated employees. I.R.C. § 414(g) contains the formula for testing whether the employer's aggregate contributions to the plan on behalf of HCEs are too high. If the plan fails to satisfy the requirements of this section, it will be disqualified, unless the excess contributions made on behalf of the HCEs, plus the earnings on the excess contributions, are returned to the company's employees by the end of the plan year after the year of the excess contribution. A 10% excise also applies to excess employee contributions (e.g., made by HCEs) that are not distributed within two and a half months of the end of the plan year.

Benefits attributable to employer contributions cannot be assigned or anticipated before they are received, except in the form of a QDRO. But employees can withdraw some or all of their voluntary contributions while continuing to be employed and to participate in the plan. Employees must always have the right to withdraw their own voluntary contributions to the plan at any time, without the accrued benefits attributable to employer contributions becoming forfeitable. [I.R.C. § 401(a)(19)] However, if the plan mandates employee contributions, I.R.C. § 411(a)(3)(D) allows the plan to provide that employer contributions will be forfeited if a participant withdraws any mandatory employee contributions at a time when he or she is less than 50% vested. If the benefits are repaid within five years after the withdrawal, or two years after the employee returns to participation under the plan (whichever comes first), the benefits must be restored.

Employees are always 100% vested in their own voluntary contributions to a pension plan. When an employer matches these voluntary contributions, EGTRRA requires vesting in the employer's matching contributions to occur either on a three-year cliff schedule, or a six-year graded schedule, beginning with 20% vesting in the second year of the employee's service.

The significant Supreme Court case of *Hughes Aircraft Co. v. Jacobson* [525 U.S. 432 (1999)] involved a defined benefit plan that mandated employee contributions (most defined benefit plans do not). A large part of the plan was attributable to employee contributions. The Hughes plan operated at a surplus. The employer suspended its contributions in light of the surplus. It also amended the plan to provide for early retirement benefits and to add a new benefit structure for new participants. Under the new structure, employee contributions were no longer required, because the plan was funded by the surplus from the older plan.

The Supreme Court did not accept the contention of the employee plaintiffs that the employer had an obligation to share the plan surplus with the employees who contributed to it, rather than using the surplus to reduce the employer's future obligations. In the Supreme Court's view, in a defined benefit plan, the employer assumes and also controls the risks. Any surplus can properly be used for other obligations—because the employer is always obligated to provide the vested benefits provided by the plan. In this analysis, Hughes did not violate ERISA, because it did not stop providing the vested benefits defined by the plan.

Nor did the Supreme Court accept the argument that Hughes had improperly terminated the old plan. Instead, the court permitted an amendment creating a new benefit structure (and did not treat it as the creation of a second plan) if only one pool of assets funds both obligations. Benefits continued to be paid to longer-serving employees on the basis of the original plan, so the old plan was not terminated merely because the additional benefit structure was added.

§ 4.18   PLAN LOANS

Under the right circumstances, plans are permitted to make loans to participants. These loans can be a useful resource if, for instance, a plan participant wishes to buy a house or pay a child's tuition. Loans to rank-and-file participants are usually permitted. However, a direct or indirect loan to a "party in interest" or a "disqualified person" is a prohibited transaction, unless a prohibited transaction exemption is available to justify the loan.

Under I.R.C. § 72(p), the general rule is that plan loans are treated as distributions—in other words, taxable income to the recipient. But there are certain exceptions. A loan will not be treated as a distribution if it does not exceed $50,000 or half the present value of the employee's nonforfeitable accrued benefit under the plan (whichever is less). (The employee can borrow up to $10,000, even if this amount is more than half the value of the accrued benefit.) Where the participant's account balance is the only security, the loan is theoretically not permitted to exceed half the pledged amount. The DOL Regulations dealing with plan loans do not forbid participants from borrowing funds from their accounts, pledging 50% of the account, and then taking hardship withdrawals, even though these steps have the effect of reducing the security below 50% of the account. [*See* Reg. § 2550.408-1(f)(2)]

The agreement to take a loan from the plan must call for repayment within five years, in payments made at least quarterly, with level amortization. Plans are permitted to impose variable interest rates on plan loans.

Tip: If the plan includes this provision, a veteran's obligation to repay a plan loan can be suspended during a period of qualified military service.

---

§ 4.19 EMPLOYER'S DEDUCTION

An employer that maintains a qualified defined benefit plan is entitled to deduct the greatest of these three amounts:

- The minimum funding standard as provided by I.R.C. § 412;
- The amount necessary to fund the cost of covering all the employees for their projected future service;
- The amount necessary to fund present and future costs, which may include liabilities stemming from service performed before the plan was established.

§ 4.20 REVERSIONS

If there were no statutory ban, unscrupulous employers might raid pension assets when they needed cash, or might terminate plans merely to recoup assets or excess assets. To prevent this, defined contribution plans (including profit-sharing and stock bonus plans) usually cannot return any assets to the employer under any circumstances. Even forfeitures (amounts contributed on behalf of employees whose employment terminates before they become vested) are to be allocated to other participants in the plan.

Under appropriate circumstances, employers can receive reversions from a defined benefit plan after satisfaction of all obligations under the plan to employees. Nor may the employer lawfully transfer assets from an overfunded plan to an underfunded plan.

Internal Revenue Code § 4980 imposes an excise tax on the amount of assets reverting to an employer from a qualified plan. The tax rate, for reversions occurring after September 30, 1990, is at least 20%. The rate rises to 50% unless the employer either transfers 25% of the assets in question to a qualified replacement plan, or increases the benefits under the terminating plan to the extent of 20% of the previous benefits to participants. A qualified replacement plan covers at least 95% of the active employees from the terminated plan who continue to be employed.

In the late 1990s, many plans became overfunded because of the strong stock market climate. If your plan is still in this condition, *see* Joanna Sammer, *When Assets Runneth Over* [(January 2001) <http://www.businessfinancemag.com/archives/appfiles/Article.cfm?IssueID=344&ArticleID=13704>], for advice about how to remove assets lawfully from an overfunded plan without triggering the ban on reversions. She notes that there are five basic approaches to utilizing plan surplus:

- Use the surplus to provide more benefits to participants and retirees, by creating a subaccount within the pension plan and crediting additional amounts to that subaccount for each affected participant or beneficiary;
- Use surplus in a I.R.C. § 204(h) retiree health benefits plan;
- Move accrued sums from an unfunded nonqualified plan into a qualified plan—as long as the nonqualified plan's benefit formula depends on years of service rather than pay; and as long as the qualified plan satisfies nondiscrimination tests;
- Expand the nonretirement benefits (e.g., disability or life insurance) offered in conjunction with a qualified pension plan—but remember that such benefits must be only "incidental" to retirement coverage;
- Merge with another company, and use plan surplus to reduce funding deficiencies in the other company's plan.

§ 4.21   FORFEITURES

Depending on the plan, at least some employees—and perhaps the vast majority of the rank-and-file workforce—will terminate employment before they become vested. The contributions made on account of such employees are known as forfeitures.

Under I.R.C. §§ 401(a)(8) and 404(a)(2), defined benefit plans are required to provide that forfeitures will not be applied to increase the benefits any employee would otherwise receive. Instead, favorable plan experience when it comes to forfeitures (or mortality or employee turnover) reduces the amount the employer has to contribute to the plan. In contrast, defined contribution plans are allowed to— and usually do—allocate forfeitures to the accounts of other participants.

If someone leaves employment, and is later rehired by the same company, the eventual retirement benefit must be adjusted actuarially to reflect both periods of employment (unless the break-in-service rules make this unnecessary). Another option is for the plan to give timely notice of its provisions for suspension of benefits, so there is no forfeiture. [Treas. Reg. § 2520.203-3(b)(4)]

When an employee dies, the plan can impose forfeiture of his or her unvested benefits, except if a Qualified Preretirement Survivor Annuity (QPSA) is required. [*See* § 12.06]

§ 4.22   DISCRIMINATION TESTING

One of the most basic plan concepts is that a plan must be operated for the exclusive benefit of its participants and beneficiaries. Furthermore, one of the main reasons for the creation of ERISA, and its elaborate structure of rules, is to prevent plans from being administered so that company owners, or major executives, get generous benefits while rank-and-file workers get little or nothing. A qualified plan must be "tested" for "discrimination." In this context, discrimination does not mean discrimination on the basis of sex, race, nationality, and so forth; it means allowing a disproportionate share of plan benefits to go to Highly Compensated Employees (HCEs).

A pension, annuity, profit-sharing, or stock bonus plan can lawfully favor HCEs in terms of contributions or benefits, but not both. [*See* I.R.C. §§ 401(a)(4), 404(a)(2)] Internal Revenue Code § 414(q) says that, for plan years after 1996, an HCE is defined as someone who owned 5% or more of the employer company's stock in either the current or the preceding year—or someone whose compensation for the preceding year was at least $80,000, as adjusted for inflation. For 2002, the applicable figure is $90,000.

The employer has the right to choose to use an alternative definition, under which HCEs are those who not only earn more than the amount of $80,000 as adjusted, but are also in the top 20% of earners in the company.

The Code used to contain rules called "family aggregation rules" (nicknamed "aggravation rules" because of their complexity) under which the compensation of several members of the family owning a family business had to be combined for purposes including discrimination testing. However, effective for plan years beginning on and after January 1, 1997, the family aggregation rules were abolished by the Small Business Job Protection Act (SBJPA) of 1996. [P.L. No. 104-188]

It does not violate the antidiscrimination rules for a plan to be "integrated" with Social Security within limits set by the "permitted disparity" rules of Code § 401(l). In effect, the employer can treat the employee's Social Security benefit (which was partially funded by the employer's FICA contributions) as part of the pension, or the employer can treat its FICA contributions as pension contributions.

The subject of discrimination testing is too complex to be fully laid out in this book. However, it should be noted that the Code includes "safe harbor" provisions for discrimination testing. Plans are not obligated to follow the safe harbor rules; they can set their own formulas. But if they do follow the safe harbor rules, they are sure not to be challenged by the IRS on this issue.

§ 4.23   LEASED EMPLOYEES

Leased employees (hired by a company from an agency that supplies workers) play a significant role in the economy. However, it is often the case that the treatment of a particular individual varies depending on the context. It is simplistic to say that a person is just an employee or a non-employee. Internal Revenue Code § 414(n) requires some people to be treated as employees eligible for plan participation even though they are formally employed by a leasing company rather than by the company for whom they perform services each day.

Section 414(n) refers to "leased employees," who are nominally employed by a "leasing organization" (e.g., an organization that furnishes temporary and contingent workers) but who "perform services" for a "service recipient." Instead of paying the leased employees directly, the service recipient pays the employees' wages (and an agency commission) to the leasing organization, which handles payroll functions including tax withholding.

However, the leased employees will be treated as employees of the service recipient when it comes to determining whether the service recipient's pension plans discriminate in favor of highly compensated employees. If the leasing organization maintains a pension plan for the employees it leases out, its contributions or benefits are treated as if they came from the service recipient for the service recipient's discrimination tests. The leasing organization's plan must count all service by leased employees for the leasing organization (even when they're leased out to a service recipient) with respect to coverage, vesting, contributions, and benefits under its own plan.

Service recipients have to count leased employees when they test their plans under the minimum participation, age and service, vesting, and top-heavy rules. They must be taken into account when computing limits on compensation and benefits and whether contributions to the plan are deductible. Furthermore, the leased employee will be treated as an employee under the Code's rules for fringe benefits such as group term life insurance, accident and health insurance, cafeteria plans, and dependent care assistance. Leased employees also have COBRA rights (they can elect continuation of health coverage).

For I.R.C. § 414(n) purposes, leased employees are those who provide services that last more than a year to a service recipient in conformity with the service recipient's agreement with the leasing organization. As a result of amendments made by the Small Business Job Protection Act of 1996, the test for 1997 and later years is whether the service recipient provides the primary direction or control for the work. (Service for related companies, such as the service recipient's controlled group of corporations, is aggregated with service for the service recipient.)

These rules relate to "substantially full-time service," which is defined as 1500 hours of service in a 12-month period, or a job that is equivalent to 75% of the hours that the service recipient's actual employees put in during a 12-month period. In other words, after a year of the recipient's full-time work, the leased employee is treated as the service recipient's employee for pension testing purposes. However, if the worker is a common-law employee for other purposes, this safe harbor cannot apply.

Even if leased employees have to be counted in determining whether the service recipient's pension plans are discriminatory, they do not have to be offered participation in the plan until they satisfy any conditions for plan participation lawfully imposed by the plan (e.g., if the employer imposes an age-21 minimum for participation, and a leased employee starts working for the employer at age 19, completing a year of service at age 20, participation can be delayed until the leased employee reaches 21).

To qualify for the safe harbor, the service recipient must get 20% or less of its rank-and-file workforce (that is, workers who are not HCEs) through leasing—and the leasing organization must have its own qualified pension plan that fits particularly stringent criteria. The leasing organization's plan must be a money purchase plan. It must not be integrated with Social Security. The leasing organization's employees must be able to participate as soon as they are hired by the organization. They must be fully vested immediately. Furthermore, the leasing organization must contribute at least 10% of compensation for each plan participant.

Although it is good practice to have individuals you believe to be independent contractors sign waivers agreeing that they are not entitled to participate in pension and benefit plans, these waivers are not sufficient if, under otherwise applicable legal principles, they really are common-law employees. The IRS will issue determination letters as to whether contingent employees are leased employees and, if so, how it affects the plan's qualification.

Bronk v. Mountain States Telephone & Telegraph Inc. [98-1 U.S.T.C. ¶50,316 (10th Cir. 1998)] holds that employees must be permitted to participate in the plan of the company that leases them, once they have satisfied the plan's age and service requirement.

However, it does not violate ERISA to draft the plan to exclude leased employees (even leased employees who count as common-law employees) from all participation. [*See* IRS Notice 84-11, Q&A 14: "[IRC] § 414(n)(1)(A) requires only that a leased employee be treated as an employee; it does not require that a leased employee be a participant in the recipient's qualified plan."]

Similarly, in the view of the Eleventh Circuit [*Wolf v. Coca-Cola Co.*, 200 F.3d 1337 (11th Cir. 2000)] it is legitimate to draft a plan to exclude certain categories of employees, even if the leased employees fit the definition of common-law employees. The Eleventh Circuit didn't find it necessary to follow *Vizcaino v. Microsoft* [159 F.3d 388 (9th Cir. 1998)], because Microsoft's plan purported to cover all common-law employees. As the *Wolf* court reads it, standing to sue under ERISA requires eligibility under the plan, not just common-law employee status.

In April 2000, the IRS released a Technical Advice Memorandum (TAM) (informational memorandum that does not have the full force of a formal regulation) about workers who claim that they were inappropriately treated as independent contractors or as employees of a leasing company or professional employer organization.

As long as plan participation is limited to employees on the payroll record, coming under specified job codes or work status codes, and as long as contingent workers are fully informed that they are not entitled to plan participation, the IRS did not see any violation of I.R.C. § 410 or Treas. Reg. § 1.401(a)-3(d), even though certain workers were excluded. The plan was not ambiguous and did not give the employer inappropriate discretion to exclude workers. The IRS inquired as to whether the job categories served an independent business purpose, and found them valid. The IRS also approved a plan provision that said that workers would not be retroactively admitted to plan participation even if an administrative agency or court treated them as employees rather than contractors. The IRS treated this provision as improving the stability and predictability of the plan.

§ 4.24   COMMUNICATING WITH EMPLOYEES

The subject of communications and notification to employees rates a chapter of its own [*see* Chapter 11], so here it will merely be noted that the plan administrator is responsible for reporting and disclosure, and can be held liable if appropriate disclosures are not made.

ERISA permits three methods of communication:

- Giving each employee a copy of the plan itself;
- Giving each employee a booklet containing the Summary Plan Description (SPD), describing the features of the plan in understandable language;
- Posting a notice on the bulletin board to inform employees that the company has adopted a plan, and where copies of the plan documents can be consulted.

Nearly all plans adopt the second alternative. The actual plan document is a lengthy, highly technical legal document, and doesn't do much to inform the average employee about rights and obligations under the plan.

§ 4.25   FIDUCIARY DUTY

A fiduciary is anyone who has charge of someone else's property or finances. Fiduciaries have legal duties to act honestly, prudently, and in the best interests of the owner of the assets. Pension plan fiduciaries have a duty to invest intelligently, selecting a diversified portfolio of appropriate investments that do not involve an excessive degree of risk.

ERISA obligates fiduciaries to administer the plan exclusively in the interests of plan participants and their beneficiaries. Specifically, if there is a situation in which one strategy would be most beneficial to the participants and another strategy would be most beneficial to the corporation sponsoring the plan, the fiduciaries must choose the first course of action, not the second.

If the plan has more than one named fiduciary, they are jointly and severally liable. Someone who alleges fiduciary impropriety can sue any one fiduciary, all of them, or any combination, and can collect the entire amount of liability from each one or from any combination of fiduciaries—no matter which fiduciary was actually at fault. The harshness of this high standard is relieved somewhat by the fact that fiduciaries who are sued can bring fiduciaries who weren't sued into the lawsuit, and can make them pay their fair share.

§ 4.26   BANKRUPTCY EFFECTS

There are two kinds of bankruptcy that may have an effect on pension plans: the employer's or an employee's. If the employer is one who seeks bankruptcy protection, an argument could be made under Bankruptcy Code § 547 that the employer's contributions to a qualified plan during the 90 days before the bankruptcy filing are "preferential transfers," and therefore should be returned to the bankruptcy estate and preserved so that creditors can make claims on them. However, the legal principle is that, if the plan participants continue to work for the employer, the employer is getting new value in exchange for the contributions and therefore the contributions are not preferences that can be reversed. [*Jones Truck Lines Inc. v. Central States, Southeast & Southwest Areas Pension, Health & Welfare Funds*, 130 F.3d 323 (8th Cir. 1997)]

When it comes to the employee's bankruptcy, the most relevant case is *Patterson v. Shumate* [504 U.S. 753 (1992)], which provides that ERISA plan law constitutes "applicable non-bankruptcy law" that will permit amounts in the plan to be excluded from the bankruptcy estate.

Internal Revenue Code § 401(a)(33) forbids certain plan amendments if the plan is covered by ERISA § 4021. Plan benefits may not be increased while the plan sponsor is a bankruptcy debtor. The plan cannot be amended to increase the plan's liabilities because of an increase in benefits, any change in the accrual of benefits, or any change in the rate at which benefits become nonforfeitable. The ban applies only if the amendments in question take effect before the effective date of the employer's plan of reorganization.

The restrictions do not apply if the plan would otherwise have a funded current liability percentage of at least 100%; if the IRS determines that the amendment is reasonable and increases benefits only slightly; or if the amendment is actually required to conform to changes in tax law.

§ 4.27   FACTORS IN CHOOSING A PLAN FORM

In deciding which form of plan to adopt, or whether to convert a plan or terminate an old plan and adopt a new one, the employer must balance many considerations, including financial and tax factors and the expected effect of a plan in motivating employee behavior (including retiring at the time most convenient for the employer).

Participants in a defined benefit plan know what their eventual pension will be if they stay with the plan until normal retirement age. If they terminate employment earlier, the vesting rules also control the size of the pension that will be paid later on, when they reach retirement age. This degree of certainty is valuable, but retirees have the problems caused by having a fixed income that does not reflect investment results.

In contrast, defined contribution plan participants know how large their account is at any given time. They can make projections of how large it will grow, based on predictions about interest rates and stock market trends. Market risk shifts from the employer to the employee and future retiree. Defined contribution plans also offer more portability: the contents of the employee's account from Plan A can simply be rolled over to Plan B when the employee stops being a Company A employee and is hired by Company B.

Defined benefit, but not defined contribution plans, are covered by the Pension Benefit Guaranty Corporation (PBGC)'s insurance program. The PBGC insures that employees will receive their pension benefits, at least the part that does not exceed a maximum figure. In exchange, employers must pay insurance premiums to the PBGC. If an underfunded defined benefit plan is terminated, the PBGC takes over part of the obligation to pay benefits. Some participants lose their pensions in this situation; some receive less than the normal amount.

§ 4.28   STRATEGIES FOR REDUCING PENSION COSTS

Large companies have devised strategies for reducing pension obligations by reducing future accruals without unlawfully reducing benefits that have already accrued. For instance, if a plan is frozen, additional service does not increase the benefit. Freezing can make an underfunded plan compliant, or even overfunded.

Companies interested in reducing pension costs can cap the number of years of service that will be counted toward a pension. The benefit can be based on high-five, last-five, last-10, or career-average compensation instead of high-three, which tends to result in a larger pension obligation. Plans can reduce the "multiplier" (i.e., set the pension as x% rather than x.5% of the chosen compensation figure, per year of service). [See also Chapter 7 for a discussion of cash balance plans, which tend to have the same effect as using a career average computation, thereby reducing the employer's obligation. *See also* Ellen S. Schultz, *Pension Cuts 101: Companies Find Host of Subtle Ways to Pare Retirement Payouts*, Wall Street Journal, July 27, 2000, at p. A1]

CHAPTER 5
DEFINED BENEFIT PLANS

§ 5.01   INTRODUCTION

This chapter deals, in detail, with issues that are specific to defined benefit plans. See Chapter 4 for background issues on pensions, Chapter 6 for defined contribution plans and 401(k) plans, and Chapter 7 for cash balance plans.

The PBGC publishes its Data Book each year. [*See* <http://www.pbgc.gov/publications/databook/databook01.pdf> for the 2001 edition] The Data Book explains the agency's operations, financial condition, and who is entitled to receive benefits from the PBGC, which now covers about 43 million workers and retirees in close to 38,000 defined benefit plans. Single copies of the Data Book can be ordered from PBGC Data Book, Suite 240, 1200 K Street NW, Washington, D.C. 20005-4026, or requests can be faxed to (202) 326-4042.

Chatham Partners (a consulting firm) reports a trend for defined benefit plans to move toward consolidated services from bundled providers—that is, companies that offer a wide range of investment options and services rather than a single service. About 25% of defined benefit assets (an aggregate of $1 trillion) are managed in bundled plans. About one-third of the surviving census of defined benefit plans (some 15,000 out of 45,000) are managed by bundled firms. [Christiane Bird, *Defined-Benefit Plans Become More "Bundled,"* Wall Street Journal, Nov. 26, 2001, at p. C1.]

§ 5.02   BENEFIT LIMITS

The limit on the maximum benefit that anyone can receive from a qualified defined benefit plan in a year is set by I.R.C. § 415(b)(1). At first, the limit was set at $90,000 a year, with provision for inflation adjustment. EGTRRA raised the annual benefit limit to $160,000, to be indexed for inflation in minimum increments of $5,000. No matter how much a person earns, only $200,000 a year in compensation can be taken into account when calculating the benefit under a defined benefit plan.

However, EGTRRA—like many complex pieces of legislation—had some unintended effects. "Technical corrections" are laws adopted to clarify difficult points or remove such unintended effects. In defined benefit plans that incorporate the legal limitations by reference, the effect of EGTRRA could be to increase the benefit automatically, even if this was not what the employer wanted to do. [*See* Rev. Rul. 2001-51, 2001-45 I.R.B. 427]

A bill signed into federal law on March 9, 2002, the Job Creation and Worker Assistance Act of 2002 (JCWAA) [Pub. L. No. 107-147] makes it clear that amendments adopted before June 30, 2002, to "freeze" the defined benefit at its pre-EGTRRA level, will be legitimate and will not be considered a forbidden cutback in benefit levels. The JCWAA also provides that if an employer has both a defined benefit plan and a 401(k) plan containing only elective deferrals (no employer matches), the limitation on benefits under overlapping plans. I.R.C. § 404(a)(7)) does not apply. [For more information about the JCWAA, *see, e.g.,*

<http://www.cyberisa.com/erisa_new_current.htm> and <http://benefitsattorney.com/child/stimulus1.html> (no www)]

§ 5.03   BENEFIT FORMS FOR DEFINED BENEFIT PLANS

All pension plans must provide the basic payment form: a life annuity for single participants, and a QJSA (qualified joint and survivor annuity) for married participants. The basic form of QJSA provides a certain level of benefits while both the former employee and spouse are still alive. When one of them dies, the payment is cut in half, because only one person remains to be supported. Although employers are allowed to offer 50% survivor annuities, they are also allowed to subsidize the survivor annuity so that it is more than 50% of the initial payment, or even so that the payment does not decline when one payee dies.

Internal Revenue Code § 401(a)(25) says that a plan that provides for alternative benefit forms (annuity, installment, lump sum, early retirement) must specify, in a definite form that precludes employer discretion, what actuarial assumptions (such as interest rates and mortality assumptions) are used to calculate equivalencies among different benefit forms. This disclosure obligation does not, however, extend to the plan's funding assumptions.

In a flat benefit plan, the pension is defined as a certain number of dollars per month, or a percentage of average annual compensation or average compensation for the "high three" years. A unit benefit plan defines the pension as compensation times years of participation times a percentage rate. Some plans of this type increase the accrual rate in later years, or are calculated using a "high five" or "final average pay" (the average of the last three years of work, when presumably earnings will be at their peak).

§ 5.04   MORTALITY TABLES

Before 2002, the IRS required defined benefit plans to use the 1983 Group Annuity Mortality (83GAM) table for making the actuarial calculations for the value of accrued benefits. [I.R.C. § 417(e)] The mortality tables must be used to make sure that the value of a lump sum benefit is at least as great as the predicted value of an annuity.

Defined benefit plans also have to calculate adjustments of the plan limitations, as required by I.R.C. § 415(b), when the benefit under the plan is paid in any form other than a QJSA, or when the employee retires before age 62 or after age 65.

However, Rev. Rul. 2001-62, 2001-53 I.R.B. 632 requires plans to switch to the 1994 Group Annuity Reserving (94GAR) table no later than for distributions with an annuity starting date on or after December 31, 2002. For nearly all participants, the new mortality table will require greater benefits for employees. The Ruling contains two model plan amendments that can be used to bring the plan into conformity.

Plans can apply 94GAR earlier than the mandatory date if they prefer, beginning with the distributions that start in January 2002. Plans that adopt the new table before December 31, 2002, have to apply it for both valuation of accrued benefits [I.R.C. §§ 417(e) and 415(b)] limitation adjustments.

Even though the IRS requires the change, adopting the new mortality table will require a plan amendment.

§ 5.05 FUNDING THE DEFINED BENEFIT PLAN

[A] Minimum Funding Standard

The process of funding a defined contribution plan is quite simple. The employer simply determines a percentage of compensation, and as long as the contribution does not exceed the Code maximum, then there are no further problems. No discretion is involved.

In contrast, funding a defined benefit plan requires subtle decisions about long-range economic and employment trends in order to deposit enough money to yield the correct stream of future benefits to plan participants and their beneficiaries.

Defined benefit, money purchase, and target benefit plans (but not profit-sharing plans, stock bonus plans, or plans under I.R.C. § 412(i) that are exclusively funded by the purchase of individual insurance or annuity contracts) are subject to a "minimum funding" requirement under I.R.C. § 412.

An excise tax of 10% is imposed by I.R.C. § 4971 for failure to meet the minimum funding standard. The excise tax rises to 100% of any deficiency that remains uncorrected a reasonable time after the plan receives notice of deficiency from the IRS.

According to the Supreme Court case, *United States v. Reorganized CF&I Fabricators of Utah Inc.* [518 U.S. 213 (1996)], the 100% assessment is a penalty (and therefore an ordinary unsecured claim) and not an excise tax entitled to seventh priority, if the company subject to it files for bankruptcy protection.

Underfunding has other implications. If the plan is covered by PBGC insurance, the PBGC must be notified whenever the minimum funding standard is not met. If the plan is terminated [*see* Chapter 17], then underfunding can make the plan liable to the PBGC for accumulated funding deficiencies.

However, complying with the minimum funding standard doesn't solve all of the employer's problems, because I.R.C. § 4972 also imposes an excise tax on excess contributions to a defined benefit plan.

Therefore, the employer should make sure that its contributions to the defined benefit plan fall within the acceptable range. Contributions should not be small enough to constitute underfunding—especially not small enough to trigger PBGC termination of the plan. But the employer will not want to contribute more than can be deducted, and will particularly want to avoid the excise tax on excess contributions.

The statutes and regulations referring to minimum funding and current liability rates refer to the interest rate on 30-year Treasury bonds. However, on October 31, 2000, the Treasury stopped issuing new 30-year bonds. Business groups such as the ERISA Industry Committee (ERIC) asked Congress to adopt more realistic benchmarks, because even before issuance of new 30-year bonds was suspended, the interest rates on the "long bond" had fallen for a number of quarters, resulting in much higher liabilities for defined benefit plan sponsors. Furthermore, declines in the stock market meant that poor investment results would also require the sponsor to contribute more—many sponsors had been able to bypass contributions to the plan for several quarters or even several years, because of strong investment returns. [*See* Craig Gunsauley, *Falling Bond Rates Inflate DB Plan Liabilities*, Employee Benefit News, December 2001 <http://www.benefitnews.com/ pfv. cfm?id=2240>]

[B] Deduction Limit

The funding standard serves another purpose: it sets an upper limit on the amount that the employer can deduct under I.R.C. § 404. If the employer overstates its pension liabilities by 200% or more, and therefore takes too large a deduction, with the result that its income taxes are underpaid by 20% or more, then a 20% accuracy-related underpayment penalty can be imposed under I.R.C. § 6662. The penalty will be suspended if the pension overstatement was less than $1,000, or if the plan relied on substantial authority such as Revenue Rulings or IRS Notices.

EGTRRA, the tax law passed in 2001, allows all defined benefit plans to deduct contributions to the plan that do not exceed the plan's unfunded current liability—even if they are greater than the FFL. Before EGTRRA, this provision was limited to plans with more than 100 participants; EGTRRA § 652(a) extended it to all defined benefit plans, adding § 404(a)(1)(D)(i) to the Code for this purpose. In order to encourage adequate funding of plans, EGTRRA § 653(a) allows the employer to make nondeductible contributions that do not exceed the accrued liability full-funding limitation for the plan.

Pensions are a form of deferred compensation, and any form of compensation is deductible only if it is reasonable and constitutes an ordinary and necessary business expense. Part of the compensation of particularly highly-paid employees may have to be disregarded for certain tax-related purposes.

For example, under I.R.C. § 401(a)(17) only $200,000 of compensation (adjusted for inflation in increments of $5,000) can be taken into account. EGTRRA increased this amount from $150,000 (adjusted for inflation). Even legitimate compensation may have to be deducted over a span of several years, not all at once. Employee compensation (including benefits and retirement plan costs) must be capitalized under I.R.C. § 263A if it is incurred in connection with production or purchase for resale of either real property or tangible personal property.

There are further requirements under I.R.C. § 404, a section included in the Code to distinguish pension and annuity plans from profit-sharing and stock bonus plans. Under I.R.C. § 404(a), the plan must have been in existence by the end of the employer's tax year for the employer to be able to deduct the contribution in the year it was made. Note that not only are plan sponsors subject to excise tax penalties if they fail to contribute enough to the plan, they are also subject to excise tax, under I.R.C. § 4972, for excess contributions.

[C] Calculating the Contribution

To set the employer's contribution level, the actuary for a defined benefit plan can use either of two basic methods (each of which has variations).

The accrued benefit method, which is also called the unit credit cost method, defines the plan liabilities on the basis of benefits that accrue in that particular year. The projected benefit cost method calculates benefits on the assumption that benefits accrue as long as a person remains a participant in the plan. ERISA § 3(31) defines variations on the projected cost method, including the entry age normal method, aggregate cost method, attained age normal cost method, and frozen initial liability cost method.

The contribution for each participant has two aspects: normal cost and supplemental liability. The normal cost for each participant is the actuarial value of the benefit units assigned for that year. The supplemental liability covers benefits for service before adoption of the plan, or between the time the plan was adopted and the time it is amended to increase coverage.

[D] Minimum Funding Standard Account

A "minimum funding standard account" must be maintained in all plan years until the end of the year in which the plan terminates. [See I.R.C. § 412(b) and ERISA § 302(b)] The minimum funding standard is met when there is no accumulated funding deficiency at the end of the year. There is no deficiency if, for all plan years, the credits to the funding standard account are at least equal to the total charges.

The minimum funding standard account consists of charges for normal costs, past service liabilities, experience losses in investments, and funding deficiencies. The general rule is that experience losses and funding deficiencies have to be amortized, not deducted currently. The charges to the account are offset by credits for, e.g., the employer's contributions to the plan, investment experience gains, and funding deficiencies that are waived by the IRS.

Internal Revenue Code § 412(l) imposes additional obligations on single-employer plans with 100 or more participants whose "funded current liability" percentage falls below 80% for the current year when it was below 90% for the preceding year. The funded current liability percentage equals the value of the plan assets divided by current liabilities. The underfunded plans are obligated to notify their participants and beneficiaries of the funding deficiency, and must pay an additional PBGC premium. In egregious cases, the PBGC may be able to bring a civil suit against the plan.

> **Tip:** If assets and liabilities of one plan are spun off to another plan, a separate funding standard account should be maintained for each plan, and adjustments will have to be made with respect to the spun-off assets and liabilities.

Thanks to I.R.C. § 405 of the Job Creation and Worker Assistance Act of 2002 [P.L. No. 107-147 (3/9/02)] for plan years beginning in 2002 and 2003 only, the plan can use slightly higher interest rates to calculate its funding requirement. The higher rates mean that they will have somewhat lower liability. The same provision also reduces the PBGC variable rate premium somewhat.

[E] Full Funding Limitation

An excise tax might be imposed whenever the employer's contribution falls below the plan's "full funding limitation" (FFL). The excise tax will not be imposed if the contribution is greater than the FFL, even if the funding standard account shows a deficit for the year. The employer's income tax deduction for plan contributions can never be more than the FFL. At all times, the FFL must be at least equal to 90% of the plan's current liability.

The FFL is a formula that can be expressed as A–B. A is the lower of the accrued liability or a percentage of the current liability. B is either the fair market value of the plan assets or the value of the assets calculated based on the I.R.C. § 412(c)(2) fixed debt obligation, whichever is lower. The "current liability" means all liabilities to participants and beneficiaries. However, "unpredictable contingent events" can be left out of the calculation.

The percentage used to calculate factor A was set at 150% for plan years beginning before 1998. The Taxpayer Relief Act of 1997 set up a new schedule. For plan years that begin within the calendar years 1999 or 2000, the limit is 155%, rising to 160% for plan years beginning within calendar 2001. Then EGTRRA made further changes. The applicable percentage is 165% in 2002 and 170% in 2003. Between 2004 and 2010 (the year in which all EGTRRA provisions expire unless Congress renews them), the percentage test is abolished. At that point, the FFL will be the difference between the plan's accrued liability (including normal cost) and the value of the plan's assets.

[F] Funding Procedures

Actual funding of the plan is done by the employer's contributing cash, non-cash property, or its own securities. The valuation of cash is simple; for property and securities, it can be difficult. The prohibited transaction rules [*see* § 8.03] must be consulted to make sure that contributions do not violate these rules. Wherever possible, transactions should be structured so that the plan trust will not have Unrelated Business Taxable Income (UBTI). In general, plan trusts are not subject to income tax—unless they have unrelated income.

Wherever possible, the employer should avoid contributing depreciated property to the plan. That's because I.R.C. § 267(b)(4) provides that the employer will have taxable gain (capital or ordinary, depending on the facts) if it contributes appreciated property to the plan. But losses on contributions of depreciated property are not recognized, because there is a transfer between the trust grantor and the trust's fiduciary.

> **Tip:** An employer that wants to use depreciated property in funding can sell the property to a third party, recognize the tax loss, then contribute the cash proceeds of the sale.

The plan will have to make quarterly payments to fund plan liability. [*See* I.R.C. § 412 and ERISA § 302] For a calendar-year plan, the due dates are April 15, July 15, October 15, and January 15 of the following year. Note that these are not the same dates as the corporation's estimated income tax payments.

Fiscal year plans modify this schedule. For instance, the dates are advanced by three months for a plan with a fiscal year ending March 31 (three months after the end of a calendar year).

Quarterly payments will be excused if the funded current liability percentage for the prior plan year was 100% or more. The purpose of the quarterly payments is to make sure that the employer contributes at least 90% of the I.R.C. § 412 funding limit for the year, or 100% of the funding liability for the preceding year (whichever is less).

If the funded current liability percentage fell below 100% in the preceding year, failure to pay a quarterly installment on time will obligate the sponsor to pay interest to the plan. Plans with more than 100 participants must include any liquidity shortfall in the quarterly payment, even if this increases the size of the payment that would otherwise have to be made.

The liquidity shortfall equals the base amount minus the plan's liquid assets on the last day of the quarter. The base amount, in turn, equals three times the adjusted disbursements from the plan for the 12 months ending on the last day of the quarter. There is also a 10% excise tax on liquidity shortfall that is not paid for any quarter as it comes due, rising to 100% of the unpaid amount if the shortfall is not paid for any quarter followed by the next four consecutive quarters. The IRS has the power to waive part or all of this I.R.C. § 4971(f)(4) excise tax if the sponsor had reasonable cause to miss the payment, was not guilty of willful neglect, and has taken appropriate steps to remedy the shortfall.

[G]   Liens Based on Funding Failures

Under I.R.C. § 412(n), a lien can be imposed against the employer, and in favor of the plan subject to PBGC jurisdiction, if the employer fails to make a required contribution to the plan when it is due.

> **Tip:** The person responsible for making the payment that was missed has an obligation to inform the PBGC within 10 days of the due date that the payment was missed.

The lien covers all of the employer's real and personal property. The lien can be imposed if the plan's funded current liability percentage fell below 100% and the unpaid balance, plus interest, was more than $1 million. It starts on the date the payment should have been made, and runs to the end of the plan year in which the liabilities go over the $1 million mark.

The PBGC can sue in federal district court under ERISA § 4003(e)(1) to enforce the lien against the employer. This power can be exercised at any time until three years after the PBGC knew or should have known of the failure to make the necessary payment (extended to six years if the employer committed fraud or concealment), or for six years after the due date from the payment.

[H] Plan Valuation Issues

An actuarial valuation must be performed at least once a year to determine the assets, liabilities, and contribution level for plans subject to I.R.C. § 412. (EGTRRA gives the Treasury the power to adopt regulations that call for even more frequent valuations.) The information is also used to prepare the Schedule B for the 5500-series form.

The basic factors in setting assumptions include:

- Employee compensation;
- Early retirement rate;
- Employee turnover;
- Disability and mortality rates (both before and after retirement);
- (For QJSAs) Life expectancy of employees' spouses;
- Expected percentage return on the plan's investments (interest assumptions may have to be adjusted in the future to reflect the plan's investment record);
- Administrative expenses, defined either as dollars per participant or a reduction in the plan's rate of return.

Within the limits set by I.R.C. § 412 and other relevant provisions, the size of the contribution can be increased or decreased somewhat based on corporate needs. However, the plan's actuarial assumptions must always be reasonable— each individual assumption, not just the aggregate. Courts have the power to overturn a plan's actuarial assumptions, even if the assumptions are not unreasonable. This is especially likely to happen if the plan has applied its own assumptions inconsistently.

> **Tip:** In general, the valuation date has to be within the plan year for which the assets are being valued, or within a month before the start of the plan year—but EGTRRA § 661(a) creates an exception under which the valuation date can sometimes be in the previous year. This exception can only be used if the plan assets, valued as of the prior plan year's date, is at least 125% of the plan's current liability.

ERISA § 302(c) provides that a plan covered by PBGC termination insurance requires IRS approval to change its actuarial assumptions, if the aggregated unfunded vested benefits of all underfunded plans maintained by the employer, or members of the same controlled group, exceed $50 million. Approval for the change is also required if the change in the assumptions raises the unfunded cumulative liability for the current plan year by more than $50 million, or more than $5 million, if this is 5% or more of the current liability.

[I]   Interest Rates

Internal Revenue Code § 412(l) sets the parameters for the interest rates used to determine the employer's contributions and the plan's current liability.

> **Tip:** As noted above, JCWAA provides some relief for 2002 and 2003 plan years.

The "permissible range" is within 10% of the weighted average of rates on 30-year Treasury obligations for the four years ending the day before the beginning of the plan year. Now that issuance of new 30-year Treasuries has been discontinued, however, another official benchmark eventually will have to be substituted.

The Department of the Treasury has the power to issue Regulations that lower the permissible range [*see* I.R.C. § 412(b)(5)] but it is not allowed to fall beneath 80% of the weighted 30-year average Treasury rate.

Factors in the interest rate assumption include:

- The economic components of interest rates;
- Current long-term interest rates;
- The plan's individual actuarial and investment factors;
- Long-range economic trends, especially in the money supply and interest rates throughout the economy.

[J]   Funding Changes

Rev. Procs. 2000-40 and -41, 2000-42 I.R.B. 357 and 371, provide the procedures under which the sponsor or administrator of a defined benefit plan subject to

I.R.C. § 412 or ERISA § 302 can get the Secretary of the Treasury to approve a change in the plan's funding method under I.R.C. § 412(c)(5)(A):

- A shift from the entry age normal method to the unit credit method of complying with the minimum funding obligation;
- Setting the normal cost level as a dollar amount instead of a level percentage of compensation under the aggregate method;
- Changing the method of valuing assets;
- Changing the valuation date from the first day of the plan year to the last day;
- Changing the plan year (which has the incidental effect of changing the valuation date);
- Changing the software used to perform valuation, if this changes the actual computations;
- Changing the method of determining the cost of ancillary benefits.

The IRS has jurisdiction to review the appropriateness of any change that significantly affects the plan's minimum funding requirement or full funding limitation. The agency will approve a change in funding method only if the proposed new method and the form of the transition are both acceptable.

Requests for change should be directed to the IRS Commissioner, TE/GE Attention: T:EP:RA PO Box 27063 McPherson Station, Washington, D.C. 20038. The due date is the end of the plan year in which the change will be effective. The IRS has discretion to extend the due date by up to two and a half months if the plan submits a statement giving adequate reason for the delay.

[K]   Minimum Funding Waivers

What can a company do if it is unable to satisfy its funding obligations and meet other business debts? ERISA and the Code give the employer various options. It may be possible to amend the plan retroactively to reduce the accrued benefits. [See I.R.C. § 412(c)(8)] DOL and the IRS might grant a variance from the minimum funding standards. The amortization periods used in the funding standard account can be extended. The funding method can be changed.

Internal Revenue Code § 412(d) allows employers to apply for a waiver of the minimum funding standard in any year. The due date for the application is the fifteenth day of the third month after the end of the plan year for which the waiver is requested. To get a waiver, the employer must show that meeting the standard would create "temporary substantial business hardship." The IRS considers factors such as conditions in the employer's industry, if the employer has an operating loss, and whether the plan can continue without a waiver.

A retroactive plan amendment can be adopted within two and a half months after the close of the plan year, with the effect of reducing benefits that accrued during the plan year for which the amendment is effective. [I.R.C. § 412(c)(8)] Notice must be given to the IRS and to the plan's interested parties. The IRS has a

90-day period to review the proposed plan amendment. If the IRS does not disapprove, then the amendment takes effect at the end of the 90-day period.

If the application is granted, the IRS will waive part or all of the funding deficiency for the year. The employer may have to provide security if the amount in question is substantial. But the IRS does not have the power to waive amortization of funding deficiencies that were waived in earlier years.

The IRS can grant up to ten additional years to amortize items such as unfunded past service liability and net experience losses. The IRS can grant this relief only if it concludes that the extension serves the purposes of ERISA and protected participants and beneficiaries in the long run by making the plan more stable.

ERISA § 302(c) requires that a defined benefit plan that is subject to PBGC termination insurance must get IRS approval to change its actuarial assumptions if all of the employer's plans (including all plans within its controlled group of corporations) have an aggregate unfunded benefit in excess of $50 million, or if the proposed change in assumptions decreases the unfunded current liability by $50 million or more for the current plan year—or by more than $5 million, representing more than 5% of the current liability.

Plans can't have it both ways. If they are granted minimum funding relief (other than a change of funding methods), as long as the relief continues, the plan is limited in its ability to adopt plan changes that increase benefits, change benefit accrual, or change the rates at which benefits become nonforfeitable. [*See* I.R.C. § 412(f)] However, amendments will be permitted if the IRS agrees that they are reasonable and increase plan liabilities only by a minimal amount, if they are actually required for the plan to remain qualified, or if the amendment merely repeals one that would have retroactively decreased accrued benefits under the plan.

§ 5.06   BENEFIT ACCRUALS

Another issue in plan administration and compliance is the schedule on which benefits are contributed on the individual's behalf, being added to the pension account so that eventually the participant will receive his or her defined benefit. Vesting is a separate but related concept. Vesting determines the extent to which employees will be entitled to receive the accrued benefit when they retire or employment otherwise terminates.

Defined benefit plans must accrue benefits using one of the three permitted mechanisms:

1. The 3% rule: at all times, the accrued benefit must be at least 3% of the maximum benefit calculated under the plan's formula, multiplied by the number of years of participation.
2. The 133.5% test: the accrued benefit payable at Normal Retirement Age equals the normal retirement benefit, and accrual in any plan year does not exceed 133.5% of the accrual for any prior year. In other words, benefits must accrue in a fairly level manner in each year.

3.   The fractional rule: the annual benefit an employee has accrued at the time of separation from service must be proportionate to what he or she would have received by remaining employed until normal retirement age.

Under § 412(i), insured plans whose accrued benefit is always at least equal to the cash surrender value of the insurance are exempt from the minimum funding rules.

§ 5.07   NOTICES OF REDUCTION OF BENEFIT ACCRUALS

Defined benefit plans (and other plans subject to the I.R.C. § 412 full funding rules) have an obligation under ERISA § 204(h) and I.R.C. § 4980F (a new provision added by EGTRRA) to provide notice of plan amendments that significantly reduce future benefit accruals. The notice must contain the text or a summary of the plan amendment, and the effective date of the amendment. Notice must be given at least 15 days before the effective date of the plan amendment. [*See* the JCWAA § 411(u) for technical corrections to this provision]

Not only is an excise tax ($100 per day) imposed on the failure, but in "egregious" cases (where the employer intentionally refused to give notice, or failed very badly to disclose the needed information) the plan amendment will not be given effect. Therefore, participants will be entitled to the unreduced benefit that was in effect before the plan was amended.

§ 5.08   PBGC COMPLIANCE

[A]   PBGC Organization

Formally speaking, the Pension Benefit Guarantee Corporation (PBGC) is organized as a corporation, but it's really a quasi-governmental agency that draws its powers from ERISA § 4002. The PBGC's Board of Directors consists of the Secretaries of Labor, Treasury, and Commerce. The federal court system gives the agency special deference, by giving its cases the earliest possible calendar dates. Employers sued by the PBGC in connection with a plan termination can be required to pay part or all of the agency's litigation costs.

The main task of the PBGC is to guarantee that participants in defined benefit plans will receive a basic benefit even if their plan is insufficiently funded, or if it is terminated.

The PBGC operates like an insurance company: It collects premiums from employers who maintain defined benefit plans, to create a fund that can be used to pay out guarantees.

[B]   PBGC Premiums

The PBGC stays afloat by charging a premium to employers who maintain defined benefit plans. The PBGC premium is $19 per plan participant, plus $9 for every $1000 of vested but unfunded benefit for which the plan is responsible. Un-funded benefits means the unfunded current liabilities determined by counting only vested benefits. The plan can use the information from Form 5500, Schedule B, instead of making a separate calculation.

> **Tip:** If a plan has fewer than 500 participants, it can submit a certificate from an enrolled actuary stating that there are no unfunded vested benefits. Nor is it necessary to calculate unfunded vested benefits if the plan is fully insured, or if the plan was fully funded in the year before the year in question. When a plan terminates, the PBGC premium is payable until the plan assets have been distributed, or until a trustee is appointed (whichever comes first). When the business of winding up the plan is completed, the PBGC refunds any unearned part of the premium.

The premium is charged for each participant, terminated vested participant, and beneficiary already receiving benefits, other than "lost" beneficiaries (the plan knows they may be entitled to benefits, but can't find them) for whom an insurance company has an irrevocable commitment to pay all the benefits. All defined benefit plans that are subject to PBGC insurance must file Form PBGC-1 each year as a combined annual report and declaration of premium payments.

The premium is paid with Form 1-ES (if the plan has more than 500 participants) or with Form 10-SP (short form for smaller plans). The contributing sponsor and the plan administrator are both liable for the PBGC premium. If the premium is not paid on time, interest runs from the due date, plus a late charge of 5% per month (capped at 100% of the original unpaid premium). The PBGC is also empowered to collect unpaid premiums from what would otherwise be the employer's federal tax refund. If the employer is a federal contractor, the PBGC can seize federal contract payments.

> **Tip:** The forms are available online as PDF files. [*See* <http://www.pbgc.gov/plan_admin/paypol/PREMPKG.htm>] Forms and instruction booklets can be ordered by telephone at (800) 736-2444 or (202) 326-4242, by fax at (202) 326-4250, or by mail from the PBGC, PO Box 64916, Baltimore, MD, 21264-4916. The PBGC suggests that a laser or inkjet printer with resolution of at least 300 Dots Per Inch be used to print out the forms. Thermal and dot matrix printers should not be used. The PBGC says that "Fit to Page" or other printer options that change the size of the image should not be used either.

A PBGC Final Rule appearing in the Federal Register of December 14, 1998 [63 Fed. Reg. 68684], amends 29 C.F.R. Part 4007 to provide that the final filing due date for a calendar-year plan's premium declaration will be October 15. In other words, the date is the same for the declaration as the extended date for the Form 5500. The Final Rule makes corresponding changes in the treatment of the declaration for fiscal-year plans. It is now due the fifteenth day of the tenth full calendar month of the premium payment year. (Adjustments are made if the plan changes its plan year, or if it is a new or newly covered plan.)

See also 65 Fed. Reg. 75160 (Dec. 1, 2000), which simplifies administration of premium payments. The administrator can pay a prorated premium for a short plan year, instead of paying the full premium and getting a refund or claiming a credit against future premium payments. A short plan year might occur during a plan's first, partial year; in the year of termination; or when a trustee is appointed under ERISA § 4042. The December 2000 rule also changes the definition of "participant." The plan can exclude from the count—and therefore not pay premiums for—a person who has no accrued benefits and to whom the plan has no other benefit liabilities. The bottom line is that a new plan doesn't have to pay premiums for its first year unless it credits service before the beginning of the plan.

Under the Job Creation and Worker Assistance Act of 2002 [Pub. L. No.107-147], for variable rate premiums for plan years beginning post-December 31, 2001, and before January 1, 2004, the interest rate is increased to 100% of the 30-year Treasury rate for the month before the start of the plan year. The higher the interest rate, the lower the actual premium the employer has to pay, so this is a relief provision.

A PBGC news release from November 23, 1999 [<http://www.pbgc.gov/news/press_releases/1999/pr0008.htm>], announces additional safe harbor relief for plans that would otherwise be subject to late payment penalties on their estimated payments of PBGC premiums. The interest payments will still be due, because the PBGC doesn't have the authority to waive interest on underpayments. The news release says that plan administrators will not face late payment penalties based on undercounting the number of plan participants, if they rely on the participant count for the previous year's premium payment.

Furthermore, if a plan corrects its underpayment before receiving a PBGC notice about it, the penalty is only 1% a month, not the 5% a month imposed on companies that do not self-correct.

[C]   Accounting Issues

On the fifteenth of every month, the PBGC updates its Web site [<http://www.pbgc.gov.services/interest/interest.htm>] to give the interest rates that should be used in that month for:

- Valuation of lump-sum payments made by the plan;
- Variable rate premiums;
- Valuation of annuity benefits;
- PBGC charges imposed with respect to employer liability, unpaid contributions, and unpaid premiums.

PBGC staff can be reached by e-mail to answer compliance questions about:

- Premium calculations and payments: premiums@pbgc.gov;
- Coverage and standard terminations: standard@pbgc.gov;
- Distress terminations: distress.term@pbgc.gov;
- Early warning program: advance.report@pbgc.gov;
- ERISA § 4010 reporting: EISA.4010@pbgc.gov;
- Reportable events: post-event.report@pbgc.gov;
- General legal questions: AskOGC@pbgc.gov;
- Problem resolution officer: practitioner.pro@pbgc.gov;
- Other: Ask.PBGC@pbgc.gov.

§ 5.09 REPORTABLE EVENTS

The PBGC doesn't want to be caught by surprise when a plan fails. To this end, plan administrators have a duty to report unusual events to the PBGC that might eventually require the agency to take over payment of pensions. Depending on the seriousness of the event, the PBGC might merely maintain a watchful attitude; or it might seek the appointment of a temporary trustee to manage the plan, or even go to the appropriate federal District Court to seek authority to terminate the plan.

The PBGC Regulations list 17 reportable events. Some of them must be reported 30 days before the event is scheduled to occur; others may be reported after the fact:

- The plan's bankruptcy or insolvency;
- The sponsoring employer's bankruptcy or insolvency;
- The sponsoring employer's liquidation under the Bankruptcy Code or any similar law (or that of a member of its controlled group of corporations);
- Notice from the IRS that the plan has ceased to be a qualified retirement plan;
- IRS determination that the plan has terminated or partially terminated;
- Failure to meet the minimum funding standard;
- Receiving a minimum funding waiver from the IRS;
- Inability to pay benefits as they come due;
- DOL determination that the plan fails to comply with ERISA Title I;
- Adoption of a plan amendment that decreases any participant's retirement benefit (except for certain decreases relating to integration with Social Security);
- A reduction in the number of active participants in the plan, to the extent that the number is less than 80% of the census at the beginning of the year or 75% of the number of active participants at the beginning of the preceding plan year;
- Distributing $10,000 or more to a participant who is a "substantial owner" (a definition roughly equal to 10% shareholder in the employer corporation) if the plan has any unfunded, nonforfeitable benefits after the distribution. Distributions made on account of the death of the substantial owner are not counted for this purpose;
- Merger or consolidation of the plan, or transfer of its assets;
- DOL requirement of an alternative method of compliance under ERISA § 110;

- A change of plan sponsor (or the same plan sponsor leaving a controlled group of corporation), if the plan has $1 million or more in unfunded nonforfeitable benefits;
- A "person" involved with the plan leaving a controlled group of corporations;
- The controlling sponsor, or a member of its controlled group, engages in a highly unusual transaction, such as declaring an extraordinary dividend or redeeming 10% or more of its stock;
- Transfer of a total of 3% or more of the plan's benefit liabilities outside the sponsor's controlled group within a 12-month period (whether or not the transferee is another plan).

At one time, the sponsoring employer had a duty to report the events to the plan administrator, but now it is only required that the events be reported to the PBGC. ERISA § 4043 requires advance notice of liquidating bankruptcy, extraordinary dividends, transfer of 3% of plan liabilities, or leaving a controlled group of corporations.

In addition to the required report to the PBGC, whenever a defined benefit plan fails to satisfy the minimum funding standard, and there has been no waiver of minimum funding granted, then participants must be notified. Form 200 must be filed with the PBGC within 10 days of the time a failure to meet the minimum funding standard involves $1 million or more.

CHAPTER 6

DEFINED CONTRIBUTION AND 401(k) PLANS

§ 6.01   INTRODUCTION

As explored in Chapters 4 and 5, the defined benefit plan not only places the investment risk on the employer (because the employer must adjust its contributions to provide the promised level of benefits—and if the value of the plan's assets declines, and its investment return goes down, the employer must supply additional funds) but also subjects the employer to complex and expensive administrative requirements.

In the 1990s, therefore, the trend was to shift from defined benefit to defined contribution or 401(k) plans. The 401(k) plan form grew fast, because (although employer matches are permitted) the predominant form of funding for these plans is deferral of employee compensation. Early in 2002, however, the Enron scandal (see below) cast doubt on the role of employer stock in funding 401(k) plans.

§ 6.02   DEFINED CONTRIBUTION PLANS

At one time, the defined benefit plan was the standard form of pension plan, but it has been replaced in this role by the defined contribution plan. Between 1980 and 1996, the number of participants in defined contribution plans went up 155% (from 20 million to 51 million). The number of participants in defined benefit plans rose only 8% in this time period (38 million to 41 million). [*See* Investment Company Research Institute, *Defined Contribution Plan Distribution Choices at Retirement*, <http://www.ici.org/pdf/rpt_annuitization.pdf>]

The defined contribution plan has comparatively few administrative requirements and offers greater portability than a defined benefit plan, because there is a separate account for each participant. Once a person becomes eligible for participation, the employer merely makes contributions, using a simple formula based on compensation, to each employee's account. Although defined contribution plans are legally required to offer QJSA payments, it is more typical for employees to elect payment of their balances as a lump sum at retirement.

The accrued benefit for a participant in a defined contribution plan equals the balance in the account. The balance, in turn, consists of employer contributions, any mandatory employee contributions that the plan requires, plus any voluntary contributions that the plan permits and the employee chooses to make. Defined contribution plans usually maintain separate subaccounts for the employer and employee component of each employee's account, but this is not a legal requirement.

ERISA § 404(c) allows the participant to control the assets in a defined contribution account, including directing the investment of the account. If the participant assumes control, the plan's fiduciaries will not be liable for losses that result from participant control over the funds. Section 404(c) requires the plan to disclose adequate information about their investment alternatives. The plan must offer at least three diversified investment types, with materially different risk and return characteristics.

According to the GAO [*Private Pensions: Issues of Coverage and Increasing Contribution Limits for Defined Contribution Plans*, GAO-01-846 (Sept. 2001)], 36% of all full- and part-time workers participated in a pension plan. The higher a person's salary, the more likely it was that he or she was a plan participant. About one-third or 38% of people earning under $40,000 were plan participants in 1998, and 28% of those earning under $40,000 participated in a defined contribution plan. The GAO predicted that about three million people (about 8% of all participants in defined contribution plans) would benefit directly from EGTRRA's increase in the defined contribution plan limitation. The agency predicted that about 11% of those eligible (about 721,000 defined contribution plan participants) would benefit directly from the ability to make catch-up contributions.

Using constant 1998 dollars as a measure, the average balance in women's defined contribution plans went from $15,372 in 1992 to $25,020 in 1998 (a 53% increase). In the same time period, the average balance for men went from $41,149 to $57,230 (an increase of only 39%). [EBRI Issue Brief No. 227, (Nov. 2000) <http://www.ebri.org/ibex/ib227.htm>]

It should be noted that this average is quite modest, and even a balance of $50,000, if invested safely in the current low-interest climate, would throw off only a few thousand dollars a year. Therefore, either a QJSA pension would be small, or the employee would earn only a few thousand dollars a year by investing a lump sum. If the employee uses the lump sum to enhance Social Security retirement benefits, even to the modest extent of $10,000 a year, the lump sum would be exhausted in only a few years. [For consequences of lump sum payouts, *see* Leonard E. Burman and Norma B. Coe, *What Happens When You Show Them The Money? Lump-Sum Distributions, Retirement Income Security, and Public Policy*, Urban Institute's Report #06750-003 (November 1999)]

§ 6.03   NEW COMPARABILITY PLANS

On October 6, 2000, the IRS published Proposed Regulations at 65 Fed. Reg. 59774-59780 setting the nondiscrimination requirements for "new comparability plans." These are defined contribution plans that are allowed to perform cross-testing and demonstrate nondiscrimination under Treas. Reg. § 1.401(a)(4)-(8) by reference to their benefits rather than the employer's contributions, although they must satisfy a "gateway" requirement preserving at least a minimum rate of accrual for non-HCEs. In practice, this is usually done by finding a defined benefit equivalent for the allocations and then arranging them in rate groups.

Some employers find new comparability plans attractive because these plans allow a much higher allocation rate for highly compensated employees than for other employees. For example, a medical group might use three allocation rates in its new comparability plan: the highest for doctors who are also shareholders in the group, the lowest for nonphysician employees, and one in the middle for physicians who are not shareholders in the practice. [The Regulations were finalized by T.D. 8954, R.I.N. 1545-AY36, 66 Fed. Reg. 34535–34545 (June 29, 2001). *See also* Notice 2000-14, 2000-10 I.R.B. 737 (Feb. 24, 2000) for the IRS opinions on issues raised by new comparability plans]

§ 6.04   401(k) PLANS

[A]   Overview

The Cash or Deferred Arrangement (CODA), also known as the 401(k) plan, has achieved prominence as one of the leading forms of plans for providing post-retirement income. Such plans were authorized by a 1978 amendment to the Internal Revenue Code and first became available in 1981. At the end of 2001, many commentators used the perspective of two decades to consider the role of the 401(k) plan in retirement planning, and in the economy as a whole. Another level of analysis was required in 2002 with the Enron scandal, discussed below.

Although 401(k) plans are subject to the rules for defined contribution plans, strictly speaking 401(k)s are not conventional pension plans. In a 401(k) plan, the employee agrees to have part of his or her salary, up to the limitation provided by the plan (which, in turn, is subject to limitations under the Tax Code) deferred and placed into an individual account instead of being paid in cash as it is earned. The advantage to the employee (apart from the forced savings aspect) is that the appreciation in value of the account is not taxed until withdrawals begin.

Many 401(k) plans feature an "employer match" (the employer contributes a percentage of what the employee contributes) but this is not a mandatory feature of this type of plan.

> **Tip:** Employers have an incentive to "match" if it increases deferrals by non-HCEs, because the increased deferrals make it easier to satisfy the ADP test. Some plans also allow employees to make after-tax contributions to their accounts, subject to the § 401(m)(2) limits.

The aggregate assets in all 401(k) plans declined for the first time in 2000; so did the average 401(k) plan balance. In 1999, there were 327,624 401(k) plans, covering 42.1 million participants; overall assets fell $72 billion in 2000, and the average balance fell from $46,740 in 1999 to $41,919 in 2000. [These figures come from Leigh Strope, *Retirement Plans Take Hit in Downturn*, (July 30, 2002) <http://news.excite.com/printstory/news/ap/010730/01/retirement-worries> (no www.) (posted to www.excite.com on July 30, 2001)] The 401(k) plan had become the predominant vehicle for retirement savings, with more money under investment than defined benefit plans or IRAs.

Consultants Watson Wyatt & Co. suggest that, to secure a comfortable retirement, a person covered by a 401(k) plan (but no other plan) will have to deposit the equivalent of about seven years' pay into the account. At least four years' pay will be required in the account if it supplements other employer plans. That's the conclusion of "Benefit Adequacy in the Age of 401(k)" [<http://www.watsonwyatt.com/us/pubs/insider/backissues.asp>]. The article includes an "adequacy matrix" for calculating the necessary savings level on the basis of the employee's age and years of service.

[B] Deferral Limits

Thanks to EGTRRA, the amount that employees can defer will increase greatly between 2001 and 2006. EGTRRA also includes other novel 401(k) provisions. Participants in 401(k) plans who are over 40 are permitted to make additional "catch-up" contributions, and low-income plan participants are allowed to take a tax credit and not a mere deduction in connection with part of their 401(k) deferrals.

For 2002, the maximum elective deferral in a 401(k) plan is $11,000. This amount increases $1,000 per year until 2006 (when it reaches $15,000). Between 2007 and 2010 (the entire EGTRRA statute is scheduled to sunset on January 1, 2011, unless Congress makes it permanent in whole or in part) the $15,000 amount will be indexed for inflation, but only when changes in the index mandate increases in $500 increments.

The limitation on deferrals is applied on the basis of the individual employee's tax year (and not the plan year). Furthermore, it applies to all CODAs in which the individual participates, not merely those relating to corporations in the same controlled group as the employer. However, the Job Creation and Worker Assistance Act of 2002 (JCWAA) [Pub. L. No. 107-147] provides that if the employer has a 401(k) plan with elective deferrals only (no employer match) and also a defined benefit plan, the I.R.C. § 404(a)(7) "overlapping limitation" does not apply.

Participants in 401(k) plans are always 100% vested in their deferrals at all times. Employees must be allowed to participate in the cash or deferred part of the plan starting with the first entry date after they have one year of service with the employer. Participants must be re-admitted to the plan immediately if they terminate their jobs but are re-employed at the same company before they have undergone a one-year break in service.

[C] Catch-Up Contributions

EGTRRA adds a new I.R.C. § 414(v), which allows employees who are age 50 or older to order additional deferrals, over and above the normal limits. These additional amounts are referred to as catch-up contributions. The intent is to make sure that older employees will come closer to getting the same benefit from the enhanced opportunities for deferrals over the course of their careers as younger employees who can make the greater deferrals for a greater number of years. Catch-up contributions can be made for taxable years beginning after December 31, 2001.

The maximum catch-up contribution for 2002 is $1,000; for 2003 it's $2,000, rising to $5,000 in 2006. Between 2007 and the time EGTRRA sunsets, the $5,000 catch-up amount will be indexed in increments of $500.

EGTRRA § 631 provides that, if all employees who have reached age 50 are permitted to make catch-up contributions, the amount of the catch-up contributions will not be used in calculating the contribution limits. Nor will the catch-up amounts be used in nondiscrimination testing.

In October 2001, the IRS issued proposed regulations for I.R.C. § 414(v). [*See* 66 Fed. Reg. 53555 (Oct. 23, 2001)] Under these rules, any 401(k) plan participant who reaches age 50 at any time during a year is considered eligible to make catch-up contributions for the entire year. [*See also* Notice 2002-4, 2002 I.R.B. 298 for guidance on catch-up contributions (and hardship distributions from 401(k) plans)]

[D] Other EGTRRA 401(k) Changes

Also as a result of EGTRRA, the Internal Revenue Code is amended by adding a new section, I.R.C. § 402A, authorizing "qualified plus contribution programs" permitting 401(k) accounts to be treated like Roth IRAs. That is, employees will be able to make elective salary deferrals. Unlike ordinary contributions to 401(k) plans, these Roth-type deferrals will be taxable income when they are placed in the account—but can qualify for tax exemption when they are withdrawn from the account.

To prevent taxation of the withdrawn amounts, the employee must leave the elective-deferral contributions in the account for at least five years after the date of contribution. Tax-free distributions can be made only to a participant who has reached age 59½ or become disabled, or to the estate of a deceased participant.

Low-income 401(k) plan participants are entitled to a tax credit for their deferrals, for tax years beginning after December 31, 2001, and before January 1, 2007. For this purpose, a low-income employee is one whose income is below $50,000 for a joint return, $25,000 for a single person's return. The maximum credit is $1,000 (50% of the first $2,000 deferred under the 401(k) plan.

§ 6.05   401(k) ANTIDISCRIMINATION RULES

Understandably, highly compensated employees are in a better position to bypass immediate receipt of part of their salaries than rank-and-file employees. Therefore, the Internal Revenue Code includes detailed provisions for determining whether the plan is excessively unbalanced in favor of deferrals by HCEs.

There are two antidiscrimination tests: the ADP test (Actual Deferral Percentage) and the ACP test (Aggregate Contribution Percentage). A full discussion is beyond the scope of this book; you should just be aware that the 401(k) plan will be scrutinized for compliance with at least one of these tests.

According to Treas. Reg. § 1.401(k)-1(f)(6), if the plan fails both those tests for a plan year, the excess contribution percentage must be corrected within the first two and a half months after the end of the plan year. Failure to correct makes the employer liable to a 10% excise tax on the amount of excess deferral that is not corrected. [I.R.C. § 4979] If the failure continues for 12 months, the plan will be disqualified.

The employer can correct the situation in three ways:

- Distributing the excess contributions (and the income allocated to them) out of the plan before the end of the following plan year;
- Recharacterizing the excess contributions as after-tax contributions;
- Making qualified nonelective or qualified matching contributions.

Given the complexity of these rules, the IRS has recognized various safe harbor mechanisms that employers can use to simplify compliance. [*See* IRS Notices 98-52, 1998-46 I.R.B. 16 and 2000-3, 2000-4 I.R.B. 413. *See also* EGTRRA §§ 663 and 666 for provisions making it somewhat easier to benefit HCEs without rendering the plan discriminatory]

§ 6.06   DISTRIBUTIONS FROM THE 401(k) PLAN

[A]   General Rule

Pre-tax deferrals from a 401(k) plan cannot be distributed to the participant until:

- Retirement,
- Death,
- Disability,
- Separation from service [see below for the abolition of the "same desk" rule],
- Hardship,
- The participant reaches age 59½.

Although profit-sharing plans can make distributions purely because of the number of years the participant has worked for the employer, or the number of years the funds have remained in the account, these are not acceptable rationales for distributions from a 401(k) plan. [I.R.C. § 401(k)(2)(B)(ii)]

[B]   Hardship Distributions

Treas. Reg. § 1.401(k)-1(d)(2)(i) defines hardship as an immediate and heavy financial need that cannot be satisfied by reasonable access to the participant's other assets. The hardship withdrawal from the plan must not exceed the amount of the need plus any taxes and penalties that the participant can reasonably expect to incur.

Certain categories have been identified as automatically satisfying the financial needs test:

- Medical expenses of the employee, spouse, and dependent children;
- Purchase of a principal residence (but not routine mortgage payments);

- Staving off eviction or foreclosure of the mortgage on the principal residence;
- Tuition, room, board, and related expenses for the next 12 months for post-secondary education of the employee, spouse, or dependents.

Employees are expected to seek insurance reimbursement wherever it is available to cope with financial hardship; to liquidate their other assets to the extent this is reasonable; to cease further elective contributions to pension plans; to seek other distributions and nontaxable loans from employer plans; and to engage in commercial borrowing on reasonable terms, before they take hardship distributions from their 401(k) plans.

Note that, because of IRS Notice 99-5, 1999-3 I.R.B. 10, hardship withdrawals from 401(k) plans cannot be rolled over to other plans unless the employee is at least 59½ or has separated from service. Therefore, an in-service hardship distribution is not subject to 20% withholding like other one-time distributions from qualified plans. However, the plan must withhold at a 10% rate unless the employee waives the application of withholding.

[C] Elimination of "Same Desk" Rule

One basis on which employees can get distributions from a 401(k) plan is separation from service—i.e., ceasing to be an employee. Before EGTRRA was passed, the "same desk" rule was applied. Under this rule, a person would not be considered separated from service if the original employer had gone through a merger, consolidation, or liquidation, but the employee continued to carry out the same job for the successor company, and thus would not be entitled to a distribution from the plan.

EGTRRA provides, for distributions made after December 31, 2001, that if a corporation sells "substantially all" (defined as 85% or more) of its business assets to an unrelated company, or sells a subsidiary to an unrelated person or company, the selling company's employees have separated from service even if, in practice, they carry out the same tasks for the new employer. [This provision is subject to the EGTRRA sunset date of January 1, 2011. *See also* Rev. Proc. 2000-27, 2000-21 I.R.B. 1016]

§ 6.07 ADMINISTRATION OF THE 401(k) PLAN

The employer has an obligation to deposit deferrals and after-tax employee contributions into the plan no later than the fifteenth business day of the second month after the funds were withheld from payroll or turned over to the employer.

Rev. Rul. 2000-8, 2000-7 I.R.B. 617 settles the question of "opting in" versus "opting out." It's permissible to draft a plan that automatically defers a fixed percentage of the employee's compensation in the plan, unless the employee chooses to opt out.

The DOL's Pension and Welfare Benefit Administration (PWBA) released guidance about 401(k) plan fee structures in order to improve plan participants' decision making. [*See* <http://www.dol.gov/pwba/pubs/401kfe~1.htm>] The PWBA groups fees into three categories: plan administration fees, investment fees, and individual service fees for optional features such as plan loans or investment advice. The fees may be payable either to the employer (if it furnishes services directly) or to outside service providers. In a bundled arrangement, all the fees are funneled through one provider that coordinates the services. An unbundled arrangement has separate charges for the fees of the trustee, communications firm, investment manager, and other service providers.

§ 6.08   INVESTMENT ADVICE FOR PARTICIPANTS

PWBA Advisory Opinion 2001-09A [(Dec. 14, 2001) <http://www.dol.gov/pwba/programs/ori/advisory2001/2001-09A.htm>] says that it would not be a prohibited transaction for a company that provides financial services to retain an independent professional to use computer modeling and modern portfolio theory to offer discretionary asset allocation services and recommended asset allocation services in connection with individual account plans—i.e., 401(k) plans. Participants will be given advice about how to allocate assets within their accounts, but would be permitted to either accept or reject the advice.

The company upon which the Advisory Opinion is based, SunAmerica Retirement Markets Inc., stated that the fiduciary for the 401(k) plan would be given detailed information about the independent financial expert's role in developing model portfolios to be recommended to plan participants—and how the expert's involvement will affect the fee structure that SunAmerica charges for its services. The financial expert's compensation is not affected by participant's decisions about how to allocate the assets in their accounts (although SunAmerica's earnings from the 401(k) plan can increase based on these choices). SunAmerica will pay fees to the financial expert, but to preserve the expert's independence, the fee from SunAmerica will not be more than 5% of the expert's annual gross income.

SunAmerica applied for a prohibited transaction exemption. The PWBA went one further by issuing an Advisory Opinion. The difference is that only SunAmerica would have been able to use an exemption, whereas the advisory opinion can be relied on by others. [*See* Tom Lauricella, *Decision Allows 401(k) Investors To Have Pros Call the Shots*, Wall Street Journal, Dec. 26, 2001, at p. C1]

§ 6.09   401(k) PLANS RESPOND TO THE ECONOMY

[A]   Market Effects

In the 1990s, 401(k) plans rose to prominence. Balances in 401(k) plans grew during the bull market—and 401(k) plan participants were often first-time or novice stock market investors, so they brought a new group of investors to the market. At the peak, there were 42 million 401(k) plan participants, with a total of $1.8 trillion invested in their accounts.

Unfortunately, however, when the stock market declined in March 2001, and when the attack of September 11, 2001, made the economy's problems worse, 401(k) plans were also adversely affected. The average plan balance peaked at $47,000 in 1999, and declined for the first time in 2000 to $42,000. In 1997, close to 79% of eligible employees participated in their company's 401(k) plan—dropping to 75% in late 2001.

In the declining economy, some large companies experienced adverse results—even bankruptcy. Employees whose contributions and employer matches were heavily invested in company stock saw a precipitous drop in the value of their 401(k) accounts. Employees at Lucent Technologies, Ikon Office Solutions, and other companies have sued their employers or ex-employers for securities law violations (based on fiduciary breaches in the form of failure to inform employees of the vital need to diversify their accounts). [This is not a new phenomenon: It occurred in conjunction with corporate failures in the past. *See* Ellen E. Schultz, *Employers Fight Limits on Firm's Stock in 401(k)s*, Wall Street Journal, Dec. 21, 2001, at p. C1]

Major companies such as Ford Motor Co. and Bethlehem Steel announced in 2001 that they would cut back or eliminate employer matches to 401(k) accounts, to save money.

ERISA limits the amount of employer stock in a plan account to 10%, but this limit does not apply to 401(k) plans. Throughout the economy, an average of 19% of 401(k) funds are invested in employer stock—but this proportion rises to 50% in plans where employees can invest in employer stock and also get employer matches in this form. [Paul J. Lim and Matthew Benjamin, *The 401(k) Stumbles*, (Dec. 24, 2001) <http://www.usnews.com/usnews/issue/011224/biztech/24401k.htm>] Qualified defined benefit plans are subject to a 10% limit on employer stock, but under current law, this does not apply to 401(k) plans.

[B] Enron Effects

Enron, a Texas energy trading firm, filed for bankruptcy protection on December 2, 2001, triggering not only a huge scandal (because of faked audit reports and document destruction) but also a broader appraisal of the role of company stock in 401(k) plans, and indeed in retirement saving in general.

During the bull market, publicly traded companies had very strong incentives to use their own stock to compensate employees. Not only could they save cash by offering stock or stock options, but distributing stock to employees reduces the risk of unfriendly takeovers, increases employees' stake in the company and therefore at least theoretically their loyalty, and gives employees the chance to benefit from increases in the value of the stock. The problem is that, in a bear market, employees suffer correspondingly as a result of decreases in the value of the stock.

Although the general rule is that corporations do not get a tax deduction for dividends they pay to their stockholders, sometimes a dividend deduction is available in connection with stock ownership by employees. Technical tax rules sometimes also allow companies to use Employee Stock Ownership Plans (ESOPs) as a vehicle for low-cost borrowing. [Ellen E. Schultz and Theo Francis, *Companies' Hot Tax Break: 401(k)s,* Wall Street Journal, Jan. 31, 2002, at p. C1.]

> **Tip:** If employers provide proper disclosure, they can set their own rules about diversification and limitations on resale of stock, because these are considered business decisions by management that are not subject to fiduciary duty. However, there is a fiduciary duty to offer prudent investment options to employees (whether or not they choose to take advantage of them!).

Nearly all 401(k) plans offer several investment options, and some plans offer more than a dozen options; the most popular number of options is somewhere between eight and twelve. Nevertheless, despite the availability of diversification, most 401(k) investors do not diversify their accounts.

In 2001, according to Hewitt Associates, 55% of plans offered the option of investing in the employer company's own stock, and 30% of 401(k) assets were invested that way. Nearly all plans (85%) allowed investment in large capitalization stock funds, but only 19% of funds were invested there. About two-thirds of plans offered the chance to invest in stable value funds or stock index funds (69% and 70%, respectively), but these were the recipients of only 16% and 11% of 401(k) funds respectively. Although about half of 401(k) plans offered money market funds and bond funds as investment alternatives, only about 2% of assets were invested in each of them. [Aaron Lucchetti and Theo Francis, *Dangers of Not Diversifying Hit Investors*, Wall Street Journal, Feb. 15, 2002, at p. C1; Steven Greenhouse, *Response to 401(k) Proposals Follows Party Lines*, New York Times, Feb. 2, 2002, at p. C1; Kathy Chen, *Pension Plans Are Adjusted After Enron*, Wall Street Journal, Jan. 29, 2002, at p. A2; Daniel Altman, *Experts Say Diversify, But Many Plans Rely Heavily on Company Stock*, New York Times, Jan. 26, 2002, at p. A26]

According to the Employee Benefits Research Institute, the average 401(k) plan is 19% invested in employer stock, but 32% is invested this way in plans that include the employer's stock, and 53% in plans where the employer company has some influence over investment choices. [Richard A. Oppel Jr., *The Danger in a One-Basket Nest Egg Prompts A Call to Limit Stock*, New York Times, Dec. 19, 2001, at p. C1]

Many employees hold a belief that their company's stock is more likely to prosper or at least offer stable value than the stock market at large. Others may hold a large position in employer stock because they're afraid that selling their shares and re-investing will be viewed as a lack of confidence in the employer. It's common for employer matches to be made in company stock rather than cash, and to forbid employees to sell such stock before reaching age 50, or until they have been with the company for a certain number of years, which also encourages build-up of company stock in 401(k) accounts. However, some companies have been criticized for imposing restrictions on rank-and-file employees, while making large stock option grants or compensation payments in stock form to top executives. [Ellen E. Schultz and Theo Francis, *Why Company Stock Is a Burden For Many—And Less So For a Few*, Wall Street Journal, Nov. 27, 2001, at p. A1]

However, diversification is not necessarily the cure to all 401(k) planning ills. It should be noted that in a broad stock market decline, like the one that marked late 2001 and early 2002, even a diversified portfolio is likely to suffer losses in many of its components.

Congress responded with the introduction of many pieces of legislation taking differing approaches to protecting retirement savings, such as limitations on concentration in employer stock and limitations on the length of time employees could be compelled to hold matching stock contributions in their accounts.

[C] "Lockdowns" and Other Transaction Limits

One reason the Enron situation spiraled out of control so fast was that the company imposed a "lockdown" that prevented employees from selling the stock in their retirement plans. Transaction limits are also called "blackouts" and "quiet periods." Typically, lockdowns are imposed when a plan is in the process of implementing procedural changes, such as changing its schedule for valuation or adopting a new service provider.

A balance must be struck between managers' desire to preserve the stock price of the company versus the employees' need to maintain the value of their retirement savings accounts. It is illegal securities fraud to deceive employees in order to prevent them from selling their stock in the corporation; if it is part of a pattern, it could also violate the Racketeer Influenced and Corrupt Organizations Act (RICO).

Enron's woes made it natural to ponder the effect of lockdowns on other plans. [Ellen E. Schultz, *"Lockdowns" of 401(k) Plans Draw Scrutiny*, Wall Street Journal, Jan. 16, 2002, at p. C1] In January 2002, the Profit Sharing/401(k) Council of America (PSCA) posted questions and answers about lockdown issues on its Web site, <http://www.psca.org>. The PSCA explains that lockdowns are necessary when a plan changes its fund managers or other record-keeping entity, so that the participants' records can be reconciled and the accuracy of the records can be checked after the transition. [*See* <http://www.spencernet.com/Archive/News013102.html>]

CHAPTER 7
CASH BALANCE PLANS

§ 7.01   INTRODUCTION

A cash balance plan is a hybrid pension plan that shares features of a conventional defined benefit plan with characteristics more like a profit-sharing or 401(k) plan. Cash balance plans are subject to the defined benefit plan rules.

The IRS's definition of a cash balance plan, found at 64 Fed. Reg. 56579, is "a defined benefit pension plan that typically defines an employee's retirement benefit by reference to the amount of a hypothetical account balance." In a typical cash balance plan, this account is credited with hypothetical allocations and interest that are determined under a formula set out in the plan.

The plan is drafted so that the corporation's books reflect an individual account for each participant. The employer funds the plan each year, based on a percentage of pay, and subject to the I.R.C. § 415 limit on employer contributions. The pension the employee will eventually receive reflects two elements: an annual benefit credit (a percentage of pay) and annual interest credited at the rate specified by the plan. Because cash balance plans provide individual accounts, the plans are more portable than ordinary defined benefit plans.

At retirement, the employee's retirement annuity is based on the vested account balance. In practice, although in most defined benefit plans accrual is greatest in the later years of employment, in cash balance plans accrual is greatest in the early years. Defined benefit plans often provide early retirement subsidies; cash balance plans seldom do.

Changing an existing defined benefit plan to a cash balance plan, via plan amendments, is called a conversion. Generally, the new cash balance benefit formula applies to new employees, and may also apply to employees who had already earned benefits under the plan before the conversion.

Although plan amendments cannot reduce benefits earned before the conversion, some conversions have the effect that employees who already earned benefits do not earn additional retirement benefits for varying periods of time after the conversion. This effect, often referred to as "wearaway" or "benefit plateau," continues until the employee's benefit under the ongoing cash balance formula catches up with the employee's protected benefit.

A report from the ERISA Advisory Council defines wearaway as an effect of plan transitions. The employee can get either the frozen benefit under the old plan formula or the total benefit under the cash balance plan—whichever is greater. But for employees who are close to early retirement age, the frozen benefit may be so much larger than the accruals under the new cash balance formula that, in effect, little or nothing will be accrued for a long time, until the benefit under the old rules is "worn away."

§ 7.02   CASH BALANCE PLANS: PROS AND CONS

Cash balance plans are authorized by a sentence in the preamble of IRS Proposed Regulations that were published on September 11, 1991, creating a safe harbor. Under this proposal, changing the accrual pattern of a defined benefit plan "will not cause a cash balance plan to fail to satisfy the requirement of I.R.C. § 411(b)(1)(H)." This proposal was never finalized, but the IRS has permitted many cash balance conversions, including some involving major corporations. [For the history of cash balance plans, *see* Ellen E. Schultz, *Inquiry Sought Into History of Pension Rule*, Wall Street Journal, Jan. 14, 2000, at p. A4, and *How a Single Sentence From IRS Paved Way to Cash Balance Plans*, Wall Street Journal, Dec. 28, 1999, at p. A1]

Cash balance plans are attractive to employers because the employer can retain any difference between the plan's actual investment return and the rate of return promised to employees. The plan can become self-funded if the gap is large enough so that the employer will not have to make further contributions.

Cash balance plans have been criticized because of the possibility of "wearaway," and on the grounds of alleged unfairness to older and longer-tenured employees. However, proponents of cash balance plans say that the traditional defined benefit plan doesn't respond to the current needs of the work force. By encouraging early retirement, the traditional plan makes it hard for employers to keep mature workers whose skills are needed.

Some employers also like cash balance plans as incentives for a younger, more mobile work force, who would value the ability to roll over a lump sum from the cash balance plan to an IRA or to another qualified plan. But it should be noted that cash balance plans could still impose participation and vesting requirements. Therefore, employees who leave before vesting, or when they are only partially vested, get little or no benefit from cash balance plans. [*See* Ellen E. Schultz, *Young and Vestless*, Wall Street Journal, Dec. 16, 1999, at p. A1. Arguments in favor of cash balance conversions are summed up by Hugh Forcier, *Understanding the Assault on Cash Balance Plans*, <http://www.faegre.com/articles/article_349.asp>. Contrary arguments can be found at <http://www.cashpensions.com>]

In 1999, IRS Chief Counsel Stuart Brown testified before the Senate Committee on Health, Education, Labor, and Pensions. [The hearing transcript was published at <http://www.senate.gov/~labor/hearings/septhear/092199wt/body_092199wt.htm>] Mr. Brown stated that mere correlation between age and benefit reduction is not necessarily unlawful age discrimination. A plan is not discriminatory for tax purposes unless the accrual rate is reduced because of the attainment of a particular age. Mr. Brown testified that there is no legal protection for the employee's expectation that the plan will not change its accrual formulas.

§ 7.03 "WHIPSAW" AND FINANCIAL FACTORS

The "whipsaw" issue arises because I.R.C. § 417 specifies the interest and mortality assumptions that must be used in converting from annuity to lump sum payment. When a worker covered by a defined benefit plan terminates employment, the sponsor must calculate the present value of any lump sum distribution.

This is done by projecting the account balance that would be available at normal retirement age, using PBGC-authorized interest rate assumptions. The next step is to find the value of the annuity that could be purchased with that sum. Finally, the PBGC interest rate assumptions are used again, to reconvert the annuity to a lump sum that represents the present value of the participant's account.

Applying this so-called whipsaw calculation to some cash balance plans increases the lump sum available to some plan participants. The participants who benefit naturally argue that the calculation has to be applied—and plan sponsors want to argue that they can bypass the whipsaw calculation. The higher the interest rates used, the less likely participants are to complain. Therefore, the whipsaw problem is most acute for disputes about plan actions taken before 1995, because in 1994 the PBGC raised its interest rate assumptions significantly.

§ 7.04   CASE LAW ON CASH BALANCE PLANS

According to *Eaton v. Onan Corp.* [117 F. Supp. 2d 812 (S.D. Ind. 2000)], converting a defined benefit plan to a cash balance plan does not violate either the ADEA or ERISA's ban on age discrimination in benefit accruals. The court said that the ERISA provisions do not apply to employees younger than the plan's "normal retirement age."

Late in 2001, the company and the plaintiffs reached a settlement of that case, and of a companion tax court case, *Arndt v. Comm'r* [Docket No. 334-9912 (Tax Ct. 2001). *See* Lee A. Sheppard, *Settlement Reached in Cash Balance Plan Case,* 2001 Tax Notes (Oct. 1, 2001) (law.com)] Under the settlement, Onan Corp. agreed to compensate 1500 early retirees and over-40 employees for their losses stemming from the conversion to a cash balance plan. Onan did not admit to age discrimination, but did agree to make changes in plan design favorable to older employees. All participants can elect to receive a lump sum that is equal to the present value of the minimum annuity they would receive at the plan's normal retirement age—even if this is greater than their cash balance account.

Esden v. Bank of Boston [229 F.3d 154 (2d Cir. 2000)], a class action against a pension plan, tackles some important issues. The plaintiffs alleged that the plan's calculation of lump sum distributions violated the ERISA antiforfeiture rule.

The plan projected cash balances that would be taken as lump sums using a 4% interest rate, well below the 5.5% rate used to accrue interest credits. When the projection was discounted back to present value, participants received less than the actuarial equivalent of the normal balance. Part of the benefit was also contingent on the distribution option chosen, which was alleged to violate ERISA § 203(a) and I.R.C. § 411(a)(2).

The Second Circuit agreed with the view expressed by the IRS in Notice 96-8, 1996-1 C.B. 359, that "whipsaw," the result of projecting the account value using a rate below the guaranteed rate, violates ERISA because the participant is entitled to the present value of the accrued benefit. The Second Circuit view is that a variable interest rate is permissible as long as it is definitely determinable and does not grant discretion to the employer to set the amount after establishing the plan.

Lyons v. Georgia-Pacific Corp. [2000 WL 1140673 (11th Cir. Aug. 11, 2000)] holds that the lump sum benefit under a defined benefit plan must be calculated by using the PBGC discount rate to discount the normal retirement benefit to present value. Although the district court treated the IRS Regulations about the discount rate [Treas. Reg. § 1.411(a)-11] as "unreasonable," the Eleventh Circuit upheld the validity of the regulations.

In *Berger v. Xerox Corp. Retirement Income Guarantee Plan* [2001 WL 930142 (S.D. Ill. 2001)], the judge says that improper interest rate calculations were used to arrive at the pre-retirement lump sum payments for terminated vested participants. Therefore, the court ordered recalculation for everyone who received such a distribution since January 1, 1990. Like *Esden* and *Lyons*, the *Berger* court required the use of the interest crediting rate in effect as of the date of the disposition.

§ 7.05   THE CONVERSION PROCESS

At least 15 days' notice must be given in advance of adoption of a plan amendment that significantly reduces the rate of benefit accruals in the future. [*See* § 11.05 for a discussion of EGTRRA rules increasing the amount of disclosure that participants are entitled to in this situation] The plan may also have to issue a revised SPD and/or a Summary of Material Modification in connection with the conversion.

The PWBA (part of the Department of Labor) published a document, "Cash Balance Plans Questions & Answers." [<http://www.dol.gov/pwba/pubs/cashbq &a.htm>] Question 11 says that neither ERISA nor the Tax Code obligates employers who convert to a cash balance plan to give employees the option of remaining in the old plan. The employer can simply replace the old formula with the new formula for all participants, as long as the benefits already accrued as of the date of the conversion are not reduced. Or the employer can keep current employees under the old plan formula, applying the new formula only to those hired after the change. Another option is for some employees to be "grandfathered in," or allowed to receive their pensions under the old formula.

Tip: If the converted plan does offer choices to participants, and if they have to sign a waiver as part of the option process, make sure that the waiver conforms to the standards of the Older Workers Benefit Protection Act. [29 U.S.C. §621 *et seq.*]

For accounting purposes, even though a cash balance plan has hybrid features, it is treated as a defined benefit plan. [*See* Alex T. Arcady and Francine Mellors, *Cash Balance Conversions: Assessing the Accounting and Business Implications*, <http://www.aicpa.org/pubs/jofa/feb2000/arcady.htm>] Therefore, its accounting treatment is controlled by FASB Statement No. 87 (Employers' Accounting for Pensions), No. 88 (Employers' Accounting for Settlements), and No.

132 (Employers' Disclosures About Pensions and Other Postretirement Benefits). An actuary will be required to calculate the new assumptions and the effect of the changed assumptions on plan balances. The company's financial statements may require footnotes to reflect the conversion.

The conversion is a negative plan amendment for accounting purposes. The financial benefits to the company must be recognized prospectively on financial statements, because the prior service cost of the pension plan is reduced.

CHAPTER 8
NONQUALIFIED PLANS

§ 8.01   INTRODUCTION

[A]   Generally

One of the most important aspects of maintaining a qualified plan (and therefore obtaining a tax deduction for related costs) is satisfying the Internal Revenue Code's tests for nondiscrimination. It is not illegal for an employer to set up a discriminatory plan, and in fact many types of nonqualified plans have evolved for companies that want to recruit, retain, or motivate senior management and/or persons who own significant amounts of stock in the corporation. Nonqualified plans are also used to provide post-retirement income higher than the levels that can be generated through a qualified plan.

In contrast with the elaborate rules required to get a current deduction for contributions to a qualified plan, the rules for nonqualified plans are much simpler. The employer is allowed to discriminate in both contributions and benefits in favor of highly compensated employees (HCEs). The plan does not have to be operated through a trust.

In fact, the employer doesn't even have to fund the plan in advance. Payments can be made as they come due, out of the employer's general assets instead of from a special trust. Insurance policies can also be used to fund nonqualified plan benefits. The ERISA funding requirements don't apply to nonqualified plans, so promises and forms of securities can be used for funding a nonqualified plan even if they would not be acceptable in a qualified plan.

In a qualified plan, a "bad boy" clause (one that removes entitlement to benefits) is allowed only for fraud or abuse of fiduciary duty. In a nonqualified plan, benefits can be forfeited by an executive who leaves the company.

Under a qualified plan, the employer gets a current deduction each year as it makes contributions to the plan. The employer's deduction for nonqualified plan expenses is not available until the year in which the participant receives money from the plan and includes it in income. The corporation's general creditors are entitled to make claims against reserves set aside to pay nonqualified plan benefits, but the qualified plan trust is protected against creditors' claims.

[B]   Structures for Nonqualified Plans

Various structures have evolved for providing nonqualified plan benefits to executives, managers, and other favored corporate employees.

[1]   SERP

A Supplemental Executive Retirement Plan (SERP), also known as an excess-benefit plan, can be used to defer amounts that exceed the qualified plan limits.

[2]   QSERP

A Qualified Supplemental Executive Retirement Plan (QSERP) is a qualified plan used to enhance retirement benefits for executives. The plan must satisfy non-discrimination requirements and is subject to the I.R.C. § 415 limits. However, the employer's contributions can be integrated with Social Security, reducing the amount the employer has to contribute on behalf of lower-paid employees. To adopt a QSERP, the employer corporation can simply amend the plan documents to include an annual list of people or job titles entitled to additional benefits of $X/year. Usually, QSERP amounts are subtracted from the amounts that would otherwise be payable under nonqualified plans. Because the QSERP is a qualified plan, the employer gets a current deduction, and the employee is not taxed until benefits are actually paid (and the employee has some certainty that they will be paid because of prefunding). If the QSERP is a defined contribution plan, it is subject to the overall limitation on contributions to all defined contribution plans; if the employer is already making close to the maximum contribution under other qualified plans there is little leeway for the QSERP.

[3]   Rabbi Trust

A rabbi trust (so-called because the first one was created by a synagogue for its clergyman) sets aside assets in an irrevocable trust to pay the benefits, although the corporation's creditors can reach the assets. The assets in the trust cannot revert to the employer until all of the obligations to pay deferred compensation have been satisfied. Executives are not taxed until they receive benefits from the trust, because of the risk that creditor claims will prevent benefit payments. A "springing" rabbi trust is set up with only minimal funding. However, if the control of the corporation changes (for instance, because of a merger or acquisition), then the trust provides for funding for payment of benefits. The rabbi trust will not be considered "funded" for ERISA purposes just because it has a spring provision.

> **Tip:** For a plan to get an IRS ruling on the validity of a rabbi trust arrangement, it must use the model form published in Rev. Proc. 92-64, 1992-2 C.B. 422. The standard form must be adopted verbatim, although additional provisions can be included if they are consistent with the standard provisions.

[4]   Secular Trust

A secular trust is an irrevocable trust whose assets cannot be reached by the employer's creditors, including its bankruptcy creditors. It offers more protection to the executive's right to receive deferred compensation than a rabbi trust, but has less favorable tax consequences. The price of increased protection for the employee is that the employee has taxable income (taxed using the I.R.C. § 72 annuity rules) equal to the employer contributions to the trust on the employee's behalf.

The employer can deduct its contributions to the trust, to the extent they are ordinary and necessary business expenses, in the tax year in which the contributions become taxable income for the employee.

[5] Top Hat Plan

A top hat plan is an unfunded deferred compensation plan limited to managers and/or HCEs. Top hat plans that are pension plans must file a brief notice each year with the Department of Labor, although less disclosure is required than for a qualified plan. An unfunded top hat pension plan is not subject to the ERISA participation, vesting, funding, or fiduciary responsibility rules. The plan must have a claims procedure. Top hat plans that are not pension plans are probably exempt from ERISA Title I. The modest role that ERISA plays in regulating top hat plans is probably enough to preempt state law, so suits cannot be brought in state court involving claims against top hat plans.

[6] Excess Benefit Plan

An excess benefit plan exists simply to provide benefits greater than I.R.C. § 415 would allow under a qualified plan. Unfunded excess benefit plans are exempt from ERISA Title I—but this means that they are vulnerable to regulation by the states.

[7] Integrated Plan

An integrated plan provides additional benefits over and above the 401(k) plan, but subject to the same employer match provisions and offering the same investment options. The participant directs the deferral percentage. First, transfers (of both elective deferrals and employer matches) are made to the qualified plan, then to the nonqualified plan

[8] Tandem Plan

Tandem plans combine with qualified plans to generate larger retirement accruals; they generally offer different investment choices and features from the regular qualified plan

[9] Wrap Plan

Wrap plans accumulate funds on behalf of top executives throughout the year, then make an annual transfer to the qualified plan of the maximum amount that can be accrued for those executives without violating the nondiscrimination rules. [*See New Options in Nonqualified Retirement Plans*, <http://institutional. vanguard.com/cgi-bin/INewsPrint/101179341> (no www)]

§ 8.02 TAXATION OF NONQUALIFIED PLANS

[A] General Considerations

Nonqualified plans can create some subtle tax problems for plan participants. The mere fact that the employer promises to pay benefits in the future doesn't create income for the plan participants, until plan benefits are either actually or constructively received. Constructive receipt is a tax concept roughly equivalent to deliberately turning down money that the taxpayer is entitled to.

Employees are taxed on benefits from nonqualified plans as they are distributed. To the extent that the employee already had to pay tax on amounts not yet distributed, employees are entitled to compute an exclusion ratio (percentage of a distribution that has already been taxed and will not be taxed again).

Nonqualified plan participants are taxed in the year in which rights to property become transferable, or the substantial risk of forfeiture ends, whichever comes first. Sometimes, property rights depend, directly or indirectly, on the plan participant continuing to perform services for the employer. If there is a covenant not to compete, however, property rights might depend on not performing services! Under the IRS Regulations, the facts of each case must be examined to determine whether there is a substantial risk of forfeiture because of a requirement of continued employment or noncompetition.

As for the trust income, there are complex factors (centering around the extent of the employer's contributions and degree of control) that determine ownership of the trust, and therefore whether the employer, the employee, or the trust itself should be taxed on income earned by a secular trust arrangement.

> **Tip:** If the employer is concerned about having to pay income tax, funding could be done with no-income or low-income assets such as zero-coupon bonds or insurance policies.

[B] I.R.C. § 83 Issues

Tax planning for nonqualified plan participants also requires a look at I.R.C. § 83, which sometimes requires employees to include in income amounts that have not been distributed from the nonqualified plan. Section 83 provides that whenever property is transferred to anyone except the employer for the provision of services, the employee's taxable income includes the fair market value of the transferred property, minus any amount paid for the property.

Section 83 doesn't apply to transfers to qualified plan trusts, or to a deferred compensation arrangement that gives the employee a mere contractual right to receive compensation in the future. Many stock option transactions are also exempt from this section. However, § 83 does apply to assets set aside in trusts, escrows, or similar arrangements that are not subject to the claims of the corporation's general creditors.

Where § 83 applies, the employee's tax is based on the value of the employee's income on the plan trust at the time of taxation, and not on the fair market value of the employer's contributions from the trust.

In 1996, the Tax Court decided that § 83(a) requires inclusion in income as soon as vacation and severance pay benefits are secured with a letter of credit, on the theory that the employee should be deemed to have received those amounts. [*Schmidt Baking Co. v. Commissioner*, 107 T.C. 271 (1996)]

Congress passed legislation to overturn that result: Internal Revenue Service Restructuring and Reform Act of 1998 (IRSRRA) [Pub. L. No. 105-206 § 7001], which adds a new I.R.C. § 404(a)(11). This section makes it clear that deeming is not proper. Amounts secured in this way must not be included in taxable income until they are actually received. IRS Notice 99-16, 1999-13 I.R.B. 10 provides information about accounting changes required to conform to the IRSRRA requirements.

[C] Employer's Tax Deduction

The employer gets a tax deduction for contributions made to a secular trust (as long as they are ordinary and necessary business expenses) in the year in which the contributions are taken into the employee's taxable income. Internal Revenue Code § 404(a)(5) gives the rules for deferred compensation plans for employees. Similar rules are found for the deferred compensation of independent contractors in I.R.C. § 404(d)(2).

Employer contributions to a plan that provides deferred compensation for shareholders who are not employees or independent contractors are not deductible. Treasury Regulation § 1.404(a)-12(b)(1) provides that the employer deducts only the amount of the actual contribution, even if employees have to include a larger sum in income (because of appreciation on amounts within the plan).

When deferred compensation is paid directly to the employee under an unfunded arrangement, the employer gets the deduction in the year of the payment—not the year of the contribution, which would be the rule in a qualified plan. If the deferred compensation obligations are merely contractual, and not funded or otherwise secured, then the employer doesn't get a deduction until the employee actually receives the compensation. If the deferred compensation exceeds the reasonable amount that would constitute an ordinary and necessary business expense, the excess is not deductible.

The employer cannot receive a deduction unless it maintains a separate account for each employee covered by a funded deferred compensation arrangement that is not a qualified plan.

Most employers use accrual-basis accounting (whereas nearly all employees use the cash method). If an accrual-basis employer defers payment of compensation to a year other than the year in which it was earned, the deduction must be delayed until the year of actual payment, unless the company is financially unable to pay, or unless it is impossible to determine the correct amount to be paid until after the year ends. [*See* Treas. Reg. §§ 1.404(a)-1(c), 1.404(b)-1]

Distributions from nonqualified plans (unless the distributions are made on account of death, sickness, accident, disability, or disability retirement) are considered wages for FICA and FUTA purposes. Internal Revenue Code § 3121(v)(2) provides that, for the purposes of paying the employer's share and withholding the employee's share of FICA and Medicare tax, amounts deferred under a nonqualified deferred compensation plan are taken into account only once. This is either the time when the services are performed or when there is no longer a substantial risk of forfeiture—whichever occurs later.

In general, income taxes must be withheld at a rate of 10% of the lump sum or benefits paid from the nonqualified deferred compensation arrangement. However, I.R.C. § 3405 gives the payee of the benefits the option of telling the plan not to withhold.

> **Tip:** Many nonqualified plans contain a provision that benefits become payable as soon as the corporation undergoes a change in control (e.g., merger or sale of the corporation's assets or stock). Deferred compensation that becomes due at this time could be an "excess parachute payment" subject to a 20% excise tax. So the value of a provision of this type in providing reassurance (and therefore motivation) for senior management must be balanced against the risk of greater corporate excise tax liability.

§ 8.03   PROHIBITED TRANSACTIONS

ERISA § 502(i) gives the DOL power to assess a civil penalty against a "party in interest" who engages in a prohibited transaction with a nonqualified plan. The penalty, which is usually assessed in connection with top hat plans, is 5% for every year or partial year in which the prohibited transaction continues in effect. There is an additional 100% penalty if DOL issues a notice of violation, but the violation is not corrected within 90 days (or whatever extension of time DOL grants).

CHAPTER 9

EARLY RETIREMENT AND RETIREE HEALTH BENEFITS

§ 9.01 INTRODUCTION

One goal of the legal system is to permit employers and employees to work out arrangements under which their mutual economic needs are met. Employers are not allowed to mandate retirement purely on the basis of age (except in a few safety-related occupations), and must accommodate employee's wishes to continue working after normal retirement age, if the employees are still capable of tackling the job.

However, although some individuals have personal reasons for wanting to stay at work, and others would prefer to retire but are financially unable to do so, there is a large group of employees who, on the contrary, prefer to retire before normal retirement age (NRA). The employer may also wish to reduce its payroll, without dismissals or layoffs. One way to do so is by offering incentives for voluntary early retirement.

Early retirement incentives have a business downside, however. In many cases, the employees who accept the offer are those who have the best prospects for getting another job. The employees who stay put may be "deadwood" who recognize that no one else would want to hire them.

Without careful planning and drafting, early retirement programs can also have a legal downside. The employer must make sure that incentives are available without unlawful discrimination. Furthermore, although it makes sense to ask early retirees to waive their claims against the employer, the waiver must be drafted with due attention to the Older Worker's Benefit Protection Act (OWBPA).

> **Tip:** Although the OWBPA mandates a 21-day period during which employees can consider whether to take an early retirement offer, the employer can still cancel the offer—it doesn't have to remain irrevocable during that period. [*Ellison v. Premier Salons Int'l Inc.,* 164 F.3d 1111 (8th Cir. 1999)]

An early retirement program can create risks from two directions. Employees who are eligible may charge that the plan is a subterfuge for forcing them into involuntary retirement. On the other hand, employees who are not offered the incentives can charge that the unavailability of the program was the result of discrimination against them. Furthermore, if the early retirement program changes over time, employees who accepted a first offer may claim that the company should have informed them of the potential for getting a better offer by waiting longer. [This topic is discussed in more detail in Chapter 15, § 15.07, as an issue of fiduciary responsibility to make full disclosure to plan participants]

The questions of early retirement programs and retiree health benefits need to be examined in tandem, because one of the most important questions in deciding whether to retire early is the availability of health coverage. Medicare eligibility depends on age (65 or over) or disability, not employment status. Furthermore, the Medicare system does not provide spousal benefits: each spouse must qualify independently. Therefore, a potential early retiree who is younger than 65 will need retiree health coverage, COBRA coverage, or private insurance.

§ 9.02   ADEA ISSUES OF EARLY RETIREMENT INCENTIVES

At what point does an incentive provided to motivate early retirement turn into pressure that adds up to "constructive discharge" (the equivalent of firing the employee)? The relevant statute is the Older Worker's Benefit Protection Act, which allows voluntary early retirement incentives but only if they satisfy the objectives of the ADEA: promoting employment opportunities for qualified and willing older workers.

The OWBPA allows employers to subsidize early retirement via flat dollar benefits, extra benefits, or percentage increases. Employees who retire early can be offered a more favorable benefit formula (e.g., adding a certain number of years to the number of years actually worked). It does not violate the OWBPA to impose a "window" period that is the only time that the incentive is available.

A defined benefit plan can pay a "Social Security supplement" starting at the date of early retirement, extending until the first date the retiree will be able to receive reduced Social Security benefits—or, if the employer prefers, until the retiree will be eligible for a full unreduced Social Security benefit.

> **Tip:** The employer can amend the pension plan to raise the NRA from 65 to 67 (a change that the Social Security Administration is gradually implementing), as long as accrued early retirement benefits, including subsidies, are preserved.

A university offered early retirement incentives to both tenured professors and top-level administrators. The North Dakota district court said (and the Eighth Circuit agreed) that payments to the faculty members were not "wages" (and therefore not subject to Social Security taxes) because the payments were made in exchange for property rights in university tenure. The payments to administrators, although similar, were subject to FICA, because the administrators were at-will employees, whereas the tenured faculty could only be dismissed for grave cause. [*North Dakota State Univ. v. United States*, 85 A.F.T.R.2d ¶2000-332 (D.N.D. Nov. 19, 1999), *aff'd,* Unempl. Ins. Rep. (CCH) ¶16,568 (8th Cir. June 18, 2001)]

§ 9.03   DISCLOSURES TO EMPLOYEES

An employee can't make a meaningful decision about whether or not to retire without understanding the choices that will be available in the near future. If the terms of the early retirement program change, people who were not eligible for the improved terms, or who elected early retirement without knowing that they could have gotten a better deal by waiting longer, may charge the employer with fraud, and may charge various parties involved with the plan with violations of fiduciary duty.

The Third Circuit announced a rule in *Fischer v. Philadelphia Electric Co.* [96 F.3d 1533 (3d Cir. 1996)] that a revised early retirement incentive has received "serious consideration," and therefore must be disclosed to potential early retirees, once senior managers discuss the proposal for purposes of implementation.

Bins v. Exxon Co. [189 F.3d 929 (9th Cir. 1999)] reached a similar conclusion. The *Bins* case was reheard in 2000. [*Bins*, 220 F.3d 1042 (9th Cir. 2000)] The mandate to the fiduciary to give complete and accurate information about plan changes under "serious consideration" in response to employee queries, was affirmed. But the Ninth Circuit did not impose a duty to volunteer information employees have not asked for. Nor did the court require the employer to report changes to employees who made inquiries in the past—unless the employer volunteered to supply updated information.

Another Ninth Circuit case, *Wayne v. Pacific Bell* [189 F.3d 982 (9th Cir. 1999)], ruled that discussion of a particular early retirement proposal during collective bargaining constitutes serious consideration—even if that particular proposal is never adopted.

Hudson v. General Dynamics Corp. [118 F. Supp. 2d 226 (D. Conn. 2000)] found a breach of fiduciary duty with respect to two employees who asked, but were not told, that an early retirement program was under consideration. However, claims were dismissed with respect to 87 other employees who did not ask, or whose inquiries came before the company seriously considered the program.

McAuley v. IBM Corp. [165 F.3d 1038 (6th Cir. 1999)] permits retirees to sue for breach of fiduciary duty when their ex-employer adopted an early retirement plan more favorable than the one they accepted and relied on in making retirement plans.

It is a breach of fiduciary duty to inform potential early retirees that lump-sum payouts are available, without also disclosing the I.R.C. § 415 limitations on rollovers and explaining the tax consequences. [*Farr v. U.S. West Communications, Inc.*, 58 F.3d 1361 (9th Cir. 1998)] Given that the fiduciaries' common-law duty of loyalty requires them to deal fairly and honestly with plan participants, it is a violation to give them incomplete information.

§ 9.04   EEOC MANUAL ON EARLY RETIREMENT INCENTIVES

Late in 2000, the EEOC updated Section 3 of its Compliance Manual to deal with benefits. [No. 915.003, (Oct. 3, 2000) <http://www.eeoc.gov/docs/benefits.html>] The agency's position is that an early retirement incentive (ERI) program is lawful as long as it's voluntary. The EEOC will not get involved if the employer chooses to:

• Set a minimum age or minimum number of years of service for employees who participate;
• Have a window (i.e., the incentive is only available for a limited time period);
• Limit the ERI to a manager, a department, a particular facility, etc.

However, ERI benefits can't be reduced or denied for older employees versus similarly situated younger employees unless the employer qualifies for one of five defenses:

- Equal cost;
- Subsidizing a portion of the early retirement benefit;
- Integrating the incentives with Social Security;
- (For a university) incentives for a tenured faculty member;
- The plan is consistent with the objectives of the ADEA.

According to the EEOC Compliance Manual (the Manual), an ERI is not voluntary if a reasonable person informed of its terms would conclude that there was no choice but to accept. Relevant factors in the analysis include, e.g., adequate time to decide; absence of coercion; lack of negative consequences for older employees who turn down the offer; and whether a particular employee had legal advice when making the decision.

The Manual provides that it is not coercion for the employer to state that layoffs will be required unless enough people accept the incentives—unless older workers are the only ones at risk of layoff. Nor is it coercion for the employer to make an offer that is "too good to refuse."

The equal cost defense probably will not be available in connection with ERIs, because the cost of early retirement benefits generally does not increase with the employee's age.

The EEOC allows the employer to limit the ERI or pay higher ERI benefits to younger employees where the benefits are used to bring early retirees up to the level of the unreduced pension they would receive at the NRA from a defined benefit pension plan. But the subsidized pension can't be greater than the pension of a similarly situated older employee who has reached NRA.

It is also permissible to offer an ERI to bridge the gap to Social Security eligibility, for a person who has not yet reached the Social Security early retirement age (currently slightly over 62). The supplement can't exceed the Social Security benefit that the employee will eventually receive as an early or normal-age retiree.

According to the EEOC, equal severance benefits are required for all similarly situated employees irrespective of their age. Employers may not deny severance on the grounds that the employee is eligible for a pension, although sometimes pension benefits can be offset against the severance pay. Denying recall rights to older workers operates as unlawful involuntary retirement. The cost of providing severance does not rise with the employees' age, so employers are not allowed to assert an equal cost defense in this context.

Retiree health benefits can legitimately be offset against severance if the retiree is eligible for an immediate pension; the retiree actually receives health benefits; and the retiree benefits are at least comparable to Medicare in type and value.

If the retiree is over 65, the benefits must be at least comparable for one-fourth the value of Medicare benefits. The offset itself must be reduced by any percentage by which the pension is reduced for retirement before the NRA, and any percentage of the retiree health coverage premium that the retiree has to pay.

In the EEOC view, an ERI ignores age as a criterion (and therefore is consistent with the ADEA's objectives) as long as it gives all employees above a certain age:

- A flat dollar amount (e.g., $20,000);
- Additional service-based benefits, for instance, $1,000 for each year of service;
- A percentage of salary;
- A flat dollar increase in pension benefits, such as an extra $200 a month;
- A percentage increase (e.g., 10%) in pension benefits;
- Extra years of service and/or age used in pension computations.

§ 9.05 ERISA ISSUES

[A] Generally

Because one of the primary purposes of ERISA is to make sure that retirement benefits will be paid in accordance with the terms of the plan, ERISA issues often arise when early retirement plans must be construed. Sometimes, ERISA welfare benefit plans will also be involved.

[B] Preemption

It is very likely that ERISA will be held to preempt state-court cases about group health plans. [*See* § 15.18] Preemption is much less likely to be found in the early retirement context. According to the Sixth Circuit, ERISA does not preempt age discrimination claims merely because the plaintiff had already retired and was collecting a pension as of the time of the suit. [*Warner v. Ford Motor Co.*, 46 F.3d 531 (6th Cir. 1995)]

The Ninth Circuit held that ERISA does not preempt claims that the employer was guilty of fraud and negligent misrepresentation in connection with the information it gave the employee about the tax consequences of taking early retirement. On the other hand, the Eleventh Circuit found that ERISA preempted state-law claims of fraudulent misrepresentation about the availability of an early retirement program. [*Compare Farr v. United States West, Inc.*, 50 F.3d 1361 (9th Cir. 1995) and *Forbus v. Sears, Roebuck & Co.*, 30 F.3d 1402 (11th Cir. 1994), *with Sanson v. GM*, 966 F.2d 618 (11th Cir. 1992)]

The 1996 case of *Lockheed v. Spink* [517 U.S. 882 (1996)] found (among other issues) that it is not a prohibited transaction (as defined by ERISA § 406) to establish an early retirement program that is conditioned on waiving enforcement of employment claims. Under this analysis, paying benefits under any circumstances shouldn't be treated as a prohibited transaction.

A plant closed, then was reopened by a new owner who cut wages, reduced benefits, changed the seniority schedule, and required employees to reapply for their old jobs. According to the Tenth Circuit, there was no "permanent shutdown" of the plant. [*Dycus v. PBGC*, 133 F.3d 1367 (10th Cir. 1998)] Therefore, the original employer's provisions about "forced termination" did not come into play, and the plaintiffs were not entitled to early retirement benefits.

[C]   Fiduciary Duty

The Seventh Circuit said that it is not a violation of ERISA fiduciary duty for early retirement benefits to be limited to only one of the employer's business locations. This was treated as a business decision (a management prerogative), not a decision taken in the capacity as an ERISA fiduciary. [*Fletcher v. Kroger Co.*, 942 F.2d 1137 (7th Cir. 1991)]

In contrast, the Southern District of New York held that a benefit committee violated its fiduciary duty, by improperly delegating to the employer the power to decide which units will be eligible for early retirement incentives, and also by failing to make the incentives available throughout the company. [*Siskind v. Sperry Retirement Program*, 795 F. Supp. 614 (S.D.N.Y. 1992)]

The plaintiffs in *Piner v. DuPont* [2000 U.S. App. LEXIS 29016 (4th Cir. Nov. 14, 2000)] were ineligible employees who sued for fiduciary breach and failure to provide disclosure documents. Their claim was that all employees should have been eligible for the program. However, their ERISA claims were dismissed: "ERISA simply does not prohibit an employer from offering some employees and not others access to separate, additional plans with enhanced benefits." [*Id.* at *6] There is no obligation under ERISA to provide documents to employees who are not eligible for the plans covered by the documents.

It does not violate ERISA to deny early retirement to employees who are deemed especially valuable to the company, if the plan gives management discretion as to whether early retirement is in the company's best interests. A company's standards (as opposed to rules) are supposed to be applied flexibly and with discretion. According to the Seventh Circuit, the way this standard was implemented was not arbitrary or capricious enough to violate ERISA. [*McNab v. General Motors*, 162 F.3d 959 (7th Cir. 1998)] Another General Motors case says that the LMRA and NLRA do not preempt an early retiree's state-law claims that the employer fraudulently induced acceptance of early retirement. [*Voilas v. General Motors*, 170 F.3d 367 (3d Cir. 1999)]

[D]   Anticutback Rule

ERISA § 204(g) forbids cutbacks in benefits. In *Bellas v. CBS* [221 F.3d 517 (3d Cir. 2000)], the plaintiff was terminated for lack of work after employment between 1964 and 1997. Before 1994, the predecessor employer's pension plan offered permanent job separation benefits to employees terminated for lack of work. A 1994 amendment narrowed the definition of "permanent job separation," and the benefit was eliminated entirely for terminations occurring after September 1, 1998.

The plaintiff charged that the change in the benefit definition, and eventual elimination of the benefit, violated the anticutback rule. The Third Circuit agreed with him, finding that payment of any benefit greater than an actuarially reduced normal retirement benefit, triggered by an unpredictable contingent event such as being laid off, is a retirement-type subsidy. The benefit accrues when the benefit program is created. The Fifth and Ninth Circuits take this position, but the Sixth and Eleventh Circuits hold that job separation benefits do not accrue until the lay-off actually occurs.

The practical significance of the *Bellas* decision is that, in circuit courts that follow this theory, employers can only decrease early retirement benefits prospectively. That is, once a person satisfies plan requirements, the plan cannot be amended to reduce or eliminate the early retirement benefit that has already accrued. [*See* Joseph S. Adams, *Court Rules Supplemental Benefits Must Stay in Plan*, <http://www.benefitslink.com/articles/mend001012.shtml>] The employer may have to budget a much larger amount than anticipated when the plan was amended.

A "suspension" of benefits (for exceeding the plan's limitation on employment after retirement) is not a "reduction" in benefits subject to the ERISA anticutback rule. Therefore, tougher restrictions on employment, adopted six years after the plaintiff retired, entitled the employer to suspend retirement benefits without violating ERISA. [*Spacek v. Maritime Association*, 134 F.3d 283 (5th Cir. 1998)]

[E] Other ERISA Issues

Whether a severance plan is an ERISA welfare benefit plan depends on the nature and extent of the employer's role. There is no plan without ongoing administrative responsibility for determining eligibility and calculating benefits. In *O'Connor v. Commonwealth Gas Co.* [251 F.3d 262 (1st Cir. 2001)] the employer wanted to reduce its census before a merger. The plaintiffs charge they were deceived into retiring early because the employer lied about future retirement incentives. The employer provided a one-time severance bonus calculated based on years of service. The First Circuit found that there was no ERISA "plan" because the program lasted only 15 weeks, covered only 300 workers, and involved only simple arithmetic, not discretionary judgment.

§ 9.06 PHASED RETIREMENT

In many instances, the needs of both employer and employee would be well served by the option of "phased retirement" (a gradual transition out of the workforce) rather than a bright-line test of being either fully active or retired. Employers would certainly save money if they could reduce the full-time payroll yet continue to receive part-time services from older workers, instead of offering them early retirement subsidies.

Assume that a phased retiree takes a lump sum pension payment but continues to work part-time. The one-time payment will probably be less than what the company would have to pay if the employee continued full-time work for an additional period of time. In a recent article, the author uses the example of a person who would have an annual pension of $36,286 by retiring at age 65 after a 40-year career with the same company, earning $50,000 a year. [Ellen E. Schultz, *"Phased Retirement" Option for Workers Is Mainly a Boon for Their Employers*, Wall Street Journal, July 27, 2000, at p. A6] If that person takes a $263,250 lump sum at 55 and works for 10 more years, the pension will be based on only 10 years' service, not 40, so the employer will have to pay only $9,071 a year.

Current law makes it especially difficult to retire and begin taking distributions from a defined benefit or 401(k) plan prior to normal retirement age, because of limitations on "in-service distributions" that are not made on account of disability or other hardship.

§ 9.07   RETIREE HEALTH BENEFITS: INTRODUCTION

At one time, it was very common for part of the incentive for early retirement to come in the form of health benefits to replace the employer's group health plan. Employers often promised "lifetime health benefits at no cost." However, health care costs rise significantly every year, and employees in poor health are more likely to be interested in health benefits than employees in good health. Therefore, a retiree health benefit program can become a major burden on the employer.

According to the Employee Benefits Research Institute (EBRI), the prevalence of retiree health benefits began to diminish seriously in December 1990. One of the precipitating factors was the Financial Accounting Standards Board (FASB)'s release of a standard called SFAS 106, requiring employers to record their unfunded retiree health benefit liabilities on their financial statements.

This reporting has the effect of reducing reported corporate earnings, so it is an undesirable phenomenon from the corporate accounting point of view. In response, some employers stopped providing retiree health benefits altogether; others put their plans on a defined contribution basis, added age and service requirements, or maintained the level of benefits for current retirees but reduced the benefits that would eventually be available to people retiring in the future.

Nevertheless, the EBRI found that as of 1999, most of the "near elderly" population (people aged 55-64) had some form of health coverage. Two-thirds had employment-based benefits, 9% bought individual policies, about one-sixth were covered by public programs such as Medicare and Medicaid, and 14.5% were uninsured. [*See* EBRI Issue Brief Executive Summary No. 236 (August 2001) <http://www.ebri.org/ibex/ib236.htm>]

According to research released in 2002 by the Kaiser Family Foundation (performed in conjunction with the Commonwealth Fund and the Health Research and Educational Trust), between 1999 and 2001 retiree health benefit availability declined to its lowest level of the period 1996–2001. Although the largest firms (those with 5,000 or more workers) were likely to provide retiree health benefits—two-thirds of such firms did so in 2001—only 3% of firms with under 200 workers provided such benefits in 2001. In 1999, 41% of firms with 200 or more workers provided retiree health benefits, but this percentage dropped to 34% in 2001. [*Erosion of Private Health Insurance Coverage for Retirees: Findings from the 2000 and 2001 Retiree Health and Prescription Drug Coverage Survey,* (April 2002), <http://www.cmwf.org/programs/medfutur/gabel_retiree_cb_506.pdf>]

In testimony before the House of Representatives [*The Future of Retiree Health Benefits: Challenges and Options,* testimony of Nov. 1, 2001 <http://www.kff.org/content/2001/6010/retireetest.pdf>], Kaiser Family Foundation executive Patricia Neuman had some suggestions for cost-effective modifications to the current system:

- Make termination of retiree health benefits a COBRA event;
- Grant a tax credit for early retirees who buy individual insurance;
- Let retirees "buy in" to Medicare before the normal age of eligibility by paying premiums;
- Enhancing the Medicare program, e.g., by adding prescription drug benefits.

Private insurance is not always an option for retirees who do not have coverage through their former employers. More than half the uninsured adults between ages 55-64 (i.e., not yet eligible for Medicare) have incomes below 200% of the poverty line. According to the Urban Institute, a 60-year-old man with one health problem would have to pay almost $7,000 a year for health insurance—which would represent 40% of the income of a person with income about twice the poverty level.

Even if cost is not an object, many senior citizens and older adults have health problems such as arthritis, angina, and kidney stones, which can prevent underwriting of health insurance or raise the premiums even further. [*Id.*]

As of 2030, even the youngest members of the massive Baby Boom generation will be senior citizens. At that point, it's estimated that there will be 70 million senior citizens—20% of the population. The incidence of chronic (and expensive) illnesses such as high blood pressure, heart disease, arthritis, and diabetes increases significantly with age. In 1995, when senior citizens were "only" 10% of the population, they accounted for 41% of health expenditures. [These figures come from The Segal Company, *Timing is Everything,* (June 2001) <http://www.segalco.com>]

§ 9.08   THE RIGHT TO ALTER OR TERMINATE RETIREE HEALTH BENEFITS

The general rule is that, as long as the employer drafts the plan to provide that the employer retains the right to amend, modify, or terminate the health benefits, the employer can do so unilaterally. ERISA has rules about vesting of pension benefits (i.e., the circumstances under which the right to a pension becomes nonforfeitable) but ERISA does not provide for vesting of welfare benefits such as retiree health benefits. Furthermore, ERISA preempts state law on this subject, so the states do not have the power to impose vesting requirements.

However, there are circumstances under which an employer's promise of retiree health coverage will become an enforceable contract. Under the "promissory estoppel" theory, if the employer makes an unambiguous promise of lifetime benefits, it will no longer be permitted to change the plan.

A limitation on this theory is that the plaintiff might be required to prove that he or she would have obtained comparable medical insurance at his or her own expense if the plan had not been misleading about future health benefits. Employers might also be bound by a promise of lifetime no-cost retiree health benefits if employees actually traded cash compensation or some other benefit in exchange for the employer's promise.

Another argument that employers can make to cut back or eliminate retiree health benefits is that the benefits were provided under a particular collective bargaining agreement and do not survive the expiration of that agreement unless the agreement specifically calls for their survival. Retirees are no longer employees, and therefore are not part of the bargaining unit. The bargaining agent does not have a duty to represent retirees—and there is a real potential for conflict of interest between current employees and retirees. Retiree benefits are not included among the mandatory subjects of bargaining. [*See* § 30.07[A]]

When a collective bargaining agreement determines retiree benefit rights "for the term of the agreement," it is not a violation of ERISA to terminate retiree health and life insurance benefits after a contract ends. In other words, it's a new ball game each time the CBA is renegotiated. [*Pabst Brewing Co. v. Corrao,* 161 F.3d 434 (7th Cir. 1998)]

ERISA's fiduciary duty was not breached by transferring the obligation to provide some retiree health benefits to a new company formed when a corporate division was spun off. [*Sengpiel v. B.F. Goodrich,* 156 F.3d 660 (6th Cir. 1998)] To the Sixth Circuit, the new entity's reduction of retiree health and life insurance benefits was lawful, because the power to alter benefits was retained in the plan documents. The reduction should be analyzed as a plan amendment, modification, or termination—i.e. a business decision—rather than a fiduciary decision involving discretionary issues in plan administration.

The employer's course of conduct (such as increasing health benefits for retirees when benefits for active workers increase) is probably not enough to make it unlawful for the employer to cut back on retiree benefits, especially if the benefit increases were provided gratuitously by the employer and the employees did not have to surrender anything to get them.

In 1988, the Second Circuit identified the Summary Plan Description (SPD) as the major source of information about the plan, so booklets issued by the employer, promising "lifetime benefits at no cost" [to the retiree], could not serve to modify the SPD and other plan documents that reserved the employer's right to modify or terminate the plan. [*Moore v. Metropolitan Life Ins.*, 856 F.2d 488 (2d Cir. 1988)]

Similar considerations apply when the employer wants to increase costs to retirees (premiums, deductibles, coinsurance) instead of eliminating the entire plan. Unless there is a contract or estoppel theory that prevents this characterization, the right to terminate the plan will probably be considered a retained right to increase retirees' obligations later on. [*See* § 37.04[A] for the Older Worker's Benefit Protection Act provisions about offsetting retiree health benefits against severance pay]

§ 9.09   TAX ISSUES FOR RETIREE HEALTH BENEFITS

Internal Revenue Code § 419A(c)(2) permits the employer to deduct the cost of retiree health benefits as part of a nondiscriminatory funded welfare plan. Key employees' retiree health benefits must be drawn from separate accounts, not the main account. Failure to maintain the separate accounts, or discrimination in furnishing retiree health benefits, is penalized by the 100% excise tax on disqualified benefits imposed by I.R.C. § 4976.

A funded welfare plan can maintain a reserve for future retiree health benefits, funded over the work lives of employees, without violating the account limit. The reserve must use a level-basis actuarial determination, making use of reasonable assumptions and current medical costs.

The Voluntary Employees' Beneficiary Association (VEBA) [I.R.C. § 501(c)(8)] is a possible funding vehicle for retiree health benefits. Caution must be exercised. The VEBA is a tax-exempt organization, so its investment income is subject to taxation. VEBAs are required to use current health costs to calculate the contributions to be made for future retirees. So if costs increase more than anticipated, or if retirees use more health care than expected, the VEBA may be exhausted.

§ 9.10   MEDICARE INTERFACE

There are two ways a person can qualify for Medicare: either being completely and permanently disabled for a period of at least two years—or reaching age 65. Income and assets are irrelevant—and so is employment status. In other words, people who are still working can be entitled to Medicare benefits (although the employer's group health plan will usually be the primary payor) but a person under 65 who is not disabled will not qualify for Medicare merely because he or she is retired. Nor does Medicare provide benefits for the under-65 spouses of retirees (or retirees' dependent children, if the unusual case but not impossible case that they have any).

The Medicare system includes "secondary payor" rules under which retirees can elect to make Medicare the primary payor for their medical care, with the employer group health plan merely the secondary payor. However, the employer does not have this option, and is not permitted to draft the health plan to make Medicare the primary payor.

Although most senior citizens get their Medicare in fee-for-service form, there is also a managed care system. Medicare HMOs are being phased out in favor of various forms of plans described under the general heading of Medicare + Choice plans.

An August 1998 survey of 350 employers, performed by Hewitt Associates, shows that about one-third of the companies had experience with Medicare HMOs for older employees and retirees. Two-thirds of the respondents planned to sponsor at least some medical coverage for retirees.

Three-quarters of them considered offering coverage under a Medicare + Choice HMO plan; 60% considered offering a Point of Service HMO. PPOs were under consideration by 55% of respondents, but very few were interested in offering the other Medicare + Choice alternatives (private fee-for-service plans; medical practices sponsored by the employers; or Medical Savings Accounts).

The Third Circuit in *Erie County Retirees Association v. County of Erie* [220 F.3d 193 (3d Cir. 2000)] ruled that the ADEA applies to retiree benefits, including health benefits. Therefore, an employer violates the ADEA by offering Medicare-eligible retirees health benefits that are inferior to those offered to employees who are not yet eligible for Medicare, unless the employer can demonstrate that it incurred equal costs or provided equal benefits for both retiree groups. On April 16, 2001, when the case was remanded to the lower court, the Western District of Pennsylvania decided that the plan did not satisfy the equal cost/equal benefit test. [*Erie County*, 140 F. Supp. 2d 466 (W.D. Pa. 2001)]

Initially, the EEOC adopted the Third Circuit's position in Chapter 3 of its Enforcement Manual. However, in an August 2001 interview, an EEOC spokesperson told EBIA that the agency was reassessing its policy based on legitimate concerns raised by commentators. The EEOC set up a task force to examine the issue fully, and agreed not to pursue the issue in litigation until the task force had reported. [*EBIA Weekly* (Aug. 2, 2001) <http://www.ebia.org>]

The University of Rhode Island offered early retirement incentives to eligible employees, with two health options. Under the first option, the plan paid money directly to the insurance company. If the actual insurance premium was lower than the stipend, the employee got the difference in cash, but if the premium was higher, the employee had to make up the difference. In the second option, the stipend ($5,000 a year for people aged 58–64, $2,000 a year for those who had reached 65 and Medicare eligibility) went directly to the employee.

Retirees who took the second option sued under the ADEA, but lost. The District of Rhode Island said that it does not violate the ADEA to coordinate retiree health benefits with Medicare, as long as the employer-provided benefits plus Medicare are equal to the benefits for younger employees. [*Gutchen v. Board of Governors of the Univ. of Rhode Island,* 148 F. Supp. 2d 151 (D.R.I. 2001)] It's unlawful to reduce the benefits of an active employee because of Medicare entitlement—but it's allowed for a retiree.

§ 9.11   SOP 92-6 REPORTS

The American Institute of Certified Public Accountants (AICPA) requires health and welfare benefits to prepare SOP 92-6 reports. SOP stands for "Statement of Position." Originally, the reports were supposed to start in 1996, but so many extensions were granted that many plan trustees didn't have to do their first SOP 92-6 report until 2001. Although the report is a lot of work to prepare, and involves many calculations that are not otherwise useful, at least the report establishes the plan's obligation for post-retirement benefits for the current year, and sets a benchmark for comparing the obligation to prior years' experience and trends in the plan. [*See* the online newsletter by the Segal Company, *Timing Is Everything: Anticipating and Preparing for Higher Retiree Health Expenditures,* (June 2001) <http://www.segalco.com>]

The cash flow projections for the 92-6 project the amount of money needed every year to pay health costs. Although prefunding of welfare benefits is not required, it is often a good idea to create an asset pool (e.g., using a VEBA) to generate tax-free investment income that can be used for future costs.

The 92-6 report can answer questions like:

- The fund's projected trend rates for medical, drug, and dental coverage costs for future years;
- The number of active employees, retirees, spouses of retirees, and surviving spouses covered by the plan;
- Average ages of active versus retired employees;
- Average number of years of service for active employees;
- Average expected retirement age for the current crop of active employees;
- Actual retirement rate by age;
- Cost of plan benefits;
- Number of active employees eligible for full retiree health benefits;
- The postretirement benefit obligation for current retirees, dependents, and beneficiaries;
- A projection of the postretirement obligations for active workers who have not yet satisfied the requirements for full eligibility;
- Whether there have been any changes in plan design that altered the obligation for postretirement benefits;
- Total current retiree contributions;
- Expected annual rate of increase for retiree contributions;
- Percentage of total cost that comes from employee and retiree cost-sharing (deductibles and coinsurance); expected changes over the next five years.

The Segal Company suggests that retiree health plans are likely to make radical design changes in the future. The "contribution allowance" approach offsets the cost of health benefits for each retiree by a contribution allowance based on a unit benefit formula or other accrual ratio (a certain number of dollars per month or year or service). At retirement, the individual's accrued allowance is calculated. That amount is paid out in increments for health coverage under the welfare fund or to buy Medigap insurance. The retiree pays the difference between the full cost of coverage and the contribution allowance.

In contrast, the account balance approach creates and manages individual accounts used exclusively to pay for retiree health coverage. The effect of both designs is to shift the risk of outliving the benefits, and the inflation risk, to plan participants.

§ 9.12   IMPLICATIONS OF THE EMPLOYER'S BANKRUPTCY

The basic rule, as created by *In re White Farm Equipment Co.* [788 F.2d 1186 (6th Cir. 1986)] is that vesting of welfare benefits is not automatic. It is a subject of bargaining, to be contracted for. In that case, the bankrupt company maintained a no-contributory, non-collectively-bargained plan that provided retiree benefits. The plaintiffs were retirees who wanted a declaratory judgment (an official statement) that their claims were both valid under ERISA and allowable as bankruptcy claims.

They also asked the court to order the employer to reinstate the plan retroactively and to resume funding it. But the court found that employee benefits regulation is strictly a federal concern. Furthermore, the employer had reserved the power to terminate the plan and could do so at that time.

Ironically, retirees of bankrupt companies may have more protection for their benefits than retirees of solvent companies. Conversely, bankruptcy may solve some of a company's problems while creating others.

Under 11 U.S.C. § 1113, a company that has filed for Chapter 11 status can ask the bankruptcy court for the right to reject an existing collective bargaining agreement, including provisions covering retiree health benefits. The company must disclose the relevant information to the union and bargain in good faith about the termination.

If the company in Chapter 11 was already paying retiree benefits, the Retiree Benefits Bankruptcy Protection Act of 1988 (RBBPA) [Pub. L. No. 100-334] requires medical and disability payments to retirees to continue, on their original terms, either until the parties agree to modify the benefits or the bankruptcy court orders a modification.

The Act includes standards for bankruptcy courts to use in deciding whether a modification is appropriate. Any modifications proposed by the bankruptcy trustee must be equitable, not just to current and former employees, but also to the company's creditors. The retirees must not have had good cause to reject the proposals. The proposed modifications must be necessary to permit the employer to reorganize in bankruptcy on fair terms.

The RBBPA also requires the employer to negotiate with retiree representatives and to disclose the best available information about the employer's financial condition. Generally speaking, the union will serve as the representative of the retirees, unless the union refuses to do so or unless the court rules that a different representative should be appointed. Any party can petition the court to appoint a committee of retirees to represent benefit recipients who are not covered by a collective bargaining agreement.

The court considering the trustee's proposal does not have the power to order benefits lower than the proposed schedule. Once the parties reach an agreement, or once the court orders changes in the benefits, the authorized representative of the retirees can petition the court for an increase, which will be granted if it appears clearly just to do so.

Tip: The RBBPA's protection does not apply to retirees, their spouses, or dependents if the retiree's gross income was $250,000 or more in the year before the employer's bankruptcy petition. The only exception is retirees who can prove they are unable to get comparable individual health care coverage. Nor does the RBBPA require bankrupt employers to maintain retiree health benefits that were provided by the union, not the employer, prior to the bankruptcy.

---

§ 9.13   401(h) PLANS

[A]   Basic Principles

The basic principle is that assets must remain within a qualified pension plan until they are distributed to participants or beneficiaries. However, the Code permits transfers of certain assets of overfunded plans to special funds known as 401(h) plans that are segregated to provide retiree health benefits.

A 401(h) plan is a pension or annuity plan that also provides incidental health benefits for retirees: benefits for sickness, accident, hospitalization, or medical expenses. The health-type benefits must be subordinate to the plan's main business of offering retirement benefits. The incidental (insurance and health) benefits must not cost more than 25% of the employer's total contributions to a defined benefit plan.

An employer that maintains a 401(h) plan must maintain separate accounts for retiree health benefits and pension benefits. The employer must make reasonable and ascertainable contributions to fund the retiree health benefits. These contributions must be distinct from the contributions to fund pension benefits.

Internal Revenue Code § 420(b)(5) permits one transfer per year to a 401(h) account for tax years beginning between January 1, 1991, and December 31, 2005.

Such transfers are not considered reversions to the employer; therefore the I.R.C. § 4980 excise tax is not imposed.

Under these Code provisions, the employer is obligated to use the transferred assets only for current retiree health liabilities. All transfers must come from excess pension assets. Excess pension assets means the fair market value minus A or B (whichever is greater) or C.

- A = 150% of the current liability under the plan;
- B = the accrued liability, including normal cost, under the plan;
- C = 125% of all liabilities under the plan to employees and their beneficiaries.

Before making a transfer to a 401(h) plan, the plan administrator must give the DOL at least 60 days' notice, and must also notify participants, beneficiaries and any union representing the participants.

[B] Final Regulations

Effective June 19, 2001, the IRS issued Final Regulations on the I.R.C. § 420 minimum cost requirements. [T.D. 8948, R.I.N. 1545-AY43] An employer that significantly reduces its retiree health coverage during a cost maintenance period does not satisfy the I.R.C. § 420(c)(3) minimum cost requirement. This requirement institutes a five-year period during which the employer has an obligation to maintain a minimum dollar level of expenditures for covered retirees, spouses, and dependents. The period begins with the taxable year in which a qualified transfer occurs. If the requirement is satisfied, the employee doesn't have taxable income, and the employer doesn't have gross income, to the extent that funds are transferred into the 401(h) plan. The transfer is neither a prohibited transaction nor a reversion to the employer.

The Uruguay Round Agreements Act of 1994 [Pub. L. No. 103-465] shifted the focus in regulating 401(h) plans from health costs to health benefits, allowing the employer to take into account cost savings recognized in managing retiree health benefit plans, as long as the employer keeps up substantially the same level of coverage for the four years after the transfer as for the year of the transfer itself and the year before the year of the transfer.

When it was first enacted, I.R.C. § 420 was supposed to be temporary. However, the Tax Relief Extension Act [Pub. L. No. 106-170], extended it from the anticipated expiration date of December 31, 2000, to December 31, 2005. The Tax Relief Extension Act reinstated minimum cost as the appropriate test of whether the employer was handling the 401(h) plan properly.

This bill also added I.R.C. § 420(c)(3)(E), requiring the Secretary of the Treasury to adopt Regulations to prevent employers from maintaining the same average cost but reducing the number of people covered under the plan. Proposed Regulations were published at 66 Fed. Reg. 1066 on January 5, 2001, and then finalized with some modifications.

Under the Final Regulations, the employer will not satisfy I.R.C. § 420(c)(3) if it significantly reduces retiree coverage during the cost maintenance period. A determination is made, on both an annual and a cumulative basis, of the number of retirees, spouses, and dependents who lose coverage because of employer actions. If employer actions reduce the number of covered individuals by more than 10% in any year, or more than 20% over the course of the cost maintenance period, the employer will fail the test.

Naturally, plan amendments will count as employer action—but so will sale of all or part of the business, or anything that operates "in conjunction with the existing plan terms to have the indirect effect of ending an individual's coverage."

In an acquisition situation, the Final Regulations provide that the employer may (but does not have to) treat retiree coverage as not having ended if the buyer provides coverage. For the year of the sale and the rest of the cost maintenance period, the employer must apply I.R.C. § 420(c)(3) by including people receiving benefits provided by the buyer in the denominator of the applicable employer cost equation. The buyer's spending on health benefits from those individuals must be treated as qualified current retiree health liabilities.

Once the buyer starts providing the benefits, the buyer's action is attributed to the employer when determining if "employer action" terminates coverage. So if the buyer starts providing retiree health benefits but then amends the plan to stop providing the benefits, the employer has to treat the affected individuals as having lost coverage per employer action. The definition of "sale" in Final Regulation includes other transfers of business; the transferee is treated as the buyer.

The 20% cumulative test applies to transfers of excess pension assets made on or after December 18, 1999. However, coverage can be reinstated by an employer that reduced coverage by more than 20% before the first taxable year that began on or after January 1, 2002. The annual test for significant reduction applies only to taxable years beginning on or after January 1, 2002.

PART III

PENSION PLAN ADMINISTRATION

CHAPTER 10

ADOPTING AND ADMINISTERING A PLAN

§ 10.01   INTRODUCTION

The process of creating a plan and getting it approved by the IRS and Department of Labor is exacting. Many alternatives are permitted, and choosing one of them requires projections about the future of the business, the future of the workforce, trends in the economy as a whole, and the laws, court decisions, and regulations that will come into effect in the future.

Employers always have a duty to notify their employees when they adopt a plan. If the plan will be subject to ERISA Title I, the Department of Labor must be notified. It is not strictly necessary to notify the IRS of the intention to establish a qualified plan, until and unless a determination letter is sought. A determination letter is evidence of the plan's qualification, but a plan that satisfies the various requirements of the Code is entitled to tax deductions, even if there has been no determination letter.

§ 10.02   DETERMINATION LETTERS

A determination letter is the IRS' determination that a proposed plan is qualified under I.R.C. § 401(a) or 403(a)—and, if the plan is operated through a plan trust, whether the plan trust is qualified under I.R.C. § 501(a).

A plan that has a determination letter and that is amended on a timely basis to conform to changes in the law will probably be able to rebut IRS attempts at retroactive disqualification of the plan.

The application for a determination letter is made to the IRS District Director's office. Interested parties (current employees who will be eligible to participate if the plan is implemented) are entitled to notification that an application has been made. If the plan is collectively bargained, all employees covered by the CBA are entitled to notice. Notice to unionized employees can be given in person (e.g., printed and handed to all employees; slips placed in all pay envelopes), by mailing, or by posting in the usual place for posting employer and/or union notices. The appropriate time for giving notice to employees is 7–21 days before the IRS gets the application. If the employees are notified by mail, the notices should be mailed 10–24 days before submission of the application.

Employees must be notified because interested parties have the right to comment directly to the IRS about the application. The PBGC or a group of interested parties can also invite the Department of Labor to comment on the application. The PBGC has standing to submit its own comments directly. The comment period runs for either 45 or 60 days after the IRS receives the request for a determination letter.

After 60 days have elapsed, the IRS does its own investigation of the qualification of the proposed plan, including consideration of any comments that have been submitted. A reviewing agent in the relevant IRS Key District Office issues the determination letter (or denies the application). If there are questions about the application, the agent tries to resolve them by telephoning or writing to the company that applied for the determination letter.

If the IRS refuses to issue the letter, there are several levels of review within the IRS, and then the employer has the right to appeal to the Tax Court.

Determination letters are requested on official IRS forms. The IRS charges user fees, depending on the nature of the application. Furthermore, a particular plan may have to apply several times. The relevant forms are:

- Form 4461: application for a determination letter for a master or prototype defined contribution plan;
- Form 4461-A: for a defined benefit plan;
- Form 5300: application for a determination letter for an individually drafted defined benefit plan;
- Form 5302: defined contribution plan;
- Form 5309: ESOP;
- Form 5307: Prototype or master submission.

Schedule Q, demographic materials demonstrating conformity with the non-discrimination requirements, must be attached to Forms 5300, 5303, 5307, and 5310.

The application for a determination letter must disclose:

- Information about the plan;
- Information about the employees who will be covered;
- A copy of the plan;
- Power of attorney.

[*See* Rev. Proc. 2000-8, 2000-1 C.B. 230, for user fees for these applications]

The IRS has announced many times that it will not issue determination letters about the changes required by EGTRRA. *See, e.g.,* Notice 2001-57, 2001-38 I.R.B. 279, 281: "until further notice, the Service will not consider EGTRRA in issuing determination, opinion and advisory letters." However, Notice 2001-55 includes sample plan provisions that can be adopted and that will operate as acceptable good-faith interpretations of EGTRRA until the IRS provides official guidance.

§ 10.03   PROTOTYPE AND MASTER PLANS

The IRS publishes prototype and master plans to assist employers in drafting plans that satisfy all the manifold requirements imposed by the Code. There are several forms, to suit various employer needs. [*See* Rev. Proc. 2000-20, 2000-6 I.R.B. 553] These standard documents either integrate the basic plan and the trust document into a single document, or keep the trust agreement separate from the plan, with an adoption agreement that covers matters such as participation, benefit formulas, and vesting.

> **Tip:** In this context, the plan "sponsor" is not the employer whose employees are covered by the plan, but the institution such as bank, insurance company, trade organization, or professional organization that manages the funds. The general rule is that a sponsor must reasonably anticipate that at least 30 employers will adopt its document within 12 months of its approval by the IRS, but Rev. Proc. 2000-20 allows a party that could be a sponsor except for not having 30 members to adopt a "mass submitter prototype plan."

The difference between a prototype and a master plan is that a prototype plan has a separate funding mechanism for each employer. A master plan, however, has a single trust or other funding mechanism that covers multiple employers.

§ 10.04   ROUTINE TAX COMPLIANCE

[A]   Necessary Forms

A "Q and A for Businesses Filing Taxes Electronically," can be found at <http://www.irs.gov>. Day-to-day administration of a plan involves creation of tax records and submission of many forms to the IRS and state taxing authorities, including:

- Form W-2: for each individual employee, this lists the compensation paid. The form must be submitted to the IRS and also to the employee. The normal due date for employee W-2s is January 31 following the end of the year of employment. However, employees who leave during the year have a right to demand that they get a W-2 form within 30 days of the last paycheck (or of the request, if made at a later date). The employer can use IRS Form 8809 to request additional time to file W-2s;
- Form W-3: a transmittal form filed with the Social Security Administration consolidating all the W-2 and W-2P forms for the entire company. The regular due date for any year's W-3 is February 28 of the following year;
- Form W-4P is used by employees to opt out of withholding or increase withholding on their pension and annuity payments. This form goes straight from employer to employee, no IRS filing is required;
- Forms 941/941E: these are the forms for quarterly returns of federal income tax. 941 is used if there are FICA taxes withheld or paid, 941E otherwise. The due date is the end of the month after the close of the calendar quarter being reported on;
- Form 945: the report on withheld taxes that are not payroll taxes (e.g., withholding on retirement plan distributions);
- Form 1041: trust income tax return, required if the plan's trust becomes disqualified (or otherwise does not operate as a tax-exempt organization) and if it

also has income equal to or greater than $600. The due date is the fifteenth day of the fourth month after the end of the trust's tax year;

- Form 1099-R: 1099-series forms are used to report miscellaneous sums that might otherwise escape the attention of the taxing authorities. The 1099-R is used to report lump sums and periodic distributions. The entire group of a company's transmittal forms requires its own transmittal form, Form 1096. The filing is due by February 28 each year for the preceding year;

Tip: Within two weeks of making a distribution, the plan administrator must provide each recipient with a written explanation of the tax consequences of taking a lump sum, including how to elect lump-sum tax treatment and how to roll over the sum to another qualified plan or to an IRA.

- Form 5308: form filed in connection with a change in the tax year of a qualified plan or trust;
- Form 5330: excise tax form for failure to meet the minimum funding standard, or for receipt of an impermissible reversion of plan assets. Disqualified persons who engage in prohibited transactions are also required to file this form. There is no fixed due date: the timing depends on the nature of the transaction subject to excise tax. Form 5558 is used to request additional time to file this form;
- Form 8109: the quarterly estimated tax return when a plan trust has unrelated business taxable income (UBTI) [*see* I.R.C. § 512(a)(1)] from operation of an unrelated trade or business. UBTI is limited to business net income (after deducting the costs of generating the income). It does not include dividends, interest, annuities, loan fees, or royalties.

[B]   Investment-Related Costs

The Department of Labor's Letter 2001-01A (Jan. 18, 2001) includes an advisory opinion and six hypotheticals explaining which expenses can properly be charged to a plan. Expenses to maintain tax qualification, perform nondiscrimination testing, or obtain an IRS determination letter can properly be charged to the plan, even though the employer does obtain financial benefits from the plan's tax-qualified status. [*See DOL Provides New Guidance on Payment of Expenses From Plan Assets*, [http://www.benefitslink.com/articles/expenses010123.shtml]

Rev. Rul. 86-142 says that employers are entitled to deduct (as I.R.C. § 162 ordinary and necessary business expenses) the recurring expenses of plan operation and administration directly paid by the employer. However, design studies, amendments required by corporate transitions, costs of negotiating with a union, cost studies to assess new benefits designs, and FASB 88 statement costs are not chargeable to the plan.

A Tax Court case, *Sklar, Greenstein & Scheer, PC v. Commissioner* [113 T.C. 9 (1999)], allows an employer maintaining a money purchase plan to deduct the expenses of suing the plan's investment manager. The Tax Court agreed with the company that such expenses are ordinary and necessary. The court did not agree with the IRS that only "recurring" expenses are deductible, as long as they satisfy the "ordinary and necessary" criterion.

§ 10.05   ERISA COMPLIANCE ISSUES

The Summary Plan Description (SPD) for a newly created plan must be filed with the Department of Labor within 120 days of the plan's adoption. (If this is later than the date of establishment, filing must be made within 120 days of the first time the plan covers common-law employees and therefore becomes subject to ERISA Title I.) It is wise to include a disclaimer in the SPD, to the effect that the plan instrument and not the SPD will govern in case of conflict.

ERISA § 104(a)(4)(A) gives the DOL the power to reject an incomplete SPD filing. The plan administrator has 45 days to file again to answer the DOL comments. If the second filing is not made, DOL has the power to sue for legal or equitable relief, or any other remedy authorized by ERISA Title I.

Many plans are insurance-based, so the employer will have contracts with health and liability insurers. However, insurance policies and other documents that set out the business relationship between the insured and the insurer do not always contain all of the terms and conditions mandated by ERISA for administration of a plan (including the required disclosures to plan participants). The solution is to adopt a "wrap" document that supplements the contractual language of the insurance policy with the statutory and regulatory language needed for an ERISA plan. [*See* EBIA Weekly (Feb. 7, 2002) <http://www.ebia.org>]

CHAPTER 11

COMMUNICATIONS WITH EMPLOYEES AND REGULATORS

§ 11.01   INTRODUCTION

Although ERISA does not require corporations to have employee benefit plans at all, if they choose to implement plans, there are many rules that must be followed, including procedural rules. Plan participants must be given enough information from the plan itself to understand their benefits—especially benefits available in multiple forms—so that informed choices must be made.

The Summary Plan Description (SPD) is the main document for communications between the plan and its participants, although other documents may also be required, for example when the terms of the plan are altered. If the plan is materially modified, or if there are changes in the information given in the SPD, the plan administrator has a duty to give participants a Summary of Material Modifications (SMM).

For a calendar-year plan that has undergone a material modification, the SMM must be sent to participants and beneficiaries by July 27 of the following year. Fiscal-year plans have until the 210th day after the end of the plan year.

The due date for the Form 5500 is July 31 (calendar-year plans) and the last day of the seventh month of the plan year after the plan year being reported, for plans that have a fiscal year. This is also the reporting schedule for individual statements of deferred vested benefits, to be sent to plan participants whose employment terminated during the plan year and who were entitled to deferred vested benefits at the time of termination.

For defined benefit plans only, the PBGC Form 1 is due on September 15 (calendar year plans) or eight and a half months after the close of the plan fiscal year being reported on. For all plans, the Summary Annual Report must be given to participants and beneficiaries by September 30 (or the last day of the ninth month of the plan year after the plan year in question). That is also the date that participants and beneficiaries of defined benefit plans that are less than 90% funded should be given notice of the plan's funding status and the limits on the PBGC guarantee.

In recent years, the Department of Labor has stepped up its enforcement activities against plans (especially small defined contribution plans and 401(k) plans) that fail to make the necessary disclosures. [*See Avoid Litigation by Informing Participants*, <http://www.benefitslink.com/articles/mend010625.shtml>]

§ 11.02   SUMMARY PLAN DESCRIPTION (SPD)

[A]   Basic Requirements

ERISA § 102 imposes a duty on the plan administrator to furnish a copy of the Summary Plan Description (SPD) to each participant and to each beneficiary receiving benefits under the plan. The SPD must be furnished within 90 days of the time a person becomes a participant or first receives benefits. (For a new plan, the SPD can be furnished within 120 days of the time the plan comes under Title I of ERISA, if this is later than the 90-day period.)

ERISA § 102 requires the SPD to be written in a way that can be understood by the average plan participant. The document must be accurate and comprehensive enough to inform them of their rights and obligations. The Pension and Welfare Benefits Administration published a Final Rule governing SPDs for pension, health, and welfare benefit plans on November 21, 2000. [*See* 65 Fed. Reg. 70226] The rule is effective on the first day of the plan's second plan year that begins on or after January 22, 2001. The PWBA estimated that up to 1.2 million plans, with 36 million participants (about 50% of health plans, 30% of pension plans) would have to make amendments to comply.

ERISA requires the following items to be included in the SPD:

- The formal and common names of the plan;
- The name and address of the employer (or of the organization maintaining a collectively bargained plan);
- The employer's EIN and the plan's IRS identification number;
- What kind of plan it is;
- How the plan is administered—e.g., by contract or by an insurer;
- The name and address of the agent for service of process (the person designated to receive summonses, complaints, subpoenas, and related litigation documents);
- A statement that process can be served not only on this designated agent, but also on the plan's administrator or trustee;
- The name, address, and title of each trustee;
- Disclosure of whether the plan is a collectively bargained plan, and a statement that the participant can examine the collective bargaining agreement or get a copy of the agreement from the plan administrator;
- Rules of eligibility for participation;
- The plan's normal retirement age;
- Circumstances under which plan benefits can be altered or suspended;
- How to waive the normal payment mechanism (the Qualified Joint and Survivor Annuity) and elect a different payment form, such as a lump sum;
- Procedures for QDROs and QMCSOs, either through a description in the SPD itself or disclosure that a free copy of a separate document will be provided on request;
- A description of the circumstances under which the plan can be terminated, the rights of participants and beneficiaries after termination occurs, and the circumstances under which benefits can be denied or suspended; what will happen to the plan's assets upon termination. (All amendments must be made with the necessary corporate governance steps, such as adoption of a resolution by the Board of Directors);
- If the plan benefits are insured by the PBGC; if they are not, the reason why insurance is not required; if they are, a disclosure that PBGC insurance is in place, how it works, and where to get more information (from the plan administrator or the PBGC; the PBGC's address must be given in the SPD);

- An explanation of the plan's rules for determining service to calculate vesting and breaks in service;
- Do the contributions to the plan come exclusively from the employer, or are employee contributions accepted or mandated?
- Method of calculating the contribution. (A defined benefit plan is allowed to simply say that the amount is "actuarially determined");
- The funding medium and entity for the plan. Usually this will be a trust fund, but sometimes an insurance company is involved;
- The plan's fiscal year;
- How to present a claim for plan benefits;
- If the plan will use the "cutback" rule to change the vesting or accrual rules described in the SPD, participants must be informed which provisions of the plan are subject to modification; when modified, the nature of the modification must be explained;
- Remedies that are available if a claim is denied;
- A statement of the rights of participants and beneficiaries and what protections are available for those rights. A model statement that can be used for this purpose is published at 29 C.F.R. § 2520.102-3.

After reviewing public comments, the PWBA decided that the current disclosure requirements give enough information about cash balance conversions and operations, so it was not necessary to impose any special requirements.

SPDs must be given to participants and beneficiaries within 90 days after they achieve that status. For a new plan, all participants must get an SPD 12 days after the plan becomes subject to ERISA reporting and disclosure requirements. If a company offers different benefits to different groups of SPDs, the company can issue a separate SPD for each group.

The best distribution methods are handing the SPDs to the employees at the workplace, or mailing them to employees' homes. It isn't enough to put them out in the workplace, because there's no guarantee that employees will take them.

The SPD can also be distributed as an insert in an employee periodical such as one published by the company or the union. If you choose this option, be sure to put a prominent notice on the front page of the periodical, stating that this issue contains an insert that has important legal consequences, and that it should be retained for reference and not discarded.

> **Tip:** The statement of participant rights required by ERISA can be incorporated into the SPD.

If a plan is amended—and most are, sooner or later—the plan administrator must issue an updated SPD every five years (measured from the time the plan first became subject to ERISA) reflecting the changes of the past five years. Even if there are no changes at all, the administrator must provide an updated SPD to all participants every 10 years.

If there are any false statements in the SPD, ERISA disclosure regulations have been violated, and the employer could face penalties from the Department of Labor. Most plan participants never see the trust documents for the plan, so they get their information from the SPD.

Furthermore, if the SPD is ambiguous, lawsuits might be decided in favor of the employee-plaintiffs, because it is a basic legal doctrine that ambiguous documents are interpreted in the manner least favorable to the party that issued them.

The Second Circuit said that the SPD should have given information, including examples, of the effect of the plan's rules on participants who retired and later were rehired by the employer. Circumstances that could result in disqualification, ineligibility, forfeiture, or suspension of benefits must be disclosed. [*Layou v. Xerox Corp.*, 238 F.3d 205 (2d Cir. 2001)]

[B] Health Plan SPDs

ERISA § 104(b)(1)(B) requires that plan participants and beneficiaries be notified within 60 days of a material reduction in the services provided under an Employee Group Health Plan (EGHP). Or the plan sponsor can simply provide notices at regular intervals, not more than 90 days apart, of changes in the interim. The SPD for an EGHP must indicate if a health insurer is responsible for financing or administration (including claims payment). If an insurer is involved, the insurer's name and address must appear in the SPD.

In 1998, the Pension and Welfare Benefit Administration issued a major statement on the SPD requirements for health plans [62 Fed. Reg. 48376 (Sept. 8, 1998)], including disclosures relating to COBRA, insurance portability, and the Newborns' and Mothers' Health Protection Act, and followed it up with a Final Rule. [65 Fed. Reg. 70226 (Nov. 21, 2000)] Calendar-year plans must be in compliance with the Final Rule no later than in the SPDs distributed January 1, 2003.

Group health plans SPDs must include the following:

- Participants' responsibility for cost-sharing (premiums, deductibles, coinsurance, copayments);
- Lifetime or annual caps on plan benefits; any other benefit limits;
- Procedures for Qualified Medical Child Support Orders (QMCSOs);
- Coverage of preventive services;
- Coverage (if any) of established and new drugs;
- Coverage of medical tests, devices, and procedures;
- Which health care providers are part of the network, and how the network is created;
- Circumstances under which network providers must be used; coverage, if any, for out-of-network services;
- How primary care and specialty providers must be selected;
- Conditions for getting emergency care;
- Requirements for preauthorization of treatment and utilization review;
- Information about the required length of hospital stays for childbirth, including

descriptions of the federal law and any additional protection furnished by state law;

- Either a description of claims procedures or a statement that a free copy of the claims procedure is available on request. [*See* § 13.03 for a discussion of claims procedures, including another Final Rule issued on November 21, 2000];
- The role of health insurance in the plan; the PWBA says "particularly in those cases where the plan is self-funded and an insurer is serving as contract administrator or claims payor, rather than as an insurer";
- Extent to which the sponsor has the right to eliminate benefits or terminate the plan;
- Participants' rights under ERISA.

The SPD can include only a general description of the provider network, as long as the SPD explains that a separate document, available without charge, lists all the network providers.

A health plan's SPD must describe employees' and their families' COBRA rights:

- What constitutes a qualifying event;
- Premiums ex-employees must pay for continuation coverage;
- Notice procedures;
- How to make a COBRA election;
- How long coverage will last.

The SPD for an EGHP must either describe the plan's procedures for validating Qualified Medical Child Support Orders, or must inform participants that a free copy of the plan's QMCSO procedures is available on request. The description should be complete enough to assist potential alternate payees in asserting their rights. [*See* James T. Herod, *New Requirements for Health Plan SPDs*, Milliman USA Benefits Perspectives (Summer 2001) <http://www.milliman.com>]

> **Tip:** Although SPDs are often prepared by insurers, HMOs, or Third Party Administrators, the plan administrator is still legally responsible for compliance—so it makes sense to review the SPD form before it is distributed to employees, to make sure it satisfies all relevant requirements.

According to *Cooperative Benefit Plan Administrators Inc. v. Whittle* [989 F. Supp. 1421 (M.D. Ala. 1997)], a manual drafted for a welfare benefit plan's administrative staff was not an SPD, even if the plaintiff relied on it—it was designed as an internal plan document, not a tool for employees to understand their benefits.

In *DeBartolo v. Blue Cross/Blue Shield of Illinois* [2001 U.S. Dist. LEXIS 18363 (N.D. Ill. Nov. 8, 2001)], patients assigned their rights under the plan to a doctor, who then approached two health plans to collect his fees. The doctor sought statutory penalties under ERISA § 104(b), on the grounds that the plan administrator refused to give him a schedule of the plan's usual and customary charges. Section 104(b) requires disclosure not only of specific documents but "other instruments under which the plan is established or is operated."

The court ruled that § 104(b) does not mandate disclosure of usual and customary charges. The category of "other instruments" is limited to formal plan documents. At any rate, the focus of the section is informing participants, and giving the doctor access to the fee schedule wouldn't further that objective. Although there is a Department of Labor advisory opinion [DOL 96-14A, July 31, 1996] that requires disclosure of the fee schedule, the court did not think that it had to follow this opinion.

§ 11.03 SUMMARY ANNUAL REPORT (SAR)

One of the administrator's more complex tasks is preparing the plan's annual report, usually on Form 5500. This information is then used to draft the Summary Annual Reports (SARs) that must be distributed to plan participants.

The administrator has nine months from the end of the plan year (or two years after the end of the extension, if an extension was granted for filing the underlying Form 5500). DOL regulations [29 C.F.R. § 2520.104b-10(d)] provide a simple "fill in the blanks" form that must be used for the SAR.

The SAR form consists of a basic financial statement about the plan and its expenses, the net value of plan assets, and whether the plan's assets appreciated or depreciated in value during the year. If the plan is subject to the minimum funding standard, the plan must disclose either that contributions were adequate to satisfy the requirement, or the amount of the deficit. Participants must also be informed of their right to receive additional information, including a copy of the full annual report, a statement of the plan's assets and liabilities, or a statement of the plan's income and expenses. Plans that have simplified reporting requirements can use alternative compliance methods to satisfy the SAR requirement.

Some plans (such as unfunded welfare plans, top-hat plans, and pension or welfare plans that are financed by employee dues) are not required to furnish SARs.

§ 11.04 INDIVIDUAL ACCOUNT PLAN DISCLOSURES

The modern trend is for plans to provide participants with a greater degree of control over the way their pension plan accounts are invested. DOL Reg. § 2550.404c-1(b), dealing with "participant directed individual account plans" (profit-sharing, stock bonus, and money purchase plans) obligates plans to offer at least three diversified categories of investments, with materially different risk and return characteristics, so that overall the participant can choose the balance between risk and return that he or she prefers. Plan fiduciaries are not liable if the participant's own investment choices result in losses, unless obeying the participant's instructions violates the terms of the plan.

Participants are entitled to receive a great deal of information in connection with individual account plans. The burden is on the plan to supply the information, not on the individual participant to request it. The mandated disclosures include:

- A description of the available investment alternatives available under the plan; the general risk and return characteristics of each, including the composition of each portfolio and how they are diversified;
- The designated investment managers for each alternative;
- When and how participants can give investment instructions; any limitations imposed on those instructions (for instance, only four changes in investment per year);
- Fees and expenses that affect the participant's account balance;
- Contact information for a fiduciary (or designee of a fiduciary) who can provide additional information about plan investments on request;
- The fact that fiduciaries are not liable if they follow the participant's investment directions, even if losses result;
- (If participants can invest in securities of the employer) Procedures to maintain confidentiality about the participant's voting and tendering shares of employer stock, and contact information for the fiduciary who monitors the confidentiality provisions.

When a participant invests in publicly traded securities and other assets subject to the Securities Act of 1933 [15 U.S.C. § 77a], the participant must be given a prospectus for the investment either before or right after making the investment. If the plan "passes through" to participants the rights to vote and/or tender the shares, the plan must provide the participant with the proxy materials and other relevant documents, and must provide instructions on how to exercise the rights.

The plan further has a duty to disclose, based on the latest information available to the plan, at least this much information (either to all participants, or on request by a participant):

- For each investment alternative, the fees and operating expenses as a percentage of the average net assets of the investment alternative;
- Whatever prospectuses, financial statements, and reports the plan has about the investment alternative;
- A description of the portfolio of each alternative;
- The value of shares in each alternative;
- The current and past performance of each alternative, net of expenses, calculated on a "reasonable and consistent basis";
- The value of the shares in the individual participant's account.

§ 11.05   NOTICES OF REDUCTION OF BENEFIT ACCRUALS

Under ERISA § 204(h), plan administrators are required to notify participants, alternate beneficiaries under QDROs, and any union representing the workers whenever a plan amendment significantly reduces future benefit accruals under any qualified plan that is subject to ERISA's minimum funding standards (e.g., defined benefit plans).

The notice must contain the text or a summary of the plan amendment, and the effective date of the amendment. Notice must be given at least 15 days before the effective date of the plan amendment. [*See* T.D. 8795, Final Regulations published at 65 Fed. Reg. 68678 (Dec. 14, 1998)] The notice requirement applies even if the amendment also triggers the need to issue a Summary of Material Modifications that is actually issued to participants.

The plan administrator can use any method reasonably calculated to get the notice to employees: hand delivery, first class mail to the employee's last known address, or delivery in combination with any other required notice.

The plan amendment cannot become effective as to any plan participant if the administrator intentionally refuses to provide the necessary notice. If only some of the necessary people were notified, the amendment does not become effective as to those who were not notified.

Example 2, Question 5 of the Final Rule says that if a plan is amended to modify the actuarial factors used to convert an annuity to a lump-sum distribution, notice is not required because the amendment does not affect the annual benefit commencing at normal retirement age.

Question 6 defines the plan provisions that must be taken into account to determine whether the rate of future accruals has been reduced:

- Dollar amount or percentage of compensation on which benefit accruals are based;
- Amount of disparity (in a plan using permitted disparity);
- Definition of service or compensation taken into account in accruing benefits;
- Method of calculating average compensation;
- (Defined benefit plan) Definition of normal retirement age;
- Denial of future participation to current participants;
- Benefits offsets;
- Provisions for minimum benefits;
- Formulas for contributions to, and forfeitures in, individual account plans.

Although this provision was an original part of ERISA when the statute was passed in 1974, disclosure was not required under the Internal Revenue Code until EGTRRA added a new I.R.C. § 4980F imposing an excise tax of $100 per day for failure to give the required notification. The employer, not the plan, is liable for the tax.

The excise tax will not be imposed if the employer didn't know that there had been a failure to meet the notice requirement, or if the failure is cured within 30 days of the employer's discovery of the failure (or the time when the employer should have known that failure occurred). The excise tax is capped at a maximum of $500,000 per tax year, but the cap does not apply if the employer did not exercise reasonable diligence in complying with this provision.

The notice must give "sufficient information," in plain English, for participants and alternate payees to understand the effect of the plan amendment. The IRS will issue regulations about what adds up to sufficient information. The agency can allow plans with fewer than 100 participants, or plans that give participants a choice between new and old benefit formulas, to give a simplified notice. It can even exempt such plans from the notice requirement.

The IRS also has the power to require a longer notice period than the 15 days provided by ERISA, and to adopt regulations that allow "new technologies" (e.g., the company Intranet) to be used to provide the notice.

If a plan "egregiously" fails to meet the notice requirement, then the affected participants and alternate payees will be entitled to receive whatever benefits they would have received if the plan had never been amended to cut back the benefits. An "egregious" failure is intentional refusal to provide notice, or simple failure to provide most of the affected individuals with most of the information they are entitled to receive.

Additional regulations have been proposed [*see* 67 Fed. Reg. 19714] on April 23, 2002, to conform to recent legislation.

§ 11.06   OTHER NOTICES AND DISCLOSURES

[A]   Notice of Deferred Benefits

Frequently, an employee will leave for one reason or another ("separation from service") at a time when he or she is entitled to a deferred vested benefit, but is not yet entitled to a retirement pension. The person in that situation is entitled to a notice containing:

- The name and address of the plan administrator;
- The nature, form, and amount of the person's deferred vested benefit;
- An explanation of any benefits that are forfeitable if the employee dies before a certain date.

The notice must be given no later than the date Schedule SSA is to be filed with the IRS. [Schedule SSA is the annual report that I.R.C. § 6057 requires of pension plans and other plans that are subject to the vesting requirements of ERISA Title I, Part 3] The IRS has the power to impose a penalty of $50 per erroneous statement or willful failure to furnish a statement.

Not less than thirty, or more than ninety, days before the annuity start date of any benefit that is immediately distributable before the participant reaches 62 or normal retirement age, the participant must also be given notice of any right he or she has to defer distribution. [*See* Treas. Reg. § 1.411(a)-11(c)(2)]

[B] Rollovers; Withholding Certificate

Not more than 90, and not less than 30, days before making a distribution, the plan administrator must notify the participant of the potential consequences of receiving a distribution that could be made the subject of a rollover. The notice should inform participants of their right to have the distribution deposited into an IRA, or to another qualified plan that will accept it.

Participants must be warned about the 20% withholding that will be imposed on all taxable distributions that are neither rolled over nor transferred—and that the sums that are received are taxable in the year of receipt. Participants must also be told that they can roll over the distribution within 60 days of its receipt to an IRA or another qualified plan. The notice must also provide information about capital gains treatment of lump sums, and the limited circumstances under which five-year averaging will be permitted. IRS Form 1099-R is used to report the taxable component of a designated distribution.

There is also a corresponding notice obligation before a plan makes a distribution that is *not* an eligible rollover distribution; the plan must send the participant IRS Form W-4P, Withholding Certificate for Pension or Annuity Payments. The W-4P informs the participant of the options he or she has with respect to withholding:

- Direct the plan not to withhold;
- Direct withholding based on marital status or the number of allowances;
- Increase withholding on periodic payments (for instance, if the participant has high outside income and might otherwise owe a large balance at the end of the tax year).

[C] QJSA/QPSA Notice

Thirty to ninety days before receipt of benefits, a plan that permits payouts in annuity form must provide all participants with a plain English statement. [All participants—vested or otherwise—are entitled to the statement. *See* I.R.C. § 417(a)(3), Treas. Reg. §§ 1.401(a)(11), and 1.417(e)-1(b)(3)] The notice should contain:

- The terms and conditions of the joint and survivor annuity;
- The participant's right to waive the annuity, including a description of the consequences of the waiver;
- Rights of the participant's spouse;
- Description of the right to revoke the election, and consequences of the revocation.

A comparable explanation must be given about the Qualified Preretirement Survivor Annuity (QPSA), although the timing requirement is more complicated. The notice is due by the latest of:

- The period that begins on the first day of the plan year in which the participant reaches age 32, and ends at the end of the plan year before the participant reaches 35;
- A reasonable time (deemed to mean no more than a year) after a person becomes a plan participant;
- A reasonable time after the employer stops subsidizing the survivor benefit;
- A reasonable time after the I.R.C. § 401(a)(11) survivor benefit provisions become applicable to the participant. This might happen, for example, if a single or divorced person marries and acquires a spouse who could become entitled to a QPSA;
- A reasonable time after separation from service. If the employee leaves before he or she is 35, the period runs from one year before to one year after the separation.

> **Tip:** The plan can accept waivers at earlier stages (as long as the spouse consents), but the plan must give the participant a written explanation of how QPSAs work. The waiver becomes void at the beginning of the plan year in which the participant reaches age 35. If a new waiver is not signed, and the participant dies before retirement age, then the spouse gets a QPSA despite the attempt to waive this form of benefit.

The plan can omit the notice of the right to waive the QPSA/QJSA if the benefit is fully subsidized by the plan, and the participant can neither waive the QPSA/QJSA nor name a nonspouse as beneficiary. The benefit is fully subsidized if not waiving neither lowers the benefit nor results in higher costs for the participant.

An IRS Notice of Proposed Rulemaking Reg.-109481-99, R.I.N. 1545-AX34, 66 Fed. Reg. 3916 (Jan. 17, 2001)] deals with consent to non-QJSA distribution methods. The Small Business Jobs Protection Act (SBJPA) [Pub. L. No. 104-188] enacted I.R.C. § 417(a)(7), allowing the QJSA disclosure statement to be provided after the annuity starting date, as long as the period for electing to waive the QJSA is at least 30 days after the notice is rendered. The 2001 proposal (effective for plan years beginning on or after January 1, 2002) permits the explanation to be furnished either on or after the annuity starting date, and permits a retroactive starting date if the plan makes provisions for it and the participant so elects.

[D] QDRO Notices

The general rule is that no one can garnish or otherwise get hold of plan benefits before they are paid. The exception to the rule is that a plan administrator not only has the right, but has the obligation, to comply with valid court orders that direct part of the benefit to the participant's separated or divorced spouse. However, not every divorce-related order must be treated as a Qualified Domestic Relations Order (QDRO).

Once a plan receives a court order, I.R.C. § 414(p) obligates the administrator to review it to see if it is qualified. The plan participant and the alternate payee (nearly always the spouse) must be notified that the plan has received an order and what the plan will do to assess its qualification. Then the administrator carries out that procedure and sends another notice to the participant and alternate payee, if the order has been determined to be qualified and therefore must be obeyed by the plan.

[E]   Break-in-Service Notice

ERISA's break-in-service rules are complex and difficult for participants to understand. Participants have the right to make a written request (although only once a year) when they are separated from service, or have a one-year break in service. The notice defines their accrued benefits under the plan, and the percentage of the accrued benefits that is nonforfeitable.

[F]   "Saver's Credit"

One effect of EGTRRA was to increase substantially the amount that taxpayers can contribute to IRA accounts (or defer in 401(k) or 403(b) accounts). *See* the IRS Announcement 2001-106 [2001-44 I.R.B. 416] for a description of the "saver's credit," which is an income tax credit under I.R.C. § 25B for low-income taxpayers who contribute to an IRA or pension plan. The Announcement contains a sample notice that can be given to employees explaining the credit.

[G]   FASB Changes

In 1998, the Financial Accounting Standards Board (FASB) revised three of its existing statements: No. 87, Employers' Accounting for Pensions; No. 88, Employers' Accounting for Settlements and Curtailments of Defined Benefit Pension Plans and for Termination Benefits; and No. 106, Employers' Accounting for Postretirement Benefits Other Than Pensions. The statement effecting the revisions, No. 132, Employers' Disclosures About Pension and Other Postretirement Benefits, streamlines the reporting process by eliminating some noncritical disclosures but increases the amount of information that must be disclosed about changes in the employers' benefit obligations and the fair values of plan assets. Statement No. 132 also aims to improve standardization of retiree benefit disclosures. It is effective for fiscal years beginning after December 15, 1997. If a company includes comparative information about years before 1998, it must restate the disclosures for earlier periods as long as the information is readily available.

[H]   Notices About Funding Problems

If the plan is underfunded, ERISA § 4011 generally requires the administrator to notify participants and beneficiaries of the funding standards and the limitations on the PBGC's guarantee of payment of benefits. A model notice that can be used for this purpose is published at 29 C.F.R. § 2627.1-.9. The notice must be given within two months of the plan's deadline for filing its annual report for the prior plan year. (If an extension was granted, the two-month period runs from the extended deadline.) However, certain plans are not required to give this notice, even if they are underfunded: plans in their first year of PBGC coverage and plans that are exempted by ERISA § 302(d)(8) because they do not have to make deficit reduction contributions.

ERISA § 502(c)(3) imposes a penalty of up to $110 a day, or whatever relief the court deems proper, for failure to give this notice.

[I] Notice of Termination

Between 60 and 180 days before the scheduled date of a standard or distress termination of a pension plan the administrator must give written notice to the parties affected, e.g., the amount and form of the benefit due of the proposed termination date. The notice must explain how the benefit was calculated (e.g., length of service, participant's age, interest rate and other assumptions, and other factors that the PBGC requires to be disclosed).

However, in *Thompson v. Bridgeport Hospital* [2001 Conn. Super. LEXIS 1755 (June 8, 2001)], an employee lost group health coverage when she was terminated. She sued in state court under a state law requiring employers to provide 15 days' advance notice of cancellation or discontinuation of group health coverage. She also sued under ERISA for penalties, fines, and damages for failure to provide COBRA notice. The state law claim was dismissed as preempted by ERISA § 514, on the grounds that the state law relates to the ERISA plan because it creates significant administrative duties for the employer.

§ 11.07 DISCLOSURE ON REQUEST

In addition to disclosures that must be made, and documents that must be furnished, automatically to all plan participants and beneficiaries, ERISA and the Internal Revenue Code require certain disclosures to be made only if a participant or beneficiary requests them.

Materials that can be requested include:

- A complete copy of the plan's latest Form 5500;
- The plan instrument (that is, the Collective Bargaining Agreement or trust that actually creates the plan);
- The latest updated SPD;
- A report on plan termination;
- Statement of accrued benefits (but the administrator only has to furnish this once in every 12-month period);
- Percentage of vesting; and, for participants who are not fully vested, the schedule on which full vesting will occur.

If a request is made, the information should be mailed within 30 days to the last known address of the requester. The plan is allowed to impose a reasonable charge for the information, based on the least expensive available means of reproducing the documents.

The plan documents, plan description, and latest annual report must be kept on file for participants who want to inspect them, at the plan administrator's principal office. If there is a request to make them available there, copies of the documents must also be kept at the employer's principal office and at each of the employer's locations where 50 or more employees work.

According to the Third Circuit in *Daniels v. Thomas & Betts Corp.* [263 F.3d 66 (3d Cir. 2001)], the plan administrator has a duty to provide a copy of the plan instrument to a participant or beneficiary based on a written request from the participant or beneficiary's attorney, although the Tenth Circuit says that the request has to come directly from the participant or beneficiary.

§ 11.08   ELECTRONIC COMMUNICATIONS

The Taxpayer Relief Act of 1997 (TRA '97) [Pub. L. No. 105-34] ordered the IRS to create rules for integrating computer technology into plan administration and the disclosure process. Proposed Rules at 63 Fed. Reg. 70071 (Dec. 18, 1998) make it clear that a pension plan, including a 401(k) plan, will not lose its qualified status merely because it uses paperless electronic methods to give notice and secure consents. However, the electronic notice must:

- Be at least as comprehensible to the average plan participant as the written notice it replaces;
- Contain as much information as the paper version;
- Be written (for instance, on a Web site or as e-mail) and not oral (e.g., automated telephone system) unless it is so simple that a writing is not required;
- Advise the recipient that a paper version of the notice is available on request, at no charge. The participant must get a personal copy—posting one copy on a bulletin board is not sufficient;
- Use any technology (even if it was not available at the time the rule was proposed) that satisfies these standards.

These proposals were finalized as T.D. 8873, published as 65 Fed. Reg. 6001 (Feb. 8, 2000) and also 2000-9 I.R.B. 713, effective for years beginning on or after January 1, 2001, for using electronic media to provide notifications to plan participants (and get their consents) with respect to distributions from a qualified plan. Specifically, paperless electronic methods of communication can be used to transmit:

- I.R.C. § 411(a)(11) notice of distribution options, right to defer distribution, and the participant's consent to a distribution;
- I.R.C. § 402(f) rollover notice;

- I.R.C. § 3405(e)(10)(B) withholding notice.

Furthermore, the plan is allowed to give the notices under I.R.C. §§ 411(a)(11) and 402(f) more than 90 days before a distribution, as long as the plan offers a summary of the notices within the 90-day period before the distribution. Plans that use electronic notices must always give participants the option of getting a paper version of the notice at no charge.

Also Notice 99-1, 1999-2 I.R.B. 8 explains electronic techniques for performing administrative tasks such as enrolling participants and designating beneficiaries. Announcement 99-6, 1999-4 I.R.B. 24 allows electronic transmission of W-4P forms.

In April 2002, the Department of Labor published an additional Final Rule as a safe harbor method of communicating employee benefit information electronically. (In other words, employers will not be penalized if they follow these procedures, but they are not the only acceptable procedures.) *See* 67 Fed. Reg. 17263 (4/9/02).

To use the safe harbor, the employer must get the employee's voluntary consent to providing the information electronically. The individual must provide an address (e.g., an e-mail address) for receiving the communications. The employer must give the individual a clear and conspicuous statement, before consent is rendered, explaining the documents to which the consent applies. Employees must be informed that they can withdraw their consent to electronic notification at any time, and must be told how to update their information and/or withdraw consent. They must also be told how to obtain paper hard copies of the documents.

Tip: Under the safe harbor, employers must communicate individually with employees. Using computer kiosks in the workplace is not an acceptable method of providing the information.

---

§ 11.09   DISCLOSURE OF DOCUMENTS TO THE DOL

ERISA required plan administrators to file all SPDs and SMMs with the Department of Labor (DOL) until it was amended by the Taxpayer Relief Act of 1997. The current version of ERISA § 104(a) requires plan administrators to respond to DOL requests by providing documents relating to an employee benefit plan—including the latest SPD, a summary of plan changes not reflected in the SPD, and the plan instrument.

However, the DOL sees its primary role in this arena as helping participants and beneficiaries get documents from the plan, so the DOL can ask for documents that participants or beneficiaries are entitled to, have requested, but have not received. But the DOL will not ask for documents that the participants and beneficiaries are not entitled to see.

If the plan administrator doesn't respond to the request within 30 days, the DOL has the power (under ERISA § 502(c)(6)) to impose civil penalties of up to

$110 a day (but not more than $1,100 per request). Penalties will not be imposed if factors beyond the administrator's control prevent compliance.

The DOL's Final Rule about document disclosure and civil penalties is set out at 67 Fed. Reg. 777-789 (Jan. 7. 2002).

§ 11.10   FORM 5500

Qualified plans must report each year to the IRS, DOL, and PBGC so that these agencies can monitor plan operations and see if the plans remain qualified, are financially sound, and are operated in accordance with all applicable requirements. The basic Form 5500 covers plans with 100 or more participants; smaller plans can use the less complex Form 5500-C/R or Form 5500-EZ. Only one filing is necessary—the IRS transmits the information to the DOL and PBGC. [The toll-free telephone hot line for questions about plan coverage, premiums, or terminations is (800) 736-2444]

Form 5500, like the Form 1040, consists of a basic form and various schedules that provide additional information. Form 5500 deals with four main subjects: the plan's financial statements, actuarial data, administrative data, and any benefits covered by insurance.

The annual report is due at the end of the seventh month following the end of the plan year. A plan that does not seem likely to complete the report in time should file IRS Form 5558, Application for Extension of Time to File Certain Employee Plan Returns, to get an extension of up to two and a half months. The extension will be granted automatically, until the due date for the employer's income tax return, as long as the plan year is the same as the employer's tax year, the income tax deadline has been extended to a date after the normal due date for the Form 5500, and a copy of the income tax extension is attached to the Form 5500.

Starting with the 2001 plan year, single-employer plans can use the 1-EZ form instead of Form 1 and Schedule A, as long as they are exempt from the variable rate premium. [*See* PBGC Tech. Update 00-6, (Dec. 20, 2000) <http://www.pbgc.gov/laws/techupdates/tech00_6.htm> explaining the simplified premium form, 1-EZ] A plan is exempt if it has no vested participants on the premium snapshot date; if it is funded exclusively by individual insurance contracts; if it has fewer than 500 participants and has no unfunded vested benefits; if the sponsor's contributions for the prior plan year were at least as great as the full funding limitation; or if the plan is terminating via a standard termination on or before the snapshot date.

Once again, the IRS is supervising a transition from paper-based to electronic filing. The Troubleshooter's Guide to Filing the ERISA Annual Report (Form 5500) [(May 2001) <http://www.dol.gov/pwba/pubs/troubleg.pdf>] provides valuable information about EFAST (electronic) filing of Form 5500. This publication contains Checklists and Quick Reference charts and general guidelines for completing the form and its schedules. [The PWBA has a toll-free line (Monday through Friday, 8 A.M. to 8 P.M. Eastern Time) at 866-463-3278, for questions about completing Form 5500, or if you need help with PWBA correspondence about the EFAST processing of a form already filed]

A "large plan" is one with 100 or more participants as of the beginning of the plan year, and a "small plan" has fewer. If the number of participants at the beginning of a plan year was 80 to 120 and a Form 5500 was filed for the previous plan year, the plan has the right to elect to complete the Form 5500 and the schedules using the same category as the previous year.

Under current rules, the Form 5500 can be filed in two formats: machine print (completed by software from EFAST approved vendors) or hand print (filled out by typewriter, or by hand; for the 2000 version, hand print forms can also be filled out with software from an EFAST-approved vendor). Individual hand print forms can be ordered from 800-TAX FORM (829-3676) and can't be filed electronically. Machine print forms can be filed by modem, by mailing magnetic tape, floppies, or CD-ROMs with the data to the IRS, or by mailing a paper version of the machine form.

Instructions for filing by modem are available at <http://www.efast.dol.gov>. Paper forms and magnetic media should be mailed PWBA, P.O. Box 7043 Lawrence, KS 66044-7043. One of the private delivery services designated as adequate by the IRS can also be used: Airborne Express, DHL Worldwide Express, FedEx, or UPS. In that case, the address is PWBA/NCS Attn: EFAST 3833 Greenway Drive Lawrence, KS 66046-1290.

The annual return for a large pension plan must include:

- Form 5500, with all applicable plan characteristics code entered on Line 8;
- As many Schedule As as are needed to report information about the plan's insurance contracts;
- (For defined benefit or money purchase plans) Schedule B actuarial information;
- Schedule C, the list of the 40 most highly compensated providers of services to the plan, including disclosure if any accountants or actuaries were terminated;
- Schedule D, reporting various investment entities in which the plan participated or invested, such as master trust investment accounts, common/collective trusts, pooled separate accounts, investment entities, or group insurance arrangements;
- Schedule E (information about ESOPs);
- Schedule G (there isn't any Schedule F) to report any loans, leases, or fixed income obligations that are uncollectable or in default;
- Schedule H financial information about the plan, including schedules of assets held for investment purposes and reportable transactions;
- Schedule P for reporting fiduciary information; this schedule must be filed to start the statute of limitations running under I.R.C. § 6501(a);
- Schedule R retirement plan information;
- Schedule SSA data about separated plan participants who have vested benefits;
- Schedule T (information on coverage of tax-qualified pension plans).

Unless Line 3b(2) of Schedule H is checked, the report of an independent qualified public accountant must be submitted with the form.

The filing requirement for a large welfare plan is Form 5500 (including the plan codes on Line 8) plus Schedule A for insurance contracts, Schedules C, D, G, and H, and schedules of assets and an accountant's report.

A fringe benefit plan described in I.R.C. § 6039D (a cafeteria plan, or a plan providing educational assistance or adoption assistance) has to file an information return on Form 5500, checking the boxes at lines 8c and 10c, plus Schedule F. However, a Form 5500 is not required for an educational assistance program that is limited to job-related training that is deductible as an ordinary and necessary business expense.

There are many problems that Form 5500 filers often encounter:

- Omitting necessary information; all lines on the form must be filled in (entering $0 if necessary);
- Attaching inappropriate documents; nothing should be attached unless the form specifically requires it;
- Attaching information that is not properly completed and labeled with the name of the plan, the sponsor's Employer Identification Number, the plan number, the type of attachment, and the schedule and line number the attachment relates to;
- Failure to use acceptable forms; entering information outside the lines or boxes.

The DOL can assess civil penalties of up to $1,100 per day per annual report, running from the date of the failure or refusal to file and until a satisfactory report is filed, against plan administrators who fail or refuse to comply with the annual reporting requirements. A report that is rejected for failure to provide material information has not been "filed".

However, voluntary compliance is usually sought before penalties are imposed. The PWBA sends correspondence asking for additional information if data is omitted, or if the agency thinks corrections are necessary in light of the instructions or to be internally consistent with other data on the form.

The PWBA has discretion to waive all or part of the penalty based on submission of a timely statement showing reasonable cause for failure to file the complete report at the time it was due. Penalties are not assessed during the time when the DOL is considering the statement of reasonable cause.

There's also a Delinquent Filer Voluntary Compliance Program (DFVC) that reduces penalties for voluntary compliance. The contact number is (202) 219-8818. To participate, the plan administrator must approach the program before being detected by the DOL as a late filer. The IRS can still impose penalties on the administrators of pension plans (but not of welfare benefit plans) if filings are omitted, even if the DOL abates its enforcement.

CHAPTER 12

PLAN DISTRIBUTIONS

§ 12.01   INTRODUCTION

One of the major tasks of plan administration is to distribute benefits from the plan to participants and their designated beneficiaries—although sometimes determining the proper beneficiary is not as easy as it sounds. The plan administrator must communicate with participants and beneficiaries of their distribution options with respect to accrued benefits. The plan administrator has a duty to provide whatever forms are necessary to make an election.

The standard form of distribution is a single-life annuity for single participants and a Qualified Joint and Survivor Annuity (QJSA) for married participants. The plan must also provide for a Qualified Preretirement Survivor Annuity (QPSA) for married persons who die before their pension enters pay status.

But plans can permit other payment forms: lump sums and annuities offering other provisions (but not extending for a term longer than the life expectancy of the employee or the joint life expectancy of the employee and designated beneficiary). [See I.R.C. § 401(a)(9)(A)(ii)] It's up to the plan whether to offer these alternate forms, or just the standard annuities. [See §§ 12.03, 12.09]

In most cases, defined contribution plans satisfy their distribution obligations by purchasing commercial annuities with the balance in the employee's account, although the plan itself might make payments for a simple annuity for a term of years. Defined benefit plans often buy annuities, although some plans handle distribution in house to save some fees.

> **Tip:** Choosing an annuity insurer is a fiduciary decision. DOL Interpretive Bulletin 95-1 includes a list of criteria to be used in making an appropriate choice.

The normal payment method for a profit-sharing plan or stock bonus plan is a lump sum, not a periodic payment. When a participant in one of these plans dies, the entire vested balance remaining in the account must go to the beneficiary designated by the participant. The spouse's consent is required if a married participant is to designate anyone other than the spouse as beneficiary.

For plans other than pension plans, I.R.C. § 401(a)(11)(B)(iii) requires that, unless the balance in a married participant's plan is distributed before his or her death, the remainder must be paid to the surviving spouse unless the surviving spouse waives this right.

§ 12.02   CASHOUT

Although it is burdensome for a plan to make periodic payments of a very small sum, and it would be convenient to simply close the books by making a one-time payment, participants cannot be forced to "cash out" (take a lump sum instead of a stream of payments) unless their vested balance is very small—$5,000 or less. [See T.D. 8794, 63 Fed. Reg. 70335 (Dec. 21, 1998)] Rev. Rul. 2000-36, 2000-31 I.R.B. 140 allows a plan to make a direct rollover under I.R.C. § 401(a)(31), the default method of handling involuntary cashouts, as long as the plan participants get adequate notice that they can get the cash instead.

The calculation of the accrued benefit under I.R.C. § 411(a)(7)(B)(i) does not have to include any service with respect to which the employee has already been cashed out at a level below $3,500.

Notice 2000-11, 2000-6 I.R.B. 572 explains how to notify employees when they receive a plan distribution that is eligible to be rolled over. The notice includes a standard form that the plan can use; if it is claimed that notice was inadequate, using the form provides a safe harbor.

The 2002 technical corrections bill, the Job Creation and Worker Assistance Act of 2002 [Pub. L. No. 107-147] provides that employers can disregard rollovers when they determine whether or not the balance exceeds $5,000 and therefore whether or not it is subject to cashout.

§ 12.03   LUMP SUMS

There is no legal requirement that plans offer lump sum distributions, although it is very common for them to do so for the convenience of retirees who either need a lump sum (to pay the entrance fee to a Continuing Care Retirement Community, for example) or who believe that they can achieve better investment results than a qualified plan, subject to fiduciary requirements, can muster. The second motivation may become less common if stock market conditions continue negative!

A Proposed Regulation, I.R.C. § 1.402(e)-2(e)(3) says that an employee must have at least five years' participation in the plan as a prerequisite for taking a lump-sum payout.

If a plan offers both lump sums and early retirement subsidies, the plan should specify whether the subsidy can be included in the lump sum, or must be taken in annuity form.

Unless the plan provides to the contrary, the federal "mailbox rule" (evidence of timely mailing creates a presumption of timely receipt; the presumption can only be overcome with convincing evidence the document was not received) applies to an ERISA plan to determine whether a participant made a timely election of a lump-sum supplemental benefit. The plan required submission of a written election at least one year before retirement to qualify for the lump sum. In *Schikore v. Bankamerica Supplemental Retirement Plan* [269 F.3d 956 (9th Cir. 2001)], the plaintiff could prove that she mailed the election. The plan refused to pay the lump sum because it claimed it never received the election form. The Ninth Circuit said that she should get the lump sum by application of the mailbox rule.

§ 12.04   ANTI-ALIENATION RULE

The underlying purpose of pension plans is to provide income to retirees and their families once the individual is no longer able to work. This purpose could not be satisfied if the pension became unavailable for some reason. Therefore, pension, annuity, stock bonus, and profit-sharing plans are subject to anti-alienation requirements under I.R.C. §§ 401(a)(13) and 404(a)(2). The benefits under such plans may not be assigned or alienated in advance. But, just as with any legal rule, there are certain exceptions to what seems to be a blanket prohibition.

Federal tax liens under I.R.C. § 6331 can be enforced; they are not considered to violate this provision. [Treas. Reg § 1.401(a)-13(b)(2)]

Once a benefit is in pay status, a participant or beneficiary can make a voluntary revocable assignment of up to 10% of any benefit payment. However, assignments of this type cannot be used to defray the costs of plan administration.

A plan loan is not an improper alienation if:

- The plan includes a specific loan provision;
- Loans are available to all participants on a nondiscriminatory basis;
- The loan is not a prohibited transaction;
- The plan imposes a reasonable interest rate on plan loans;
- The loan is secured by the accrued nonforfeitable benefit. [*See* I.R.C. § 4975(d)(1) and § 4.18]

The Supreme Court's decision in *Patterson v. Shumate* [504 U.S. 753 (1992)] holds that ERISA's anti-alienation provisions are "applicable non-bankruptcy law" under Bankruptcy Code § 541(c)(1). Therefore, benefits from an ERISA-qualified plan can be excluded from the employee's bankruptcy estate, and will not be available to the employee's creditors.

But because of an earlier Supreme Court decision, *Mackey v. Lanier Collection Agency & Service* [486 U.S. 825 (1988)], pension benefits are protected from creditors, but welfare benefits are not. Creditors are sometimes entitled (within limits) to garnish the wages of debtors, but they cannot garnish future pension benefits. If the plan itself is terminating, creditors cannot garnish employees' interests in the plan, even if one consequence of the termination is that they will receive a lump sum instead of ongoing annuity payments.

Once the benefits are paid, the anti-alienation provision no longer applies. [*See Robbins v. DeBuono*, 218 F.3d 197 (2d Cir. 2000)] So, unless there is a state law that offers additional protection, the funds can be attached by creditors.

ERISA's anti-alienation provisions do not prevent imposition of a constructive trust—for instance, when a family court order has been violated. [*Central States Southeast & Southwest Area Pension Fund v. Howell*, 227 F.3d 672 (6th Cir. 2000)]

The State of Illinois said that, under its Uniform Disposition of Unclaimed Property Act, $125,000 in unclaimed pension benefits reverted to the state treasury. But the Seventh Circuit held that ERISA preempts the state law governing unclaimed property. [*Commonwealth Edison Co. v. Vega*, 174 F.3d 870 (7th Cir. 1999)] Therefore, unclaimed benefits remain plan assets until a participant or beneficiary accesses them. It would violate ERISA to entitle states to seize unclaimed benefits, because that would give the state a role in plan management that is contrary to the interests of participants and beneficiaries.

Kopec v. Kopec [70 F. Supp. 2d 217 (E.D.N.Y. 1999)] allows the IRS to levy against the entire balance of an IRA account that an employee-spouse funded with rollovers from a qualified plan. Although the suit (brought by the employee's wife, who claimed that she was entitled to a 50% interest because she had not waived her survivorship interest) was brought under ERISA, the court treated it as a tax enforcement case. Under 26 U.S.C. § 7426(a)(1), a wrongful levy claim requires proof of title or ownership in the levied property. The court said that the wife was still entitled to collect a survivorship annuity from the plan, and therefore had no ownership interest in the IRA account and could not object to the IRS levy.

§ 12.05   QJSA PAYMENTS

The normal method of paying pension plan benefits to married participants is the QJSA, payable for the lives of both the employee and his or her spouse. Once the first spouse dies, the plan can reduce the annuity payable to the survivor—although not more than 50% of the initial payment. Employers can also choose to subsidize the survivor annuity at some level between 50% and 100% of the original payment.

In addition to the QJSA/QPSA, a plan can offer term annuities and/or life annuities, and life annuities can include term certain guarantee features.

Why would a couple be willing to waive the standard form and take a payment other than a QJSA? For one thing, the payments might be larger in the short run. The participant might be the first spouse to retire, with additional funds expected in the future from the other spouse's pension. If the spouse who is expected to survive will have ample funds (e.g., from personal assets and insurance on the life of the other spouse), then a reduced or absent survivor annuity may not create problems.

I.R.C. § 417(d) provides that QJSAs are required only if the participant was married for one year or more before plan payments begin, with an exception for participants who marry in the year before payments begin and remain married for one year. To avoid tracking problems, most plans simply offer QJSAs to all married participants whatever the duration of the marriage.

Because of a 1984 federal law, the Retirement Equity Act, the employee spouse cannot waive the QJSA without the written consent of the other spouse. There is a 60-day window for making the waiver, starting 90 days before the annuity start date (the first day of the employee spouse's first benefit period under the plan), ending 30 days before the annuity start date. However, the Small Business Job Protection Act [Pub. L. No. 104-188] amended the Internal Revenue Code to allow QJSA disclosures to be given even after the annuity starting date.

The final regulations are promulgated at T.D. 8796, 63 Fed. Reg. 70009 (Dec. 18, 1998), that loosen up the notice requirements somewhat. Distributions from the plan can be made less than 30 days after the notice is given, but participants and beneficiaries still must be given at least seven days notice. QJSA disclosure can be deferred until after the annuity starting date. However, the participant can revoke the election until the annuity starting date or seven days after notice is given—whichever comes later. [*See also* Treas. Reg. 109481-99 R.I.N. 1545-ZX34, effective for plan years beginning on or after January 1, 2002, the QJSA explanation can be furnished on or after the annuity starting date]

A waiver of the right to receive the pension in QJSA form must be in writing, and must either be notarized or witnessed by a representative of the pension plan. [*See* Treas. Reg. § 1.417(e)-1(b)(3)] Furthermore, the waiver must be expressed in a document specifically related to the plan; a prenuptial agreement between the employee and his or her spouse won't work for this purpose. [Treas. Reg. § 1.401(a)-20, Q&A 28] The waiver binds only the spouse who signs it; if the employee and spouse divorce, any subsequent spouse is still entitled to a QJSA unless he or she waives it. [I.R.C. § 417(a)(4)] Sample "safe harbor" language for QJSA (and QPSA) waivers can be found in IRS Notice 97-10, 1997-2 I.R.B. 40.

In this context, ERISA preempts community property law [*Boggs v. Boggs*, 520 U.S. 833 (1997)], so a spouse who waives the right to a QJSA can't later assert community property rights in those benefits.

Internal Revenue Code § 417(a)(1)(A)(ii) allows the plan participant to revoke the waiver of QJSA payment at any time before payments begin. The spouse's consent is not required for the revocation, because it has the effect of increasing, not decreasing, the spouse's rights.

§ 12.06   POST-DEATH PAYMENTS

The terms of the plan, and the fact situation, determine whether payments must continue after the death of the plan participant. For instance, if the employee was unmarried and received a life annuity, or if the employee was married and the employee and spouse validly waived the QJSA in favor of a life annuity, the plan will have no post-death obligations. Usually, however, the plan will be required to make a single or ongoing distributions to a beneficiary designated by the employee, or named as beneficiary under the terms of the plan.

Internal Revenue Code § 401(a)(9)(B) provides that if an employee dies when an annuity or installment pension with a survivorship feature is in pay status, the plan continues distributions in the same manner, but to the beneficiary rather than the retiree. The general rule is that the plan has five years from the death of the employee to complete distribution of the decedent's entire interest.

The five-year rule does not apply if the decedent's interest is payable to a designated beneficiary in life annuity form, or in installments that do not extend past the beneficiary's life expectancy. In this situation, the plan must begin the distributions no later than December 31 of the year following the date of the employee's death.

Qualified plans are required to provide Qualified Preretirement Survivor Annuities (QPSAs) if a vested plan participant dies before benefits begin. [I.R.C.

§ 401(a)(11)] The QPSA for a defined benefit plan participant who was eligible to retire at the time of death must be at least as great as what the spouse would have received if the employee had retired with the QJSA on the day before the actual date of death.

In the case of a person who was not yet retirement-eligible on the date of death, the defined benefit plan must calculate the survivor annuity that would have been available if the employee had separated from service on the date he or she died, and survived until the plan's earliest retirement date. The QPSA must be at least equivalent to the QJSA that would have been payable if the employee spouse had died the day after retiring with a QJSA on the plan's earliest retirement date.

In a defined contribution plan, the QPSA must be actuarially equivalent to at least 50% of the nonforfeitable account balance as of the time of death.

The designated beneficiary can also be an irrevocable trust that is valid under state law and has identifiable beneficiaries. It's the responsibility of the employee who wants to take this option to provide the plan with a copy of the trust.

According to I.R.C. § 401(a)(9)(B), if an employee dies once payment of an annuity or installment pension has begun, the plan simply continues the distributions in the same manner—unless, of course, they are supposed to stop at the employee's death.

Plans are allowed to reduce pension benefits to fund the QPSA. Therefore, participants (with the consent of the spouse of a married participant) have the right to waive the QPSA in order to prevent this reduction in the pension amount.

The plan must notify participants of the right to waive the QPSA. The notice must be given in the period that starts on the first day of the plan year in which the participant reaches age 32 and ends with the close of the plan year before the plan year in which the participant reaches age 35. [I.R.C. § 417(a)(3)(B)]

The notice must disclose:

- The terms and conditions of the QPSA;
- The effect of waiving it;
- The spouse's right to invalidate the waiver by withholding consent;
- The participant's right to revoke the waiver and reinstate the QPSA.

§ 12.07   THE REQUIRED BEGINNING DATE

[A]   Theory and Application

Congress' initial reasons for passing ERISA, and for allowing Individual Retirement Accounts (IRAs) revolved around providing current income for workers for the time period between retirement and their death. Not only was estate planning with qualified retirement benefits not considered important, it was not even considered a worthwhile objective—the benefits were supposed to be used up during the individual's lifetime. Therefore, distributions from qualified plans and IRAs were required to start no later than a Required Beginning Date (RBD). The RBD was defined as April 1 of the year after the year in which the individual reached age 70½. An excise tax penalty was imposed on the failure to make at least the Minimum Required Distribution (MRD) each year.

Over the years, theories in Congress and at the IRS have changed. Estate planning for benefits is now treated as a legitimate objective. Furthermore, although the RBD/MRD requirements remain in effect for IRAs, and for qualified plan participants who are corporate officers or directors, or who own 5% or more of the stock in the employer corporation, they have been abolished for rank-and-file employees. If plan participants choose to defer retirement and remain at work past age 70½, they will no longer suffer a tax penalty for doing so.

For plan years beginning on or after January 1, 1997, I.R.C. § 401(a)(9)(C) sets the RBD for a rank-and-file employee at the later of April 1 following the year in which the individual reached age 70½ or that person's actual retirement date. The plan must make actuarial adjustments to the pensions of persons who continue to work after age 70½.

The eventual pension must be at least the actuarial equivalent of the benefits payable as of the date the actuarial increase must begin, plus the actuarial equivalent of any additional benefits that accrue after the starting date, reduced by the actuarial equivalent of whatever retirement benefits are actually distributed after the annuity start date. Employees who stay at work after age 70½ can be given the option of suspending distributions from the plan until they actually retire.

[B] Excise Taxes

The basic tax rule is that amounts received by a plan participant from a plan are taxable income for that year. (Any after-tax contributions made by participants were not deductible when they were made, and will not be taxed again when they are withdrawn. Participants who made after-tax contributions are therefore allowed to calculate an exclusion ratio, so part of each distribution is tax-free to the extent that it can be traced back to past after-tax contributions.)

A 10% excise tax (over and above the normal income tax) is imposed on "premature" distributions. The general rule is that a distribution made before age 59½ is premature. Distributions under a QDRO are not subject to this excise tax. Nor is a distribution considered premature if it is made to a person who has reached age 55 and separated from service. Distributions are not subject to the 10% penalty if they are made after the participant's death, or to employees who are so totally disabled as to be unable to engage in any substantial gainful activity.

The premature distribution excise tax is imposed on lump sums, but not on distributions made over the life, lives, or joint life expectancies of the participant or the participant and one or more beneficiaries. Defined benefit plans are subject to additional rules on this topic. Finally, if a plan participant's unreimbursed medical expenses are high enough to be tax-deductible (over 7.5% of adjusted gross income), plan distributions are not considered premature, even if the participant does not actually use the distributions to pay the medical bills.

Before 1996, plan participants could find themselves between a rock and a hard place. Not only was an excise tax penalty placed on premature withdrawals; a different penalty was imposed on excess lifetime withdrawals from a pension plan but also on excess accumulations of pension benefits within the estate. The SBJPA suspended the tax on excessive distributions for the period 1996–1999, but retained the tax on excessive accumulation in the estate. The Taxpayer Relief Act of 1997 permanently repealed both excise taxes, greatly increasing the financial and estate planning flexibility available to plan participants.

[C] 2001–2002 Rules

An IRS Proposed Regulation [66 Fed. Reg. 3928-3954 (Jan. 17, 2001)] covers required minimum distributions from qualified plans, IRAs, and I.R.C. § 403(b) and § 457 (government and nonprofit-organization) plans. The Proposal substantially simplifies earlier Proposed Regulations issued in 1987 under I.R.C. § 401(a)(9). The 2001 Proposal is effective for distributions for 2002 and subsequent calendar years. [*See* Announcement 2001-18, 2001-10 I.R.B. 791, for more guidance on timing issues]

The 1987 rules did not allow a participant who had designated a beneficiary before the Required Beginning Date (RBD) to change the designation after the RBD, even if there were sound planning reasons to make a change. Under the 1987 rules, unless the designated beneficiary was the employee's spouse, the balance remaining as of the employee's death would have to be distributed relatively quickly. Yet many financial plans favor "stretching out" the distribution, to provide income over a longer time while also reducing the amount of taxable income received in each year.

The 2001 proposal enacts a single Minimum Distribution Incidental Benefit (MDIB) table, in Treas. Reg. § 1.401(a)(9)-2, to be used to calculate the RMD. The table provides for distributions during the employee's life, ranging from 25.2 years (at age 70) to 1.8 years (at ages 115 and older!). The same table can be used whether the beneficiary is a natural person (the employee's spouse or otherwise), or an entity such as a spouse or charity. Under prior law, the balance would have to be distributed faster after death if the beneficiary was an entity, because entities do not have a life expectancy over which the balance can be distributed.

The MDIB table uses the same assumption in all cases: that the beneficiary is 10 years younger than the employee (no matter what their actual ages are). Distributions are made over the predicted life expectancy of a person 10 years younger than the employee. Even greater "stretch-out" is allowed if the beneficiary is the employee's spouse, and is actually more than 10 years younger than the employee, because in that case the calculation of the RMD can be based on the spouse's actual life expectancy. If the employee fails to designate a beneficiary, the RMD is calculated based on the employee's own life expectancy, reduced by one year every year.

With respect to post-death distributions, the 2001 Proposed Regulations allow a beneficiary to be designated even after the RBD, up to the end of the year following the year of the employee's death, in case the employee's executor wants to do post-mortem estate planning. Beneficiaries now have the right to cash out small account balances. If receiving the benefits is financially not advantageous to them, they can disclaim their status as beneficiaries.

The general rule for post-death distributions is that the benefits remaining when the employee dies must be distributed over the life expectancy of the designated beneficiary. The calculation is made in the year the employee dies. If more than one beneficiary is designated (for instance, two or more of the employee's children), then the beneficiary with the shortest life expectancy is treated as the designated beneficiary—whether the employee dies before or after the RBD. If the employee dies without designating a beneficiary, then distribution must be made to his or her intestate distributees, over a period of five years.

In May 2002, the proposals were finalized in substantially the proposed form. However, the final rule, Notice 2002-27, 2002-18 I.R.B. 814, makes it easier to distribute benefits to separate accounts with different beneficiaries, slightly simplifies the RMD calculation by eliminating some of the mathematical factors used in the calculation, and requiring the beneficiary of a decedent's account to be named by September 30 (rather than December 30) of the year of death. This last change was made to make it clear that distribution to the beneficiaries must start in the year of death. IRA trustees must begin to inform beneficiaries of the RMD as of January 31, 2003.

§ 12.08   DIVORCE-RELATED ORDERS

[A]   QDROs and QMCSOs

For many couples, one spouse's interest in a retirement plan is a major marital financial asset. In fact, it may be the only significant marital financial asset. Given our society's high divorce rate, plan administrators are often confronted with court orders incident to an employee's separation or divorce—or are faced with conflicting claims after the death of an employee who divorced, remarried, and eventually died without having changed the beneficiary designation from the first to the second spouse.

Although the general rule is that plan benefits cannot be anticipated or alienated, there is an important exception for family law orders that fit the definitions of Qualified Domestic Relations Orders (QDROs) or Qualified Medical Child Support Orders (QMCSOs). [On QMCSOs, see the HHS/DOL Final Rule on National Medical Child Support Notice, 65 Fed. Reg. 82128 (DOL) and 65 Fed. Reg. 72154 (HHS), as discussed at § 18.16]

Once the administrator determines that a court order has the status of a QDRO, payments can legitimately be made to the alternate payee: i.e., the separated or divorced ex-spouse of an employee.

A QDRO is a court order based on a state domestic relations law (including community property law) dealing with child support, alimony, or marital property rights. No court is allowed to use a QDRO to order a plan to make payments in any type or form not allowed by the plan documents. A QDRO cannot force a plan to pay benefits that have already been assigned to someone else under an earlier QDRO, or to increase the actuarial value of benefits to be paid. The Department of Labor's introduction to the subject of plan administration of QDROs can be found at <http://www.dol.gov/pwba/pubs/qdro.htm>. [*See also* Jeffrey J. Lane, *QDROs: What You Need to Know*, Milliman USA Benefits Perspectives, (Summer 2001) <http://www.milliman.com>]

To be entitled to recognition by the plan, a QDRO must contain at least this much information:

- The recipient's right to plan benefits;
- The names and addresses of the parties;
- The amount or percentage of the plan benefit to be paid to the alternate payee named in the order;
- The time period or number of payments covered by the order;
- The plan(s) it applies to (the same employee might be covered by more than one plan).

Generally, the alternate payee does not receive distributions under the QDRO before the date the employee would be entitled to them. However, distributions can be made from any plan on the earliest date the participant could get the distribution after separation from service, or when the participant reaches age 50—whichever is later. If the plan is drafted to allow it, QDROs can require immediate distribution, or at a time that is not related to the age of the employee spouse.

For QDROs issued when the employee spouse is still working and has not retired, the payments are calculated based on the present value of the normal retirement benefits already accrued as of that time. Early retirement subsidies are not taken into account. The QDRO can provide for recalculation at the time of retirement, in case an early retirement subsidy is actually paid.

The question of who should get benefits under an ERISA welfare benefit plan is a question of federal law. Therefore, the Sixth Circuit says that ERISA preempts state-law claims that undue influence was exercised to get an employee to change his beneficiary designation. [*Tinsley v. General Motors*, 227 F.3d 700 (6th Cir. 2000)]

Under the January 2001 proposals, as implemented in 2002, the ex-spouse who is entitled to some or all of the benefits will be considered a spouse for distribution purposes, even if the QDRO does not make explicit reference to I.R.C. §§ 401(a)(11) and 417—and even if the employee has more than one ex-spouse. Distributions to the alternate payee named by the QDRO must begin no later than the employee's Required Beginning Date. However, the calculation will be based on the employee's life expectancy. If the ex-spouse is more than 10 years younger than the employee, the actual joint life expectancies of the employee and ex-spouse will be used in the calculations.

Where a QDRO transferred a portion of the lifetime annuity but did not specify that the ex-spouse was to be treated as the surviving spouse for the survivor annuity, it was proper for payments to stop after the participant's death. [*Dorn v. IBEW*, 211 F.3d 938 (5th Cir. 2000)]

Although ERISA explicitly covers only QDROs dealing with pension plans, courts sometimes use a similar rationale to divide welfare benefits such as life insurance. [*See, e.g., Deaton v. Cross*, 184 F. Supp. 2d 441 (D. Md. 2002); *Seaman v. Johnson*, [184 F. Supp. 2d 642 (E.D. Mich. 2002). In both these cases, the court held that the divorce-related court order should prevail over the beneficiary designation filed with the plan.]

[B] QDRO Methodology

Under the "separate interest" method of distribution under a defined benefit plan, the alternate payee gets future payments based on his or her life expectancy, not that of the plan participant. [*See, e.g., In re Marriage of Shelstead*, 66 Cal. App. 4th 893 (1998)] The nonemployee wife was awarded a 50% community property interest in the employee husband's pension plan. The order said that, if the wife died before the husband, she would be able to designate a successor in interest to receive her community-property share. But the California Court of Appeals decided that, although this was a divorce-related order, it was not a QDRO because it did not settle the rights of an alternate payee, and she could leave her share to anyone, not just another acceptable alternate payee.

Under the "shared payment" method, the alternate payee gets a portion of each pension payment made to the plan participant, so both the participant and the alternate payee use the same timing schedule and form of annuity. The alternate payee gets to take advantage of any early retirement incentives elected by the participant. The enhanced benefit under an early retirement plan is actuarially reduced if the alternate payee is younger than the participant (this is often the case, especially if the participant is male and his ex-wife is younger than he is), but is not increased if the alternate payee is older than the participant.

In *Rich v. Southern California IBEW-NECA Pension Plan* [1999 Daily Journal D.A.R. 6965 (Cal. App. 1999)], the QDRO divided the community property portion of the employee spouse's pension equally between employee and nonemployee spouses, with payments continuing until the death of one of them. When the nonemployee spouse died, the employee spouse applied to the plan to receive the entire benefit. The survivor lost at trial, because the court held that the nonemployee spouse had received a separate interest in the plan. However, the appellate court disagreed, treating the QDRO as a shared payment division.

In a defined contribution plan, the beneficiary is always named, usually at the time of plan enrollment, and remains the same until and unless the participant changes it. Defined contribution plans always use the separate interest method. A plan participant can make his or her subsequent spouse a named beneficiary, but an alternate payee who remarries does not have the right to choose a joint-and-survivor payment option with respect to the participant ex-spouse's pension. [*See* Darren J. Goodman, *Transferring the Alternate Payee's Retirement Benefits at Death: A Look at* Shelstead, <http://www.qdroprep.com/benefit.htm>]

Under a defined benefit plan, unless the QDRO stipulates a preretirement death benefit for the ex-spouse, the ex-spouse will receive nothing if the participant spouse dies before the benefit starts. On the other hand, the effect of the death of the nonparticipant spouse before benefits begin is that the participant spouse will be entitled to 100% of the benefit.

A valid QDRO gives the alternate payee the status of an ERISA "beneficiary." Sometimes the alternate payee gets even more protection, as a "participant." If the QDRO is issued when the employee spouse's pension is already in pay status, the shared payment method will be used. If the nonemployee spouse dies first, his or her share of the QJSA reverts to the surviving employee spouse. The alternate payee is just a beneficiary, and can only dispose of his or her interest in the plan by naming another alternate beneficiary as contingent alternate beneficiary in the QDRO.

But where the separate interest method is available (in defined contribution and 401(k) plans, or if the divorce occurs before benefits are in pay status), the alternate payee's status is more like that of a plan participant, because he or she can choose the form of pension payment. Some forms of payment (e.g., an annuity for a term certain) allow the payee to designate someone to receive unpaid benefits at the payee's death.

[C] The Administrator's Response

When a plan administrator receives a court order, the first step is to determine whether the order is entitled to QDRO status. However, once ERISA compliance is determined, the administrator must comply with the QDRO, without inquiring as to its acceptability under state law. An employee who opposes the terms of the QDRO has to litigate with the ex-spouse in state court; the plan administrator is not liable for complying with the QDRO. [*Blue v. UAL Corp.*, 160 F.3d 383 (7th Cir. 1998)]

If the administrator believes that a document described as a QDRO is a sham, or at least questionable, PWBA Advisory Opinion #99-13A [(Sept. 29, 1999) <http://www.dol.gov/pwba/programs/ori/advisory99/99-13a.htm>] provides guidance. The administrator who requested the opinion received a series of 16 purported QDROs, many of them from the same lawyer. The documents gave the same address for the plan participant and the alternate payee, although they were supposed to be separated or divorced. The administrator was aware of a publication suggesting sham divorces as a means of accessing ESOP benefits during employment.

The advisory opinion says that administrators are "not free to ignore" information casting doubt on the validity of an order. If the administrator finds that evidence credible, the administrator must make a case-by-case determination of the validity of each order, "without inappropriately spending plan assets or inappropriately involving the plan in the state domestic relations proceeding."

The PWBA Advisory Opinion says that appropriate action could include informing the court of the potential invalidity of the order; intervening in a domestic relations proceeding; or even bringing suit. However, an administrator who can't get a response within a reasonable time from the agency that issued the order "may not independently determine that the order is not valid under state law." [PWBA Advisory Opinion #99-13A (Sept. 29, 1999) <http://www.dol.gov/pwba/programs/ori/advisory99/99-13a.htm>] ERISA Opinion Letter 94-32A says that it is improper to charge either the participant or the alternate payee a fee for processing a QDRO.

This determination must be made within a reasonable time. The employee and the proposed alternate payee must be notified promptly that the order was received. The administrator must explain to them how the plan will determine the validity of the alleged QDRO. The funds in question must be segregated, and separately accounted for, until the determination has been made. There is an 18-month limit on keeping the funds in the segregated account. [*See* PWBA Advisory Opinion 2000-09A, (July 12, 2000) <http://www.dol.gov/pwba/programs/ori/advisory2000/2000-09a.htm> for a discussion of what to do when an alternate payee is named under a plan that limits beneficiary designations to spouses, minor children, and parents—but not former spouses]

[D]   QDRO Case Law: *Egelhoff* and After

In 1997, the Fourth Circuit ruled that unless the QDRO is issued before the date of retirement, benefits will vest in the current spouse, not the divorced spouse, because pensions are distributed in QJSA form unless there is either a QDRO or a proper waiver by the participant and current spouse during the 90-day period before the pension's annuity start date. [*Hopkins v. AT&T Global Info. Sys.*, 105 F.3d 153 (4th Cir. 1997)]

According to a PWBA Advisory Opinion 2001-06A [(June 1, 2001) <http://www.dol.gov/pwba/programs/ori/advisory2001/2001-06A.htm>] an income-withholding notice issued by a welfare department or county child support agency can be treated as a "judgment, decree, or order" dealing with state family or domestic relations law. In the PWBA's view, ERISA does not absolutely insist that valid QDROs be issued by a court, as long as they relate to child support, enforce an order, and are issued by an agency with jurisdiction over child support matters.

The Supreme Court decided, in *Egelhoff v. Egelhoff* [532 U.S. 131 (2001)] that ERISA preempts a Washington State law that made all beneficiary designations (in life insurance as well as qualified plans) invalid when the employee or insured person divorced. The Supreme Court decided that the state law "relates to" ERISA plans, and therefore is preempted, because qualified plans can be regulated only by federal, and not state, law.

Other courts soon applied the *Egelhoff* decision. An ex-spouse tried to use California community property law to collect benefits under an employee benefit plan providing life insurance. The Ninth Circuit held, in *Metropolitan Life Insurance v. Buechler* [2001 U.S. App. LEXIS 21390 (9th Cir. Sept. 25, 2001)] that the disposition of insurance proceeds is a core ERISA concern, where community property laws are preempted. Therefore, the postdivorce designation of a new beneficiary governed.

In a California case, a participant remarried but failed to change the designation of the ex-spouse as beneficiary. [*Araiza-Klier v. TIAA*, 2001 Cal. App. LEXIS 2794 (Nov. 29, 2001)] Both the ex-spouse and the surviving spouse filed claims for the employee's annuity, and the annuity company went to court for guidance about whom to pay. An intermediate appellate court ruled that *Egelhoff* requires preemption of the state law that awards the benefit to the surviving spouse. However, the court still ordered payment of the benefit to the surviving spouse, because the ex-spouse waived her interest as beneficiary in the divorce decree, and federal common law allows divorcing spouses to waive their interests in the employee spouse's benefits.

In a similar Texas case, the plan participant died before his divorce was final. He named his estate as beneficiary. [*Barnett v. Barnett*, 67 S.W.2d 107 (Tex. 2001)] The surviving spouse could not recover a community property interest in the life insurance proceeds that had already been paid to the estate—once again, because *Egelhoff* requires preemption of state law, including community property law.

Delaware had a slightly different law: one that said that property (here, a 401(k) account) could not be transferred before a divorce-related property settlement became final. The plan participant tried to remove his ex-spouse as beneficiary of his 401(k) plan and make his children the beneficiaries. The Family Court said that ERISA preempts the state law. But to remove incentives to violate state law, the court decided that the 401(k) account should be considered marital property for division as part of the divorce. [*Jones v. Jones*, 789 A.2d 598 (Del. Fam. Ct. 2001)]

ERISA doesn't rule out payments made on the basis of a QDRO approved after the plan participant's death, because the purpose of the statute is to protect ex-spouses and children (even if sometimes this will defeat the plan participant's preferred estate plan). [*Trustees of the Directors Guild of America-Producer Pension Benefit Plans v. Tise*, 234 F.3d 415 (9th Cir. 2000); *Hogan v. Raytheon Co.*, No. C00-0026 (N.D. Iowa July 9, 2001)]

§ 12.09   REDUCTION OF BENEFIT FORMS

Qualified plans must always offer payments in the form of QJSAs and QPSAs. What if a plan originally adopts additional, optional forms of benefit payments, then later finds that some of them are unpopular or hard to administer? For years beginning after December 31, 2001, as a result of EGTRRA, I.R.C. § 411(d)(6) and ERISA § 204(g) have been amended to make it easier for defined contribution plans to cut back on the number of benefit options that they offer, especially in connection with plan mergers and other transitions.

A defined contribution plan will not be penalized for reducing participants' accrued benefits if the plan adopts amendments that reduce the number of benefit options—provided that the participant is always entitled to get a single-sum distribution that is based on at least as high a proportion of his or her account as the form of benefit that is being eliminated under the plan amendment. EGTRRA obligates the IRS to issue new regulations no later than December 31, 2003, to this effect, applying to plan years beginning after December 31, 2003 (or earlier, if the IRS so specifies).

§ 12.10   ROLLOVERS

Because of termination of employment, or termination of a plan itself, a person of working age may become entitled to a plan distribution. If he or she does not need the funds immediately, and would encounter an unwelcome income tax liability, one solution is to "roll over" the funds by placing them into another qualified plan or an IRA within 60 days.

The funds that are rolled over are not available to be spent by the plan participant, and therefore the participant is not taxed.

Tip: Although employees have a right to roll over these funds, the qualified plan that is the intended recipient does not have an obligation to accept rollovers. So it makes sense for the distributing plan to require employees to submit a statement that the potential recipient is not only qualified to take rollover contributions, but is willing to do so. The recipient plan is allowed to impose conditions, such as the form in which it will accept rollovers and the minimum amount it will accept as a rollover. The recipient plan is also entitled to set its own distribution rules and does not have to follow the rules of the original plan.

A direct rollover is considered a distribution, not a transfer of assets. [Treas. Reg. § 1.401(a)(31)-1] Therefore, the participant and spouse may have to sign a waiver because plan benefits are not being paid in QJSA form.

Rollovers can be carried out either by the plan administrator of the first plan sending a check or wire transfer to the trustee or custodian of the transferee plan, or by giving the participant a check payable to the IRA, plan trustee, or custodian.

A distribution to a spouse, or a QDRO distribution to an ex-spouse, can also be rolled over, but only to an IRA, not to a qualified plan.

EGTRRA increased the number of circumstances in which funds can be rolled over between plans. One result is that the notice given to employees about their rollover rights became obsolete. The IRS therefore drafted a new version of the Safe Harbor Explanation. [Notice 2002-3, 2002-2 I.R.B. 289] It is permissible to adapt the safe harbor notice by leaving out portions that do not apply to the plan.

The Notice advises, "even if a plan accepts rollovers, it might not accept rollovers of certain types of distributions, such as after-tax amounts. If this is the case, and your distribution includes after-tax amounts, you may wish instead to roll your distribution over to a traditional IRA or split your rollover amount between the employer plan in which you will participate and a traditional IRA."

The notice must explain:

- The rules for transferring a distribution to another qualified plan;
- The requirement for withholding income tax on amounts that are eligible for rollover but are not rolled over;
- The obligation to make a rollover within 60 days of receiving the funds;
- Any applicable information about early withdrawal penalties, hardship withdrawals, withdrawals to buy a house or pay medical or education expenses, and distributions of the employer's own securities.

If a plan provides for cash out of benefits that do not exceed $5,000 (remember, it is illegal to impose a mandatory cash out if the plan balance is greater than $5,000), EGTRRA requires the plan to make a direct rollover the default distribution method for cash outs that fall between $1,000 and $5,000. [*See* I.R.C. § 401(a)(31)(B)]

Also see I.R.C. § 411(a)(11)(D), which was added by EGTRRA, providing that when determining whether someone's balance is low enough to be subject to involuntary cash out, rollover contributions and interest on rollover contributions don't have to be included in the calculation. The Job Creation and Worker Assistance Act of 2002 [H.R. 3090, Pub. L. No. 107-147] made technical corrections to make it easier for the employer to disregard rollovers in cash out calculations.

A recent survey shows that each year, people who change jobs take approximately $33 billion to $39 billion in cash distributions from their retirement plans. [Putnam Investments, *Retirement Savings in an Unsettled Economy*, <http://news.excite.com/printstory/news/bw/010522/ma-putnam-investments> (posted to news.excite.com on May 22, 2001)] Thirty percent of participants (and an even higher percentage—39%—of young participants, aged 18–34 do this) take cash instead of rolling over their distributions into IRAs. The result is that unnecessary income taxes and penalties are incurred, perhaps as much as $8.3 billion a year. If the funds had been rolled over and left to appreciate tax-free until withdrawal, the plan participants would have much larger accounts at retirement.

§ 12.11 WITHHOLDING

A designated distribution is any amount of $200 or more that the participant could roll over, but chooses not to. Under I.R.C. §§ 401(a)(3) and 3405(c), plan administrators have to withhold a mandatory 20% of any designated distribution.

All or part of an employee's balance in a qualified plan is eligible for rollover, except:

- A series of substantially equal periodic payments, made at the rate of at least one payment a year, over the life of the employee or the joint lives of the employee and designated beneficiary;
- Payments made for a term of at least ten years [*See* I.R.C. § 402(c)(4)];
- The RMDs under I.R.C. § 401(a)(8) for officers, directors, and 5% stockholders.

In the case of a partial rollover, withholding applies only to the part that the employee withdraws from the plan, not the part that is rolled over.

For amounts that are neither annuities nor eligible rollover distributions, optional withholding can be done at a rate of 10%. The employee can direct the plan not to withhold. During the six months immediately preceding the first payment, and at least once a year once benefits are in pay status, the plan must notify participants of their right to make, renew, or revoke a withholding election. The employer can either include the withheld amounts in each quarterly Form 941 filing, or use Form 941E to report withholding.

The plan administrator is responsible for withholding unless the administrator directs that the insurer or other payer of benefits perform this task. [Treas. Reg. § 31.3405(c)-1]

Whenever designated distributions (i.e., those eligible for withholding) are made, the employer and plan administrator become responsible for making returns and reports to the IRS, participants, and beneficiaries.

A penalty of $25 per day is imposed by I.R.C. § 6047(e), up to a maximum of $15,000, for failure to meet this requirement, although the penalty can be waived if the plan has a good excuse for noncompliance. [*See* I.R.C. § 6047(b) for the required records; record-keeping violations can be penalized by up to $50 per failure per year, up to a maximum of $50,000 per year.]

CHAPTER 13

PROCESSING AND REVIEWING CLAIMS AND APPEALS

§ 13.01   INTRODUCTION

All pension and welfare benefit plans that are subject to ERISA Title I are required to maintain a "reasonable claims procedure." An appropriate claims procedure is one that is described in the SPD: does not place undue restrictions or inhibitions on the processing of claims, and satisfies the relevant regulations about filing claims, reviewing submitted claims, and informing participants when a claim is denied. [DOL Reg. § 2560.503]

At the very least, the procedure must give claimants (or their authorized representatives) the right to apply to the plan for review, see the pertinent documents, and submit written comments and issues for resolution.

The plan must give a specific reason if it denies a claim. Claimants must be referred to the relevant plan provision. They must be given information about how to appeal the denial. [*See* § 13.03, below, for further discussion of the PWBA Final Rule adopted in November 2000]

§ 13.02   THIRD-PARTY ADMINISTRATORS (TPAs)

[A]   Use and Benefits of TPAs

About two-thirds of covered workers in the United States get their benefits from plans that use some degree of third-party administration instead of handling all plan administration in house.

A TPA is an outsourcing firm that handles administrative tasks. It could be a consulting firm or a broad-based benefits administration firm. There are no federal licensing rules for TPAs, although some states impose their own requirements.

If the plan has unexpectedly high claims, TPAs usually provide stop-loss protection with back-up insurance that benefits the plan itself (rather than the employees with high expenses). Having a stop-loss plan doesn't turn a self-insured plan into an insured plan for ERISA purposes. [*See* Frederick D. Hunt, *Everything You Wanted to Know About TPAs but Were Afraid to Ask*, <http://users.erols.com/spba/p0000010.html> (no www.)]

[B]   TPA Case Law

A plan sued its TPA for making an improper payment. Benefits were paid to a plan participant who was badly hurt in an automobile accident while he was driving under the influence of alcohol (however, no criminal charges were brought against him). The plan excluded coverage of injuries occurring in the course of illegal acts, including DWI. The plan had stop-loss coverage, but the stop-loss insurer refused to pay because the injured person's blood alcohol level had been three times the legal limit. The plan sued the TPA for breach of contract and breach of fiduciary duty (for making the improper payments), and also sued to make the stop-loss carrier pay if the TPA did not.

The TPA said that the illegal-acts provision was ambiguous, because it was not clear whether a conviction was required. The Eastern District of Arkansas disagreed. [*SGI/Argis Employee Benefit Trust Plan v. The Canada Life Assurance Co.*, 151 F. Supp. 2d 1044 (E.D. Ark. 2001)] DWI is illegal whether or not there is a conviction. The court held that the stop-loss insurer was not required to reimburse the plan for the payment made by the TPA, but allowed the case to continue to determine whether the payment was in fact improper.

§ 13.03   HEALTH PLAN CLAIMS

The Department of Labor's Pension and Welfare Benefits Agency (PWBA) published a wide-ranging Final Rule on claims procedures for health and disability plans, amending 29 C.F.R. Part 2560. [*See* 65 Fed. Reg. 70246-70271 (Nov. 21, 2000)]

In early July, however, the DOL rules that were supposed to apply to health plan claims filed on or after January 1, 2002, were extended, so that plans could defer compliance until plan years beginning on or after July 1, 2002, but must comply not later than January 1, 2003. The rules for claims processing in disability, pension, and welfare benefit plans are not affected by this announcement. [Press release, *PWBA Extends Date for Group Health Plans to Comply with Claims Procedure Requirements*, <http://www.dol.gov/pwba/media/press/pr070601.htm>]

The Final Rule applies to ERISA health and disability plans, dental and vision plans, and health Flexible Spending Accounts, but not to plans offering long-term care benefits. The Final Rule requires plans to speed up decision making and appeals, especially in situations where an employee files a claim for urgent care.

The Final Rule draws a distinction between preservice claims (advance approval of health care services) and postservice claims (where medical care has already been provided). The distinction is made because postservice claims are much less urgent. The employee has already been treated, so the question becomes who will pay the bill, not whether potentially necessary care will be available or not.

Under the Final Rule, a plan must make a decision within 15 days on ordinary preservice claims, and within 72 hours for urgent care claims. (The plan is bound by the treating physician's characterization of a claim as urgent.) Decisions on postservice claims can wait for 30 days. For adjudicating pre- or postservice claims (but not urgent claims), the plan can get one extension of time of up to 15 days. If a defective claim is filed (for instance, some of the information fields have been left blank), the plan must notify the claimant and can't reject the claim because of procedural defects.

In comparison, before the Final Rule, the plan gave employees 60 days to appeal; the Final Rule not only gives them 180 days to appeal, but expands their right to sue based on claims denials.

For "concurrent care decisions" about continued reimbursement for treatment that has already started, the plan participant must be given a right to request review before the plan terminates or even reduces the benefits. Employees must be given enough advance notice to use the appeal rights under the plan. If the employee's treating physician considers the request to extend benefits to be urgent, then the plan must resolve the dispute within 24 hours.

The Final Rule also increases the amount of disclosure the employer must provide. Employees are now entitled to a detailed explanation of the plan's claims procedures and why a claim has been denied. Internal protocols used to make decisions must be disclosed. Plans must also have a mechanism for making sure that claims are decided uniformly by the different decision makers.

Plans are not allowed to impose any fees or costs for appealing a denial. The reviewer cannot be either the person who made the initial denial or someone who works for that person. Whenever there is an issue of medical judgment, such as when treatment is necessary, the plan must consult appropriate health care professionals. The reviewer must examine the claim de novo (from the beginning), not just to see if the initial decision involved an abuse of discretion. The employee is allowed to introduce new facts that they did not provide earlier—even if these facts would not be admissible as evidence in a suit.

Plans are entitled to two options. They can have either a single level of review of denied claims, or two sequential levels of review (like a trial court and an appeals court). But plans that impose a second level of review don't get any additional time. Both levels of review must be completed within the normal time frame.

Health plans are allowed to include an arbitration requirement as part of the process. Employees are entitled to full disclosure of how the arbitrators are chosen and how the procedure works. The claimant must agree to arbitration, and can't be compelled to arbitrate unwillingly. Arbitration can only be used as an intermediate step after the plan's own internal appeals procedure has been completed.

The Pension and Welfare Benefit Administration has summed up the various queries it has received about the claims standards in a Frequently Asked Questions page at <http://dol.gov/pwba/faqs/main.html>.

The FAQ clarifies that the regulation only applies to coverage determinations that are part of a claim for benefits; a question about eligibility that does not also apply for benefits accordingly is not covered. However, if a plan requires "preservice" claims (e.g., requests for preauthorization) to be submitted, then it "is not entirely free" to ignore inquiries (especially from an attending physician, and especially if specific medical conditions and specific treatments are mentioned) that might involve preservice claims, even if the procedure is not fully followed.

The claims standards apply to dental benefits and prescription drug benefit programs, whether they are a stand-alone plan or part of an EGHP. However, contract disputes between health care providers and insurers or managed care organizations are not covered by the requirements unless the dispute affects claimants' rights to benefits.

The regulation sets up time frames for making claims decisions—but does not govern the timing for actual payment of benefits. However, failure to make payments within a reasonable time may trigger ERISA fiduciary liability issues.

If a claimant authorizes someone else to act as a representative, then the plan should provide information and notifications directly to the authorized representative—although the plan can legitimately communicate with both the claimant and the authorized representative.

The FAQ says that the time for making an initial claims determination starts when the claim is filed under the plan's reasonable filing procedures—even if it is not a "clean claim" (one that contains all the necessary information). The plan may have to make a decision even before certain information (such as "coordination of benefit" information) has been submitted. However, for a nonurgent claim, the plan administrator can unilaterally decide that an additional 15-day period is needed for reasons beyond the control of the plan, such as the claimant's failure to supply required information.

The direct supervisor of the person who makes initial claim determinations can serve as the fiduciary who reviews claims on appeal—the regulation merely bans the person who made the initial determination, or his or her subordinates, from performing the review.

§ 13.04   HIPAA EDI STANDARDS

One reason for high medical costs is that a lot of time and effort is devoted to processing, transmitting, and analyzing information. A number of different standards evolved for storing and displaying health information. To streamline this process, HIPAA requires a uniform set of EDI standards to be placed into effect for health and welfare funds.

Standard code sets, such as the HCFA Common Procedure System and the CPT-4 [Physicians' Current Procedural Terminology, 4th ed. (Celeste G. Kirschner et al., American Medical Ass'n Annual)] must be applied uniformly. The standards cover both the format and the content of electronic files used to submit health care claims, transmit payment information, coordinate benefits among plans, enroll and disenroll plan beneficiaries, and related tasks.

HIPAA's EDI standards apply to insured and self-insured EGHPs, health insurers and HMOs, but not to small, self-administered health plans with fewer than 50 participants. Employers are covered only if they administer their own health plans.

Failure to comply can be penalized by up to $100 per plan per violation, up to a maximum penalty of $25,000 per calendar year for each transaction standard to which a plan is subject.

> **Tip:** Even plan sponsors that are not directly subject to the rule will probably have to make changes in their computer systems to exchange information with their health insurers and managed care organizations.

The original requirement was compliance no later than October 16, 2002. However, the Administrative Simplification Compliance Act [Pub. L. No. 107-

105] extended the deadline to October 16, 2003, for all plans (there are no special relief rules for small plans) as long as they submit a compliance plan to the Department of Health and Human Services no later than October 16, 2002. The compliance plan must explain the extent of, and reasons for, any noncompliance, show how the entity will move toward compliance, and how it will test its system (the testing period must begin by April 16, 2003).

§ 13.05 CASE LAW ON CLAIMS

[A] Generally

Many cases have been litigated over questions of the proper way to handle and process claims within a plan—and especially over the standard of review that courts should apply when reviewing the decisions of plan administrators.

[B] Experimental Treatment

EGHPs typically refuse to cover experimental treatment, and new forms of treatment are very often more expensive than the ones they replace. There is a long line of cases attempting to distinguish between experimental treatments and those that are novel but are accepted as scientifically valid by the medical community.

A mid-1997 Fourth Circuit holds that a plan did not abuse its discretion in denying reimbursement for high-dose chemotherapy and bone marrow transplants for cancer patients because they were deemed experimental. The plaintiff went ahead with the treatment after pre-authorization was denied; she also signed a medical disclosure statement that the treatment was experimental, not accepted as conventional. [*Martin v. Blue Cross/Blue Shield*, 115 F.3d 1201(4th Cir. 1997)]

A Tenth Circuit case says that if a plan's definition of experimental treatment is treatment not generally accepted by the medical community, then the plan is entitled to exercise its discretion as to which treatments are in this category. [*Healthcare America Plans Inc. v. Bossemeyer*, 166 F.3d 347 (10th Cir. 1998)] When the decision is reviewed, the court should not examine the evidence de novo; it should merely determine whether the plan's decision was arbitrary and capricious.

In *Zervos v. Verizon New York, Inc.* [277 F.3d 635 (2d Cir. 2002), the insurer refused to pre-authorize a new kind of high-dose chemotherapy and blood cell transplant, based on an independent medical expert's opinion that this procedure was only as effective as conventional chemotherapy. The Second Circuit said that the insurer had improperly imposed a requirement that experimental treatments be superior to more accepted treatments—treatment should be covered as long as there is scientific evidence of their validity.

[C] Other Exclusions

A plaintiff's treating physician sent her to a rehabilitation facility after she suffered severe head injuries. The program provided daily structured retraining in basic physical and cognitive skills. The health plan administrator denied the claim as a custodial service that was not covered under the plan. The district court affirmed the denial of benefits, holding that the plan had not abused its discretion. However, the Ninth Circuit reversed. [*Castillo v. CIGNA Healthcare*, 2001 U.S. App. LEXIS 13307 (9th Cir. June 7, 2001)]

All of the doctors treating the plaintiff agreed that the services were needed to gain functional improvement and independence, so the care was not custodial in nature. The services also met the plan's definition of rehabilitation therapy likely to result in clear and reasonable improvement in normal, necessary physical movement, within a three-month time frame.

In the case of *Mitchell v. Dialysis Clinic, Inc.* [2001 U.S. App. LEXIS 19439 (6th Cir. Aug. 24, 2001)], the plaintiff and her husband were covered by the employer's self-funded medical plan. The plaintiff submitted a claim when her self-employed husband was injured while working. The plan denied benefits under its exclusion for on-the-job injuries or illnesses. The plaintiff said that the exclusion was inapplicable because her husband did not have Worker's Compensation insurance. The Sixth Circuit upheld the benefits denial. It is true that the plan excluded work-related injuries "for which the covered person is entitled to benefits under any Worker's Compensation law," a category that did not include the plaintiff's husband. However, coverage was also limited to nonoccupational injuries (injury that "does not arise out of (or in the course of) any work for pay or profit"), with no mention of Worker's Compensation. Therefore, the plan did not act arbitrarily or capriciously in denying the claim.

[D] Timing

A Ninth Circuit case, *Chappel v. Laboratory Corp. of America* [232 F.3d 719 (9th Cir. 2000)], involves a plan that required a claimant who challenged a claims denial to request arbitration within 60 days. The arbitrator's decision would be final and binding, and would completely preclude an ERISA suit. Claimants had to pay part of the cost of arbitration, and they were not entitled to recover attorneys' fees even if they prevailed against the employer.

The Ninth Circuit found the arbitration clause (which was disclosed in the plan's SPD) was valid. But it reversed the District Court's dismissal of the plaintiff's claim for breach of fiduciary duty. The plan administrator should not have relied completely on the SPD to inform plan participants of their obligation to arbitrate claims instead of litigating them. Claimants who can show that they did not get timely and effective notice of the duty to arbitrate can get another chance to arbitrate. Once arbitration is completed, the claimant has exhausted administrative remedies under the plan and will be permitted to sue.

ERISA's guarantee of the right to appeal benefit denials includes the right to review pertinent documents. The plan participant who sued in *Simpson v. Ameritech Corp. Inc.* [2000 U.S. Dist. LEXIS 14607 (E.D. Mich. Aug. 30, 2000)] said she was denied access to documents relevant to her claim for LTD benefits. The District Court denied relief, because she didn't even ask for the documents until the appeals procedure was complete. *But see* an earlier case, *Ellis v. Metropolitan Life Insurance Co.* [126 F.3d 228 (4th Cir. 1997)], holding that the DOL regulations imply a requirement that the plan administrator or fiduciary inform participants of their right to review documents.

[E] Other Issues

Health plan fiduciaries have a duty to consider all pertinent available information and to make a decision based on substantial evidence. The District of Connecticut ruled [*Crocco v. Xerox Corp.* [65 L.W. 2567 (D. Conn. Feb. 5, 1997)] that the employer failed to provide the required "full and fair review" when it relied on its Utilization Review firm and therefore approved payment for only 30 days of a four-month psychiatric hospitalization. The plan administrator had a duty to review the medical records and make an independent determination of the correctness of the Utilization Review firm's decision. It wasn't good enough to permit an appeal after denial of the claim.

Prevailing plan participants who succeed in challenging a benefit denial are entitled to attorneys' fees in any case unless there are special circumstances that rule out a fee award. [*Martin v. Arkansas Blue Cross/Blue Shield*, 270 F.3d 673 (8th Cir. 2001)]

§ 13.06   THE STANDARD OF REVIEW

If and when a plan participant sues in connection with plan benefits, one of the most important questions is the "standard of review" the court will use to assess the plan administrator's decision. The two possibilities are "de novo" review, under which the court considers the question as if it were a new case, or review to see if the administrator abused his or her discretion. Many more plan decisions will be reversed—and many more claimants will win their cases—if the court can look at all the factors underlying the matter, and not just to see if there was an abuse of discretion.

The basic rule, as set by the seminal case of *Bruch v. Firestone Tire & Rubber* [489 U.S. 101 (1989)], is that plan administrators' decisions will be reviewed on a de novo basis, unless the plan itself is drafted to give the fiduciaries discretion over the way the plan operates. If the plan sponsor reserved this discretion, the court's only role is to see whether the administrators abused their discretion.

However, if the fiduciary that made the decision had a conflict of interest, then de novo review might be imposed, or the conflict might be treated as a factor in determining whether discretion was abused. [*Anderson v. Blue Cross/Blue*

Shield of Alabama, 907 F.2d 1072 (11th Cir. 1990); *Baker v. Big Star Division of Grand Union*, 893 F.2d 288 (11th Cir. 1989)]

In a plan where the insurer is also the administrator, the potential conflict of interest means that a person whose claim was denied can present additional evidence to show that a conflict of interest did exist and therefore that de novo review is appropriate. [*Dorsey v. Provident Life and Accident Ins. Co.*, discussed in Shannon P. Duffy, *Judge Constructs Higher Standard for ERISA Review*, The Legal Intelligencer (Oct. 10, 2001) (law.com). This case finds that the denial—including two reviews by the same doctors—was invalid even under the "arbitrary and capricious" standard, because the reviewing doctor didn't pay proper attention to the pattern of the plaintiff's symptoms.]

Under the de novo standard of review, the court will not give special deference to either the plaintiff's or the plan's interpretation of the plan language. On the other hand, if the plan reserves discretion for the fiduciary, then the court will probably assign more weight to the fiduciary's interpretation of the plan language. Unless the plan specifically gives the administrator discretionary authority, courts should use a de novo standard not only to see if the administrator interpreted the plan language correctly, but whether the administrator determined fact issues correctly. [*Kinstler v. First Reliance Standard Life Ins. Co.*, 181 F.3d 243 (2d Cir. 1999)]

According to the Ninth Circuit, a disability plan that required "satisfactory written proof" of disability, but did not say in so many words that the administrator had discretionary authority, was subject to de novo review. [*Kearney v. Standard Ins. Co.*, 175 F.3d 1084 (9th Cir. 1998)]

In contrast, the Seventh Circuit case of *McNab v. GM* [162 F.3d 959 (7th Cir. 1998)] involved an early retirement plan giving management discretion to reject early retirement applications from employees who were deemed so valuable that their early retirement was contrary to the employer's best interests. The Seventh Circuit interpreted this as a standard rather than a rule—standards can be applied flexibly and with discretion. Denying early retirement to the plaintiffs was not sufficiently arbitrary or capricious to violate ERISA.

A later Seventh Circuit case says that, for a sponsor to reserve discretion, the plan documents must demand more than claimants prove or give satisfactory proof of entitlement to benefits. The rationale of *Herzberger v. Standard Insurance Co.* [205 F.3d 327, 331 (7th Cir. 2000)] is that an ERISA plan is a contract, to be interpreted by the courts and not by the party who drafted the language. But the court approved this language as enough to trigger the arbitrary and capricious standard: "Benefits under this plan will be paid only if the plan administrator decides in his discretion that the applicant is entitled to them."

The Eastern District of Wisconsin found that it was arbitrary and capricious for a plan to deny coverage of a medically necessary feeding tube, for a patient who was unable to swallow, using the theory that meals were available in the hospital: "An administrator is not free to give ordinary words bizarre or obscure interpretations." [*See Schneider v. Wisconsin UFCW Unions*, 985 F. Supp. 848, 850 (E.D. Wis. 1997)]

§ 13.07   CASE LAW ON CLAIMS PROCEDURAL ISSUES

A fiduciary, including a life insurance company, has a right under ERISA § 502(a) to seek appropriate equitable relief from the courts in order to enforce plan provisions. Therefore, the fiduciary can bring an interpleader action (a suit asking for court guidance on how to dispose of funds whose ownership is disputed) if there are conflicting claims to insurance proceeds—for instance, based on a beneficiary designation and community property law. [*Aetna Life Ins. Co. v. Bayona*, 223 F.3d 1030 (9th Cir. 2000)]

An Eleventh Circuit case arose when a self-insured health plan imposed a 90-day time limit for filing suits based on internal appeals of claims denials. [*Northlake Regional Med. Ctr. v. Waffle House Sys. Employee Benefit Plan*, 160 F.3d 1301 (11th Cir. 1998)] The Eleventh Circuit found this requirement to be valid. The court would not impose a general rule that a 90-day time limit is always valid, but under the facts of the case, and given the plan's procedures for expediting decision making, the court deemed this to be a reasonable time limit.

In *Santino v. Provident Life and Accident Ins. Co.* [276 F.3d 772 (6th Cir. 2001)], the insurer classified a doctor as having suffered a "residual" rather than a "total" disability, because he could no longer practice his medical specialty, but he could do administrative work. After about four years, the doctor sued to increase his benefit to the level appropriate for total disability. The plan, however, imposed a three-year statute of limitations on filing suit.

The similar case of *Alcorn v. Raytheon Co.* [175 F. Supp. 2d 117 (D. Mass. 2001)] involves discontinuance of disability benefits because of the employer's determination that disability had lasted only one month. Once again, the plan required suit to be brought within three years; the plaintiff did not sue for four and a half years.

A number of plaintiffs, including a group of participants in several self-insured medical plans, brought suit against several TPAs. The plans paid for out-of-network services on the basis of usual, customary, and reasonable amounts (UCR). If the actual out-of-network charge was higher than the plan's UCR, the participant had to pay the difference. The TPAs set the charges based on typical charges in the same or a similar area, whereas the plaintiffs alleged that the plan language required the UCR to be supported by appropriate data.

The Southern District of New York dismissed the suit, treating it as a claim for benefits due and fiduciary breach claim [*AMA v. United Healthcare Corp.*, 2001 U.S. Dist. LEXIS 10818 (S.D.N.Y. July 30, 2001)] The claim for benefits due was inappropriate, because such claims can only be made against a plan or a plan administrator, not a TPA. In the Southern District view, the cause of action for fiduciary breach exists to protect plan assets, not to benefit individuals. Even if the allegations are correct, in effect the plan paid less than it should have, so plan assets would be preserved, not dissipated. The plaintiffs also said that their denial notices were not specific enough, but the Southern District ruled that this is not the TPA's responsibility: The plan itself has to provide such information, including information about UCRs.

Tip: People who are insured under an employer-sponsored plan do not have standing under ERISA to charge that a health insurer used "clandestine" restrictive utilization review policies to reduce the value of the insurance coverage. The District Court for the District of Maryland said that this type of alleged financial injury is not covered by ERISA. [*Doe v. Blue Cross/Blue Shield,* 70 L.W. 1240 (D. Md. Sept. 28, 2001)]

CHAPTER 14
AMENDING A PLAN

§ 14.01   INTRODUCTION

It is very likely that, no matter how carefully a plan was drafted, amendments will be required over the course of time. The company's line of business or workforce may change. The business may suffer reverses. And it's more than likely that ERISA and the tax code will change in ways that require corresponding amendments to the plan. Each new tax bill that requires amendments includes a schedule for when plans are required to make their conforming amendments. In particular, *see* Rev. Proc. 2001-6, 2001-1 I.R.B. 194, and Announcement 2001-12, 2001-6 I.R.B. 526, for requirements for conforming to various pieces of pre-EGTRRA tax legislation.

Plan amendments can be adopted either prospectively or retroactively. Retro-active amendments can be made until the last day (including extensions) for filing the income tax return for the year the plan was adopted.

The Department of Labor must be notified whenever a plan is materially modified or the information called for by ERISA § 102(b) changes. The DOL must receive an updated SPD when the participants and beneficiaries do. The DOL can reject an incomplete submission, giving the plan administrator 45 days for corrections. The 5500-series form filed with the IRS also requires reporting of the plan amendments and changes in the plan description that occurred during the year.

In most cases, the Internal Revenue Code does not require that employees be notified in advance that the plan will be amended. So they don't have a right to comment on the proposed amendment (although they do have a right to comment on the plan's initial application for a determination letter). The exception is that advance notice is required if the amendment changes the vesting schedules of participants who have three years or more of plan participation, because they have the right to choose between the new and the old schedules. However, ERISA does impose a notice requirement. Once a plan is amended, ERISA §§ 102(a)(1) and 104(b)(1) require participants to get a Summary of Material Modifications (SMM) within 210 days of the end of the plan year in which the change is adopted.

§ 14.02   FLEXIBILITY THROUGH AMENDMENT

To preserve flexibility, it's a good idea for the sponsor to draft the plan re-serving the right to amend the plan in the future. Plans can be amended to change or eliminate:

- Ancillary life insurance provided in connection with a pension plan;
- Accident or health insurance that is incidental to a pension plan;
- Some Social Security supplements;
- Availability of plan loans;
- Employees' ability to direct investment of their plan accounts or balances;
- The actual investment options available under the plan;

- Employees' ability to make after-tax contributions to the plan, or to make elective salary deferrals to a plan that is not a 401(k) plan;
- Administrative procedures for the plan (although even after the amendments, participants must have a right to fair redress of their grievances);
- Dates used to allocate contributions, forfeitures, earnings, and account balances.

But any amendment must take into account I.R.C. § 411(d)(6), which forbids amendments that reduce accrued benefits, including early retirement benefits and retirement-related subsidies—even if the employees affected by the change consent to it. Furthermore, the general rule is that protected benefits cannot be reduced or eliminated when a plan is merged or its benefits are transferred to another plan.

A current, but not a former, employee can go to court to get a declaratory judgment that a plan has lost its qualification after an amendment. [*Flynn v. C.I.R.,* 269 F.3d 1064 (D.C. Cir. 2001)] The D.C. Circuit considers ex-employees "interested parties" only with respect to termination of a plan.

However, a plan that is subject to the I.R.C. § 412 minimum funding standard can be amended retroactively to reduce accrued benefits—as long as the plan sponsor can prove to the DOL that the sponsor is undergoing substantial business hardship that mandates a cutback in benefits. The amendments must be adopted within 2½ months of the end of the plan year. They must not reduce anyone's accrued benefit for plan years before the beginning of the first plan year that the amendment applies to. IRS approval is required for amendments of this type, and the DOL may have to be notified.

A plan can be amended to change its vesting schedule as long as no participant loses any nonforfeitable accrued benefits.

Even if an amendment is allowed, participants who have at least three years of service with the plan must be given a chance to choose between the new and the old schedules. [I.R.C. § 411(a)(10)(B)] The plan can provide that, once employees make this election, it is irrevocable. The period for making the election must start by the date the amendment is adopted. It cannot end before 60 days after the date the amendment is adopted, the date it becomes effective, or the date the participant gets written notice of the amendment—whichever comes last. *See* the Proposed Regulations published by the IRS on April 23, 2002, at 67 Fed. Reg. 19713, explaining how to give notice of reduction in early retirement subsidies or other benefits.

A defined benefit plan can lose its qualified status if it adopts an amendment that increases plan liabilities, if the result is that the funded current liability falls below 60% for the plan year. The employer can preserve the plan's qualification by posting "adequate" security. Either the corporation must place cash and securities in escrow, or it must obtain a bond from a corporate security company that is acceptable under ERISA § 412. [*See* I.R.C. § 401(a)(29) and ERISA § 307]

§ 14.03   CHANGE IN PLAN YEAR

IRS Determination letters are not limited to initial qualification of a plan: They can also be obtained for plan amendments. The current employees who are eligible for plan participation are "interested parties" and must be notified of the application for a determination letter. If the proposed amendment changes eligibility for participation, then all employees at the same workplace as the original interested parties must be notified.

The request for change in a retirement plan's plan year is made on Form 5308. IRS approval is automatic as long as:

- No plan year is longer than 12 months. In other words, a year can be broken up into two short years, but two short years can't be consolidated into a long one;
- The change does not have the effect of deferring the time at which the plan becomes subject to changes in the law;
- The plan trust (if any) remains tax-exempt and does not have any Unrelated Business Taxable Income in the short year;
- Legal approval for the change is granted before the end of the short year;
- (Defined benefit plans) The deduction taken for the short year is the appropriate prorated share of the costs for the full year.

§ 14.04   REDUCTION IN FORMS OF DISTRIBUTION

Although it is not permitted to amend a qualified plan in any way that reduces any participant's accrued benefit, it is permissible to amend a plan to eliminate optional forms of benefits (such as periodic payments other than the required QJSA/QPSA). EGTRRA provides that, for plan years beginning after December 31, 2001, defined contribution plans can eliminate certain forms of benefit payout.

In particular, if funds are transferred from one qualified plan to another (e.g., in connection with a merger or acquisition), the transferee plan will not be required to provide all the payment options that the transferor plan provided. [See I.R.C. § 411(d)(6)(D) and ERISA § 204(g)(4)] However, if payout forms are eliminated, the plan participants must be allowed to take their distributions in lump-sum form.

EGTRRA orders the IRS to issue regulations no later than December 31, 2003, to explain when a plan amendment has a significant impact on plan participants. According to the report issued by Congress when EGTRRA was passed, the factors in the decision include:

- Effect of the plan amendment on early retirement benefits and subsidies;
- The number of years before a particular participant reaches normal retirement age (or early retirement age, if the plan offers an early retirement option);
- The amount of benefits affected by the amendment;
- The percentage of the overall benefit affected by the amendment;
- Length of time between adoption of the plan amendment and its effective date.

§ 14.05   EGTRRA CONFORMING AMENDMENTS

It is common for plans to require amendments to conform to changes in tax and labor law (or to take advantage of additional options that have opened up for employers). The Economic Growth and Tax Relief Reconciliation Act of 2001 (EGTRRA) [Pub. L. No. 107-16] made many sweeping changes in pension administration and taxation. Areas in which plan amendments may be required, or may be desirable, include:

- Higher limits on amount of employer contributions to both defined benefit and defined contribution plans;
- Higher elective deferrals in 401(k) plans;
- Extra catch-up contributions made by employees age 50 and over;
- Faster vesting for employer's matching contributions to a qualified plan;
- Changes in the way 401(k) plans are tested to make sure they do not discriminate in favor of highly compensated employees;
- Higher deductions for employers on account of their contributions to qualified plans;
- Changes in the minimum funding rules that apply to defined benefit plans;
- Greater mobility between plans because rollovers between plans have been liberalized.

Because of the sweeping nature of these changes, the IRS has tried to dam the flow by refusing to issue determination letters with respect to EGTRRA compliance. However, Notice 2001-57, 2001-38 I.R.B. 279, contains sample provisions that sponsors can rely on to demonstrate their good-faith compliance attempts, until the IRS issues final Regulations about the EGTRRA provisions.

§ 14.06   ERISA 204(h) NOTICE

The plan administrator has a duty to notify employees when a defined benefit plan (or any other plan that is subject to the minimum funding requirement) is amended in a way that significantly reduces the rate at which future benefits will accrue. In effect, this is an early warning system that signals to employees that their eventual pensions may be smaller than anticipated.

EGTRRA supplements the rules found at ERISA § 204(h) with a comparable Internal Revenue Code provision, I.R.C. § 4980F, which also imposes an excise tax on failure to make the required notification. *See* 67 Fed. Reg. 19714 for additional Proposed Regulations on this topic.

§ 14.07   AMENDMENTS TO A BANKRUPT SPONSOR'S PLAN

The general rule is that plan benefits may not be increased while the plan sponsor is a bankruptcy debtor. [*See* I.R.C. § 401(a)(33)] Amendments are forbidden if the plan's liabilities rise because of the benefit increase, or because of a change in the rate of accrual or nonforfeitability of benefits. However, amendments that take effect after the effective date of the plan of reorganization are allowed. So are amendments to plans, whose funded current liability percentage is 100% or more, or amendments approved by the IRS, or amendments required to maintain compliance with tax law changes.

§ 14.08   ISSUES HIGHLIGHTED BY THE IRS

IRS' Employee Plans division listed more than a dozen issues that frequently require plan amendments. These issues often prevent the IRS from closing a case until the issues are resolved to the agency's satisfaction:

- Defined benefit plans that do not apply I.R.C. §§ 415(b)(2)(E) and 417(e) properly;
- Defined contribution plans that do not reflect changes in the calculation of the maximum contributions;
- Plans that use the wrong procedure to waive the QJSA;
- Plans that don't meet the effective date requirements of amendments to the Code;
- Plans that can't prove that they complied with earlier tax and pension laws;
- Plans that have not been amended to forbid rollovers of 401(k) plan hardship distributions;
- Plans that do not define "highly-compensated employee" properly;
- Top-heavy plans that have not been updated in view of current laws.

[*See Recurring Plan Issues in Determination Case Review*, <http://www.irs.gov/irs/display/0,,il%3D46%26genericId%3D6928,00.html>. For technical advice about getting letter rulings, Revenue Rulings, and determination letters about plans, *see* Rev. Proc. 2002-4, 2002-1 I.R.B. 127, and Rev. Proc. 2002-6, 2002-1 I.R.B. 203. The IRS updates these areas of technical advice in new rulings every year. *See also* Announcement 2001-72, 2001-28 I.R.B. 39, for more information about determination letters]

CHAPTER 15

ENFORCEMENT AND COMPLIANCE ISSUES FOR QUALIFIED PLANS

§ 15.01   INTRODUCTION

The underlying purpose of ERISA, and of various later pieces of legislation, is to make sure that plan participants and their beneficiaries receive the promised benefits. Therefore, the focus of enforcement is to make sure that plans remain sound, and that participants and beneficiaries do not fall victim to outright fraud, mistake, negligence, poor administration, or declines in the sponsoring company's financial fortunes. Certain types of transactions are prohibited—although "prohibited transaction exemptions" can be obtained in cases where payment of benefits is not placed at real risk. [*See* § 15.15[C]]

In addition to private suits by participants and beneficiaries, the Department of Labor (DOL) and the IRS carry out administrative enforcement efforts and become involved in litigation about plan compliance and participant and beneficiary rights.

A pension plan is a legal entity that can sue or be sued under ERISA Title I. [*See* ERISA § 502(d)] Unless somebody is found liable in an individual capacity, the plan is responsible for paying all money judgments.

Because the management of plan assets for the sole benefit of participants and beneficiaries is so central to plan operation, the identification, duties, and liabilities of fiduciaries are central to plan enforcement.

ERISA § 402(a)(1) requires all plans either to have a named fiduciary, or to explain in the plan document how fiduciaries will be selected. Under ERISA § 411, a convicted felon is not permitted to serve as plan administrator, fiduciary, officer, trustee, custodian, counsel, agent, consultant, or employee with decision-making authority for 13 years after his or her conviction or the end of his or her prison term, whichever comes later.

§ 15.02   WHO IS A FIDUCIARY?

In general legal terms, a fiduciary is anyone responsible for another party's money or property. Fiduciaries have a legal duty to behave honestly and conscientiously, and to avoid promoting their own self-interest at the expense of the owner of the assets.

Many types of people who deal with pension and benefit plans are considered fiduciaries under ERISA—including some people who do not think of themselves in that way or do not understand their responsibilities and potential liabilities.

Fiduciary liability extends far beyond embezzlement and other criminal acts. It is even possible for one fiduciary's mistake or wrongdoing to get a group of other fiduciaries into trouble.

An individual, business, or institution that deals with a plan becomes a fiduciary whenever, and to the extent that, he or she:

- Exercises any discretionary authority (i.e., is able to make decisions) or control over the management of the plan;

- Exercises any authority (even if it isn't discretionary) over the management and disposition of plan assets. The distinction is made because the greatest potential for abuse exists when money is at stake;
- Receives direct or indirect compensation for giving the plan investment advice about its assets;
- Has any discretionary authority or responsibility for day-to-day plan administration (as distinct from plan management).

In other words, if a plan hires attorneys, accountants, or actuaries to provide advice, those professionals will usually not become fiduciaries of the plan, because they do not control the direction that the plan takes. They merely provide technical information that the administrator and other fiduciaries use to make decisions.

However, in *L.I. Head Start Child Development Services v. Frank* [165 F. Supp. 2d 367 (E.D.N.Y. 2001)], the court held that attorneys can be liable for breaches of fiduciary duty committed by an insolvent health fund, if the lawyers knew that their legal fees were paid from funds improperly accumulated by the fund and not used for the exclusive benefit of participants and beneficiaries. In effect, nonfiduciary professionals can become liable through knowing participation in a fiduciary's breach of duty.

> **Tip:** If the professional adviser is not a fiduciary, ERISA probably will not preempt state-law malpractice suits brought by the plan.

Similarly, a stockbroker who simply executes the fiduciaries' orders to adjust the plan's investment portfolio is not a fiduciary—but an investment manager who has a role in setting the plan's investment policy is very definitely a fiduciary.

In October 2001, a Tennessee district court ruled that an insurer acting under an Administrative Services Only (ASO) contract could be sued for breach of fiduciary duty, even though it was not named in the plan documents as a fiduciary, because of the discretion it exercised in managing the plan's assets and keeping its records. [*Guardsmark Inc. v. Blue Cross and Blue Shield of Tennessee*, 2001 WL 1352231 (W.D. Tenn. Oct. 19, 2001)]

The court treated the insurer as a "functional fiduciary" subject to claims that it wrongfully approved some claims and lost documentation for other claims, and that it overcharged the plan for its services and failed to provide proper documentation. The District Court also ruled that state-law claims were not preempted by ERISA, to the extent that some of the plan's claims against Blue Cross were not covered by ERISA.

The owner of a grocery store was held personally liable, to the tune of more than $5 million, for wrongfully terminating a voucher program that provided groceries to retirees. The program was treated as an ERISA pension plan. The store owner was not liable as an administrator, but he was liable as a fiduciary, for failure to fund the plan and for terminating it without making provision for rights already funded under the plan. [*Musmeci v. Schewgmann Giant Super Markets*, No. 97-2757 (E.D. La. Jan. 22, 2002)]

Harold Ives Trucking Co. v. Spradley & Coker Inc. [178 F.3d 523 (8th Cir. 1999)] holds that, even though its service contract had language to the contrary, a Third Party Administrator (TPA) became a fiduciary by making an independent determination that a rehab facility was covered under an Employee Group Health Plan.

Fiduciary conduct is examined on two levels. Fiduciaries must satisfy their affirmative obligations (to choose proper investments for the plan; to diversity investments unless diversification itself is imprudent; to maintain proper liquidity; to obtain a reasonable yield on plan investments; and to make proper administrative decisions). They are also forbidden to engage in prohibited transactions.

The Pension and Welfare Benefit Administration published a Final Rule on January 5, 2000 [65 Fed. Reg. 615], creating a safe harbor for insurance companies that manage pension funds as part of their general accounts. Insurance policies do become plan assets, but for policies issued on or before December 31, 1998, the insurance company will not be an ERISA fiduciary as to the plan, if the insurer provides adequate annual disclosure to plan participants. Furthermore, if the insurer unilaterally modifies the policy in a way that has a material adverse effect on the policyholder, 60 days' advance notice is required.

§ 15.03 FIDUCIARY DUTIES

[A] ERISA Requirements

ERISA imposes four major duties on fiduciaries:

- Loyalty;
- Prudence;
- Acting in accordance with the plan documents;
- Monitoring the performance of anyone to whom fiduciary responsibility has been delegated.

The source of the duty of loyalty is the ERISA mandate that plan assets be held for the exclusive benefit of participants and beneficiaries. Once assets have been placed into the plan trust, or used to buy insurance, they can no longer be used for the benefit of the employer.

The duty of prudence requires fiduciaries to behave with the level of care, skill, prudence, and diligence that a hypothetical prudent person would use to handle the same tasks. This hypothetical prudent person is familiar with the plan and its situation—not the "man on the street" who lacks specialized knowledge.

Although trust law requires every asset within a trust to satisfy the prudent person test, DOL Reg. § 2550.404a-1(c)(2) allows the fiduciary to select assets by considering the relevant facts and circumstances, including the role of the individual investment within the portfolio. Relying on expert advice is encouraged, but it does not guarantee that an investment choice will be considered prudent.

[B] Diversification

The general rule is that ERISA requires fiduciaries to diversify unless diversification is imprudent (the fiduciary has to prove this). The fiduciary is supposed to select a balanced portfolio that is responsive to current conditions. The portfolio's liquidity and current return must be considered in light of anticipated needs for cash flow. Fiduciaries are not restricted to a "legal list" of investments, and are permitted to take a certain amount of risk, as long as the risk is reasonable in the context of the entire portfolio.

In early 2002, the failure of Enron Corporation highlighted the entire question of investment in employer securities. The basic ERISA rule is that plans can invest in employer securities only if they are "qualifying employer securities" such as stock and eligible debt instruments. Defined benefit plans are subject to additional limitations on holdings of employer securities. [*See* § 6.09[C] for additional discussion of this issue in the context of 401(k) plans]

A Fifth Circuit case held that a pension administrator did not breach fiduciary duty by investing 65% of the plan's assets in undeveloped land. [*Metzler v. Graham*, 112 F.3d 207 (5th Cir. 1997)] The court decided that there was no real risk of a large loss, so the investment was prudent at the time it was made. Most of the plan participants were young, so there was enough time to make up for losses if they did occur, and there was plenty of time for appreciation in the land's value. The fiduciary was familiar with the local real estate market and thus able to select good investments. Historically, real estate has played an important portfolio role as an investment hedge.

[C] Investments

The question of how to invest plan assets becomes even more salient in a down market, when many plans face losses, than during a roaring bull market.

The Ninth Circuit not only found a fiduciary breach, but also held a plan manager personally liable for the plan's losses when he used plan assets to buy complex derivative securities that were illiquid and very risky. This was held to be imprudent because fiduciaries must investigate their purchases in advance. Relying on a trusted broker isn't good enough. [*Gilbert v. EMG Advisors Inc.*, 1999 U.S. App. LEXIS 4719 (9th Cir. March 17, 1999)]

But fiduciaries are not liable merely because adverse consequences happened on their watch. An employer's purchase of Guaranteed Investment Certificates (GICs), for individual pension accounts, from a company that was eventually seized by regulators, was not a breach of fiduciary duty. [*In re Unisys Savs. Plan Litig.*, 173 F.3d 145 (3d Cir. 1999)] The employer acted with adequate prudence by delegating investment responsibility to appropriate parties, who made an adequate investigation before recommending the purchase. [*Bussian v. RJR Nabisco Inc.*, 21 F. Supp. 680 (S.D. Tex. 1998), reaches a similar conclusion for annuities purchased from an insurer that later became bankrupt]

[D]   Fiduciary Duties in Health Plans

The Department of Labor issued a letter on February 19, 1998, stating that it may constitute a breach of fiduciary duty for health plan trustees to choose health providers purely on the basis of the lowest bid, without consideration of quality. Quality involves issues such as the provider's scope of operations; the qualifications and accreditations of its doctors and facilities, how easy it is for plan beneficiaries to gain access to a doctor; and consumer satisfaction scores the provider has already achieved. [*See* RIA Compensation and Benefits Update, May 25, 1998, at p. 3.]

According to the Supreme Court, an HMO is not acting as a fiduciary when, acting through its doctors, it makes a "mixed" decision about medical treatment and health plan eligibility. [*Pegram v. Herdrich*, 530 U.S. 211 (2000)] Therefore, even if plan participants are right that the plan refused them necessary treatments in order to increase its profits, they have not stated a cause of action for breach of fiduciary duty; they have not stated a cause of action for breach of fiduciary duty.

A health plan participant was not informed that, after losing an internal appeal of a denied claim, his only further redress was to file for arbitration within 60 days. However, he would have known this if he had consulted the SPD. The Ninth Circuit ruled that failure to disclose the arbitration requirement violated ERISA § 404(a), which obligates fiduciaries to act solely in the interests of plan participants and beneficiaries. [*Chappel v. Laboratory Corp. of Am.*, 232 F.3d 719 (9th Cir. 2000)] The fiduciary must provide written notice of the steps that must be taken to invoke arbitration.

A health plan can recover the "reasonable" value of services provided to injured employees, which means the fee-for-service fee schedule. The right of subrogation is not limited to the actual amount that the health care providers received because the health plan paid a discounted amount. [*Ince v. Aetna Health Mgmt., Inc.*, 173 F.3d 672 (8th Cir. 1999)]

§ 15.04   DUTIES OF THE TRUSTEE

Usually, pension and welfare benefit plans will be organized in trust form. Every trust must have at least one trustee. ERISA § 403(a) provides that the trustee can be named in the instrument itself, appointed under a procedure set out in the plan, or appointed by a named fiduciary.

The trustee has exclusive authority and discretion to manage and control the plan's assets. If there are multiple trustees, they must jointly manage and control, although ERISA § 403(a) permits them to delegate some duties. Certain fiduciary duties can be delegated—it depends on whether trustee responsibility or other duties are involved.

A plan can be drafted to make its trustee subject to a named fiduciary who is not a trustee—for example, to make the trustee report to an administrative committee. If this is done, the trustee must comply with "proper" directions given by the named fiduciary, if they are in accordance with the plan's procedures and not contrary to law.

If there has been a proper appointment of an investment manager, the trustee does not have to manage or invest the assets placed under the investment manager's control. Crucially, the trustee will not be liable for the acts or omissions of the investment manager. The trustee has a duty to make sure that the manager charges reasonable fees; performance-based fees, rather than flat fees determined in advance, are allowed.

§ 15.05   THE EMPLOYER'S ROLE

Although it might be predicted that the heaviest liability for plan misconduct would fall on the company that sponsors the plan, this is not always the case. The corporation might not be a fiduciary, or might not be acting in a fiduciary capacity in a particular case.

The first question is what role the corporation was playing. Businesses decisions, such as amending or terminating an unduly expensive plan, are not considered to be fiduciary decisions subject to ERISA. For instance, the decision not to provide severance benefits to laid-off workers has been held to be a nonfiduciary decision. [*Aminoff v. Ally & Gargano*, 65 L.W. 2400 (S.D.N.Y. Nov. 21, 1996)]

To prevent conflicts of interest, ERISA §§ 403, 4042, and 4044 allow fiduciaries to perform certain actions without violating the duty to maintain the plan for the sole benefit of participants and beneficiaries. Employer contributions can be returned if:

- The contributions were made based on a mistake of fact;
- The plan is not qualified under I.R.C. §§ 401(a) or 403(a);
- The income tax deduction for part or all of the contribution is disallowed;
- The contribution could be treated as an excess contribution under I.R.C. § 4975.

Nor is there a conflict of interest if the fiduciary follows PBGC requirements for a distribution incident to a plan termination.

§ 15.06   INVESTMENT MANAGERS

[A]   Qualified Managers under ERISA

If the plan so permits, ERISA allows fiduciaries to delegate their investment duties to a qualified investment manager.

There are four categories of qualified investment managers:

- Investment advisers who are registered under the federal Investment Company Act—whether they are independent consultants or in-house employees of the plan;
- Trust companies;
- Banks;
- Qualified insurance companies.

ERISA requires the manager to acknowledge in writing that he, she, or it has become a fiduciary with respect to the plan.

DOL Reg. § 2510.3-21(c) explains who will be deemed qualified to render investment advice:

- Those who give advice about the value of securities or recommend investing, buying, or selling securities (or other property, such as real estate);
- Those who are given discretion to buy or sell securities for the plan;
- Those who give advice, on a regular basis, under an oral or written agreement, if the advice is intended to serve as a primary basis for investing plan funds.

As long as the fiduciaries were prudent when they chose the manager (and continued to review the manager's performance), the fiduciaries will not be liable for acts and omissions committed by the manager.

A broker-dealer, bank, or reporting dealer does not become a fiduciary if its only role is to take and execute buy and sell orders for the plan. [DOL Reg. § 2510.3-21(d)(1)] The investment manager is a fiduciary only as to whatever percentage of the overall investment he or she can influence (except in situations where ERISA § 405(a) makes the investment manager responsible for breaches by co-fiduciaries).

[B]   The Role of the Insurer

The Supreme Court's decision in *John Hancock Mutual Life Insurance v. Harris Trust* [510 U.S. 86 (1993)] holds that assets held in an insurer's general account and not guaranteed by the insurer are plan assets subject to ERISA's fiduciary requirements.

DOL issued interim regulations covering insurance contracts sold before December 31, 1998; later contracts are all covered by ERISA fiduciary rules. DOL's Interpretive Bulletin 95-1 says that a fiduciary who chooses annuities to distribute plan benefits has a fiduciary duty to choose the safest available contract, based on factors such as the insurer's size and reputation, the insurer's other lines of business, and the size and provisions of the proposed contracts.

§ 15.07   DUTY TO DISCLOSE

Employees have a right to information about their benefit options, and fiduciaries have a corresponding duty to make complete, accurate disclosure. Furthermore, they need information about the way the plan is expected to evolve, so they can make future plans.

The classic test, stemming from *Fischer v. Philadelphia Electric Co.* [96 F.3d 1533 (3d Cir. 1996)] is that plan participants who inquire must not only be informed about the current structure of the plan—they must be informed of proposals that are under "serious consideration" by management. [Some cases say that, although information must be provided to those who ask for it, it need not be volunteered if there is no request, e.g., *Bins v. Exxon Co.,* 220 F.3d 1042 (9th Cir. 2000); *Hudson v. General Dynamics Corp.*, 118 F. Supp. 2d 226 (D. Conn. 2000). But other cases say that there is a fiduciary duty to give information whenever silence could be harmful to beneficiaries' financial interests. *See Krohn v. Huron Mem. Hosp.*, 173 F.3d 542 (6th Cir. 1999).]

The fiduciary must provide complete and accurate information about the tax consequences of options under a plan. [*Farr v. U.S. West Communications Inc.*, 58 F.3d 1361 (9th Cir. 1998)] But it is not a fiduciary breach to distribute benefits in accordance with the participant's own instructions, even if the fiduciary allegedly gave inaccurate tax advice. [*Glencoe v. TIAA*, 69 F. Supp. 2d 849 (S.D.W.V. 1999)]

Failure to provide this information on request is a breach of fiduciary duty. [*McAuley v. IBM Corp.*, 165 F.3d 1038 (6th Cir. 1999)] The fiduciaries' common-law duty of loyalty requires honest, fair dealings with plan participants. The Second Circuit position is that even long-range contingency plans must be disclosed. In *Caputo v. Pfizer* [267 F.3d 181 (2d Cir. 2001)], the court held that the fiduciary breached his duty by saying "a golden handshake (early retirement incentive) will never appear in your lifetime" when the fiduciary knew that the company was considering additional downsizing, and early retirement incentives are common in downsizing companies.

In *Mullins v. Pfizer Inc.* [147 F. Supp. 2d 95 (D. Conn. 2001)], the court found that there was a specific proposal (including cost calculations and predicted acceptance rates) because senior managers with authority to implement the change had seen the proposal. Therefore, ERISA was violated by not informing the plaintiff, although apparently the benefits representative hadn't been informed of it yet. The fiduciary duty is owed by the employer as plan administrator, not by the office staff, and the administrator has the additional duty of informing the people who run the plan.

According to *Wayne v. Pacific Bell* [189 F.3d 982 (9th Cir. 1999)], discussion of a particular early retirement proposal during collective bargaining is tantamount to serious consideration, even if the proposal is not adopted. Therefore, the company has an affirmative duty to inform employees accurately about the proposal actually accepted by the union.

Although many cases have arisen in the context of early retirement programs, fiduciary disclosure issues can come up in other contexts as well. There is a clear fiduciary duty to provide employees with copies of certain plan documents. According to the Second Circuit, ERISA § 104(b)(4) requires the plan administrator to provide copies of "plan documents" on request. However, actuarial evaluation reports do not fall into this category, and need not be disclosed. The Sixth Circuit reached the opposite conclusion. [*Compare Board of Trustees of CWA/ITU Negotiated Pension Plan v. Weinstein*, 107 F.3d 139 (2d Cir. 1997), *with Bartling v. Fruehauf Corp.*, 29 F.3d 1062 (6th Cir. 1994)]

In *Simeon v. Mount Sinai Medical Center* [159 F. Supp. 2d 598 (S.D.N.Y. 2001)], the plaintiff charged that she was not informed about the tax-sheltered annuity plan maintained by the employer. ERISA § 104(b)(1) requires administrators to provide SPDs within 90 days of the date a person becomes a plan participant; ERISA § 3(7) defines this to mean when the person becomes eligible to participate. The employer said that she was sent a certified letter a month after she was hired, describing the plan and giving the date for a meeting at which she could enroll. The District Court held that the letter didn't accompany an SPD, and didn't count as an SPD in and of itself. In this reading, pension plan eligibles must get an SPD within 90 days of eligibility, whereas welfare benefit participants don't have to get an SPD until they're "covered."

§ 15.08   PENALTIES FOR FIDUCIARY BREACH

A fiduciary that breaches the required duties can be sued by plan participants, plan beneficiaries, and/or the Department of Labor. Penalty taxes can be imposed for improper transactions involving the plan. Generally speaking, ERISA § 509 grants relief to the plan itself; participants and beneficiaries find their remedies under ERISA § 502(a)(3).

A fiduciary who is guilty of a breach of duty is personally liable to the plan and must compensate it for any loss in asset value caused by the violation. The fiduciary must also "disgorge" (surrender) any personal financial advantage improperly obtained: see ERISA § 409. However, there is liability only if there is a causal connection between a breach and the loss or the improper profits. Fiduciaries are not expected to guarantee that the plan will never lose money.

A plan can get a court order removing a faithless fiduciary from office. The removed fiduciary can be ordered to pay the plan's attorneys' fees plus interest on the sum involved. But plan participants cannot get an award of punitive damages, no matter how outrageous the fiduciary's conduct (although some courts will order punitive damages payable to the plan itself). In the most serious cases, a fiduciary can be subject to criminal charges instead of, or in addition to, civil penalties.

Plans can have "bad boy" clauses. For example, under ERISA § 206(d) and I.R.C. § 401(a)(13)(C) fiduciaries who are also plan participants can have their pensions reduced if they breach fiduciary duty, if they are convicted of crimes against the plan, or if they lose or settle a civil suit or enter into a settlement with the Department of Labor or PBGC.

Unless the crime involved an ERISA pension plan, and restitution to the plan is ordered, a federal court sentencing a person convicted of a crime does not have the power to order that undistributed funds from the convicted person's pension plan be used to pay restitution. [*United States v. Jackson*, 229 F.3d 1223 (9th Cir. 2000). *See* <http://laws.findlaw.com/9th/9950302v2.html>]

§ 15.09   ERISA § 502

ERISA § 502 gives participants and beneficiaries, the DOL, and fiduciaries many remedies against abuses and risks to the plan. In fact, an important part of litigation planning is deciding which subsection of ERISA § 502 to invoke—defendants can get a case dismissed if the wrong subsection is charged or if the plaintiff asks for remedies that are unavailable under that subsection.

Under ERISA § 502, "participant" means an employee or ex-employee who is or may become eligible to receive any benefit under the plan. "Beneficiary" either means someone eligible or potentially eligible to receive benefits under the plan terms, or as designated by a participant.

Participants and beneficiaries (but not the DOL, the employer, or the plan itself) can use ERISA § 502(a)(1)(B) to sue for benefits due under the terms of the plan, to enforce rights under the terms of the plan, or to clarify rights to future benefits under the terms of a plan.

Civil actions under ERISA § 502(a)(2) can be brought by participants, beneficiaries, or the DOL when a breach of fiduciary duty is alleged.

The DOL, participants, beneficiaries, or fiduciaries can sue under ERISA §§ 502(a)(3) and (a)(5) to enjoin violations of ERISA Title I, to get equitable relief under Title I, or to impose penalties on PIIs for engaging in prohibited transactions. The remedies under ERISA § 502(a)(3) can include ordering return of misappropriated plan assets, plus the profits improperly earned on them—but this remedy is not available in situations where the defendant did not hold or profit from plan assets.

An ERISA § 502(a)(3) suit for individual equitable relief can be maintained against a company that deceived its employees about benefit safety if they were transferred to a new division that was spun off by the company. The Supreme Court ruled that the corporation was acting as a fiduciary when it lied about benefit security. [*Varity Corp. v. Howe*, 514 U.S. 1082 (1996)]

A party in interest to a prohibited transaction with a plan can be liable under ERISA § 502(a)(3), even if the defendant is not a fiduciary [*Harris Trust v. Salomon Brothers*, 530 U.S. 238 (2000)]

A health plan and its administrator cannot sue under ERISA § 502(a)(3) to be reimbursed for benefits paid to a plan beneficiary who collects tort damages from the person responsible for his or her injuries. [*Great-West Life & Annuity Ins. Co. v. Knudson*, 534 U.S. 204 (2002)] Section 502(a)(3) lets fiduciaries sue for equitable relief only, not legal relief, when beneficiaries violate the terms of the plan. In this case, the beneficiary was crippled in a car accident. The health plan paid more than $400,000 for her medical care. She settled with the manufacturer of the car she was driving at the time of the accident for $650,000, but only $13,289 of the settlement was allocated to medical expenses, so that was all that the plan received as reimbursement.

The Third Circuit ruled that an employee can sue under ERISA § 502(a)(3) for breach of fiduciary duty for failure to disclose pertinent information, even where the employee did not specifically ask for it. [*Jordan v. Federal Express Corp.*, 116 F.3d 1005 (3d Cir. 1997)] In this case, a married employee opted for a joint and survivor annuity, but was not informed that this election was irrevocable. He divorced and remarried. The pension plan agreed to remove his first wife as an annuitant, but refused to either substitute his second wife or recast the annuity as a single-life annuity for the employee's life. The Third Circuit applied trust principles in an ERISA context to decide that a fiduciary must provide information where silence could be harmful to a beneficiary's interest.

Beneficiaries who are wrongfully deprived of coverage can be reinstated in the plan—but they can get only the benefits that would have been payable if they had been covered all along. They are not entitled to "disgorgement" of the money the employer saved by failing to provide the benefits at the appropriate time. [*LaRocca v. Borden, Inc.*, 276 F.3d 22 (1st Cir. 2002)]

Usually, an employer is not acting as a fiduciary when it amends a plan, but if benefits were vested, reducing them violates the plans and breaches fiduciary duty. [*Devlin v. Empire Blue Cross/Blue Shield*, 274 F.3d 76 (2d Cir. 2001). This case, and the similar case of *Abbruscato v. Empire Blue Cross/Blue Shield*, 274 F.3d 90 (2d Cir. 2001) are discussed in Nixon Peabody Benefits Briefs, (January 2002) <http://www.nixonpeabody.com>.]

The Third Circuit says that a grant of interest on benefits wrongfully withheld is proper, because it is "other appropriate equitable relief," but the Eighth Circuit disagrees. [*Compare Fotta v. Trustees of UMW Health Retirement Fund*, 165 F.3d 209 (3d Cir. 1998), *with Kerr v. Charles V. Vatterott & Co.*, 184 F.3d 939 (8th Cir. 1999)] However, if benefits are denied under a long-term disability plan, the plaintiff cannot recover the expenses of medical treatment, because this is the kind of extracontractual, compensatory damages that the *Mertens* case rules out. [*Rogers v. Hartford Life & Accident Ins. Co.*, 167 F.3d 933 (5th Cir. 1999)]

If the ERISA § 105 requirement of providing benefit statements is violated, the DOL, participants, or beneficiaries can sue under ERISA § 502(a)(4). Only participants or beneficiaries can sue, under ERISA § 502(a)(1)(A), to collect a penalty of $110 a day when a plan fails to supply the information required by Title I. The DOL can sue under ERISA § 502(a)(5) for equitable relief for employees who were misclassified as project, supplementary, or temporary rather than permanent workers, even though the employees can use ERISA administrative proceedings to obtain benefits themselves. [*Herman v. Time Warner*, 56 F. Supp. 2d 411 (S.D.N.Y. 1999)]

Section 502(a)(6) authorizes civil actions by the DOL to collect the excise tax on prohibited transactions or the penalty tax on fiduciary violations. State governments (but NOT the DOL) can sue under § 502(a)(7) to enforce compliance with a Qualified Medical Child Support Order (QMCSO). The states have a role to play here because they have traditionally been empowered to deal with family law issues such as child support.

Funds from an insurance contract or annuity purchased in connection with termination of participant status can be secured by a suit under § 502(a)(9). Suit can be brought by the DOL, fiduciaries, or persons who were participants or beneficiaries at the time of the violation—but suit can only be brought if the purchase of the policy or annuity violated the terms of the plan or violated fiduciary obligations.

ERISA § 502(c) allows the Department of Labor to impose a penalty of $110 per day (dating from the date of failure or refusal to furnish the documents) against a plan administrator who doesn't comply with a participant's or beneficiary's request for plan documents within 30 days. Administrators can be penalized even if the failure is not deliberate—but not if it is due to matters beyond their reasonable control.

Both the federal and the state courts have jurisdiction under § 502(e) when participants or beneficiaries bring suit to recover benefits, clarify their rights to future benefits, or enforce rights under any plan that falls under ERISA Title I. Although ERISA does not rule out binding arbitration of claims, any other Title I claim can only be heard in a federal, not a state, court.

ERISA § 502(i) requires the DOL to impose a civil penalty on fiduciaries who violate the fiduciary responsibility provisions of Title I. A nonfiduciary who knowingly participates in a fiduciary violation can also be penalized under this section. The base penalty is 20% of the penalty that the court orders under ERISA § 502(a)(2) or (a)(5). If the fiduciary or person who assisted the fiduciary in the breach settled with the DOL to avoid being taken to court, the base penalty is 20% of the amount of the settlement. The penalty can be reduced or even waived if the person acted reasonably and in good faith. Because the main objective of this section is to safeguard the plan, a reduction or waiver can also be obtained if the fiduciary or helper would not be able to reimburse the plan without severe financial hardship if the full penalty were assessed.

Section 502(k) permits plan administrators, fiduciaries, participants, and beneficiaries to sue the Department of Labor itself in district court in order to compel the agency to undertake an action required by ERISA Title I, to prevent the Department from acting contrary to Title I, or to review a final order of the Secretary of Labor.

Section 502 also permits fiduciaries to ask the court to remove another fiduciary from office, or to issue an injunction against anyone who has violated ERISA Title I or the plan's own terms.

It is mandatory for the DOL to impose civil penalties, under § 502(l), against a fiduciary who knowingly violates the Title I provisions on fiduciary responsibility, and also against anyone who knowingly participates in a violation. The basic penalty is 20% of the court order under §§ 502(a)(2) or (a)(5), or the settlement with DOL in such a case. However, any penalty imposed under § 502(i), or any prohibited transaction excise tax, can be used to offset the § 502(l) penalty. The Secretary of Labor has discretion to reduce or waive the penalty in two circumstances: if the fiduciary acted reasonably and in good faith—or if waiver permits the fiduciary to reimburse the plan for its losses.

§ 15.10   ERISA § 510

ERISA § 510 makes it unlawful to interfere with ERISA rights, or to discharge or discriminate against a participant for exercising ERISA rights. The typical examples are firing an employee to prevent benefit accrual, or firing someone in retaliation for making a claim for plan benefits. ERISA preempts state-law wrongful termination claims in these circumstances. [*Ingersoll-Rand v. McClendon*, 498 U.S. 133 (1990)] Section 510 applies to welfare benefit plans as well as pension plans. [*Inter-Modal Rail Employees v. Atchison, Topeka & Santa Fe Railroad*, 520 U.S. 510 (1997)]

However, refusal to rehire laid off workers who have credited service, as part of a policy of reducing pension obligations, does not violate § 510 because the people who seek to be rehired have not yet been hired or promised benefits. [*Becker v. Mack Trucks Inc.*, 281 F.3d 372 (3d Cir. 2002). *See* Shannon P. Duffy, *Failure to Rehire Workers Doesn't Violate ERISA*, The Legal Intelligencer (Feb. 22, 2002) (law.com)]

The McDonnell Douglas Corporation got a large federal contract, in part because the company said it would stay in Tulsa, Oklahoma (providing jobs!) for at least three years. When the company decided to shut down the plant just after receiving the order, the Northern District of Oklahoma said that the closure violated ERISA § 510 because it was motivated by desire not to pay benefits under two pension plans and a retiree health plan.

The company asserted unsuccessfully that it had a business justification for closing the plant because of excess capacity. The court in *Millsap v. McDonnell Douglas Corp.* [162 F. Supp. 2d 1262 (N.D. Okla. 2001)] found that there was no documentary evidence to support this defense, and the company failed to produce documents that were sought in discovery. Although courts usually defer to business judgment, the Northern District found that there had been a history of deception and bad faith.

The Title VII "burden-shifting" analysis discussed in Chapter 42, § 42.10[A] applies to ERISA cases as well. First the plaintiff must prove a prima facie case; failure to do this will result in dismissal of the case. If the plaintiff's prima facie case is proved, the defendant gets a chance to explain its legitimate, nondiscriminatory reason for its action. Finally, the plaintiff gets another chance, to prove by a preponderance of the evidence that the employer's explanation is actually a pretext for discrimination.

A group of employees brought suit unsuccessfully under ERISA § 510. According to the Eastern District of Pennsylvania, the employer was not liable under § 510, because that section requires an ongoing employment relationship, and thus does not apply to initial hires or rehires.

In *Baker v. O'Reilly Automotive, Inc.* [2001 U.S. Dist. LEXIS 15085 (N.D. Tex. Sept. 20, 2001)], the employer had a policy of firing anyone who had less than a year of service (and therefore was not eligible under the FMLA) and who was absent for 14 days for any reason. Therefore, the plaintiff was fired after breast cancer surgery. She received a COBRA notice but did not elect continuation coverage.

She sued under ERISA § 510 for damages (including her medical expenses related to cancer treatment), claiming that she was fired to relieve her employer of the obligation to pay her medical bills. However, she lost her case, because § 510 requires proof of the employer's specific intent to interfere with an ERISA right. Although the court found the employer's policy to be harsh and unreasonable, it was not illegal, and it was uniformly applied to all employees.

§ 15.11   OTHER ENFORCEMENT ISSUES

Criminal penalties can be imposed under ERISA § 511, making it a crime, punishable by up to one year's imprisonment and/or a fine of $10,000, to use or threaten force, fraud, or violence to restrain, coerce, or intimidate a participant or beneficiary, in order to interfere with or prevent exercise of any right under the terms of the plan or under Title I.

ERISA § 409(a) makes a breaching fiduciary personally liable to the plan to make up for losses caused by the breach (such as the difference between what the plan would have earned given appropriate investments, minus its actual earnings). The breaching fiduciary is also liable for any other legal and equitable remedies the plan chooses to impose.

However, in *Peacock v. Thomas* [516 U.S. 349 (1996)], the plaintiff won an ERISA case against his employer, but could not collect the judgment, allegedly because a corporate officer who was not a fiduciary misappropriated the funds that could have been used to satisfy the judgment. The plaintiff could not "pierce the corporate veil" and make the corporate officer personally liable, for various technical legal reasons. For one thing, the case was not closely enough related to ERISA for the federal courts to get involved. Anyway, a federal court cannot enforce a judgment against someone who was not liable for it in the first place.

The Department of Labor has authority under ERISA § 504(a)(2) to investigate whether a Title I violation has occurred so the employer might be ordered to submit books, papers, and records for DOL examination. This can be done only once per 12-month period unless the DOL has reasonable cause to believe that Title I was violated. The DOL also has subpoena power over books, records, and witnesses under § 504(c), but the subpoena can be enforced only if the agency shows that the investigation has a legitimate purpose, the inquiry is relevant to that purpose, and the government does not already have the information.

ERISA § 515 permits a civil action against an employer for delinquency in making contributions. This section does not have a statute of limitations, so most courts that have considered the issue use a six-year statute of limitations (typical for contract cases). The statute of limitations is clear under a similar provision, ERISA § 4003(e)(1) (which correlates with I.R.C. § 412(n)). If an employer fails to make a required contribution to the plan, at a time when the plan's funded current liability percentage is lower than 100% and the employer owes the plan more than $1 million (including interest), then all of the employer's real and personal property becomes subject to a lien in favor of the plan.

The plan that was supposed to, but didn't, make the payment has an obligation to notify the PBGC within 10 days of the payment due date. The PBGC has six years from the date of the missed payment, or three years form the time it knew or should have known about the missed payment, to sue in federal District Court to enforce the lien. Fraud or concealment by the employer extends the statute of limitations to six years from the PBGC's discovery of the true state of affairs.

Although confidential communications with an attorney, for the purpose of getting legal advice, generally are privileged, there is a "fiduciary exception" to this rule. Under the fiduciary exception, fiduciaries are supposed to act on behalf of the plan's participants and beneficiaries, so an attorney advising a fiduciary about plan administration is really working for the participants and beneficiaries. [*See Coffman v. Metropolitan Life Ins. Co.*, 24 F.R.D. 296 (S.D.W.V. 2001)]

ERISA gives the federal courts subject-matter jurisdiction to hear interpleader actions (a case in which the holder of disputed property asks the court for guidance about what to do with the property) when an insurance company needs to determine the proper beneficiary under a benefit plan. The insurance company is acting as a fiduciary, and interpleader is one of the types of equitable relief that can be granted to a fiduciary in order to enforce the terms of the plan. [*Aetna Life Ins. v. Bayona*, 227 F.3d 1070 (9th Cir. 2000)]

Schleibaum v. Kmart Corp. [153 F.3d 496 (7th Cir. 1998)] involved a claim that the employer breached ERISA by failing to give adequate notice of benefit denial when it ceased payment of life insurance on behalf of an ex-employee whom the employer claimed was not permanently and totally disabled. After the ex-employee's death, his family sued under ERISA § 503 (failure to provide mandated appeal information). The defendant prevailed at the District Court level, on the theory that the plaintiff should simply have bought his own insurance after the denial. The Seventh Circuit, however, found for the plaintiffs, on the grounds that the employee should not have been forced to purchase this coverage. The Seventh Circuit also held that a plaintiff in such a situation is not required to mitigate (reduce) damages by investigating his or her rights, given that the employer is in control of information about the benefit plan.

In general, standing to sue under ERISA, as a participant or beneficiary, is determined as of the time the suit is filed. However, in *McBride v. PLM Int'l Inc.*

[179 F.3d 737 (9th Cir. 1999)], a whistleblower employee objected to the termination of an ESOP plan and to using the value of common rather than preferred stock in making termination distributions from the ESOP. According to the Ninth Circuit, the plaintiff was a plan participant, despite being fired and despite the termination of the plan. Therefore, he was a whistleblower, as defined by ERISA § 1140, with standing to sue. As the Ninth Circuit pointed out, a contrary result would actually encourage employers to fire dissident employees and terminate plans—not exactly the results ERISA was supposed to achieve!

§ 15.12   LIABILITY OF CO-FIDUCIARIES

If a plan's assets are held by more than one trustee, the general rule is that all the trustees are jointly responsible for management, unless the plan's trust instrument either makes a specific allocation of responsibility, or sets up a procedure for allocating responsibility.

Every trustee has a legal duty to use reasonable care to make sure the other fiduciaries do not breach their duties. Any fiduciary's misconduct implicates all the others. Fiduciaries are liable for the acts and omissions of their fellow fiduciaries if:

- They knowingly participate in, or knowingly conceal, a breach on another party's act;
- They facilitate someone else's breach by failing to perform their own fiduciary duties as stated by § 404(a)(2);
- They know about a breach by another fiduciary, but fail to take reasonable steps to remedy it.

Under a 1993 Supreme Court case, the plan can also get equitable remedies (but not damages) from a nonfiduciary who cooperated with a fiduciary who breached fiduciary duty. [*Mertens v. Hewitt Assocs.*, 508 U.S. 248 (1993)] An attorney who knowingly participates in a fiduciary breach may have to make restitution to the plan, or have a constructive trust imposed on his or her legal fees received as a result of the fiduciary's breach—even if the attorney is not a fiduciary him- or herself. [*Long Island Head Start Child Dev. Servs. v. Frank*, 165 F. Supp. 2d 367 (E.D.N.Y. 2001)]

Some courts have applied *Mertens* to prevent any claims by plans against nonfiduciaries. This only puts more pressure on the fiduciaries, because then they are the only possible defendants if something goes wrong. But fiduciaries cannot be liable for other fiduciaries' conduct occurring before they themselves became fiduciaries. Nor do they have a duty to remedy breaches that occurred before their tenure or after they cease to be fiduciaries.

ERISA § 405(c)(1) allows a plan to make an explicit allocation of fiduciary responsibility (other than the responsibility of trustees) among the named fiduciaries. The plan can also have procedures for fiduciaries to designate a party other than a named fiduciary to carry out fiduciary responsibilities under the plan. In general, a fiduciary who designates someone else will not be responsible for the acts or omissions of the designee. The two major exceptions occur when making or continuing the designation violates the designor's duties under ERISA § 404(a)(1), or when ERISA § 405(a) makes the designor responsible for the co-fiduciary's breach.

§ 15.13   BONDING

The basic rule set down by ERISA § 412(a) is that all fiduciaries, and plan officials who are not fiduciaries but who handle plan assets, must be bonded. Generally, the employer will maintain a single bond covering all of its plans that are subject to ERISA Title I. Recovery on behalf of one plan must not be allowed to reduce the amount available to the other plans below the minimum requirement.

The exceptions are some banks and insurance companies with assets over $1 million, and administrators, officers, and employees who deal with unfunded plans. (An unfunded plan is one whose assets come from the general funds of the employer or a union, even if the funds derive in part from employee contributions.) A bond is not required for amounts characterized as general assets of the employer until they are transferred to the insurers that pay the actual benefits.

Various forms of bonds are acceptable:

- Blanket bond (covering all the fiduciaries and everyone who handles the plan's money);
- Individual bond;
- Name schedule bond (covering a group of named individuals);
- Position schedule bond (covering whoever fills certain jobs or stands in certain relationships to the plan).

The bond must be issued by a corporate surety that holds a Department of Treasury Certificate of Authority. To be acceptable, the bond must not have a deductible, and must cover claims discovered after termination or cancellation of the bond. The amount of the bond must be large enough to cover the plan's potential losses caused by plan officials' dishonesty or fraud. In general, the bond must be 10% of the funds handled, but not less than $1,000 or more than $500,000.

> **Tip:** A company in sound financial condition can save the cost of the bond by applying to the DOL for an opinion that payments are not at risk, and therefore the administrators of funded plans need not be bonded.

§ 15.14   INDEMNIFICATION

ERISA § 410 says that language in a plan, or in a side agreement with a fiduciary, is void as against public policy if it limits the fiduciary's liability for breach of fiduciary duty. However, the employer (as distinct from the plan) can permissibly indemnify the fiduciary or buy insurance covering the fiduciary. The fiduciary can also buy his or her own insurance coverage. [*See* § 43.08 for more discussion of fiduciary liability insurance] The sponsor corporation can also agree to use corporate assets to indemnify the fiduciary. This is allowed by the Department of Labor, and it is not considered a prohibited transaction.

§ 15.15 PROHIBITED TRANSACTIONS

[A] Generally

Objectivity is one of the most important fiduciary characteristics. ERISA bans certain types of transactions between a plan and parties who might lose objectivity because of those transactions. "Parties in interest" and "disqualified persons" are blocked from certain categories of transactions, even if a particular transaction is fair.

Title I of ERISA makes any one of these a prohibited transaction if it occurs between the plan and a party in interest:

- Sale, exchange, or lease of property, including the plan's assumption of a mortgage, or a mortgage placed on the property by a party in interest during the 10 years before the transfer of the property to the plan;
- Extensions of credit;
- Furnishing goods or services;
- Transfers or uses of plan assets for the benefit of a party in interest;
- Acquisition or holding of employer securities that are not qualified, or in excess of the normal limit (usually 10% of the fair market value of the plan assets);
- Use of plan income or assets by a fiduciary in her or her personal interest or for his or her own account;
- Payments to a fiduciary for his or her own account, made by anyone who deals with the plan;
- Conflict of interest: the fiduciary acts on behalf of a party, or representing a party, in any transaction representing the plan—if the interests of the party the fiduciary represents are adverse to the interests of the plan or of its participants and beneficiaries.

Tip: After the September 11 attack, the PWBA proposed amendments to Prohibited Transaction Exemption 80-26. [*See* 66 Fed. Reg. 49703 (Sept. 28, 2001)] PTE 80-26 is a class exemption allowing interest-free loans from parties in interest to a plan to pay the plan's ordinary operating expenses for up to three days for purposes incidental to ordinary operations. PTE 80-26 was extended to cover Y2K expenses; this proposal was made by the DOL on its own motion to help companies handle liquidity problems that the 9/11 attack created for benefit plans.

[B]   Parties in Interest

ERISA § 3(14) defines "party in interest" (PII) very broadly:

- Any fiduciary or relative of a fiduciary;
- Plan employees or persons who provide counsel to the plan—or their relatives;
- The plan's service providers and their relatives;
- Any employer or employee organization (e.g., union) whose members are covered by the plan;
- Anyone who owns 50% or more of the employer corporation, whether ownership is direct or indirect; relatives of the 50% owner;
- A corporation, partnership, trust, or estate that is 50% or more controlled by anyone in one of the categories above (unless they are involved only as relatives of a person involved with the plan);
- Employees, officers, and directors of organizations in the list (or anyone with similar powers and responsibilities without the formal title);
- Employees, officers, and directors (or those with similar rights and duties) of organizations in the list;
- Employees, officers, and directors of the plan;
- Anyone who has a direct or indirect 10% share ownership in the plan or an organization closely related to the plan;
- Anyone with a direct or indirect 10% interest in the capital or profits of a partnership or joint venture with anyone on the list.

Any participant, beneficiary, or plan fiduciary can bring suit for "appropriate equitable relief" under ERISA § 406 when an individual or business that is a "party in interest" (e.g., the employees and service providers of the plan) enters into a prohibited transaction—even if this individual or business is not an ERISA fiduciary. [*Harris Trust & Savings Bank v. Salomon Smith Barney*, 530 U.S. 238 (2000)] Therefore, the party in interest can be enjoined by a court, or required to make restitution to the plan, if the prohibited transaction results in financial losses to the plan.

A disqualified person who engages in a prohibited transaction can be required to pay an excise tax, even if he or she didn't know the transaction was prohibited. The excise tax is 15% of the amount involved per year. An additional tax of 100% of the amount involved is imposed when the IRS notifies the disqualified person that the transaction is prohibited, but the transaction is not rescinded within 90 days of receipt of the notice. The excise tax is payable to the IRS. In addition, the Department of Labor can impose a civil penalty that is more or less equivalent to the excise tax if a plan that is not qualified under Title I engages in a prohibited transaction.

The rules for welfare benefit plans are slightly different: The excise tax, under ERISA § 502(i) and I.R.C. § 4975(f)(5), is 5% of the amount of the prohibited transaction, and this amount is cumulated if the prohibited transaction continues over several years. There is a 100% excise tax for failure to correct a prohibited transaction after receipt of notice from the IRS.

[C]   Prohibited Transaction Exemptions

Because the prohibited transaction rules are so broad, the DOL has the power to grant "Prohibited Transaction Exemptions" for technically improper transactions that in fact are advantageous to the plan and benefit the plan's participants.

Exemptions fall into two main categories: the specific exemptions set out in ERISA § 408, and those granted by DOL and the Treasury after conferring. Before granting an exemption, the federal agency must decide that the proposed exemption is administratively feasible; serves the best interests of participants and beneficiaries; and protects the rights of participants and beneficiaries.

To get an individual exemption, a plan must apply to the relevant agency or agencies, and also give notice to affected parties and publish a notice in the Federal Register. Affected parties can place their comments (positive or negative) on the record. In some cases, a hearing will be required before the exemption is granted (e.g., when a fiduciary seeks permission to deal with the plan for his own account or to represent an adverse party).

ERISA includes statutory exemptions for loans to PIIs who are also plan participants or beneficiaries, as long as the loans are made on fair terms; for payment of reasonable compensation to PIIs for services they provide to the plan, rental of real estate to the plan at reasonable rates, and other deals that are the equivalent of arm's length transactions. There is also a statutory exemption for investing more than 10% of the plan's assets in qualifying employer securities and real property, as long as the plan purchases these items at a reasonable price and does not have to pay a commission to acquire them from the employer. Depending on the type of security, the plan will not be permitted to hold more than 25 to 50% of the entire issue.

"Class exemptions" have also been adopted for frequent transactions that are not harmful to the plan or its participants. Class exemptions have been granted, for instances, in connection with interest-free loans; mortgage loans to PIIs; and hiring PIIs to provide investment advice to the plan.

§ 15.16   PAYMENT OF PLAN EXPENSES

One of the PWBA's top enforcement priorities, starting in 2000, has been getting plan sponsors to reimburse plans for expenses that were paid out of plan assets but should have been paid by the sponsors themselves. [*See* Gerald E. Cole, *Paying Employee Benefit Plan Expenses*, Milliman & Robertson Benefits Perspectives Update (April 2001)] The DOL said that its regional offices would be conducting more plan expense audits than before. If a violation is found, not only must the employer reimburse the plan, but anyone involved in the transaction is subject to a 20% penalty. The Department of Labor can refer the case to the IRS for collection of the excise tax on prohibited transactions.

"Settlor functions" (decisions about establishing a plan or about plan design) are discretionary and not subject to the ERISA fiduciary requirements. Therefore, the expenses of performing settlor functions are not expenses of plan administration, and it is improper to use plan assets to pay them.

DOL Advisory Opinion 97-03A says that plan assets can be used to pay the expenses of terminating the plan itself, if the plan was silent about paying expenses, or if the plan permitted the payment of necessary administrative expenses. Plans that required the sponsor to pay such expenses can be amended to make the plan responsible for the expenses—but only expenses incurred after the amendment.

The DOL provided additional guidance in Advisory Opinion 2001-01A and a separate group of fact patterns. Under this Opinion, formation of a plan is a settlor activity, and the plan should not pay for it. Maintaining qualified status could involve fiduciary activities that the plan can pay for. Depending on whether they are incurred before or after a plan amendment, and whether they are reasonable and necessary for plan administration, these expenses could be legitimate plan expenses:

- Minimum funding valuations;
- Requests for determination;
- Processing fees;
- Preparation and submission of reports required by government agencies;
- Sending copies of such reports to participants;
- Making disclosure to, and communicating with, plan participants;
- Gathering information to make investment decisions for the plan;
- Amending the plan when complying with the law requires an amendment;
- Asset valuations in connection with a plan merger or spinoff (as long as the valuation is done after the plan is amended to cope with the transition);
- Winding up a terminated plan (including preparing valuations for the PBGC and distributing the plan's assets);
- Paying PBGC premiums;
- Preparing and auditing the plan's financial statements;
- Paying investment expenses.

Advisory Opinion 2001-01A says that the following are not allowable expenses that can be charged against the plan:

- Comparing benefit structures;
- Studies for outsourcing services that were previously performed by the sponsor at no cost to the plan;
- Preparing plan amendments that are not required for the sake of compliance;
- Preparing the financial disclosures that the sponsor is required to make under accounting standards;
- Getting valuations as part of deciding whether a merger or spinoff is worthwhile;
- Penalties imposed on the plan administrator;

- Analyses of whether to adopt early retirement incentives;
- Analyses of whether to terminate the plan.

Tip: Although plans are not allowed to charge participants or beneficiaries for processing Qualified Domestic Relations Orders (QDROs) or other documents relating to statutory rights, it is probably acceptable to charge a fee in connection with discretionary matters such as hardship distributions and plan loans.

---

§ 15.17   SERVICE PROVIDERS

Part of the fiduciary's duty of prudence is intelligent and informed selection of service providers for the plan, followed by monitoring of the job that the service providers do. [*See* Tess J. Ferrera, *Procedural Due Diligence in the Selection and Monitoring of Plan Service Providers*, 9 Journal of Pension Benefits (Autumn 2001), available at <http://www.kilstock.com/site/print/detail?Article_ID=1031>] Although it is understandable that fiduciaries will think first of their friends, colleagues, or relatives in selecting a service provider, the baseline is that they must deal only with people who have at least the minimum qualifications and experience to do the tasks they are hired for. A thorough reference check should be performed.

Compensation must be at least reasonably comparable to market rates for the same work. Selection by competitive bidding is helpful. Before retaining a service provider, it is vital to determine whether the fee that is quoted covers all the necessary services, or whether it is possible or likely that additional fees will be incurred, based on the predicted activities of the plan. The fiduciary doesn't always have to select the low bidder, but must be able to justify the selection as providing the best value on balance.

§ 15.18   ERISA LITIGATION

[A]   Generally

In ERISA litigation, as in many other types of cases involving plans, the basic questions include who can be sued, the proper court for the case, when the suit must be filed to be timely, and what remedies can be ordered if the case is proved.

In 1997, the district court for the District of Colorado ruled that plan participants' ERISA claims to recover benefits under a severance plan are legal, not equitable. Therefore, a jury trial would be available. But this was very much a minority view—nine Circuits had already ruled that jury trials are not available in such cases. In 1998, the Tenth Circuit joined the others. [*Adams v. Cyprus Amax Mineral Co.*, 149 F.3d 1156 (D. Colo. 1997)]

Jury trials are usually unavailable in ERISA § 502(a)(1)(B) and (a)(3) cases. Another possibility is that a jury will be empanelled in these cases, but it will only determine the part of the case relating to breach of contract. The judge in the case will decide claims of breach of fiduciary duty.

By and large, ERISA cases are treated like contract cases. Therefore, the damages available to a winning plaintiff basically put the plaintiff in the position he or she would have been in if the contract had been complied with. "Extra-contractual" damages (like damages for negligent or intentional infliction of emotional distress) will probably not be available. In most ERISA cases, punitive damages are also ruled out.

In any ERISA action brought by participants, beneficiaries, or fiduciaries, the winning side (whether plaintiff or defendant) can be awarded reasonable costs and attorneys' fees if the court thinks this is appropriate. Usually the attorneys' fee award starts out with the "lodestar" figure. This is the number of hours the winning lawyer spent on the case, multiplied by an hourly rate the court considers reasonable. In rare cases, the lodestar is reduced: if the court thinks the lawyer wasted time, for instance. Sometimes the fee award is greater than the lodestar amount, if the case was especially difficult, the lawyer broke new ground with innovative legal theories, or took on an unpopular case.

[B] Preemption

In many instances, cases involving benefits will have to be brought in federal rather than state courts, because of ERISA preemption. According to the Tenth Circuit, ERISA does not preempt claims about promises of job security, but it does preempt claims about promises involving employee benefits. [*Wilcott v. Matlack Inc.*, 64 F.3d 1458 (10th Cir. 1995)]

Another question is removal—whether a state case can be removed to the federal court system. In the view of the Eleventh Circuit, the employer cannot get the case removed to federal court, even for the limited purpose of deciding the preemption issue, if the plaintiff's state claims relate to benefits that are not covered by ERISA, even though they are bundled with an ERISA plan. [*Kemp v. IBM*, 109 F.3d 708 (11th Cir. 1997)]

[C] Exhaustion of Remedies

The court system is supposed to handle major conflicts, not minor everyday disputes that can and should be addressed in less complex and less socially expensive ways. Therefore, plaintiffs often have a legal duty of "exhaustion of remedies." That is, they will not be permitted to bring court cases until they have pursued all the administrative remedies within the system they are challenging. ERISA requires every plan to have a system for pursuing claims and appealing claims denials. So the general rule is that would-be plaintiffs must go through these steps before filing suit. This is not stated in so many words in ERISA itself, but judges have looked to ERISA's legislative history and other labor laws to determine when this requirement should be implied.

Plaintiffs clearly have to exhaust their remedies within the plan when their case involves benefits. Courts are split as to whether ERISA § 510 plaintiffs (interference with protected rights; see above) are required to exhaust their remedies. Exhaustion of remedies will not be required if:

- Going through channels would be futile;
- It was impossible to pursue plan remedies because the defendant wrongfully denied the plaintiff access to the plan's claims procedures;
- Irreparable harm would ensue if exhaustion of remedies was required;
- Participants and beneficiaries did not know how to enforce their rights, because they were deprived of information about claims procedures.

[D]   Statute of Limitations

ERISA § 525 permits a civil action against an employer for delinquency in making contributions. This section does not contain an express statute of limitations; most courts use a six-year statute of limitations, treating the case as the equivalent of an action to enforce a written contract.

The statute of limitations for an ERISA § 409 case (breach of fiduciary duty) derives from ERISA § 413. The suit must be brought within three years of the time the plaintiff discovered the alleged wrongdoing, or six years from the date of the last breach or the last date on which the omission could have been cured—whichever is earlier.

ERISA has an explicit statute of limitations for claims of breach of fiduciary duty, but not for participants' claims for plan benefits. According to *Wetzel v. Lou Ehlers Cadillac Group Long Term Disability Insurance Program* [222 F.3d 643 (9th Cir. 1999)], the crucial issue is whether the plaintiff provided proof of continuing disability for each month. The general federal rule is that a claim accrues as soon as a claimant knows or had reason to know that his claim had been denied. This rule would apply in any month in which adequate proof of loss was provided. But a separate three-year statute of limitations would be applied to determine whether claims were timely or time-barred for each month in which adequate proof of loss was not submitted.

ERISA § 413 requires a claim to be filed within six years of the event, or three years of the plaintiff's actual knowledge of the event. The District of New Jersey said that a claim filed about five years after the plaintiff learned about an early retirement plan was time-barred. [*Higgins v. Exxon Co.*, Civ. No. 98-cv-05797 (D.N.J. 2001)] The plaintiff learned about the program about three months after he retired. He had actual knowledge of the plan because he knew that additional benefits had been provided, and that he didn't qualify for the benefits.

Because § 510 does not include an explicit statute of limitations, the First Circuit held that the *state* statute of limitation for the most similar type of case should be applied in § 510 cases. Furthermore, the First Circuit used the state's three-year statute of limitations for personal injury cases, not the six-year statute of limitations for contract cases—so the plaintiff's suit was dismissed as time-barred. [*Muldoon v. C.J. Muldoon & Sons Inc.*, 278 F.3d 31 (1st Cir. 2002). *See* <http://www.spencernet.com/Archive/News022002.html>]

According to the First, Third, Seventh, Eighth, Ninth, and District of Columbia Circuits, the six-year statute of limitations under ERISA § 413 "in case of fraud or concealment," can be applied only when both fraud and concealment are charged. The Second Circuit disagrees, allowing the six-year statute of limitations for claims of either fraud or concealment [*Caputo v. Pfizer Inc.*, 267 F.3d 181 (2d Cir. 2001)]

If the source of the suit is a fiduciary's omission rather than a wrongful action, the time limit is six years from the last date the fiduciary could have cured the problem.

§ 15.19   CORRECTION PROGRAMS

[A]   Plan Deficiency Aids

One of the central tenets of tax and ERISA enforcement for plans is that, wherever possible, plans should be encouraged to determine where they fall short of compliance, and to correct the problems before regulators detect them. The IRS publishes Alert Guidelines, Explanations, & Plan Deficiency Paragraphs [<http://www.irs.gov/faqs/display/0,,i1%3D54%26genericId%3D50216,00.html>] so businesses can see the standards that IRS reviewers use when they review retirement plans for compliance. Each worksheet comes with explanatory text. The IRS Checksheets, also known as Plan Deficiency Paragraphs, are standardized text that plans can use to draft provisions that will satisfy IRS requirements.

[B]   FastTrack

In late 2001, the IRS announced the Large and Mid-Size Business Division FastTrack Dispute Resolution Pilot Program, a one-year experiment designed to reduce the time needed to resolve disputes with corporate taxpayers. The goal was resolution within 120 days. When the program is used, the taxpayer and IRS can implement either mediation by IRS appeals officials, to resolve the factual issues, or dispute resolution by an appeals official who recommends settlement terms. Any proposed resolution requires the agreement of the taxpayer and the IRS team manager to become effective. Participating in the program does not foreclose the taxpayer's other legal or appeal rights. [*IRS Launches "Fast Track" Dispute Resolution Program,* Spencernet Newsservice, (Nov. 27, 2001) <http://www.spencernet.com/Archive/News112701.html>]

[C] Voluntary Correction

The IRS has engaged in ongoing efforts to allow plans to correct failures without losing qualification. The Department of Labor encourages voluntary return to compliance by plan administrators. Penalties are reduced under the Voluntary Fiduciary Correction Program (VFCP) and Delinquent Filer Voluntary Compliance Program (DFVCP) if plans file late forms or reverse improper transactions before the DOL engages in enforcement activity.

Rules for these programs are published at 67 Fed. Reg. 15052 and 15062 (both 3/28/02). For DOL Fact Sheets about the two programs, *see* <http://www.dol.gov/pwba/pubs/0302afact_sheet.html> and <http://www.dol.gov/pwba/pubs/0302fact_sheet.html>. The Frequently Asked Questions about the programs appear at <http://www.dol.gov/pwba/faqs/faq_dfvc.html> (no www).

[D] Removing Assets

Although Rev. Proc. 2001-17, 2001-7 I.R.B. 589 describes limited circumstances under which assets can be removed from the plan to effect correction of a qualification failure, the better strategy is to prevent excess assets from entering the plan in the first place. Section 6.02(2)(c) of the Procedure permits removal of the assets only if the Code, Regulations, or other generally applicable guidance allows correction by way of distributing assets or participants or beneficiaries, or returning assets to the employer or plan sponsor. This section also says that if an excess allocation is made for a plan participant (other than a 401(k) participant), and the allocation does not exceed the I.R.C. § 415 limit, then the excess allocation should be corrected by reallocating it to other participants or reducing the sponsoring employer's future contributions. [*Removing Assets from a Plan to Effect Correction*, BenefitsLink Correcting Plan Defects Q&A, (Dec. 3, 2001) <http://www.benefitslink.com/cgi-bin/qa.cgi?database_id=164&mode=read&database=qa_plan_defects>] The funds should not be returned to the sponsor. If the funds are excess because the plan fails the ADP antidiscrimination test, funds may be returned to participants. The funds must be returned to participants if a deferral is greater than the I.R.C. § 402(g) maximum (which is $10,500 for 2001 and $11,000 for 2002) and the required minimum distribution is not made under I.R.C. § 401(a)(9).

CHAPTER 16

EFFECT OF CORPORATE TRANSITIONS ON PENSION AND BENEFIT PLANS

§ 16.01 INTRODUCTION

A qualified plan can change its form for several reasons: by amendment, by termination, or as a response to a change in form in the corporation that sponsors the plan. The sponsoring corporation can merge with or be acquired by another company, and some or all of the first plan's employees can become employees of the new or surviving corporation. The transition may be primarily motivated by corporate needs or primarily to change the form or operation of the plan (e.g., combining several existing plans for ease of administration or to cut costs).

Basic fiduciary principles continue to apply during a transition, and plans must still be maintained for the sole benefit of participants and beneficiaries. Therefore, the Supreme Court decided that plan participants and beneficiaries can sue under ERISA § 502(a)(3) to get equitable relief for themselves, when a company spun off its money-losing divisions to a new, financially unstable corporation and then lied to employees about the safety of their benefits if they transferred to the new corporation. [*Varity Corp. v. Howe,* 516 U.S. 489 (1996)]

However, because pension benefits vest but welfare benefits (including retiree health and insurance benefits) do not, ERISA fiduciary duty is not violated by transferring the obligation to pay nonpension retiree benefits to a new company spun off from the former employer. Nor will the courts hear an ERISA contract claim.

The Sixth Circuit's analysis in *Sengpiel v. B.F. Goodrich Co.* [156 F.3d 660 (6th Cir. 1998)] is that ERISA requires prefunding of pensions, but not of welfare benefits. Because the spun-off entity retained the right to reduce benefits in the plan documents, reduction in benefits had to be analyzed as a business decision, and not a discretionary administrative decision by a fiduciary.

Part of the due diligence that must be undertaken prior to purchasing another business, or selling a business, is the effect of the change on each corporation's employee benefit plans. For example, if it is discovered that the seller's plan is underfunded, the sales documents might be redrafted to obligate the seller to correct the underfunding—or the sales price might simply be reduced accordingly. Sometimes, the deciding factor in structuring the deal will be the way the deal partners intend to treat their benefit plans.

A change in corporate structure can have unintended effects on plans, such as violation of nondiscrimination, minimum participation, and anticutback rules. The buyer must be particularly careful to find out if defined contribution plans are unfunded, or defined benefit plans are underfunded. The presence or absence of golden parachutes, retiree health benefit obligations, and COBRA obligations must be determined. Worker Adjustment and Restraining Notification Act (WARN) [29 U.S.C. § 2101 *et seq.*] notification may also be required if there is a significant reduction in the workforce after the corporate transition. [*See* § 30.10] Plan discrimination testing must also be repeated after a change of corporate organization. [*See* § 4.22]

Changes in ownership or the form of ownership of a corporation sponsoring a plan will frequently be "reportable events" of which the PBGC must be notified (in case the plan is unable to meet its payment obligations and the PBGC has to take over).

The reorganization of a plan's contributing sponsor makes the successor corporation responsible for certain plan liabilities such as the plan's accumulated funding deficiencies, including those previously waived by the IRS. [*See* ERISA §§ 4062(f) and 4069(b)] A party that engages in a transaction within five years before a plan termination, if the transaction was intended to evade liability in connection with the plan, becomes a contributing sponsor who is liable for those amounts. In other words, the effect of the transaction is precisely the opposite of what was intended.

When operations are terminated at a facility and 20% or more of the participants separate from service, the employer must either fund the plan's guaranteed benefits immediately or make provisions for the funding. There is also likely to be a WARN Act event. [*See* § 30.10]

The test of whether two companies are alter egos (and therefore one must make up for the other's delinquent contributions to a pension plan) comes from basic corporate law. Does one company control the other so closely that the second corporation has no independent existence? Is the second corporation only a sham used for fraudulent purposes? [*See also* Ellen E. Schultz' reporting, *Raw Deals: Companies Quietly Use Mergers and Spinoffs to Cut Worker Benefits*, Wall Street Journal, Dec. 27, 2000, at p. A1 showing that a corporate division that is up for sale can be made to seem more attractive to potential buyers by reducing liability for employee medical coverage, making the pension plan less generous, or freezing pension benefits while retaining control over plan investments]

There are also tax, labor law, and unemployment insurance consequences of corporate transitions.

§ 16.02   CHOICE OF FORM

[A]   Generally

Although there are almost infinite variations, there are several basic ways to structure a transaction. Two companies could merge, either creating a new successor company or with one company merged into the other. One company could buy all of the other's assets, or one company could buy all of the other company's stock. The consequences of stock and asset purchases are different.

In either a merger or a stock purchase, the buyer acquires the seller's liabilities as an automatic part of the deal. The buyer will become the sponsor of the seller's employee plan benefits unless:

- Action is taken to terminate or freeze the plan. Both corporate action (resolution of the Board of Directors; perhaps affirmation by the stockholders) and pension plan action (plan amendment) will be required;

- The plan is transferred away from the acquired entity (e.g., to a parent corporation that is selling one of its subsidiaries);
- The transaction is set up so the seller retains plan sponsorship.

In this situation, if the plan is not assumed, employees might end up forfeiting benefits that had not vested as of the time of the sale. But if the transaction has the legal effect of a partial termination of the plan, vesting will be required.

In contrast, in an asset sale, the buyer is traditionally deemed to assume only the specific liabilities it agrees to assume. Thus, the buyer becomes a successor plan sponsor only if it takes action to become one, such as adopting the existing plan or a plan that is a spinoff of the existing plan. A spinoff divides one plan into two or more, for instance by assigning a spun-off plan to each of several divisions. There are many reasons why an asset buyer might prefer to avoid adopting the seller's plan—because of underfunding or other liability triggers, or a bad match with the buyer's existing deferred compensation plans.

But asset purchases have their own risks. Some recent court cases make the purchaser liable for pension liabilities such as the asset seller's unpaid pension contributions and termination liability. This could occur even if the asset buyer did not expressly assume the obligations, and even if it is not a successor under the general principles governing corporate transitions, as long as there is continuity of operations and the seller bought the assets knowing that the liabilities existed.

[B]   T.D. 8928

T.D. 8928, 66 Fed. Reg. 1843 (Jan. 10, 2001), provides that, when a corporation makes an asset sale (of substantially all the assets of a trade or business, or an asset as substantial as a factory or a corporate division), it is treated as the successor employer if the seller entirely ceases to provide group health plans, and the buyer maintains business operations using the assets. A transfer (e.g., in bankruptcy) is considered an asset sale if it has the same effect as a sale would have.

The plans that the seller maintained before the transaction could be retained, frozen, or terminated. A buyer who adopts an existing plan could agree to assume liability only going forward, with the seller retaining liability for violations of the plan rules that occurred before the sale. As for plans maintained by the buyer before the transaction, the buyer's and seller's plans could merge. [*See* below for the anticutback rules and the requirement of crediting prior service to the new plan]

Like all rules, this has exceptions. If the transaction is in effect a merger rather than an asset sale, liabilities will be characterized as they would be in a merger. If the buying corporation is a mere continuation of the selling corporation, or if the transaction is a fraud intended to escape liability, the transaction will be disregarded.

If only plan assets, and not the operating terms of the two plans, are merged, then the transaction is not considered a plan amendment that has the effect of reducing plan accruals. However, if the plans merge and one adopts the other's formulas and definitions, the original plan is deemed to have been amended. If benefits are reduced, notice must be given under ERISA § 204.

[C] Labor Law Implications of Choice of Form

Labor law follows the basic rule that a merger or sale of stock obligates the acquiring company to assume the liabilities of the acquired or selling company. This includes the Collective Bargaining Agreement (CBA). But in an asset sale, the CBA is not assumed unless the purchaser voluntarily takes it on, or unless there is another reason to view the buyer as a successor or surrogate of the seller.

Yet even if the company is not fully bound by its predecessor's CBA, it could still have a duty to bargain in good faith with the existing union, based on continuity linking the old and new enterprises. If a transaction lacks real substance, the successor could be forced to assume the predecessor's labor-law obligations. The main test is whether there has been a significant practical change or whether operations continue despite a nominal change in ownership.

In addition to situations in which one entity replaces another, two or more enterprises can be treated as a "single employer" for labor-law purposes. One might be treated as an alter ego (surrogate) of the other. If a parent company and its subsidiary engage in the same line of business, the NLRB will probably treat them as a single enterprise, not two. Furthermore, "joint employers" that are separate entities but share decision making about labor issues may be treated together by the NLRB.

Either a purchaser must be prepared to take on the predecessor's union contracts and other labor-law obligations, or must structure the transaction to be free of such obligations. Also note that a change in corporate ownership (even if corporate structure remains the same) can lead the state to revoke the privilege to self-insure against Worker's Compensation claims.

A new company that adopts an existing operation can unilaterally change the wage scale, unless it's "perfectly clear" that the new owner will hire all of the old employees. In a "perfectly clear" case where the new owner does not consult with the union and there is no evidence of what would have emerged if there had been negotiations, the employees are given the benefit of the doubt. It is assumed that the former wage rate would have continued and would not have been diminished. So new ownership in a "perfectly clear" case cannot lead to wage cuts unless the union agrees.

According to the Third Circuit, a bankrupt company remained liable for retroactive wage payments under a CBA, even though the CBA was supposedly assigned in conjunction with the sale of the company's assets. [*American Flint Glass Workers Union v. Anchor Resolution Corp.*, 197 F.3d 76 (3d Cir. 1999)] Bankruptcy Code § 365(k) lets a debtor avoid liability for contract obligations only if there has been a complete assignment of both rights and duties under those contracts. In this case, the purchaser specifically disavowed responsibility for those retroactive payments. The transaction was deemed an attempt to unilaterally amend the CBA, which is forbidden by Bankruptcy Code § 1133(f).

The labor law doctrine of "CBA bar" says that another representation election will not be held during the existence of a valid, ongoing collective bargaining agreement. A CBA bars a new election in a merger or acquisition if the new operation carries on the old business. It is not a bar if the transaction produces an entirely new company that makes major personnel changes. A CBA is not a bar when a successor employer comes in and does not issue a written assumption of the existing agreement.

[D] Transitions and Unemployment Insurance

Although it is a comparatively minor cost, the acquiror of a business may wish to take advantage of the amount of FUTA tax already paid by the transferor of the business for the part of the year before the transition. The successor employer can rely on wages paid (and therefore on FUTA payments made) by the predecessor if either one of two circumstances exists. The first is that the transferee acquires substantially all the property used in the transferor's entire trade or business (or in a separate unit of the trade or business). The other is that, whether or not the property was acquired, at least one employee from the old business remains employed immediately after the transfer.

> **Tip:** A multistate operation will usually be permitted to combine wages paid in the various states for FUTA purposes.

The IRS' view, for FICA and tax withholding as well as FUTA purposes, is that, in a statutory merger or consolidation, the surviving corporation is the same taxpayer and the same corporation as the predecessor corporation(s). Of course, that means that the successor will have to pay any taxes due but unpaid by the predecessor—unless the successor gives the local administrative agency adequate written notice.

However, most state unemployment laws provide that companies remain subject to unemployment insurance laws for at least two years once they have acquired an experience rating—with the result that the transferor may remain liable in a year after it ceases operations, unless it applies to the local administrative agency for a determination that it is no longer an employer.

If the predecessor has acquired a good experience rating, the successor will probably be able to take over the experience rating with the rest of the operation, as long as operations remain more or less the same, at the original business location, and the workforce remains stable. Altering these important factors in effect creates a new enterprise, which will have to acquire its own experience rating.

§ 16.03   THE ANTICUTBACK RULE

Internal Revenue Code § 411(d)(6) forbids amendments that reduce accrued benefits, including early retirement benefits and the availability of additional forms of payment over and above the required QJSA and QPSA. But according to *Board of Trustees of the Sheet Metal Workers Nat'l Pension Fund v. C.I.R.* [117 T.C. 220 (2001)], only employees, not retirees, can "accrue" benefits. Therefore, eliminating post-retirement Cost of Living Increases doesn't violate the anticutback rule, because the benefits weren't "accrued." In contrast, *Michael v. Riverside Cement Co. Pension Plan* [266 F.3d 1023 (9th Cir. 2001)] says that the employer violated the anticutback rule by eliminating a provision that gave re-employed employees full benefits (without reduction for benefits paid at their first retirement) when they finally retired for a second time.

If a plan is spun off, the spin-off plan is required to maintain the old plan's payment options as to benefits accrued before the spinoff.

In a merger, employees are permitted to retain their premerger pay-out options. In practice, this means that if a merged plan wants to have a single pay-out structure, it must improve the less-favorable plan to equal the options under the more-favorable plan.

Section 411(a)(10)(B) requires that individuals who had three years of service before the corporate transition will be entitled to keep the old vesting schedule, if it is more favorable to them than the newly adopted one. Employers have an obligation to inform employees of this option.

According to I.R.C. § 414(l), if plans (even plans maintained by the same employer) merge or consolidate, or if a plan's assets and liabilities are transferred to another plan, each participant's benefit immediately after the transition, calculated on a termination basis, must be at least as great as his or her benefit would have been if the plan had terminated immediately before the transition.

The regulations for this section say that a transfer of assets and liabilities from one plan to another will be treated as a spinoff followed by a merger. This usually means that Form 5310-A has to be filed at least 30 days before the merger, spinoff, or asset transfer.

Section 414(l) requires a plan's actuaries to make reasonable assumptions about expected retirement age, mortality, and interest rates before and after the asset transfer. The termination assumptions that the PBGC uses offer a safe harbor because using them is always deemed reasonable, but their use is not mandatory.

According to *Systems Council EM-3 v. AT&T Corp.* [159 F.3d 1376 (D.C. Cir. 1999)], a plan sponsor can spin off part of a plan to another corporation in the same controlled group, and keep some or even all of the assets of the original plan. The participants in the spun-off plan are not entitled to a share of the surplus assets, even though they would have been distributed in a termination.

The Secretary of the Treasury has the power to enforce ERISA § 208, which is very similar to I.R.C. § 414(l). The Department of Labor has indirect enforcement powers under ERISA § 208, because of its enforcement powers over fiduciary conduct. [*See* Lonie A. Hassel, *Asset Transfer Under 414(l)*, (March 18, 2001) <http://www.groom.com>]

Internal Revenue Code § 414 has separate rules for merging two defined contribution plans; two defined benefit plans; and one plan of each type to make sure that participants' entitlement to benefits is not reduced as a result of the transaction. There are further requirements to be observed if one of the plans is fully funded but the other is underfunded. For defined benefit plans, this section serves two policy purposes. It avoids manipulation of funding by means of moving plan assets between the plans of a controlled group of corporations, and it prevents the dilution of benefits within the ERISA § 4044 priority order for categories of assets during a termination.

The priority order is as follows:

- Assets are allocated to benefits coming from participant contributions;
- Benefits going to individuals who were already getting benefits during the three years before the termination;
- Benefits to persons who could have been getting benefits during that three-year period;
- PBGC-guaranteed benefits;
- Other nonforfeitable benefits;
- Everything else.

§ 16.04 NOTICE OF REDUCTION OF BENEFITS

ERISA § 204(h) requires notices of reductions in future benefits. This provision was amended by EGTRRA. Now, notice must be given before the effective date of any amendment that eliminates or reduces an early retirement benefit or early retirement subsidy. An excise tax is imposed on failure to provide proper notice.

Notice is due a reasonable time before the effective date of the plan amendment. The notice can be given before the formal adoption of the amendment, as long as there is no material change before the amendment is finally adopted. If there is an "egregious" failure to provide notice, then the amendment cannot take effect, and individuals affected by the change get the larger of the pre- or postamendment form of the benefit.

The Pension and Welfare Benefits Administration (PWBA) has its own provision for informing employees of the effect of a transition on their benefits. [The agency has published a 32-page booklet, *Pension and Health Care Coverage: Questions and Answers for Dislocated Workers* at <http://www.dol.gov/pwba>]

§ 16.05 THE MINIMUM PARTICIPATION RULE

Initially, minimum participation rules were applied to both defined contribution and defined benefit plans. However, the Small Business Job Protection Act of

1996 [Pub. L. No. 104-188] eliminated this rule for defined contribution plans—now only defined benefit plans are required to have a minimum number or percentage of participants. This is significant in the context of corporate transitions because asset buyers often decline to adopt the seller's plan. If the plan is not adopted, there is a risk that the new plan will fail to cover the mandated number or percentage of employees.

Some relief is available under I.R.C. § 410(b)(6)(C), which allows one year after an acquisition or the disposition of a corporation to satisfy the minimum participation requirement. But after that, the plan is likely to become disqualified—unless it has been terminated in the interim.

A possible strategy is to freeze the plan. However, if too many participants choose to cash out, that creates difficulties. Two or more plans can be merged into a larger plan, offering a benefit structure at least as favorable as the most favorable of the merged plans, no later than the fifteenth day of the tenth month after the end of the plan year.

§ 16.06   IN-SERVICE DISTRIBUTIONS AND REHIRING

The underlying purpose of pension plans is to provide postretirement financial security. Therefore, "in-service distributions" (distributions from the plan while the individual is still working) are severely discouraged by the Code. There is some interest in modifying this requirement in order to make it easier for workers to make a transition out of the workforce by taking "phased retirement" rather than terminating workforce participation entirely.

There are some special rules governing taxation of in-service distributions during a transition. Treasury Regulation § 1.401-1(b)(1)(i) provides that defined benefit plans cannot make in-service distributions before the employee's retirement or termination of employment—unless the plan itself is terminated. But a defined contribution plan that is not a 401(k) plan can use the two-year/five-year rule. That is, contributions can be withdrawn from the plan after the contributions have been in the plan for two years, or the participant has five years of plan participation.

Tip: EGTRRA eliminates the "same desk" rule for 401(k) plans. In other words, when there is a merger consolidation, or liquidation, participants in a 401(k) plan will be entitled to take a distribution from the plan even if the successor company hires them and they have not separated from service. Congress intended to increase the portability of pensions in this situation.

Because of the abolition of the same desk rule, distributions can be made from the seller's plan in either an asset or a stock sale, to employees who go to work for the buyer or stay at the subsidiary that has been sold, as long as that subsidiary drops participation in the plan by the time of the sale. Distributions are not allowed if the subsidiary that is the subject of the sale retains the plan, the buyer takes over as plan sponsor, or assets are transferred to a plan maintained by the buyer corporation. In most cases, a plan amendment will be required. It probably makes sense to permit distributions to any participant who is transferred out of the seller's controlled group as a result of a stock sale, sale of assets, or other corporate transaction. Note that, because this is an EGTRRA provision, it is subject to the January 1, 2011, sunset date of the entire statute.

In *Dycus v. PBGC* [133 F.3d 1367 (10th Cir. 1998)], a plant closed and then was reopened by a new owner, who required employees to reapply for their jobs, cut wages, reduced benefits, and changed the seniority schedule. Notwithstanding these changes, employees were not entitled to early retirement benefits under the plan's forced termination provision. The Tenth Circuit ruled that there had not been a permanent shutdown triggering the entitlement to early retirement benefits.

§ 16.07   TAX ISSUES

[A]   Attributes of Successor Plans

If, after a merger, liquidation, or reorganization, the surviving company maintains the predecessor corporation's qualified plan, I.R.C. § 381 generally provides that the original plans' tax attributes are passed on to the successor plan. If two qualified plans consolidate, the deductions taken by each employer before the consolidation will not be retroactively disqualified by the consolidation.

The acquiring corporation can keep up the plan for the benefit of those covered by it under the old ownership—with no obligation to cover the workers who were its own employees before the acquisition.

Revenue Procedure 99-50, 1999-52 I.R.B. 757 sets forth the basic and a separate elective procedure for preparing tax forms (e.g., Form 1099; Form 5498) when a successor business acquires substantially all of the assets used in a trade or business. The standard procedure is that both predecessor and successor companies have to file the relevant forms for the year of the acquisition. But, to relieve burdens, the alternate procedure allows the predecessor and successor companies to agree that the successor company will take over the entire reporting burden for the year of the acquisition.

[B]   Golden Parachutes

The risk of acquisition or merger makes corporate recruitment more difficult, because top candidates have a realistic fear that they will lose their jobs during a shake-up. [*See* Paul L. Gilles, *Gaining Control during Changes in Control*, HR Magazine, June 1999, at p. 98] Employment agreements with prominent candidates often include "golden parachutes" (providing generous compensation if the job is lost because of a corporate transition) and "golden handcuffs" (retention bonuses that are forfeited if the individual quits shortly after being hired).

Most of these programs have a double rather than a single trigger. That is, they do not take effect when the employees quit voluntarily, only if they have involuntary job loss. A modified double trigger plan contains a window period, during which payments will be made even if the employee quits voluntarily. The window is often placed in the thirteenth month of the agreement, when the 20% excise tax on excess parachute payments can be minimized. In fact, if a company is particularly insistent on hiring a particular top executive, it may even agree to "gross up" the payment—that is, to take over payment of the excise tax on the excess parachute payment.

Parachute payments deal with the risk that current top management will be ousted if there is a change in control. The acquirer may face the opposite problem: Managers whose skills are needed for success may quit because of the transition. A "stay bonus" for remaining with the new owner is a fixed benefit (and therefore a fixed incremental cost for the business buyer). The bonus is paid after the employee has remained for a certain period of time. It could also be combined with a golden parachute. For instance, the executive could be offered two months' salary as a bonus for staying a year, or given a severance package of three months' salary and outplacement assistance if terminated without good cause within 18 months of the transition.

Internal Revenue Code § 280G does not allow corporations to deduct "excess parachute payments." Any "disqualified person" who receives an excess parachute payment is subject to a 20% excise tax, under I.R.C. § 4999. A parachute payment is a payment of compensation, contingent on a change in ownership, and equal to three times or more of the base amount (roughly speaking, the base amount is the individual's normal compensation).

In Rev. Proc. 2002-13, 2002-8 I.R.B. 549, the IRS proposed new regulations for tax treatment of golden parachute payments, in connection with corporate transitions that occur on or after January 1, 2004. Taxpayers can use the rules that were proposed by the Treasury in 1989 for transitions occurring before that date.

A parachute payment is compensation (including cash, the right to receive cash, or a property transfer—including a stock option) that is contingent on a change in corporate ownership or control. Under Rev. Proc. 2002-13, a person is a shareholder if he or she owns 1% or more of the fair market value (FMV) of all of the corporation's outstanding shares of stock. A person is a highly compensated individual if he or she earns $90,000 or more (this is the 2002 figure; it will be adjusted for inflation).

§ 16.08   THE PBGC EARLY WARNING PROGRAM

PBGC's Early Warning Program is supposed to reduce the agency's risk of loss in the context of corporate transitions. PBGC's Technical Update 00-3 (July 24, 2000) explains that the program focuses on below-investment-rated companies that have plans with current liability over $25 million, or plans with over $5 million in unfunded current liability. The PBGC gets to review the transactions of these companies to see if a transaction weakens the plan's financial support to the extent that the PBGC might become liable to take over benefit payments.

The early warning program is designed to identify transactions that significantly increase the PBGC's risk of loss. Although the agency has never published standards for what it considers a significant increase in risk, certain types of transactions have been identified as potential problem areas: the breakup of a controlled group; a leveraged buyout; major divestiture by a company that retains significantly underfunded pension liabilities; or transfer of significantly underfunded pension liabilities in connection with sale of a business.

§ 16.09 STOCK OPTIONS

During the late lamented Internet boom, stock options were greatly cherished by employees because of the possibility of purchasing stock for a few dollars and being able to resell it at a much higher price—especially if the company was a start-up with the potential for a high-flying Initial Public Offering. Under current depressed stock market conditions, far fewer employees hold options that can be exercised profitably. However, in the hope that conditions will turn around again, the topic is worth discussing.

The Financial Accounting Standards Board (FASB) tackles the treatment of stock options after an acquisition. [*See Stock Compensation: Interpretation of Opinion 25,* at <http://www.rutgers.edu/Accounting/raw/fasb/project/stockcom.html>]

Question 17, which says that when one business purchases another, and the acquiring corporation grants stock options in exchange for outstanding vested options of the acquired corporation (or options that vest precisely because a change of control has occurred), the fair market value of the options in the acquiring corporation's stock is part of the purchase price for the acquired corporation.

Therefore, accounting treatment is determined by APB Opinion 16, "Business Combinations," not Opinion 25, which covers most stock option issues. But nonvested options granted by the acquiring corporation in exchange for nonvested options in the acquired corporation's stock are governed by Opinion 25.

One article says that mergers raise many questions about stock options, including:

- Do employees of the acquired company forfeit their outstanding options?
- Are their options bought out?
- Do they receive options in the acquiror company in exchange?

[Robbi Fox, Ed Hauder, and Mike Jones, *What Happens to Outstanding Stock Options in a Merger or Acquisition*, J. of Compensation and Benefits, March 2001, at p. 16]

One of the most important factors in the answer is whether the transaction is considered a "pooling of interest" or a "purchase." (For most transactions initiated after June 30, 2001, pooling is unavailable.) Pooling of interest means that the companies exchange equity securities, and the two companies pool their bookkeeping and accounting.

The recorded assets and liabilities carry over to the books of the new entity, and income from both companies is also pooled. There is no premium for goodwill on the balance sheet, and goodwill doesn't have to be amortized as an expense. The net result is that the company's reported earnings will be higher, and the surviving company will be more attractive to investment bankers and the stock market.

In contrast, under the purchase method, the acquirer purchases the acquired company. The financial statements of the combined entity must reflect the fair value of the acquired company's assets and liabilities.

Only certain types of securities can be used in a pooled transaction. That prevents employees from cashing out their stock options. As a result, companies usually will either exchange options of the combining company for options of the surviving company, or carry out a "stock out" (rather than a "cash out") of the options on the basis of their fair market value. Instead of getting options, the employees get full value shares, based on an "option pricing model" created by economists. (The best known model is called Black-Scholes.) The number of shares equals the full value of the options divided by the stock price.

In a transaction that is accounted as a purchase, there is more flexibility for the treatment of the acquired company's outstanding options. If the acquiring company decides not to do anything about these options, then the terms of the plan under which they were granted determines the treatment. Most plans provide that all outstanding stock options become vested when there is a change in control. If the people who own the options have lost their jobs because of the change in control, they usually get a limited period of time (such as 30–60 days) to exercise the vested options. They will probably lose all unvested options. Furthermore, they will probably get no value for "underwater" options (i.e., options whose exercise price is higher than the actual value of the stock at the time they would wish to exercise the option).

The acquiring company can also buy out the outstanding options, a choice that it might make if it doesn't want to exchange its own shares, or doesn't have shares to exchange, and if it is necessary to compensate employees for the lost future value of their options. Yet another possibility is for the acquiring company to exchange options on its own stock for options on the acquired company's stock. This choice doesn't require spending any cash, allows employees of the acquired corporation to get something for unvested options, and preserves the potential to realize future value.

§ 16.10   CORPORATE CULTURE AND HR'S ROLE IN TRANSITION PLANNING

In economic boom times, there tend to be a lot of corporate transitions, because corporations with high-valued stock can take on aggressive acquisition programs. In bad times, there tend to be a lot of transitions, because that is often the only way a weakened company can survive! In 1998, there were almost 11,500 merger or acquisition transitions, with an aggregate value of more than $1.6 trillion, and in 2000, the aggregate value of mergers was about $1.8 trillion (12.9% higher than the corresponding figure for 1999).

Some business combinations fail for lack of business logic, but in many cases, the problem is irreconcilability of the corporate cultures. [On issues of reconciling corporate cultures, see Bill Leonard, *Will This Marriage Work?*, HR Magazine, April 1999, at p. 35; Robert J. Grossman, *Irreconcilable Differences*, HR Magazine, April 1999, at p. 42] Getting both HR departments involved earlier, and giving them a larger role, could have smoothed the transition. In some cases, analysis by HR can point to potential problems that rule out a transaction.

The corporation's board of directors has a duty of due diligence: Transactions that can affect the corporation's continued existence or that can change its form must be studied thoroughly. A transaction can be recommended only if it is in the best interests of stockholders. It may be legally necessary to consider other constituencies as well, such as employees, retirees, and the community as a whole.

Therefore, it is important to determine if a potential merger partner has committed discrimination, labor-law violations, or wage and hour violations. Even if the potential partner has behaved lawfully in every respect, it may have a more generous pension or benefit structure that will have to be maintained for current employees. If the partner's investment performance is poor, or its actuarial assumptions are defective, then additional funds may be required to prop up its pension plans.

PLAN TERMINATION

§ 17.01   INTRODUCTION

When companies start a pension plan, they usually do so in good faith, and with the intention of keeping the plan in operation as long as it is necessary to provide benefits. However, ERISA and the Internal Revenue Code recognize that sometimes it will be necessary to terminate a pension plan—usually because the sponsoring corporation is ceasing operations, being absorbed by another company, or has financial difficulties so severe that it cannot continue to meet its obligations. There are even some rare circumstances under which the plan is *over*funded, and the employer is able to terminate the plan, distribute its assets, and retain the plan surplus for its own benefit.

Plan termination is usually voluntary, premised on the employer's decision to shut down the plan. However, courts, based on a determination that the economic security of plan participants is at risk, can order involuntary terminations. The legal system provides structures for winding up pension plans in an orderly way. Usually, the plan's assets are applied to purchase annuities that will pay participants' pensions as they become entitled to receive them.

Under the relevant legal and tax rules, a plan termination can be either complete or partial. When a termination occurs, all accrued benefits vest immediately—including benefits that would not vest until later under the plan's normal vesting schedule. This requirement is imposed to reduce the temptation to terminate expensive and inconvenient plans!

Terminating a plan involves both the IRS and the Department of Labor (DOL). Both ERISA and the IRC must be consulted. There are forms to be filed, consents to be secured, and disclosure obligations to the participants and beneficiaries of the plan. Then, the plan's assets are distributed within an "administratively reasonable time" (generally defined as one year or less). But if the process continues for too long, the plan may be treated as if it had not terminated, and reports under I.R.C. §§ 6057-6059 will still be required. Section 6059 applies only to defined benefit plans.

> **Tip:** Under some circumstances, a Reduction in Force (RIF) is deemed to cause a partial termination (for which vesting will be required). Therefore, before implementing an RIF, the company should determine the pension implications of the program.

A federal agency called the Pension Benefit Guaranty Corporation (PBGC) plays an important role in the termination of defined benefit plans. When a plan termination is contemplated, the plan notifies the PBGC, which has 60 days (or longer, if the plan consents to an extension) to review the proposed termination for any improprieties.

The PBGC also has the power to ask the federal court system to close down a pension plan (even if the employer has not sought to terminate the plan) and supervise the orderly distribution of its assets. The PBGC is not involved in the termination of defined contribution plans, because each participant in such a plan has an individual account that can be distributed to him or her.

There are certain exceptions to these general rules. Benefits are not guaranteed if they become nonforfeitable only because of the termination; nor does the agency guarantee benefits in full if the plan was in effect for less than 60 months before it terminated. If a benefit was scheduled to increase under a plan amendment that was either made or took effect within 60 months prior to the termination, the PBGC will not guarantee the increase. The benefits of "substantial owners" (those owning 10% or more of the company's stock) are not guaranteed. In April 2002, the PGBC liberalized its rules, giving participants in terminated plans more alternatives for receiving benefits. [*See* 67 Fed. Reg. 16949 (April 8, 2002). *See* § 17.03[B] below]

§ 17.02   TERMINATION TYPES

[A]   Generally

There are two types of voluntary termination: standard and distress. A standard termination, governed by ERISA § 4041, is used by plans that have at least enough assets to pay the benefits guaranteed by the PBGC. All terminations are handled as standard terminations unless the PBGC permits a "distress termination," which imposes lower obligations on the plan.

Under ERISA § 4044, there are six priority categories of accrued benefits. When the plan's assets are distributed, all Category-1 claims must be paid, then all Category-2 claims, and so on, until the assets are exhausted. Therefore, in many instances some of the classes will go unpaid. The categories, in descending order of priority, are:

- Voluntary employee contributions made to the plan. (NOTE: These amounts are NOT guaranteed by the PBGC, because they fall outside the definition of "basic benefits";
- Mandatory contributions that employees made to the plan, plus 5% interest;
- Annuity benefits that derive from employer contributions, if the annuity was or could have been in pay status three years or more before termination of the plan. ("Could have been" refers to the situation in which employees continue to work despite their eligibility for early retirement);
- All other PBGC-guaranteed benefits;
- All other nonforfeitable benefits;
- All benefits that are accrued but forfeitable.

Before a plan administrator can actually make any distributions, there is a legal obligation to determine the plan's ability to pay benefits at the level deemed appropriate by the PBGC. The plan administrator must notify the PBGC if the plan is unable to pay the guaranteed benefits. The PBGC makes its own determination and issues notices. If, on the other hand, the administrator determines that the

PBGC-guaranteed benefits, but not all the guaranteed liabilities, can be paid, then the plan should distribute the assets but notify the PBGC.

If the PBGC affirms the administrator's characterization, it will issue a Notice of Liability resolving the issue of the plan's sufficiency. The plan administrator is obligated to provide a new valuation of the plan's liabilities and guaranteed benefits. An enrolled actuary must certify the valuation.

Tip: The date of the final distribution can be extended by filing IRS Form 5310 (Application for a Determination Letter), and the PBGC must be notified of this filing. [*See* IRS Announcement 97-81 1997-34 I.R.B. 12]

Hughes Aircraft Co. v. Jacobson [525 U.S. 432 (1999)], which involved several other pension issues, also affects plan termination. This case involves a plan partially funded by mandatory employee contributions. The employer suspended its own contributions at a time when the plan had a surplus. The employer created a new, noncontributory plan for new plan participants. Participants in the existing plan charged the employer with ERISA violations in connection with the amendment.

The Supreme Court's ruling is that the changes in the plan structure did not constitute a voluntary termination under ERISA § 4041(a)(1), and the employees were not entitled to an order terminating the plan voluntarily. The employees asserted a "wasting trust" theory (that the original plan had been wound up because it satisfied all of its objectives), but the Supreme Court refused to accept this theory, deeming it inconsistent with ERISA's detailed provisions for terminating a plan. [*Id.*]

The Supreme Court ruled that neither a standard nor a distress termination is appropriate as long as a plan continues to provide benefits to participants and to accumulate funds to make payments in the future. [*Id.*]

A qualified plan must provide protection for its beneficiaries whenever the plan is merged or consolidated with another plan, or when its liabilities are transferred to another plan. [*See* I.R.C. §§ 401(a)(13), 404(a)(2), and 414(l), and ERISA § 206(d)] Each participant must receive a benefit immediately after a hypothetical merger, consolidation, or transfer of the plan at least as great as the participant would have received if the plan had terminated before the transaction occurred.

[B] Standard Termination

The appropriate PBGC form for carrying out a standard termination is Form 500 (Standard Termination Notice).

Within 120 days after the proposed termination date, the plan administrator must submit a Schedule EA-5 of the Form 500, a certificate prepared by a PBGC-enrolled actuary to the PBGC. The certificate estimates the value of the plan assets and the present value of plan liabilities, so that the actuary can certify that assets are adequate to satisfy the liabilities. The administrator must also furnish any other information the PBGC requests. The plan administrator must certify under penalty of perjury that the actuary's certificate is correct, and that the information given to the PBGC has been accurate and complete.

Once all the assets are distributed, the administrator must file PBGC Form 501 within 30 days of the final distribution, to prove that the assets were distributed. The penalty for a late form can be up to $1,100 a day. [*See* 29 C.F.R. § 4010.13] Late filing can also have the effect of creating a last, short plan year for the plan—thereby reducing the refund of the PBGC premium that the employer would otherwise be entitled to receive.

Also see 63 Fed. Reg. 68676 (Dec. 14, 1998) for a Final Rule applicable to amendments adopted on or after December 12, 1998. It contains an example showing the application of ERISA § 204(h) to some situations of defined benefit plans that cannot be terminated on the proposed termination date because of failure to satisfy all the requirements of ERISA Title IV. If all of the title IV requirements are not satisfied, accruals can still cease as long as the plan adopts an amendment ending accruals as of a particular date.

The ERISA § 204(h) notice of the amendment (including disclosure of its effective date) must be given. Question 16 in the Q&A for the Final Rule explains that an amendment providing for the end of benefit accruals on a specific date is subject to ERISA § 204(h). A plan terminated in accordance with Title IV is deemed to have satisfied ERISA § 204(h) no later than its termination date, so no additional benefits have to accrue after the date of the termination. But if the amendment reducing future accruals is effective earlier than the termination date, then ERISA § 204(h) does apply. [*See* § 5.07 for further discussion of this issue]

[C]   Notification

At least 60 days but not more than 90 days before the proposed date of a voluntary termination, the plan administrator must provide notice of the intended termination. [ERISA § 4041(a)(2)] Notice must be given to plan participants; their beneficiaries; alternate payees under domestic relations orders; and the employees' collective bargaining representative (if the workplace is unionized). The notice must give the date of the termination and must explain that the PBGC guarantee ends as soon as the benefits are distributed. The notice must also disclose the name and address of the insurance company chosen to provide annuities to participants. (If the choice has not yet been made, the names and addresses of possible choices must be disclosed.)

Tip: Selection of the insurer is a fiduciary decision, subject to the normal rules of fiduciary duty. The notice must also identify a contact person who will answer questions about the termination process.

Items to be disclosed include:

- The name of the plan and of its sponsor;
- The plan's tax number;
- The sponsor's Employer Identification Number;
- A statement that service credit and benefits will continue to accrue until the termination, or that benefit accruals have been frozen or will be frozen on a specified date—whichever is applicable;
- A promise to provide written notification of the benefits each affected party will receive under the termination;
- A promise to each retiree that retirement benefits in annuity form will not be affected by the termination;
- Disclosure that standard termination is available if and only if the plan has adequate assets to cover its liabilities to all participants and all beneficiaries of deceased participants;
- A statement that further notice will be given if the termination does not occur as contemplated.

When a distress termination rather than a standard termination is intended, the disclosure requirements [ERISA § 4041(c)] are fundamentally similar. However, parties must be informed whether the plan's assets are sufficient to pay all guaranteed benefits or all benefit liabilities. Notice is also required of the extent to which the PBGC guarantees payment of benefits, and an explanation of any benefit reductions that may be imposed, based on the PBGC's maximum guarantee.

The plan's filing of PBGC Form 500 (Standard Termination Notice) triggers the obligation to issue another notice to participants and beneficiaries, in a comprehensible, nontechnical form. This Notice of Plan Benefits [PBGC Reg. § 4041.23] explains the factors determining benefit entitlement (e.g., age, length of service, wages, interest assumptions), and how payments will be made. It is also necessary to disclose that benefits might be either higher or lower than the estimate.

For benefits already in pay status, disclosure is required of the amount and form of benefits that will be payable. For individuals who have named a retirement date and elected a form for the payout, but whose benefits are not yet in pay status, the projected benefit start date must be announced, with disclosure of the form and amount of benefits payable as of that date, and the date for any scheduled increase or reduction in benefits. If the benefit start date is not known for benefits not in pay status, disclosure is required of the benefits available at normal retirement age or after the death of a participant, with special attention to any benefits that can be paid as lump sums.

Another notice is required when underfunding is very significant: e.g., $50 million or more in the plan year before the year of the notice. Notice is also required if a lien could be imposed on plan assets, or the IRS granted a minimum funding waiver covering more than $1 million. The notice informs plan participants about the financial status of the plan, its sponsor, and the sponsor's controlled group of corporations. [*See* PBGC Reg. § 4010] The information must be provided within 105 days of the end of the corporation's information year.

ERISA § 4011 calls for notification of funding status when plans fail to meet their full funding limitation, and their PBGC premium is increased to compensate for the underfunding. The PBGC Regulations include a model notice. Participants and beneficiaries must be warned of the underfunding and of the limitations on the PBGC's obligation to insure benefits. This notice is due two months after the deadline for filing the annual report for the year in which the plan was underfunded.

Information about plan termination must also be provided in the Summary Plan Description (SPD) furnished to plan participants. The Pension and Welfare Benefits Administration (PWBA) Final Rule about SPDs [65 Fed. Reg. 70226-70244 (Nov. 21, 2000)] requires disclosure of:

- A summary of the plan's provisions authorizing the sponsor, or other party, to terminate the plan or eliminate some or all of its benefits;
- Circumstances that might trigger termination or elimination of some benefits;
- The benefits, rights, and obligations of plan participants and beneficiaries if and when the plan is terminated. In pension plan SPDs, the accrual and vesting consequences of plan termination must be disclosed. (This is not an issue in welfare plan SPDs, because such benefits do not vest);
- How the plan assets will be disposed of on termination.

[D] Distress Termination

A plan that does not have enough assets to pay all the benefit liabilities can apply to the PBGC for a "distress" termination, which is available only if the plan's sponsors (and the other corporations that are part of a controlled group of corporations with the sponsor) can prove financial hardship, e.g., involvement in voluntary or involuntary bankruptcy or insolvency proceedings. If a company makes a Chapter 11 filing, seeking bankruptcy reorganization, a distress termination will be permitted only if the bankruptcy court decides that terminating the plan is necessary, or that the company cannot remain in business and pay its debts if it maintains the plan.

Distress termination might also be permitted if the sponsor proves to the PBGC that terminating the plan is essential to paying its debts and remaining in operation. A distress termination might also be available if pension costs have become intolerable only because of the decline in the covered workforce—loss of stock market value of the plans' assets would not be considered an acceptable rationale.

To request a distress termination, the plan must file PBGC Form 601, not more than 120 days after the proposed distress termination date. The duty to notify participants is more or less the same for standard and distress terminations.

A distress termination calls for actuarial certification, using Schedule EA-D of the Form 601.

If the plan has enough assets to pay the guaranteed benefits, the PBGC issues a "distribution notice." Within 15 days of receiving this notice, the plan administrator must give each participant and beneficiary a notice of impending distribution. Unless an extension has been granted, the distribution must begin within 60 days and be completed within 240 days. Then PBGC Form 602 (Post-Distribution Certification) must be filed within 30 days of the completion of distribution of the assets.

As soon as possible after receiving an application for a distress termination, the PBGC is supposed to rule on the application. If the agency turns down the application and the plan has enough assets to satisfy its liabilities, a standard termination is carried out. But if the assets are inadequate and the PBGC is not cooperative, the plan cannot go through a voluntary termination at all.

[E] Partial Termination

Full vesting is required when a plan is terminated or partially terminated, but there is no simple definition of "partial termination." The IRS says that partial termination occurs when there is a substantial reduction in the number or percentage of plan participants. Partial termination is presumed not to occur at 20%, presumed to exist at 50% reduction. In between, the facts and circumstances of the case are determinative.

The problem is that RIFs usually target higher-paid, long-tenure employees, so the question of whom to count is very important. For example, if there are 100 participants in a plan, 60 of whom are fully vested and the rest unvested or partially vested, and 50 people are RIFed (40 fully, 10 partially vested) then there has been a 50% reduction and a partial termination if you count all participants, but only 10 out of 40 partially vested employees have been RIFed. [*See* Nixon Peabody, LLP Benefits Briefs Vol. 14, No. 5 (December 2001) <http://www.nixonpeabody.com>]

The Seventh Circuit rule is that events from more than one plan year can be used to determine if a partial termination has occurred, when an employee alleges that his balances should vest fully because of the termination. [*Matz v. Household Int'l Tax Reduction Investment Plan*, 227 F.3d 971 (7th Cir. 2000). *See also Sea Ray v. Robinson*, 164 F.3d 981 (6th Cir. 1999)] The Sixth Circuit's rationale in this situation is that, if review was limited to a single year, employers would be able to escape liability by firing some employees in December, some in January. [*Sea Ray*, 164 F.3d 981]

On a related issue, the *Matz* court required counting of both vested and nonvested participants to determine whether a partial termination occurred. However, the Supreme Court ordered the court to reconsider its opinion because of *United States v. Mead Corp.* [53 U.S. 218 (2001)], a Supreme Court case about the extent to which courts have to abide by the rules of administrative agencies. This time, the Seventh Circuit decided that only nonvested participants should be counted in deciding if there has been a partial termination. [*Matz v. Household Int'l Tax Reduction Investment Plan*, 265 F.3d 572 (7th Cir. 2001)] This ruling makes it less likely that a partial termination will be found, especially in close cases where the percentage of terminated participants is close to the 20% threshold.

§ 17.03   THE PBGC'S ROLE

[A] PBGC Guarantee

Defined benefit plans pay premiums to the PBGC annually, providing funds for the federal agency to supervise plan terminations and, if necessary, assume payment of a terminating or terminated plan's obligations to its participants. For information about PBGC operations and the availability of benefits after a plan termination, *see* the Pension Insurance Data Book 2000 (Aug. 21, 2001). Single copies can be ordered from PBGC Data Book, Suite 240 1200 K Street NW Washington, D.C. 20005-4026, or by fax at (202) 326-4042.

The PBGC guarantee is intended to protect the employers of the plan, not the sponsor corporation. If the assets of a terminating plan are not large enough to pay the benefits, the PBGC makes the payments and then seeks recoupment from the corporation. However, an employer's liability to the PBGC is capped at 70% of its net worth, or 75% of the unfunded guaranteed benefits.

In the case of a single-employer plan, the PBGC guarantees payment of all nonforfeitable benefits. However, the PBGC guarantee is subject to a maximum limitation, with the result that some participants will not receive the full benefit they would have received had the plan not terminated. For plans terminating in 2000, the monthly maximum guarantee is $3,221.59/month ($38,659.08/year); for terminations in 2001, the monthly maximum guarantee is $3,392.05 per month ($40,704.60/year), and for terminations in 2002, it is $3,579.55/month, or $42,954.60 a year. [*See* <http://www.pbgc.gov/news/press_releases/2001>]

The PBGC guarantees "basic benefits." (The PBGC has legal authority to set up a separate trust fund to guarantee nonbasic benefits, but it has chosen not to do so.) The basic benefit guaranteed by the PBGC is a monthly life annuity that lasts for the participant's life. (This is in contrast to the joint and survivor annuity that is the normal payment form for a married participant to receive under an ongoing plan.) The annuity begins at age 65. The annuity is equal to either $750 a month (adjusted for increases in the FICA wage base) or the employee's average monthly gross income for the five consecutive years with the highest income, whichever is less.

When a plan is to be terminated, the PBGC:

- Determines if the benefit is nonforfeitable and payable in periodic install-ments; if so, it is a guaranteed basic benefit;

- Performs actuarial calculations to convert benefits in other forms to straight life annuities commencing at age 65.

The PBGC has the power to assess penalties if an employer was late in paying its PBGC premiums, or if the employer failed to provide the required notices to employees.

[B] Proposal on Payment Forms

PBGC No. 02-14 (Dec. 22, 2000) [65 Fed. Reg. 81456 (Dec. 26, 2000)] announces proposed regulatory changes for payments to participants when the PBGC takes over a plan. Under the proposal, participants would be allowed to select alternative annuity benefit forms. (The spouses of married participants would have to consent.) Nonspouse beneficiaries could be named. The proposal distinguishes between separation from service and retirement, and determines who will inherit benefits that are payable to a deceased participant. The proposal also simplifies the application of the maximum guaranteed benefit rules if the same individual is entitled to benefits both as a plan participant and as a survivor of another participant (e.g., a deceased spouse who was a co-worker).

Under the proposal, the PBGC would make benefits available as straight life annuities and annuities for five, ten, or fifteen years certain and continuous. The proposal also includes joint and 50, 75 or 100% survivor annuities and joint and 50% survivor "pop-up" annuities. (in a pop-up annuity, the participant's benefit increases to the unreduced level if the beneficiary dies before the participant). Joint life annuities would only be available to two natural persons—not a person plus a trust or a charity.

The PBGC's intention is to make all of these payment forms available on termination of a plan, even if the plan did not offer all of them while it was in operation. The proposal gives the PBGC the power to promulgate further regulations that add additional forms of benefit payment, although it does not plan to do so for particular plans, only overall.

The proposal defines the Earliest PBGC Retirement Date (EPRD)—a concept that is needed because some plans allow participants to receive a lump sum well before normal retirement age. The EPRD is the earliest retirement date allowed by ERISA Title IV—i.e., the earliest date to receive an immediate annuity, or to receive a lump sum if the plan permits this. The EPRD is either the earliest annuity date or, for dates before age 55, either 55 or the time when the participant could retire, given consideration of all facts and circumstances.

The proposal calls for the PBGC to adjust the survivor's benefit under a joint and survivor annuity if the agency determines that there was an underpayment or overpayment as of the time of the first spouse's death.

Under current law, the PBGC sets an aggregate limit on the amount of benefits it will guarantee in three situations:

- Benefits payable to the same person under multiple plans;

- Benefits payable to the same person relative to two or more participants;
- Benefits with respect to a participant who has more than one beneficiary.

Under the proposal, the PBGC will waive the limit with respect to a person who is dually entitled to benefits as both worker and survivor, but aggregation will continue for multiple beneficiaries, who will have to divide the benefit.

The PBGC finalized these proposals more or less intact in April 2002: 67 Fed. Reg. 16949 (April 18, 2002). Some changes were made in the definition of "earliest PBGC Retirement Date." The Final Rule defines this as the earliest date the plan participant could retire for the purposes of ERISA Title IV. Usually, this will mean either age 55 or the first date the participant could retire and collect an immediate annuity, whichever is later.

[C]   Penalties and PBGC Enforcement

Revenue Procedure 2000-17, 2000-11 I.R.B. 766 explains how a plan can get a waiver of the IRC § 4971(b) 100% tax that is imposed when accumulated funding deficiencies under I.R.C. § 412 remain even after the 10% tax has been imposed. The Secretary of the Treasury can waive the 100% tax for certain terminated single-employer plans, even if the accumulated funding deficiency has not been reduced to zero.

A PBGC Proposed Rule, R.I.N. 1212-AA95 [66 Fed. Reg. 2857, also available at <http://www.benefitslink.com/pbgcregs/4071-proposed-2001.shtml>] centralizes all the PBGC rules about penalties as 29 C.F.R. Parts 4003, 4007, and 4071. Under the proposal, the PBGC agrees to waive all or part of a late payment penalty if the employer had reasonable cause for lateness. The PBGC also has discretion to waive the penalty even if the employer is unable to make the "reasonable cause" showing.

In general, the PBGC debt collection rules found at 29 C.F.R. Part 4903 allow the agency to collect penalties by diverting tax refunds or other amounts the federal government would otherwise owe the employer. But under the proposal, this collection technique will not be applied if there is a safe harbor or other law or regulation that allows a waiver; if the employer had a reasonable cause for not making the payment or for making only a partial payment; if the employer's failure to pay was based on an incorrect interpretation of the law; or if collection would violate the purposes of ERISA.

Section 32 of the proposal defines reasonable cause as circumstances beyond the employer's control, which the employer could not have avoided by exercising ordinary care and prudence. Section 34 goes into more detail: Reasonable cause includes the absence of the person who was supposed to make the payment; fire or other casualty; or reasonable reliance on incorrect evidence given by the PBGC (either orally or in writing).

But the larger the size of the organization and its staff, the higher the standard of care it will be expected to satisfy. Of course, the larger the amount of premium that the government seeks to collect, the greater the enforcement effort that will be expended.

[D]   QDROs in Plans Under PBGC Control

Qualified Domestic Relations Orders (QDROs) are discussed in detail at § 12.08 If the PBGC takes over a plan some of whose benefits must be paid to alternate payees (ex-spouses and separated spouses of participants), it issues two standard QDRO forms (Model Separate Interest; Model Shared Payment) for use by domestic relations courts. PBGC QDROs either specify or give the alternate payee discretion to control the time at which benefits begin, how the benefits are paid, the percentage of the pension payment going to the alternate payee, and how long the alternate payments begin.

QDROs cannot require the PBGC to provide any benefit type or option that would not otherwise be available under the plan or that would not otherwise be offered by the PBGC. Nor can the court order increase the amount that the PBGC would have to pay relative to the employee spouse's pension account.

The PBGC's Model Separate Interest form can be used only if the order is entered before the employee's pension is in pay status. It is appropriate when the alternate payee's benefits are fixed and do not depend on when the participant starts to get benefits or the form in which the participant receives them. The effect of this form is to divide the pension account under the PBGC's control into two parts: one for the participant, one for the non-employee alternate beneficiary. The Shared Payment form, in contrast, operates at the level of each individual payment. As each payment comes due, it is divided between the employee and the alternate beneficiary. The alternate beneficiary will not receive benefits after the employee's death unless the order specifically provides for survivor benefits.

§ 17.04   INVOLUNTARY TERMINATION

[A]   Basic Procedure

ERISA § 4042 governs involuntary termination proceedings brought when the plan assets are less than the total of guaranteed benefits. The PBGC asks the appropriate federal district court to oust the plan administrator and appoint a trustee to wind up the plan. ERISA § 4062(b)(1) makes the employer liable to the PBGC for the total amount of unfounded plan liabilities on the termination date, plus interest starting on the termination date.

The PBGC is empowered to ask for involuntary termination if:

- The plan has failed to meet its minimum funding standards;
- The plan cannot pay benefits when due;
- The plan has been required to report one or more distributions to a "substantial owner" (10% shareholder);
- The fund's liabilities will increase unreasonably if the plan is not terminated.

In those situations, it is a judgment call: The PBGC decides whether or not to seek involuntary termination. If the situation is even worse (the plan does not even have enough assets to pay its current benefits, much less to keep paying benefits as they come due; the plan has applied for a distress termination but lacks money to fund the guaranteed benefits), the PBGC has an obligation to seek involuntary termination.

> **Tip:** Although the bankruptcy "automatic stay" prevents most forms of litigation against anyone who has applied for bankruptcy protection, the PBGC has the power to apply for involuntary termination even if a bankruptcy case is pending. In fact, the bankruptcy case might be delayed to straighten out the pension situation.

[B]   The Role of the Trustee

If the district court appoints a trustee, the plan must be terminated. The PBGC can also force termination of a plan even without such an appointment. If a trustee is appointed, his or her duty is to keep the plan administrator, participants, beneficiaries, unions, and employers with potential ERISA liability informed about the progress of the termination. The trustee has the power to demand turnover of some or all of the plan's records and assets. The trustee has a choice of either continuing the pattern of benefit payments in place before the trustee's appointment, or limiting payment of benefits to the basic benefits.

Under ERISA § 4062(d), the employer is liable for the unpaid contributions to the trustee plan. The employer must provide the trustee with cash, or securities acceptable to the trustee, in an amount equal to:

- The accumulated funding deficiencies under I.R.C. § 412(a);
- Any funding deficiencies that the IRS waived under I.R.C. § 412(c) before the termination date;
- All decreases in the minimum funding standard permitted by I.R.C. § 412(e) before the termination date, plus interest running from the termination date.

Under certain circumstances outlined in ERISA § 4069(b), a successor corporation can become liable for such amounts, if the sponsor reorganizes; the purpose of the reorganization was to evade liability; and reorganization occurred within the five years before a plan termination that would have caused liability. In this context, reorganization means a merger, consolidation, or becoming a division of another company; changing identity, form, or place or organization; or the liquidation of a subsidiary into its parent.

Also note that ERISA § 4062(b) provides that when an employer ceases operations at a facility, leading to separation from service of 20% or more of the total number of plan participants, the employer either has to fund the guaranteed benefits immediately, or make provision for their funding.

[C]   Calculations for Involuntary or Distress Terminations

Under 29 C.F.R. Part 4044 (Appendix D, Table I-02), benefits under a plan going through an involuntary or distress termination are calculated based on a determination of the likelihood (low/medium/high) that the participant will retire early in various years. Then, once early retirement benefits are computed, the total value of benefits under the plan can be computed. The process uses the Unreduced Retirement Age, which is either the normal retirement age or the earliest age at which a pension can be paid without actuarial reduction—whichever is earlier.

These figures, which are updated by the PBGC each year, come from 66 Fed. Reg. 59,694 (Nov. 30, 2001):

Year of Retirement	Low	Medium	High
2003	<458	458–1936	>1936
2004	<471	471–1988	>1988
2005	<483	483–2042	>2042
2006	<497	497–2097	>2097
2007	<510	510–2154	>2154
2008	<524	524–2212	>2212
2009	<538	538–2272	>2272
2010	<552	552–2333	>2333
2011	<567	567–2396	>2396
2012, later	<583	583–2461	>2461

§ 17.05   PLAN REVERSIONS

Before ERISA, it was legal for an employer to simply wind up a plan and take back its assets. But under current law, a plan provision that calls for reversion (or increased reversion) cannot become effective until the end of the fifth calendar year following the year of adoption. In other words, employers have to wait at least five years to take advantage of a reversion opportunity. Furthermore, if the plan called for mandatory contributions, once the benefits are paid off, assets must be allocated to mandatory contributions before the reversion occurs.

An employer that is entitled to a reversion must pay 50% of the reversion amount as an excise tax. However, if the employer establishes a qualified replacement plan or amends the terminating plan to increase benefits, the excise tax is reduced to 20%. IRS Form 5330 is used to pay the excise tax. It is due the last day of the month after the month in which the reversion occurred.

The defined benefit plan involved in *Shepley v. New Coleman Holdings Inc.* [174 F.3d 65 (2d Cir. 1999)] was 100% employer-funded; no employee contributions were accepted. The employer terminated the plan and satisfied all of its liabilities, and $14 million remained. Participants sued under ERISA § 1344(d) (1)(C) to prevent the money from reverting to the employer. They were successful at the district court level. However, the Second Circuit ruled in favor of the employer, because the plan documents authorized reversion of any funds remaining post-termination.

§ 17.06 EFFECT ON BENEFITS

[A] Forfeit of Benefits

Benefits become nonforfeitable when a plan terminates or partially terminates. A defined contribution plan's benefits become nonforfeitable if and when the employer completely ceases its contributions to the plan. If a defined benefit plan terminates within 10 years of its creation, I.R.C. § 411(d)(2) imposes limits on the benefits that can be paid to the 25 highest-compensated individuals covered by the plan. This rule prevails even if it results in the loss of some accrued benefits.

[B] The Anticutback Rule

Whether deliberately or inadvertently, employers sometimes make cutbacks in a plan, or scale it down. The effect can be inadvertent if the employer lacks the money to make a required deposit, or simply is ignorant of what the legal requirements are. The consequences are not always those intended by the employer. The worst-case scenario is that the plan will be treated as partially terminated, and then retroactively disqualified, obligating the employer to pay back taxes for prior plan years. Retroactive disqualification also harms employees, who are likely to owe back taxes. Furthermore, distributions from a disqualified plan cannot be rolled over to a qualified plan.

A plan is frozen if it is amended to keep the plan trust in existence, but without further contributions or accrual of benefits. A frozen plan is still subject to the top-heavy plan rules, and still has to provide QJSAs and QPSAs on the same terms as if it had not been frozen.

Most plans are subject to I.R.C. § 412, so whenever a plan is partially terminated as defined by I.R.C. § 411(d)(3)(A), immediate 100% vesting is required. Full vesting for employees makes it more likely that the plan will discriminate in favor of HCEs or will yield reversions to the employer. That's because employees in a frozen plan are often given the choice of withdrawing their accrued benefits immediately, or keeping them within the plan until the normal time for distribution. But if too many rank-and-file employees choose withdrawal, the unintended result could be that the plan becomes discriminatory because too high a proportion of HCEs keep their benefits within the plan.

A plan is usually deemed partially terminated if more than 20% of the plan's participants lose their jobs. A "vertical partial termination" occurs when a group of employees lose coverage under the plan. A "horizontal partial termination" occurs when the potential for reversion of plan assets to the employer increases unduly.

If it is uncertain whether there has been a partial termination, Form 5300 can be filed to request an IRS determination letter. If the IRS rules that there has been a partial termination, the event must be reported to the PBGC (as must a 20% cut in the workforce, or a plan amendment that reduces the accrual of benefits by 50% or more for 50% or more of the workforce).

§ 17.07 REPORTING AND COMPLIANCE

When a plan is terminated, IRS Form 5310 is used to request an IRS determination letter stating that the associated plan trust did not become disqualified or lose its exempt status. Form 6088 must be filed in conjunction with this form, listing up to 25 owners or 5% shareholders of the employer corporation who received any distribution from the plan during the preceding five years.

The general rule is that Form 5310-A must be filed 30 days or more before a transfer of plan assets to another qualified retirement plan because of a merger, consolidation, or change in ownership of assets or liabilities. When two defined contribution plans merge or a defined contribution plan is spun off, or a defined benefit plan engages in a merger or spinoff that has only minimal effects, the Form 5310-A filing is not required.

In the somewhat unlikely case that the trust of a terminating plan has more assets than are needed to pay all the plan benefits, and therefore the employer recovers those excess assets, Form 5319 must be filed by the last day of the month after the month in which the employer recouped the assets. This is also the form the employer uses to pay the excise tax on the recouped funds.

The Form 5500-series annual report must be filed for the year of the merger, consolidation, division, or termination. If a trust is frozen (the plan maintains its assets, although benefit accruals have stopped), the 5500-series filing is required in every year until all the assets have been distributed.

§ 17.08 PAYMENT OF EXPENSES

It is appropriate for fiduciaries to use plan assets to pay the expenses of an ongoing plan. However, the decision to terminate a plan is a business decision made by the plan's settlor, and not a fiduciary decision. That means that some of the termination expenses relate to settlor functions—and it violates ERISA to use plan assets to pay settlor expenses. Therefore, allocation is necessary. DOL's ERISA Opinion Letter No. 97-032A (February, 1997) recommends that the allocation be made by an independent fiduciary.

These expenses are considered fiduciary expenses that can properly be paid out of plan assets:

- Getting an audit;
- Preparing and filing the final annual report;
- Amending the plan to carry out the termination;
- Calculating benefits;
- Preparing benefit statements;
- Notifying participants and beneficiaries about their rights incident to termination.

However, the cost of maintaining the plan's tax-qualified status—including the cost of getting determination letters—is a settlor expense.

Part IV

BENEFIT PLANS

CHAPTER 18

EMPLOYEE GROUP HEALTH PLANS (EGHPs)

§18.01 INTRODUCTION

What started out as a modest Depression-era plan to make sure that doctors got paid for their services (and not in chickens or home-made preserves, either) has had immense implications for the American workplace and the economy as a whole.

The first health insurance plan was originated at the behest of doctors. During World War II, workers were very hard to find (because of military and defense-plant needs), and the federal government froze wages but not benefits. Therefore, offering health insurance was one of the few ways in which employers could compete to offer incentives to recruit workers. After the war ended, unions had a powerful role in an industrialized economy, and negotiations for health plans were an important part of negotiations for each new Collective Bargaining Agreement.

For many years, health care costs, and therefore insurance costs, rose much faster than inflation, until employers faced a heavy burden. In the 1970s and 1980s, there was a vast shift from indemnity insurance [*see* § 18.12] to some form of managed care. The promise of managed care was that eliminating waste and keeping employees healthier would reduce costs.

However, by the end of the twentieth century, managed care was a problem in and of itself. Insurers began to charge the kind of double-digit annual premium increases that caused so much pain in the 1970s. Many patients were dissatisfied with managed care, charging that they were often denied access to necessary care. Doctors were dissatisfied, with the restrictions on their freedom to prescribe, with the amount of paperwork they had to do, and with both the size and speed of their reimbursement from managed care organizations (MCOs).

Just as there has been a transition from defined-benefit to defined-contribution or employee-funded retirement plans, health plans have shifted from the once-predominant indemnity plan to a heavy dominance of some form of managed care. Some employers have always chosen to self-insure rather than purchase insurance; others have switched to self-insurance to cut costs. A new form that is emerging is the so-called defined contribution or consumer-oriented health care plan.

One of the most important differences between ERISA's pension plan provisions and its welfare benefit plan provisions is that, by and large, welfare benefits do not vest, and can be altered or terminated if the plan document retains the sponsor's discretion to do so. However, in some situations, the employer will be deemed to have a contractual obligation to maintain the plan. In a unionized company, the CBA will impose further limitations on the employer's ability to alter the health plans it maintains. [For the requirements for Summary Plan Descriptions (SPDs) for health plans, *see* § 11.02[B]]

§18.02 THE HEALTH CARE LANDSCAPE

Although initially the employer group health plan market was divided only between self-insured and indemnity insurance plans, today managed care is dominant. There are many types of managed care plans. At one time the Health Management Organization (HMO) was the dominant managed care form, but today its predominance is yielding to plans that provide somewhat more flexibility and provider choice for patients.

Although questions of how states and the federal government can regulate managed care are very important in our legal system, these fast-moving issues are by and large outside the scope of this book.

> **Tip:** Two Web sites that contain excellent current information about state regulation of managed care plans are Families U.S.A. <http://www.familiesusa.org> and the Kaiser Family Foundation <http://www.kff.org>. Many states require managed care organizations to maintain review processes so neutral outsiders who do not have a financial interest in restricting the plan's costs can review claims denials. State laws also deal with issues such as access to emergency care, access to specialists, and limits on financial incentives given to doctors to induce them to reduce the number of treatments.

A Department of Labor Information Letter says that it may be a breach of fiduciary duty for the trustees of a health plan to choose health care providers merely on the basis of cost, without considering quality. Measures of quality include how many doctors the plan has; their qualifications; access to doctors; the provider's past records; accreditation and third-party ratings of the plan, its providers, and its facilities; and consumer satisfaction. Therefore, to satisfy their fiduciary duty, health plan trustees must examine a managed care organization's track record, not automatically select the low bidder. [The DOL letter is discussed in the RIA Compensation and Benefits Update, March 25, 1998, at p. 3]

§ 18.03   BENEFITS MANDATES

[A]   Generally

Although as a general rule, employers have complete discretion to determine which benefits will be included in the plan, and the ratio between benefits, there are certain legislative mandates that temper this discretion.

The regulations call for penalties of up to $100 per day per person affected by noncompliance if states fail to enact, or enact but fail to enforce, consumer health statutes such as the ones discussed in this section. [*See* 45 C.F.R. Part 150, Interim Final Regulations issued by the agency then known as HCFA (now it is called CMS, for The Centers for Medicare and Medicaid Services) on August 20, 1999; 64 Fed. Reg. 45786] For a database about state laws on mandated health benefits, sorted by state and type of benefit, *see* <http://www.insure.com/health/lawtool.cfm>.

[B] Maternity Stays

The Newborns' and Mothers' Health Protection Act of 1996 (NMHPA) [Pub. L. No. 104-204] and the Taxpayer Relief Act of 1997 [Pub. L. No. 105-35] combine ERISA and tax code provisions to mandate that group health plans (both insured and self-insured, whatever the number of participants) provide at least a minimum hospital stay for childbirth. The minimum is 48 hours after a vaginal delivery, 96 hours after a Caesarian section.

Mother and child can be discharged earlier if, after consulting the mother, the mother's attending physician allows it. However, the plan is not allowed to offer financial incentives to the physician or the mother to shorten the stay. If the plan does not provide hospitalization benefits for childbirth, it is not required to add those benefits because of this legislation. The NMHPA does not preempt state laws that require an even longer maternity stay.

Rules to implement the NMHPA were jointly issued by the IRS, Pension and Welfare Benefit Administration, and Health Care Financing Administration (now renamed Centers for Medicare and Medicaid Services). [*See* 63 Fed. Reg. 57,545 and 57,565 (both published on October 27, 1998), adopted as Labor Reg. § 2590.711]

Under the interim rules, when a baby is delivered in the hospital, the stay begins at the time of the delivery (or the last delivery, in a multiple birth). If the mother is admitted to the hospital after giving birth elsewhere, the stay begins at the time of admission. These rules forbid health plans to penalize health care providers for complying with the NMHPA. It is permissible to offer post-discharge follow-up after an early discharge, as long as the services offered do not exceed those that would be provided during the 48- or 96-hour stay required by the NMHPA.

Violation of the NMHPA is subject to the I.R.C. § 4980D penalty of $100 per participant per day, starting when the failure occurs and running until it is corrected. No penalty will be imposed if the failure to provide an adequate postpartum stay was unintentional, and is corrected within 30 days. If the failure is unintentional but is not corrected, the maximum penalty is $500,000 a year, or 10% of the EGHP's expenses for the year before the failure—whichever is less.

[C] Women's Health and Cancer Rights Act (WHCRA)

The Women's Health and Cancer Rights Act (WHCRA) [Pub. L. No. 105-277], became law on October 21, 1998, effective for plan years beginning on or after that date. The Act provides that if an EGHP covers mastectomies, it must also cover reconstructive breast surgery if the patient wants it and her attending physician prescribes it. This includes reconstruction of the mastectomized breast; surgery on the other breast to balance the patient's appearance; prostheses; and treatment of physical complications of mastectomy. Deductibles and co-insurance for reconstructive surgery must be comparable to those imposed on other procedures.

EGHPs (and the insurers and HMOs that provide the medical and surgical benefits) have an ongoing obligation to notify new plan participants of their WHCRA rights, and to renew the notice annually. (It is not necessary for both the EGHP and insurer or HMO to furnish the notice, as long as one of them does.) The notice must satisfy the DOL requirements for Summary Plan Descriptions. [*See* 29 C.F.R. § 2520.104b-1] The annual notice doesn't have to be given in the first year of enrollment, because it would only duplicate the initial enrollment notice.

Annual notices must be delivered by a method that is reasonably likely to get the information to the plan participant: e.g., first-class mail or e-mail. The notice can be included with an SPD, Summary of Material Modification, or Summary Annual Report; with a benefits newsletter or union newsletter; open enrollment information for the plan; or other written plan communication.

The DOL has furnished this model notice that will satisfy the compliance burden: "Did you know that your plan, as required by the WHCRA, provides benefits for mastectomy-related services including reconstruction and surgery to achieve symmetry between the breasts, prostheses, and complications of mastectomy (including lymph edema)? Call your Plan Administrator [insert phone number] for more information." [<http://www.dol.gov/pwba/pubs>]

After a double mastectomy, the plaintiff had problems with the implants and tissue expanders used in reconstructive surgery. Her insurer approved a new implant at a university hospital, but refused a request to have the surgery performed at a hospital closer to her home. She brought suit under the WHCRA and also asserted state-law claims. The state-law claims were dismissed (as preempted by ERISA). The WHCRA claim was dismissed because she brought suit directly under this suit; the court held that the WHCRA does not have any separate enforcement mechanisms apart from ordinary ERISA enforcement. [*Howard v. Coventry Health Care of Iowa, Inc.*, 158 F. Supp. 2d 937 (S.D. Iowa 2001)]

[D] Contraceptives

A December 14, 2000, EEOC decision [available at <http://www.eeoc.gov/docs/decision-contraception.html>] agrees with the charging parties, a group of female employees, that it violates Title VII for a plan to fail to cover prescription contraceptive drugs and devices when it covers other types of preventive medical care, and when it covers vasectomy and tubal ligation (permanent surgical methods of contraception). The EEOC treats the distinction as discrimination on the basis of sex (in that only women use birth control pills, diaphragms, and IUDs) and pregnancy.

The EEOC's rationale is that the Pregnancy Discrimination Amendment (PDA) [42 U.S.C. § 2000e(k). *See* § 34.06] forbids discrimination on the basis of potential as well as actual pregnancy. Employers can lawfully exclude coverage of abortion, but not of contraception. In this case, the employer said that contraception was not covered because only abnormal health conditions were covered—but the plan covered sterilization of healthy persons based on their desire not to procreate in the future.

The EEOC also noted that plans frequently cover vaccination and preventing examinations, which, like contraception, prevent healthy employees from developing unwanted health conditions. The EEOC required the plan to cover the full range of available prescription contraceptives, because a woman employee's needs might change in the course of employment.

In June 2001, the Western District of Washington granted summary judgment for the plaintiff in the first federal case after the EEOC ruling. In other words, the employer had an obligation to cover contraceptives under the EGHP. [*Erickson v. Bartell Drug,* No. C00-1213L (W.D. Wash. June 12, 2001). *See* Erin Van Bronkhorst, *Federal Judge Rules Employer Must Include Contraceptives in Health Insurance Plan*, Associated Press (June 13, 2001) (law.com)]

[E] Mental Health Parity

A very controversial 1996 federal statute, the Veterans' Affairs, Housing and Urban Development and Independent Agencies Appropriations Act [Pub. L. No. 104-204] imposed a requirement of parity in EGHPs with more than 50 participants. Under the parity provision, plans that did not impose lifetime or annual limits on medical and surgical benefits could not do so on mental health benefits. Most plans do impose limits—so the limits would have to be the same for mental and physical ailments. In 1996, this requirement was made part of ERISA.

The 1997 budget bill made the requirement part of the Internal Revenue Code, for services furnished between January 1, 1998, and September 30, 2001. [*See* I.R.C. § 9812] The IRS, DOL, and Department of Health and Human Services jointly published extensive interim regulations. [62 Fed. Reg. 66931 (Dec. 22, 1997)] The three agencies announced early in 2002 that they would draft further guidance.

The Mental Health Parity Act was permitted to expire in 2001. One of President Clinton's last acts before leaving office was an Executive Order requiring phasing in of mental health parity in federal employment no later than January 1, 2001. This is significant because of the large size of the federal workforce.

However, the parity requirement was restored by the 2002 Appropriations Act [Pub. L. No. 107-116 (Jan. 10, 2002)] for various federal departments including DOL and HHS, reinstating the parity requirement up through December 31, 2002. The Job Creation and Worker Assistance Act of 2002 [Pub. L. No. 107-147] extends the parity requirement for an additional year, up through December 31, 2003. However, the JCWAA makes it clear that employers will not be penalized for noncompliance with the parity requirement if the noncompliance occurred between the September 30, 2001, expiration date and January 10, 2002, when the parity requirement was reinstated.

As of 2000, 22 states imposed their own mental health parity requirements (although some of the statutes cover only specific biologically-based mental illnesses such as schizophrenia): Arkansas, California, Colorado, Connecticut, Delaware, Indiana, Maine, Maryland, Massachusetts, Minnesota, Montana, New Hampshire, New Jersey, New Mexico, North Carolina, Oklahoma, Rhode Island, South Carolina, South Dakota, Texas, Vermont, and Virginia. [*HR Update*, HR Magazine, Feb. 2002, at p. 27]

[F]   Other Inclusion Issues

The Supreme Court affirmed, without opinion, the Seventh Circuit's decision in *Doe v. Mutual of Omaha.* [179 F.3d 557 (7th Cir. 1999)] The Seventh Circuit ruled that it is not a violation of Title II of the Americans With Disabilities Act for either an insured or a self-insured health plan to impose a lower lifetime cap on AIDS-related conditions than on other conditions (e.g., $25,000 versus $1 million). The rationale is that Mutual of Omaha didn't refuse to sell policies to people with AIDS, although the policy was worth far less to a person with AIDS or an AIDS-related condition than someone with other health problems.

EGHPs are forbidden to discriminate against employees or their dependents who suffer from end-stage renal disease (ESRD). Internal Revenue Code § 5000 imposes a heavy penalty: 25% of the employer's health care expenses (not just the amount that would have been paid for ESRD coverage in the absence of discrimination). Also note that ERISA § 609(d) requires plans to maintain their coverage of pediatric vaccines at least at the May 1, 1993, level.

§ 18.04   DENTAL PLANS

Many medium-sized and large companies offer some form of dental coverage. As with most health-related benefits, the prevalence of the benefit increases directly with the size of the company. In 1997, 93% of companies in a William M. Mercer survey offered dental plans, although 37% made it an optional rather than a standard benefit. Eighty-six percent provided dental coverage on a fee-for-service benefit; 29% combined fee-for-service and managed care features within the plan. [Nancy Hatch Woodward, *Less Painful Dental Plans*, HR Magazine, Sept. 1999 at p. 92]

Most dental plans offer fee for service coverage, although some plans use HMOs or PPOs. An emerging new form, endorsed by the American Dental Association in 1996, is the direct reimbursement plan: a fee-for-service plan where employees choose their own dentists. The plan sets a limit; up to the limit, the employee is entitled to payment of a percentage of dental expenses, e.g., full coverage of the first $100 in expenses, 50% reimbursement of the next $1,800, phasing out at a plan limit of $1,000 in benefits. [*Id.*]

Dental plans are subject to COBRA's continuation coverage requirement.

The basic structure of a dental plan is a schedule of covered procedures and payments for each (which might be defined as dollar amounts or percentages). The dentist who renders the care is paid for each service to covered employees (in a fee-for-service plan) or receives capitated or other prearranged compensation under an HMO or PPO plan. There is an increasing trend to require advance approval of large non-emergency claims.

The general rule is that the percentage of coverage is inversely related to the expected cost of the service. Low-cost procedures like X-rays and examinations get a higher percentage of reimbursement (often, 100%, but limitations to two exams and cleanings per year are also common) than fillings, root canals, and dental surgery (typically reimbursed at an 80% level). Prosthetics and orthodontia are typically reimbursed at a 50% level. Dental plans typically exclude cosmetic dentistry, hospitalization for inpatient dental procedures, and amounts that would be covered by other insurance (including Worker's Compensation). Usually, dental plans impose an annual maximum.

§ 18.05   PRESCRIPTION DRUG COVERAGE

Many companies' EGHPs provide at least some coverage of prescription drugs, as a complement to medical treatment. Some employers offer separate prescription drug plans with the objective of saving money by ordering in bulk. Some prescription drug plans also cover employees' dependents—often, with some degree of financial responsibility on the employee's part.

The typical prescription drug plan covers only outpatient drugs; drugs taken by hospital patients come under the hospital care benefit. The usual plan imposes a copayment on each prescription (e.g., $5–$25). Overall dollar limitations on reimbursement per plan year are common. However, many plans are bedeviled by high increases, such as 15–20% a year, in prescription drug costs.

Some plans allow repeat prescriptions to be dispensed by mail, allowing savings due to centralized cost processing. However, a mail order plan is not well suited to short-term, acute medications. A mail order plan can be combined with a nationwide panel plan, where a network of pharmacies agrees to sell prescription drugs at the panel's schedule prices. Participating pharmacies accept membership cards from enrolled employees; the pharmacies submit their claims for payment directly to the plan.

About 60% of retail drug prescriptions are handled by Pharmacy Benefit Management (PBM) companies that permit economies of scale. Plans often try to reduce costs by encouraging the use of generic rather than brand-name drugs (e.g., by imposing higher copayments on brand-name drugs; limiting reimbursement to drugs appearing on a formulary set in advance; refusing reimbursement for drugs that are not deemed safe and effective or cost-effective; and requiring prior approval of prescriptions so doctors will test the less expensive drug before prescribing the more expensive alternative. [*See* Miles Z. Epstein and David G. Epstein, *Prescription for Success*, HR Magazine, June 1999, at p. 73]

In 2000 and later years, in response to major increases in prescription drug costs (they rose 20% in 2000), some plans are moving toward two- or three tier copayment systems, where participants pay the lowest percentage for generic drugs, the highest percentage for proprietary drugs that are not included in the plan's formulary, and an intermediate amount for proprietary drugs on the formulary. According to Towers Perrin's 2001 Health Care Cost Survey, in the preceding two years 65% of employers initiated drug cost control measures, with an additional 26% considering taking such steps. [National Underwriter, *Soaring Drug Costs Alter Benefit Plans* (April 20, 2001) <http://www.benefits link.com>]

§ 18.06   DOMESTIC PARTNER BENEFITS

[A]   Current Trends

Not all employees fit neatly into the categories of "married" or "single." Some employees live with a domestic partner, whether in a nonmarital cohabitation relationship or with a same-sex partner. An increasing number of companies are offering health or other benefits to the unmarried domestic partners of employees.

The general rule is that the employer has discretion to offer—or refuse to offer—domestic partner benefits. The advantage is that the plan can be a powerful motivator; the disadvantages are cost, administrative complexity, and possible offense to employees and recruitment candidates who are offended by nonmarital relationships.

EBRI notes that the most usual definition of "domestic partner" includes several elements:

- The partners are adults;
- They are not close blood relatives;
- They have a committed, exclusive personal relationship;
- They share their financial lives, e.g., by owning property together or having joint bank accounts.

By and large, employers find that domestic partner benefits are not a large expense, because most employees do not have domestic partners—and some domestic partners have their own employment-related coverage. [*See Basic Facts About Domestic Partner Benefits* <http://www.lambdalegal.org/cig-bin/iowa/documents/record?record=17>; *Facts from EBRI: Domestic Partner Benefits*, (March 1999) <http://www.ebri.org/facts/0399afact.htm>]

According to the Human Rights Campaign Foundation, the number of companies offering domestic partner benefits increased 20% between 2000 and 2001. As of August 2001, there were 4,284 companies, government agencies, and academic institutions offering domestic partner benefits. Among the Fortune 500, 29% offered domestic partner benefits in 2001—versus only 12% in 1998. Two-thirds of companies that offer domestic partner benefits provide them to both same-sex and heterosexual couples; the other third use the rationale that same-sex couples are entitled to domestic partner benefits because they don't have the option of marrying their partners. [*U.S. Domestic Partner Benefit Offerings Up—Report*, (Oct. 2, 2001) <http://news.excite.com/printstory/news/r/011002/19/rights-benefits> (no www.) (posted to news.excite.com on November 2, 2001)]

A state university's denial of health insurance benefits to the same-sex domestic partners of faculty members has been held to violate the Oregon state Constitution. *Tanner v. Oregon Health Sciences Univ.* [971 P.2d 435 (Ore. App. 1998)] holds that unmarried same-sex couples constitute a true class. They are not permitted to marry, and therefore discrimination against them represents unconstitutional discrimination on the basis of sexual orientation and not, as the university claimed, a distinction on the basis of marital status.

According to the Southern District of New York, neither Title VII nor the Equal Pay Act is violated when a company grants domestic partner benefits to same-sex couples but denies them to unmarried heterosexual couples. [*Foray v. Bell Atlantic*, 56 F. Supp. 2d 327 (S.D.N.Y. 1999)] The court's rationale is that male-female couples who want access to family benefits have the option of getting married to secure them, whereas same-sex couples do not have this choice.

According to *Irizarry v. Chicago Board of Educ.* [69 L.W. 1128 (N.D. Ill. July 26, 2000)], the practice of limiting domestic partner benefits to same-sex furthers the legitimate government interest of recruiting and retaining qualified employees who have same-sex life partners.

[B] Taxation of Domestic Partner Benefits

Under Treas. Reg. § 1.106-1, employees are not taxed on coverage provided to their spouse or dependents. However, there is no regulatory language about domestic partners. Therefore, unless the relationship is recognized by the state as spousal, or unless the domestic partner qualifies as a dependent under I.R.C. § 152(a)(8) (i.e., the employee domestic partner provides at least half the support for the other domestic partner), the employee will have taxable income equal to the value of the dependent coverage. However, if the cohabitation relationship is illegal under local law, I.R.C. § 152(b)(5) forbids treatment of the non-employee domestic partner as a dependent of the employee domestic partner.

If the non-employee domestic partner can be claimed as a dependent of the employee domestic partner, then the cost of domestic partner benefits is exempt from FICA and FUTA. But if the cost is taxable to the employee, both FICA and FUTA will apply in addition to income tax. Under Treas. Reg. § 1.61-21(b)(1), the gross income for the employee is the fair market value of the taxable fringe benefit, minus any amount the employee paid for it. Because the employee was taxed at the time the coverage was provided, neither the employee nor the domestic partner will be taxed if, for instance, health insurance or other reimbursement is provided later on. [*See also* PLR 971708 and PLR 200108010 (Nov. 17, 2000), Private Letter Rulings (IRS)] on tax issues involving domestic partner benefits]

§ 18.07   TAX ISSUES IN EGHPs

For both the employer and the employee, the major EGHP tax issues fall under I.R.C. §§ 104–106. It is often in the best interests of both employer and employee for benefits to be provided under a plan of accident and health insurance (A&H). This result is desirable because the employer can deduct its costs of offering such a plan, and the employee does not have taxable income because the plan exists.

Section 104 provides that an employee does not have gross income when he or she receives A&H insurance benefits that the employee paid for, or that derive from employer contributions that have already been taxed to the employee. For years after 1996, amounts paid under other arrangements having the effect of A&H plans will be taxed as if they did, in fact, come from an A&H plan.

Section 105 provides that amounts an employee receives from an A&H plan are taxable if they are paid by the employer or stem from employer contributions not already taxed to the employee. If the employer reimburses medical expenses incurred by the employee for him- or herself and family, if the expenses would be deductible under I.R.C. § 213 (medical diagnosis and treatment, rather than cosmetic or experimental procedures), and if they have not already been deducted by the employee, then the employee has no gross income as a result of the medical expense reimbursement.

The employee can rely on I.R.C. § 105 to exclude amounts that were not received from an insurance policy, as long as they were received under a "plan." For this purpose, a plan is a structured arrangement—although it need not be legally enforceable or even written. The purpose of the plan must be to provide benefits to common-law employees (not independent contractors or self-employed persons) in the event of personal injury or sickness. If the plan is not legally enforceable, Treas. Reg. § 1.105-5 imposes the additional requirement that it be communicated to employees before they encounter any covered health expenses.

The third section of the trilogy, I.R.C. § 106, provides that employees do not have gross income if their employers provide them with A&H insurance.

Rev. Rul. 2002-3, I.R.B. 2002-316 (Dec. 12. 2001), disapproves a widely marketed tax avoidance scheme. Promoters of the scheme claim that the employer can reimburse employees for health insurance premiums they pay via pre-tax salary reduction, without creating taxable income for the employee, so that after-tax pay is the same as it would be if there had been no salary reduction and no reimbursement payments. For example, if an employee earns $800, and gets free health insurance, and if the employee's rate of income tax and FICA is 20%, then the employee's take-home pay would be $640 (80% of $800). The tax shelter scheme calls for imposing a $200 salary reduction on the employee's salary, so that his or her take-home pay becomes $480 (80% of $800 minus the $200 salary reduction), and then reimbursing the employee $160 for health insurance premiums. The employee then has the same amount of cash as the original after-tax amount, but the employer has saved $40 and paid a smaller FICA amount—which constitutes the motive for tax avoidance and the reason why the IRS disapproves of the plan.

The Revenue Ruling says that the salary reductions are actually insurance premiums paid by the employer, and therefore are excluded from gross income under I.R.C. § 106, and excluded form withholding under I.R.C. § 3401. However, the reimbursements are not excluded from income, because the employee has not actually paid a premium that the employer can reimburse. Nor are the amounts excluded under I.R.C. § 105, because they do not reimburse the employees for medical expenses. They are also subject to FICA and FUTA tax.

Also see IRS Private Letter Ruling 9814023, holding that distributing "medical consumer cards" was a fringe benefit. The cards provided discounts on items such as dental and vision care that were excluded from the basic health plan. Employees do not have gross income when the card is issued, because it is part of an I.R.C. § 106 accident and health plan. Using the card to get a discount is not income because the employer doesn't pay the employee; instead, participating health providers extend a discount.

§ 18.08   HEALTH-BASED DISCRIMINATION

On January 5, 2001, HHS, the PWBA, and the IRS jointly issued an interim final regulation on discrimination based on health factors. For questions and answers about the rule, *see* <http://www.dol.gov/pwba/faqs/main.html>. Note that whether a plan provision complies with HIPAA doesn't determine whether or not it violates the Americans with Disabilities Act (ADA).

The interim final rule implements I.R.C. § 9802/ERISA § 702 (added by HIPAA), which prohibits discrimination in health coverage. Group health plans and insurers are not allowed to discriminate against—or charge a higher premium to—individual participants or beneficiaries on the basis of any individual "health factor":

- Health status;
- Mental or physical condition;
- Claims experience;
- Past health care;
- Medical history;
- Genetic information;
- Disability;
- Insurability.

Group and self-insured plans must make coverage uniformly available to all similarly situated individuals, whether or not they have health factors. Restrictions on benefits must apply uniformly to all similarly situated individuals. Benefits can legitimately be limited or excluded in relation to a specific disease or condition, for certain types of drugs or treatments, or based on a determination that a procedure is experimental or is not medically necessary—just as long as all similarly situated individuals, not just those with health factors, are affected by the limitation.

The interim final rule says that modifying a plan to restrict benefits for the treatment of a condition for which an individual has already filed a claim violates HIPAA if the plan amendment takes effect before the beginning of the next plan year—unless there are other facts on record to show that the plan was changed for reasons independent of the claim.

"List billing" (using separate individual rates that vary by health factors in connection with a group health plan) is forbidden by the interim final rule, even if the employer absorbs the higher cost and does not pass them along to employees who have health factors. Underwriting can still be used to set group premiums, but the insurer must use claims experience as part of rate-setting for the group as a whole.

Employees can be placed in valid employment-based classifications consistent with the employer's usual business practices: e.g., full-time versus part-time employees, unionized and non-unionized, participants and beneficiaries, beneficiaries of full-time or part-time employees, and employees in different occupational classes or work locations. In fact, health benefits can differ by occupation or geographic location, even if this is based on health factors of the entire group. What is forbidden is taking individual health factors into account.

The general rule is that plans may not deny enrollment or increase premiums or copayments because a person is unable to engage in normal life activities. Permissible distinctions can be drawn between employees on the basis of the services that they render to the company.

Tip: It would not violate the interim final rule to offer benefit packages to current employees that are not available to COBRA "qualified beneficiaries," but it would violate COBRA. Both COBRA and the antidiscrimination rules allow the plan to impose a higher premium for COBRA coverage during the disability extension than during other COBRA election periods.

"Nonconfinement clauses" (provisions that deny eligibility to a participant or beneficiary who is hospitalized on the date coverage would otherwise become effective) are forbidden under the interim final rule. "Actively at work" clauses that deny coverage or raise copayments for people out sick on the day coverage would otherwise begin are also improper. However, the plan or insurer can legitimately require the individual to begin work before coverage actually becomes effective.

The interim final rule permits employers to provide more favorable treatment to people who have above-average health care needs. It is acceptable to extend the period of coverage for disabled former employees, or to cover a disabled dependent child who has reached an age at which dependent coverage would ordinarily terminate.

Certain plans are exempt from the interim final rule, such as benefits that are not covered by HIPAA (e.g., long-term care insurance); single-participant plans; and self-funded plans that elect under 45 C.F.R. § 146.180 to opt out of the non-discrimination requirements.

> **Tip:** The interim final rule's objective is to prevent discrimination against employees who have health problems. But HCFA (now known as the Centers for Medicare and Medicaid Services, or CMS) permits employers to maintain bona fide "wellness" (health promotion) programs. [*See* 66 Fed. Reg. 1420-1435 (Jan. 8, 2001)] It is not considered discrimination against employees in poor health to offer favorable treatment (such as premium discounts; rebates; reduced copayment responsibilities) to employees who engage in health promotion practices such as exercise or quitting smoking.

§ 18.09 MEDICAL SAVINGS ACCOUNTS (ARCHER MSAs)

In addition to imposing health insurance portability requirements, HIPAA enacted I.R.C. § 220, which adds a new type of health plan for taxable years that begin after December 31, 1996. The "Medical Savings Account" (MSA), started out as a small-scale pilot project for the years 1997–2000, designed to terminate once 750,000 accounts had been created. A limited number of individuals were permitted to open accounts that combine an IRA-like savings account (contributions are tax-deductible, within limits) with a high-deductible health insurance policy but no other health insurance coverage.

The MSA account is tax exempt as long as it remains an MSA. Account owners do not get a tax deduction when they withdraw funds from the account to pay medical expenses, because the contributions have already received favorable tax treatment. Funds taken from the account for any other purpose are not only taxable income but subject to a 15% excise tax.

IRS Announcement 99-95, 1999-42 I.R.B. 520, extended the MSA project. The Community Renewal Tax Relief Bill of 2000 (H.R. 5652), passed on December 15, 2000, renamed the account the Archer MSA (after Representative Bill Archer, Republican of Texas) and extended its lifetime for a further two years. Then the Job Creation and Worker Assistance Act of 2002 [Pub. L. No. 107-147], extended the availability of Archer MSAs until December 31, 2003.

However, the MSA did not achieve popularity. According to IRS Announcement 2001-99, 2001-42 I.R.B. 340, only 36,250 MSA returns were filed for the year 2000, and only 76,035 were expected for 2001—far below the cut-off amount of 750,000. Rev. Proc. 2001-59, 2001-52 I.R.B. 623 sets the MSA limits for the year 2002.

A high-deductible plan covering only one person has an annual deductible that falls between $1,650 and $2,500, and imposes a stop-loss so that the participant will not have out-of-pocket expenses over $3,300. A high-deductible family policy is one that has a deductible in the range between $3,300 and $4,950, and stops out of pocket losses at a figure not above $6,050.

§ 18.10   MEDICAL EXPENSE REIMBURSEMENT PLANS

Maintaining a medical expense reimbursement plan is yet another option employers have to coping with employees' health care needs. The plan must cover employees, although it is not a legal requirement that it cover all employees. The plan can be informal. There is no legal requirement that the plan be in writing, unless it is an "welfare benefit plan" for ERISA purposes. In any case, employees must be given reasonable notice of the plan's existence and of how it operates.

Medical expense reimbursement plans usually reimburse employees directly for their medical expenses. Payment comes from the employer's resources, not from an insurance policy. Usually, the plan sets a maximum: e.g., only claims of $X per year will be covered. The plan can also be coordinated with insurance, so that the employer pays up to a certain amount, with insurance covering the rest.

For tax purposes, the most important question is whether the plan shifts risk to a third party (other than the employer and employee). A plan that uses a third-party administrator (TPA) to handle administrative or bookkeeping services does not shift risk to the TPA. The employer's costs of maintaining a self-insured plan will probably be deductible, as ordinary and necessary business expenses.

Internal Revenue Code § 105(h) governs self-insured medical expense reimbursement plans—those whose benefits are not payable exclusively from insurance. Plans of this type must satisfy coverage and nondiscrimination tests to qualify:

- The IRS issues a determination letter stating that the plan is nondiscriminatory;
- The plan covers at least 70% of all employees;
- At least 70% of all employees are eligible for the plan, and 80% or more of the eligible employees are actually covered.

However, the plan need not count employees who are younger than 25 years old, those who have been working for the company for less than three years' service, part-time or seasonal employees, or employees covered by a collective bargaining agreement that made accident and health benefits the subject of good-faith bargaining.

The plan is not discriminatory if the benefits provided for highly compensated employees (HCEs) and their dependents are also provided for other employees. The plan can impose a dollar maximum on the benefits paid on behalf of any individual, but cannot set the maximum at a percentage of compensation, because that would improperly favor HCEs.

If a self-insured medical reimbursement plan is discriminatory, then the HCEs (but not the rank-and-file employees) will have taxable income equal to the employer's plan contributions on their behalf. If taxable income does result from a self-insured medical expense reimbursement plan, the income will be subject to income tax withholding, but not to FICA or FUTA. [*See* I.R.C. § 3121(a)(2)(B)]

§ 18.11 FLEXIBLE SPENDING ACCOUNTS (FSAs)

[A] Generally

An FSA is an arrangement under which an employer diverts some cash compensation into a separate account, which must be identified for specific use: either for dependent care expenses, or for medical expenses that are not reimbursed by insurance or directly by the employer.

The amount that can be placed into a dependent care FSA is limited by the Internal Revenue Code's limits on deductible dependent care expenses. Funds targeted for medical care cannot be used for dependent care, and vice versa. A medical expense FSA must last at least twelve months, although a short first year, when the plan is initially adopted, is allowed. Premiums for other health coverage cannot be reimbursed by the FSA.

An FSA can either be part of a cafeteria plan or a separate plan. Stand-alone FSAs are subject to the same nondiscrimination rules as cafeteria plans.

IRS regulations define an FSA as a benefit program that reimburses an employee for specified, incurred expenses. The maximum amount of reimbursement that can be made "reasonably available" to a participant during a period of coverage is limited to 500% of the total premium for the coverage. FSA reimbursement must be made available at least monthly, or when the level of expenses reaches a reasonable minimum amount such as $50.

To receive reimbursement, the FSA participant must submit a written statement from an independent third party (such as the doctor or medical office administrator) to confirm that a medical expense of $X has been incurred, and that this expense was neither reimbursed by nor eligible for reimbursement under any other plan.

All FSA plans (stand-alone or in cafeteria plans) must operate on a "use it or lose it" basis. In other words, if an employee puts $3,000 into a medical expense FSA, but has only $1,000 in unreimbursed medical expenses, the other $2,000 is forfeited. Forfeitures can be refunded to the participants as a whole, based on a reasonable and uniform method of allocation, based on the amount of contributions to the plan, but not based on reimbursement from the plan. Unofficial IRS statements hint that forfeitures can be used to pay the plan's administrative expenses, or can be returned to participants pro rata.

[B] HIPAA Exemption for FSAs

In 1997, the IRS, the Department of Labor's Pension and Welfare Benefits Administration, and the Department of Health and Human Services joined to publish a "clarification of regulations" that appears at 62 Fed. Reg. 67688 (Dec. 29, 1997).

Under this document, health insurance portability is not required for certain health FSAs, because they rank as "excepted benefits" under ERISA §§ 732 and 733(c) and I.R.C. §§ 9831 and 9832(c).

According to this document, a health FSA is a "benefit program that provides employees with coverage under which specified, incurred expenses may be reimbursed (subject to reimbursement maximums and any other reasonable conditions) and under which the maximum amount of reimbursement that is reasonably available to a participant for a period of coverage is not substantially in excess of the total premium (including both employee-paid and employer-paid portions of the premium) for the participant's coverage." FSAs usually cover medical expenses excluded by the primary EGHP.

An FSA is not "creditable coverage" subject to the HIPAA portability requirements if the employee's maximum FSA benefit for the year is not greater than twice the employee's salary reduction election under the FSA for the year, as long as the employee has other EGHP coverage, and as long as the FSA provides at least some benefits that are not "excepted benefits."

According to Hewitt Associates (call (847) 295-5000 for more information), about 17.5% of the workforce participates in health care FSAs. The survey of about 500 employers showed an average 1997 FSA contribution of $744 per employee for health care accounts, $2,848 for dependent care accounts.

§ 18.12   EGHP STRUCTURES

Originally, indemnity plans were the standard; now, that role is held by managed care plans of various types. Within the managed care category, HMOs were once dominant, but now must share the spotlight with other plan forms that offer greater choice of health care providers. Recently, attention has been given to defined contribution and voucher plans.

Indemnity plans were the original model for EGHP coverage. In response to uncontrolled increases in health care costs, most plans switched to some form of managed care (see below). However, now that managed care costs are rising out of control, there may be renewed interest in indemnity plans.

Usually, indemnity plans are divided into "basic" and "major medical" models. Basic coverage encompasses surgery, hospitalization, and care provided by physicians during a hospital stay. A major medical plan pays when other coverage is exhausted. A comprehensive major medical plan combines basic and major medical features, whereas a supplemental plan offers pure excess insurance.

The standard model for indemnity insurance calls for the patient to be responsible for paying a deductible each year (e.g., $X, or $X per family member) before the plan has any responsibility for payments. Most plans also impose a coinsurance responsibility: In an 80/20 plan, for example, once the deductible is satisfied, the patient is responsible for 20% of the bill—or 20% of the "schedule amount" that the plan pays for the service, plus the full difference between the actual charge and the schedule amount. It is also typical for indemnity plans to include a "stop-loss" provision that represents the maximum out-of-pocket spending an individual or family will incur under the plan. But the plan, in turn, usually limits its exposure by imposing overall limits on each employee's coverage, whether per year or over a lifetime.

Reimbursement to providers under indemnity plans is generally made on the basis of the table of "usual, customary and reasonable charges" promulgated by the insurer. These are either historical figures or a schedule of charges for various items.

§ 18.13   MANAGED CARE

[A]   Concepts and Models

Managed care was a response to the climate of the 1970s and 1980s, when employers were faced with explosive increases in insurance premiums. The general concept of managed care includes many kinds of entities and relationships among patients, employers, and health care providers. The theory is that adding management skills to the health care equation will save money by increasing cost-consciousness and reducing employees' tendency to extravagant health care consumption. However, the analogy between health care and other forms of consumption is rather strained, because the doctor or other health care provider, and not the patient, determines the services that the patient will attempt to claim from the health plan. Furthermore, it is hard to imagine anyone jeopardizing his own health—much less the health of his children—merely to save money for an insurance plan.

A common feature of managed care plans is utilization review. Patients may be required to consult a "gatekeeper" primary care physician before they can be referred to a specialist. Nonemergency procedures may have to be approved in advance by a claims reviewer. Patients' operations and hospital stays will be assessed for medical necessity.

In some managed care models, the employee is required to get all care within a closed network of providers; otherwise, reimbursement will not be available for out-of-network care (except in emergencies or when necessary care is not available within the network). But the trade-off is that the employee either gets care within the network at no additional charge, or pays only a small amount per visit, per prescription, or per service.

Managed care plans typically have their own payment schedules, which may be significantly lower than actual health care costs encountered in the community. The managed care plan's reimbursement to the patient may be defined in terms of this schedule, with the result that the patient has very significant copayment responsibilities. If a patient has satisfied the deductible and is charged $1,000 for a procedure and the health plan's schedule amount is $800; it pays 80% of the schedule amount, or $640, making the patient responsible for the remaining $360.

Generally, employees will be given one open enrollment period a year. During this time, employees who have just become eligible will be able to select one of the options available under the plan. Employees who have already selected a plan option will be able to change their selection. Once made, a decision is usually irrevocable until the next open enrollment period. Most open enrollment periods occur in the autumn, but this is by custom; it is not a legal requirement.

[B] Health Maintenance Organizations

The Health Maintenance Organization, or HMO, is both a network of providers and a mechanism for financing health care. The theory is that participating providers are paid on a "capitated" basis. That is, they receive a fee "per head" covering all medical services under the plan for a particular employee or dependent of an employee. The theory is that, because providers do not receive more if their patients get additional health services, they will not be motivated to order unnecessary services for purely financial reasons.

In a "staff model" HMO the health professionals are salaried employees of the HMO. In the more prevalent Individual Practice Association (IPA) model HMO, the health professionals enter into contracts with the IPA, and the IPA negotiates with the HMO to set a reimbursement schedule for each service on the schedule.

Under the "group model," the HMO enters into contracts with independent group practices that are responsible for administrative tasks and are usually paid on a capitated basis. The "network model" HMO's doctors practice primarily in fee-for-service mode, However, they also agree to provide certain services to HMO patients, once again generally in exchange for a capitation fee.

Employees who want HMO coverage can sign up with the HMO during a stated open enrollment period each year. There are also rules for switching from one HMO to another if several are available in the relevant geographic area, and rules for disenrolling from the HMO and returning to an indemnity plan (if the employer still offers one).

A federal law, the Health Maintenance Organization Act of 1973, imposes some degree of uniformity and federal regulation (by the Department of Health and Human Services) on HMOs that wish to call themselves "federally qualified." (It is legal for a state-licensed HMO to do business even if it is not federally qualified.)

Federally qualified HMOs must provide an obligatory package of services including both primary and specialty physician services; hospital inpatient and outpatient care; emergency medical treatment; short-term outpatient mental health treatment; referrals and treatment of substance abuse; home health care; and preventive health care. Federally qualified HMOs can also provide additional, optional services such as long-term care, longer-term mental health treatment, dental and vision care; physical therapy; and prescription drugs. Optional services do not have to be provided on a capitated basis, and the HMO can impose fees on such services.

[C] Preferred Provider Organizations (PPOs)

A PPO is an administrative structure under which health care providers become "preferred" by affiliating with the structure. Employers negotiate with the PPO to set the rate scale for specified health services.

There is no set enrollment period for employees to join a PPO. Nor is there a single centralized entity that has complete financial responsibility for the enrollees' care. Sponsorship of PPOs is quite diverse: they might be created by a hospital or other health care provider, a health insurer, entrepreneur, or group of doctors.

[D] Point of Service (POS) Plans

A point of service plan is a hybrid of indemnity and HMO concepts. Participants can select their providers from a network, but they are not obligated to get their care within the network. If they do, their only copayment responsibility is a small amount per visit. Indemnity concepts such as an annual deductible and a co-insurance percentage apply when they choose out-of-network care. POS plans usually impose a high coinsurance percentage, such as 40%, on out-of-network care.

[E] Managed Care Cost Reduction Techniques

Utilization review (UR) is a cornerstone of managed care cost-cutting. In traditional fee-for-service medicine, the health care provider determines which treatments will be used, and the payor reimburses for part or all of the care ordered by the provider.

Managed care adds "gatekeepers"—reviewers who determine whether a claim satisfies the requirements of the plan. In many instances, the plan will require prior approval of claims, and will deny or reduce claims for non-emergency services that did not receive this approval in advance. UR also includes concurrent review (e.g., reviewing the need for continued hospitalization while the patient is still in the hospital) and retrospective review (after treatment is completed).

Procedural controls are common. Most plans will pay for a second opinion prior to surgery, but will not pay for surgery unless the second opinion confirms the recommendation for surgery. Cost-cutting techniques also include adopting a fixed payment schedule, and favoring outpatient and home care over hospitalization.

A carve-out is a discount mechanism under which particular forms of medical expense, or high-cost conditions, are managed separately from the rest of the health plan.

It should be noted that HMO limitations on hospital stays for childbirth led to the passage of federal law. [*See* the discussion of the Newborns' and Mothers' Health Protection Act [Pub. L. No. 104-204]

[F] Cost Trends

Managed care became popular because of undesirable increases in the cost of indemnity health plans. However, managed care has not lived up to its promise of reducing health care costs. Furthermore, participants in indemnity plans decide how much health care they want to receive. Managed care participants often feel (whether accurately or not) that they are denied access to medically necessary care so that the plans can increase their profits.

A complicating factor in the equation was the ongoing development of more and more sophisticated drugs. This is good, to the extent that it saves lives, reduces suffering, and allows people to be treated at home instead of in a hospital—but it is bad, to the extent that the new drugs are even more expensive than the older ones they replace. Therefore, for many plans, increases in prescription drug costs drove health care cost inflation.

Health care costs remained fairly level between 1994 and 1997, but went up 6.1% in 1998. Employers, especially small employers, faced even larger price increases in 1999. The January 1999 increases for businesses with over 100 employees averaged 6%, but small businesses faced 10–13% increases.

According to the Bureau of Labor Statistics, benefit costs for private employers went up about 2.25% a year between 1994 and 1999, but went up 6% between September 1999 and September 2000. National health spending went up 5.7% in 1999 and 6.9% in 2000, reaching the stratospheric level of $1.3 trillion for that year. The economy as a whole grew only 6.5%, so once again health care spending outpaced growth. In 2000, health care represented 13.2% of the domestic economy. [*See, e.g.*, Ron Winslow, *Health-Care Inflation Kept in Check Last Year*, Wall Street Journal, Jan. 20. 1998, at p. B1; Jennifer Steinhauer, *Health Insurance Costs Rise, Hitting Small Business Hard*, New York Times, Jan. 19, 1999, at p. A1; The Towers Perrin Health Care Cost Survey at <http://www.towers.com>; Hewitt Associates figures at <http://www.hewitt.com/news/pressrel/1999/11-08-99.htm>; Robert Pear, *Propelled by Drug and Hospital Costs, Health Spending Surged in 2000*, New York Times, Jan. 8, 2002, at p. A14; Jill Carroll, *Health-Care Outlays Accelerated in 2000 With a Jump of 6.9% to $1.3 Trillion*, Wall Street Journal, Jan. 8, 2002, at p. A4]

In many companies, the 2001 plan year was marked by 15% increases in employee copayments—while employers absorbed an equal percentage increase. Pundits predicted more cost-shifting, with employees expected to pay more for their prescription drugs and perhaps other services. Large companies were often hit with 15–17% increases in HMO premiums, 9–12% for PPOs (plans that do not require pre-approval to see a specialist), and 12–15% in fee-for-service plans. [Milt Freudenheim, *The High Cost of Being Well: Benefits at a Premium*, New York Times, Oct. 16, 2001, at p. C1]

For the years between 1997 and 2001, the January/February 2002 issue of the journal Health Affairs reports that the percentage of employees getting employment-related coverage continued to grow, even though costs were also going up. In 1997, for instance, 75.1% of employees had access to job-related health insurance, and 62.4% actually had coverage.

In 2001, 77.4% of employees could have been covered at work, and 63.5% actually were. However, that time period included several years of economic prosperity, when employers had to compete to recruit and retain workers—some commentators believe that as unemployment increases, more and more people will lose coverage, either because they are no longer employed (and cannot afford COBRA coverage), because the employer no longer offers coverage, or because they cannot afford the copayments that would be involved if they accepted the coverage.

Access to health insurance is much greater for full-time than part-time workers. In 2001, full-time workers were offered health benefits 84.7% of the time, versus 50.4% for people who worked 21-34 hours a week. [*See* press release, *Number of Americans With Job-Based Health Benefits Grew Through Early 2001, Despite Higher Benefit Costs* at <http://130.94.25.113/press/janfeb0202.htm> (no www.); Todd Zwillich, *Report: 725,000 in U.S. Lose Health Coverage*, Health From Reuters (Dec. 4, 2001) <http://news.excite.com/news/4011204/17/health-coverage> (no www.) (posted to news.excite.com on December 4, 2001)]

Ironically, employees who do not accept coverage under EGHPs tend to have worse health than those who accept—probably because the less-healthy employees miss more days of work, have lower income, and are less able to afford copayments. [*See* Kaiser Daily Health Policy Report, *Study Finds That Those Who Decline Employer-Sponsored Coverage Are in Worse Health Than Employees Who Take Up Coverage* at <http://www.kaisernetwork.org/daily_reports/print_report.cfm?DR_ID=9057&dr_cat=3>]

The Kaiser Family Foundation 2001 Employer Health Benefits Survey [*see* <http://www.kff.org/content/2001/20010906a/>] shows that the average monthly premium in 2001, for all plans, was $191 (employer share) plus $30 (employee share) for single employees, and $438 plus $150, respectively, for family coverage. Within this average, HMOs had the lowest premium costs ($168/month from the employer, $32/month from the employee for singles, $387 and $158 for families) and indemnity plans the highest ($219, $19, $537, and $103, respectively).

The Kaiser survey showed that, although 73% of employees were covered by indemnity insurance plans in 1988, by 2001 this had plummeted to a mere 7%. In 1996, 28% of employees were covered by PPOs—but this became the dominant form in 2001, when 48% of employees belonged to PPOs. HMOs had a 31% share of the market in 1996, but only 23% in 1996.

According to Watson Wyatt's research from 2001, only about 40% of employees are satisfied with the overall performance of their EGHP [Brendan McKenna, *Employees Kept in the Dark Are Dissatisfied With Health Insurance* at <http://www.insure.com> (posted on www.insure.com on September 1, 2001)] Less than half of those surveyed trust the employer to design a plan that meets their needs. About two-thirds of employees underestimate the amount that the employer pays in premiums—and about the same percentage overestimates their share of the cost of health care! Only one-seventh of employees who have communications problems with their plan are satisfied with the way that plan performs; whereas two-thirds of employees who have good communications are also satisfied with their benefits.

[G]   Choosing a Managed Care Plan

Most employers can choose among several or many managed care plan vendors (although they won't be able to take advantage of this to bargain for low prices!). When an employer chooses a plan, cost considerations are important, but they don't tell the whole story.

Employees may initially be glad to sign up with an HMO that imposes low copayments, but they will be dissatisfied if they have to travel too far to find a network provider, or wait too long for appointments. Other possible sources of discontent are difficulties in getting referrals to specialists, and denial of access to prescriptions, tests, and treatments that the patients and/or doctors think are likely to be beneficial.

When an HMO account representative approaches you, collect as much information as you can about the plan, its history, and its results (including references from other subscribers). A telephone or face-to-face appointment with the HMO's medical director is useful to research staff quality. The medical director can let you know how the HMO chooses its affiliated physicians and how much input physicians have on HMO policies. Also find out if the plan is good at keeping its physicians, or whether it has a problem of high turnover. An important issue to explore is how doctors in the network resolve problems among themselves—and with the HMO—about preferred treatment methods.

Your state insurance department will probably have information about the HMO's operations, loss ratios (percentage of premiums used to pay claims rather than profits or administrative expenses) and how complaints have been resolved in the past.

There are various objective measures of HMO quality. The National Commission on Quality Assurance accredits HMOs. The standard survey instrument for managed care plans is HEDIS (Health Plan Employer Data and Information Set); plans should provide their HEDIS results on request.

Factors to consider are:

- Number of health care providers in the network or participating in the plan;
- Qualifications of health care providers (board certification or eligibility; hospital affiliations; any past complaints or suits);
- How the provider pattern fits your employee census (are there too many obstetricians and not enough cardiologists, or vice versa?);
- Quality of hospitals and other facilities involved with the plan;
- Utilization review and other cost-control measures;

- Availability of primary care physicians at off hours (to cut down on the number of emergency room visits);
- Use of claims management to coordinate treatment of serious illness and injury to promote rehabilitation;
- How premiums compare to those of other MCOs—however, a low premium may simply mean that you will face exceptionally large increases in the future;
- Measures the plan takes to promote consumer satisfaction (telephone help lines, clear explanations of claims procedures, swift resolution of claims disputes, periodic surveys to assess consumers' reactions to the plan.

A good HMO should have plenty of staff to respond to patients' questions (whether to go to the doctor; how to handle minor ailments or accidents; claim and benefit questions).

[H] Self-Insured Plans

As insurance premiums increase, more and more employers adopt, or at least consider adopting, self-insured plans. However, a self-insured plan has a heavy administrative and disclosure burden. Reinsurance is vital, because even a young and healthy group of employees can incur catastrophically high claims if even one employee is in a serious accident or has a child with major health care needs. Furthermore, health care providers tend to shift costs onto self-payors.

One coping mechanism is to use a Blue Cross or other entity as a Third-Party Administrator (TPA), which could give your plan access to the insurer's discount structure.

> **Tip:** A self-insured plan risks conflict of interest if it gets its stop-loss coverage from the same company that provides TPA services, because a party in control of the plan and plan assets provides the coverage. [*See* Michael A. McKuin, *The Stop-Loss Shuffle* at <http://members.aol.com/mmckuin/stop-loss-page1.html> (no www.)]

In a specific stop-loss plan, the insurer agrees to reimburse the employer or other plan sponsor for any claim that exceeds a specified amount (the "retention"). An aggregate stop-loss plan covers all claims above the retention in a particular year. In effect, a stop-loss plan works like an insurance policy with a very high deductible. But from the insurer's viewpoint, a specified stop-loss plan is more favorable, because although the insurer collects premiums in either case, it has no direct liability to the employees covered by a stop-loss plan, and cannot be sued by them for allegedly improper denials of claims or refusals to pre-approve treatment. A stop-loss plan ends on a particular date, and the insurer is not responsible for claims that accrued by that date but have not yet been filed. In contrast, an insured plan is responsible for these "tail" or IBNR (Incurred But Not Reported) claims.

[I]   Defined Contribution and Voucher Plans

Some employers prefer to avoid the difficulties, expenses, and controversy involved in EGHP management, and prefer to give employees health care vouchers so they can purchase their own coverage. The employer agrees to give the employee a fixed amount that can be applied to a menu of health care choices. The employer's exposure is limited and is not subject to health care price increases. In effect the voucher works like a defined contribution or 401(k) plan, shifting control to the employees—but also putting them at risk of bad or simply unlucky decisions.

A defined contribution health plan, also known as a "consumer-driven" plan, is another way of limiting the employer's exposure to cost increases. [*See* the Employee Benefits Research Institute Fact Sheet at <http://www.ebri.org/conclave/fact3.pdf>; Jill Elswick, *Consumer-Driven Plans Counter Criticism*, Employee Benefit News, (February 2002) <http://www.benefitnews.com/pfv.cfm?=id=2459>]

In a fixed-dollar contribution plan, the employer offers a choice of health plans and gives each worker a certain amount of compensation to buy insurance. Employees who want a more expensive policy must use their own pretax dollars to pay the difference. In a fixed-percentage contribution plan, the employer's contribution is defined as a percentage of the premium, with the rest paid by the employee.

Employers could also combine a high deductible health plan with a funded or unfunded account for medical expenses. The employer might set up an account in which funds are accumulated on behalf of active employees, to be used for their eventual retiree health expenses. [Christine Keller, *Recent Trend in Health Care: Defined Contribution Health Care Arrangements* (Feb. 14, 2002) <http://www.groom.com/articles_display.asp?display=161>]

The example cited in an article by Barbara Martinez [*Health Plan That Puts Employees in Charge of Spending Catches On*, Wall Street Journal, Jan. 8, 2002, at p. B1] is a plan where each employee gets a $2,000 medical account that covers all kinds of medical bills (including prescription drugs). After exhaustion of the $2,000, the employee is personally responsible for the next $1,000 in health care costs. An employee who has expenses over and above $3,000 would be 100% covered by the employer for in-network care, 80% for out-of-network care. An employee who didn't use the full $2,000 could roll it over to the next year. These plans are usually designed so that preventive care is fully paid for by the employer and does not require drawing down the account.

Defined contribution plans are touted as means of improving employees' consumerism and health care shopping behavior, although that was also an argument used in favor of managed care, which is now failing to control costs.

It should be noted that the IRS has never clarified the tax status of funds that remain within a defined contribution plan from one year to the next—and, in fact, this is a subject on which the IRS has announced it will not issue rulings. I.R.C. § 105 says that a benefit is not tax-free if the employee receives the benefit whether or not a medical expense is incurred. [*See* Jill Elswick, *Tax Risks Cloud DC Health Plans*, Employee Benefit News, (December 2001) <http://www.benefitnews.com>]

The Keller article cited above points out that employers that want to establish defined contribution plans must resolve many tax questions. If the arrangement constitutes a Flexible Spending Account, then Internal Revenue Code requirements will have to be satisfied. If the arrangement is trust-funded, it may become an ERISA welfare benefit plan, with additional requirements to meet. Very possibly, the IRS will treat the arrangement as a self-insured medical plan, in which case there may be nondiscrimination, COBRA, and HIPAA compliance obligations. Questions of dependent coverage will have to be worked out.

§ 18.14 EMPLOYER LIABILITY FOR HMO ACTIONS

The managed care relationship has three parts: the HMO or other managed care organization (MCO) that provides care; the employer that enters into a contract with the MCO; and the employee or dependent that receives health care. When there is a bad result (whether or not malpractice occurred), the employee might want to sue the employer as well as the MCO.

One of the most controversial topics in our legal system is precisely how much control the legal system should have over medical practice, and the extent to which physicians, HMOs, and employers can be held liable for the results of HMO coverage decisions. Initially, employers usually avoided liability because the HMO provided the actual treatment (or claims denial). In many cases, HMOs escaped liability as well, because ERISA preempts state law but says virtually nothing about HMOs' obligations. This state of affairs led to many demands for increased regulation (especially state regulation) of HMO operations in the interests of protecting health care consumers. Many of these explosive issues are beyond the scope of this book, because they involve the employer and the EGHP only indirectly.

The Supreme Court has tackled some of these issues. *Humana Inc. v. Forsyth* [525 U.S. 299 (1999)] permitted EGHP members to bring a RICO suit for insurance fraud when they alleged that they were overbilled as part of a conspiracy to force them to make excessive copayments. The significance of a RICO suit is that treble damages can be ordered. The defendant claimed that the McCarran-Ferguson Act [15 U.S.C. §§ 1011–1015] (which exempts "the business of insurance" from antitrust regulation) preempts the RICO suit. However, the Supreme Court held that RICO does not invalidate or supersede state insurance laws, so the McCarran-Ferguson Act does not bar the RICO suit.

The Supreme Court returned to EGHP ERISA issues in April 1999, finding in *UNUM Life Insurance Co. of America v. Ward* [526 U.S. 358 (1999)] that ERISA does not preempt state "notice-prejudice" laws. These laws prevent insurers from denying claims because they were filed late, unless the delay actually prejudiced the insurer's interests. This decision does not harm employers who administer EGHPs, because it says that although the employer is the insurer's "agent," the employer's role "relates to" an ERISA plan and therefore ERISA preempts suits against the employer with respect to this role.

In mid-2000, the Supreme Court decided, in *Pegram v. Herdrich* [530 U.S. 211 (2000)], that when an HMO, acting through its doctors, makes a mixed decision about medical treatment and health plan eligibility (rather than a purely medical decision about what kind of operation is proper for a particular diagnosis, or a purely financial decision), then the HMO is not acting as a fiduciary. Therefore, even if patients are correct that the HMO refused them necessary and medically valid treatment because the HMO wanted to increase its profits by cutting the amount of care available to subscribers, this would not state a cause of action for breach of fiduciary duty.

When an insurance policy is converted from an EGHP to an individual policy, state law claims about that policy no longer "relate to" a benefit plan, and therefore are not preempted by ERISA. [*Waks v. Empire Blue Cross/Blue Shield*, 263 F.3d 872 (9th Cir. 2001)]

To reduce its liability exposure, the employer should negotiate and draft its contracts with MCOs accordingly:

- Have doctors and other individual health care providers acknowledge that they are independent contractors, not employees of the corporation sponsoring the plan, and that they are fully responsible for their own professional actions;
- Make sure that patients can use an alternative dispute resolution procedure to handle their complaints;
- Set up a feedback mechanism so providers can protest UR-related denials of services the providers deem necessary;
- Require providers to maintain at least a specified minimum level of malpractice coverage, because the less coverage the provider has, the more likely a dissatisfied patient is to feel that additional defendants need to be brought into a dispute;
- Make sure that medical specialists are consulted about all decisions involving specialty referrals;
- Maintain adequate documentation of the disposal of each claim.

[*See* Chapter 13 for federal requirements about health care claims. To learn more about legal issues affecting MCOs, *see, e.g.*, Families USA, *State Managed Care*

Patient Protections at <http://www.familiesusa.org/media/updates/hitmisup.htm>, detailing state laws requiring coverage of emergency care, access to providers, continuity of care, consumer protection, and appeal rights when claims are denied. *See also* the Kaiser Family Foundation Web site, <http://www.kff.org>, for ongoing coverage of HMO legal issues]

§18.15 LABOR LAW ISSUES IN THE EGHP

A 1996 NLRB ruling holds that an employer's reservation of the right to "amend or modify" the health plan did not give the employer the power to replace the existing fee-for-service plan with a managed care plan. Such a change is so sweeping that the employer cannot implement it unilaterally without bargaining. [*Loral Defense Systems-Akron*, 320 NLRB No. 54 (Jan. 31, 1996), *aff'd*, 200 F.3d 436 (6th Cir. 1999)]

When negotiations reach an impasse, the employer cannot replace the union-sponsored health (and retirement) plans with employer-proposed plans that did not form part of the pre-impasse negotiations. [*Grondorf, Field Black & Co. v. NLRB*, 107 F.3d 882 (D.C. Cir. 1997)]

A unionized company that wants its employees to pay 30% of the premium thereby has an obligation to release information to the union about the health care claims of non-union employees and their dependents. The information is not confidential, because the employer has opened up the issue of health care costs and cost containment. [*Carr v. Gates Health Care Plan*, 195 F.3d 292 (7th Cir. 1999)]

§18.16 QUALIFIED MEDICAL CHILD SUPPORT ORDERS (QMCSOs)

Divorce courts often issue orders explaining how to divide an employee spouse's retirement benefits with the divorcing non-employee spouse. These orders are called Qualified Domestic Relations Orders, or QDROs. [*See* §12.08] The counterpart for the EGHP is the QMCSO, which supplements COBRA continuation coverage as an additional means of protecting children against loss of health care coverage as a result of their parents' divorce. [*See* §12.08[A]] A QMCSO is a court order that requires a parent covered by an EGHP to take whatever steps are necessary to enroll the child ("the alternate recipient") in the health plan—whether that includes notifying the plan or paying insurance premiums.

A valid QMCSO must identify:

- Every plan it applies to;
- The period of time covered by the order;
- The type of coverage the plan must give each alternate recipient (or a method of determining the coverage);
- The name and last known mailing address of the employee parent and each alternate recipient.

When a health plan receives a document described as a QMCSO, the plan has an obligation to review it to see if it is a valid order. Every health plan must have a written document setting out its procedure for reviewing QMCSOs. Courts do not have the power to order benefits that are not provided under the plan—so, for instance, if a plan does not offer dependent coverage, a QMCSO cannot create this coverage.

The plan administrator must notify the participant and the alternate recipients that the order has been received, and how the plan will analyze the order's validity. If, as usually happens, the plan approves the order as valid, then the participant and alternate recipients must be notified. Because the alternate recipients are children, they can designate a parent, stepparent, or attorney to receive copies of the notice on their behalf.

State governments (but NOT the DOL) can sue under I.R.C. § 502(a)(7) to enforce compliance with a Qualified Medical Child Support Order (QMCSO). The states have a role to play here because they have traditionally been empowered to deal with family law issues such as child support.

A 1998 law, the Child Support Performance and Incentives Act [Pub. L. No. 105-200], requires state child-support enforcement agencies to protect children's rights to medical coverage. The DOL and HHS published a Final Rule giving the text for the National Medical Child Support Notice. [*See* 65 Fed. Reg. 82128 and 82154 (Dec. 27, 2000)] State agencies have been required to use the form to enforce child support orders since October 1, 2001.

The Notice includes Parts A and B. Part A, the Employer Withholding Notice, informs the employer of the facts of the medical child support order. The employer must either:

- Inform the child-support enforcement agency that forwarded the order that the employer doesn't provide health care coverage to the employee who is the subject of the order;
- Inform the agency that the person named in the order is no longer an employee (the agency must also be notified if the employee is subsequently terminated); or
- Forward Part B of the form to the plan administrator within 20 business days, if health care coverage for a child is applicable.

The next step is for the plan administrator to decide whether the child(ren) covered by the order is or are enrolled in the health plan. If so, any appropriate withholding amount is taken from the employee's wages to provide medical coverage for the children. These deductions cannot exceed the amount of medical support specified by the order. They are also subject to federal and state limitations on wage assignments.

Employers can be sanctioned under ERISA and state law if they fail to carry out the wage deductions—or, on the other hand, if they fire or discipline employees because they have medical child support obligations.

It is the plan administrator's responsibility to send Part B to the child support enforcement agency. The form indicates whether the administrator deems the notice to be a valid QMCSO and, if so, what coverage options are available and which options the child(ren) has or have been enrolled in. The administrator has 40 business days to assess the validity of an alleged QMCSO.

§ 18.17   THE EMPLOYER'S RIGHT OF SUBROGATION

Subrogation is a legal concept under which a party that advances expenses can recover them when the person who received the funds is reimbursed for those expenses. More specifically, if an EGHP covers the medical treatment of an injured employee, or dependent of an employee, the EGHP will have a legal right to part of the verdict or settlement that the employee receives from suing whoever caused the accident or manufactured the dangerous product.

For the plan to have a right of subrogation, the plan language, or the insurance covering the plan, must provide this right explicitly. State law must also be consulted to see if limitations are imposed on subrogation.

California, for example, has a state antisubrogation statute that says that a health insurer is not entitled to reimbursement out of a victim's medical malpractice recovery. The statute has been upheld as enforceable and not preempted by ERISA (which has an exception for laws under which states regulate the business of insurance). [*Medical Mutual of Ohio v. deSoto*, 234 F.3d 298 (6th Cir. 2000)]

By contrast, some state laws facilitate subrogation: for instance, by requiring the participant to agree to subrogation as a condition of receiving benefits under the plan.

The Supreme Court decided a subrogation case. [*Great-West Life & Annuity Ins. Co. v. Knudson,* 534 U.S. 204 (2002)] In this case, the plan called for recovery from plan beneficiaries if they recovered any payments from third parties. The plan paid most of the $411,157.11 in medical expenses when a car crash rendered an employee quadriplegic. She settled her tort case; the settlement allocated only $13,828.70 to past medical expenses. The Supreme Court refused to allow the plan to sue under ERISA § 503(a)(3) (civil action to enjoin an act or practice violating the terms of the plan), or to obtain equitable relief to collect more of the funds it had advanced. The Supreme Court refused to permit the plan to bring such a suit, ruling that compelling payment of money due under a contract is not an "equitable" remedy.

Shortly after this decision, the Northern District of Illinois ruled that ERISA does not preempt a suit brought by a health plan against a plan participant who still has continuing control over the money that the health plan wants to recover. [*Administrative Committee of Wal-Mart Stores Health and Welfare Plan v. Varco*, 2002 U.S. Dist. LEXIS 530 (N.D. Ill. Jan. 14, 2002)] Therefore, the concept of "constructive trust" (segregating funds that legitimately belong to someone else) can be applied. This does not conflict with *Great-West*, because in that case the funds had already been placed into a trust to be used for future medical care, and had been used to pay attorneys' fees; the funds did not remain in the injured person's hands.

A plan participant was a passenger in a car when he was injured by an uninsured drunk driver. [*Lasky v. State Farm Mutual Auto Ins. Co.*, 2001 U.S. Dist. LEXIS 13636 (W.D. Mich. Aug. 31, 2001)] The EGHP paid about $30,000 of medical expenses. The plaintiff's automobile insurer paid $6,800 under the uninsured motorist coverage. After arbitration, the driver's insurer paid $100,000 for pain and suffering. The health plan sought reimbursement of what it had paid. The plaintiff's contention was that the automobile insurer should have been the primary payor, so it should reimburse the ERISA plan (i.e., that the amount the plaintiff received should not be reduced).

The court ruled that interpretation of the policies shows that the ERISA plan was the primary insurer. The plan language said that if there was automobile insurance coverage, the language of that policy would control; and the automobile insurance policy made the ERISA plan primary. However, the plan's reimbursement clause did not clearly rule out the application of the "make-whole" doctrine (i.e., the purpose of insurance is to make the injured person financially whole), and therefore the ERISA plan was not entitled to reimbursement out of the $100,000 award.

If the plaintiff had been required to reimburse the plan, he would not have been fully compensated for all of his injuries. The legal system calls for subrogation to prevent injured persons from getting double or multiple recoveries for a single injury, but that was not a possibility here.

According to the Eighth Circuit, a health plan can recover the "reasonable" value of the services it provided to injured employees. This is defined as the fee-for-service fee schedule. The employer's right of subrogation is not limited to the actual amount that the health plan paid to the health care provider (health plans typically pay providers less than the schedule amount). [*Ince v. Aetna Health Management Inc.*, 173 F.3d 672 (8th Cir. 1999)]

In another case involving discounted rates, the district court for the District of Rhode Island awarded more than $4 million in damages, plus interest, to plan participants who challenged an HMO's practice of imposing copayments based on billing rates, even though the HMO actually had negotiated a lower, discounted rate that it paid to health care providers. [*Corsini v. United HealthCare Servs. Inc.*, 145 F. Supp. 2d 184 (D.R.I. 2001)]

In a Sixth Circuit case, the employee received about $18,000 in medical expense reimbursement after a car accident. [*Smith v. Wal-Mart Assocs. Group Health Plan*, 2000 U.S. App. LEXIS 33993 (6th Cir. Dec. 27, 2000)] She got a tort judgment of $25,000 against the other driver. One-third went to her lawyer as a contingent fee. The plan's subrogation clause allowed the plan to recover benefits already paid, to the extent of "any payment resulting from a judgment or settlement." However, the Sixth Circuit said that the attorney's one-third share of the judgment should have the effect of reducing the amount the plan could receive: The employee had received only two-thirds of the $25,000. The plan would have to sue the lawyer to recover the rest.

Tip: The problem in the case mentioned above can be avoided by drafting the subrogation clause to clarify that the plan can recover against the full, unreduced amount of any settlement or judgment.

CHAPTER 19

HEALTH INSURANCE CONTINUATION AND PORTABILITY (COBRA AND HIPAA)

§ 19.01   INTRODUCTION

The two dominant mechanisms for providing health insurance coverage in our society are employee group health plans (EGHPs) and the Medicare system for senior citizens and the disabled. However, there are many instances in which a person has lost coverage under one EGHP and is not (or is not yet) covered by another one, and is not eligible for Medicare. Individual health coverage is expensive—and furthermore, the ex-employee or a member of his or her family might have a medical condition that makes insurance harder to obtain or raises its cost even higher.

Two federal statutes, the Comprehensive Omnibus Budget Reconciliation Act (COBRA) and the Health Insurance Portability and Accessibility Act (HIPAA) work together to make the transition between EGHPs, or from EGHP coverage to individual health coverage, at least somewhat smoother. Both statutes impose responsibilities on the employer, so the health plan administrator must be aware of these duties.

§ 19.02   COBRA CONTINUATION COVERAGE

[A] Qualifying Events

Continuation coverage is the right of a "qualified beneficiary" (i.e., a former employee or his or her spouse and dependents) to maintain coverage under the employer's group health plan after a "COBRA event." A COBRA event is either personal or work-related and poses a threat to coverage under the ordinary circumstances:

- The employee is terminated or has hours reduced (unless termination is for gross misconduct);
- The employee divorces or becomes legally separated;
- The employee's dependent child ceases to be covered by the plan (usually because of "aging out");
- The employee's employer files for bankruptcy protection;
- The employee becomes Medicare-eligible (which entitles the employee's spouse to COBRA coverage);
- The employee dies (obviously, this is only a COBRA event for the survivors).

Although COBRA does not define "gross misconduct," the standard is probably the same as "willful misconduct"—substantial and willful disregard of the employer's best interests. [*Chatterjee v. School Dist. of Philadelphia,* 170 F. Supp. 2d 509 (E.D. Pa. 2001). *But see Lloynd v. Hanover Foods Corp.,* 72 F. Supp. 2d 469 (D. Del. 1999) (a factory worker fired for ruining a batch of product was merely negligent, and therefore was entitled to COBRA notice; the plan had to pay $3,000 of her medical expenses, plus a $25,250 civil penalty ($50 a day) for failure to give notice.]

Whenever a "qualifying event" occurs, anyone who performs services for the employer and is covered by the EGHP must be given COBRA rights—including partners, self-employed people who are allowed to participate in the plan, and eligible independent contractors.

> **Tip:** Continuation coverage is also available if the ex-employee's child is no longer a dependent because he or she has reached age 19 and is not a full-time student.

If a cafeteria plan includes health benefits, COBRA applies only to benefits actually elected by a plan participant, not those that he or she declines. COBRA does not apply to Flexible Spending Accounts, Medical Savings Accounts, or to plans that are substantially limited to qualified long-term care services, because these are not deemed to be conventional health plans.

When a person makes a COBRA election, health insurance coverage continues under the EGHP—but the employee, not the employer, pays the premium. (The employer can also agree to subsidize the COBRA premium, e.g., as an early retirement incentive.) The employer can impose an administrative charge of up to 2% of the premium, but no other fees or charges. The COBRA premium is set once a year, in advance.

[B] Covered Businesses

Businesses are subject to COBRA if they have 20 or more employees on a typical workday, and if they maintain a group health plan (either insured or self-insured). Most of the states (all except Alabama, Arizona, Delaware, Hawaii, Idaho, Indiana, Michigan, Montana, Pennsylvania, Virginia, and Washington) have COBRA expansion statutes that require companies with fewer than 20 employees to provide the equivalent of the federal COBRA notice and continuation coverage rights.

The length of the continuation coverage period can be anywhere from 30 days (in Oklahoma) to 24 months (Connecticut); the most common duration is 18 months, required in California, Colorado, Florida, Kentucky, Maryland, Massachusetts, Minnesota, Nevada, New Hampshire, New York, North Carolina, Rhode Island, South Dakota, West Virginia, and Wisconsin. [This information comes from State Health Facts Online: State Continuation Coverage for Small Firm Employees (COBRA Expansions) on the Kaiser Family Foundation Web site, <http://www.kff.org>]

Note, however, that employees probably will not be able to sue in state court if they allege that COBRA claims were denied in bad faith, because this is an area in which ERISA preempts state enforcement. [*Estate of Coggins v. Wagner Hopkins Inc.*, 183 F. Supp. 2d 1126 (W.D. Wis. 2001); *Harrelson v. Blue Cross/ Blue Shield of Alabama*, 150 F. Supp. 2d 1290 (M.D. Ala. 2001). The *Coggins* case also says that the ex-employee cannot sue the employer, insurer, or plan administrator to recover medical expenses that she had to pay out-of-pocket when her COBRA coverage was improperly terminated.]

Self-insured plans are subject to COBRA, too. The "premium" for them is a reasonable estimate, using reasonable actuarial assumptions, of the cost of providing health coverage for employees similarly situated to the qualified beneficiary.

Continuation coverage must be the same as active employees receive, although continuation coverage can change as the underlying plan changes. If the employer terminates or reduces coverage in an EGHP, qualified beneficiaries must be allowed to elect coverage under whatever plan the employer continues to maintain for similarly situated active employees. The employer cannot condition continuation coverage on submission of evidence of insurability. [See I.R.C. § 4980B(f)(2)(D)]

[C] Family Rights

The employee's spouse and children may also have independent rights to maintain coverage: for instance, after a divorce, when the former employee dies, or when the former employee becomes eligible for Medicare. (In this situation, the former employee no longer has COBRA rights—but, because Medicare does not cover spouses or dependents, these family members have COBRA rights.)

Continuation coverage is available if the ex-employee's child is no longer a dependent (e.g., reaches age 19 and is not a full-time student).

The one-time employee can exercise the COBRA election on behalf of his or her spouse and children, and the spouse can exercise the election on behalf of the children. However, only plan participants, not their beneficiaries, are entitled to receive penalties if the plan administrator fails to provide COBRA notice. [*Wright v. Hanna Steel Corp.*, 270 F.3d 1336 (11th Cir. 2001)]

[D] Duration of Coverage

COBRA specifies minimum obligations that employers must meet; they always have discretion to provide additional coverage.

The basic duration of COBRA continuation coverage for ex-employees is 18 months, starting with the qualifying event. However, if the ex-employee satisfies the Social Security Administration definition of total disability (basically, is incapable of substantial gainful activity), the employee and family members are entitled to 29 months of continuation coverage not 18. But for the 11 months after the end of the normal 18-month term, the employer can lawfully charge the employee 150% of the premium, not just the normal 102%.

Qualified beneficiaries can get 29 months of continuation coverage with respect to the same qualifying event if they are qualified with respect to a termination of employment or a reduction in hours; they became disabled within the first 60 days of COBRA continuation coverage; and they give the plan administrator a copy of the determination of disability within 60 days of the date it was issued and also within the initial 18-month COBRA period.

If the qualifying event is the ex-employee's becoming eligible for Medicare, his or her qualified beneficiaries are entitled to 36 months of continuation coverage.

However, COBRA entitlement ends if:

- The employer terminates and does not replace the EGHP for active employees (in effect, there is no longer any plan whose coverage can be continued);
- The qualified beneficiary fails to pay the COBRA premium;
- The employee becomes eligible for Medicare (although family members still have COBRA rights);
- The qualified beneficiary gains coverage under another EGHP.

The Supreme Court ruled, in *Geissal v. Moore Medical Group* [524 U.S. 74 (1998)], that the employer can terminate COBRA coverage if the employee gains access to other coverage AFTER making a COBRA election, but cannot terminate COBRA eligibility on the basis of coverage (for instance, coverage under a spouse's plan) that the employee had access to before the COBRA election.

By the time the case was remanded to the district court, the plaintiff had died, and his estate maintained the litigation. The estate contended that the plan was unjustly enriched by refusing to provide benefits, so ERISA § 502(a)(3) entitled it to equitable relief. The district court disagreed saying that the estate sought money damages, which are not considered "equitable relief" for this purpose. [*Geissal v. Moore Med. Group*, 158 F. Supp. 2d 957 (E.D. Mo. 2001)]

[E] COBRA Regulations

The IRS published important Proposed Regulations at 63 Fed. Reg. 708 (Jan. 7, 1998), adopted as 26 C.F.R. § 54.4980B-1 to conform COBRA to HIPAA (see below), the Small Business Job Protection Act [Pub. L. No. 104-188], and various other statutes. As a result of these changes, qualified beneficiaries can get 29 months (rather than the basic 18 months) of COBRA coverage with respect to the same qualifying event if:

- They are all qualified with respect to a termination of employment or a reduction in hours;
- They became disabled (as defined by the Social Security Administration) within the first 60 days of COBRA continuation coverage;
- They gave the plan administrator a copy of the determination of disability within the initial 18-month COBRA period and also within 60 days of the date the determination was issued.

During the 11-month extension, the employer can charge a premium that is 150% of the applicable premium, whereas the employer is limited to charging

102% of the premium during the 18-month basic COBRA period. Charging 150% is not considered premium discrimination on the basis of health status, so I.R.C. § 9802(b) is not violated. If there is a second qualifying event during a disability extension, then COBRA coverage can last for 36 months, with the 150% premium charged until the end of the 36-month period.

HIPAA entitles children born to, or adopted by, covered employees during a period of COBRA coverage to be covered by COBRA. The child's maximum coverage period runs from the date of the employee's qualifying event, and not from the child's birth or adoption. The effect is that the child's COBRA coverage ends at the same time as the coverage of other family members.

Under the January 7, 1998 rule, Medical Savings Accounts and plans substantially all of whose coverage is for qualified long-term care services (as defined by I.R.C. § 7702B) are not subject to the COBRA continuation coverage obligation.

The IRS' next move was to finalize regulations first proposed in 1987. The Final Rule at 64 Fed. Reg. 5160 (Feb. 3, 1999) includes rules for coping with EGHPs during corporate transitions. [See § 16.01] It is effective for qualifying events that occur in plan years beginning on or after January 1, 2000. If the EGHP provides both core health coverage and noncore coverage (e.g., vision and dental), it is no longer necessary to allow qualified employees to elect only the core coverage.

Treasury Decision 8928, 66 Fed. Reg. 1843 (Jan. 10, 2001) supplements the February 1999 Final Rule. Treasury Decision 8928's effective date is January 10, 2001, and it applies to qualifying events that occur on or after January 1, 2002. Under this Treasury Decision, all benefits offered by a business are treated as a single plan, unless the governing instruments make it clear that the benefits come from separate plans.

If a plan claims exemption from COBRA on the grounds that it has fewer than 20 employees, part-time employees will be reflected in the calculation on the basis of Full-Time Equivalents (i.e., 80 persons working 10 hours a week = 20 FTEs), no matter how they are scheduled. This provision was included to deter employers from manipulating scheduling.

Treasury Decision 8928 also finalizes rules about COBRA requirements in business reorganizations. The purchaser of a substantial asset such as a plant or corporate division or of substantially all the assets of a trade or business will be treated as a successor employer if the seller entirely ceases to provide group health plans, and the buyer continues business operations involving the assets. A transfer that has the same effect (including a bankruptcy-related transaction) can be treated as an asset "sale" even if it takes some other form for official purposes. Under the T.D., in an asset sale, employees have a qualifying event if they terminate employment and do not receive continuation coverage from the successor—even if they are then rehired in the same job.

§ 19.03   COBRA AND THE FMLA

Taking FMLA leave [*see* Chapter 38] is not in and of itself a COBRA-quali-fying event. But if an employee who was covered by the EGHP before or during the FMLA leave fails to return to work after the FMLA leave, there is a qualifying event for this person (and any dependent at risk of losing health coverage) as of the last day of the FMLA leave. The employer is not allowed to make the ex-employee reimburse the employer for health premiums paid during the leave.

However, there is no qualifying event if, while the employee is on leave, the employer eliminates EGHP coverage for the entire group of workers the person on leave belonged to. The rationale is that the worker would have lost health coverage even if he or she had not taken leave.

The qualifying event for an employee who does not return to work occurs on the last day of the FMLA leave, and the regular COBRA notice must be given. The qualifying event occurs even if the employee had an obligation to pay health insur-ance premiums during the leave but failed to do so. State laws that require a longer leave than the 12-week FMLA period are disregarded in determining whether a qualifying event has occurred.

§ 19.04   COBRA NOTICE

[A]   Generally

One of the most important tasks in COBRA administration is timely issuance of the proper notices, as provided by I.R.C. § 4980B(f)(6)(A) and ERISA § 606. The employer has an obligation to notify the plan administrator when employ-ment-related qualifying events occur, such as when an employee is terminated or laid off, or when the company files in Chapter 11 for bankruptcy protection. The responsibility for reporting personal qualifying events, such as divorce or separa-tion, rests on the qualified beneficiary.

Notice must be given to the administrator within 60 days of the qualifying event. The plan administrator then has 14 days from receiving notice to notify the qualified beneficiary of COBRA rights and how to elect them.

The notice should explain:

- Who can be a qualified beneficiary;
- What events trigger the right to continuation coverage;
- How and when to elect coverage;
- The right to reject the coverage (e.g., for financial reasons);
- Rights of the other qualified beneficiaries if one qualified beneficiary waives the election;
- Obligation to pay the premiums on time;
- How long the coverage will last;
- Events that will allow the employer to terminate continuation coverage.

Although the COBRA notice must be written, an oral waiver of the election has been held to be valid and enforceable. [*Hummer v. Sears, Roebuck & Co.*, 1994 WL 116117 (E.D. Pa. March 21, 1994)]

> **Tip:** Under Department of Labor Final Rules published on April 9, 2002, COBRA notices can be given electronically (for instance by e-mailing employees who consent to receive notice in electronic form), [*See* 67 Fed. Reg. 17263].

The employer's business records, showing that COBRA notice was mailed, are adequate evidence to prove that notice was given, even if the employer cannot produce a copy of the actual letter that was sent to the employees. [*Roberts v. National Health Corp.*, 133 F.3d 916 (4th Cir. 1998)]

According to the Fifth Circuit, the employer satisfies its duty by sending the notice by certified mail to the employee's last known address—even if the employer learns that the employee did not actually receive the notice [*Degruise v. Sprint Corp.*, 279 F.3d 333 (5th Cir. 2002); *see* <http://www.spencernet.com/Archive/News012902.html>]

If the ex-employee clearly fails to make a timely election, this will excuse the plan administrator's mistake in putting an incorrect return date on the notice. [*Deering v. O.K. Indus.*, 2001 U.S. App. LEXIS 8923 (8th Cir. May 11, 2001)]

Department of Labor Advisory Opinion 99-14A allows the health plan to satisfy the notice requirement by sending a single notice to multiple beneficiaries living at the same address: e.g., one first-class letter covering the employee, spouse, and dependent children. But there must either be a separate election notice in the mailing for each qualified beneficiary, or an explanation of their independent rights to elect coverage. [*See* <http://www.corbel.com/newssftu25.asp>]

Qualified beneficiaries must be given a period of at least 60 days to either accept or waive continuation coverage. The election period must begin no later than the time EGHP coverage would end if there were no election. In other words, notice must be given early enough to prevent any gap in coverage. The Eleventh Circuit has ruled that if the COBRA notice fails to specify the 60-day period, then the right to make the election extends indefinitely. [*Branch v. G. Bernd Co.*, 955 F.2d 1574 (11th Cir. 1992)]

If an ex-employee needs only a certain number of months of COBRA coverage (usually the waiting period for eligibility in a new plan), COBRA does not permit the ex-employer's plan to require the ex-employee to pay for a full 18 months of retroactive coverage. [*Popovits v. Circuit City Stores Inc.*, 185 F.3d 276 (7th Cir. 1999)]

The first premium payment is not due until 45 days after the election. Qualified beneficiaries get an automatic grace period of at least 30 days, during which coverage cannot be terminated for nonpayment of premiums—even if the underlying EGHP has a shorter grace period. But if the plan provides a longer grace period, the employee must be permitted to take advantage of it.

A plan that permits retirees to continue coverage at their own expense for an indefinite time (after the COBRA requirement ends) nevertheless must issue COBRA notices at retirement, because retirement is a COBRA event. [*Mansfield v. Chicago Park Dist. Group Plan*, 997 F. Supp. 1053 (N.D. Ill. 1998)]

In *Fallo v. Piccadilly Cafeterias Inc.* [141 F.3d 580 (5th Cir. 1998)], an employee was entitled to an 11-month COBRA extension, after the normal 18-month period, because his wife became disabled during the 18-month period. The terms of the plan echoed the COBRA statute, requiring that notice of the Social Security Administration's determination of disability be given before the initial 18-month period expired. But the SPD merely required that notice be given to the plan within 60 days of the SSA disability determination and did not rule out extensions for disabilities beginning late in the 18-month period. The SPD was the document given to employees, and therefore the document that the Fifth Circuit chose to enforce.

A terminated employee indicated an intention to elect COBRA coverage, but never paid the initial premium. When she incurred medical expenses, she asked the plan to reimburse her but deduct the continuation coverage premium from the reimbursement she requested. The plan refused to do so, and the court agreed. [*Goletto v. W.H. Braum Inc.*, 1999 WL 1096042 (D. Kan. Nov. 8, 1999)] It is legitimate for a plan to terminate coverage retroactive to the date of the qualifying event. Otherwise, employees could gamble by applying for continuation coverage, then withholding premium payments until they encountered medical expenses that they wanted the plan to cover.

An employer that mistakenly extended continuation coverage longer than the collectively bargained date could lawfully terminate the coverage as soon as it discovered the mistake, even though the former employee's wife had encountered $45,000 in hospital bills in the meantime. The case of *Coker v. TWA* [165 F.3d 579 (7th Cir. 1999)] holds that it was not reasonable of the plaintiff to rely on the employer's mistake, because the plaintiff received an accurate written explanation of the benefits when he was laid off.

COBRA-qualified beneficiaries have been treated as unsecured creditors of the employer, if the employer sells its assets and then goes bankrupt. [In re *ABC Fabrics of Tampa, Inc.*, 2001 WL 261785 (M.D. Fla. Feb. 8, 2001)]

[B] Penalties for Notice Failure

The Internal Revenue Code and ERISA § 502(g) impose a penalty of $110 per day per beneficiary for noncompliance, subject to a maximum of $220 per family per day. There is also a limit of the smaller of $500,000 or 10% of the amount the employer paid (or incurred obligations for) its EGHPs in the preceding year. Furthermore, a health plan that does not conform to COBRA does not generate I.R.C. § 162 "ordinary and necessary business expenses." Therefore, the employer is denied a deduction for health plan costs.

The penalty is imposed on the employer. It can also be imposed on the individuals responsible for administering the plan or providing benefits under it, if those individuals have contractual responsibility for running the plan. A third-party administrator (TPA) would fall into this category unless factors beyond the administrator's control prevented the notice from being given. There is a cap of $2 million for all plans administered, for an administrator who fails to satisfy all the COBRA requirements, but who is not guilty of willful neglect and who did have reasonable support for his or her decisions.

The penalty can be reduced or waived if no one had reason to know that the appropriate notices were not given, or if the failure to notify was corrected within 30 days after a responsible person became aware of the failure.

Statutory penalties are not available in a suit for denial of benefits, only for refusal or failure to provide the necessary notice. [*Moreno v. St. Francis Hosp. & Health Ctr.*, 2001 U.S. Dist. LEXIS 17206 (N.D. Ill. Oct. 17, 2001)]

The Southern District of Ohio imposed $1,020 in statutory penalties on a plan that failed to send a COBRA notice. The court rejected the employer's argument that the ex-employee could not afford the premiums and therefore was not damaged by the notice failure. [*Chenoweth v. Wal-Mart Stores Inc.*, 159 F. Supp. 2d 1032 (S.D. Ohio 2001)]

In addition to the statutory penalties, any person or organization can be sued under ERISA Title I by someone who lost coverage because of the defendant's actions or inaction.

For instance, *Wright v. Hanna Steel Corp.* [270 F.3d 1336 (11th Cir. 2001)] affirms the District Court's award of $75/day penalties to the participant when the employer failed to provide COBRA notice. However, the Eleventh Circuit reversed the District Court's award to the participant's spouse and children.

In this case, the plaintiff quit his job at the end of 1996, and did not receive a COBRA notice. He started a new job right away and applied to transfer his family's coverage to the new employer's plan. The transfer application was denied because the insurer's records showed that he was still covered by the former employer's plan. A couple of months later, the plaintiff told the former employer about the situation and asked it to check its records, but he got no reply. Several months after that, the plaintiff's wife was diagnosed with cancer. The insurer treated her illness as a noncovered preexisting condition. Eventually, the insurer agreed to cover the wife's cancer treatment. The plaintiff sued the employer for statutory penalties for failure to provide notice, for failure to provide the notice, and for attorneys' fees. The District Court awarded a total of $93,000: $75/day to the employee and his wife, $10/day to the children for a period of 18 months, plus $24,000 in attorneys' fees.

When a plan administrator is aware that a COBRA notice was not delivered, the good-faith requirement is not satisfied if the administrator fails to send another notice. [*Wooderson v. Am. Airlines, Inc.*, 2001 U.S. Dist. LEXIS 3721 (N.D. Tex. March 23, 2001)]

The same court held that it is not necessary to exhaust administrative remedies within the plan before suing for failure to provide COBRA notice (although it is required before an ERISA claim). An employer cannot get a failure-to-notify case dismissed because it acted in good faith. Statutory damages can be awarded whether or not the plaintiff has actual damages, and whether or not the employer acted in good faith, although these factors can affect the amount of damages. [*Thompson v. Origin Technology in Business*, 2001 U.S. Dist. LEXIS 12609 (N.D. Tex. Aug. 20, 2001)]

§ 19.05   HEALTH INSURANCE PORTABILITY

[A]   Coverage

The Health Insurance Portability and Accountability Act of 1996 (HIPAA) [I.R.C. Chapter 100, §§ 9801-9806], also known as the Kennedy-Kassebaum Act, copes with the situation in which a person leaves employment with one employer, gets another job, and experiences health care bills before he or she is covered by the new employer's plan, or where the new plan might exclude coverage of the ailment as a preexisting condition.

For plan years beginning after June 30, 1997, the HIPAA "creditable coverage" requirement in effect allows coverage to carry over from one plan to the other, as long as employees use COBRA (or other means) to make sure that there is never a gap of 63 days or more in coverage.

Although plans can control costs by imposing pre-existing condition limitations, the scope of the limitation is restricted. Under HIPAA, the most stringent definition of "pre-existing condition" that a plan can apply is a mental or physical condition for which medical advice, diagnosis, care, or treatment was sought during the six-month period before the enrollment date. In general, the maximum duration for a pre-existing condition limitation is 12 months from the enrollment date for the current health plan. The enrollment date is the earlier of the first day of the waiting period for enrollment or the date of actual enrollment. Late enrollees (who fail to enroll in the plan during the open enrollment period, or the first period of eligibility) can be subject to an 18-month rather than a 12-month pre-existing condition limitation.

The fact that someone underwent genetic testing is not a "pre-existing condition" (even if susceptibility to a disease or condition is revealed), as long as there is no actual diagnosis of an existing illness. Pre-existing condition limitations cannot be imposed on pregnancy. There are very few situations in which newly born or adopted children can be deemed to have a pre-existing condition. Plans that include dependent coverage must offer a "dependent special enrollment period" lasting at least 30 days during which a new dependent acquired by marriage, birth or adoption can be added to the plan.

"Creditable coverage" means coverage from another EGHP, from individual health insurance, from Medicare Part A or B, or from Medicaid. Health plan coverage ceases to be creditable, and therefore is not portable to a new plan, if there is a break of 63 days or more during which the employee is completely without health insurance. The so-called affiliation period (the waiting period after a new employee enrolls in a new health plan) is not considered a period of being uninsured.

> **Tip:** HIPAA obligates EGHPs to provide a certification of the dates creditable coverage began and ended, whenever a former participant gains or loses entitlement to COBRA continuation coverage. The ex-participant can also request the certification at any time within 24 months of the COBRA event, so he or she can submit it to a new plan to prove the existence of creditable coverage. Insured (rather than self-insured) plans are exempt from the certification requirement if they have a procedure for having the insurer issue the certificates.

The mental health parity requirement applies to HIPAA. [*See* PWBA rules at 62 Fed. Reg. 66957 (Dec. 22, 1997)]

[B] Nondiscrimination Requirements

HIPAA forbids discrimination in benefits in health plans. (In this context, discrimination is closer to the Title VII sense than the pension plan sense of not favoring highly compensated employees.) Under HIPAA, it is unlawful for a plan to base its rules for eligibility or continued eligibility, or its definition of the waiting period, on an employee's or dependent's:

- Health status;
- Physical or mental health condition;
- Claims experience;
- Past receipt of health care;
- Medical history;
- Genetic information;
- Evidence of insurability;
- Disability.

None of these factors can be used to increase the premium or other contribution that an individual plan participant has to pay, when compared to other similarly situated participants. HIPAA does not limit the premiums or copayments that employers can require participants to pay. It is also legitimate to offer employees discounts, rebates, or reductions in their copayment obligations based on their participation in health promotion and disease prevention programs (such as smoking cessation or weight loss programs).

[C] Insurers' Obligations

One of Congress's rationales in passing HIPAA was that employers, especially small companies, often had difficulty getting insurance—and once they had insurance, they often faced cancellation of coverage or at least excessively high rate increases.

HIPAA imposes obligations on insurers with respect to group health policies. The rules are different for "small employer" coverage (2–50 employees) and "large employer coverage" (groups of more than 50 employees). HIPAA's general requirement is that insurers who sell small employer coverage within a state must sell to all small employers who want to purchase the coverage, although there is no corresponding obligation to sell to would-be large-group buyers.

In either the small or the large-group market, the insurer has an obligation to renew coverage or continue it in force as long as the purchase chooses, unless the purchaser:

- Stops paying the premiums;
- Commits fraud related to the policy;
- The insurer withdraws from the relevant market within the state;
- Plan enrollees move outside the service area for a network plan;
- (In a plan based on association membership) enrollees cease to be members of the association;
- The purchaser violates the rules on participation or contributions to the plan.

If an insurer discontinues one kind of group coverage but maintains others, all affected plan sponsors, participants, and beneficiaries are entitled to 90 days' notice of the discontinuance. The plan sponsor must be given the option to purchase the other coverage that the insurer offers in that market.

The insurer must act uniformly, without considering the existing or potential health problems of plan participants and beneficiaries, or the claims experience of the plan sponsor. An insurer that chooses to discontinue all of its coverage in the small- or large-group market must give state insurance regulators 180 days notice of intent to discontinue. An insurer that withdraws will be barred from re-entering the market for five years. This requirement is imposed to prevent insurers from leaving and re-entering the market purely based on their own needs.

[D] Exceptions to the Portability Rule

Plans of certain types are not subject to the portability rules, because they are not deemed to be health benefit plans:

- Plans that offer accident and/or disability insurance;
- Liability insurance plans;
- Insured plans that provide medical benefits that are secondary or incidental to other benefits;
- Limited scope plans providing, e.g., dental, vision, or long-term care benefits;
- Coverage that is limited to a specified disease or illness;
- Fixed-indemnity plans (e.g., hospitalization insurance);
- Medicare Supplementary (Medigap) insurance.

Plans that cover only a single current employee are not subject to portability requirements.

Flexible Spending Accounts (FSAs) are "excepted benefits" under ERISA §§ 732 and 733(c) and I.R.C. §§ 9831 and 9832(c). Therefore, health insurance portability is not required for these plans. [*See* the "clarification of regulations" jointly issued by the IRS, the Pension and Welfare Benefit Administration, and the Department of Health and Human Services at 62 Fed. Reg. 67688 (Dec. 29, 1997)] The FSA is excepted from HIPAA if the employee's maximum FSA benefit for the year does not exceed twice the employee's salary reduction election for the year, as long as the employee has other EGHP coverage and as long as the FSA provides at least some benefits that are not "excepted benefits."

Another IRS/DOL/HCFA joint clarification, published at 62 Fed. Reg. 67689 (Dec. 29, 1997) does not allow plans to establish rules for initial or continued eligibility on the basis of health status (including medical condition, claims experience, receipt of health care, medical history, genetic testing, insurability, or disability. Employees and their dependents (even late enrollees) cannot be required to pass a physical examination in order to enroll in the health plan.

HCFA's Program Memorandum 00-04 says that HIPAA forbids the use of "actively at work" provisions (i.e., limiting coverage under a new plan to people who were working on the day on which a plan changes its carrier) to discriminate on the basis of disability or other health factors.

[E] Penalties and Enforcement

Health plans are subject to a penalty tax, under I.R.C. Chapter 100, for failure to comply with the HIPAA portability rules. The basic penalty rate is $110 per person per day of noncompliance. The maximum liability that a single-employer plan can incur is the smaller of $500,000 or 10% of the amount paid or incurred by the EGHP for the preceding year.

Liability can be waived or reduced if the person responsible for the error or omission did not know, and could not have known, of the defect; if the cause of the failure was reasonable; and no willful neglect was involved. Penalties can also be avoided if the failure is corrected within 30 days of the first date it could have been detected. If the source of the problem is the insurer's error or misconduct, plans with 2–50 employees will not be subjected to the penalty tax.

However, a minimum tax that cannot be waived is imposed if the HIPAA compliance failure is found after the plan has received notice of income tax examination. In that case, the tax is the lesser of $2,500 or the tax that would otherwise be imposed.

CHAPTER 20

DISABILITY PLANS

§ 20.01 INTRODUCTION

Because of an acute illness, a chronic illness, or an injury (work-related or otherwise), many working-age individuals will go through brief, extended, or permanent periods during which they are unable to do their normal job.

Almost one-eighth of the people between ages 16–65 had a physical problem that limited their work capacity in some ways. That means almost 20 million people nationwide. Over 5 percent of adults—almost nine million people—had a disability severe enough to prevent them from working. Between 6 and 12% of the average corporate payroll goes to disability-related costs.

There are both public (Social Security Disability Income; Worker's Compensation) and private systems for dealing with disability. Some states require employers to provide disability benefits; in other states, employers often do this as an employee benefit.

In 2001, a survey by the Consumer Federation of America and the American Council of Life Insurers found that 40% of workers have no long-term disability coverage. Among those who have the coverage, 41% consider it inadequate. Workers feel less secure that they understand disability coverage than other benefits such as pensions and health benefits. [Marcy Gordon, *Study Finds Worker Coverage Lacking*, (April 23, 2001) <http://news.excite.com/news/ap/010423/18/workers-disability> (posted to news.excite.com on April 23, 2001)]

§ 20.02 EMPLOYMENT-BASED PLANS

As of 1993, the Bureau of Labor Statistics found that 87% of mid-sized and larger companies offered some form of short-term disability coverage (25% sickness and accident insurance; 49% paid sick leave but no other provision, 26% offering both). But long-term disability (LTD) coverage was less common, offered to 41% of the employees of those businesses.

Usually, a short-term disability (STD) is defined either as one that lasts less than six months, or one that lasts less than a year. Long-term disability benefits typically terminate after a period of years (e.g., five years) or at age 65, when the employee would presumably be retiring anyway.

A typical arrangement is for the employer to self-insure for short-term disability, but to buy LTD insurance (possibly with the covered employees contributing part of the cost). It is also typical for STD and LTD plans to use different definitions of disability. The long-term plan has more restrictive definitions, because the employer's possible exposure is greater.

Using an "own occupation" definition (the person is disabled when unable to carry out the duties of the predisability occupation) makes it easier to qualify for benefits than using an "any occupation" definition (benefits stop as soon as the person is able to return to any work, or any work suitable to his or her education and training). Another frequent plan design is for the definition to start out as "own-occ" but switch after two years to inability to perform any occupation suitable to the individual's education and training.

337

LTD plans usually replace 60–70% of predisability income; 60% is the most common level. The plan may also limit income replacement from all sources, including Worker's Compensation and Social Security, to a percentage such as 75% of predisability income. Many plans offset (reduce) disability benefits to account for government benefits and damages received from tort suits or settlements (e.g., if the employee was injured in an accident or by a defective product).

Another cost-saving measure is to have benefits start after a waiting period, so that the plan covers situations in which work ability is impaired for a long time, but not ordinary illnesses and minor injuries (which are probably covered by sick leave anyway).

A Taft-Hartley plan is a temporary disability plan jointly run by employers and a union. The plan's goal is to assist employees who are in financial need because of a disability, while also helping them return to work as soon as possible (if they can be rehabilitated adequately).

As an incentive for rehabilitation, the plan may continue benefits at a low level while the individual engages in a trial period of re-employment, or undertakes part-time or lower-level work in an attempt to re-enter the workforce. [*See* Chapter 37 for a discussion of Age Discrimination in Employment Act (ADEA) [29 U.S.C. § 621 *et seq.*] implications of disability plans]

Many companies have succeeded in controlling costs through integrated disability management (whether or not the disability is occupational in origin). Using a single source to manage rehabilitation of injured workers and administer disability and Worker's Compensation benefits can be an effective tactic. [*See, e.g.,* Dianne Dyck, *Disability Management Best Practices*, <http://www.benefits canada.com/departments/disability/disability.html>]

§ 20.03   STATE MANDATES

In five states (California, Hawaii, New York, New Jersey, Rhode Island), employers are required to provide TDI (Temporary Disability Insurance) coverage for between 26 and 52 weeks of non-occupational temporary disability for industrial and commercial workers. Either the state administers a fund from which employer contributions are distributed to disabled employees, or the state maintains a fund but gives employers the choice of self-insuring, buying insurance, or paying into a union-sponsored disability plan.

TDI benefits are offset (that is, reduced) by Worker's Compensation and unemployment benefits.

§ 20.04   COMPLIANCE ISSUES

[A]   ERISA Compliance

For ERISA purposes, most disability arrangements are welfare benefit plans, and therefore subject to disclosure, filing, and fiduciary requirements. Some disability plans, however, are top-hat plans that only cover executives, so the employer's disclosure obligations are more limited. If a plan is maintained only to comply with Worker's Compensation or state mandates, then ERISA § 4(b)(3) exempts the plan from ERISA compliance obligations. ERISA compliance is also excused in situations where an employer makes payments out of its general assets to an employee who is out of work for medical reasons. [*See* 29 C.F.R. § 2510.3-1(b)(1)]

If the employee pays all the premiums for LTD insurance, and the employer's only role is to administer the payments (without giving its approval of the policy), then ERISA does not preempt a suit by the employee against the insurer claiming bad faith termination of benefits. There are three tests for deciding whether ERISA preempts litigation about a disability policy:

- Was there a "plan, fund or program"? In this case, a plan was clearly present—but it was not an ERISA plan;
- Does the arrangement qualify for the ERISA safe harbor? The safe harbor is available if the employer does not make any contributions to the plan; the plan is completely voluntary; the employer does not profit from the plan (although it can legitimately receive a reasonable administrative fee); and the employer allows one or more insurers to publicize the availability of the program, but does not endorse or recommend it;
- Is the employer's sole function under the plan collecting premiums, or does it have deeper involvement? [*Bagden v. Equitable Life Assurance Society of the United States*, 1999 U.S. Dist. LEXIS 7066 (E.D. Pa. March 11, 1999), discussed in Shannon P. Duffy, *Employee-Paid Disability Policy Falls Under ERISA Safe Harbor*, <http://www.law.com/servlet/ContentServer?pagename= OpenMarket/Xcelerate/View&c=LawArticle&cid=1015973950606&live=true &cst=1&pc=0&pa=0]

ERISA does not preempt an employee's state-law claims about denial of benefits under an individual policy that was converted from a group policy. The employer is no longer involved, so neither is ERISA. [*Demars v. CIGNA Corp.*, 173 F.3d 443 (1st Cir. 1999)]

ERISA does not preempt state "notice-prejudice" laws. Such laws prevent insurers from denying a claim on the basis that the insured person did not give timely notice of the covered event, unless the delay really causes harm to the insurer. [*Daug v. UNUM Life Ins. Co.*, 1999 WL 238236 (10th Cir. 1999); *Cisneros v. UNUM*, 134 F.3d 939 (9th Cir. 1999)]

According to the Seventh Circuit, the plaintiff in *Feldman v. American Memorial Life Insurance Co.* [196 F.3d 783 (7th Cir. 1999)] was not totally disabled throughout the 90-day elimination period in her disability insurance policy. Therefore, her ERISA § 510 claim, that the employer fired her to prevent her from collecting benefits, had to fail. She never became eligible for the benefits, and therefore the employer could not have been motivated to terminate her to prevent payment of benefits she had earned.

The Northern District of Georgia would not allow a Long Term Disability insurer to recover three years of overpayments made to a partially disabled person who gave the insurer proper notice that he was working part-time (which would have justified termination of payments). But ERISA does allow termination of the payments on a prospective basis.

A plan participant who was denied benefits under a LTD plan sued under ERISA § 502(a)(3). The participant got a default judgment covering disability expenses, medical benefits, prejudgment interest, and attorneys' fees. [*Rogers v. Hartford Life & Accident Ins. Co.*, 167 F.3d 933 (5th Cir. 1999)] The plan got the court to reopen the case. The Fifth Circuit reduced the damages, on the grounds that the cost of medical treatment lay outside the disability plan's terms. The *Mertens* case [508 U.S. 248 (1993)] says that the I.R.C. § 502(a)(3) remedies are all equitable, so therefore compensatory damages are not available.

[B] Tax Issues

Whether an employer can get a tax deduction for the cost of its disability plan depends on satisfying I.R.C. § 162 (ordinary and necessary business expenses). The employer's contributions must also satisfy I.R.C. § 104.

From the employee's viewpoint, the key section is I.R.C. § 106, which excludes employer coverage under an accident and health insurance (A&H) plan from the employee's gross income. This section is usually interpreted to include the premiums that the employer pays to maintain an insured disability plan, as well as the value of coverage under a self-insured disability plan. After a disability occurs, the benefits received by the employee under A&H or disability insurance must be included in income to the extent that they are attributable to previously excluded employer contributions. Amounts paid directly by the employer to the employee are also includible in gross income.

However, benefits paid for permanent loss (or loss of use) of a body part or its function, or for disfigurement, are not included in the employee's income, as long as the benefit is computed without regard to absence from work.

The I.R.C. § 22 tax credit, often referred to as the Credit for the Elderly, also applies to individuals who retired at a time when they were permanently and totally disabled.

In *Thomas v. Commissioner* [2001 T.N.T. 173-7 (2001)], the employer sponsored an insured disability plan. It was a "premium conversion plan" (this type is also known as a premium-only or premium-payment plan). Participants could pay with pretax dollars, but the plaintiff elected to pay with after-tax dollars. He suffered several months of disability and collected about $5,000 in disability benefits, which he did not report as taxable income. However, because he used after-tax dollars, the benefits were tax-free under I.R.C. § 104(a)(3).

Tip: Enrollment materials for the plan should explain the consequences of paying with pretax versus after-tax dollars.

[C]   ADA Compliance

It should also be noted that a disability plan that imposes lower limits for mental health care than for care of physical ailments may violate the Americans with Disabilities Act (ADA). [Pub. L. No. 101-336] The Mental Health Parity Act [42 U.S.C. § 300gg], which expired in 2001 but was renewed in 2002, makes it unlawful for employee group health plans to set lower limits for mental health care than for treatment of physical illnesses. This statute, however, was not applicable to disability plans.

Early in 2000, the Supreme Court affirmed (without opinion) [528 U.S. 1106 (2000)] the Seventh Circuit's decision in *Doe v. Mutual of Ohio.* [179 F.3d 557 (7th Cir. 2000)] It does not violate the ADA's public accommodations title for an insured or self-insured health plan to impose a lower cap on benefits for AIDS-related illnesses or conditions than for other ailments. The Supreme Court would not grant privileged status to diseases that cause ADA disability over other diseases that do not.

ADA Title IV immunizes insurer and benefit plan decisions based on underwriting, classifying, or administering risk, as long as the decisions are not a subterfuge to escape ADA compliance. Decisions that have actuarial support are likely to qualify for this safe harbor. However, *Lewis v. Aetna Life Ins. Co.* [7 F. Supp. 2d 743 (E.D. Va. 1998)] does not allow safe harbor characterization for a distinction between mental and physical disabilities for which actuarial support was not proven.

Friedrich v. Intel Corp. [181 F.3d 1105 (9th Cir. 1999)] involved a self-funded LTD plan that excluded "mental, emotional or psychiatric illness or disorder of any type," but covered disability confirmed by "objective medical findings" such as lab tests and diagnostic scans. The plaintiff was terminated in October 1993. At that time, he suffered from symptoms that were diagnosed both as major depression and as Chronic Fatigue Syndrome (CFS). Eventually, he qualified for Social Security disability benefits.

Five doctors retained by his ex-employer reported that the plaintiff suffered from a noncovered psychiatric illness, with no objective evidence of organic illness. However, the Ninth Circuit required LTD benefits to be paid, on the grounds that Intel had failed to provide an adequate appeals procedure. It was also held that the plaintiff presented appropriate evidence that CFS is a coverable organic illness; that there was objective proof of his health status; and that any psychiatric problems were secondary to physical illness.

According to *Weyer v. Twentieth Century Fox Film Corp.* [198 F.3d 1104 (9th Cir. 2000)], ADA Title I was not violated by imposing different caps for mental and physical ailments. In this case, the plaintiff was totally disabled and could not perform essential functions of the job even with accommodation. Title III was not violated because there was no public accommodation involved, and insurance underwriting decisions are protected by the Title IV safe harbor.

Disability insurers seldom litigate mental disability cases until the second year. They may take a more proactive stance if they face the potential of claims with the same limits as physical disability claims, or without any limits at all.

[D] EEOC Compliance Manual

EEOC directives do not have the force of law. Even Regulations promulgated by this agency have often been invalidated by court decisions. However, you should consult Section 3 of the EEOC's Compliance Manual, issued October 3, 2000 [<http://www.eeoc.gov/docs/benefits.html>] for EEOC policy on what constitutes discrimination on the basis of age or handicap, and what "equal" benefits mean in the context of disability benefits.

The revised Compliance Manual permits employers to reduce long-term disability benefits to account for Social Security Disability Income, Worker's Compensation, and other non-age-based government benefits. LTD benefits paid to older workers can also be reduced by pension benefits that come from employer contributions, under two conditions. Either the employee voluntarily opts to receive the pension (at any age) or has reached age 62 of the plan's normal retirement age (whichever is later) and is eligible for a full, unreduced pension. In plans partially funded by employee contributions, the employer is only permitted to reduce benefits that can be traced back to its own contributions, not employee contributions.

The EEOC position is that disability retirement benefits are not equal if they are calculated on the basis of the number of years the employee would have worked until NRA, because that approach favors younger employees. But disability benefits under government programs can legitimately be used to reduce disability benefits paid by the employer.

[E] Other Compliance Issues

Disability benefits are not considered "medical care," so when an employee is terminated, the right to COBRA continuation coverage [see Chapter 19] extends to the employee group health plan but not to the long-term disability plan.

The Family and Medical Leave Act [Pub. L. No. 103-3. See Chapter 38] may entitle the employee to claim unpaid leave for personal medical needs.

In the view of the Ninth Circuit, the ADEA may be violated by calculating disability retirement benefits using the age at the time of hiring. The plan at issue calculated the benefit on the basis of years of service lost as a result of disability, based on the length of service between age 55 (presumed retirement date) and the date the claimant became a public employee. Under *Hazen* [see § 42.11[D]], calculations based on actual years of service are acceptable, because a younger person might have more years of service, and vice versa. But this is a slightly different question, because the age at hire had a strong effect on the potential disability benefit. The Ninth Circuit remanded the case to the District Court for disposition. [*Arnett v. California Public Employees Retirement Sys.*, 179 F.3d 690 (9th Cir. 1999)]

At least according to the First Circuit, a Social Security Disability Insurance (SSDI) determination is relevant to the question of whether a person receiving LTD benefits continues to be disabled. But the SSDI determination is not controlling, because ERISA-regulated disability plans and SSDI have different standards. [*Pari-Fasano v. ITT Hartford Life and Accident Ins. Co.*, 230 F.3d 415 (1st Cir. 2000)]

§ 20.05   CASE LAW ON "TOTAL DISABILITY"

In many instances, the question is not how to interpret the plan—the question is whether or not the claimant satisfies the plan's definition of "total disability." It may be inability to perform the applicant's own occupation, or any occupation for which his or her education and training qualifies him or her—or the definition may shift depending on the length of the period of disability.

Even if the question is ability to engage in "any gainful occupation," most courts will require consideration of the individual's earnings history and the availability of jobs in the relevant geographic area. [*See, e.g., Mossa v. Provident Life & Casualty Ins. Co.*, 36 F. Supp. 2d 524 (E.D.N.Y. 1999)]

It was permissible for the insurer to terminate LTD benefits, based on its conclusion that an actuary/business executive with hearing loss in both ears was able to do a variety of jobs appropriate for his experience and physical limitations. He submitted a report that there was no job available to him paying more than $45,000 a year, but the insurer reasonably relied on the Chicago Society of Actuaries' conclusion that there were many jobs, some of them paying six figures, that a hearing-impaired person could perform. [*O'Reilly v. Hartford Life & Accident Ins. Co.*, 272 F.3d 955 (7th Cir. 2001)]

The Ninth Circuit found that the plaintiff was not "totally disabled," under the plan's standard of inability to engage in any occupation or employment, when several doctors testified that the plaintiff could do most sedentary or light-duty jobs. [*Goodberry v. Northrop Grumman Long Term Disability Income Plan*, 1999 U.S. App. LEXIS 29507 (9th Cir. Nov. 4, 1999)] The plan did not grant discretionary authority, so the court performed de novo review. The court did not find it necessary for the plan to consult a vocational expert, because the expert would not be able to contribute to the determination of inability to perform any occupation.

The employee in *Whatley v. C.N.A. Insurance* [189 F.3d 1310 (11th Cir. 1999)] lost his job on September 29. Later, he applied for disability benefits, claiming that he became totally disabled on October 3. The benefits were denied, on the theory that he could not have been disabled on September 29 (because he worked on that day), so any disability must have arisen after employment was terminated. According to the Eleventh Circuit, however, he might have been totally disabled at the end of September. Summary judgment should not have been granted—fact questions remained to be settled, including medical evidence about the actual onset of total disability.

Riedl v. General American Life [248 F.3d 753 (8th Cir. 2001)] holds that the plaintiff should not have been granted summary judgment against the insurer: there was no clear evidence that he was totally disabled. The plan imposed a six-month waiting period. After that, an applicant would be deemed totally disabled if, for 24 months after the injury or illness, the applicant would be unable to work at his or her regular job or another reasonable job available within the employer company. After that 24-month period, the applicant would be considered totally disabled if unable to work at any occupation.

The plaintiff (a shift supervisor) went on medical leave in April 1995 and had surgery in August 1995. In September 1995, his cardiologist cleared him to return to work without restrictions. Soon thereafter, he accepted an early retirement severance package. In November 1995, he applied for LTD benefits. In December 1995, his attending physician and his cardiologist said he was totally disabled for his own job, but could do other work. The Eighth Circuit said that summary judgment was inappropriate, because the finder of fact would have to hear all the facts to decide the question of disability.

§ 20.06   EFFECT OF PLAN AMENDMENTS

In late 1999, the Eighth Circuit offered yet another lesson in the importance of careful drafting of plan documents. Ceridian Corporation used to pay insurance premiums for disabled individuals as part of its long-term disability plan. When it discontinued this practice, a group of disabled ex-employees sued. The SPD reserved the right to amend the plan, but did not specify whether it could be amended with respect to people who were already disabled at the time of the change. [*Barker v. Ceridian Corp.*, 193 F.3d 976 (8th Cir. 1999)] The Eighth Circuit held that the SPD provision was ambiguous. That opened the way for testimony about the company's intentions. The Eighth Circuit ordered Ceridian to continue paying for insurance for the group of ex-employees already disabled at the time of the change in the plan.

Another employer fared better in amending its disability plan. [*See Anderson v. Intermountain Power Serv. Corp.*, 1999 U.S. App. LEXIS 25629 (10th Cir. Oct. 14, 1999)] After the plaintiff became disabled and began to collect long-term disability benefits, the plan informed him that he would have to pay health insurance premiums to maintain his health coverage. He made partial but not full payments, and his health insurance was canceled. The District Court and Court of Appeals denied his ERISA and disability discrimination claims. Canceling coverage for late payment was not a breach of fiduciary duty. The plan had no legal obligation to accept partial payments. Accepting some partial payments as an accommodation to the ex-employee did not waive the right to enforce the payment provisions at a later time.

§ 20.07   CLAIMS PROCEDURES AND THE STANDARD OF REVIEW

See Chapter 13 for a discussion of claims procedures. The Department of Labor's final rule on claims procedures [65 Fed. Reg. 70246 (Nov. 21, 2000)] sets the time frame for resolving disability claims. At the initial level, claims must be resolved within 45 days of the time the plan receives the claim. But, as long as the claimant receives a notice explaining the reason for the delay, resolution can be deferred for 30 days due to factors beyond the control of the plan. A second 30-day extension is possible. If the decision is adverse to the claimant, the appeal usually has to be decided within 45 days. If the plan is unable to complete review within the original time period, a 45-day extension is possible.

According to the Eighth Circuit, former employees must go through all the internal review procedures provided by a disability plan before bringing suit to collect disability benefits. This is true even if the plan does not explicitly refer to exhaustion of remedies. The court's position is that employees should be expected to know that the plan's rules have to be followed before involving the court system. [*Kinkead v. Southwestern Bell Corp.*, 111 F.3d 67 (8th Cir. 1997)]

The LTD plan involved in *Guerrero v. Lumberman's Mutual Casualty Co.* [174 F. Supp. 2d 1218 (D. Kan. 2001)] had two levels of appeal after a denial or termination of benefits. Plan documents expressed forbade a suit until remedies had been applied in a timely fashion and then exhausted. The plaintiff sued after the first level of appeal. Her suit was dismissed because she had not requested a second appeal within 60 days of the denial of her claim at the first appeal. The District Court said that failure to meet the plan's time limits is also a failure to exhaust remedies. The court rejected the plaintiff's argument that the second appeal would have been futile—there would have been different reviewers handling the second appeal.

The plan document for the insured ERISA disability plan involved in *Hess v. Hartford Life & Accident Ins. Co.* [274 F.3d 456 (7th Cir. 2001)] defined the disability benefit as a percentage of regular monthly pay, excluding commissions. The employee's predisability compensation, however, had been almost entirely commission-based. The employee asserted that her employment contract called for the use of average commissions for the prior two years in computing benefits.

The Seventh Circuit said that although the employer had discretion to interpret the terms of the plan—and although the court would review its interpretation deferentially—it acted arbitrary and capriciously, and should have used a higher base figure for computing disability benefits. It is arbitrary to ignore highly relevant information such as the employment contract.

Tip: If the case had arisen after the effective date of the recent DOL regulation on claims procedure, the insurer would not even have been entitled to deferential review. The Regulation requires consideration of "all comments, documents, records and other information" submitted by claimants. The Preamble to the regulation says that courts should not defer to decisions contrary to the procedure set out in the regulation.

The Ninth Circuit applied the Social Security Administration "treating physician rule" to ERISA plans—in other words, that the opinion of a physician who actually treats the patient carries more weight than that of a physician who merely reviews the paperwork. [*Regula v. Delta Family-Care Disability Survivorship Plan*, 266 F.3d 1130 (9th Cir. 2001)]

Connors v. Connecticut General Life Insurance Co. [272 F.3d 127 (2d Cir. 2001)] holds that the opinion of the plaintiff's own doctor, whom he had seen for five years, should have been given at least as much weight with respect to whether the plaintiff continued to be disabled, as the opinion of the insurer's experts. However, the Second Circuit declined to apply the "treating physician" rule in this case, limiting its use to cases where the court defers to the plan administrator's decision and reviews the case with an "arbitrary and capricious" standard. Here, the standard of review was de novo.

An LTD plan directed the administrator to pay benefits if the participant submits "satisfactory proof of total disability." According to the Eighth Circuit, courts must review these determinations using a de novo standard of review. [*Walke v. Group Long Term Disability Ins.*, 256 F.3d 835 (8th Cir. 2001)] The Ninth Circuit made a similar ruling in *Kearney v. Standard Insurance Co.* [175 F.3d 1084 (9th Cir. 1998)] The Eighth Circuit view was that this was ambiguous language, normally found in non-ERISA contexts; if the insurer chose to include this language, it must deal with consequences of the administrator not being awarded discretion.

To the Fourth Circuit, the arbitrary and capricious standard of review applies only if the plan gives the administrator discretion. De novo review is required for all other plans. The long-term disability plan construed in *Feder v. Paul Revere Life Insurance Co.* [228 F.3d 518 (4th Cir. 2000)] said that a physician was eligible if he or she was totally disabled and unable to perform professional duties. Total disability meant injury or sickness that completely precluded work and made the doctor unable to perform the central duties of the medical specialty.

The plaintiff, a surgeon, was terminated in 1993, and submitted a LTD claim for disabling mental illness. Benefits were paid as of February 1994. In June 1996, the insurer gave notice that benefits were being terminated because the doctor no longer qualified. The Fourth Circuit reversed the grant of summary judgment for the plan, because its insurer did not reserve discretion—it merely required submission of written claims, which is an inevitable part of all insurance claims processes.

According to the Seventh Circuit, for a sponsor to reserve discretion, the plan documents must say more than that claimants must prove or give satisfactory proof of entitlement to benefits. The rationale of *Herzberger v. Standard Insurance Co.* [205 F.3d 327 (7th Cir. 2000)] is that an ERISA plan is a contract, which is interpreted by courts and not the party who drafted the language. However, the court approved this language as adequate to secure deferential review: "Benefits under this plan will be paid only if the plan administrator decides in his discretion that the applicant is entitled to them."

§ 20.08   APPEALS OF CLAIM DENIALS

The insurer (which also administered the plan) denied plaintiff's initial LTD benefit claim. The initial denial letter stated that the participant was not "totally disabled" under the plan's definition, and advised her to submit additional information. She appealed the denial, providing more medical data. The administrator denied the claim once again, in a more detailed letter. [*Olive v. American Express LTD Benefit Plan*, 183 F. Supp. 2d 1191 (C.D. Cal. 2002)] The Central District ruled that the initial denial letter was inadequate because it was ambiguous and failed to inform the claimant whether her claim was substantively defective (her medical condition wasn't really totally disabling), procedurally defective (she didn't submit all the necessary records), or both.

A plan that has only one level of review has to be especially careful to be precise in its initial denials, so claimants will know how to prove meritorious claims. Furthermore, because of the administrator's conflict of interest (as an insurer, it would have to pay any claims that were granted), the standard of review was de novo. [*See also* Shannon P. Duffy, *Judge Scolds Insurer, Gives Lawyer Disability*, The Legal Intelligencer (May 22, 2001) (law.com), discussing two other cases where insurers' decisions were subjected to additional scrutiny when they also administered the plans]

CHAPTER 21

INSURANCE FRINGE BENEFITS

§ 21.01   INTRODUCTION

In addition to plans in which insurance operates behind the scenes (health plans; pension plans funded by insurance contracts), some fringe benefit plans exist to provide insurance coverage to employees. This chapter covers life insurance and long-term care insurance (LTCI) fringe benefits.

§ 21.02   LIFE INSURANCE FRINGE BENEFITS

[A]   Favorable Tax Treatment

Life insurance plays a valuable part in employees' financial planning through their entire planning cycle. For young employees who have not accumulated many assets, insurance is valuable as the source of a potential "instant estate." Older employees with greater accumulation of assets nevertheless value the benefits that life insurance can provide for survivors. Traditionally, life insurance was given favorable treatment for estate tax purposes, although as a result of EGTRRA, a larger number of estates will be exempt from estate taxation, making this a less important consideration.

The Internal Revenue Code authorizes several mechanisms under which employers can provide life insurance to employees at little or no income tax cost to the employees. (These mechanisms are distinct from the "key-person" insurance coverage that pays benefits to the corporation itself when it becomes necessary to replace a top executive or creative person.) The basic rule is that, if the employer pays the premiums and the insurance proceeds go to the beneficiary designated by the employee, the employee will have taxable income and the employer will be able to deduct the cost of providing the insurance. (The employer gets a deduction only for "ordinary and necessary business expenses.") However, the Code also provides certain relief measures that limit or eliminate the tax cost of these fringe benefits.

[B]   Employee-Owned, Employer-Paid Insurance

It is common for employers to pay the premiums for life insurance owned by the employees covered by the plan. Treas. Reg. § 1.1035-1 gives the employer an income tax deduction for the cost of the plan, provided that the employer is not the beneficiary, and also limited by the I.R.C. § 162 "ordinary and necessary" rule.

The premiums that the employer pays are taxable income for the employee, but the insurance proceeds are not taxable income for the beneficiary who receives them. [*See* I.R.C. § 101)] If the employee borrows against the policy, interest on the loan (unlike most forms of personal interest) is deductible.

> **Tip:** Employer-pay life insurance plans are not subject to nondiscrimination requirements, so it is perfectly legitimate for the employer to furnish insurance to the employees the employer particularly wants to motivate, without making the plan available to the whole workforce.

[C]   Company-Owned Life Insurance (COLI)

Under this variation, the policies are owned by the company itself, and can be used to finance death benefits paid under the employer's benefit plans. Cash-value insurance can be used to finance retirement benefits. The beneficiary of the plan, or the estate of the deceased employee, does have income under I.R.C. § 101(a), because the death benefits are deemed to be paid directly by the employer and not by an insurer.

When the employer owns the COLI policy and uses it only to fund the death benefit, the employee does not have taxable income during his or her life from either the policy's cash surrender value or the premium payments that the employer makes—as long as the employee's beneficiary is only an unsecured creditor with respect to the proceeds of the policy.

The employer can take policy loans against the COLI policies to pay current benefits under a nonqualified plan, but cannot deduct the interest if more than $50,000 is borrowed from a policy covering an individual. [*See* I.R.C. § 264(a)(4)]

Usually, the corporation is not entitled to a deduction for the premiums it pays for COLI, because of the employer's interest as a beneficiary. However, there is an exception to this rule for premiums paid for certain annuity contracts used in connection with COLI plans.

In 2002, a series of articles in the *Wall Street Journal* severely criticized COLI (calling it "janitor insurance" or "dead peasant insurance"), because in some instances, a corporation collects significant insurance benefits on the lives of low-paid workers who had little or no personal or company-provided insurance and whose families therefore were left poorly provided for. Insurance benefiting the company when nonkey employees die was criticized as unfair, because the insurance is sometimes maintained on retirees and other ex-employees, so companies benefit by the death of persons who are no longer employees at all, much less key employees. (Initially, corporations were only deemed to have an insurable interest in the lives of key employees, but this rule was changed in the 1980s.)

This type of insurance can also be used by corporations for financial manipulation. Corporations can deduct the insurance premiums they pay for this purpose; and, because they are insurance policies, the buildup of cash value is not taxed, and increase in cash value can be used to improve the financial results on the company's books. The insurance proceeds are not taxable income, so the company can get a windfall if someone dies after a short period of employment. The insurance can also be used as collateral for loans, or policy loans can be taken against the insurance. [Ellen E. Schultz and Theo Francis, *Worker Dies, Firm Profits—Why?*, Wall Street Journal, Apr. 19, 2002, at p. A1; Ellen E. Schultz and Theo Francis, *Why are Workers in [sic] Dark?* Wall Street Journal, Apr. 24, 2000 at p. C1; Theo Francis and Ellen E. Schultz, *Why Secret Insurance on Employees Pays Off,* Wall Street Journal, Apr. 25, 2002, at p. C1]

> **Tip:** Although federal controls on the use of COLI may be imposed in the future, they are not yet in effect. Texas does not permit companies to get insurance on nonkey employees, and California, Illinois, Michigan, Minnesota, New York and Ohio require the consent of the employee whose life is insured.

[D] Section 79 (Group-Term Life)

Internal Revenue Code § 79 allows an employer to establish a written, non-discriminatory plan to provide term life insurance policies to a group of employees. (Term life insurance is pure insurance, with no cash value.) Employees can receive up to $50,000 worth of coverage under the plan with no tax consequences to them. But if the employer provides coverage over $50,000, the employee does have taxable income. The calculation is based on an official IRS table. The excess coverage is subject to FICA tax but not FUTA tax or income tax withholding. [I.R.C. § 3121(a)(2)]

The table was revised effective July 1, 1999. [*See* 64 Fed. Reg. 29788 (June 3, 1999)] The new rates are much lower than the old ones—especially for older employees:

Employee's Age	Prior Law	Revised Rates
Up to 25	.08	.05
25–29	.08	.06
30–34	.09	.08
35–39	.11	.09
40–44	.17	.10
45–49	.29	.15
50–54	.48	.23
55–59	.75	.43
60–64	1.17	.66
65–70	2.10	1.27
>70	3.76	2.06

A Section 79 plan must either be available to all employees, or to groups of employees defined in a way that does not allow selection of employees based on individual characteristics. So the plan can condition eligibility on factors related to age or employment, but not on the amount of the corporation's stock that the person owns. Nor can the amount of coverage be based on individual factors (although it can be proportionate to compensation). As a general rule, Section 79 plans must cover at least ten employees.

To satisfy the nondiscrimination test, the plan must benefit at least 70% of the sponsoring company's employees, and not more than 15% of the participants may be key employees. If the group-term life insurance plan is part of a cafeteria plan, it must also satisfy the I.R.C. § 125 rules. If the plan fails the nondiscrimination test, then highly compensated employees will have to include the full cost of coverage (not just the coverage over and above $50,000) in income.

[E] Split Dollar

A split dollar plan is a benefit arrangement under which the ownership, and possibly payment of premiums, is divided between the employer and the employee. Each year, the employer contributes an amount equal to the policy's increase in cash value for the year. Under the "endorsement method," the employer owns the policy, and the policy is endorsed to explain the allocation between employer and employee. Under the "collateral assignment" method, the employee or a third party owns the policy, which is then assigned to the employer, using the collateral endorsement.

When the employee dies, the employer receives the cash value, or an amount equivalent to the premiums paid, while the rest of the benefits go to the beneficiary designated by the employee. In an equity split-dollar plan, the employer is repaid for the premiums it paid; the rest of the proceeds go to the beneficiary designed by the employee.

In a reverse split-dollar plan, however, the employee owns the policy and its cash value, and at the employee's death, the employer receives the basic death benefit (the death benefit minus amounts attributable to whatever investment component the life insurance contract had). The employer usually reimburses the employee for the annual term costs of the death benefit. The employee's current compensation might also be increased to provide funds to pay the premium. This additional compensation is taxable income for the employee; as is any premium payment made by the employer that is equivalent to compensation. The employer does not get a deduction for the annual term cost of the policy. Other payments by the employer in connection with a split-dollar plan are probably deductible as compensation (as long as they are ordinary and necessary business expenses). Internal Revenue Code § 101 provided that neither the employer nor the employee's beneficiary has taxable income when the proceeds are received.

The IRS' first rulings on taxation of split dollar, Rev. Rul. 64-328 and Rev. Rul. 66-110, were limited to the endorsement and collateral assignment types of split dollar. They did not tackle the equity form, which gained popularity over the years. In 2001, the IRS attempted to reform the taxation of split dollar by issuing Notice 2001-10, 2001-5 I.R.B. 1.

Notice 2001-10 applied I.R.C. §§ 83 and 7872 in the split-dollar context. A life insurance contract is property to the extent of its cash surrender value. The IRS' position, in Notice 2001-10, was that the employee has gross income from his or her beneficial interest in cash surrender value, because I.R.C. § 83 says that there has been a transfer in connection with provision of services.

Notice 2001-10 also raised the issue of whether the employer makes loans to the employee (an area that is taxed under I.R.C. § 7872 if the employer makes loans at below-market interest rates; the interest that the employee doesn't have to pay is taxed as compensation). If the plan involves a reasonable, bona fide expectation that the employer will be repaid for its share of the premiums in the future, then the arrangement can be treated as loans from employer to employee to acquire life insurance. Notice 2001-10 contained guidelines for determining if there is a below-market loan, and if so how large it is.

Before Notice 2001-10, the IRS allowed the use of either the P.S. 58 rates or lower one-year term rates published by insurers to be used to value split-dollar arrangements. But in Notice 2001-10, the IRS published a new table, Table 2001, to be used both in split-dollar valuations and in valuations for qualified retirement plans.

This discussion is phrased in the past tense, because the IRS reversed its position on split dollar, withdrawing Notice 2001-10 and replacing it with Notice 2002-8, 2002-4 I.R.B. 398. Notice 2002-8 sets out a simple method of categorizing split-dollar arrangements as either "transfer" or "loan" arrangements.

In a transfer arrangement, the employer owns the policy and pays the premiums, making a transfer of insurance and cash value to the employee. In contrast, in a loan arrangement, the employee owns the policy; the employee makes low- or no-interest loans to the employee so the employee has funds to pay the premiums. If the employer makes premium payments that are not loans to the employee, then these payments are taxable income for the employee in the year in which they are made.

Under Notice 2002-8, the most important factor in split-dollar taxation is the ownership of the policy. If the employer is the formal owner of the policy, then the transfer rules apply (endorsement method). If the employee owns the policy (collateral assignment method), then the loan rules determine taxation of the split-dollar arrangement.

When it changed its position, the IRS did not abolish Table 2001. Table 2001 can be used to value split-dollar insurance, but so can the one-year term rates published by the insurance company that sells the policies used in the split-dollar program.

Tip: Notice 2002-8 allows especially favorable treatment for certain amendments adopted before January 28, 2002, so check to see whether your plan qualifies. Arrangements that were in existence before January 28, 2002, can also be terminated before January 1, 2004, without the IRS taxing a transfer of property to the employee. [*See A Fresh Start for Split-Dollar*, Kilpatrick Stockton Legal Alert, (January 2002) <http://www.kilstock.com/site/print/detail?Article_Id=1013>]

In July 2002, the IRS issued a lengthy set of Proposed Regulations, RIN 1545-BA44 covering the income tax, employment tax, and gift tax implications of split-dollar plans, including those used in life insurance trusts rather than an employment context. Like Notice 2002-8, the Proposed Regulations call for taxation under either an economic benefit theory or a loan theory. Under the economic benefit theory, the transfer of value can be taxable compensation, a Code § 301 distribution, or a gift, depending on the relationship between the parties to the split-dollar arrangement.

Under the proposal, the economic benefit theory applies if the owner of the contract provides economic benefits to the non-owner, which will generally be true in an endorsement arrangement. The economic benefit theory also applies if the arrangement is created in connection with performance of services, but the employee does not own the contract, or if the insurance is placed in a life insurance trust.

When the loan theory applies (which is generally true in collateral assignment situations), the non-owner of the contract is deemed to make loans of the premiums to the contract's owner.

The Proposed Regulations give rules for determining who is the owner—the person named in the policy as the owner; but the first person named is generally treated as the owner if there are two or more designated owners.

[F] Case Law on Life Insurance Fringe Benefits

Cehrs v. Northeast Ohio Alzheimer's Research Center [155 F.3d 755 (6th Cir. 1998)] involves an employer that had a life insurance plan. A disabled employee was told that he did not fit the plan's definition of disability, so the employer would not maintain his life insurance coverage. However, the employer did not give any reason for the determination or explain how to appeal it. After the ex-employee's death, his family brought suit under ERISA § 503. The employer's litigating position was that the family failed to mitigate (reduce) his damages by investigating and discovering that the employer's position was incorrect. The Sixth Circuit rejected this argument, taking the position that when a plan fails to provide the notices required by law, employees are not able to mitigate their damages. Requiring mitigation would actually reward the plan for failing to provide the mandatory notices.

The estate of a wrongfully terminated employee was entitled to recover the face value of employer-provided insurance that was lost as a result of the discharge, minus the proceeds of the insurance policy that the deceased ex-employee bought as a replacement. [*Sposato v. Electronic Data Sys. Corp.*, 188 F.3d 1146 (9th Cir. 1999)] The Ninth Circuit used the amount of insurance, not just the premiums that the employer would have paid, as the standard of measurement.

A plan participant who had an employer-sponsored life insurance policy died during medical leave. The insurer refused to pay, saying she was not an "active employee" at the time of her death. The employee's widower sued the insurer for wrongful denial of benefits and breach of fiduciary duty. The Fourth Circuit did not reach the fiduciary claim because it found that benefits were wrongfully denied. [*Tester v. Reliance Ins. Co.*, 228 F.3d 372 (4th Cir. 2000)] In the court's analysis, the term "active" was ambiguous, and if applied too strictly would terminate coverage for any employee who ever missed work because of illness. Furthermore, the insurer continued to accept premiums on behalf of the employee; the employer's position was that the employee was on an approved leave of absence.

When Kenneth Howell died in 1966, he had a life insurance policy under a welfare benefit plan. In 1994, his second wife (he already had three children from a prior marriage) sued for divorce. In 1995, a family court ordered both spouses to refrain from transferring or otherwise disposing of marital assets during the divorce proceedings. Proceedings were still pending when he died. However, contrary to the court order, he had changed the beneficiary designation from his second wife to his children. The pension fund brought an interpleader action under ERISA. [*Central States, Southeast & Southwest Areas Pension Fund v. Howell*, 227 F.3d 672 (6th Cir. 2000)] The court order did not qualify as a QDRO, because it did not have mandatory information such as the number of payments and how the participant's benefits were to be allocated. Because there was no QDRO, ERISA preempted state-law allocation principles. The beneficiary card filed with the plan, directing payment to the children, governed. However, the case was remanded to the District Court to see if a constructive trust should be imposed—i.e., whether the benefits should be treated as if a trust had been established with provisions reflecting equity and justice.

When an employee died, his spouse filed claims for unpaid benefits and compensation against the employee's employer (who was also the plan administrator) and the insurer that issued the life insurance for the ERISA plan. [*Everhart v. Allmerica Fin. Life Ins. Co.*, 275 F.3d 751 (9th Cir. 2001)] The widow settled her claims against the employer and released all claims against the plan and against the employer in its role as plan administrator. The widow sued the insurer to collect the life insurance. The Ninth Circuit agreed with the insurer: releasing claims against the plan administrator meant that there was no longer any legal right to sue the insurer, because ERISA claims have to be brought against the plan and/or its administrator.

§ 21.03   LONG-TERM CARE INSURANCE PLANS

There are many widespread misconceptions about the Medicare system. One of them is that Medicare covers nursing home care. Although the Medicare system includes limited nursing home coverage (only 100 days or less, of recuperation after a hospital stay, in a specialized skilled nursing facility) and limited home care coverage (in most instances, also linked to hospitalization), it specifically excludes coverage of "custodial care." Many elderly people need custodial care because of physical and/or mental frailty, and this care is very expensive. (Some younger disabled people also need long-term care.)

Long-term care insurance (LTCI) is private insurance, sold by life and health insurers, that covers the cost of home and institutional care for the frail elderly and disabled. There is an increasing trend for employers to offer group long-term care insurance plans as an employee benefit—and to permit employees not only to purchase coverage for themselves and their spouses, but for their parents. Individual coverage for senior citizens can be difficult to find, and is often expensive when it is available.

Unlike most types of employee benefit, however, the typical LTCI plan is completely paid for by the employee. The employer's role is purely to administer the plan, and make it easier for employees to get insurance (frequently without proof of insurability) and at lower, group rates than if they purchased policies individually.

As of 2001, less than 2% of all workers were enrolled in group LTCI plans. At the end of 2000, there were approximately 929,000 employees covered by group LTCI plans. In 2002, the federal government became the largest sponsor of group LTCI, and the huge federal workforce (20 million active and retired workers) became eligible to elect such coverage. According to a study done by HIAA, the average employee enrolled in a group LTCI plan is 50 years old. Enrollees typically have higher income, more assets, and more education than non-enrollees. Employees who choose to participate in group LTCI are more likely than non-enrollees to agree that it is important to plan now for future long-term care needs; they think the risk of needing care is greater than non-enrollees do, and they are less likely to think that the government will pay for whatever care they do need. [SpencerNet News Service, *Study Finds Potential For Growth in Long-Term Care Market*, (Dec. 12, 2001) <http://www.spencernet.com>; National Underwriter Co., *HIAA Survey Reveals Buyer-Nonbuyer Attitudes in the Group LTC Market*, <www.nationalunderwriter.com/archives/>]

CHAPTER 22
OTHER FRINGE BENEFITS

§ 22.01   INTRODUCTION

This book has already dealt with issues of setting and administering current compensation (pay planning), deferred compensation (pension planning), and the provision of several of the major types of fringe benefits: health plans, disability coverage, and life insurance plans.

It is common, however, for employers to provide other forms of benefits as compensation and as incentives. This chapter traces their tax, ERISA, and state-law consequences.

For tax purposes, the most relevant sections include I.R.C. § 162 (allowing a deduction for all of the employer's ordinary and necessary business expenses, including the employer's contributions to unfunded welfare benefit plans) and I.R.C. §§ 419 and 419A, which set limits on the deductions.

In general, employers will be able to deduct direct payments of benefits or expenses. Employers can make contributions that bear a reasonable actuarial relationship to the amounts that will be needed to pay benefits in the future. In some circumstances, a statutory safe harbor allows deductible contributions.

If a funded welfare plan earns income (e.g., from investments), that income will probably be taxed to the employer that maintains the plan. Unrelated business taxable income (UBTI) earned by the plan will almost certainly be taxed to the employer. [*See* Chapter 1, §§ 1.08, 1.12 for a discussion of some of the issues of determining who is an "employee" who is or might be eligible for plan participation]

§ 22.02   STOCK OPTIONS

[A]   Generally

Both the corporation and its employees benefit when the price of the company's stock increases. This common-sense observation inspired widespread creation of plans under which employees are awarded stock options, with the intention that employees would be able to purchase stock in the employer corporation at below-market rates, and would have a personal incentive to work hard so the value of the stock would continue to climb. Depending on the company's circumstances, and the incentives it wants to provide, stock options could be granted widely, or restricted to top executives.

Giving stock options to employees, or allowing them to participate in a stock purchase plan, is also a way to create incentives, give additional compensation, and qualify for a tax deduction, without actually spending cash from the corporate coffers. Stock option plans were also very popular among startup companies that had little cash but high hopes.

For practical and tax reasons, the employer will probably want to impose some limitations on the options. A typical restriction is the employee's obligation to put (resell) the stock back to the corporation on termination of employment. An arrangement like this includes a method of calculating the put price (e.g., book value or a set P/E ratio).

A stock bonus plan is very similar to a profit-sharing plan from both the labor law and tax perspectives. However, distributions are generally made in the employer's common stock rather than in cash. Employees must be given put options obligating the employer to repurchase shares of stock that are not readily tradeable on an established market.

An Employee Stock Ownership Plan (ESOP) is a stock bonus plan or a plan combining stock bonus and money-purchase features. ESOPs invest primarily in the employer's common stock. The Internal Revenue Code contains additional rules for leveraged ESOPs that borrow the funds used to purchase the stock. ESOPs are often adopted as a defense against hostile takeovers of the issuing corporation. [*See* Prop. Reg. § 31.3121(a)-1(k) and 31.3306(b)-1(e)]

In 2001, the IRS proposed to require corporations to withhold and pay FICA and FUTA taxes whenever ISOs or ESOP options were exercised, starting in 2003. [Notices 2001-72 and 2001-73, 2001-I.R.B. 49, at 548 and 549] However, the proposal attracted a great deal of unfavorable comment from Congress as well as the business community, and it was withdrawn in 2002. [Notice 2002-47, 2002-28 I.R.B. 97] If the IRS issues additional guidance in the future (i.e., changes its mind again), the new rules will not apply to exercise of a statutory stock option at any time before January 1 of the year two years after publication of the final rule. However, Notice 2002-47 does not alter the individual employee's obligation to report and pay tax on gains on selling optioned stock—it just relieves employers of withholding and tax payment obligations in this context.

Revenue Procedure 2002-50, 2002-29 I.R.B. 173, sets out the conditions under which it is not necessary for a broker who carries out a stock sale to issue an IRS Form 1099-B when an employee exercises a stock option to purchase stock and then sells the stock on the same day.

Stock appreciation rights (SARs) are really a form of cash compensation. The grantee of SARs gets money from the corporation, based on the price of the company stock. If, for instance, a corporate Vice President has SARs for 1,000 shares, the corporation will pay him or her the difference between the FMV of those shares at the time of exercise and the FMV at the time of grant. SARs are not usually issued by themselves. Generally they accompany qualified or nonqualified stock options. Often, they can be exercised with the stock options, giving the employee some of the cash needed to pay for the optioned shares.

A junior stock plan is another motivational device. Executives are given the right to buy junior stock (stock in the employer corporation with reduced dividend rights and voting powers). Owners of junior stock can convert it to ordinary common stock by achieving specified performance goals.

[B] Incentive Stock Options (ISOs)

Internal Revenue Code § 422 creates a specially tax-favored category of Incentive Stock Options (ISOs). An ISO plan is permitted to discriminate in favor of highly compensated employees. However, favorable tax consequences are available to the employee only if he or she retains the shares for at least one year from the exercise of the option or two years from the grant of the option.

ISOs must be granted pursuant to a plan that states the aggregate number of shares that can be issued under option, and indicates which employees can receive them. The corporation's shareholders must approve the plan, during the time period running from 12 months before to 12 months after the adoption of the plan. Options can only be granted during the 10-year period after the adoption of the plan, but the corporation can simply adopt further ISO plans after the initial 10-year period expires.

The option price must be at least equal to the fair market value of the stock at the time the option is granted. In other words, ISOs cannot be issued at a bargain price, although NQSOs can be. The employees must wait for the stock's value to appreciate to benefit from the options.

Employees themselves can only exercise ISOs, during their lifetimes. Employees are only allowed to transfer ISOs by will or intestacy. If, at the time of the grant, the grantee owns 10% or more of the corporation's stock, the option price must be set higher, and only five years can be given to exercise the option, not ten.

Furthermore, the aggregate fair market value of each employee's stock cannot exceed $100,000 (measured as of the date of the grant of the option) in the first calendar year for which the options are exercisable. The $100,000 limit does not have to be written into the ISO plan document. It is applied automatically, and amounts over $100,000 simply are not characterized as ISOs.

[C] Nonqualified Stock Options (NQSOs)

Nonqualified stock options (NQSOs) are stock options that do not satisfy the I.R.C. § 422 rules. Sometimes NQSOs are issued "in the money": that is, the price at which the option can be exercised is lower than the current value of the stock, not just the anticipated future value of the stock at the time the option can be exercised.

There is no tax effect at the time of the grant of an NQSO, as long as the option itself does not have a readily ascertainable market value (i.e., the options are not traded actively). When the option is exercised, the employee has taxable income, equal to the FMV of the stock minus the consideration paid for the option. However, if the stock received by exercising the option is not transferable, and is subject to a substantial risk of forfeiture, then income is not taxed until the condition lapses. At that time, the amount of gain is determined, using the then-current FMV of the stock.

The FMV of the stock at the time of the exercise of the option, minus the price of the option, is a preference item for Alternative Minimum Tax purposes.

[D] Option Taxation under I.R.C. § 83

Internal Revenue Code § 83 governs all transfers of property in exchange for performance of services, so it is important to stock option taxation but also has broader applicability. Under I.R.C. § 83, the person who performs the services has taxable income, at ordinary income (not capital gains) rates at the time that the rights in the property become transferable or are no longer subject to a substantial risk of forfeiture.

The amount of ordinary income to be recognized equals the fair market value (FMV) of the property minus any amount the employee paid for it. The options can be made forfeitable if the employee leaves before a certain number of years of employment. That motivates the employee to stay longer by offering tax incentives: There is no taxable income until the restriction lapses.

The point at which an option becomes subject to I.R.C. § 83 depends on whether it has an ascertainable market value (for instance, if it is traded on an established market). If so, and if the option is vested, it is taxed as soon as it is granted—not at the later point when it is exercised. Options that have no ascertainable FMV do not become subject to I.R.C. § 83 until they are exercised, on the theory that an option with an FMV can be sold as a separate asset.

Therefore, the employee faces taxation at two stages. The first is when the option can be exercised and the stock purchased; the second is when the stock is sold. (Gains from the sale of stock are capital gains; they do not generate ordinary income.)

Stock options are vested when the stock is transferable and there is no longer a substantial risk of forfeiture. (Sometimes stock awarded to employees is endorsed on its face to prevent transfer.) Section 83 holds that property is subject to a substantial risk of forfeiture if the right to receive the property is conditioned on future performance of substantial services ("earn-out restriction").

There's no bright-line test for when services are substantial; it depends on factors such as the regularity with which services are supposed to be performed and the amount of time needed to perform them. A retiree whose consulting agreement allows him or her to keep the stock while failing to perform the services is not performing substantial services.

Under I.R.C. § 83, refraining from performing services (e.g., under a noncompete clause) can also give rise to a substantial risk of forfeiture.

If the employer company's stock is publicly traded and it is a "reporting" company under the Exchange Act of 1934 [15 U.S.C. §§ 77b-e, etc.], major executives who are corporate officers, directors, or 10% shareholders will probably be subject to the Exchange Act's ban on "short-swing" profits earned by corporate insiders who trade in the company's stock. Internal Revenue Code § 83(c)(3) provides that rights are not vested at any time that the person receiving stock options cannot sell the stock without violating the short-swing profit rules. That means that the insider who gets a stock option has no income either for six months or until the first day that the stock can be sold.

In the usual stock option situation, until the option vests, the corporation is still considered the owner of the stock. The dividends on the stock are considered additional compensation for the employee. On the other hand, the corporation can deduct these dividends (as employee compensation) even though under ordinary circumstances a corporation cannot deduct the dividends that it pays.

The employee has the right to elect immediate taxation in the year of the transfer of the property, even if I.R.C. § 83 would not otherwise impose tax. This is a reasonable choice where otherwise the appreciation on the stock would be taxed as compensation.

> **Tip:** If the employee pays the tax right away and later has to forfeit the options (e.g., by quitting his or her job), the tax already paid is not refundable.

The employer can deduct the compensation that the employee includes in income under I.R.C. § 83 (as long as the compensation is reasonable). The deduction is taken in the employer's tax year that includes the year in which the employee includes the sum in his or her income. Nearly all employees pay taxes on a calendar-year basis, whereas most corporations operate on a fiscal year. The employer gets an immediate deduction if the property is vested as soon as it is transferred, or if the employee exercises the election to be taxed immediately.

To sum up the ISO/NQSO distinction, when an individual is granted NQSOs:

- (At time of grant) If there is no readily ascertainable FMV, there is no tax effect;
- (At time of grant) If there is an ascertainable FMV, § 83 governs taxation;
- (At time of exercise) The employee has taxable income equal to the FMV of the stock minus consideration paid for the option. However, if the stock received on exercise of the option is nontransferrable and subject to a substantial risk of forfeiture, taxable income is not a factor until the condition lapses. At that point, gain is determined based on the FMV at the time of the lapse. If the employee actually sells the stock purchased under the option, then he or she will have capital gain or loss on the sale;
- The employer gets a deduction equal to the individual's gain.

If the employee gets ISOs instead of NQSOs:

- (At time of grant) The employee has no taxable income;
- (At time of exercise) The employee has no income;
- (At time of disposition of stock) The employee has capital gain or loss, with consequences depending on the length of the holding period;
- The employer does not get a deduction. [I.R.C. § 421(a)(2)]

If an employee disposes of shares obtained under an ISO within two years of the grant of the option or one year of exercising the option, any gain is ordinary income, and the employer is entitled to a tax deduction equal to this amount.

The value of a publicly traded stock at a particular time can easily be determined by consulting published price quotations. However, options are (or at least used to be) often issued by nonpublic companies, especially startups. In 2002, the

IRS issued two documents about valuations of stock options. Rev. Proc. 2002-13, 2002-8 I.R.B. 549, creates a "safe harbor" method for valuing stock options that generates acceptable values by considering the volatility of the stock; the exercise price of the option; the value of the stock at the time of valuation, and the term of the option as of the valuation date. Rev. Proc. 2002-13 applies to the tax on "excess golden parachutes" [*see* § 3.03[D]] and therefore must be taken into account when a company is acquired and its golden parachutes are triggered.

Later in 2002, the IRS modified Rev. Proc. 2002-13 in Rev. Proc. 2002-45, 2002-27 I.R.B. 40. Rev. Proc. 2002-45 includes a valuation table, superseding the Rev. Proc. 2002-13 valuation table. In order to use the safe harbor method, the corporation must base the volatility factor on the most recent year used for complying with accounting requirements, and disclosed in the company's most recent financial statements.

Under Rev. Proc. 2002-45, a corporation (whether or not its stock is publicly traded) can use the safe harbor method of valuation. It can also use any method consistent with GAAP and with the spirit of IRS Regulations, or the method used to value options for gift and estate tax purposes. However, Rev. Proc. 2002-45 forbids use of the "spread method" (i.e., the option exercise price minus the market value of the stock when the option is exercised)—and this has historically been the most common method of valuing options. The effect of Rev. Proc. 2002-45 is to increase the value assigned to most options, and therefore more corporations will be subject to the tax on excess parachutes payments; companies that were already subject will have to pay more. Rev. Proc. 2002-45 is effective June 13, 2002, but can be applied retroactively to transactions on or after April 26, 2002.

[E]   Securities Law Issues for Stock Option Plans

Federal securities laws and state Blue Sky Laws must be consulted before offering stock options (or any other form of securities-based compensation). Public companies have an established obligation to disclose option transactions to their shareholders, and to reflect them in SEC filings and on proxy statements. The Exchange Act also forbids insiders to take short-swing profits.

For fiscal years ending on or after March 15, 2002, and for proxies for shareholder meetings or shareholder actions on or after June 15, 2002, the SEC has imposed additional disclosure requirements on reporting companies that offer stock compensation plans. Disclosure is now required of plans offering equity compensation, whether or not approved by security holders.

For each category, the reporting company must put a table in the Form 10-K (the annual report) and in the proxy statement whenever shareholders are asked to approve a compensation plan that includes securities. The table should have three columns:

- Number of securities to be issued on exercise of outstanding options, rights, and warrants;

- The weighted average exercise price for the outstanding options, rights, and warrants;
- Securities not reflected in the first column, still available to be issued in the future under equity compensation plans. [*See New Disclosure Rules for Stock Plans*, Watson Wyatt Insider, <http://www.watsonwyatt.com/us/pubs/insider/showarticle.asp?ArticleID=9588&Component=The+Insider>]

§ 22.03 CAFETERIA PLANS

[A] Plan Characteristics

A cafeteria plan, as defined by I.R.C. § 125, is a written plan under which the employer offers a "menu" of benefits, permitting employees to choose between cash and a group of benefits. The plan must offer at least one taxable and one nontaxable benefit. Other than a 401(k) plan, the cafeteria plan may not offer any pension or deferred compensation benefits.

The I.R.C. § 125 requirements for a valid cafeteria plan are

- All plan participants are employees (although the Proposed Regulations allow ex-employees to be included in the plan, as long as it is not predominantly for their benefits. Spouses and children of employees can receive benefits under the plan, but cannot actively participate (e.g., by choosing the benefits);
- The participant chooses between cash and one or more benefits, although the amount of cash does not have to be as great as the entire cost of the nontaxable benefit [Prop. Reg. § 1.125-1];
- The plan does not discriminate in favor of highly compensated employees (HCEs);
- The benefits provided to HCEs do not exceed 25% of the total benefits for the year;
- The election to take benefits rather than cash must be made before the beginning of the plan year;
- Changes in the election must conform to the Regulations.

The allowable benefits include:

- Accident and health plans;
- Group-term life insurance;
- Disability coverage, including accidental death and dismemberment (ADD) plans;
- Dependent care assistance;
- Benefits that fail nondiscrimination tests and therefore are not part of a qualified plan;
- Vacation days;
- Group automobile insurance or other taxable benefit purchased by the employee with after-tax dollars.

Cafeteria plans are not permitted to include long-term care insurance. Neither can Flexible Spending Accounts [*see* § 18.11] because FSAs are not allowed to be used to pay insurance premiums.

The nontaxable benefits that can be included in a cafeteria plan are group-term life insurance, medical expense reimbursement, and accident and disability benefits as defined by I.R.C. § 106, dependent care assistance, and paid vacation days.

In a pretax premium plan, a "mini cafeteria" salary reduction plan is used to provide after-tax dollars for the employees to pay insurance premiums. The most common application is health insurance coverage for dependents, in plans where the employer covers employees but dependent coverage is on an "employee pay all" basis. The employer adopts a plan that allows the employee, before the start of the plan year, to elect a reduction in compensation sufficient to pay the employee's share of the premium. These salary reductions are not subject to the employer share of FICA.

A cafeteria plan must be designed as a "use it or lose it" plan: Unused benefits cannot be carried over to subsequent years. Participants can be given a chance to use their vacation days, sell them back to the employer for cash, or buy extra vacation days—as long as the plan is not used to defer the receipt of compensation to a later plan year. [*See* Prop. Reg. § 1.125-1, Q&A 7]

In a 1996 Private Letter Ruling, the IRS said that employers can contribute the value of unused vacation days to an employee's 401(k) plan. A contribution of this type will not reduce the amount of compensation that the employee can defer or that the employer can match.

If a cafeteria plan fails nondiscrimination testing, then the HCEs will have taxable income. The test for discrimination in benefits is whether contributions are made for each participant in a uniform relationship to compensation. If contributions for each participant are equal to the cost of coverage that the plan incurs for HCEs, or if contributions for each participant are at least equal to 75% of the cost for the similarly situated plan participant who has the highest cost of benefits, the plan satisfies the nondiscrimination tests.

Nontaxable cafeteria plan benefits are not subject to employer or employee FICA taxes. However, amounts placed into a 401(k) plan are subject to both employer and employee shares of FICA and FUTA.

Generally, participants will be given a 30-day period at the end of every year to make the election for the following year. The period might close a few days, or even a month, before the end of the year to give the plan administrators time to process the election request.

ERISA § 403 does not require cafeteria plans to be managed by a trust (although the terms of the plan itself can require trust management). However, if the plan allows after-tax contributions for the purchase of benefits, such contributions must be placed into trust unless they are used to buy insurance policies.

[B]   Cafeteria Plans After HIPAA

Proposed and Temporary Regulations for bringing cafeteria plans into conformity with HIPAA were published at 62 Fed. Reg. 60165 and 60196 (Nov. 7, 1997). Then, in March 2000, the IRS replaced the 1997 Temporary Regulations with T.D. 8878, 65 Fed. Reg. 15548, 2000-15 I.R.B. 857 (March 23, 2000). These Regulations, which were supposed to be final, clarified the circumstances under which employees participating in cafeteria plans can change their elections in connection with accident, health, or group-term life insurance coverage. For example, a change might be needed when a Qualified Medical Child Support Order (QMCSO) is granted, or when the person gains or loses eligibility for Medicare or Medicaid.

At the beginning of 2001, the IRS revised this Treasury Decision. [*See* T.D. 8921, 66 Fed. Reg. 1837 (Jan. 10, 2001)] T.D. 8921 modifies the T.D. 8878 Final Regulations by allowing cafeteria plan participants to increase or decrease their coverage whenever they have a change-of-status event.

Changes were always allowed on the basis of marriage or divorce. Thanks to T.D. 8921, changes are also permitted when a dependent is born or adopted. An employee who decreases or cancels coverage under the cafeteria plan because of coverage under a spouse or dependent's plan has to certify that he or she is getting other coverage.

The cafeteria plan election can be changed to conform to a domestic relations order, but only if the spouse or former spouse actually provides coverage for the child; T.D. 8921 also allows elections to be changed when the employee's responsibility for payments under the plan increases or decreases significantly. The plan's payment for dependent care cannot be greater than what the employee earns.

§ 22.04   EDUCATION ASSISTANCE

Employers offer education assistance both because anything that employees consider a valuable benefit is a good motivator, and because a better-educated workforce promotes efficiency and productivity. However, the tax status of this benefit has fluctuated over the past decades.

There were no Code provisions allowing employees to receive educational assistance tax-free before I.R.C. § 127 was enacted in 1978, as a five-year pilot project. Under I.R.C. § 127, employees did not have taxable income because of qualified employer educational assistance. The employer was entitled to a deduction for maintaining a qualifying educational assistance plan. Even without a plan, educational assistance spending might be deductible as a working condition fringe benefit under I.R.C. § 132. Internal Revenue Code § 127 contains a dollar limitation ($5,250 a year). [*See* IRS Publication 508, *Tax Benefits for Work-Related Education*]

Since 1983, the provision has been saved from expiration several times. The Small Business Job Protection Act of 1996 [Pub. L. No. 104-188] allowed employees to exclude qualified educational assistance received during the period January 1, 1995–May 31, 1997. The income exclusion was extended again, for courses beginning before June 1, 2000, by the Tax Relief Act of 1997. [Pub. L. No. 105-34] The Ticket to Work Act [Pub. L. No. 106-170] extended the exclusion for undergraduate (but not graduate-level) education assistance until the end of 2001.

EGTRRA not only made the exclusion permanent, it repealed the earlier limitation of assistance to undergraduate-level education. Congress intended to resolve employers' insecurities about establishing a plan that could be eliminated by later tax legislation.

§ 22.05   EMPLOYEE ASSISTANCE PROGRAMS (EAPs)

The purpose of the Employee Assistance Program (EAP) is to help employees cope with stress and other problems. The theory is that sympathetic listening, and referrals for whatever professional services are needed, will ease employees' anxieties and make them more productive. EAPs can offer any combination of one-on-one counseling, information and referral, hotlines and crisis intervention, and informational seminars.

EAPs typically deal with problems such as substance abuse, dependent care, and problems with spouses and children. Many companies have found that early intervention makes it possible to shorten the damage and amount of time that would otherwise be involved, for instance, when the employee "hits bottom" with a drug or alcohol problem, or when an untreated mental illness requires inpatient hospitalization in a crisis. Each dollar invested in EAP services is estimated to return anywhere from two to eight dollars in health and productivity savings.

EAPs also take a role in coordinating an employee's return to work after recuperating from an accident or illness (which may include a shortened or flexible schedule, intermittent FMLA leave, or other accommodations).

The services can be provided in house by the HR department, or contracted out to outside vendors. The second course is more expensive, but it may make the EAP more credible to employees, or may reassure employees that their confidentiality will be protected.

§ 22.06   MISCELLANEOUS FRINGES

Employees do not have taxable income if they receive certain minor fringe benefits provided by the employer on a nondiscriminatory basis to all employees. Under I.R.C. § 132, the benefits are not taxed to the employees. FICA, FUTA, and federal income tax withholding are not required, and the employer share of these taxes does not have to be paid. Generally, the employer will be able to deduct the cost of the program (which is supposed to be nominal, in any case) as long as it fits the definition of an ordinary and necessary business expense.

The categories of miscellaneous fringe benefits authorized under I.R.C. § 132 are:

- No-additional-cost services of the employer company (e.g., air travel for an airline employee; a simple will prepared by a law firm for a non-attorney staffer). The employee must gain access to services normally sold to customers, but the employer must not incur any substantial cost. In effect, the employees are given access to the business's excess capacity;
- Employee discounts; the discount must not exceed the gross profit percentage for goods, or 20% of the cost of services;
- De minimis fringe benefits, such as free beverages at work or small Christmas presents—anything too trivial to account for separately;
- An on-premises eating facility such as a low-cost cafeteria that prepares meals on premises for the convenience of the employer (because employees can take shorter meal breaks because the subsidized dining facility is available). The facility must be owned or operated by the employer, must generate revenue at least equal to its operating costs, and must provide meals during the workday or right before or right after it. It must also be in or near the workplace, and must be operated by the employer (possibly through a contract with a third-party management company);
- Working condition fringe benefits—goods or services the employee could deduct if he or she paid for them personally. Typical examples are business travel and the use of company cars;
- Up to $180 a month (2001 level) or $185 a month (2002 level) for parking, and up to $65 (2001) or $100 (2002) a month for transit passes or highway vehicle transport (i.e., van pooling);
- An on-premises gym for the exclusive use of employees and their families;
- Reimbursement of employment-related moving expenses that would be deductible if the employee paid them directly (but have not in fact been deducted by the employee).

Another Code section, I.R.C. § 119, governs meals and lodging furnished on premises for the convenience of the employer: e.g., a room for a hotel manager who must be around to handle problems as they arise. Such benefits are not taxable income for the employee.

§ 22.07   VOLUNTARY EMPLOYEE BENEFIT ASSOCIATIONS (VEBAs)

A Voluntary Employee Benefit Association (VEBA), as defined by I.R.C. § 501(c)(9), is a trust that is funded by employer contributions (with or without employee contributions) and is used to pay benefits to employees who voluntarily exercise the option to participate in the association. VEBAs provide life, sickness, accident, or similar benefits to employee members and their dependents and designated beneficiaries. Benefits that can be offered by a VEBA safeguard or improve health or protect against a contingency that threatens the employee's earning power. But VEBAs are not allowed to offer reimbursement of commuting expenses, profit sharing, or stock bonuses.

The trust itself is not a taxable entity, but VEBA benefits constitute taxable income to the employee unless they are specifically exempted.

The VEBA must be controlled by its employee membership, by a bank or other independent trustee, or by fiduciaries chosen by or on behalf of the membership. A VEBA is considered a welfare plan under ERISA, and therefore is subject to ERISA Parts 1 (notice and reporting), 4 (trust and fiduciary responsibility), and 5 (enforcement).

The Sixth Circuit ruled that the portion of the VEBA contribution used to fund long-term disability benefits was deductible, but the portion used to fund post-retirement benefits and medical benefits for union members was not deductible, because the employer failed to satisfy the I.R.C. § 419A(c)(2) requirements for accumulating assets to prefund the benefits. [*Parker-Hannifin Corp. v. Commissioner,* 139 F.3d 1090 (6th Cir. 1998)]

§ 22.08   FRINGE BENEFIT PLANS: TAX COMPLIANCE

[A]   Reporting Requirements

The reporting requirements for a fringe benefit plan are set out in I.R.C. § 6039D. The plan must report:

- Number of employees at the employer company;
- Number of employees eligible to participate in the plan;
- Number actually participating;
- Number of highly compensated employees in each of the above categories;
- The plan's total cost during the year;
- The employer's name, address, and Employer Identification Number;
- The nature of its business.

If any fringe benefits are taxable, the employer can either add them to the regular wages for a payroll period, or withhold federal income tax at the rate for supplemental wages. [The relevant IRS publication is 15-B, Employer's Tax Guide to Fringe Benefits. The January 2002 edition can be accessed at <http://www.irs.gov/pub/irs-pdf/p15b.pdf>]

[B]   The Employer's Tax Deduction

When it comes to pensions, the tax rules are devised to make sure that the employer contributes enough to fund the plan. In contrast, when it comes to welfare benefits, the tax focus is preventing excessive prefunding of benefit plans. So the relevant Code sections (I.R.C. §§ 419 and 419A) specify a maximum funding level for welfare benefit trusts. If this level is exceeded, the trust is no longer tax-exempt.

Although the employer receives a tax deduction for maintaining a welfare benefit trust, the deduction is limited to the "qualified cost" of the benefit plans for the year. That means the direct cost of funding benefits, plus whatever amount I.R.C. § 419A permits to be added to the account for the year as a safety cushion.

Reference should also be made to I.R.C. § 4976, which imposes a 100% excise tax on disqualified benefit distributions made from funded welfare benefit plans. For instance, retiree health and life insurance benefits for highly compensated employees are supposed to be kept in a separate account from comparable contributions for rank-and-file employees.

Therefore, benefits paid to HCEs from the general account would be disqualified. VEBA benefits to HCEs that violate nondiscrimination requirements are also disqualified, as are amounts that revert to the employer. (An erroneous contribution which is withdrawn by the employer after a determination that it is not deductible is not considered a reversion.)

§ 22.09   ERISA REGULATION OF WELFARE BENEFIT PLANS

[A]   Creation and Administration

Although most of the attention goes to ERISA's regulation of pension plans, ERISA also covers welfare benefit plans—a category roughly equivalent to fringe benefit plans. An ERISA welfare benefit plan is created (generally by a corporate resolution passed by the Board of Directors and managed by the relevant corporate officials) and administered to provide one or more of these benefits to plan participants and their beneficiaries:

- Medical benefits;
- Health care;
- Accident insurance;
- Disability benefits;
- Death benefits;
- Supplemental unemployment benefits;
- Vacation benefits;
- Training (e.g., apprenticeship);
- Day care centers (but not dependent care spending reimbursement accounts);
- Scholarships;
- Prepaid legal services;
- Any benefit described in the Labor-Management Relations Act § 302(c) [29 U.S.C. §§ 141–144, etc.] other than death benefits, pensions, or insurance coverage for pensions or death benefits.

The people receiving the benefits must be common-law employees and not independent contractors. For this purpose, employee status depends on agency principles such as who controls and supervises the person, and whether the person can recognize profit or loss from the work relationship. It does not depend on the "reasonable expectations" of the parties. [*Mutual Insurance Co. v. Darden*, 503 U.S. 318 (1992)]

Welfare benefit plans are subject to ERISA Title I. The Eleventh Circuit has ruled that a Title I plan exists if circumstances lead a reasonable person to ascertain the intended benefits, intended beneficiaries, financing sources, and procedure for receiving benefits under the plan. [*Donovan v. Dillingham*, 688 F.2d 1367 (11th Cir. 1982)] A plan can be deemed to exist even if the ERISA rules are not observed, and in fact, even if there is no written instrument.

Severance pay plans are sometimes treated as pension plans, but are more likely to be characterized as welfare benefit plans. DOL Advisory Opinion 84-12A says that a severance pay plan is not a pension plan if:

- Its benefits are not contingent on the employee's retirement;
- Total payments do not exceed twice the employee's compensation for the year before the termination;
- Payments are completed within 24 months after termination of service for the employer.

Under a similar analysis, bonus programs are not treated as pension plans for ERISA Title I purposes unless the payments are systematically deferred at least until termination of employment. DOL Reg. § 2510.3 says that an employer plan that supplements retirement benefits (e.g., until early retirees can qualify for Social Security benefits) can be either a pension or a welfare benefit plan, depending on its terms and how it is administered.

ERISA Title I does not apply to certain payroll practices:

- Extra pay for nonstandard working hours (overtime, shift premiums, holiday premiums);
- Compensation paid when the employee is on sick leave, taking a sick day, or otherwise medically unable to work;
- Compensation paid for other absences, such as vacation days, sabbaticals, and military leave.

[B] ERISA Case Law on Welfare Benefits

A brokerage firm created an association of small firms (under 225 employees) so the members could maintain a self-funded health benefit plan. The Third Circuit ruled that the members lacked the requisite commonality of interest, and therefore the plan was not an "employee welfare benefit plan" as defined by ERISA. [*Gruber v. Hubbard Bert Karle Weber Inc.*, 159 F.3d 780 (3d Cir. 1998)]

Where failure to make complete disclosure could be harmful to benefit participants, a benefit plan administrator had a fiduciary duty to give complete and accurate information about the plan. If it is clear that a participant is unaware of important features of the plan, it is not enough simply to answer questions. [*Krohn v. Huron Mem. Hosp.*, 173 F.3d 542 (6th Cir. 1999)]

Vega v. National Life Insurance Services Inc. [188 F.3d 287 (5th Cir. 1999)] involved a plan sponsored by a married couple that owned a business. The plan administrator (which was a subsidiary of the insurer that wrote the plan's policies) denied a health claim for the wife. The administrator relied on information from the wife's doctor that the claim was for surgery planned before the policy was obtained.

The Fifth Circuit decided that even if a plan administrator has a conflict of interest when it denies a claim (which, in this case, would have been paid by the administrator's parent company) ERISA does not impose an additional duty of reasonable investigation before denying the claim. Even an administrator who has a conflict of interest can reach a valid decision, but when a court reviews the transaction for abuse of discretion, the conflict of interest is evidence.

PART V

THE HR FUNCTION

CHAPTER 23
HIRING AND RECRUITMENT

§ 23.01 INTRODUCTION

Efficient hiring practices benefit the company at all levels. Prompt, economical selection of the best person to do the job (whether from inside the company or brought in from outside) will keep operations running smoothly and encourage innovation that will keep the business competitive.

On the downside, bad hiring practices create many kinds of risks.

The most obvious risks are employment discrimination charges brought by ex-employees or job applicants. The employer might be held liable for negligence in hiring or retaining a person who commits a crime in the workplace, or who sexually harasses other workers.

Subtler risks come from poorly chosen employees who absorb too much training time, drag down the efficiency of an entire department, make costly mistakes—or who must be discharged and replaced, setting the whole cycle in motion again.

§ 23.02 PRODUCTIVE HIRING

Unless the plan is specifically to hire someone for a short-term or temporary assignment, an important objective is to find someone who will develop loyalty and will want to stay with the company for a long time. Training is both expensive and inconvenient, and it takes time for a new hire to get used to the job, so turnover is very harmful to productivity.

The best candidate is not necessarily the one with the most impressive resume. In fact, someone with great credentials might be constantly "head-hunted" and inclined to jump ship when a better offer comes along. The company is probably better off hiring someone who is suited to the job as it exists now and as it will develop in the future.

Current employees can be a great starting point for recruitment (and many companies offer bonuses if a current employee recruits someone who is hired and completes a minimum period satisfactorily), but they should not be the only source of recruitment—especially if you want a diverse workforce.

College and graduate school recruitment should not be restricted to those nearby, or only to a small class of Ivy League schools. If nationwide recruitment is a cost problem, the Internet allows nationwide recruiting and low cost. However, resumes posted on the Internet are no more or less truthful than those delivered by traditional means, so reference checks are still required.

§ 23.03 ANALYZING JOB REQUIREMENTS

In many cases, poor hiring decisions are made because of lack of insight into the real demands of the job. A candidate is chosen who matches the formal, written job description, but there's a mismatch, because the real job isn't very much like the job description. Often, people are hired on the basis of technical skills, but those skills are seldom used on a day-to-day basis.

The job should be analyzed to see how much time is actually spent on tasks such as:

- Meeting and conferring with others;
- Using specific computer hardware and software;
- Selling the company's products;
- Working with machinery;
- Supervising other people's work;
- Writing and analyzing reports;
- Creating policy for the organization;
- Carrying out policy set by others;
- Heavy lifting or repetitive stress;
- Driving;
- Business travel.

It is important to understand the physical demands of the job, to see who can meet them without accommodation, and what accommodations can reasonably be made to the needs of individuals with disabilities. [*See* § 36.05 for a discussion of reasonable accommodation.]

The job's role within the organization should also be analyzed. Maybe the whole operation could become more productive if the responsibilities assigned to the job were changed, or if the job were moved higher or lower on the grading system or organization chart. Maybe there have been problems because the job reports to one person, when it would make more sense to report to someone else.

The job must be identified as exempt or non-exempt for wage and hour purposes. Sometimes it makes economic sense to restructure job duties so that the job becomes exempt from overtime requirements. However, the change must be real, not just a meaningless title.

Reasons for job turnover should also be analyzed and steps taken to improve retention. In the late 2000s, companies faced a serious seller's market, and had to compete heavily to attract and retain good workers. The current economic downturn makes it more of a buyer's market, but it is still a good idea to remain competitive with the working conditions, salary, and benefits available elsewhere.

The job interview, and especially follow-up interviews with various people in the corporate hierarchy, should be used to give the potential employee strong insight into the resources available and what will be expected if he or she is offered, and accepts, the job.

There should be a written job description indicating:

- Job title;
- When it has to be filled;
- Why the organization needs someone for that position at all (perhaps the duties could be delegated to existing employees, outsourced, or assigned to temporary or part-time employees);
- Required educational qualifications;

- Necessary skills;
- Standards for defining inadequate, satisfactory, good, and excellent performance; the educational qualifications, skills, and experience that are really needed to perform the job; and standards (as objective as possible) for defining inadequate, satisfactory, good, and excellent performance.

The job description should indicate reporting relationships (whom the jobholder reports to; who reports to him or her). It should explain the promotion potential for the job, including conditions (such as getting an MBA or meeting performance goals). If your company has a grading system, the job grade should be indicated. The job description should also include the salary range.

§ 23.04   RECRUITMENT

[A]   Generally

It is probably worthwhile to consider promoting existing employees to fill important positions, although sometimes it is necessary to look outside—or desirable to get new skills and viewpoints. Even a policy of promoting from within requires recruiting, to fill entry- and mid-levels that have been vacated by the promoted employees.

[B]   Recruitment from Within

Many companies create incentives for employees to do well by stressing internal transfers and promotions. These workers do not have to leave (or threaten to leave) to advance or earn more money if they are given access to job postings and given a real chance to compete for jobs. Internal recruitment also saves money that would otherwise go to advertisements and search firm fees. The company can get a detailed view of the employee's past performance by consulting their own records. Internal promotion also means that the person selected will be familiar with the corporate culture. However, sometimes supervisors deliberately torpedo the promotion chances of their best employees, because they don't want to lose them!

In most companies, job postings literally are posted on a bulletin board, leaving the notice up for five to ten days. More and more companies are using the corporate Intranet for this purpose. The posting should explain the nature of the job (although another advantage of recruiting from within is that the applicants will be fairly familiar with it already); the qualifications required; and whether there are any limitations. For instance, seniority is a very significant factor in promotions in a unionized workplace. Some companies have a policy that employees are not allowed to apply for internal vacancies unless they have held their current job for at least six months with satisfactory or better performance appraisals. The usual policy is to keep the application confidential from the applicant's immediate supervisor, until there is the possibility that the promotion will be offered.

[C]   Competitive Recruiting

If at least some outside applications are solicited, the question becomes how to stay competitive in the job market. Attractive features can include:

- High cash compensation;
- High overall compensation package, taking health and other benefits into account;
- High job security;
- Prestige within the industry;
- Ability to work on cutting-edge projects;
- Availability of stock options;
- Pleasant working environment;
- Easy commute;
- Family-friendly policies (although these are neutral or even a disadvantage for unmarried employees).

Companies that send letters to rejected candidates often include the polite phrase, "We will keep your resume on file," but few of them actually review the filed resumes when they have another job to fill—although this can be a simple and inexpensive source of candidates.

The state employment service can be a good resource for low-level jobs, and even some higher-level technical jobs. Unemployment benefits are not available to workers who have voluntarily quit, or who were fired for wrongdoing, so workers receiving benefits are probably not unstable or a bad risk merely on account of being unemployed. Also, people who are employed but want a new job sometimes register with the state employment office because it has contacts with a wide range of employers and because it does not charge jobseekers a fee. To fill higher-level positions, if a local company has had a major downsizing recently, check with the company that handles their executive outplacement.

Tip: An automated voice-mail system, called interactive voice response (IVR), can mechanize the early stages of the recruitment process. Applicants call a toll-free telephone number and answer a series of questions. If they have the basic qualifications, the system can direct them to submit a resume or schedule an in-person interview. [*See* Ruth E. Thaler-Carter, *Recruiting Through the Web: Better or Just Bigger?*, HR Magazine, November 1998, at p. 61]

[D]   Avoiding Improprieties

If you hire someone who held a senior position at one of your competitors, it is possible that the individual had an employment contract with the company that contained a covenant not to compete. Another possibility is that, when his or her severance package was negotiated, a covenant not to compete was signed at that time. Therefore, it is important to find out if a job applicant is subject to such an agreement, and whether taking the job that is offered would violate it.

Even without a covenant not to compete, a competitor could charge that you hired its ex-employee to misappropriate the competitor's customer lists and trade secrets. If you recruited the ex-employee, you might be charged with interference with contractual relationships. So make it part of the interview process to make a record about the circumstances of the contact.

[E] Rehiring

Sometimes downsizing goes too deep, and employees can be recalled at a later time. Employees leave because of differences of opinion, personality conflicts, or because they have been offered another job. Rehiring a former employee has both advantages and disadvantages. The ex-employee needs less training than an outsider, because he or she is already familiar with procedures and the corporate culture. However, there is a risk of morale problems, both arising out of the original termination and on the part of other employees who feel that they were insufficiently rewarded for loyally sticking to the company all along.

§ 23.05 SEARCH FIRMS

For a rank-and-file job, putting out the word to employees, or within the neighborhood could be enough to fill the vacancy. For an entry-level job, recruiting from high schools, colleges, and vocational training programs often works well. Newspaper classified ads, ads in specialty journals, and to an increasing extent, Internet job search sites, can result in a good match between needs and job candidates.

However, the stakes are higher when a top executive or prominent professional has to be replaced. The successful candidate will set the company's policy and/or creative agenda. A good choice strengthens the company's long-term competitive position; the wrong choice could lead to long-term damage. The person hired might have excellent credentials and work hard, but might have a vision for the company that is incompatible with the rest of management.

For those and other reasons, businesses often look to search firms when a major job needs to be filled. This is a costly option. Search firm fees can be the equivalent of a year's salary—or more!—for a highly compensated executive. But it pays off in productivity if the right candidate is selected and gets to work quickly.

There are two main types of firms in the search professional. Contingency firms are usually used to find candidates for jobs paying $40,000–$80,000 a year; an executive search firm usually gets involved only with jobs paying $75,000 a year or more. A search firm works directly for the company seeking to hire an executive. Usually, its contracts require the company to pay for its services whether or not a candidate is hired. In contrast, a contingency firm's clients include both job seekers and companies looking to hire someone, and the company pays a fee if and only if hiring results.

A search firm's fee can be anywhere from 25–100% of the first year salary. Contingency firms usually charge less, perhaps 20–33% of the first year's salary. Only cash compensation, not bonuses or stock options, is included in the calculation. Both kinds of firms often give refunds if the new hire leaves or has to be discharged during a probationary period such as 90 days.

Many companies are not familiar with search firms, so they do not know what to expect or how to assess the quality of the firm's performance. John Marra, president of the recruitment firm Marra Peters & Partners, has some suggestions:

- Be clear on the criteria you use to judge the firm's performance;
- Get references from past clients and follow them up;
- Tell the search firm what you expect the successful candidate to accomplish the first six months and the first year after hiring, and how you will assess the new hire's performance;
- Ask the search firm to send only candidates who are a good match with your requirements;
- Get the search firm's promise to keep working with you until the vacancy is satisfactorily filled (if necessary, after someone has been hired, terminated after a probationary period, and a new search performed).

Some of the provisions to look for in a recruitment contract are:

- Clarification that the firm does not have the authority to hire someone on behalf of your company, or to promise terms and conditions of employment—only your company's authorized agent can do that;
- A statement that your company is committed to equal employment opportunity principles;
- The firm's agreement that it will be responsible if it commits discrimination in referring candidates to you—and that it will indemnify your company for any liability resulting from its discriminatory referrals;
- A clear statement of the firm's responsibilities, including screening candidates and checking their references;
- Recruiting expenses that your company agrees to pay;
- Whether you have to pay if you hire a candidate obtained through another channel, or only if the recruiter sends the successful candidate to you;
- The recruiter's promise not to contact or solicit your new hire for a period of at least two years.

§ 23.06   JOB APPLICATIONS

Frequently, the first real contact between the corporation and the potential employee occurs when the applicant submits a formal job application. The application is a legal document that can have serious consequences: both as a source of promises that the employer can be held to, and as a source of information whose correctness the applicant can be held responsible for. For example, false statements on an application can constitute "after-acquired evidence" of wrongdoing that can limit the damages available to a successful employee plaintiff. [*See* § 42.10[C]]

It often makes sense to have a candidate fill out a job application even if he or she has submitted a resume. The resume only includes the information the candidate wants to disclose. The application form is standard, and resumes are very variable, so it is easier to compare applicants if you have the same information about each. The application might ask for:

- Positions held with the last three or four employers;
- Dates of employment;
- Job title;
- Salary;
- Name of immediate supervisor;
- Why the candidate left that job (unless he or she is still employed);
- Permission to contact the supervisor for a reference.

> **Tip:** In several states (e.g., California, Delaware, Minnesota, Wisconsin), if you require applicants to sign their applications, the state privacy law also requires you to give them a copy of the completed application, or lets employees copy personnel files including job applications.

The application should make it clear that the form is a legal document that can have serious ramifications. It is important to require the applicant to state that all the information given on the application is complete and accurate—and that it will be grounds for discipline or dismissal if the applicant is hired and the employer later finds out that false information was given on the application.

There should be a separate signature line if the employer wants to get a credit report to indicate release of this information. Applicants should be informed when reference checks will be done. The form should clarify that application is being made for at-will employment. If the job offer is conditional on the applicant's passing a physical examination and/or drug and alcohol testing, this should be indicated on the application.

Check state law about which questions are permissible, and which are ruled out by antidiscrimination laws.

> **Tip:** It could make sense to indicate that applications will be rejected if the applicant includes extraneous information that was not requested on the application. Some applicants use this material tactically: for instance, if they volunteer information about union activism, they might claim that they were discriminated against by the employer. [*See* Timothy S. Bland and Sue S. Stalcup, *Build a Legal Employment Application,* HR Magazine, March 1999, at p. 129]

§ 23.07   ESTABLISHING TERMS AND CONDITIONS

The interview should stress the at-will nature of employment if your company wants the flexibility to terminate employees without a formal structure. Train interviewers to avoid statements such as "If you do a good job, you'll be set for life here" or "We never lay anybody off, no matter how tough the economy gets." Interviewers should also avoid statements about corporate procedure ("We go through all the channels before anybody gets fired") unless they accurately reflect corporate policy and practice.

Interviewers are agents of the company, and even if the employee handbook says that the company is only obligated if there are written contracts, in fact the company is likely to be held accountable for promises made by the interviewer (for instance, about vacation terms, the availability of leave, and education benefits).

Many companies set a salary range rather than an explicit pay rate for a particular job. Interviewers should understand whether or not they can negotiate a salary with a promising candidate, or if that matter will have to be referred to a higher-up. Interviewees should always be told clearly who else is involved in the interview process, what the powers are of each person, and who has the power to actually make a job offer.

§ 23.08   REFERENCE CHECKS

Not every statement made on an application or in an interview is strictly accurate! At the worst, criminals may seek a job where they can plunder the corporate funds, so it is often worthwhile to have an arrangement with a third-party provider that checks criminal record databases. In the case of an especially unusual or sensitive job, it can make sense to do a detailed investigation, or even hire a private investigator, before extending a job offer.

On a less dramatic scale, basically honest people often exaggerate their credentials, turn attendance at a program into a degree, or claim more credit for results than they are entitled to. Companies that are sensitive to the risk of defamation may limit the amount of information that they provide about former employees, but they should at least be able to confirm the dates of employment and the positions held.

Reference checks on employees (rather than applicants) can also be useful. A lack of candor can be a valid reason for denying a raise or promotion, and "after-acquired evidence" discovered as late as the preparation for a discrimination suit can be used to reduce the recovery a plaintiff can obtain.

According to American Background Information Services Inc., between January 1998 and October 2000 about one-eighth (12.6%) of the people it screened had undisclosed criminal backgrounds. Blair Cohen, the CEO of InfoMart Inc., another employment screening company, says that 8.3% of those screened have a criminal record, and nearly one-quarter (23%) misrepresented their education or work credentials.

Usually, a criminal-record check starts with a trace on the applicant's Social Security number, which generates a list of previous addresses. (Of course, this implies that the applicant was operating "on the books" and using his or her own name!) A complete search looks for outstanding wants and warrants (misdemeanors as well as felonies), motor vehicle reports, credit reports, academic qualifications, and verification of past employment.

Firms that perform checks charge an average of $35–$50 for a basic search for a low-level candidate, and perhaps $150–$200 for a more senior employee; it could cost about $300 for a three-to-five-day turnaround on a search.

> **Tip:** Make sure that the outsourcing firm fully understands the Fair Credit Reporting Act limitations on use of investigative credit reports—and make sure they have plenty of liability insurance if they could be required to indemnify your company!

A good criminal record check goes back at least seven years. Because many court systems have automated records going back only one to six years, it is often necessary for the research firm to do a manual search (which often costs extra). It is also common for misdemeanor and felony records to be kept in different places, which could also lead to higher fees for separate searches. [Merry Mayer, *Background Checks in Focus*, HR Magazine, January 2002, at p. 59]

§ 23.09 NONDISCRIMINATORY HIRING

Federal law bans discrimination in employment, which definitely includes hiring. Discrimination on account of age, sex, race, disability, religion, and/or national origin is banned. However, even a company that strives to avoid deliberate prejudice can find it hard to eradicate "disparate impact"—apparently neutral practices that actually disadvantage members of one group more than others. For instance, a minimum height requirement screens out more women and certain ethnic groups than white males. That does not mean that employers cannot impose height requirements, as long as it really is necessary to be taller than a certain height to do the job properly.

Other potential sources of disparate impact include:

- Educational standards;
- Preemployment testing;
- Requirements of military service;
- Referrals from your current workforce (who tend to know people of their own ethnic group);

- Rules about facial hair (which could disadvantage religious applicants, or black men who have ingrown hairs that make shaving painful);
- Refusing to hire anyone who has ever been arrested, filed for bankruptcy, or had a child out of wedlock.

Your attorney should review hiring practices to make sure that they are not discriminatory and that all requirements can be justified in terms of the practical needs of the business and skills that will actually be used on the job. For each position, you should also determine the physical capacities that are central to the job, those that are sometimes used but are peripheral, and those that are never invoked by the job.

If employees request flextime (for parenting needs, as an accommodation to disability, as a religious accommodation, or simply for convenience), you should either be able to grant the request or demonstrate a legitimate business reason why conventional business hours or standard shifts must be observed.

There are two important criteria for assessing interview questions:

- Do the questions relate to legitimate workplace issues, rather than just satisfying curiosity?
- Are they asked uniformly, rather than only to a group of people chosen on the basis of preconceived notions? For instance, it is discriminatory to ask a woman if her husband "lets" her travel on business, but not discriminatory to discuss the amount of travel required with all applicants, including the number of overnight or prolonged stays required, and to ask all candidates if they are able to travel that much.

Equal employment opportunity law assumes that many candidates will be interviewed for each opening, and there are many reasons why the successful candidate will be selected. There is no reason to collect a great deal of information about candidates who have no real chance of selection. Therefore, some questions are acceptable when a conditional job offer is made that would not be allowed at a first-stage interview.

For instance, marital status and having children are very relevant to participation in an employee group health plan, but irrelevant if the person is not going to get a job offer. So this information should either be requested only after hiring, or collected on a separate sheet of paper and not consulted until after hiring. [*See* § 36.09 for a discussion of acceptable and unacceptable pre-employment inquiries and tests in the disability context]

It is not acceptable to ask an interviewee about his or her history of receiving Worker's Compensation benefits, but anyone who gets a conditional job offer can be asked about past injuries that may require accommodation.

There are also circumstances under which the company's commitment to equal employment opportunity must be put into writing: if the company is a federal contractor, for instance.

§ 23.10 PRE-EMPLOYMENT TESTING

[A] Permissible Testing

It is legitimate for an employer to test job applicants to see if they have relevant skills. Title VII permits the use of professionally developed ability tests that are not designed or administered with a discriminatory motive. A valid test is one that is neither explicitly nor implicitly discriminatory against protected groups; one that tests skills that are actually used in the job; and one that has been validated by psychologists or other experts so that it really offers insight into the issues needed for effective hiring.

A Supreme Court case, *Albemarle Paper Co. v. Moody* [422 U.S. 407 (1975)] holds that if a test has a disproportionate negative effect on a minority group, the test is permissible only if professionally accepted methods verify the test's ability to predict important elements of work behavior. As *Griggs v. Duke Power Co.* [401 U.S. 424 (1971)] says, the point of pre-employment testing is to measure the applicant's performance in the context of a specific job, not in the abstract. Even if the company's pre-employment test is valid, it is discriminatory to give the test only to minority-group members.

[B] Validating a Test

If your company adopts a pre-employment test and monitors the results, discovering that the test has an adverse impact on women and/or members of minority groups, then you should either get rid of the test, change it to remove the adverse impact, or do a validity study that confirms both that the test is a business necessity and that it accurately predicts the skills needed for successful job performance. The Civil Rights Act of 1991 [Pub. L. No. 102-166] says that it is not acceptable to grade minority applicants' tests on a "curve," or to have a lower passing grade for minorities.

Publications about psychological testing are good for finding out which tests have already been validated. Three types of validation are accepted:

- Criterion-related (the test is an accurate predictor of work behavior or other criteria of employee adequacy);
- Content-related (the test accurately duplicates the tasks that will actually be called for in the workplace);
- Construct-related (the test identifies general mental and psychological traits needed to do the job, such as the ability to remain cool under pressure and respond courteously to angry customers).

§ 23.11   IMMIGRATION ISSUES

[A]   Employment Requirement

Before the September 11 attack, the focus was on making sure that employers hired only noncitizens who were permitted to work in this country. Since then, the focus has shifted more in the direction of security, and there has been a crackdown on people who overstay their visas.

If an alien wishes to enter this country on the basis of employment, he or she must not only have a definite job offer from a U.S. employer, but the employer must have "labor certification." That is, the Department of Labor must certify that the job is "open" because the company cannot recruit a qualified U.S. worker at the prevailing wages. First, the employer must use the State Employment Service and post and advertise the job opportunity. The employer must interview any applicants who come through that route, and must file a recruitment report with the DOL explaining why none of those applicants was suitable for the position.

However, certain occupations are considered "shortage" occupations because of a documented difficulty in filling the jobs: nursing, physical therapy, and people of demonstrated exceptional ability in business, science, or the arts. Multinational executives, outstanding university-level teachers, researchers, and people whose jobs are in the national interest do not displace American workers, so labor certification will not be required for such jobs. [*See* <http://www.ins.usdoj.gov/graphics/services/residency/obl25.htm>]

[B]   Immigration Categories

Employment-based immigration is regulated under the Immigration Act of 1990. [Pub. L. No. 101-649] There are seven categories of employable immigrants:

- Priority workers individuals of extraordinary ability and/or vocational responsibility;
- Professionals with advanced degrees and/or exceptional ability;
- Other workers (skilled workers, professionals without advanced degrees; unskilled workers who have DOL certification that there is a shortage of U.S. workers with similar skills);
- Special immigrants (e.g., religious workers sent to the U.S. by a religious hierarchy);
- Immigrants who have the financial capacity to invest at least $1 million within the United States, employing at least 10 U.S. workers;
- H-1B "specialty occupation" workers who reside temporarily within the United States, and work here, but do not become citizens;
- H-2 temporary non-agricultural workers.

[C] Employer Responsibilities

U.S. labor and immigration law places a burden on the employer (or on an agency that gets a fee for recruitment or making referrals) to determine whether job applicants are legally permitted to work in this country. No later than three business days after hiring, the employer must ascertain if the new hire is a U.S. citizen or a legal immigrant who is not only permitted to reside in this country but to work here.

The employer responsibilities stem from the Immigration Reform and Control Act of 1986 (IRCA). [7 U.S.C. § 1324a] The employer is responsible for checking documents presented by potential new employees to demonstrate their identity and authorization to work within the United States. (There are people who are lawfully permitted to enter and reside in this country, but not to work here, so there is more to the matter than distinguishing illegal aliens from lawful immigrants.)

The information must be obtained in a way that is not discriminatory against dark-skinned people, or people whose first language is not English.

Once someone is eligible to work in the United States, IRCA makes it an unfair employment practice to discriminate in hiring, recruitment, or retention on the basis of national origin (but this provision is applicable only to companies that have between four and 15 employees; if there are 15 or more employees, Title VII bans national origin discrimination).

The employer reviews the documents submitted by the new hire and completes Part 2 of the Form I-9 ("Employer Review and Verification"). Documents must be checked within three days of hiring someone, using Form I-9; and records of the document checks must be kept for three years, or one year after employment terminates.

The employer cannot avoid this responsibility by having workers supplied under a contract (e.g., with an employment agency or leasing company). It will not get the employer off the hook to have new hires indemnify the employer if they are not actually permitted to work within the United States However, if the employer gets referrals from a state employment service, and the service furnishes certification that it has verified employee eligibility, that will insulate the employer from liability.

Both the Immigration and Naturalization Service (INS) and the DOL are entitled to inspect a company's I-9 forms, but to enter a workplace they must either have a warrant or give 72 hours' notice.

Civil and criminal penalties of anywhere from $250 to $2,000 (depending on the circumstances) can be imposed for a first offense of hiring persons who are not permitted to work in the United States. Repeat offenses can be penalized by $3,000 to $10,000. Even failure to maintain the appropriate paperwork and records can be penalized by up to $1,000. Anyone (including an employer) who is guilty of document fraud can be fined $250 to $2,000 per document per instance in which it was used; up to $5,000 per document for repeat violations.

It is illegal to knowingly hire an ineligible person. Knowledge includes constructive knowledge (reasonable inferences from facts and circumstances, to the degree that a person acting with reasonable care would have to be aware). According to INS regulations [*see* 8 C.F.R. § 274a], these circumstances create an inference of constructive knowledge:

- The employer actually has some information that the person is not eligible for U.S. employment;
- The applicant refuses to complete the I-9 form, or does it improperly;
- The employer acts with "reckless and wanton disregard" of the consequences of hiring ineligible persons.

However, accent and appearance are not acceptable sources of constructive knowledge. Once the employer knows that the hiree is (or has become, because of a change of status) ineligible to work in the United States, continuing employment is unlawful. [*See* 8 U.S.C. § 1324a]

Presidential Executive Order 12989 [61 Fed. Reg. 6091 (Feb. 13, 1996)] debars federal contractors from getting further federal contracts after they have been caught knowingly hiring illegal aliens.

[D]   Employment Verification Documents

Hired individuals prove their eligibility to work within the United States either by showing that they are U.S. citizens (e.g., showing a U.S. passport or birth certificate evidencing birth within the United States) or by showing that they have a so-called green card. (The document is no longer actually green.)

Since 1997, the Immigration and Naturalization Service has issued Form I-766, a tamper-resistant card issued to aliens whose immigration status permits work within the United States. The I-766 is a List A Employment Authorization Document (EAD): that is, it establishes both the job applicant's identity and his or her entitlement to work.

There are three categories of documents. List A documents can be used to prove both identity and employability:

- U.S. passport (even if expired; all other documents must be current to be usable for this purpose);
- A current passport from another country, stamped to show permission to work here (Form I-551);
- (If authorization is based on working for a specific employer) a current foreign passport with the Form I-94 Arrival-Departure Record;
- INS Form I-766, I-688, I-688A or I-688B (employment authorization documents).

The employer must at least examine the documents to see if they appear to relate to the person offering them as proof.

List B documents prove identity only:

- A U.S. or Canadian driver's license, especially if it has a photograph;
- A voter registration card;
- A university photo I.D.;
- A U.S. military card or service record;
- I.D. issued by a state or local government (as long as it has either a photograph or comparable identification information).

List C documents prove employability only:

- A Social Security card (unless it is stamped to indicate work ineligibility);
- Form FS-545 or DS-135 (two forms of certification of birth outside the United States);
- An original birth certificate from the United States, or a certified copy of a birth certificate that bears an official seal;
- A current INS employment authorization document;
- INS Form I-197 (U.S. citizen I.D. card);
- INS Form I-179 (I.D. card for the use of residents).

The potential employee, not the employer, decides which of these documents to present. The employer must accept any combination of original documents that establishes both identity and employment status. The Immigration and Nationality Act calls for a transition to a secure system to prevent fraud under which one person claims the identity of another, or fraud via document counterfeiting.

The INS has several experimental programs to help employers verify the employment status of noncitizens who apply for jobs. So far, these programs are only available in selected states. [*See* <http://www.ins.usdoj.gov/graphics/services/SAVE.htm> or call toll-free, (888) 464-4218] The INS gives employers free software that they can use in their computer systems to see if the individual appears on a database of persons who should not be in the United States or who should not be employed. Pub. L. No. 107-128 (Jan. 16, 2002) extends the main pilot program until 2004.

In the wake of the September 11 attack, there were many calls for greater surveillance of noncitizens, and for issuance of a national I.D. for both citizens and noncitizens, so expect developments in these areas.

[E]   H-1B Visas

The H-1B visa is a non-immigrant visa for temporary workers in "specialty occupations." This means jobs that apply a highly specialized body of knowledge in both a theoretical and a practical way. Most H-1B visa holders work in high-tech businesses, such as software development. The initial duration of the visa is three years, although it can be extended for three more years. The worker must have at least a bachelor's degree in his or her specialty field, or must have equivalent qualifications and expertise. If the job requires a state license, the visa holder must have the license.

H-1B workers must be paid either the salary the employer would otherwise pay for the job, or the prevailing wage in the area. This requirement is designed to prevent employers from hiring foreign workers simply to lower wage costs. Willful violation of this requirement or the layoff requirement can be penalized by a $35,000 fine and three years' debarment from federal contracts.

Employers usually recruit workers from foreign students in the United States on student visas and about to graduate from a program that gives them the necessary specialized skills. Immigration law requires the employer to wait until the student graduates before making a job offer. You can get around this problem by having the student get permission from the Immigration and Naturalization Services to add a year of PGPT (post-graduate practical training) to his or her student visa, so you can apply for the H-1B visa during this extra year. The holders of student visas are required to leave the United States by July of the year in which they graduate, unless they have PGPT authorization.

The American Competitiveness and Workforce Improvement Act of 1998 (ACWIA) [Pub. L. No. 105-277] modifies the H-1B visa process. [*See* DOL Interim Final Regulations, 65 Fed. Reg. 80109 (Dec. 20, 2000)] The H-1B visa quota for fiscal years 2001, 2002, and 2003 is set at 195,000 visas a year. Until October 1, 2003, "non-displacement" requirements are imposed on employers who are H-1B dependent (get 15% or more of their work force from this source) or who have already violated the visa rules.

H-1B visa holders may not be hired until the employer has first attempted to recruit qualified U.S. workers, although a more qualified H-1B applicant can legitimately be preferred to a less-qualified U.S. citizen. Employers are also forbidden to terminate U.S. workers for the purpose of replacing them with H-1B workers. Temporary agencies and other suppliers of contingent workers are forbidden to make any placements of H-1B workers with any company that has displaced U.S. workers.

The DOL regulation not only protects U.S. jobs, it protects the H-1B workers from exploitation. They must be given benefits on the same basis as their U.S. counterparts. Whenever their employer places them in a nonproductive category (e.g., there is a temporary lull in work), they must be kept at full salary. It is unlawful for employers to require H-1B workers to reimburse them for the cost of filing the employment petition, or to penalize workers for terminating their work assignment prematurely.

To encourage reporting of misconduct, protection is extended to applicants, employees, and ex-employees who assist the Departments of Labor and Justice in their investigations. In fact, H-1B whistleblowers can be permitted to remain in the United States for up to six years.

There were 342,035 applications for H-1B visas in 2001, 14% higher than the 2000 level. About half of the visas granted go to the computer industry, and about half of the nonimmigrant workers who use these visas come from India. [*Tech Downturn Doesn't Slow H-1B Visas*, <http://news.findlaw.com/ap/ht/1700/ 1-28-2002/200201281012235107.html> (no www.)]

Since March 30, 2000, all H-1B petitions have required the attachment of Form I-129W to the Form I-129 ("Petition for Nonimmigrant Worker"). The form collects information (e.g., the job for which a nonimmigrant worker will be hired, the employer's industry, the worker's background, and his or her compensation) that the INS uses for statistical and reporting purposes. The form also determines whether the petitioning employer will be required to pay the $1,000 fee for expedited processing (within 15 calendar days) enacted by the American Competitiveness and Workforce Improvement Act of 1998 in addition to the standard petition fee of $110. [For details, see *Information for Employers*, <http://www.ins. usdoj.gov/graphics/services/employerinfo/index.htm>. Premium processing customers can also contact the four service centers:

> California, CSC.Premium.Processing@usdoj.gov, telephone (949) 831-8550;
>
> Nebraska, NSC.Premium.Processing@usdoj.gov, (402) 474-5012,
>
> Texas, TSC.Premium.Processing@usdoj.gov, (214) 275-4415, and
>
> Vermont, VSC.Premium.Processing@usdoj.gov, (802) 527-3192]

[F]   Case Law on Immigration Issues in Employment

Undocumented aliens are employees entitled to vote in representation elections, even if their status has been challenged under the IRCA. [*NLRB v. Kolkka*, 170 F.3d 937 (9th Cir. 1999)] But an illegal alien is not an "employee" for Worker's Compensation purposes, and therefore cannot receive Comp benefits for an on-the-job injury. [*Granados v. Windson Development Corp.*, 257 Va. 103, 509 S.E.2d 290 (1999)], or back pay in a suit alleging unlawful layoff. [*Hoffman Plastic Products Inc. v. NLRB*, 00-1595 (Sup. Ct. March 26, 2002)]

It was an unfair labor practice to contact the INS right after the union won an election, telling eleven employees that they could not work until they straightened out their immigration status. This was a departure from the employer's normal practice. The NLRB said that, although IRCA compliance is important, it must not be used as a smokescreen for anti-union animus. [*Nortech Waste*, 336 N.L.R.B. 79 (2001)]

[G]   EEOC/DOJ Memorandum of Understanding

Under the Memorandum of Understanding (MOU) between the EEOC and the Department of Justice's Office of Special Counsel for Immigration Related Unfair Employment Practices [*see* 63 Fed. Reg. 5518 (Feb. 3, 1998)] each agency can act as the other's agents to receive complaints about immigration-related discrimination charges. The two agencies will coordinate to limit duplication of efforts. Document abuse, intimidation, and retaliation will be treated as immigration-related unfair labor practices. The EEOC has agreed not to ask if the charging party is a U.S. citizen, national, or work-authorized alien as a condition for referring charges to the DOJ.

However, according to the Fourth Circuit, only a citizen or an alien with a valid work visa is a "qualified" employee who can make out a Title VII prima facie case. [*Egbuna v. Time-Life Libraries Inc.*, 153 F.3d 184 (4th Cir. 1998)]

The EEOC's "Enforcement Guidance on Remedies for Undocumented Workers Under Laws Prohibiting Employment Discrimination" [No. 915.002 (Oct. 26, 1999), at <http://www.eeoc.gov/docs/undoc.html>] says that undocumented workers who suffer discrimination contrary to Title VII, the ADEA, ADA, or EPA can be entitled to back pay, hiring, and reinstatement, whenever this can be granted without direct conflict with IRCA and other immigration laws. People hired under IRCA can be entitled to remedies unless the employer knew that they were not eligible to work in the United States. If the employer did know, hiring and reinstatement remedies are available only for individuals who are now able to provide work documentation. (The NLRB mentions in a footnote that it disagrees with the Fourth Circuit's ruling in *Egbuna*.)

The EEOC's contention is that the purpose of federal antidiscrimination remedies is to control the behavior of employers, and also to compensate workers for discrimination they have suffered. It is so important to deter discrimination that discrimination victims should be able to get at least some remedies even if their own behavior has not been above reproach. On the other hand, the purpose of immigration laws is to prevent illegal immigration, a purpose that can be served without immunizing employers who discriminate.

The EEOC view is that injunctions and other remedies that forbid future discrimination are compatible with immigration laws. Sometimes, however, awarding back pay and damages will not be proper because it will conflict with immigration laws. Under this interpretation, the employer will be liable for back pay, except for periods when the undocumented worker was outside the United States, or except for the situation in which the worker is either reinstated or unable to document work eligibility within a reasonable time after being offered a job or reinstatement.

However, remedies can be restricted if the worker's undocumented status represented part of the employer's mixed motive, or if the worker's true status was after-acquired evidence for the employer. Only attorneys' fees and injunctive relief, not reinstatement, back pay, or damages, are available in mixed-motive cases.

The EEOC also takes the view that employers are never justified in using a worker's undocumented status as a reason for discriminatory terms of employment or failure to promote, so back pay is appropriate in all such cases. Employers are also liable for retaliation damages if they reported, or threatened to report, undocumented workers to the INS to punish them for enforcing their rights as employees.

§ 23.12   ADA COMPLIANCE IN HIRING

The ADA protects qualified individuals with a disability. The employer must determine whether to extend a job offer to a candidate with a disability, a question that includes consideration of accommodations that may be needed in the course of employment. Some pre-employment inquiries are simply unacceptable; others are permissible only after a conditional job offer has been made.

The EEOC's Technical Assistance Manual for implementation of the ADA defines these pre-hire questions as improper:

- Have you ever been treated for these diseases?
- Have you ever been hospitalized? Why?
- Are there any health factors that prevent you from doing the job you applied for? (However, if the inquiry is restricted to specific job functions, it is permissible to ask about ability to perform those particular functions, and about potential accommodations.)
- How much sick leave did you take last year?
- Are you taking any prescribed medications?
- Have you ever been treated for substance abuse?

When it comes to pre-employment testing, it is discriminatory to give a test in a form or manner that requires the use of an impaired sensory, speaking, or manual skill, unless the point of the test is the degree to which that skill is present. So an assembly-line job may legitimately require manual dexterity. But if the point is to test keyboarding speed, a hearing-impaired person may have to be given a test that includes nonverbal commands as to when to start and stop. It may be necessary to have a test read aloud to a blind or dyslexic person, or to have a sign language interpreter. Every effort should be made to administer the test in a room that is wheelchair-accessible.

> **Tip:** Tell applicants if there will be a test as part of the interview process. Then it is up to them to explain the nature of any accommodation they need to take the test.

Pre-employment medical examinations are allowed only if the candidate has already met the other criteria, and a conditional job offer has been extended. The examination must be required of everyone in that job category who gets a conditional offer. Once the offer has been made, it is acceptable to ask about past injuries and Worker's Compensation claims.

Post-offer medical examinations are considered nondiscriminatory, and therefore it is not necessary to provide proof of business necessity. But if the applicant with a disability is in fact qualified for the job, and the offer is withdrawn subsequent to the examination, the employer must show job-related business necessity for canceling the offer, and must also prove that reasonable accommodation to the disability could not be made without undue hardship.

For active employees, medical examinations and inquiries about the nature and severity of disability can be required only if they are job-related and consistent with business necessity: For instance, someone has been ill or injured, and the question is fitness to return to work.

The ADA also requires disability-related information to be kept confidential. In fact, it should be collected and maintained on separate forms, and even stored in files separate from general personnel information, although there are certain exceptions to the general rule of confidentiality:

- Supervisors and managers can be informed about work restrictions or accommodations that are needed;
- If emergency treatment might be required for a disabled employee (e.g., an epileptic might have a seizure; a diabetic might go into insulin shock or coma), first aid and safety personnel can be informed, so they will be prepared;
- A special post-September 11 rule allows collection of information about special needs for evacuation in an emergency;
- Government officials investigating ADA compliance are entitled to information about the number of employees with disabilities, and the nature of the disabilities.

§ 23.13   CREDIT REPORTING IN THE HIRING PROCESS

A federal law, the Fair Credit Reporting Act (FCRA) [15 U.S.C. § 1681a *et seq*.], as amended by the Consumer Credit Reporting Reform Act of 1996 (CCRRA) [Pub. L. No. 104-208], governs the use of credit reports and investigative credit reports not only for making loans and approving credit card applications, but in the employment context as well.

The FCRA provides that a consumer report is a written or oral communication from a consumer reporting agency, dealing with a consumer's entitlement to credit, "character, general reputation, personal characteristics, or mode of living."

An investigative credit report is different in that it involves personal interviews with people who have personal knowledge of the individual. The CCRRA requires employers to give job applicants a written disclosure statement, and to get their consent in writing, before requesting either a consumer report or an investigative consumer report. Furthermore, if the employer wants an investigative report, it must explain to the applicant (via a written disclosure mailed no later than three days after the report is requested) that this type of report covers matters like character and conduct.

The FCRA [*see* 15 U.S.C. § 1681b(3)(B)] says that "employment purposes" are legitimate reasons for requesting a credit report or investigative credit report. "Employment purposes" means "evaluating a consumer for employment, promotion, reassignment or retention as an employee." Because the FCRA specifically authorizes the use of credit reporting information in the hiring process, doing so is not employment discrimination.

An "adverse action" includes "denial of employment or any other decision for employment purposes that adversely affects any current or prospective employee." When the credit report is negative, leading to adverse action, the employer must provide oral, written, or electronic (for instance, fax or e-mail) notice of the adverse action. It must also explain how to review the credit report file, correct errors (the negative report might refer to someone else with a similar name, or someone who has appropriated the job applicant's identity) and contest items that the consumer believes to be untrue. Notice must be given after the employer makes the decision, but before the adverse action is implemented.

The CCRRA also imposes an obligation on the employer. Before it gets any reports from a reporting agency, it must give the agency a statement that the employer complies with the various consumer protection requirements of credit reporting law.

CHAPTER 24

RECORDKEEPING

§ 24.01   INTRODUCTION

Employee records are important in setting compensation, assuring that it is paid appropriately, and administering benefit plans. Proper records are necessary to handle insurance matters, comply with court orders, fill out tax returns and other government documents, and demonstrate EEO and immigration compliance.

In addition to determining its internal needs for gathering, processing, and deleting information, the company must be aware of legal requirements for record retention, and limitations on document destruction. Destroying documents that are subject to discovery in a court case is at least a civil offense, and may constitute contempt of court or even a criminal offense, depending on circumstances.

All documents in personnel files should be date-stamped when they are received, because it may be necessary to determine what was in the file at a particular time.

Tip: If it is legal and practical to destroy a document, make sure that all paper copies have been destroyed, as well as all computer files (including back-ups, copies on disks, and data uploaded to an Internet site for safekeeping). Just because someone has deleted a file does not mean that it has even been removed from that computer, much less from the entire network.

Many of the states have laws that guarantee employees access to their own employment records. If your state has such a law, check to see if ex-employees are entitled to access, or if only current employees do.

§ 24.02   OSHA RECORDS

[A]   Injury and Illness Recordkeeping

Complying with the Occupational Safety and Health Act [*see* Chapter 31] requires constant accumulation of data on a day-by-day basis, followed by compilation of annual records.

Effective January 1, 2002, OSHA changed the reporting requirements found in 29 C.F.R. Part 1904 ("Recording and Reporting Occupational Injuries and Illnesses"). The new requirements are simplified, streamlined, and work better with computer technology than the old requirements. The new forms can be downloaded from <http://www.osha.gov> or ordered by telephone from the OSHA publication office at (202) 693-1888. The Final Rule appears at 66 Fed. Reg. 5916 (Jan. 19. 2001). Although most of the changes went into effect as scheduled, the effective date of the rules about hearing loss and reporting of musculoskeletal disorders were delayed until January 1, 2003. [*See* 66 Fed. Reg. 35113 (July 3, 2001)]

Under the prior rules, employers were required to make incident reports on Form 101, Supplementary Record of Occupational Injury and Illnesses. The replacement form is Form 301, the Injury and Illness Incident Report.

The prior rules called for the employer to collate all the 101 forms to create the annual Form 200, Log and Summary of Occupational Injuries and Illnesses. The new forms are 300, Log of Work-Related Injuries and Illnesses, and 300A, Summary of Work-Related Injuries and Illnesses. [*See* 29 C.F.R. § 1904.4]

The forms are used to report new cases of work-related illness or injury. The OSHA 301 Incident Report must be completed within seven calendar days of receiving information about the incident. The OSHA 300 log requires a short description of each incident. The OSHA 300-A summary is compiled at the end of the year, using this log.

All businesses have to make a report of OSHA if an incident in the workplace results in a death, or if three or more workers are hospitalized. However, it is not necessary for companies in low-hazard businesses such as retail, service, finance, real estate, or insurance to maintain OSHA illness and industry records unless OSHA specifically requests such records. [*See* <http://www.osha-slc.gov/OshStd_data/1904_New/1094_0002.html> for information about the exemption]

OSHA enforcement guidance, dated November 21, 2001 [*Recordkeeping Policies and Procedures Manual CPL 2-0.131*, discussed at 70 L.W. 2334 (Dec. 4, 2001); the manual is available only at <http://www.osha-slc.gov>] imposes penalties of $1,000 for each year that the OSHA 300 form is not properly maintained. If the form is not filled out at all, a separate penalty of $1,000 per form, subject to a maximum of $7,000, can be imposed. OSHA agreed, however, not to issue citations for violating the recordkeeping rule during a four-month transition period after January 1, 2002, as long as the employer makes a good-faith effort to report properly. OSHA also ordered the states to adopt their own equivalents of the OSHA recordkeeping changes.

[B] Asbestos, Lead, and Noise Monitoring Records

If the workplace noise level is high, the employer not only must monitor exposure, but must maintain records for two years. Records of employees' hearing tests must be retained at least as long as they work for the employer. Exposure monitoring records and asbestos and lead medical surveillance records should be retained for at least 30 years after termination of employment of the individual monitored.

Asbestos monitoring records should indicate:

* Each monitored employee's name, Social Security number, extent of exposure;
* If a respirator was worn; if so, what kind;
* Date the asbestos level was monitored;
* The workplace operation or process that was monitored;
* How the samples were taken and evaluated;
* Evidence supporting the scientific validity of the sampling methodology;
* How long the sampling process lasted; number of samples taken; sampling results.

For each employee subject to medical surveillance, the record should give his or her name and Social Security number, the employee reports of asbestos-related medical conditions; and a written report from the doctor who performs the surveillance, indicating whether the employee actually is suffering effects of asbestos exposure.

For testing of lead rather than asbestos, the employer must maintain written records of tests determining whether the ambient lead level exceeds the Permissible Exposure Limit (PEL). The test record should indicate:

- Name and Social Security number of each monitored employee;
- Date of the test;
- Area that was monitored;
- Previous airborne lead readings taken at the same place;
- Employee complaints that might be related to lead exposure;
- Any other evidence suggestive of lead exposure.

[C] OSHA Postings

Employers must post a notice of OSHA rights, as mandated by 29 C.F.R. § 1903.2(a). Failure to post is subject to a civil penalty of up to $7,000 per violation, but normally the penalty will be $1,000.

An employer who receives an OSHA citation must post a copy of the citation near each place where a violation occurred. The copy must be left in place for three working days or until the violation is corrected—whichever comes first. Posting is also required if the employer contests a citation or files a petition for modification of abatement. Failure to make these postings can result in a $1,000 fine.

§ 24.03 TITLE VII RECORD-KEEPING AND NOTICE REQUIREMENTS

The Equal Employment Opportunity Commission (EEOC) requires companies with 100 or more employees to file an annual report. The Employer Information Report (EEO-1) is a simple two-page form that tracks the composition of the workforce. The due date is September 30 of each year. A copy of the most recent report must be kept on file at every company required to file (either at the "reporting unit" or the company's or division's headquarters). The EEOC also has the right to require other reports about employment practices if the agency thinks additional reports are necessary to carry out Title VII or the Americans With Disabilities Act.

Records of application forms, requests for accommodation, and other employment-related data must be preserved for one year. The one-year period starts either when the data is collected or the personnel action is taken, whichever is later. Personnel records of fired employees must also be kept for one year after employment ends.

If a discrimination charge is made, all records relating to the employment action involved in the charge must be retained until there has been a final disposition of the charge. According to 29 C.F.R. § 1602.14, this means that either the case is over, or the employee's time to sue has elapsed.

Users of pre-employment tests must maintain records about the validation of the test, including statistical studies to determine if the test has adverse impact on protected classes of applicants and employees.

Employers also have to make records that are relevant to charges of unlawful employment practices and maintain those records. [*See* 42 U.S.C. § 2000e-8(c)]

One of the many notices that must be posted in the workplace is the official EEOC notice about equal employment opportunity and how to file a charge. [42 U.S.C. § 2000e-10] If the employer willfully violates this requirement, a fine of up to $100 can be imposed for each separate offense.

§ 24.04   FMLA RECORDS

Federal law does not impose any specific form for keeping FMLA records, so any paper or electronic method can be used to record the necessary information:

- Basic payroll data for each employee, such as hours worked; pay rate; supplemental wages or wage deductions; total compensation paid;
- Dates on which FMLA leave was taken;
- Hours of leave (if less than a day was taken);
- Copies of the employee's notice to the employer of impending leave;
- Copies of the employer's disclosure materials about FMLA rights;
- Documentation of the employer's leave policy;
- Records of payment of premiums for employee benefit plans;
- Records of any dispute about when employees are entitled to leave or reinstatement after a leave.

> **Tip:** Because employee medical records, including certification of serious medical condition and fitness to return to work, are confidential, they should be kept physically separate from the employee's other records, to prevent unauthorized access to the data. [*See* § 26.07 about privacy requirements]

§ 24.05   IMMIGRATION RECORDS

The information collected to verify identity and eligibility to work in the United States [*see* § 23.11[D]] must be retained for three years after the date of hiring. Records should be retained for three years from the date of recruiting or referral with respect to applicants who were not hired or who did not accept a job offer. Certifications of employment eligibility furnished by state employment services must also be retained for three years. For former employees, the record-retention period is the later of three years after hiring, or one year after termination.

§ 24.06   EMPLOYMENT TAX RECORDS

Newly hired employees should be asked to provide a W-4 (withholding exemptions) form, so the appropriate number of exemptions can be used to withhold income taxes. An employee about to retire should be asked for Form W-4P to determine whether pension withholding should be done, and if so, in what amount.

IRS Publication 15, Employer's Tax Guide, requires at least the following information to be collected by the employer and made available for IRS review on request:

- Dates and amounts of all payments of wages and pensions;
- Fair market value of any wages paid other than in cash (e.g., in merchandise or services);
- Each employee's name, address, Social Security number, and job title;
- Dates each employee started and terminated employment;
- Dates and amounts of any payments made by the employer, or by an insurer or other third party, to employees who were out sick or injured;
- Copies of W-4 and W-4P forms;
- W-2 forms sent to employees but returned as undeliverable;
- Copies of all tax returns;
- Records of dates and amounts of tax deposits.

§ 24.07   UNEMPLOYMENT INSURANCE RECORDS

FUTA records must show the total amount of remuneration to employees in the calendar year, the amount of wages subject to tax, and the contributions made to the state unemployment insurance funds of each state in which the company does business. The records must be kept open to inspection by the IRS and state unemployment tax officials.

Records must be organized by pay period (dates the period starts and ends; total remuneration including commissions paid in the period) and by employee. The records to be kept for each worker include:

- Name;
- Social Security number;
- Date of hiring (or rehiring) and termination;
- Place of work;
- Wages for each payroll period;
- Wage rate;
- Date wages were paid;
- Amount of expense reimbursement granted;
- Time lost when worker was unavailable for work.

Although unemployment insurance information can be released to government agencies other than the employment security agency (child support enforcement agencies, for example), in general the information is confidential and should not be disclosed to unauthorized parties.

§ 24.08 RECORD-RETENTION REQUIREMENTS

Various state and federal laws require retention of records (about individual employees and summaries reflecting the entire corporate experience). The enterprise should draft its record-retention policies to comply with statutory requirements:

- Title VII: Personnel and employment records as well as EEO-1 reports must be kept for six months. Records relating to a discrimination charge must be retained until the charge is disposed of;
- Equal Pay Act: Records of a pay differential imposed on the basis of sex must be kept for two years;
- FMLA: Records must be retained for three years;
- FICA/FUTA: Records of withholding and paying these taxes must be retained for four years;
- ERISA: The record-retention period is six years;
- Federal contractors: Information about the employer's contractor status must be retained for three years;
- OSHA: The record-retention requirement for employee exposure to toxic substances is very long: 30 years;
- Tax records: The minimum retention period is four years;
- ADEA: 29 C.F.R. § 1627.3(b)(2) requires a benefit plan that is subject to the ADEA to be kept on file while the plan is in operation, and for at least one year after its termination.

CHAPTER 25

CORPORATE COMMUNICATIONS

§ 25.01   INTRODUCTION

Communications within the corporation, and from the corporation to outsiders, have tremendous practical and legal consequences. To avoid trouble, everyone in a position to speak for the corporation should be aware of these potential ramifications and should be very careful about what is communicated (because not only are there things that should not be said, but items that must be accurately disclosed in various contexts) and in what form.

§ 25.02   EMPLOYMENT CONTRACTS

[A]   Basic Considerations

Labor law aspects of Collective Bargaining Agreements between an employer and a union are discussed in Chapter 30. For employees who are not union members, there are both advantages and disadvantages to entering into a written employment contract. The written contract reduces uncertainty, and that is good—but it also limits flexibility, and that can create problems. If an employee has a written employment contract, disputes with the employer must be handled as contract cases; a suit for wrongful termination will not be available. [*Claggett v. Wake Forest Univ.*, 486 S.E.2d 443 (N.C. App. 1997)]

An individual written employment contract should cover issues such as:

- Duration of employment;
- Renewal provisions (including the amount of notice to be given);
- The duties the employee will perform;
- Promotion possibilities;
- Compensation and benefits, including contingent compensation—contingent on results and/or bonuses and stock options;
- Rights in inventions and other intellectual property developed by the employee during the contract term; treatment of intellectual property developed while the contract is in force but not during working hours, or not of the type the employee was hired to produce;
- Covenant not to compete with the employer, and agreement not to solicit its employees and customers, even after termination of employment. To be enforceable, these agreements must be reasonable in both duration and geographic scope, and must not be so severe that they prevent the individual from earning a living;
- Severability: If any contract provision is invalid, that provision will be removed from the contract, and the rest of the contract will remain valid and enforceable;
- Alternative Dispute Resolution: Whether disputes about the contract will be resolved by an arbitrator, mediator, or other decision maker other than a court.

[B] Employment Contract Case Law

A California case from mid-2000 allows a company to alter its established employment policies, as long as:

*   Vested benefits are preserved;
*   Employees get reasonable notice of the change;
*   There is a reasonable phase-in period for the new rules.

According to *Asmus v. Pacific Bell* [23 Cal. 4th 1, 999 P.2d 71 (Cal. 2000)], the employer does not have to provide additional consideration to employees to support the change. [*See* Kevin Livingston, *Employers Win Right to Rescind Job Promises*, The Recorder (June 5, 2000) (law.com)]

The case arose when Pacific Bell established a policy in 1986 giving job security to managers who satisfied the company's business expectations. The company said it would maintain the policy as long as "there is no change that will materially alter Pacific Bell's business plan achievement." The job security policy was canceled in 1992 in a memo saying the company needed greater flexibility in order to stay competitive in its economic environment. Sixty ex-managers sued for an injunction against implementation of the changes. They also sought ERISA damages and damages for breach of contract, breach of fiduciary duty, and fraud. The California Supreme Court held that the company had a right to change its policies, and the managers accepted the changed policy by continuing to work.

In contrast, another California case, *Guz v. Bechtel National Inc.* [100 Cal. Rptr. 2d 352 (Cal. 2000)], finds that there was an implied contract, creating triable issues at to whether the employee still worked at will, because of contradictory statements in the employer's personnel policies. The policies said that the employee worked at will—but also said they could be terminated only for cause, which is a contractual concept.

The Statute of Frauds is another fundamental contract rule, one that says that a contract that lasts a year or more can only be enforced if it is in writing. In a Washington State case, the employee had an oral five-year contract, allowing either party to end the contract on six months' notice. The employee was fired after spending about eleven months with the company.

When he sued for breach of contract, his argument was that the Statute of Frauds should not apply because the contract could have been wrapped up in less than a year, and that is what happened. He lost his case—the court said that the Statute of Frauds applies only to employment contracts with an indefinite duration, not those with a specific term such as five years. With no written agreement, he also did not have a case against the employer. [*French v. Sabey Corp.*, 134 Wash. 2d 547, 951 P.2d 260 (1998)]

Oral promises that an employee who relocated would be fired only for good cause did not add up to a contract. Therefore, as an at-will employee, she could be fired even without cause. Here, the problem for the employee wasn't the Statute of

Frauds, but the failure to form an enforceable contract at all. [*Montgomery County Hosp. Dist. v. Brown*, 965 S.W.2d 501, 41 Tex. Sup. Ct. J. 537 (Tex. 1998)]

An employee was orally promised a bonus of a percentage of the employer's profits. The bonus could not be figured out until after the year ended. The employer said that the Statute of Frauds prevented enforcement of the contract, because the calculation required a period of more than a year. The employee's argument (which prevailed in a New York court which allowed enforcement of the oral contract) was that he worked at will and certainly could be fired in less than one year. [*Cron v. Hargo Fabrics, Inc.*, 91 N.Y.2d 362 (N.Y. 1998)]

[C] Noncompete Case Law

Contract terms also become significant after termination of the employment relationship, in the context of covenants not to compete.

An accounting firm's employment contract, requiring ex-employees to compensate the firm if they worked for any of the firm's clients during the 18 months following termination of employment, was too broad, and therefore unenforceable. [*BDO Seidman v. Hirshberg*, 93 N.Y.2d 382 (N.Y. App. 1999)] The court considered it inappropriate to forbid ex-employees to work for clients they had not had contact with during their employment tenure, or to forbid them to work for personal clients they had brought to the ex-employer firm.

In a fast-moving business such as information technology, for instance, a one-year term (that might be acceptable in a conventional retail environment) could be deemed unreasonable and unenforceable. [*See, e.g., EarthWeb v. Schlack*, 71 F. Supp. 2d 299 (S.D.N.Y. 1999), *remanded without opinion* 205 F.3d 1322 (2d Cir. 2002)]

California law actually forbids noncompete agreements, although, in the right case, California might agree with the 20 states that accept the "inevitable disclosure" doctrine—i.e., that an ex-employee can be enjoined from going to work for a competitor of the former employer, if the inevitable result would be disclosure of the ex-employer's trade secrets, even if the ex-employee does not intend to do so.

The general rule is that employees who are not bound by employment agreements or termination agreements containing noncompete clauses are free to compete with the employer after they leave. A top executive may be considered a fiduciary as to the employer. A principle of corporate law called the "corporate opportunity doctrine" imposes a duty on a current employee to disclose to the employer whenever a business opportunity arises that is appropriate for the corporation.

It is improper for an executive to take advantage of the opportunity personally. [*See Hanover Ins. Co. v. Sutton*, 46 Mass. App. 153, 705 N.E.2d 279 (1999)] In this analysis, the opportunity is an asset of the corporation, and the executive is no more permitted to take advantage of it without the corporation's knowledge than he could help himself to one of the office computers.

It can be considered improper to contact the employer's customers while still employed—especially if the employee worked in a position of special confidence that provided contact with the customers and access to information about them. [*Dalton v. Camp*, 519 S.E.2d 82 (N.C. App. 1999)]

You might guess that an employee with a good memory would not be allowed to memorize the employer's customer list and use it after leaving employment if an employee with a bad memory would not be allowed to write down or photocopy the information. However, a Washington State trial court refused to treat a memorized list as a protectable trade secret. But then the state's Supreme Court granted protection to the information itself. [*Ed Nowogroski Ins. Inc. v. Rucker*, 137 Wash. 2d 427, 971 P.2d 736 (1999)]

In a Minnesota case [*Kallok v. Medtronic, Inc.*, 573 N.W.2d 356 (Minn. 1998)], a company that hired a person away from a direct competitor was found liable for tortious interference with the covenant not to compete. It was ordered to reimburse the first employer for the $90,000 in attorneys' fees it encountered when suing the employee to enforce the covenant. When the recruited employee got the job offer, he informed the recruiting company about the covenant, which barred employment in a field in which he had worked or had access to confidential information in the preceding year. The term of the agreement was two years. The recruiting company asked its outside attorney if hiring the competitor's employee would create legal problems. The lawyer said that it would be acceptable because the employee worked in a different field and did not have confidential information.

Once the employee changed companies, the first employer got a court order forbidding the employee to work for the new company. The competitor was also penalized for interfering with the employment contract. Proving a case of tortious interference requires proof of five elements:

- Existence of a contract that could be breached;
- The defendant's knowledge that the contract existed;
- Intentional action breaching or promoting breach of the contract;
- Lack of justification for the action;
- The injured contracting party suffers damages.

The Minnesota court decided that the competitor did not investigate enough. Simple inquiries would have uncovered the real provisions of the noncompete agreement. Therefore, the hiring company was not justified in its actions. Its actions forced the first employer to sue its ex-employee, so the hiring company was rightly ordered to reimburse the first employer for legal fees directly resulting from this wrongdoing.

Cameco Inc. v. Gedicke [157 N.J. 504, 724 A.2d 783 (N.J. Sup. 1999)] holds that an employee can be liable for breach of the duty of loyalty for assisting the employer's competitors, even if there is no direct competition. It depends on the nature of the employer/employee relationship. It also depends on the level of assistance the employee provided to competitors. Under this analysis, an employee has a duty to inform the employer of his or her plans before establishing a moonlighting business that could conflict with the employer's business. Appropriate damages for the breach of the employee's duty of loyalty could include the injury to the employer's business plus the profits the employee earned from inappropriately competitive moonlighting.

§ 25.03   EMPLOYEE HANDBOOKS

[A]   Generally

Employee handbooks are traditional in large corporations, as a means of creating a uniform culture and distributing information to what can be a large, diverse, and widely disseminated group of employees. Handbooks are useful in training new hires about the employer's expectations. They provide a ready reference about work rules—and employee discipline often revolves around claimed infractions of these rules, so employees must be informed of the rules.

Not all handbooks are printed; more and more companies are using the Web or an intranet to provide information.

Employee handbooks can be extremely useful, but unless they are drafted carefully and kept up to date, they can create at least as many problems as they solve. Sometimes, statements made in a handbook will be deemed to create a binding contract—although this is not necessarily what the employer wished to do.

Furthermore, once the employer is deemed to have created a contract, some courts will say that the employer can no longer amend that contract whenever it wants to, without providing additional consideration to the employees in return for the change. Although some courts say that the fact that the employee continues to work for the employer provides consideration, others require the employees to get some additional benefit if the employer wants to alter the contract.

> **Tip:** Many federal and state statutes limit the policies that employers can adopt. For example, a policy against leaves of less than one day could violate the Family and Medical Leave Act, or might be a refusal to make a reasonable accommodation required by the Americans With Disabilities Act.

Typical subjects for coverage in the handbook include:

- Training;
- Benefits (health plan, dental plan, disability, etc.);
- Access to profit-sharing plans;
- Defined benefit, defined contribution, 401(k), and other pension plans;
- Stock options;
- Vacations, leave (including sick leave, pregnancy, and military leave), holidays, and time off;
- Explanation of employees' rights under the Family and Medical Leave Act (FMLA) (the Department of Labor's Wage and Hour Division publishes a

standard FMLA Fact Sheet, if you don't want to have to draft your own explanation);
- Employer's policy of checking all references provided;
- Policy of employing only U.S. citizens and noncitizens who can lawfully work within the United States;
- Drug-free workplace policy, including circumstances under which drug testing will be required;
- Policies about e-mail and Internet use in the workplace;
- Policies about employment of both spouses in a couple, or more than one family member;
- Antiharassment policy; commitment to investigate charges; alternative reporting procedures if the supervisor is the alleged harasser;
- Policies about conflict of interests and acceptance of gifts from suppliers;
- Confidentiality of the employer's intellectual property;
- Employees' patent rights (if any) in inventions they develop while they are working for the employer;
- What will be considered a disciplinary offense;
- Discipline procedure (e.g., oral reprimand, followed by a written warning; suspension after two written warnings for the same offense; retention of warnings in the personnel record for at least a year; and termination; immediate termination will be permitted in the case of a serious, dangerous, or criminal act);

[B] At-Will Employment

For employees who are not unionized, and who do not have individual employment contracts, it is often a good idea to put a disclaimer in the handbook:

- Employees are hired at will;
- They can be fired when the employer sees fit; it is not necessary for the employer to demonstrate good cause for the discharge;
- The information in the handbook is for guidance only, and does not bind the employer to a contract.

To be legally effective, a disclaimer must be clear and conspicuous. It cannot be buried in small print somewhere in the back of the book. In fact, the first page is an excellent location. When a disclaimer is issued, it does not apply to people who were already employees and working under the old policy.

The mere fact that the employer has a system of progressive discipline, spelled out in the handbook, does not mean that the employee is no longer an at-will employee. However, it makes sense to include a disclaimer explaining the function of the disciplinary system.

The more specific a provision is, the more likely that courts are to construe it as creating a formal contract. However, in order to win when they charge breach of this implied contract, employees may have to show detrimental reliance (i.e., that they relied on the provision, and this reliance was harmful for them). At the very least, employees will have to prove that they read the handbook, because it is hard to claim reliance on an unread provision.

[C] Orientation Checklists

It is a good idea to provide orientation to train new hires. It is even better to standardize the orientation process, with standard documents for welcoming and instructing new employees. Both the employee and the supervisor handling the orientation should sign the document, so that later on the employee will not be able to claim that lifetime employment was promised if the document clearly states that employment is at will.

The orientation checklist should cover subjects such as:

- The company's equal employment opportunity policies;
- The company's position on unionization and union activity (get legal advice before promulgating a policy!);
- Which unions (if any) that are already recognized as bargaining agents for the employees;
- The terms of the formal probation process (if there is one);
- What a new hire has to do to become a permanent employee, but make sure that no promises are made of indefinite tenure or lifetime employment;
- The new employee's job title, duties, and promotion path;
- The compensation and benefit package for the job (including vacation days, vacation banking, disability benefits, sick leave, options under the group health plan, and severance pay);
- Work rules;
- Circumstances under which the employee can be terminated.

Even if the manual indicates the employees will be on probation for a certain length of time after being hired, they will still be entitled to good faith and fair dealing from the employer. In fact, some courts will allow probationary employees to sue for wrongful termination, if the employer did not offer them long-term employment after the end of the probation period.

[D] Legal Consequences of Handbooks

When a union challenges one provision in a handbook, then it can open the door to a challenge from NLRB that involves the handbook as a whole. In the case of *Lafayette Park Hotel* [326 N.L.R.B. 69 (1998)], the handbook included a ban on false, vicious, profane, or malicious statements about the hotel or its employees. The NLRB struck down this rule, on the grounds that the employees were not given adequate notice of what constituted improper conduct. The NLRB also invalidated another rule that required employees to leave the premises as soon as they finished their shift. This rule was unacceptable because it restricted access to nonwork areas such as the parking lot.

In earlier NLRB cases, the agency allowed employees to reveal wage and benefit information to the union during contract negotiations, despite a work rule prohibiting disclosure of confidential information. A work rule against "derogatory" statements could not be enforced to prevent the union from making truthful statements that questioned the quality of care provided by the employer (a hospital). [*See* A. Michael Weber, *Unions Challenge Employee Handbook Language*, National Law Journal, Feb. 8, 1999, at p. S7]

Two Indiana workers were fired when a supervisor found them on the roof of the plant. They said, probably truthfully, that they had been ordered up to the roof to clean the gutters. However, the supervisor smelled marijuana in the attic through which the roof was reached. After their discharge, the workers sued the employer because the grievance procedures given in the handbook were not followed before their discharge. Not only did the employer win, but the case was dismissed without a full trial. In Indiana, handbook provisions create a contract only if the employee provided some consideration over and above merely taking the job. Anyway, the handbook didn't promise that the procedures would be followed in every case. In fact, it said that immediate dismissals could occur when necessary. [*Orr v. Westminster Village N.*, 689 N.E.2d 712 (Ind. 1997)]

In May 1999, an Arizona court decided that handbook provisions requiring good cause for termination implied that the employees had a contract. Therefore, even though the handbook contained a provision stating that it was not an employment contract, and even though the employer reserved the right to amend the handbook, the employer lost the power to make unilateral amendments. Employees had to be notified, and give their individual consent, for the changes to become operative. [*Demasse v. ITT Corp.*, 194 Ariz. 500, 984 P.2d 1138 (Ariz. 1999)]

§ 25.04   WORK RULES

Some organizations are small enough, informal enough, or simple enough in operation that they do not need written work rules. But in the larger organization, or even a small operation where the work rules could become an issue, a written list of rules (in the handbook or set out separately) can be very useful.

The work rules document should make it clear that the employer is the only one to make work rules and that the employer has the right to modify them at any time. The rules themselves are not a contract with the employees that has to be negotiated, or that has to be maintained in its original form.

Work rules deal with issues such as:

• Workplace safety and security (not letting in unauthorized persons; wearing protective equipment in construction areas or where hazardous chemicals are present);

• Emergency procedures in case of fires, chemical spills, etc.;

- Where (if anyplace!) smoking is allowed in the workplace; if smoking is banned inside the workplace, limitations on going outside for smoking breaks;
- Requirement of on-time arrival and staying until the end of the work day or shift;
- Dress and grooming rules—are uniforms required for any job titles? Which days are "casual" days, and what is acceptable business casual clothing? Are there any limitations or bans on facial hair, hairstyles, makeup, or jewelry? (Make sure that these rules do not violate employees' rights to reasonable accommodation of their religious practices);
- Availability of paid and unpaid leave; how to request leave. Some companies maintain a no-fault absence policy, under which employees get a certain number of days off no matter what the reason is, but discipline can be imposed for excessive absence. A paid leave bank is similar, but allows unused days to be carried over or cashed out. Get legal advice about harmonizing your leave policy with legal requirements for disability and unpaid family leave;
- Bans on horseplay, substance abuse, possession of alcohol in the workplace, and removing products or materials (even waste or spoiled items) without permission;
- Bans on harassment, fighting, and weapons;
- Control of solicitation within the workplace. A "no-solicitation" rule can be very helpful, not only in restricting union activity, but in improving efficiency and avoiding conflict among employees. It can get pretty expensive to come to work each day if you are asked to contribute to everyone's favorite charity and chip in for presents for people who are getting married, leaving the company, having a baby, in the hospital...) An effective no-solicitation rule must be appropriately communicated to employees, it must be nondiscriminatory, and it must be applied uniformly. So if one employee is given permission to sell raffle tickets for the Catholic Church, while another is denied permission to raise money for the NAACP (or vice versa), it will appear that the employer is guilty of discrimination;
- The extent to which employees are permitted to inspect their own personal records or show them to an attorney, union representative, etc. Check your state law: It probably requires employees to have access to their records, and also protects privacy rights by limiting disclosure of personal information to anyone except the employee without the employee's consent. [See § 26.07 for rules on privacy of health records];
- Ethical standards imposed on employees: for example, when they are allowed to accept gifts from a potential supplier; use of inside information; lobbying, political activities, and donations;
- How to find additional work-related information and answers to questions: for instance, through the HR department, the Employee Assistance Program, or the corporate intranet.

> **Tip:** Even though the work rules are not contractual in nature, it is a good idea to have employees sign a notice stating that they received a copy of the work rules and had a chance to read and become familiar with them. The notice may come in handy later if the employee claims that he or she never saw the rules and didn't understand them.

§ 25.05   SYSTEMS OF PROGRESSIVE DISCIPLINE

One approach to at-will employment is for the employer to take and maintain a consistent position that only the employer determines the quality of the employee's work performance. Employees can therefore be disciplined or fired based on the employer's sole determination that their work is unsatisfactory. In a unionized workplace, it is almost certain that the collective bargaining agreement will require a system of progressive discipline, where all the steps, from a verbal warning through levels of reprimands, must be followed before the employee can be fired.

There are various reasons why even a nonunion workplace might have a progressive discipline system. It could improve efficiency. Sometimes, employees really do not know that their work is below par, so it is better to show them how to improve instead of firing them. Also, if the employer voluntarily adopts a progressive discipline system, this could make employees less interested in unionizing.

The downside is that having specific rules to follow limits the employer's flexibility. Even in a nonunion setting, the disciplinary system may be treated by courts as a contractual obligation, so that once the system is set up, it has to be maintained in the future.

Usually, a system of progressive discipline begins with an oral warning explaining why the supervisor is dissatisfied with the employee's performance. The next step is a written warning. If performance is still unsatisfactory, discipline proceeds to a probationary period or suspension (usually unpaid, lasting three–five days), then demotion or termination.

All the steps, including oral warnings, should be documented in the employee's personnel record. The written warning should include a place for the employee's signature, indicating that the document has been read. The employee should be given a copy for reference. It is often helpful to let the employee include a brief written statement giving his or her side of the story.

> **Tip:** It has always been permitted for unionized workers to bring a representative to interviews that could result in disciplinary action; the NLRB's position is that even nonunionized workers have the same right.

It is important to monitor the reasons for an employee's lateness or absence. Discipline or discharge could constitute a violation of a statute if the employee has been injured (and qualified for Worker's Compensation), is disabled as defined by the ADA, or is taking care of a sick family member and therefore is entitled to FMLA leave.

All investigations should be documented, to show that the employer is acting on the basis of facts and not discrimination against members of a protected group.

An objective party should review all termination decisions. The best time is after tempers have had a chance to cool, but promptly enough to demonstrate the employer's efficiency and involvement. Before a termination, review the process to see that the employee received the appropriate warnings; the investigation gave enough weight to the employee's explanation; and the employee was treated fairly, objectively, and on a par with other similarly situated employees.

In general, employees who are discharged for cause are not entitled to severance pay [*see* Chapter 3] However, the employee handbook may have been written in such general terms that it constitutes a contract to pay severance benefits, even in connection with a discharge for cause. Severance policies that are written and communicated to workers may become welfare benefit plans subject to ERISA. If there is no formal plan, and the employer has not entered into an express or implied contract, then it is completely at the employer's discretion to grant or withhold severance benefits.

§ 25.06 EMPLOYEE EVALUATIONS

Regular evaluations of employee performance can be critical in making sure that the organization meets its goals. Employees who are not performing up to par can be identified and given the training, encouragement, or whatever they need to improve. When it's time to award merit raises and bonuses, the performance appraisal should identify the stars.

A well-done performance appraisal identifies real problems in employee performance and gives insights into solutions. Some of the basic issues for performance reviews include:

- Whether the quantity of work performed by the employee has been satisfactory;
- Quality of the work;
- The employee's knowledge of the job;
- His or her dependability, initiative, and adaptability;
- The extent to which the employee has learned new skills, and seems likely to be able to acquire the skills that will be needed in the future;
- The extent of the employee's cooperation, attendance, and punctuality;
- Areas in which the employee needs to improve.

However, performance appraisals must be carefully done. If they're mishandled, the result is often to subject the employer to liability for wrongful termination or employment discrimination. There are many reasons why the appraisal process itself doesn't work well:

- Managers do not have time to do a thoughtful job of appraising performance, so they decide to err on the side of generosity;
- The appraisals do not seem to actually be used for anything, so managers put down whatever seems uncontroversial—or simply update the previous year's forms without much thought;
- In a large work group, managers may not know very much about what individual employees are doing;
- Managers want to be liked by the employees who report to them; they're afraid that a tough-minded appraisal could create hostility and reduce motivation;
- Ambitious managers want to give themselves an indirect pat on the back, hoping that they will be seen as outstanding leaders if all their subordinates are doing a great job;
- A bad appraisal could be attacked as the product of racism, sexism, sexual harassment, or retaliation. However, the answer is **not** to give everyone good marks because it looks very suspicious if the employer claims that someone who got a long line of excellent appraisals was fired for poor performance.

At a minimum, the employee should be shown a written performance appraisal, be given an opportunity to discuss it, and should be asked to sign a statement that he or she has read the document. Some states make it a legal requirement that the employee must be allowed to add comments; it is a good idea anyway.

The modern form of appraisal is the "360-degree review," which has input from more than one person, including co-workers and customers. However, it can be hard to gather all the necessary information, and not everyone will be candid. An alternative might be to have more frequent but informal reviews: for instance, at the end of every project, or every quarter or twice a year.

§ 25.07   MANDATORY PREDISPUTE ARBITRATION PROVISIONS

Employers, faced with the delay, high costs, and significant risks of employment litigation, often seek to require in advance that employees will raise any discrimination claims using the arbitration process rather than litigation. *See* Chapter 40.

However, it takes skillful drafting to use the employee handbook for this purpose. Cases like *Paladino v. Avnet Computer Technologies Inc.* [134 F.3d 1054 (11th Cir. 1998)], *Phox v. Allied Capital Advisers* [74 Fair Empl. Prac. Cas. (BNA) 809 (D.D.C. 1997)], and *Trumbull v. Century Marketing Corp.* [12 F. Supp. 2d 683 (N.D. Oh. 1998)] have refused to enforce these provisions, because they did not give the employees enough notice of their rights.

To have a chance of enforcement, a handbook provision must make it clear which statutes are covered, and clearly and explicitly indicate that arbitration is the sole remedy. It makes sense to have the employee sign a document when he or she receives the handbook—not only stating that the handbook has been received, but that the employee has read its contents and understands them.

§ 25.08   DEFAMATION

A hostile or unflattering statement that a company or one of its agents makes about a job applicant, employee, or former employee could become the focus of charges, or even a lawsuit. However, there are several circumstances under which negative statements are legally protected. For one thing, the statement might have been demonstrably true. They might have been made without malice, or in a privileged context.

Slander is defined as communicating a defamatory statement orally or otherwise informally. Libel means communicating a defamatory statement more broadly ("publishing" it). A defamatory statement is one that attributes serious misconduct to someone else. The victim of slander or libel can sue and obtain tort damages, unless the statement was privileged in some way.

The basic rule is that a plaintiff not only has to prove that defamation occurred, but also that some actual damages were suffered because of the defamation. But there are some statements so negative that they are automatically presumed to damage the reputation of the person about whom they are made. A plaintiff who proves such "defamation per se" can win without proving actual damages (concrete injury attributable to the defamation).

To support a suit, the alleged slander or libel must be a statement of fact, not a mere opinion or a general, imprecise statement ("Marcia is hard to work with"; "Steve seems to be working through some problems in his life."). A pure opinion cannot be defamatory, because it is not a statement of fact, but a statement of fact backing up that opinion can be defamatory. A corporation is liable for the statements of its employees and agents, as long as they were acting within the scope of their employment.

Truth is always a defense to a defamation charge: For instance, it is not defamatory to say that an employee was fired for stealing office supplies if this is what actually happened. If the employer believes a statement is true, and the statement is communicated without malice, then the employer is entitled to a defense. The jury, not the judge, decides whether or not a statement was communicated with malice.

A statement has not been "published" to the extent that a libel charge can be made if it is communicated only to the plaintiff, or to someone who is acting on behalf of the plaintiff (including a friend or an investigator who calls to find out what the employer is saying about the employee). Courts take different positions about communications that stay within the employer corporation. Some courts say that this is so narrow that no publication has occurred, whereas others accept the plaintiff's argument that dissemination was broad enough to constitute libel.

The idea that communication within the corporation cannot be defamatory, because the corporation is "talking to itself," has been adopted in Alabama, Georgia, Louisiana, Missouri, Oklahoma, Tennessee, Washington, and Wisconsin.

In a 2001 case from Pennsylvania, it was held that an employee cannot sue a co-worker for slander if the co-worker criticizes the plaintiff's work to a supervisor. Under Pennsylvania law, such a communication is not defamatory, because of the nature of the audience. There is no possibility of exposing someone to public censure or ridicule if the comment stays in the workplace. In this reading, statements about job performance are probably protected as opinions anyway. [*See* Shannon P. Duffy, *Criticisms of Job Performance by Co-Workers Aren't Defamatory*, The Legal Intelligencer, (June 27, 2001) (law.com)]

On the other hand, the Restatement of Torts (2d) § 577 says that expression within a corporation clearly constitutes publication, and this is the position taken by the states of California, Connecticut, Florida, Illinois, Indiana, Kansas, Massachusetts, Michigan, Minnesota, New York, Nevada, and Oregon. These states view the purpose of defamation law as protecting reputation within the business community, and an intraoffice communication could certainly endanger reputation.

§ 25.09   PRIVILEGED STATEMENTS

[A]   Generally

Some kinds of communication are essential to the operation of businesses and the legal system, so they are afforded special treatment. They are referred to as "privileged," and by definition cannot be defamatory.

For instance, a case from California holds that a supervisor's statements made in an employee's performance review generally cannot be considered defamatory unless the supervisor falsely accuses an employee of criminal conduct, lack of integrity, incompetence, or reprehensible behavior. In other words, to lose the privilege, the supervisor must actually lie, not just be wrong about the employee. Even unjustified or bad-faith statements might be treated as privileged if they are opinions held by the supervisor. [*Jensen v. Hewlett-Packard Co.*, 14 Cal. App. 4th 958 (1993)]

Restatement of Torts (2d) § 596 permits a privilege when the publisher and the recipient of the information share a common interest, such as making sure that honest, qualified individuals are hired and retain their jobs.

Information about a teacher's dismissal for sexually harassing students, and his subsequent reinstatement after arbitration, was newsworthy and of public interest. Therefore, comments by school district officials to the local newspaper were privileged and were not defamatory. [*Corbally v. Kennewick Sch. Dist.*, 973 P.2d 1074 (Wash. App. 1999)]

In addition to absolute privilege, "qualified" privilege exists in some circumstances. A qualified privilege is one that can be taken away under some circumstances, whereas an absolute privilege survives all kinds of challenges. If the employer asserts a qualified privilege, it has the burden of proving that it is entitled to the privilege.

The District of Columbia Court of Appeals ruled in 1998 that employee evaluations are not absolutely privileged. The employer is entitled to a qualified privilege when communications remain within the firm. However, the privilege can be forfeited if information is disclosed outside the firm, if too much information is communicated, or there is a malicious motivation for the communication. [*Wallace v. Skadden, Arps, Slate, Meagher & Flom*, 715 A.2d 873 (D.C. App. 1998)]

The California Court of Appeals says that there is a qualified privilege for reports of workplace harassment (as § 35.02 shows, the employer has a duty to investigate harassment charges), and dissemination of these reports is defamatory only if the person communicating the report acts with malice. [*Bierbower v. FHP, Inc.*, 70 Cal. App. 4th 1, 82 Cal. Rptr. 2d 393 (1999)]

If a corporation has an audit committee, discussion of possible embezzlement or securities violations are probably entitled to qualified privilege as long as they remain within the committee, and are not disclosed (other than to law enforcement officials, which is the subject of another privilege). If there has been an investigation about workplace matters, disclosing the results of the investigation to the employees at large would probably also be privileged.

Even though they are not law enforcement officials, the EEOC and unemployment officials are close enough so that communications to them are privileged. There is at least a qualified privilege to make statements in the course of processing a union grievance or issuing dismissal letters required under a collective bargaining agreement. In fact, in some states (Michigan, New Mexico, Louisiana, Missouri) the privilege is absolute, not qualified.

California [Cal. Civ. Code § 47(c)] gives employers a qualified privilege for statements made without malice and on the basis of credible evidence. Alaska presumes [Alaska Stats. § 09.65.160] that employers act in good faith when they discuss their employees with other prospective employers. However, if the employer acts recklessly, maliciously, or contrary to the employee's civil rights, the privilege is no longer available.

In any state, employers are probably entitled to a qualified privilege when they make good-faith comments on employee performance to someone who has a legitimate right to the information. However, some degree of caution must be exercised. Not all co-workers necessarily have a legitimate interest in performance appraisals.

There is a qualified privilege to protect the safety of employees who might hurt themselves, or might be hurt by others. (Communications that are privileged in the context of a defamation suit are probably also privileged if the employee sues for violation of privacy instead of, or in addition to, defamation.)

However, even if a privilege initially exists, it can be sacrificed—most typically, by failure to act in good faith, or by making statements without proof and with reckless disregard as to whether or not they are true.

It takes more than naïve acceptance of a statement that turns out to be false to constitute "malice." [*Sanderson v. Bellevue Maternity Hosp.*, 259 A.2d 888 (N.Y. App. Div. 1999)] However, passing along a statement whose truth the communicator finds extremely doubtful shows reckless disregard for the truth and therefore can subject the employer to liability.

[B] Attorney-Client Privilege

To do a good job, lawyers must learn all the facts of the situation, not just the facts that put their clients in a favorable light. Certain information is privileged if a client communicates it to a lawyer. The lawyer cannot be required to disclose this information—in fact, in most instances, it is unethical for the lawyer to disclose the information without the client's consent.

The factors that determine the availability of attorney-client privilege include:

- Whether the client approached the lawyer specifically to seek legal advice (as distinct from a casual chat, or when the lawyer played another role, such as giving business advice or serving as a director of a company);
- Whether the lawyer is acting as a lawyer, not a director or business advisor;
- Whether the communication relates to the lawyer-client relationship;
- Whether the client intends the information to be confidential;
- Whether the client did anything (deliberately or inadvertently) to remove the privilege; for instance, material distributed by the corporation will not be privileged.

It can be hard to determine the status of corporate documents.

A report might be confidential only if it were drafted specifically as a confidential document for transmission to the attorney.

The EEOC was not allowed to introduce a report prepared by the employer's attorneys about their investigation of a sexual harassment charge.

If the primary purpose of a communication is to get legal advice, a secondary business motive will not take away the privilege. But the privilege will be waived (that is, surrendered) if the corporation voluntarily distributes the document to non-attorneys, or discloses or allows the disclosure of a significant part of the document. For instance, if a corporation issues a press release about a development, or sends an employee to read a technical paper at an industry conference, it will not be able to argue that the press release or the technical paper is confidential.

However, a statement made by an employee who is not acting as an agent of the employer, but is simply an independent witness to an event probably will not be confidential, no matter why the statement was made.

In addition to the attorney-client privilege, the law of evidence contains a separate "work product" privilege. Work product is material prepared by attorneys and their employees as part of representing a client. Work product is also confidential and cannot become part of the discovery process before litigation.

[C] Self-Critical Analysis

Companies that want to improve diversity and eliminate discrimination often make studies of their employment and HR practices. Can discrimination plaintiffs require the company to disclose those documents, and use them to prove that the company used discriminatory employment practices?

Several federal courts have recognized a "self-critical analysis privilege": in other words, that these reports are internal documents that should not have to be revealed to plaintiffs, because companies should be encouraged to be candid about their discrimination problems instead of suppressing what they know to avoid embarrassing disclosures in lawsuits. [*See* Eric J. Wallach, Leslie Reider and Anthony C. Ginetto, *Employment Law*, National Law Journal, June 26, 1997, at p. B9; Michael Delikat and Ruth Raisfeld, *Litigation Over Corporate Diversity Programs*, New York Law Journal, July 14, 1997, at p. S5]

The opposite view is that the documents were prepared as part of the company's Title VII compliance program, would eventually be reported to the EEOC, and therefore could not reasonably be described as privileged. Even under this argument, a distinction might be drawn between a self-critical analysis that a company originated voluntarily and one that is mandated by the EEOC or by federal contract regulators. Or the court might require the company to produce hard information like statistics about workplace diversity, but permit the analytical part of the report to remain confidential.

It also helps to control dissemination of sensitive documents. The fewer people who have access to the document, and the more they agree that the company needs to analyze its performance in order to improve, the less likely they are to disclose the document in a way that is harmful or embarrassing to the corporation.

§ 25.10 DUTY TO COMMUNICATE

Not only are there situations in which an employer becomes liable for defamation or other disclosures; sometimes the employer can get into trouble for failing to communicate. There might be a duty to disclose dangerousness, so that other employers will not hire someone who puts their other employees or customers at risk. A subsequent employer may sue if the first employer fails to reveal relevant information, such as a job applicant's dismissal for stealing or workplace drug dealing.

Employers have a legal duty to protect customers and co-workers. That makes them negligent if they know that someone is dangerous, but they still retain him or her as an employee. This is true even if the risk is of conduct outside the scope of employment. An employer who knows that an employee has violent tendencies can be liable because of workplace assaults committed by that person, even if the assaults are not only not part of the job, but are contrary to the employer's policy and work rules. However, if the injured person is a fellow employee, it is very likely that the employee's only remedy will be through the Worker's Compensation system. [*See* § 33.03 for the concept of WC exclusivity]

Employers can be sued for negligent hiring or negligent entrustment if they hire someone for a safety-critical job but fail to check that person's references. In some contexts (such as hiring workers for a nursing home or day care center) there may be a duty to consult a special database maintained by the state or by a licensing organization to list individuals who are ineligible for employment because they have been convicted of a crime.

An employer will probably be exempt from liability for negligent hiring if a thorough investigation is performed before hiring; but if an employer fails to discover information that would have been disclosed by an ordinary background check, liability is a possibility. [*See* Eric J. Wallach and Mark E. Greenfield, *Negligent Hiring and Supervision Claims: The New Look*, National Law Journal, May 12, 1997, at p. S9]

Discrimination plaintiffs sometimes add a negligent hiring claim to their complaints. Their theory is that the employer was negligent in hiring and/or retaining a supervisor who was racist, sexist, or otherwise prone to engage in discriminatory conduct. The advantage to the plaintiff is that, although the discrimination claim is subject to the Civil Rights Act of 1991 (CRA '91) cap on damages [*see* § 42.12[B]], the negligent hiring claim is not. Also, it is hard to introduce evidence into a discrimination case about acts of discrimination or harassment carried out against employees other than the plaintiff, but this is relevant evidence in a negligent hiring case.

The employer might also be liable for negligent supervision, if the court or jury accepts the argument that the supervisor would not have been able to carry out the act of discrimination or harassment if the employer had managed the facility better.

§ 25.11   RESPONSES TO REFERENCE CHECKS

The employer has to steer between two hazards: neither committing defamation, nor failing to disclose information that must be divulged. One approach that often works is just to confirm the start and end dates of a former employee's employment, and then say that it is against company policy to discuss ex-employees. Another possibility is to disclose only information that is fully documented by HR files.

Tip: If your state gives employees the right to review their files and make their own comments, make sure that any response to an inquiry includes the employee's comments. For instance, "Ms. Jones was dismissed for excessive lateness and poor performance. However, she said that other people were late just as often, and we should have been more sympathetic about her performance because her mother had just died." That way, the questioner gets both sides of the story.

The Society for Human Resources Management reports that only about 19% of 850 HR staffers surveyed explain why an ex-employee left when they are contacted for a reference, and only 13% give any information about the former employee's work performance. [Jeffrey L. Seglin, *Too Much Ado About Giving References*, New York Times, Feb. 21, 1999, at p. G4]

This article cites business school Professor C. Patrick Fleener's study of federal and state court records for the periods 1965–1970 and 1985–1990. He found reports of a mere 16 defamation cases, and the employer won 12 of those. Four plaintiff victories in ten years do not seem like enough of a reason to disrupt the entire practice of using references in hiring!

If an employee's resignation or termination is being negotiated, one area of negotiation is what will be said in response to reference checks.

It may be easier to get reference check information by asking about a job candidate's strengths and accomplishments as an employee, rather than stating or implying that you want negative information. No one is going to sue for defamation for being described as "hard working," "effective," or "creative"!

A negligence suit brought by an employer against a staffing service was dismissed. The staffing service referred a bookkeeper who turned out to be a convicted embezzler, and who stole again from the employer. The staffing agency won the case because the employer did not specifically request a criminal background check, so the staffing service relied on testimonials from two other ex-employers who said the bookkeeper was honest. [*See* Joann S. Lublin, *Who Must Check a Prospect's Work History?* Wall Street Journal, July 31, 2001, at p. B1]

San Benito Bank & Trust Co. v. Landair Travels [31 S.W.3d 312 (Tex. App. 2000)] says that under Texas law, an employer does not have a duty to report embezzlement to law enforcement authorities or warn the new employer, because the first employer no longer controlled the employee's actions. There was no duty to prevent future crimes (she also embezzled funds from the subsequent employer). In fact, even a current employer does not have a duty to prevent off-duty wrongdoing by employees.

§ 25.12 NEGOTIATED RESIGNATIONS

In some cases, an employee has been guilty of misconduct so serious (securities fraud or embezzlement, for example) that immediate removal is needed to reduce the risk to the corporation. In other cases, it will be less clear that employment must be ended—situations that fall under the Hollywood euphemism "creative differences." In such a situation, both parties benefit if they negotiate a resignation. The employee will leave on a stipulated date, and will release the company from all claims of employment-related discrimination. [*See* Chapter 37, § 37.07[A] for the specific problems of drafting a release that will satisfy the provisions of the Older Workers Benefit Protection Act (OWBPA). [Pub. L. No. 101-433]

A resignation agreement is a contract and therefore is subject to the ordinary rules of contract law. For instance, if the employer deliberately misleads an employee, or subjects him or her to undue influence, the resignation agreement will be void and the employer will not be able to enforce it against the employee. The implications of the agreement are serious enough that first-line supervisors should not be allowed to negotiate. Either a trained HR staffer or an attorney should take on this role.

The agreement covers issues such as:

- The employee represents that he or she has not already filed any charges, or instituted litigation against the employer. If legal action is already in the works, settlement discussions or conciliation from the antidiscrimination agency is in order, but it is too late to negotiate a simple resignation agreement;
- The employee waives all claims against the employer. Drafting the proper, enforceable language is an intricate legal task;
- The employee agrees to treat the resignation as voluntary, and therefore not to apply for unemployment compensation;
- The employer should state that it does not admit liability of any kind, but is only using the agreement to clarify the issues;
- The employer should specify the kind of reference it will give the employee, and how it will handle reference checks from potential future employers;
- The employee should waive any merit-based bonuses that would otherwise be payable in the year of the resignation;
- The employee should agree to return all materials in his or her possession containing trade secrets or other proprietary materials of the employer, and should agree to refrain from using the employer's proprietary/trade secret information in any later employment;
- The employee should agree to keep the terms of the agreement confidential.

§ 25.13   RELEASES

An employee who has already filed discrimination charges may be willing to settle those charges, receiving some consideration in exchange for releasing the employer from further threat of suit by that employee. (However, a suit brought by another employee, or by the EEOC, continues to be a risk.) During the negotiations before a resignation, the employer and employee could agree on a severance package that winds up their relationship, making it clear that the soon-to-be-ex-employee will not bring any discrimination charges.

> **Tip:** If the terminating employee is a senior executive or creative person, and the risk of lawsuit, unfair competition, or solicitation of your employees or customers is a significant one, it could make sense to offer a consulting agreement after termination of employment. That way, at least he or she will be on your side instead of becoming an opponent.

A release is a contract, a legal agreement for surrendering claims that already exist. A release can be quite general, simply referring to "all claims" or quite specific, spelling out a whole laundry list of claims. A release of liability could be combined with reasonable covenants not to compete and provisions about the employer's intellectual property.

Courts might refuse to enforce a release that is too general, on the grounds that it is not specific enough to inform employees of their rights. But a release that is too detailed can put ideas into the heads of employees who had no real intention of bringing suit—or who didn't know the vast and exotic variety of ways in which they can make trouble for the employer!

Before payments of pensions and benefits begin, the plan might require the potential participant or beneficiary to sign a release stating that the plan has computed the amounts of benefits correctly, or that the participant or beneficiary waives all claims against the plan except the right to receive benefits as specified by the plan.

Courts are split as to whether such mandatory releases are enforceable. If all plan participants and beneficiaries have to sign, the release becomes part of ordinary plan administration, and there is no additional consideration for it. The employer gets something (freedom from suits and other claims) but doesn't give up anything in return (the benefits would be available under the plan anyway).

A release is a contract. All contracts require consideration to be enforceable. Each party must receive something under the contract. In a typical release situation, the employer provides additional benefits (e.g., extra severance pay; outplacement assistance; early retirement incentives) over and above normal severance. The employee offers the employer a release of all claims, thus sparing the employer the risk of having to defend against charges. If each party gets something of value, the court probably won't worry about exact equivalence, as long as the parties knew their rights and understood all the implications of the release.

A general release covers all claims in existence at the time of the release; a limited release covers only the types of claims named in the release itself.

> **Tip:** A release covering an injured worker who is entitled to Worker's Compensation is valid only if it is approved by a Worker's Compensation judge. Special care is required in drafting the release. If the worker releases claims relating to compensable physical injury, he or she will still have the right to bring suit on other grounds, such as claims that the employer acted in bad faith or intentionally inflicted emotional distress on the employee.

States take varying approaches about what can be covered by a general release. Some states say that they can cover all claims, known or unknown, but other states say that a general release is not effective for claims that the employee did not know about or suspect at the time the release was signed. Under this theory, people can only give up claims that they know about and decide are worth less than the benefits under the release.

CHAPTER 26
PRIVACY ISSUES

§ 26.01   INTRODUCTION

For the employee, a significant part of each working day is spent in the workplace. The employer takes on some of the roles of the government. Do employees have the same civil rights with respect to their employers as citizens have with respect to their governments? In some ways, the answer is "Yes," but in other ways, the legal system balances the employer's need for honesty, sobriety, and efficiency in the workplace against the employees' desire for privacy. Many (if not most) constitutional rights are limitations on government power, not the power of private entities such as employers.

Many of the topics in this book are either completely regulated by federal laws, or federal laws are dominant, but in the privacy arena, state laws are very significant. Most states have laws on access and copying of personnel files, so that employees can view and copy their own files, but access by outsiders is restricted.

Most states also protect privacy of medical records, especially those involving genetic testing or reports of substance abuse treatment. States often impose limitations on the extent to which employers can collect and record information about employees' lawful off-premises activities. For instance, many states make it illegal to investigate the religious, political, and social organizations that employees belong to.

§ 26.02   POLYGRAPH TESTING

There are many problems with using polygraphy ("lie detector tests") in the workplace setting. These tests are expensive and not very reliable. The real test is whether the employee is nervous, and a practiced liar may be far less nervous than a timid but honest employee.

There are outright bans on polygraph testing in the workplace in Massachusetts, Michigan, Minnesota, and Oregon. Alaska, Connecticut, Delaware, Hawaii, Maine, Nebraska, New Jersey, New York, Rhode Island, West Virginia, and Wisconsin forbid employers to require, request, or even suggest testing. In one of these states, it violates public policy to fire someone for refusing to take a polygraph test, because the test cannot be demanded as a condition of employment. In Illinois, Maine, Michigan, Nevada, New Mexico, and Virginia, testing is not forbidden, but polygraph operators have to be licensed.

The Federal Employee Polygraph Protection Act of 1988 [Pub. L. No. 100-347, 29 U.S.C. § 2001] forbids most private employers from using polygraph tests for pre-employment screening. In the workplace itself, it is permissible to polygraph employees but only the course of an ongoing investigation about economic loss or injury to the employer's business. (In this context, drug tests and written or oral "honesty tests" are not considered polygraph examinations.)

Under the federal law, an employee can be asked to submit to polygraph testing only if:

- He or she has access to the property involved in the inquiry;

- The employer has a reasonable suspicion about the employee's involvement;
- Before the examination, the employer provides the employee with a specific written statement about the nature of the investigation and the basis for the employer's suspicion of the employee.

The employer is required to keep these statements on file for three years after they are issued.

The employer must advise the employee of his or her rights:

- To refuse the test or stop it after it has begun;
- To seek representation by a lawyer or other person (such as a union representative);
- To review the questions before the test;
- To review the results before the employer uses them as a premise for adverse employment action.

The employee must be notified that test results may be turned over to prosecutors.

In the view of the Seventh Circuit, an employer may have violated the Employee Polygraph Protection Act by asking for a taped voice sample from an employee for analysis to see if he had left a threatening voice mail for another employee. Because the sample was used to analyze truthfulness, and not just for a simple comparison between the employee's voice and the threatening message, it fell under the statutory definition of "lie detector." [*See Veazey v. Communications & Cable of Chicago, Inc.*, 194 F.3d 850 (7th Cir. 1999)]

§ 26.03   DRUG USE IN THE WORKPLACE

[A]   A Pervasive Problem

Workplace drug use is a serious problem for many reasons. Some drug users are able to restrict their substance abuse to off-work hours and off-premises locations. Some of them are able to pay for drugs by legitimate means. Even in this "best-case" scenario, drug residues are likely to affect their performance during working hours. That's why many states either deny Worker's Compensation to anyone who was drunk or drug-impaired at the time of an accident, or presume that substance abuse was the cause of any accident unless the injured person can prove otherwise.

Many, if not most, drug users are unable to be so moderate in their drug consumption, and are likely to be impaired during working hours. They may use or even deal drugs in the workplace. If they can't afford to pay for their drugs, they are very likely to steal, embezzle, or commit industrial espionage to get drug money. Employees who are already breaking the law by illegal drug use may lose their inhibitions against committing other crimes as well.

The abuse of legal substances, such as alcohol and prescription drugs, also creates problems for employers. Although the problems are reduced, because laws are not violated, they are problems nonetheless, and the Employee Assistance Program should make help available for those who need a substance abuse program or support group.

Under the Federal Drug-Free Workplace Act [41 U.S.C. § 701], companies with federal procurement contracts over $25,000 (and many companies are federal contractors) must certify to the contracting agency that they will provide a drug-free workplace. The contract will not be awarded if they do not make the certification.

The contractor-employer's obligations are to:

- Notify employees that using, possessing, and selling drugs is prohibited, and what the penalties will be if these rules are violated;
- Set up a drug-free awareness program;
- Order employees to abide by the program and notify the employer if they are convicted of a drug offense (even one occurring off-premises);
- Notify the contracting agency within ten days of receiving such a report from an employee;
- Impose penalties on all employees convicted of drug violations that are related to the workplace;
- Continue to make a good-faith effort to keep drugs out of the workplace.

If the employer is a defense contractor, it must do regular drug tests on employees in "sensitive positions," in other words, those with access to classified information.

A Connecticut statute [Conn. Gen. Stat. § 31-51x], prohibits urine testing for drugs unless the employer has a reasonable suspicion that the employee is using drugs or alcohol in a way that does or could adversely affect job performance. However, this statute does not apply to tests on consent of the employee (here, because an employee accused of theft agreed to take a test to reduce the disciplinary consequences of the theft). [*Poulos v. Pfizer*, 711 A.2d 688 (Conn. 1998)]

[B] Case Law On Drug Testing

Department of Transportation rules have been held to protect the public, not transportation workers. Therefore, it is legitimate for employers to delegate the administration of the testing program to an outside company. If the outside company mixes up the urine specimens, it is liable for the mistakes, and the employer that hired it is not. [*Carroll v. Federal Express Corp.*, 113 F.3d 163 (9th Cir. 1997)]

Pre-employment drug testing is more likely to be upheld by the courts than testing of current employees, on the theory that employees have a legitimate right of privacy. In 1997, the California Supreme Court took the position that urine testing for drugs can be required of persons who have received conditional job offers, but not employees who are under consideration for promotions. The rationale is that the Fourth Amendment allows drug testing that is not connected to specific suspicion, but only if there is a special need and the employee's privacy is impaired only minimally, as compared to the special interests of public employers. [*Loder v. Glendale, California*, 14 Cal. 4th 846, 927 P.2d 1200 (1997)]

In another California case, a job offer was extended conditioned on the applicant's passing a drug test. The applicant had to move to take up the new job, and logistics kept him from actually taking (and failing) the drug test until he was already on the payroll. The employer fired him, and he claimed that he was already an employee so a suspicionless drug test was improper. The California Court of Appeals did not accept that argument. [*Pilkington Barnes Hind v. Superior Court*, 66 Cal. App. 4th 28, 77 Cal. Rptr. 2d 596 (1998)] The distinction between job applicants and employees exists because employers have a chance to observe their active employees, and in appropriate cases detect signs of drug abuse that give rise to reasonable suspicion. The employer had not yet had a chance to observe the plaintiff.

Cases in Arizona and California say that it does not violate public policy to discharge a worker based on his or her refusal to take a drug test. [*AFL-CIO v. California Unemployment Ins. Appeals Bd.*, 23 Cal. App. 4th 51, 28 Cal. Rptr. 2d 210 (1994); *Hart v. Seven Resorts Inc.*, 191 Ariz. 297 (Ariz. App. 1997)] In a Fourth Circuit case, two employees charged that, although they were nominally fired for refusing to take a drug test, the real reason was that they were union activists. The court held that neither imposing the drug testing requirement nor firing the two workers violated the National Labor Relations Act.

Even though the testing program was implemented only one week after a strike, it was applied uniformly to all employees so could not be cited as an example of anti-union animus. Furthermore, since six out of 20 employees tested positive, the employer had a valid concern about drug use in the workforce. *Eldeco Inc. v. NLRB* [132 F.3d 1007 (4th Cir. 1997)] says that drug testing policies are valid as long as they are not disparately enforced (e.g., on the basis of racial stereotyping or union membership).

In *Smith v. Zero Defects Inc.* [132 Idaho 881 (1999)], the employer's policy called for termination of any employee testing with a detectable level of alcohol or illegal drugs. The plaintiff tested positive for amphetamines during a random test; he was not impaired at that particular time. However, Idaho (like Nebraska, Nevada, Oklahoma, and Utah—but unlike Arizona, Kansas, Oregon, and Washington) considers violation of an employer's zero-tolerance policy to be misconduct that is serious enough to prevent the employee from getting unemployment insurance benefits, even if he or she was not impaired at the time of the test. In other words, off-duty drug use can be serious enough to block unemployment benefit eligibility.

It was legitimate for a school board to fire a teacher who refused to take a drug test that was ordered after a local law-enforcement sweep found marijuana in her car parked in the school parking lot. The demand did not violate the teachers' contract requirement for either consent or a search warrant for search of teachers' personal property in the school building. The demand for testing was appropriate in light of the violation of the school's drug and alcohol policy. [*Hearn v. Board of Pub. Educ.*, 191 F.3d 1329 (11th Cir. 1999)]

An arbitrator's award, requiring reinstatement of an employee who was fired after failing a drug test, could not be enforced, because it violated the well-established public policy against allowing drug users to keep safety-sensitive jobs. [*Exxon Corp. v. Esso Worker's Union*, 118 F.3d 841 (1st Cir. 1997)] However, two years later, the Tenth Circuit upheld an award reinstating a truck driver who admitted to smoking marijuana two days before an accident. The arbitrator read the CBA's requirement of discharge only for "just cause" to require proof of on-the-job drug use, drug dealing, or impairment, not just off-hours drug use. [*Kennecott Utah Copper Corp. v. Becker*, 195 F.3d 1201 (10th Cir. 1999)]

Decisions in several states (Illinois, Louisiana, New York, Wyoming) allow a person fired because of a false-positive drug test to sue the testing firm for failing to meet its duty of due care in collecting, handling, and processing the specimens, but in the views of the Fifth Circuit, and courts in Texas and Pennsylvania, testing firms do not have an enforceable duty to the employee, because the employer is the one that hires the testing company. [*Duncan v. Afton*, 991 P.2d 739 (Wyo. 1999); *Ney v. Axelrod*, 723 A.2d 719 (Pa. Sup. 1999)]

It is probably inappropriate to impose a drug testing requirement that covers lawful prescription and over-the-counter medications. The Tenth Circuit granted an injunction against an employer's drug policy that required its employees to notify, and get permission from, their supervisors if they took prescription medications. The court treated this as a violation of the Americans with Disabilities Act, as a forbidden inquiry about disability. [*Roe v. Cheyenne Mountain Conference Resort Inc.*, 124 F.3d 1221 (10th Cir. 1997)]

> **Tip:** However, the ADA's protection is limited to "qualified individuals with a disability," so if side effects of a prescription medication (such as falling asleep or losing coordination) make it unsafe for a person to perform a particular job, then that person is not qualified for ADA purposes.

Furthermore, current substance abuse is not a disability for ADA purposes (although it is unlawful to discriminate against someone who is now clean and sober because of a past history of substance abuse). "Current" drug use means use that is recent enough for the employer to conclude that drug abuse is an ongoing problem. [*Zenor v. El Paso Healthcare System, Limited*, 176 F.3d 847 (5th Cir. 1999)] Drug use several weeks prior to termination can fit this definition. [*See, e.g., Shafer v. Preston Mem. Hosp.*, 107 F.3d 274 (4th Cir. 1997); *Collings v. Longview Fibre Co.*, 63 F.3d 828 (9th Cir. 1975)]

The ADA has a safe harbor [42 U.S.C. § 12114(b)] for people who have completed a rehab program. Just entering a program isn't enough; the safe harbor is for people with a history of staying clean.

§ 26.04   CREDIT CHECKS

A federal law, the Fair Credit Reporting Act (FCRA) [15 U.S.C. § 1681], as amended by the Consumer Credit Reporting Reform Act of 1996 [Pub. L. No. 104-208] governs the access of businesses to credit reports. Although credit reports are most commonly used in the context of loans or merchandise sales, it is also fairly common for potential employers to run a credit check before making a job offer.

Under the FCRA, employers must notify applicants before they seek credit information as part of the application process. A civil penalty is imposed for ordering a credit check without the mandatory notification. The employer must also notify applicants and employees before any negative employment-related action is taken on the basis of an investigative credit report.

The FCRA allows credit reporting agencies to disclose the information they have gathered to companies that use the information for "employment purposes," i.e., evaluating the subject of the credit report for employment, promotion, retention as an employee, or reassignment. The reporting agency is allowed to furnish a report discussing the job applicant's or employee's creditworthiness, standing, character, and reputation.

In addition to federal regulation of the use of credit reports, some states (Arizona, California, Connecticut, Florida, Kansas, Kentucky, Maine, Maryland, Massachusetts, Montana, New Hampshire, New Mexico, New York, Oklahoma, and Texas) impose additional requirements on employer use of credit reports.

If a third party performs a drug test, it might be treated as a "credit report" or "investigative credit report" under the federal Fair Credit Reporting Act. However, if the employer performs the test itself, the FCRA is not involved, because the statute does not apply to transactions between a consumer and the entity that makes the report. Therefore, an employee fired after a urine test that was positive for marijuana cannot use the FCRA to sue the employer that performed the test. [*Chube v. Exxon Chem. Ams.*, 760 F. Supp. 557 (M.D. La. 1991)]

§ 26.05   GENETIC TESTING

There are already more than 500 genetic tests available, although they are too expensive for widespread use. More than half the states make it unlawful to impose a requirement of genetic testing (e.g., for sickle cell trait or susceptibility to cancer) as a condition of employment, as a condition of insurance, or as a factor in raising insurance premiums.

The state laws focus on different areas. Some of them make the results of genetic testing confidential, while others limit the extent to which insurers can deny coverage or raise premiums on that account. Another group of statutes focuses on hiring.

On February 8, 2000, then-President Clinton issued an Executive Order that prevents mandatory genetic testing, or use of genetic information in employment-related decisions, in federal workplaces. Connecticut passed a statute forbidding employers to request genetic information from employees or to discriminate against employees or applicants on the basis of genetic information (information about genes, gene products, or inherited characteristics). [1998 Conn. Acts 98-1890]

§ 26.06   SEARCHES AND SURVEILLANCE

[A]   Constitutional Limits on Employees

Although the Constitution puts limits on unreasonable searches and seizures, the focus is on the activities of public agencies such as the police and the military. Therefore, it is very unlikely that the actions of a private employer would have a constitutional dimension, or that the employee would be able to invoke the Fourth Amendment as protection against searches and seizures.

However, an employer's surveillance activities might constitute an invasion of privacy, which could furnish grounds for a suit by an employee.

An employer can legitimately order a workplace search if there is a good reason in the first place (such as getting evidence of embezzlement, theft of products, or other work-related misconduct) and the scope of the search is appropriate to satisfying that purpose. But, because the employer controls the workplace but employees control their own personal possessions such as coats and handbags, get legal advice about how to handle a search.

There is no general state or federal ban on video surveillance of nonprivate areas within the workplace (areas that are open to the public or that are open to inspection of other employees).

Surveillance programs are most likely to survive legal challenge if:

- They are created in response to a real problem (e.g., inventory shrinkage) or a real threat (e.g., potential employer liability);
- Employees are accurately informed of the purposes and content of the program;
- Surveillance is restricted to the least intrusive method that is still effective.

According to the American Management Association's 1997 survey [<http://www.amanet.org>], two-thirds of medium- to large-sized companies perform electronic surveillance, but more than half of them use only simple nonintrusive measures such as video cameras in the lobby. Only about 15% reviewed the content of employees' e-mail, and 10.4% taped phone conversations. About one-seventh of respondents reviewed computer files, but only about 5% reviewed voice mail messages.

On most subjects, job hunters and HR staffers agree about workplace privacy, but there are disagreements about e-mail monitoring and searches of employees' desks, according to a Society for Human Resource Management poll. [*See* <http://www.shrm.org>] More than three-quarters of HR professionals and nearly two-thirds of job seekers think that it is acceptable for a company to monitor employees' Internet use during working hours. More than two-thirds of HR professionals, but less than half of job applicants, thought it was appropriate for employers to monitor employee e-mail. Almost half of the HR professionals thought that employers had the right to search desks, but less than a quarter of job seekers agreed that this was appropriate.

The First Circuit says that it does not violate the Fourth Amendment for a public employer to use silent video cameras for surveillance of the work area. In this case, the work environment was an open space with no assigned offices, cubicles, workstations, or desks, so the court concluded that it would not be reasonable to assume that privacy would be available in such an environment. [*Vega-Rodriguez v. Puerto Rico Telephone Co.*, 110 F.3d 174 (1st Cir. 1997)]

However, in a unionized company, it might be an unfair labor practice to install surveillance devices, at least without the consent of the union. In 1997, the NLRB decided. [*Colgate-Palmolive Co.*, 323 N.L.R.B. 82 (1997)] that installation of hidden surveillance cameras is a mandatory bargaining subject, not a management decision. To the NLRB, only subjects like product lines and capital investments are management prerogatives.

Early in 2002, the Supreme Court permitted unionized employees to sue in state court for invasion of privacy because of video surveillance of company bathrooms. The employer, a trucking company, said that the cameras were installed to frustrate drug dealing and drug use, and were not aimed at urinals or bathroom stalls. The issue in *Consolidated Freightways v. Cramer* [122 S. Ct. 806 (2002)] was whether LMRA § 301 preempts the state law forbidding undisclosed videotaping of employees. The Supreme Court held that it does not, so state-law suits can go forward—even though the case might be interpreted as involving interpretation of a collective bargaining agreement (the usual test for LMRA § 301 preemption).

[B] Wiretapping

Wiretapping, and other forms of interception of wire, oral, and electronic communications, including e-mail (or electronic or mechanical interception of conversations) are covered by the federal Omnibus Crime Control and Safe Streets Act of 1968 [18 U.S.C. § 2511 *et seq.*] Interceptions by the employer are regulated. Interceptions are prohibited only if the employee had a reasonable expectation that the communication would not be subject to interception.

For instance, if a telephone salesperson has known from the beginning of the job that contact with customers is subject to monitoring, there would be no reasonable expectation of privacy. But even if interception of calls is legitimate, the employer must cease the interception if it is clear that a particular call is personal and not business-related. One of the parties to a communication has a right to intercept it; so does anyone with explicit or implicit consent to intercept.

The federal statute imposes penalties for improper interception that can be as high as $10,000. Punitive damages can be imposed on an employer that acted wantonly, recklessly, or maliciously.

To investigate charges of misuse of the police paging system, the city of Reno monitored pagers. The district court for the District of Nevada held [*Bohach v. City of Reno*, 932 F. Supp. 1232 (D. Nev. 1997)] that there was no search, and federal wiretap statutes were not violated, because the pager technology required centralized storage of the messages, defeating any reasonable expectation of privacy.

[C] Internet and E-Mail Monitoring

Apart from the fact that employees are not supposed to use the company computer system for personal purposes, employee e-mails can subject the employer to liability (in the context of sexual or racial harassment, for example, or concealment of improprieties).

One way to cope is to monitor employee e-mail use. [*See* Cheryl Blackwell Bryson and Michelle Day, *Workplace Surveillance Poses Legal, Ethical Issues*, National Law Journal, Jan. 11, 1999, at p. B8]

State and federal wiretap statutes typically include a "provider exception," under which the provider of communications is allowed to intercept messages on the system. An employer is clearly a provider when it owns the equipment on which the employees communicate.

In *Smyth v. Pillsbury Co.* [914 F. Supp. 97 (E.D. Pa. 1996)], an employer was held not to have invaded the privacy of an employee who was fired after sending hostile e-mail messages to a supervisor. The court applied the provider rule because the employer company owned the communications equipment, even though the employees were told that their e-mails were confidential and would not give rise to employee discipline. Therefore, this exception might not be available if an Internet service provider actually handles the e-mail service.

[D] Identification Numbers

It is convenient, but not always good policy, to use Social Security numbers as employee IDs. Business is becoming more and more internationalized, so overseas personnel will not have Social Security numbers. The European Union's privacy requirements are quite stringent, and must be obeyed when doing business outside the United States. [*See* Susan J. Wells, *You've Got Their Numbers—And They Want Them Back*, HR Magazine, Dec. 1998, at p. 3] Wells suggests choosing an identification system that does not rely on Social Security numbers or nine-digit numbers that could be confused with Social Security numbers. For most companies, a six-digit number (which allows 999,999 options!) will be satisfactory. It's better to assign numbers at random, not sequentially. If the numbers are assigned based on hiring dates, a hacker who knows when some people were hired could guess other employees' numbers. Your payroll and database programs impose standards: You may have to start each ID number with a number not a zero, blank space, or character such as an asterisk or ampersand.

[E]   How-Tos for Employers

Attorney Jonathan A. Segal, in two recent articles [Jonathan A. Segal, *Security vs. Privacy*, HR Magazine, Feb. 2002, at p. 93; *Searching for Answers*, HR Magazine, March 2000, at p. 59] provides some useful guidance for employers:

- Notify employees that working areas in the workplace are not private, and employees and their belongings are subject to search there, to rebut later charges that employees felt their reasonable expectation of privacy was violated or that private information about them was made public;
- Inform employees that their cars can be searched when they are parked on company property;
- Make it clear that the employer has the right to search employees' lockers, even if they are locked (providing the locks can reinforce this message as well as making it easier to open them when needed);
- Reserve the right to search all employees, not just individuals on the basis of reasonable suspicion. However, given the potential for hostility, in practice searches should only be done in emergencies, or on a reasonable-suspicion basis;
- Impose a work rule that refusal to be searched will be considered serious misconduct that justifies termination;
- Tell workers that they do not have an expectation of privacy in their e-mails, voice mails, computer hard drives, network access, and Web usage histories on company computers, even if they have been issued, or have chosen, a password;
- Put a message on the voice mail system indicating that messages can be recorded and reviewed. This puts outsiders as well as employees on notice that there is potential for monitoring;
- Ask employees for their written consent to monitoring of telephone conversations and voice mail;
- Inform employees that mail that they have addressed to them at the workplace can be opened by the employer—even if it is marked Personal or Confidential. (Federal law makes it illegal to obstruct mail delivery—but the Post Office's position is that once mail is delivered to the workplace, it has been delivered, so the employer does not obstruct mail delivery by opening mail before the employee gets it.)

Segal points out the need to balance reserving legal rights against employees' (and perhaps customers') reactions to a full-surveillance program. He stresses the absolute need for documentation: why a search was ordered, and what it found, for instance; or the nature of an emergency that required broad-based searches without individual suspicion.

He counsels employers to rely on observed or alleged behavior, and not profiling characteristics such as race, religion, or union advocacy. Wherever possible, searches of female employees should be performed by women, and searches of male employees by males. There should be a witness to all searches, and the shop steward should be allowed access if he or she wishes to be present.

To avoid later claims of harassment or battery, don't touch employees who refuse to be searched, and don't detain employees (which could constitute false imprisonment) except in security emergencies where it is necessary to detain the employee until the police arrive.

It is common for companies that do drug testing to appoint an independent Medical Review Officer (MRO). In fact, an MRO has to be used for all drug tests required by federal law, and some state laws also impose this requirement. Samples are sent to the testing lab, and the lab reports all the results. The MRO then contacts all employees who tested positive to see if there is a legitimate explanation—such as use of a prescription drug. If there is a legitimate explanation, then the MRO reports the result to the employer as a negative.

Even if the employer has the right to monitor conversations, or to open mail, the best policy is to terminate observation once it is clear that the communication is personal. Under the federal Electronic Communications Privacy Act [P.L. No. 99-508], messages are considered intercepted only if they are acquired in the course of transmission. It is not clear when an e-mail or voice mail is considered transmitted; it could be either when the sender completes the process of sending it, or when the receiver receives the message. *Fraser v. Nationwide Mutual Ins. Co.* [135 F. Supp. 2d 623 (E.D. Pa. 2001)] says that a message is intercepted only if it is viewed before the intended recipient accesses it.

§ 26.07 HIPAA PRIVACY RULES

Congress passed the Health Insurance Portability and Accessibility Act (HIPAA) [Pub. L. No. 104-191], covering many issues related to health insurance and health care. The statute ordered Congress to issue federal health care privacy standards by August 21, 1999. However, Congress failed to meet this deadline, which gave the Department of Health and Human Services the right to draft regulations.

The HIPAA Regulations published on December 28, 2000 [65 Fed. Reg. 82511, amending 45 C.F.R. Parts 160 and 164] initially required most entities to comply by April 14, 2003, with an extra year for small health plans to get up to speed.

With one important exception (self-insured plans) EGHPs are not directly affected by the privacy rules. The theme of the HIPAA privacy rules is that the individual must give specific authorization before a covered entity can use protected health information for any reason other than payment, treatment, or health care operations. State health care laws are not preempted if they furnish even greater protection of patient confidentiality. [*See Complying with HIPAA's Medical Records Privacy Regulations*, (6/00) <http://www.pillsburywinthrop.com>]

A covered entity is a health plan, health care clearinghouse, or health care provider that ever transmits health information electronically. Protected health information (PHI) means all individually identifiable information that is transmitted or maintained in any form by a covered entity. A group health plan is permitted to disclose PHI to a plan sponsor only if the sponsor certifies to the plan that it will comply with the privacy rules about use and disclosure of the information.

The plan sponsor has a duty to amend the plan document governing the health plan to describe its use of PHI. Once this has been done, the sponsor has a duty to certify to the group health plan that the required amendments have been made. The plan sponsor can only use PHI for plan administration activities that constitute payment or health care operations.

The plan does not need individual employees' consent to provide summary (rather than individual) health information to the sponsor for administrative activities such as getting bids from other insurers or for amending or terminating the plan. A covered entity can "de-identify" individual data by stripping out all of the 19 identifying factors (for instance, birth date, photograph, phone number, Social Security number) laid out in the regulation.

A group health plan that provides its benefits entirely through an insurer or an HMO, and that does not create, maintain, or receive PHI other than summary health information and enrollment information is not required to designate a private official/contact person or satisfy the other administrative requirements of 45 C.F.R. § 164.530.

A fully insured group health plan is not required to issue the Notice of Privacy Practices to its plan participants. The HMO or issuer of the plan has this responsibility. However, a self-insured plan does have to provide the Notice. For people already in the group, notice is required as of the plan's compliance date (and within 60 days after a material revision). New participants get the notice at enrollment.

To comply with the regulation, the notice must:

- Be written in plain English or otherwise effectively communicated (for instance, a video could be used to convey the information);
- Prominently display this header: "This notice describes how medical information about you may be used and disclosed and how you can get access to this information. Please review it carefully;"
- Describe when the covered entity can or must use PHI without authorization from the individual;
- Describe the entity's procedures for disclosing information to the plan sponsor;
- Explain when authorization is required for disclosure of information;
- Disclose the individual's right to revoke authorization; restrict uses and disclosures; get confidential communications; inspect, copy, and amend PHI; find out what disclosures were made; and get a paper copy (if the original notice was electronic);
- Disclose the entity's duty to maintain privacy;
- Reserve the right to change the privacy policy and apply the new policy retroactively;

- Explain how to file complaints about privacy right violations;
- Give contact information for a plan representative who can handle questions about, and resolve problems with, the policy;
- Contain the effective date for notice.

Enforcing this Regulation is the responsibility of the Department of Health and Human Services' Office of Civil Rights, which handles a spectrum of tasks from providing technical guidance and doing compliance reviews to complaint investigations, assessing civil penalties, and making referrals for criminal prosecution.

A covered entity that violates the rules can be subjected to civil penalties of up to $100 per incident, up to a maximum of $25,000 per person per year for each standard violated. Criminal penalties can be imposed for improper access or disclosure of information, obtaining personal health information under false pretenses, or making malicious use of confidential information, especially if there was a profit motive.

Although employers and plan sponsors of insured plans are not directly subject to these rules, they do have to restrict the way in which they collect and use personal information. When employers and sponsors receive PHI from a covered entity such as an insurer or HMO, the plan sponsor must agree to control re-use of the information. Employers are not permitted to use PHI for employment-related functions or functions for other benefit plans.

The rule requires certain information to be included in the plan document:

- A description of how PHI can be used and disclosed;
- The sponsor's access to PHI if it has provided certification as to the necessary plan amendment and conditions on the use of PHI;
- Description of security measures such as firewalls, restriction of access to authorized persons, and mechanisms for resolving charges of noncompliance with the privacy rules.

The mandatory certification is the employer's commitment not to use or disclose PHI except as permitted by HIPAA or required by law—a ban that includes not using PHI for employment-related actions. The employer must agree to make PHI accessible to the individuals involved and to let them correct mistakes. The employer must account for its disclosures, and must provide the Department of HHS with compliance information about its information practices. Any subcontractors or agents who get access to PHI must agree to abide by the same limitations. The employer must use firewalls to preserve data security. To the extent feasible PHI must be returned to the supplier of the information—or be destroyed—when the data is no longer needed.

However, it should be noted that, according to a report released in November 2001, many online health-related activities are not subject to HIPAA privacy rules. Even when applicability is fully phased in as of April 2003, activities such as making purchases and doing research on health-oriented Web sites will not be covered.

Web sites that are not health providers, insurers, or health care clearinghouses can collect and re-use or even sell personal information without triggering the HIPAA rules. [Lisa Richwine, *US Doesn't Protect Most Online Health Info* (Nov. 19, 2001) <http://news.excite.com/printstory/news/er/011119/12/net-health-privacy-dc> (Excite.com posting from Nov. 19, 2001)] The Administrative Simplification Compliance Act [Pub. L. No. 107-105], did NOT extend the compliance date for the privacy rule, only for the EDI standards [*See* § 13.04]

CHAPTER 27

THE ROLE OF THE COMPUTER IN HR

§ 27.01   INTRODUCTION

Corporate human resource functions have always been number-intensive, from calculating a payroll to preparing reports on the nature of the workforce. Therefore, the HR department was an "early adopter" of all kinds of technology, going as far back as tabulating machines, through mainframe computers using punched cards, to the desktop PC, to today's networked systems. (Ironically, computer networks have something in common with the old-style mainframe with "dumb terminals" linked to it.)

Not only are computers used within the business, and not only are functions such as payroll preparation and tax reporting compliance often outsourced by electronic means, computerized communications continue to gain in importance. The Internet provides vast information and calculation resources for the HR department.

A corporate intranet (private computer network) can be developed to transmit information to, and receive information from, employees. Instead of printing a lengthy employee manual, then reprinting it to respond to changes in laws and corporate policy, the material can be input in a form that a computer can use and displayed on the intranet, with access limited to authorized persons.

An intranet can be set up with various levels of security, possibly password-protected, so that all employees have access to basic information like the employee handbook and work rules, but only those who need to know have access to salary information and employee performance ratings. Intranets can also be used for training, for job postings within the organization, and to advise employees how to save for retirement and manage their benefits.

§ 27.02   INTERNET RESEARCH

Many Web sites specialize in providing information about the HR function. The Society for Human Resources Management (SHRM) has a secure commerce server for online book orders, so credit card orders are safe. [*See* <http://shrmstore.shrm.org> (no www)] HR Magazine's site [<http://www.hrhq.com>], has a "conference room" for online chat with other HR professionals. The articles archive for HRMagazine appears at <http://www.shrm.org/hrmagazine/articles>.

Law firm Web sites are also an excellent source of up-to-date information about court cases, new tax rulings, and compliance matters.

If you need information about outplacement, or need to find an experienced professional in your area, *see* the Association of Outplacement Consulting Firm's site, <http://www.aocfi.org>. The International Foundation of Benefit Plans can be found at <http://www.ifebp.org>.

The best government sites, such as <http://www.irs.ustreas.gov> are full of useful forms, explanations, and news summaries, as well as offering the full text of new regulations. It is worth scheduling time to regularly review the Pension and Welfare Benefit Administration and Occupational Safety and Health Administration sites to monitor ongoing developments; to see if you want to post an official comment on a proposal or testify at a hearing; or if there are new forms and publications available.

The Department of Labor has an immense bank of information online. However, the site does not always run quickly, and finding the specific information you need can be difficult. HR Magazine's home page recognizes this and helps you cope with a site map for more productive access to government information. [*See* <http://www.shrm.org>]

The Department of Labor's main site is <http://www.dol.gov>. The Bureau of Labor Statistics reports the relative strengths of various employment sectors and employment cost trends. [*See* <http://www.bls.gov>] It also disseminates statistics on occupational safety and health. [*See* <http://www.bls.gov>. OSHA's home page is http://www.osha.gov>] Federal contracting compliance information is available from the Employment Standards Administration. [*See* <http://www.dol.gov/esa/ofcp_org.htm>]

The Pension and Welfare Benefits Administration, a subagency of DOL, has its site at <http://www.dol.gov/pwba>. For Worker's Compensation information, *see* <http://www.dol.gov/esa/owcp_org.htm>. The Wage and Hour Division's Web presence is <http://www.dol.gov/esa/whd_org.htm>. *See* <http://www.doleta.gov> for the DOL's Corporate Citizenship Resource center, with profiles of companies that have implemented exceptional work-family programs. *See* <http://www.pbgc.gov> for coverage of the expansion of PBGC information technology.

There are so many HR resources available that it could be too time-consuming to use an ordinary search engine to find them all. Therefore, "meta-indexes" have been developed: Web home pages that offer links to information-rich sites. *See*, for instance,

* Labor lawyer David Rhett Baker's Web "bibliography," <http://www.benefits link.com/articles/usingweb.html>;
* Society of Human Resources Management HR Links, <http://www.shrm.org/hrlinks/>;
* Cornell University School of Industrial Labor Relations, <http://workindex.com>;
* HR Professional's Gateway to the Internet, <http://www.hrprosgateway.com/www/index2.html>;
* Nottingham Trent University (Britain) Human Resources Management Resources on the Internet, <http://www.nbs.ntu.ac.uk>;
* Employment Law Links, <http://www.contilaw.com/links.html> and <http://www.mtsu.edu/~rlhannah/employee_benefits.html>.

These are some private sites that may be helpful:

* Work/Family Forum, <http://www.workfamily.com>;
* AboutWork (career development advice and strategies), <http://www.about work.com>;

- Ross Runkel's Employment Law Page, <http://www.rossrunkel.com>;
- Payroll Guide Newsletter and other compliance products, <http://riahome. com/payrollandpension/payroll/payrollproducts.asp>;
- Wageweb (survey data on typical compensation level for various jobs—designed for use in pay planning), <http://www.wageweb.com>;
- Benefitslink Benefits Buzz shows news clips for events of the previous 48 hours, with links to the full text of articles. There is also an archive of past issues that can be searched by topic, <http://www.benefitslink.com/buzz/>. Benefitslink also has two daily online newsletters, one dealing with pensions and one with benefit issues;
- Sites by consulting firms, such as <http://www.spencernet.com> and Aon Consulting, <http://www.aon.com>;
- A group of related sites (HR Wire, EEO Advisor, Compensation & Benefits Advisor, Human Resource Advisor), <http://www.hr-esource.com>;
- For technical information about plan design, see the Enrolled Actuaries Report, <http://www.actuary.org>;
- The Employee Benefits Research Institute has a very comprehensive site at <http://www.ebri.org>, although some of the best material is members-only;
- Wall Street Journal Career Journal, <http://www.careerjournal.com>.

§ 27.03   RECRUITING VIA THE INTERNET

According to the consulting firm The Internet Business Network, more than 1.2 million job postings are already available online, and there are more than a million resumes available for search. Many of the postings and resumes involve computer and other technical jobs, but more and more people (especially recent graduates) are computer and Internet-savvy no matter what they studied.

If your corporation has a Web site, it's easy and inexpensive to add an area for posting job opportunities. You can include an electronic form so even candidates who do not have an electronic resume can submit their qualifications. The form can be used for initial screening of applicants.

§ 27.04   BENEFITS MANAGEMENT ONLINE

There are many reasons to limit the corporate content that is publicly available on the Internet: Premature disclosure of confidential information could result in loss of privacy, premature release of corporate plans, exposure of trade secrets, securities law violations, or the like. Corporations also generate a tremendous amount of information that is not security-sensitive, but is not of interest outside the organization.

Obviously many companies are already aware of this. In early 2002, Towers Perrin reported that 91% of their survey respondents use the World Wide Web to communicate with employees. Nearly half (48%) use Internet and intranet applications to allow employees to learn about benefits and perform some degree of self-management of their accounts. Virtually all the respondents (96%) say that self-service benefit management can make the HR department—and the organization as a whole—more efficient and deliver information faster and more accurately. A large majority (80%) agree that the Web can lower HR costs. [Spencernet, *Study Finds 91% of Companies Use Web for Communications* (February 20, 2002) <http://www.spencernet.com/Archive/News022002.html>]

Early in 2002, a study by University of Maryland researchers, focusing on the Ceridian Lifeworks® Online network, shows that employees reacted very positively to online delivery of EAP and work-life services. Nearly all respondents (92%) found that the site was helpful or extremely helpful. Ninety-three percent said they were likely or very likely to return to the site. Over three-quarters (79%) of the respondents went to the site to research a specific topic, rather than to surf the site. About half (48%) of respondents said they used the online service instead of calling or going to the EAP office, because they got immediate access to the information. About a quarter of respondents (28%) said using the site was faster than talking to a person. Relatively small numbers of respondents (12% and 10% respectively) said they used the site because their question was fairly minor, or because it was too embarrassing to discuss in person. [This study is discussed in *First-Ever Study Finds Employees Highly Motivated To Use Online EAP*, <http://www.ceridian.com>]

The cost of implementing an intranet depends on the scope of the project, and whether the project requires full-scale programming or can be implemented wholly or partially with off-the-shelf commercial software packages. Another important question is whether the in-house information technology staff can handle the job, or whether a consultant will be needed.

In 1999, the market for HR software and solutions totaled $2.6 billion. The estimated market for 2003 is $3.7 billion. [Joyce Slayton, *HR Made Easy*, The Industry Standard, Sept. 18, 2000, at p. 298] The trend is to use software to improve training, recruitment, and retention. The third generation of products is sophisticated enough to create a personalized analysis, setting out the alternatives, for every employee. Popular HR applications include management of payroll and benefits, recruitment, training, communication of company policies, employee profiles, and performance reviews.

The use of online enrollment for benefits and online reporting changes in personal data (e.g., an employee marries or divorces; has or adopts a child; a child stops being a dependent) has grown dramatically since 1999, and is now very common. However, most Internet users found that they could speed up transaction processing by moving from paper to electronic processing—but the HR workload didn't really decrease! [*News Briefs, More Companies Using the Internet for Human Resources*, WestGroup Employment Alert, Oct. 12, 2000, at p. 12]

The Hunter Group (a Baltimore consulting firm) surveyed major companies, with a total of over 6 million employees. More than 90% of the respondents call their implementation of self-service benefits information over an intranet "successful" or "somewhat successful." The system can provide a 100% return on investment in just a year. The average survey respondent spent about $1.5 million to install self-service benefit information systems. However, the cost per employee of deploying the system ranged all the way from $35 to $1,600, depending on the size of the workforce and the complexity of the system.

Watson Wyatt found that 85% of large companies they surveyed used an intranet in benefits management. 72% used the public Internet, 63% used an interactive voice response system (the familiar "For health benefits information press 3...") and 43% used call centers. For small companies, the dominant electronic communications tools were intranets (used by 74%) and the Internet (68%). Web solutions can also be supplemented by human operators working in call centers to answer questions or transfer calls. [Susan G. Wells, *Communicating Benefits Information Online*, HR Magazine, (February 2001) <http://www.shrm.org/hrmagazine/2001index/0201/default.asp?page=0201wells.htm>]

However, one limitation on the usefulness of a corporate intranet is limited employee access. In 41% of firms surveyed as early as 1998 by Sedgwick Noble Lowndes, 80–100% of the workforce had access to the company's intranet or were expected to gain access within a year. In 9% of the respondent companies, 61–80% of the employees had access to the intranet, but in 22% of the companies intranet access was 20% or below. [Since 1999, Sedgwick Noble Lowndes has been part of Marsh & McLennan, <http://www.marshmac.com>] However, there are ways to provide intranet access without putting a computer on every desktop. Touch-screen kiosks (like the ones used on ATMs), or a few specialized computer terminals, can be placed in the HR office, the office of the Employee Assistance Program (EAP), or the cafeteria or breakroom.

Amoco handled its intranet implementation by splitting the intranet into an HR component (including HR publications, business unit information, benefits information, volunteer information, and ads posted by employees who want to sell personal items), and a benefits component. The benefits component covers the employee handbook, personnel policies, and links to relevant Internet sites like financial planning sites.

Motorola took a dramatic but risky step: It simply eliminated all paper forms and correspondence related to HR. The upshot was a saving of $1.5 million, but there were hard-to-estimate losses with respect to employees who needed additional technical support. [*See Intranet Delivery of HR and Benefits Information*, WestGroup Employment Alert, Feb. 19. 1998, at p. 2; and *More Midsized Firms Communicate Benefits Information Through Intranets*, RIA Compensation & Benefits Update, Oct. 7, 1998, at p. 6.]

§ 27.05   LEGAL IMPLICATIONS OF E-MAIL

The benefits of e-mail in providing a simple method of communications are obvious. However, unencrypted e-mail is not secure. It is much more like a postcard that can be read by anybody than it is like a sealed letter—much less a coded message. Merely clicking a "delete" icon does not remove a message completely and permanently from the entire computer system, network, or service provider that offers e-mail service. So a message that is embarrassing or worse (e.g., one involving racial epithets, sexual harassment, or evidence of corporate wrongdoing) can be found by hostile parties—including plaintiffs' lawyers.

If a company provides e-mail access at work, it should inform employees of the company's policies with respect to e-mail. A reasonable e-mail policy might involve

- Disclosure that the company has the right to monitor employee e-mail. [*See* § 26.06[C] for a discussion of privacy issues] It would be illegal to fire, or otherwise take action against, an employee who uses e-mail to engage in protected concerted activity such as complaining about safety risks. Threatening or inflammatory messages are not protected under labor law, but a direct protest to management certainly would be. Employee-to-employee communications are probably protected unless they actually threaten the harmonious and efficient operation of the business enterprise;
- Restriction of e-mail to business use. Inexpensive software is available to uninstall or disable games on office computers or networks, and to track usage (e.g., to see if gambling or pornographic sites are being accessed). However, although such measures may increase productivity, they must be balanced against the resentment employees may experience;
- No forwarding of copyrighted materials (for example, newspaper stories or cartoons);
- No use of obscene or suggestive language or slurs against any group;
- No discussion of matters that might have legal consequences (e.g., price fixing or industrial espionage);
- Asking employees to think before they send a message if there is anything in the message that they would not want publicized, or that could put the employer in a bad light.

CHAPTER 28
WORK-FAMILY ISSUES

§ 28.01   INTRODUCTION

Work-family issues didn't arise when most people were subsistence farmers and the whole family worked together to raise crops for survival. The problems were muted when most family units consisted of a male breadwinner and a house-wife. Since World War II (when many women had to do factory and other work to replace men away at war), however, many employees have had trouble reconciling their family obligations with the needs of paid jobs.

The need for child care is not a problem limited to a small minority. According to the Bureau of Labor Statistics in 2001, among married couples who had children under 18, the mother was employed in 67.6% of the families, and both parents were employed in 63.2% of the families; in about one-third of the families (29.5%) the father had a paid job and the mother did not. Looking at families with children under six (pre-school-age children, where the children's needs and the day care problems are the greatest) the mother held a paying job in 59.5% of the families. In a majority of families with pre-school-age children, both parents worked (55.9%). In about one-third of families with children under six (37.7%), the father held a paid job but the mother did not. [Bureau of Labor Statistics, Table 4: Families With Own Children: Employment Status of Parents by Child and Family Type, 2000-01 Annual Averages, <http://www.bls.gov/news.release/famee.t04.htm>]

There are new kinds of families developing (single parents, blended families, grandparents raising grandchildren). Greater involvement of fathers in hands-on child care also increases the demand for FMLA leave or flexible hours for fathers. [*See* Chapter 38] for the FMLA; however, paternity leave has never really caught on, for reasons discussed by Melinda Ligos, *The Fear of Taking Paternity Leave*, New York Times, May 31, 2000, at p. G1]

Nor is child care the only issue. People in mid-life are sometimes called the "sandwich generation" because they have responsibilities for aging parents as well as growing children. The Department of Labor Women's Bureau is a good resource for work-family issues. [*See* <http://www.dol.gov/wb/childcare/b2bintro.htm>] So is the National Partnership for Women and Families. [*See* <http://www.nationalpartnership.org>]

§ 28.02   EMPLOYER-PROVIDED DAY CARE

One option, perhaps the most appreciated by employees, is for the employer to maintain an on-site day care center. Calculating the costs and benefits of running a day care center can be difficult. Initial expenses can be high, but this perk is valuable in recruiting good employees and retaining employees who need quality care for their children.

On-site care is only feasible for large companies—and probably is more workable outside big cities because metropolitan rents are often prohibitive. An employer-sponsored day care center has to be licensed. It will be subject to ongoing inspections. The employer company could become liable if, for example, a child were injured on the premises, or several children developed a contagious illness. The standard Worker's Compensation insurance policy also excludes injuries that occur in an employer-operated day care center.

It can be convenient for the employer to contract out daily operations to an experienced provider of high-quality child care, although this adds further expenses. The employer can also co-sponsor a nearby child care center that offers care to employees of several companies.

However, it is much more common for employers to reimburse employees for some of their child care expenses. [*See* § 28.07 for a discussion of child care fringe benefits and their tax implications. A smaller-scale program gives employees "I&R" (information and referral) to child care resources, but does not actually furnish services or funds]

In 2001, more and more employers built or participated in child care centers open 24 hours a day, to help single parents and working couples. Longer commutes also mean that parents are away from home for longer and need more hours of day care availability. Although some states have laws forbidding round-the-clock child care centers, some states endorsed this form of care as part of the welfare reform effort. The demand is high, because according to the Department of Labor, in 1997 one-sixth of employees worked on evening, night, or rotating shifts. [Barbara Carton, *Bedtime Stories: In 24-Hour Workplace, Day Care is Moving to the Night Shift*, Wall Street Journal, July 6, 2001, at p. A1. For a case study of child care options Dallas-area parents face, *see Dallas-Area Working Parents Mostly Tough Out Child Care Issues on Their Own* (no by-line), Dallas Morning News, Feb. 4, 2002, on the Society for Human Resource Management (SHRM) Web site]

The SHRM found that the percentage of small and medium sized companies (where the majority of U.S. workers are employed) offering on-site care actually declined between 1997 and 2001 (from 6% to 5%). On-site care in these enterprises is concentrated in only a few industries: education, health services, nonprofit organizations, and retail trade.

In 2001, 20% of companies provided information and referrals to help their employees locate child care—as compared to 15% in 1997. However, this is the least intensive form of child care assistance, and the least expensive for the employer. Only 4% of SHRM's survey respondents provided subsidies for child care in 2001, way down from the 6% who did so in 1997.

Hewitt Associates reports that large companies take a more active child care role (just as they typically offer more generous benefit packages than smaller companies). Twelve percent of large firms offer day care on or near the premises, 10% negotiate for discounts when employees send their children to neighborhood day care centers, and 43% provide information and referral. These percentages increased about 2% between 1995 and 2001.

§ 28.03   BREAST FEEDING IN THE WORKPLACE

Breast feeding for at least the first six months of life, and preferably a year, is the medical recommendation for newborn babies. So either new mothers must choose bottle feeding; delay their return to work until they are ready to stop breast feeding; or participate in a workplace lactation program that either allows them to feed their babies at the workplace or gives them an appropriate private place to pump and store breast milk. [*See* Kathryn Tyler, *Got Milk?* HR Magazine, March 1999, at p. 69]

Workplace lactation programs are a good value for employers, because they aid employee retention. Furthermore, breast-fed babies are often healthier than formula-fed babies, so their parents need less time off to deal with babies' illnesses. The Los Angeles Department of Water and Power found that every dollar invested in the lactation program provided a return of $3.50–$5.00. The program cut absenteeism by 27% and reduced health care costs by 35%.

The demands of a lactation program are modest. Participating employees need a private, reasonably quiet and pleasant place to express breast milk and a refrigerator or cooler to keep it cool, plus a sink to wash up. Typically, employees will need two 30-minute, or three 20-minute, breaks to express milk.

The focus of a recent article [*Breast-Feeding In the Workplace: What Should an Employer Do?* WestGroup Employment Alert, March 16, 2000, at p. 1] is that the PDA and the ADA do not cover breast-feeding. In general, courts hearing cases on this issue have not required the employer to provide personal leave, modified schedules, or changes in job routine for employees who breast feed after returning from maternity leave. In this analysis, lactation is a natural function, and is neither a pregnancy-related medical condition nor a disability.

However, there are some relevant state statutes. Hawaii has enacted a law making it unlawful discrimination to refuse to hire, or to discharge or discriminate against a woman who breast feeds or expresses milk in the workplace.

States such as California, Florida, and New York have general statutes allowing mothers to breast-feed in public places where they are not trespassing, but these laws do not specifically cover workplace issues. Hawaii, Georgia, Minnesota, Oregon, and Tennessee have statutes that require or at least allow employers to provide unpaid break time so lactating employees can express breast milk. The employer also has to make reasonable efforts to provide a more suitable place than a toilet stall to do this. A Texas law grants businesses a "mother-friendly" designation if they offer flexible work schedules, private spaces for breast-feeding and expressing milk, and hygienic storage for expressed breast milk.

§ 28.04   ADOPTION ASSISTANCE

Under I.R.C. § 137, as amended by EGTRRA, employers can establish a written adoption assistance program, providing benefits for employees who adopt children. Employees who receive such assistance may be able to exclude as much as $10,000 in employer assistance from income (and they may also qualify for an income tax credit of up to $10,000 when they adopt a child). [*See* I.R.C. § 23] Under pre-EGTRRA law, a larger amount could be excluded if the adoptee had special needs, but current law harmonizes the two.

The $10,000 amount is a maximum. The income exclusion and adoption credit are reduced for very high-income persons or families (modified adjusted gross income of $150,000 or more). The $10,000 amount is also a 2002 amount, and will be adjusted as the cost of living increases in 2003 and later tax years.

The 2002 tax bill, the Job Creation and Worker Assistance Act of 2002 (JCWAA) [Pub. L. No. 107-147] makes it clear that if an employee receives adoption assistance for a special-needs child, the full $10,000 credit can be taken even if the actual adoption expenses are less than $10,000. However, expenses incurred for pre-2002 tax years are subject to the limit prevailing in the year of the adoption. If a special-needs child is adopted in a tax year beginning after 2002, then the JCWAA provides that the $10,000 credit is reduced by any qualified adoption expenses for the same child in earlier years.

Hewitt Associates says that, among employers who provide adoption assistance, the average benefit is $3,000. Less than half of 1 percent of the workforce uses this benefit each year, but it creates a lot of good will. [*See* Gregory Weaver, *A Great Little Perk*, Indianapolis Star, (Nov. 20, 2000) <http://www.starnews.com.business/articles/adopt1120.html> (Posted to www.starnews.com on Nov. 20, 2000)]

§ 28.05   CORPORATE ELDER CARE ACTIVITIES

Everybody knows that the U.S. senior citizen population is growing, and soon the huge Baby Boom generation will reach retirement age. The vast majority of care provided to assist elderly people with their illnesses and limitations imposed by aging is unpaid, informal care from family members and friends. In 1994, there were about 5.9 million informal caregivers taking care of 3.6 million elderly and disabled people. [William D. Spector, The Characteristics of Long-Term Care Users, AHRQ Publications Clearinghouse, P.O. Box 8547, Silver Spring, MD 20907, (800) 358-9295 (free)]

Caring for the disabled elderly has an immense impact on the caregivers' family life—and on their productivity as employees. A 1995 study by AARP and the National Alliance for Caregiving estimates that U.S. industry loses at least $11.4 billion a year in productivity because employee caregivers have to take emergency time off, leave early, or are interrupted at work. The same organizations' 1996 survey estimates that there are about 14.4 million employee caregivers in the United States.

Caregivers spend an estimated average of 15 hours a week taking care of their aging relatives. Some of these tasks have to be performed during normal working hours. In some instances, caregivers have to switch from full-time to part-time work, or quit their paying jobs entirely. Stress can greatly reduce the productivity of caregiver employees when they're in the office.

"Who Cares," a 1999 study by the National Alliance for Caregiving and AARP, reports that about one-quarter of caregivers take care of a person with Alzheimer's Disease or other dementia-causing illness, and that there may be anywhere from 1.9 million to 4 million cases of Alzheimer's in the United States. That adds up to at least 2%, and maybe as much as 12%, of the senior citizen population. Caring for a person with Alzheimer's is very time-consuming and stressful. If the employer can offer supportive services for employees who have relatives with dementia, this is likely to pay off in terms of more employees retaining their jobs, and fewer quitting to become full-time caregivers—as well as greater productivity while they are still employed. [GAO/HEHS-98-16, *Alzheimer's Disease: Estimates of Prevalence in the United States*, (January 1998)]

The MetLife Mature Market Group and the National Alliance for Caregiving released a report. [*Family Caregiving in the U.S.: Findings From A National Survey*, (1997)] The survey showed that almost one-fourth of all U.S. households included one or more persons with caregiving responsibilities. Almost two-thirds of those caregivers were employed; more than 50% worked full-time. That meant 14.4 million Americans combining caregiving and employment responsibilities.

MetLife's conclusion was that lost productivity and extra supervisory time for resolving caregiving problems cost American business $11.4 billion a year (to replace employees, cope with absenteeism and partial absenteeism, and deal with interruptions during the work day). The estimated average cost to business, per caregiver employee, was $1,142 a year: $69 traced to absenteeism, $85 to partial absenteeism, $657 for workday interruptions, $189 for employees leaving work to deal with crises, and $141 for supervisory involvement. In addition, replacing employees who quit to become full-time caregivers was estimated to cost almost $5 billion a year more. Furthermore, because caregiving is so stressful, caregivers are unusually heavy consumers of health and counseling services, increasing the employer's plan costs.

The majority of caregivers are women, taking care not only of their own parents but of their in-laws. [*See* the Department of Labor's Women's Bureau White Paper, *Work and Elder Care: Facts for Caregivers and Their Employers*, <http://www.dol.gov/dol/wb/public/wb_pubs/elderc.htm> (posted May 1998). For a later, broader-based report, *see* the November 14, 2000 report of the Department of Labor's Advisory Council on Employee Welfare and Pension Benefit Plans, <http://www.dol.gov/pwba/adcoun/report2.htm>] This report notes that 41% of caregivers are responsible for children under 18 as well as for one or more elderly persons.

A small but useful study [*The MetLife Juggling Act Study: Balancing Caregiving With Work and the Costs Involved*, MMI_MetLife@metlife.com (1990)] identifies key themes in the caregiving experience:

- Caregivers often underestimate how hard it is to be a caregiver, or how much effort will be required over how long a time;

- Not only do they make informal adjustments to their work schedules, 84% of survey respondents made formal adjustments, such as leaving their jobs, taking early retirement, or using sick and vacation days;
- Caregivers lost access to promotions, training, transfers, and other avenues toward improved career status;
- Close to two-thirds of caregivers lost some income, and therefore forfeited abilities to save and build wealth. The estimated median loss over the total period of caregiving was $243,761; the estimated mean loss was $566,443;
- Caregivers' own retirement becomes precarious. If they work less, earn less, and save less, they will also be entitled to smaller pensions from their employers and smaller Social Security benefits;
- Most caregivers also provide financial assistance as well as practical help to their relatives or friends. On the average, financial help was provided over a period of two to six years, at an average figure of almost $20,000. These gifts reduced caregivers' ability to invest in home improvements, make consumer expenditures, and pay for their children's education;
- Many caregivers found that their own health deteriorated: 20% reported serious health problems related to caregiving;
- One-quarter of respondents found that their productivity at work declined because of caregiving; 10% felt it declined significantly for this reason.

§ 28.06   THE CORPORATE ELDER CARE ROLE

In 1996, Hewitt Associates found that 30% of major corporations offered elder care benefits. Of those, 79% provided information and referral, 25% had a long-term care insurance plan, and 17% provided counseling to help caregivers cope with stress and make practical plans.

Tip: When the federal Older Americans Act [Pub. L. No. 38-73] was re-authorized at the end of 2000, a new National Family Caregiver Support program was created and funded with $125 million nationwide. Be sure to work with your local Area Agency on Aging to put caregiver employees in touch with these programs.

Under an I&R (information and referral) plan, the HR department, Employee Assistance Program, or other relevant department maintains listings of nursing homes, home health agencies, government agencies for the aging, and other resources.

Other elder care resources that employers can provide include:

- Seminars about relevant topics such as Medicare and Medicaid;
- Support groups for caregivers;
- Hotlines giving elder care information;

- Subsidized phone consultations with resource or elder care experts (including those in other geographic areas, where employees' relatives live);
- Directories and other publications;
- Caregiver fairs, providing exhibits from public agencies as well as voluntary organizations and for-profit service vendors;
- Counseling from a psychologist or clinical social worker;
- Subsidies for adult day care for the parent;
- Respite care;
- Emergency care (including care in the home of the elderly person);
- Paratransit, such as wheelchair-accessible vans, to provide transportation to medical appointments and other trips that would otherwise require the employee's services as driver;
- Subsidizing the cost of pagers that the parent can use to contact the employee in an emergency;
- Case management—services of social workers or geriatric care managers (GCMs), who advise the employee about creating and managing a complete elder care plan;
- Adding elderly dependent parents to the coverage of dependent care accounts.

For the unionized workplace, *see* the AFL-CIO's worksheet, "Bargaining for Eldercare," available at <http://www.aflcio.com>.

A 1998 speech by Joy Loverde [*see* WestGroup Employment Alert, May 14, 1998, at p. 7] suggests criteria for a compassionate, cost-effective corporate elder care program:

- The program educates employees;
- It alerts them to responsibility they can take for their parents' (or other recipients') elder care;
- It teaches employees to share care giving and create an informal network;
- It motivates employees by focusing on their needs, not elders' needs;
- It gives employees psychological tools for discussing sensitive matters.

[*See* § 21.03 for a discussion of long-term care insurance (LTCI) as an employee benefit. Most employment-related LTCI plans are fully paid for by the employee, so the employer's only cost is a small amount for administration and employee communications]

The Health Insurance Portability and Accountability Act (HIPAA) of 1996 [Pub. L. No. 104-191] cleared up some previously murky tax questions. It enacted Code § 7702B, which provides for tax deductions for some LTCI purchasers. In effect, HIPAA places "qualified" long-term care insurance plans on the same footing as Accident & Health (A&H) plans, so the employer will be entitled to a tax deduction (if it does contribute to the premiums) and employees will not have taxable income on account of employer contributions. But HIPAA also makes it clear that LTCI cannot be provided through either a cafeteria plan or a flexible spending account.

§ 28.07   DEPENDENT CARE ASSISTANCE PLANS

The Internal Revenue Code recognizes, and gives favorable tax treatment to, plans under which the employer makes direct payments to provide dependent care to employees, or the employer reimburses employees for certain dependent care expenses. [I.R.C. § 129] The employer is not obligated to pre-fund the plan. It can pay benefits as they arise, out of current income, with no need to maintain a separate account. However, the employer is required to provide reasonable notice to eligible employees that the program is in existence and how it operates.

Employees do not have taxable income because of participation in an I.R.C. § 129 plan. However, the plan cannot pay more for dependent care than the employee earns. (In other words, the plan can't be set up as a perk for employees who are, in essence, on parenthood leave and earn very little.) Furthermore, in effect the plan only assists employees who are single parents, or who are part of a two-career couple, because the employee will have taxable income if the I.R.C. § 129 benefits exceed the income of the employee's spouse, unless that spouse is a full-time student or disabled.

In addition to these limitations, the maximum employer contribution to an I.R.C. § 129 plan that can be excluded from income is $5,000 per employee. This is further reduced to $2,500 in the case of married employees who file separate returns.

For this purpose, dependent care expenses are household services and other expenses that are incurred to permit the employee to hold a job outside the home. In the I.R.C. § 129 context, "dependents" means dependent children under age 15, or a spouse or other dependent (e.g., an aging parent) who is physically or mentally incapable of self-care.

The Code defines a qualified dependent care assistance plan as a written plan for the exclusive benefit of employees, subject to a classification created by the employer but approved as nondiscriminatory by the IRS. To be considered nondiscriminatory, not more than 25% of the contributions to the plan or benefits received from the plan may relate to shareholders, 5% owners, or their families. The average benefits provided under the plan to employees who are not highly compensated must be 55% or more of those provided to highly compensated employees.

If the plan fails to be qualified for this reason, then HCEs (but not other employees) will have taxable income as a result of plan participation. Every year, by January 31, employees must be given a written report of the amounts paid or expenses incurred by the plan for that employee's dependent care in the previous year. An employer-provided day care center is deemed to be a welfare benefit plan, but a dependent care plan that involves reimbursement of employees' dependent care expenses is not.

Dependent-care plans are linked to the Code provisions for a dependent care credit that taxpayers can take. As amended by the JCWAA, the I.R.C. § 21 credit is up to 35% of qualifying expenses (for tax years beginning in 2003; the limit was 30% in earlier years). The credit is a sliding-scale percentage (a higher percentage for lower-income people) of qualifying dependent care expenses up to a maximum: $3,000 for one qualifying dependent, $6,000 for two qualifying dependents. (Before the JCWAA, the limits were $2,400 and $4,800, respectively.)

CHAPTER 29
DIVERSITY IN THE WORKPLACE

§ 29.01   INTRODUCTION

At one time, most workforces were quite homogeneous, with a workforce drawn from the surrounding area. Sons would follow their fathers into the "mill" or the office, joined by their brothers and cousins, eventually retiring at 65 with a gold watch. Women worked as clerical or sales workers, or teachers or nurses—not engineers or executives. They quit their jobs when they got married, or when they had children. Handicapped people were kept out of sight. There might be a few people in the workforce who were considered too masculine (if they were women) or not masculine enough (for men). They might even be suspected of homosexuality—if so, they'd be at pains to deny it; they certainly wouldn't show up at the company picnic with a same-sex life partner.

Although the workers might be immigrants or the children of immigrants, it was a pretty safe bet that the managers would be college-educated, Anglo-Saxon white males. Whatever the problems and tensions within the operation, relatively few of them would be caused by racial, religious, nationalistic, or cultural friction—simply because different groups seldom came in contact.

Today, the picture has changed significantly! Although the majority of the U.S. workforce is male, there is a high proportion of female workers—not all of whom hold traditionally feminine jobs. There are many first- and second-generation immigrants in the work force, but now they are more likely to come from Asia and the Pacific, or from Latin America, than from the European countries that dominated earlier waves of immigration.

The expansion of diversity in the workplace has not been achieved without a struggle. Nor do all the problems come from the proverbial "angry white males." Anyone can be prejudiced, hostile, blinded by stereotypes, ignorant of other peoples' traditions, or just plain hard to work with. Furthermore, a company can be doing its best to offer equal opportunity—while women and minorities believe that they have little access to mobility within the organization, and white males simultaneously believe that they are at a disadvantage.

According to WetFeet.com, a San Francisco recruiting and consulting company that concentrates on first jobs, 16% of those surveyed consider a diverse workforce a key indicator of a company's commitment to diversity. One-third of the respondents said that they wouldn't work for a company that lacked diversity. Close to half (44%) of black job applicants say they have eliminated employers from consideration because of their lack of ethnic diversity. [*See* <http://www.wet feet.com/corporate/diversity.asp>, discussed in Bill Leonard, *HR Update*, HR Magazine, April 2001, at p. 27]

The HR department's mission is to promote efficiency and cooperation—not to eliminate differences or even prejudices. A company's workforce doesn't have to worship together, enjoy the same sporting events, celebrate the same holidays, or even like each other. They do have to understand the factors shaping other peoples' behavior, strive to avoid offending others, be tolerant of unintended offensive remarks and actions, and work together harmoniously and productively. For some tested techniques of diversity management, *see* Career Magazine's Diversity Initiative Program Web site, <http://www.careermag.com>.

§ 29.02   THE GLASS CEILING

Unfortunately, some people are actively and consciously hostile to those different from themselves. They engage in whatever discriminatory actions they think they can get away with. However, overt hatred and resentment are not the only factors that block full advancement for qualified women and members of minority groups. There are other, subtler forces at work, sometimes affecting people who on a conscious level are objective and tolerant.

The prejudices of the past cast a long shadow. If law and business schools used to discriminate against minorities and women, then the supply of members of these groups with professional degrees, and with decades of business experience, will be limited. If a company hardly ever recruits women or members of minority groups for its training program, and if its policy is to promote from within, then it will look to its (overwhelmingly white male) middle managers when it's time to fill senior posts.

These subtler barriers to advancement are sometimes called the "glass ceiling": Advancement up to a point is reasonably easy, but there are invisible barriers to achieving the really top jobs. *See* the reports of a federal commission convened under the Glass Ceiling Act, a provision of the Civil Rights Act of 1999. [Pub. L. No. 102-166]

According to the main report, "Many judgments on hiring and promotion are made on the basis of a look, the shape of a body, or the color of skin." [*A Solid Investment: Making Full Use of the Nation's Human Capital*, <http://www.ilr. cornell.edu/library/e_archive/gov_reports/GlassCeiling/documents/GlassCeiling PrelimRecommendations.pdf>] The report agrees with Ann Morrison's conclusion that prejudice is the single most important barrier to female and minority advancement into the executive ranks—or promotion once they achieve the first rungs on the ladder. [Ann Morrison, *The New Leaders: Guidelines on Leadership of Diversity in America*, <http://www.ilr.cornell.edu/library/e_archive/default.html? page=home>]

Although the Glass Ceiling report acknowledges that some factors (such as educational systems and social attitudes) are beyond corporate control, the report identifies some factors that business can control:

- Whether recruitment is narrow or broad-based;
- Extent of outreach efforts;
- Degree to which new hires are assigned to marginal areas or staff jobs that have less promotion potential than more central, line jobs;
- Presence or absence of mentors;
- Whether good performance is rewarded with access to training and prime assignments;

- Access to social events and informal networks (e.g., social and sporting events);
- Help and support from colleagues, versus hostility and demeaning treatment;
- Whether evaluations are objective or merely reflect prejudices.

Certain characteristics are shared by successful diversity programs:

- The CEO actively supports the program;
- The program is comprehensive and inclusive;
- The program has a genuine goal of advancing the most talented people, whatever their background;
- Results are reviewed, and managers are accountable for results;
- The company has long-range relationships with community organizations, not a single effort that is quickly abandoned;
- Recruitment is genuinely diverse;
- Recruiters consult sources such as www.diversityee.com, www.newsjobs.com, www.diversity-services.com, and www.HireDiversity.com to obtain resumes from people from a wide variety of backgrounds;
- The program makes out a business case for diversity and communicates it to employees.

§ 29.03 DIVERSITY TRAINING

Corporations frequently attempt to defuse hostilities within the workplace by offering (or requiring) diversity training. Usually, it is provided by outside contractors. The training could be a voluntary initiative by management, part of a negotiated settlement with the EEOC or a state antidiscrimination agency, or part of the settlement of a court case. The mission of the training is to make employees examine their assumptions and to relate to other employees in a more professional manner.

The goals of diversity training include:

- Finding areas in which the organization is defective;
- Setting goals for improvement;
- Identifying specific steps for reaching the goals;
- Training employees to carry out those steps.

However, diversity training is not without risks and disadvantages. The program can wind up furnishing evidence for a Title VII or other discrimination suit. A well-intentioned program to promote understanding and harmony can worsen the anger and resentment already simmering below the surface. Employees can feel that discussion of other religions or lifestyles is an insult to their own deeply held beliefs. [This point is raised by Simon J. Nadel, *Religion and Sexual Orientation at Work May Produce Combustible Combination*, 68 L.W. 2163 (Sept. 28, 1999)] An attempt to reach out to traditionally disfavored groups could be construed as reverse discrimination. And, in any event, a diversity training program (which could be viewed as purely cosmetic) is no substitute for effective hiring or for making sure that no one is subjected to a hostile environment in the workplace.

§ 29.04   DIVERSITY AUDITS

The prospect of performing a diversity audit raises a similar mix of questions. A company that has central-office commitment to diversity might have very different conditions at the shop-floor level. Furthermore, a multi-unit company can find it difficult to maintain uniform policies throughout.

A well-designed audit can pinpoint the problems and lead to their resolution. However, a badly designed survey does not generate any useful information, but it does generate data that could be damning if a plaintiff discovers it. Doing a diversity audit shows that management cares about the issue. However, that could backfire, if employees expect real change that doesn't come.

> **Tip:** If a lawyer performs or supervises the audit, there is at least a possibility that potentially embarrassing material can be protected by attorney-client confidentiality. But don't forget that confidentiality is sacrificed if the information is publicized.

Labor lawyers Christine Amalfe and Heather Akawie Adelman give some suggestions for an effective diversity audit:

- The first step is advice from a qualified employment lawyer;
- Concentrate on facts, not subjective comments, when collecting information;
- Destroy the individual survey responses and interview notes once statistical data has been compiled;
- Mark the finished report "privileged and confidential";
- Keep the reports separate from other HR information;
- Control distribution, and do not disclose the results to anyone who does not have a legitimate need to know.

Cummins Incorporated, a manufacturer of diesel engines and power generator products, uses an audit team to make sure that all locations stay on the same page. (The company is careful to make sure that the composition of the team is diverse in and of itself.) The team goes out to each site and interviews about 10% of the employees over a period of three to four days. The team reviews the demographics of each operation, goes over its personnel policies, and does a walkthrough to see if there are any hostile environment issues (e.g., pin-ups that could make some workers uncomfortable). The team makes suggestions there and reports back to the central office. [Lin Grensing-Pophal, *A Balancing Act on Diversity Audits*, HR Magazine, November 2001, at p. 87; Christine Amalfe and Heather Akawie Adelman, *Diversity In the Workplace: The Benefits and Shortcomings of Internal Audits and Surveys*, <http://www.acca.com>]

§ 29.05   ENGLISH-ONLY RULES

In many (if not most) workplace situations, the ability to speak and understand English fluently is a valid job qualification. However, a person can be fluent in English even though it is not his or her first language. He or she may be more comfortable speaking other languages. If the employer bans languages other than English in the workplace, it is easy for national-origin minority groups to show disparate impact.

As of early 1999, almost half the states (most of them in the South or Northwest) had passed statutes declaring English to be the official language of the state: Alabama, Alaska, Arkansas, California, Colorado, Florida, Georgia, Hawaii, Illinois, Indiana, Kentucky, Louisiana, Massachusetts, Mississippi, Missouri, Montana, Nebraska, New Hampshire, North Carolina, South Carolina, North Dakota, South Dakota, Tennessee, Virginia, and Wyoming. Most of these statutes include certain exceptions (e.g., the criminal trial of a person who does not speak English; when health and safety requires communication in another language). About 40 cities also had similar laws of their own.

According to the Federal Reserve Bank of Atlanta, in states with English-only laws, men who were not fluent in English earned an average of 9.3% less than fluent English speakers. However, the wages of women who were not fluent in English did not differ significantly in the two groups of states. [This information comes from Alejandro Bodipo-Memba, *Wage Gap Widens in "English-Only" States*, Wall Street Journal, Feb. 25, 1999, at p. A2]

An employer who imposes such a rule must be able to demonstrate job-relatedness and business necessity: for instance, that there is no other way to meet customer needs or communicate in an emergency. But it would be hard to establish business necessity for forbidding employees to converse in other languages during meals or breaks, or when they are in the restroom or a locker room.

The EEOC's National Origins Guidelines say that merely implementing an English-only rule has a disparate impact. However, the Ninth Circuit rejected these guidelines, requiring proof that the rule creates a hostile work environment for persons whose first language is not English, or proof that the rule is imposed on employees who experience difficulty in speaking English. [*Garcia v. Spun Steak Co.*, 998 F.2d 1480 (9th Cir. 1993); the EEOC guidelines are at 29 C.F.R. § 1606.7. The Northern District of Texas upheld the rule, saying that it was within the EEOC's jurisdiction to adopt it. *See EEOC v. Premier Operator Services, Inc.*, 75 F. Supp. 2d 550 (N.D. Tex. 1999)]

> **Tip:** A workplace English class, centering around work-related vocabulary and concepts, can be an excellent idea, especially if employees speak many languages, so that English becomes a central means of communication.

Where a high percentage of employees or customers speak languages other than English, or where the company does a good deal of business in non-English-speaking countries, bilingual employees (whether native speakers or those who have learned the language) can be invaluable. The question then becomes whether the pay rate should be higher for bilingual employees.

According to *Roman v. Cornell University* [53 F. Supp. 2d 223 (N.D.N.Y. 1999], it is permissible for an employer to require bilingual employees to speak English on the basis of complaints that non-Spanish-speaking employees felt excluded from conversations. The rules must be rational; they must be communicated clearly; and must cover all languages other than English instead of singling out one in particular. Furthermore, it could be hostile environment discrimination to apply a rule in a way that shows hostility toward a particular nationality. [*Velasquez v. Goldwater Mem. Hosp.*, 88 F. Supp. 2d 257 (S.D.N.Y. 2000); *Gotfryd v. Book Covers Inc.*, 1999 WL 20925 (N.D. Ill. Jan. 5, 1999)]

In September, 2000, the EEOC arranged a settlement of close to $200,000 with an Illinois company that agreed to provide back pay for seven Hispanic workers who quit or were fired under the company's English-only rule, plus punitive damages. [No by-line, "Employer's English-Only Policy Brings a Settlement of $192,500," *New York Times,* September 2, 2000, at p. A12]

§ 29.06   PROMOTING DIVERSITY

Steps to take to promote equality in the workplace—or simply to avoid getting sued—include:

- Broaden your recruitment efforts. Don't recruit only at the nearest colleges, or only at the Ivy League. Low-cost public colleges attract some excellent students who can't afford private institutions, so don't rule them out as sources of recruitment;
- Reward managers who increase the diversity of their workforces (with raises, bonuses, and promotions);
- Compare your diversity efforts to those of competitors;
- Provide newly hired female and minority candidates with the training, access to information, mentoring, and networking that they need to succeed;
- Remind employees to avoid ethnic slurs and statements that could create a hostile environment in all written documents, e-mail, and voice mail messages—and also remind them that supposedly deleted materials can often be restored!

PART VI

EMPLOYEE RELATIONS

CHAPTER 30

LABOR LAW

§ 30.01 INTRODUCTION

In the broadest sense, labor law covers the entire relationship between employers and employees. However, the term is usually used in a much narrower sense: to mean the body of law dealing with whether a union will be allowed to organize a workplace; union elections, challenges to elections, and decertification of a union that is guilty of misconduct or that no longer represents employee interests; negotiating a Collective Bargaining Agreement (CBA); interpretation of the CBA; and strikes. Labor law sets rules for conduct by both management and unions.

In most cases, labor law is a matter of federal law. Congress has preempted this issue, in the interest of creating a single, uniform body of law that prevails throughout the country.

At one time, especially during the period of industrial prosperity right after the Second World War, unions were immensely powerful. However, for many reasons, including a shift from an industrial to a service- and knowledge-based economy, union power and influence have declined steadily. In 1983, about one-fifth of U.S. wage and salary workers were union members. By 1996, that percentage had declined to 14.9%, and fell again in 1997, to 14.5%—and to a mere 9.1% in 2000. [*See* David Wessel, *Some Workers Gain With New Union Tactics*, Wall Street Journal, Jan. 31, 2002, at p. A1]

The easiest kind of operation for a union to organize is a large factory with many well-paid blue collar workers who believe they can improve their job security and enhance their pay and benefits by unionizing. The workers must be secure enough to be able to make a credible threat of going out on strike. They have to believe that they will be able to survive economically during a strike, that they will be rehired afterwards, and that the employer needs to end the strike quickly for its own economic benefit.

But there are many instances in which these conditions are not met, and either workers are afraid to unionize, or believe that they have nothing to gain (and in fact may lose by becoming the pawns of a corrupt union, or may undergo job loss if the employer goes out of business or relocates in another state or a foreign country). Recently, unions have been concentrating on organizing service workers, whose jobs can't be relocated easily, and putting pressure on employers to recognize unions by consent, rather than having a representation election. (There are still about 3,000 representation elections each year, and the results are pretty evenly divided between union and employer victories.)

§ 30.02 SOURCES OF LABOR LAW

[A] Generally

The NLRA was supplemented in 1947 by the Labor-Management Relations Act (LMRA) [29 U.S.C. §§ 141–144, etc.], popularly known as the Taft-Hartley

Act. The LMRA extends the powers of the NLRB. It outlaws certain kinds of strikes, including jurisdictional strikes, strikes to enforce unfair labor practices (rather than strikes to protest them), and secondary boycotts. A secondary boycott is an attempt to pressure a neutral company to keep it from dealing with a company that the union has a dispute with.

The Landrum-Griffin Act, known as the Labor-Management Reporting and Disclosure Act of 1959 [Pub. L. No. 86-257], forbids hot-cargo agreements (agreements not to carry the merchandise of a company involved in a labor dispute). It allows prehire agreements in the building and construction industries, and makes it an unfair labor practice to picket in order to force an employer to recognize or bargain with a union.

The Norris-LaGuardia Act severely limits the situations in which an employer can secure an injunction against a union. However, injunctions are still available in certain circumstances. In *Burlington Northern Railway v. IBT Local 174* [170 F.3d 897 (9th Cir. 1999)], for instance, an injunction was upheld to prevent a union from picketing a site where nonunionized contractors loaded goods onto trains. Because no collective bargaining agreement or organizing effort was at stake, there was no "labor dispute" as defined by the Norris-LaGuardia Act.

Although federal law usually preempts state law in the labor arena, the states do have a limited role in protecting their own legitimate interests. They can pass certain labor laws that will not be federally preempted: For instance, there is a legitimate state interest in preventing violence, so states can regulate how and when picketing can be done. States can legislate in areas such as minimum wages, child labor, and employment discrimination.

States can also cope with issues that are only peripheral to the main purposes of the LMRA. This category includes defamation suits brought by employers against unions, suits dealing with continuation of welfare benefits during strikes, and internal union affairs. States are also allowed to legislate in the area of union security, for instance by passing right-to-work laws forbidding union shops and agency shops. [*See* § 30.06]

[B]   NLRA Section 7

The National Labor Relations Act of 1935 (NLRA), also known as the Wagner Act, is one of the bedrock federal labor statutes. The NLRA establishes the National Labor Relations Board (NLRB) as a kind of referee between management and unionized labor.

Section 7 of the NLRA says that employees have the right to engage in "protected concerted activities." In other words, they can act together to form a union, join a union, present grievances, bargain collectively, go on strike, and picket peacefully.

> **Tip:** Once a union is certified, the employer is justified in doing away with its entire benefit package and negotiating "from scratch" with the union, even if the result is a less generous benefit package that the union agreed to in exchange for concessions in other areas. The employer can legitimately explain this phenomenon to workers considering whether or not to vote for the union.

[C] Unfair Labor Practices

Either a union or an employer can be guilty of an "unfair labor practice" as defined by the NLRA and the LMRA. The NLRB has the power to issue a "cease and desist" order if it deems that an unfair practice has occurred. The NLRB also has powers to order positive actions, such as ordering an employer to bargain with a union.

NLRA § 8 defines unfair labor practices to include:

- Refusal to engage in collective bargaining—whether the recalcitrant party is management or union;
- Employer domination of a union;
- Retaliation against employees for filing charges with the NLRB or testifying before the agency;
- Discrimination against employees based on either union activities or refusal to join a union. In this context, discrimination includes firing, refusal to hire, refusal to reinstate, demotion, discrimination in compensation, discrimination in work assignments. etc. However, if a union security clause is in place, employees can be required to pay union dues or the equivalent of dues, but they cannot be required to actually join the union;
- Deliberately inefficient work practices that require the employment of excessive numbers of workers ("featherbedding");
- Certain practices occurring during strikes or picketing.

The LMRA penalizes unfair labor practices by unions, including:

- Restraining or coercing employees when they exercise their right to bargain collectively, choose a representative, or vote against unionization;
- Causing an employer to discriminate against any employee;
- Refusing to participate in collective bargaining, once the union becomes the authorized bargaining representative for the employees;
- Engaging in strikes or concerted activity for the purpose of boycotting one employer, forcing another employer to recognize an uncertified union, forcing any employer to recognize a particular union when a different union is actually the

authorized bargaining representative, or when a determination of jurisdiction still has to be made;

- Requiring union members in a union shop to pay excessive initiation fees or excessive dues;
- Featherbedding.

It is not an unfair labor practice for an employer to put work rules in the employee handbook against abusive and threatening language and limiting solicitations and distributions within the workplace; pro-union employees can make their point of view known without threatening their opponents, so the rules do not interfere with protected collective activity. [*Adtranz ABB Daimler-Benz Transp. v. NLRB*, 253 F.3d 19 (D.C. Cir. 2001)]

[D] LMRA Preemption

Many cases turn on whether § 301 of the Labor-Management Relations Act (LMRA) should be applied. This section gives federal District Courts jurisdiction over suits for violations of a collective bargaining agreement, as well as suits by one union against another. This section is often applied to bring labor questions into the federal courts—and keep them out of state courts when issues such as wrongful termination and unfair employee discipline are raised.

The most important issue in deciding whether LMRA preemption exists is the relationship between the controversy and the collective bargaining agreement. State laws are preempted whenever it is necessary to interpret the CBA. However, the Supreme Court decided in 1994 that a mere need to refer to the CBA is not enough to justify preemption. The underlying dispute must really involve searching out the meaning of the terms of the contract. [*Lividas v. Bradshaw*, 512 U.S. 107 (1994)]

If the CBA includes a contractual grievance or arbitration provision (and most do), then potential plaintiffs have to exhaust their remedies (complete the entire process) before bringing suit under § 301. Plaintiffs are entitled to demand jury trials in LMRA § 301 cases. [*Nicely v. USX*, 709 F. Supp. 646 (W.D. Pa. 1989)]

In 1996, two Circuits found that state laws that penalize employers for late payment of wages are preempted by LMRA § 301. In one case, this conclusion was reached because the CBA had to be interpreted, in the other because the state law was treated as an "end run" around the limitations imposed by the LMRA. [*Antol v. Esposito*, 100 F.3d 1111 (3d Cir. 1996); *Atchely v. Heritage Cable Vision Ass'n*, 101 F.3d 495 (7th Cir. 1996)]

Other cases in which preemption was found include:

- Failure to rehire, negligent and intentional infliction of emotional distress (because deciding the case required interpretation of the CBA's seniority provisions);
- A claim that a worker was denied reinstatement after a period of disability in retaliation for filing a Worker's Compensation claim, because the issue here

was the management's exclusive right to hire and fire under the CBA "management rights" clause;

- Alleged failure to promote because of racial discrimination and union activity, because the CBA covers promotion, seniority, and training. [*Weisbart v. Hawaiian Tug & Barge Corp.*, 1994 U.S. App. LEXIS 13061 (9th Cir. May 31, 1994); *Martin v. Shaw's Supermarkets, Inc.*, 105 F.3d 40 (1st Cir. 1997); *Reece v. Houston Lighting and Power Co.*, 79 F.3d 485 (5th Cir. 1996)]

However, preemption was not found in these situations, on the grounds that the court did not have to interpret the CBA to decide the case:

- Retaliatory discharge;
- Discharge of an employee for reasons violating public policy;
- False imprisonment (unreasonable detention of an employee by a security guard);
- Claims about oral contracts other than the CBA (for instance, a verbal promise of lifetime employment) or implied contracts;
- Claims under state antidiscrimination laws on issues that are not normally bargained away during contract negotiations.

Although LMRA § 301 says that labor unions can "sue and be sued" in federal courts, that provision does not automatically provide federal jurisdiction whenever a union wants to sue in federal court. The union must abide by the normal rules of civil procedure, so there must be diversity jurisdiction (the parties are citizens of different states and the alleged damages exceed a required minimum amount) or a federal question must be involved. [*K.V. Mart Co. v. United Food & Commercial Workers*, 173 F.3d 1221 (9th Cir. 1999)]

As to what constitutes a federal question, *Textron v. UAAIW* [523 U.S. 653 (1998)] holds that an allegation of a CBA violation by an employer presents a federal question. However, a charge that the employer fraudulently induced the union to enter into a contract, and got a no-strike pledge, by promising not to subcontract out work did not come under LMRA § 301, and did not present a federal question.

The LMRA itself can be preempted by other statutes. In a Sixth Circuit case, employees and a union sued under LMRA § 301 to recover nonguaranteed pension benefits. The court ruled that ERISA, not the LMRA, prevailed, because of 1987 amendments to ERISA that make the employer liable to the PBGC for benefits that are unfunded at the time a plan terminates. [*United Steelworkers of Am. v. United Eng'g Inc.*, 52 F.3d 1386 (6th Cir. 1995)]

§ 30.03   EMPLOYEE STATUS

[A]   Definition of Employee

The NLRA defines the rights of "employees," so an important basic question is who fits into this category. Independent contractors are not employees, but common-law employees under the employer's control in terms of hiring, firing, work methods and results, provision of tools and materials, and employee discipline, are also employees for NLRA purposes.

Employee status is maintained during a temporary layoff, if the worker reasonably expects to be recalled in the future. A sick or injured worker continues to be an employee either until he or she takes another permanent full-time job, or is permanently unable to return to work for physical reasons.

In some contexts, retirees will not be considered employees once they are off the company's active payroll and have no right to be rehired or any reasonable expectation of being rehired.

[B] Part-Time and Temporary Workers

Temporary or casual workers will probably not be considered employees. Part-time workers are considered employees, although sometimes it is inappropriate to put them in a bargaining unit with full-timers, if their interests are adverse. In August 2000, the NLRB ruled that temporary workers can be included in the same collective bargaining unit as permanent employees, as long as the characteristics of the job are similar. [*M.B. Sturgis Inc.*, 331 N.L.R.B. 173 (Aug. 25, 2000) (<http://www.nlrb.gov/slip331.html>)]

This reverses earlier NLRB decisions saying that temporary workers could be organized in a bargaining unit with permanent workers only if neither the "supplier employer" (the temp agency or other company that supplied the workers) nor the "user employer" (the place where the work was actually performed) objected. As you can imagine, one or both usually did object!

The NLRB ruled that the union has the right to show that the two companies are really joint employers of the workers, because they both determine the terms and conditions of employment. However, the user employer can rebut the union's contention by showing that the supplier employer maintains the real control over the workers.

Late in 2001, the NLRB ruled that temporary warehouse workers supplied by staffing firms and jointly employed by the staffing company and Tree of Life fit the definition of "drivers and warehousemen," so it was an unfair labor practice for the company not to apply the CBA's terms on working conditions to the temporary workers. [*Tree of Life Inc.*, 336 N.L.R.B. 77 (Oct. 1, 2001)]

> **Tip:** The law firm Nixon Peabody LLP suggests that user employers avoid giving referred employees the same uniforms, badges, or ID cards as their permanent work force. They should not be given copies of the policy manual or handbook. The supplier employer rather than the user employer should be responsible for disciplining the referred employees. [Nixon Peabody LLP, Employment Law Alert Issue 71 (January 2001)]

[C] Supervisors

The text of the NLRA [29 U.S.C. § 152] says that "supervisors" such as fore-men and forewomen are not "employees," for the common-sense reason that su-pervisors promote management interests and therefore do not fit in well with rank-and-file workers, who have different and often opposing interests.

A supervisor is someone who has a formal job title indicating supervisory status, has been held out as a supervisor by management, or is perceived as a su-pervisor by rank-and-file workers. A supervisor makes independent, individual judgments, can reward or discipline employees (up to and including firing them) and has authority to adjust employee grievances.

To be a supervisor, someone must have supervisory authority on a consistent basis (whether or not it is exercised). Sporadic or limited authority, such as power to take over in an emergency, doesn't make a rank-and-file worker into a supervisor. Courts have expanded the statutory definition, so that managers are not considered employees either, because of their discretion and ability to set corporate policy.

In May 1997, the First Circuit held that a TV station's technical directors were not supervisors, and therefore should have been included in the bargaining unit. [*Telemundo de Puerto Rico v. NLRB*, 113 F.3d 270 (1st Cir. 1997)] But in late 2001, the Eighth Circuit ruled that TV producers and assignment editors are not supervisors. Although they assign work to other journalists, they do not use independent judgment, either because the assignment involves mechanical application of routine or because decisions are made collectively. [*Multimedia KSDK Inc. v. NLRB*, 285 F.3d 759 (8th Cir. 2001)]

In mid-2001, the Supreme Court resolved a conflict about the status of Registered Nurses in nursing homes. Because the RNs direct the activities of non-RN staff, they are supervisors and cannot be organized in the same unit as the other staffers. [*NLRB v. Kentucky River Community Care Inc.*, 121 S. Ct. 1861 (2001)]

In the case of *Dreyer's Grand Ice Cream, Inc. v. NLRB* [140 F.3d 684 (7th Cir. 1998)], two pro-union workers held the post of "super-coordinator." They were in charge of several work teams, including interviewing job applicants, recommending hiring and pay raises, and disciplining team members. The super-coordinator job was eliminated after a year, and the two employees kept their increased salaries but were not promoted to the newly created post of "facilitator."

There was an unsuccessful attempt to unionize the workplace, and the two former super-coordinators were fired. The NLRB ordered reinstatement. Dreyer's sought review on the grounds that even after the super-coordinator positions were eliminated, the two workers were supervisors who did not belong in the bargaining unit. However, the Seventh Circuit agreed with the NLRB, because the two did not continue to exercise authority after they had been demoted.

The NLRB said that "shift supervisors" in a college security department were not really supervisors, but the Second Circuit disagreed. There was evidence that the shift supervisors assigned work to their co-workers and directed and disciplined them. [*NLRB v. Quinnipiac College*, 256 F.3d 68 (2d Cir. 2001)]

[D] Union Organizers

A paid union organizer can qualify as a protected "employee" under the NLRA. The fact that he or she is paid a salary by the union does not deprive him or her of the protection of federal labor law. This concept has been extended to treat a volunteer union organizer who is not paid by the union as an employee. [*NLRB v. Town & Country Electric Inc.*, 516 U.S. 85 (1995); *NLRB v. Fluor Daniel*, 102 F.3d 818 (6th Cir. 1996)]

An employer is allowed to maintain a policy against moonlighting (refusal to employ anyone who holds another job)—as long as the policy is nondiscriminatory and is applied uniformly. If the employer has a policy of this type, it is not unlawful discrimination to refuse to hire someone who also works as a paid union organizer. However, the union can win in this situation by showing that the policy really was not neutral, and that the company refused to hire union organizers but tolerated other forms of moonlighting. [*Architectural Glass and Metal Co. v. NLRB*, 107 F.3d 426 (6th Cir. 1997); *H.B. Zachry Co. v. NLRB*, 886 F.2d 70 (4th Cir. 1989)]

If the NLRB charges that employees were fired for pro-union activity, and not for a legitimate reason (such as poor work performance or the employer's financial need to reduce the payroll) the NLRB has the duty of proving the anti-union motivation. It is not up to the employer to prove legitimate reasons for the discharge. [*Schaeff Inc. v. NLRB*, 113 F.3d 264 (D.C. Cir. 1997)]

On another status issue, the NLRB ruled in January 2000 that a full-time paid union organizer who was denied employment as an electrician because of his admitted intention to organize the workplace was entitled to back pay for the period of time he was unable to work at that job. Furthermore, his union salary should not be subtracted from the back pay award because the NLRB treated it as "secondary employment," not interim earnings that would offset the award. [*Ferguson Elec. Co.*, 330 N.L.R.B. 75 (Jan. 19. 2000)]

§ 30.04   ELECTIONS, CERTIFICATION, AND RECOGNITION

[A]   Generally

To gain "certification," and thereby become the bargaining agent for the employees (whom the employer must deal with), a union has to win an election supervised by the NLRB. There is a one-year period after the certification election during which no rival union is allowed to seek certification.

A union organizing campaign begins with a petition for certification. Typically, the petition is filed by the union or by an individual employee who is a union supporter. Most organizing work is done by pro-union employees, because employers can and usually do bar non-employees from soliciting on business premises during working hours. [*But see* § 30.04[H]], below, for exceptions to this rule] If there are two or more unions trying to organize the same workplace, the employer is allowed to express a preference for one over the other.

A certification petition is valid only if at least 30% of the employees in the bargaining unit indicate their interest. Acceptable indications of interest are:

- Authorization cards;
- Union membership cards;
- Applications for membership;
- Records of union dues;
- Employee signatures on certification petitions.

It is a serious unfair labor practice for employers to retaliate against workers because of their union activism, so it is important to document good business reasons for any disciplinary action taken against less-than-optimal workers who also happen to be union activists.

[B]   Consent Elections

The NLRB is responsible for determining the validity of the representation petition. If the employer does not oppose holding the election, the election is a consent election. The employer and union sign a contract permitting an election. The NLRB will probably have to accept the consent agreement's definition of the appropriate bargaining unit, unless it violates the law (for instance, by including guards in a mixed bargaining unit).

Within seven days of the time that the appropriate NLRB Regional Director approves a consent agreement, the employer has a duty to submit the "Excelsior List" to the Regional Director. This is a list of the names and addresses of every worker eligible to vote in the consent election. The Regional Director distributes the list to all interested parties. [The name comes from the NLRB case of *Excelsior Underwear Inc.,* 156 N.L.R.B. 271 (1986).]

Tip: It is an unfair labor practice for an employer to recognize a union that does not represent the majority of workers. So the employer has a duty to at least examine the authorization cards before agreeing to a consent election. But if an NLRB hearing is anticipated, it is better not to examine the cards. Disciplinary actions will be less vulnerable to challenge if the employer did not know which employees expressed pro-union sentiments, and therefore could not have retaliated against them on this basis.

Also see *Consolidated Diesel v. NLRB* [263 F.3d 345 (4th Cir. 2001)], holding that it was improper for an employer to investigate charges that antiunion workers felt harassed by pro-union workers "talking up" the union. The Fourth Circuit's interpretation is that the employer interfered with the right to organize, because it is impossible to maintain an organization campaign without saying anything that could be potentially offensive to anyone.

[C] NLRB Hearings

If the employer objects, but the NLRB finds that there is reasonable cause to believe that the union might be an appropriate representative for the employees, the NLRB holds a nonadversary hearing to determine if there is a question of representation. (Employers who are dissatisfied with the Regional Director's decision can appeal to the central NLRB for review.) This type of hearing cannot be used to raise claims of unfair labor practices by either side.

In most instances, the hearing will result in setting a date for a secret ballot election under NLRB supervision. The NLRB will then certify the result: whether or not the union has secured a majority vote.

A union will be certified as bargaining representative for the unit if it wins the votes of a majority of the voters (not a majority of those eligible to vote). But the election will not be valid unless a "representative number" of eligible employees actually voted. There is no bright-line test for whether the number of voters was representative. Many factors, such as the voter turnout, adequacy of the employees' notice of the election and opportunity to vote, and the presence or absence of unfair practices by the employer, are considered to see if there was a high enough turnout.

[D] Election Procedure

Usually, the election will be held at the workplace, because that is accessible to all employees. However, if there is good cause shown for holding an election somewhere else, or for allowing voting by mail, the NLRB will supervise the out-of-plant election. Elections are held by secret ballot. The voters enter the voting location, have their employee status checked, and then mark their ballots in a closed booth where their selections are not visible. The ballots are collected for later tallying.

According to *San Diego Gas & Electric* [325 N.L.R.B. 218 (1998)], voting by mail should be allowed not only in the tense situation of an election during a strike or picketing, but also whenever potential voters would have to travel a significant distance to the polls and are so scattered that simply relocating the polling place would not be effective. Another indicator for mail balloting is a workforce with varying schedules, so that they cannot be assembled in one place at a particular time.

Before a certification or deauthorization election, the employer must post an election notice in a conspicious place in the workplace. The notice must be up for at least three full working days before 12:01 A.M. of the day scheduled for the election. Failure to post the notice can result in the election results being set aside. The notice must give the date, time, and place of the election, and must show a sample ballot so employees will know how to mark it to indicate their choice.

If there are objections to the eligibility of certain voters, or to the mechanics of the election, either the employer or union can file an objection with the NLRB within seven days of the ballot tally. There is no absolute right to get a hearing on the validity of the election: The NLRB Regional Director decides when one is needed.

If an employer relies on the results of an invalid election to change policies within the workplace, the Ninth Circuit said that the appropriate remedy is to hold a new election. [*Gardner Mechanical Servs. v. NLRB*, 89 F.3d 586 (9th Cir. 1996)] A bargaining order is improper unless there is proof that it would be impossible to hold a valid election.

[E] Voter Eligibility

The simple answer is that all "employees" in the "bargaining unit" are entitled to vote in a representation election. However, it can be hard to determine the appropriate bargaining unit, and there are some questions about who retains employee status.

A worker who has taken a voluntary leave of absence is entitled to vote unless the relationship with the employer has been severed. If the employee on leave retains seniority and is still in the employer's pension and benefit plans, he or she is probably an eligible voter. Employees on sick leave or maternity leave are entitled to vote, unless they have been formally or constructively terminated from employment.

For laid-off workers, the question is whether they have a reasonable expectation of recall (determined as of the date of the election, not the date of the NLRB pre-election hearing). Laid-off workers with no such reasonable expectation cannot vote in an election about whether the union from the old plant can continue to represent workers after the employer's move to a smaller, more automated plant. [*Hughes Christensen Inc. v. NLRB*, 101 F.3d 28 (5th Cir. 1996)]

A person who was lawfully fired before the date of the election is not eligible to vote, but someone who is unlawfully discharged for union activity retains employee status, and therefore is entitled to vote.

Economic strikers [*see* § 30.09[B] for characterization of strikes] who have not been replaced as to the date of the election are entitled to vote. During the 12 months after the beginning of an economic strike, economic strikers are still entitled to vote if they have been replaced—even if they are not entitled to immediate reinstatement after the strike ends. Employees who are on the preferential reinstatement list are also entitled to vote. But if the election is held more than 12 months after the beginning of a strike, replaced economic strikers are not entitled to vote, even if they still have a reasonable expectation of recall.

Replacement workers hired during an economic strike are entitled to vote in the election, but only if they were employed before the eligibility cutoff date for the election. Unlike economic strikers, unfair labor practice strikers are always eligible to vote in representation elections, but their replacements are never entitled to vote.

Undocumented aliens are employees entitled to vote in representation elections, even if their status has been challenged under the IRCA [*NLRB v. Kolkka*, 170 F.3d 937 (9th Cir. 1999)], but they cannot be awarded back pay when they are laid off, even unlawfully. [*Hoffman Plastics Compounds, Inc. v. NLRB*, 00-1595 (Sup. Ct. March 27, 2002)]

[F]   Electioneering and Communications

During a certification campaign, both employer and union are entitled to communicate their viewpoints to employees. The employer is considered a "person" entitled to exercise free speech rights, subject to limitations of accuracy and fairness. If the employer overreaches, the election results will be set aside, and the employer will have to go through the whole process again, perhaps with more employee sympathy for the union. In egregious cases, the employer might have to answer charges of an unfair labor practice.

The "critical period" is the time between the filing of a representation petition and the election itself. (For a runoff or rerun election, the critical period begins at the first election, and even conduct occurring before the certification petition was filed might be considered relevant as to the fairness of the election.) The NLRB will observe the conduct of both sides, and has the power to invalidate elections, even if the misconduct is not serious enough to constitute an unfair labor practice. The employer is held responsible for the conduct of its agents, including its lawyers and labor relations consultants.

Tip: An employer can avoid liability for an inappropriate statement by an agent if it repudiates the statement promptly, admitting that it was out of line, restating it in proper form, and giving at least as much publicity to the retraction as to the original communication.

Certification elections are supposed to provide "laboratory conditions" (i.e., pure and untainted) for workplace democracy. Employers are not allowed to conduct pre-election polls, or even ask employees their opinions about unionization, if the inquiry is too close to the time of the election. However, it is accepted labor law that employers can call a meeting of workers on company time for management to assert its arguments against unionization. If the union is permitted to solicit employees during meals and other breaks, the employer can call a mass meeting without giving the union equal time to reply.

During the 24-hour period just before the election, neither management nor union is allowed to make speeches to massed employees on company time. If the employer does this, it is not an unfair labor practice, but it could lead to invalidation of the election. The employer is allowed to distribute printed materials to workers during this time. The employer can also conduct antiunion meetings away from the workplace during the 24-hour period, as long as attendance is voluntary and employees choose to come in on their own time.

These are examples that have been found to constitute unfair labor practices by the employer:

- Announcing benefits on election day;
- Explicitly promising benefits if the union loses;
- Threatening to withhold benefits if the union wins;
- Using a supervisor (even a low-level one) as an election observer [*Family Serv. Agency, San Francisco*, 331 N.L.R.B. 103 (July 24, 2000)];
- Announcing new benefits during the critical period to show that the employer offers a better deal than the union—unless the benefits were decided before the representation petition was filed, or there is economic justification for providing them at that time. The employer can increase the amount of information available about benefits [*Beverly Enters. Inc. v. NLRB*, 139 F.3D 135 (2d Cir. 1998)], even though actually increasing benefits before the election would be unacceptable;
- Delivering paychecks at the voting site for a decertification election, rather than at the workplace [*United Cerebral Palsy Ass'n of Niagara County*, 327 N.L.R.B. 14 (1998)] The NLRB requires a legitimate business reason for changing the procedure for delivering paychecks within 24 hours of an election. Usually, a higher voter turnout is good—but in a decertification election, increased turnout benefits the employer rather than the union;
- Telling employees that their yearly merit raises would end if the company unionized. [*LaSalle Ambulance, Inc.*, 327 N.L.R.B. 18 (1998)] It would have been acceptable to state that the yearly raises were a term of condition of employment that could not be altered without bargaining, not a new issue that could not be implemented without bargaining;
- Telling employees that unless they returned to work the next day without a union contract, the business would be closed down, and its equipment would be leased, was a threat (an unfair labor practice) and not just a permissible prediction of future events. It was a threat because it referred to events wholly within the employer's control [*NLRB v. Gerig's Dump Trucking Inc.*, 137 F.3d 936 (7th Cir. 1998)];
- A company-wide increase in employer contributions to the 401(k) plan was announced three days before an election to the employees participating in the election; the good news was not given to employees in the company's other units until later [*Waste Management of Palm Beach*, 329 N.L.R.B. 20 (2000)];
- Moving a security camera to videotape employees handing out union literature during the period before a representation election. [*Robert Orr-Sysco Food Servs.*, 334 N.L.R.B. 122 (2001); *National Steel & Shipbuilding Co. v. NLRB*, 156 F.3d 1268 (D.C. Cir. 1998) holds that the employer's videotaping union rallies outside the plant interferes with protected activities, unless the employer can provide objective justification for the surveillance. However, *Metropolitan*

Regional Council, United Brotherhood of Carpenters & Joiners, 335 N.L.R.B. 67 (Aug. 21, 2001) says that it is also an unfair labor practice for a union to photograph and videotape employees of a nonunion contractor as they crossed a picket line.]

It has been deemed to be an unfair labor practice by the union promising to throw "the biggest party in Texas" if the union won. [*Trencor, Inc. v. NLRB*, 110 F.3d 268 (5th Cir. 1997)] In the case of *Overnite Transportation Co. v. NLRB* [140 F.3d 259 (D.C. Cir. 1998)], pro-union employees photographed and videotaped other employees. The court refused to overturn the union's election victory because the employees were not acting as union agents, and they did not create an atmosphere of fear and reprisal that would prevent a fair election.

However, these have been held not to be improper practices by the employer:

- Delaying pay raises until after the election, as long as timing is the only issue—raises will be paid no matter who wins the election;
- Distributing fact-based (not coercive or threatening) handbills during an organizing drive, saying that unionization would lead to long, bitter negotiations and possibly an ugly strike [*General Elec. Co.*, 323 N.L.R.B. 91 (2000)];
- Announcing two new floating holidays the day before the election. The election was nevertheless valid because the holidays affected thousands of employees throughout the employer's parent company. The timing of the announcement was logical within the company's fiscal year; it was just a coincidence that it was right before the election. [*Network Ambulance Servs. Inc.*, 329 N.L.R.B. 13 (1999)]

The NLRB did not abuse its discretion by extending the certification year for an additional six months, and by ordering the employer to reinstate its bargaining proposals, where the employer withdrew all its proposals just before the certification year ended. [*NLRB v. Beverly Health & Rehab Servs. Inc.*, 187 F.3d 769 (8th Cir. 1999)]

In *Waldinger Corp. v. NLRB* [262 F.3d 1213 (11th Cir. 2001)], a supervisor advocated the union at a meeting at which many authorization cards were signed. The Eleventh Circuit held that the supervisor's actions did not taint the cards, and therefore the employer was not justified in withdrawing recognition of the union. Although there is a legal concept of "supervisory taint," it is present only if the supervisor gives a false impression that the employer favors the union, or that employees are at risk of coercion or retaliation.

[G] Buttons and Insignia

The right to free speech extends to employees in the workplace to the extent that workers must be allowed to wear union buttons. They must be allowed to wear union buttons to the poll, even though blatant electioneering like this would not be allowed in a general election.

Wearing union insignia is protected by NLRA § 7, and interfering with this right violates § 8(a)(1), unless the union materials cause a real safety hazard, or there is a real risk of violence between union supporters and opponents. The mere possibility of violence is not enough.

There is a partial exception. Employees who work with the public, and who are required to wear a uniform, can be forbidden to wear all kinds of jewelry, including union buttons. They can be required to wear the standard uniform, not a union T-shirt. But the employer must be careful to communicate the uniform policy, and to enforce it across the board, not just against union insignia.

An employer can permissibly forbid employees to display any decals not issued by the employer on their hard hats. According to the Fourth Circuit, the ban served a legitimate function. [*Eastern Omni Constructors Inc. v. NLRB*, 170 F.3d 418 (4th Cir. 1999)] The employer-issued decals promoted workplace safety by identifying workers certified to use particular pieces of equipment. The employees' free expression was not stifled because they could display union insignia on other articles of clothing.

[H]   Access by Non-Employees

In most instances, a workplace is private property, not a public space. Therefore, union organizers do not automatically have a right to leaflet or distribute literature if this is contrary to the wishes of the employer or other owner of the property.

An exception might occur in a "company town" situation, where in effect all property is owned by the employer, so there is no public space where the union can distribute literature. [*See, e.g., Lechmere v. NLRB*, 502 U.S. 527 (1991)] Another exception might be a place that is so remote geographically that the union has no reasonable means of communicating with employees outside the workplace.

The Ninth Circuit held that it was an unfair labor practice for a store to have union representatives arrested for picketing and handbilling in the store's private parking lot. [*NLRB v. Calkins*, 187 F.3d 1080 (9th Cir. 1999)] The court refused to apply *Lechmere* on the grounds that the case was decided under Connecticut law, which allows union organizers to be excluded from private property as trespassers. California law offers broader free-speech protection and allows union representatives to picket and distribute literature on private property.

The Tenth Circuit said it was legitimate for the City of Denver to bar the musicians' union from picketing and leafleting on the pedestrian walkway of the city-owned art center. The walkway was not a public forum and had no history of being used for public expressive activities. [*Hawkins v. Denver*, 170 F.3d 1281 (10th Cir. 1999)] However, in 2001 the Ninth Circuit said that a sidewalk built on private property, to replace the public sidewalk that was demolished when the street was widened, is still a public forum for First Amendment purposes, giving the union the right to picket there. [*Venetian Casino Resort LLC v. Local Joint Executive Bd. of Las Vegas*, 257 F.3d 937 (9th Cir. 2001)]

The Third Circuit has found that the NLRA is not violated when an employer denies access to its property to union representatives who want to distribute handbills accusing the employer of using underpaid nonunion labor. In this context, the employer's property rights clearly prevail over the union's free speech right—especially because general information aimed at the public, not an actual certification election, was involved. [*Metropolitan Dist. Council of Phila. v. NLRB*, 68 F.3d 71 (3rd Cir. 1995)] The employer also has a right to control the use of plant bulletin boards and to forbid the posting of union materials on those boards. [*Guardian Indus. Corp. v. NLRB*, 49 F.3d 317 (7th Cir. 1995)]

Can a business located in a shopping mall forbid the distribution of union literature in that mall? The Eighth Circuit says that a business that is just a tenant (and therefore does not have exclusive rights to the corridor outside its business location) cannot forbid union handbilling. But the Sixth Circuit says that a mall owner can ban solicitation by union representatives who are not employed at the mall, even if other kinds of solicitation (e.g., for charity) are allowed. [*O'Neil's Markets v. United Food & Commercial Workers*, 95 F.3d 733 (8th Cir. 1996); *Cleveland Real Estate Partners v. NLRB*, 95 F.3d 457 (6th Cir. 1996); *Riesbeck Food Markets Inc. v. NLRB*, 91 F.3d 132 (4th Cir. 1996)]

The NLRB says that a mall can demand that it be given advance notice of the names of people who propose to give out union handbills, but once this is done, the mall cannot forbid handbillers to refer to mall tenants by name. That strikes a balance between permitting free speech but allowing malls to exclude people who had behaved improperly in the past. [*Glendale Assocs.*, 335 N.L.R.B. 8 (Aug. 23, 2001)]

§ 30.05   THE APPROPRIATE BARGAINING UNIT

Even after winning an election, a union cannot be certified unless it is organized as the appropriate bargaining unit for the enterprise. NLRA § 9(b) gives the NLRB power to determine the appropriate bargaining unit. The basic standard is whether there is a community of interest among the unit members, not just employees in general (who can be expected to want higher wages and better benefits). Neither employer nor union can tell in advance what will be considered the appropriate unit, or how large the unit will be.

The appropriateness of a bargaining unit depends on the duties, skills, and working conditions of the employees who are supposed to have common interests. If there are competing proposed bargaining units for the same company, their relative popularity with employees is highly significant.

A union can be organized by employer, craft, or plan, or a subdivision of one of these categories. A union decision to organize as a craft unit is legally protected. The NLRB does not have the power to decide that a different unit would be more appropriate.

Employees and supervisors cannot be in the same bargaining unit. In fact, in many instances, supervisors cannot unionize at all, because they are considered a part of management. As a general rule, professionals and nonprofessionals cannot be included in a unit, but this rule can be waived if a majority of the professional employees vote to be included. (The nonprofessionals do not get veto power over inclusion of professionals.)

Determination of professional status does not depend entirely on job title. The factual determination is whether the work is predominantly intellectual, is not routine, requires discretion and independent judgment, mandates specialized knowledge, and cannot be standardized as to time. Professionals can still be unionized, but they must consent to inclusion in a nonprofessional bargaining unit instead of having their own.

If plant guards are unionized, they must have their own bargaining unit. They cannot be organized with other employees, because the employer would not feel very secure during a strike if several guards were union activists—much less if one of them was the shop steward!

§ 30.06   UNION SECURITY

[A]   NLRA Prohibitions

Closed shops (where only union members can be hired) are illegal. The NLRA also forbids "preferential hiring" situations under which the employer is obligated to hire only union members unless the union is unable to fill all vacancies with qualified workers.

However, the LMRA authorizes "union shops," where all current employees must be union members, and new hires can be required to join the union after hiring (within seven days in the construction industry, within 30 days in other industries), and "agency shops," where payment of initiation fees and union dues is mandatory, but actual membership is optional. "Union security" measures are available to a union that is the bona fide bargaining representative of the employees in the bargaining unit and there has not been a deauthorization election certified in the year preceding the effective date of the union security agreement.

It is not a breach of a union's duty of fair representation for it to enter into a CBA that contains a union security clause that echoes the wording of NLRA § 8(3)(a). [*Marquez v. Screen Actors Guild*, 525 U.S. 33 (1998)] The plaintiff claimed that she should have been notified of her right not to join the union and to pay the union only for its representational activities.

If the union wants "automatic dues checkoff" (deduction of dues from the paycheck, so the union doesn't have to bill the member), it must have its members provide a written assignment lasting until the contract expires, or for one year, whichever comes first.

Under the NLRA [29 U.S.C. § 169], employees who have a religious objection to unionization cannot be forced to join or support a union—even if the workplace is subject to a union security measure. However, to prevent financial windfalls, the employee can be required to contribute the equivalent of the initiation fee to a nonreligious charity of the employee's choice.

Tip: It's OK for the union to require independent corroboration from a reliable third party (e.g., the employee's pastor) when an employee asserts a religious objection to paying the dues; it doesn't violate the union's duty of reasonable accommodation of religious needs. [*Bashouse v. Local Union 2209*, 70 L.W. 1236 (N.D. Ind. Oct. 2, 2001)]

Communications Workers of America v. Beck [487 U.S. 735 (1988)] says that employees who do not want to join a union, but who are subject to a union security clause in the CBA, can be charged fees that can be traced back to collective bargaining, contract administration, and pursuing grievances. But they can prevent the union from using their money for political or other "nonrepresentational purposes."

A union can include organizing expenses as an element in the agency fees charged to nonmembers. The NLRB allows this [*see United Food & Commercial Workers*, 329 N.L.R.B. 69 (Sept. 30, 1999)] because of the positive effect of unionization on a company's wage scales, benefiting workers who do not join.

President Bush's Executive Order 13201 [66 Fed. Reg. 11,219 (Feb. 22, 2001)] requires federal contractors to post a "Beck notice" informing employees of their right to avoid joining a union, and their right to object to use of funds for nonrepresentational purposes—and that they can seek a refund of funds used in this way over their objections. *But see UAW-Labor Employment & Training Co. v. Chao* [70 L.W. 1410 (D.D.C. Jan. 2, 2002)], holding that Executive Order 13201 is invalid because it is preempted by the National Labor Relations Act. [This case is discussed in Steven Greenhouse, *Judge Voids a Union Rule Issued by Bush*, New York Times, Jan. 8, 2002, at p. A14]

The converse of union security is a state "right to work" law that says that unwilling employees cannot be compelled to join unions or pay dues. Alabama, Arizona, Arkansas, Georgia, Louisiana, Mississippi, Nebraska, Nevada, North Dakota, South Carolina, Texas, Utah, and Virginia have adopted such laws.

[B] Hiring Halls

Under a union security option, the employer decides who to hire, but the union may be able to get hirees to join or pay dues. A hiring hall works differently. It is a mechanism under which the union selects workers and sends them to the employer, based on the employer's requisition (for six plasterers and two electricians, for example). The union decides which union or nonunion workers will be referred for the job.

An exclusive hiring hall is a relationship under which the employer gets all its workers through union referrals. This is not considered a union security arrangement, so it is legal in the right-to-work states. A nonexclusive hiring hall makes union referral only one of the ways in which the employer can find new workers.

The NLRA provides that it is unlawful for a union to give preference to union members over equally qualified nonmembers in the operation of a nonexclusive hiring hall. The operation and structure of a hiring hall is a mandatory bargaining subject.

§ 30.07   THE COLLECTIVE BARGAINING PROCESS

[A]   Basic Issues

Under the NLRA, the purpose of certifying a union is to provide an ongoing process of collective bargaining between employer and union on important work-related issues, leading to the adoption of a union contract, or Collective Bargaining Agreement (CBA). Even after a CBA is in place, it is still necessary to bargain on "mandatory" issues, and allowable to bargain on "permissive" issues. [*See* 29 U.S.C. § 158(a)(5)] There are some subjects on which it is illegal to bargain. For instance, it is illegal to implement a closed shop, even if both employer and union are willing.

Mandatory bargaining subjects include:

- Drug testing;
- Dues checkoff (the employer's practice of deducting union dues from paychecks, then forwarding these amounts to the union);
- Work rules;
- Bans on moonlighting by employees;
- Transfers of work out of the bargaining unit;
- Contracting out work done by employees in the bargaining unit (contracting out work done by nonunionized employees is not a mandatory subject of bargaining);
- Bonuses;
- Medical insurance;
- Clauses that forbid strikes and lockouts.

Mandatory bargaining subjects are those that materially or significantly affect the terms or conditions of employment. Issues that have a remote or incidental effect on the work environment are permissible subjects of bargaining.

Where bargaining is required, the employer has a duty to meet with the union at reasonable times to confer over the terms and conditions of employment (such as wages and hours). Refusal to bargain is an unfair labor practice. On the other hand, certain issues are established as managerial prerogatives that can be decided unilaterally, without bargaining:

- Complete termination of operations;
- Sale of an entire business;

- A partial closing that has business motivations, and is not the result of antiunion animus;
- Relocation of bargaining-unit work that is motivated by a basic change in the nature of the employer's operations, where the work at the new location is significantly different from the work at the old one.

The basic rule is that bargaining is required if a decision is undertaken to save labor costs, but not if the employer takes on a program of modernization or environmental compliance that costs more than the potential savings on labor costs. Even if the employer has the right to make a decision without union involvement, it has an obligation to engage in "effects bargaining": that is, it must notify the union that the decision has been made, and must bargain about the effects the change will have on union members.

Changing the methods of production is considered a managerial prerogative, although employees who believe that they are adversely affected by the change can file a grievance or seek effects bargaining about the change.

The Seventh Circuit says that CBA management rights clauses allow the employer to unilaterally impose a policy controlling employees' use of drugs and alcohol both on and off the job. Although in general drug testing is a mandatory bargaining subject, the Fifth Circuit allows the employer to impose its policy unilaterally after a bargaining impasse. [*Chicago Tribune Co. v. NLRB*, 974 F.2d 933 (7th Cir. 1992); *Steelworkers v. ASARCO, Inc.*, 970 F.2d 1448 (5th Cir. 1992)]

Bargaining must be done in good faith. Neither side is obligated to make concessions or give in where it thinks surrender would be imprudent. If the bargaining process comes to an impasse—i.e., neither side is introducing new proposals or yielding on proposals already on the table—then the employer can lawfully cease negotiating and simply put its own proposals into place.

"Regressive bargaining"—withdrawing an offer if the union is unable to meet the employer's time frame—has been upheld by the NLRB in *White Cap, Inc.* [325 N.L.R.B. 220 (1998)], unless it is done specifically for the purpose of avoiding a contract. Where the employer has a legitimate business reason for wanting to resolve the issue quickly, regressive bargaining is permissible.

TruServ Corp. v. NLRB [254 F.3d 1105 (D.C. Cir. 2001)] holds that the NLRB was wrong: The parties had reached a bargaining impasse, and the employer was entitled to act unilaterally. Hard bargaining had gone on for eight days; the employer submitted its last, best, and final offer, but the union refused to submit this offer for a member vote; and the parties were far apart on critical issues such as wages, holidays, and health care. To establish that an impasse had occurred, the D.C. Circuit used factors such as bargaining history, good faith, length of negotiations, importance of the unresolved issues, and what the parties believed about the progress of negotiations.

After a collective bargaining agreement expires, there is nothing left to be enforced under contract law. But labor law [NLRA § 8(a)(5)] obligates the employer to maintain the status quo, at least until an impasse is reached and the employer can start implementing its own proposals unilaterally. The employer cannot take advantage of a bargaining impasse to unilaterally impose new provisions, or any provisions more favorable to its own cause than the provisions that were on the table during negotiations.

[B] Typical CBA Clauses

Although the actual contract that emerges from bargaining will reflect the individual needs of the business, and the comparative strengths of management and union, the following are issues that are often addressed in Collective Bargaining Agreements:

- Description of the bargaining unit;
- Management rights;
- Workday and workweek;
- Overtime;
- Classification of jobs for wage purposes;
- Compensation, bonuses, health, and other benefits;
- Paid time off (who is eligible, scheduling time off, who must be notified, which paid holidays are provided);
- Sick leave (number of days available; waiting period; doctors' notes; discipline for misusing sick leave);
- Seniority (what counts as a break in continuous service; effect of corporate transitions on seniority);
- Subcontracting;
- Plant closing and successorship;
- Severance pay;
- Hiring halls;
- Union security;
- Access to premises by non-employee union staff;
- Progressive discipline (the steps such as reprimands, conferences, and written warnings that will be provided before an employee is discharged);
- Drug testing;
- Grievance procedures (scope of disputes covered; how employees can present grievances; whether binding arbitration is required).

[C] Bargaining on Modification, Termination

The employer has an obligation to notify the union whenever it intends to modify or terminate a CBA. The employer must also notify the Federal Mediation and Conciliation Service of the intended action. Sixty days before the contract is scheduled to expire (or 60 days before the intended modification or termination), the employer must notify the union, inviting it to negotiate a new or amended contract. Notice to the FMCS is due 30 days after the notice to the union. Failure to give the required notice is an unfair labor practice. [29 U.S.C. § 158(d)]

The sixty-day notice period is referred to as the cooling-off period. The contract remains in effect during this period, and neither strikes nor lockouts are permitted.

Employers need not volunteer information, but they have a duty to provide the union with whatever information the union requests in order to represent the employees adequately. Information relating to wage rates and job descriptions is presumed relevant. However, employers do not have to disclose confidential or privileged information, or anything not relevant to the bargaining process. The union has to show a specific need for access to the employer's nonpublic financial information. The union can see financial data if the employer claims that it cannot afford a wage increase. In case of dispute, the NLRB determines what has to be disclosed and what is privileged.

§ 30.08   ELECTIONS AFTER CERTIFICATION

Representation elections are not the only kind that can be ordered and supervised by the NLRB. Federal labor law allows a rerun or runoff election to be held to redress an improper election. Once a union is in place, employees can ask that it be deauthorized or decertified. The employer also has the right to challenge a union's majority status.

A rerun election is held if there were election improprieties, or if two unions competed for representation; the ballot included a "no union" choice, and "no union" got as many votes as the other alternatives. (If there is only one union on the ballot, a tie vote means that the union loses, because it failed to attract a majority of the voters.)

A runoff election is held if no choice gets a majority. Only one runoff election can be held, although there could be both a rerun and a runoff election in the same organizing campaign.

A deauthorization petition is filed by a group of employees who want to remove the union's authority to enter into a union shop contract. Therefore, there are no deauthorization petitions in right-to-work states, because there aren't any union shops either. When a majority of the bargaining unit (not just a majority of the voters) vote for deauthorization, the union remains the authorized bargaining representative for the employees, but the employees no longer have to pay union dues.

The purpose of a decertification petition is to remove the union's bargaining authority. The petition can be filed by an employee, a group of employees, or someone acting on behalf of the employees. The employer does not have the right to file a decertification petition, but it does have a free-speech right to inform employees of their right to remove a union that they feel has not represented them adequately.

A decertification petition requires a showing of interest by 30% of the employees in the bargaining unit. Most petitions that are filed get the necessary vote (a majority of actual voters, not eligible voters) and therefore result in decertification of the union.

Decertification petitions cannot be filed at certain times: one year after certification of a union; a reasonable time after an employer's voluntary recognition of a union; or within 12 months of another decertification petition.

The employer has the right to petition the NLRB to determine that the union has lost its majority status. The employer must offer objective evidence of the change, such as employee turnover so heavy that few of the original pro-union workers remain; the union's failure to process employee grievances; or a strike that yielded no benefits for employees. If an employer has information that leads it to doubt the union's majority status, it is an unfair labor practice to enter into a contract with this union and then try to disavow the contract based on those doubts. The appropriate action is to refuse the contract. [*Auciello Iron Works Inc. v. NLRB*, 517 U.S. 781 (1996)]

The general rule, known as the CBA bar, is that no union election can be held while a collective bargaining agreement is in force. However, if there has been a substantial increase in personnel since the contract was signed, a new election may be proper if the union no longer represents a majority of the current workforce.

§ 30.09   STRIKES

[A]   Right to Strike

The NLRA gives employees the right to engage in "protected concerted activities"—joining together to organize, protest, and otherwise assert their interests in a lawful manner. This includes going on strike if a new contract cannot be negotiated, or based on a union's claim that working conditions are bad enough to justify a strike.

A striking union's gamble is that the employer will need to maintain continuous operations and therefore will grant significant concessions before the employees lose too much income by stopping work. But at other times employers actually benefit from strikes, if they can save payroll for a while, shut down an unproductive location, relocate to a lower-cost area (in another state or even another country) or bringing in "striker replacements."

Violence, sabotage, and threats are not protected activity. If a threatened strike would imperil the national health or safety, the President of the United States can order the U.S. Attorney General to petition the appropriate federal court for an 80-day cooling-off period, during which the strike is enjoined.

Secondary strikes and secondary boycotts—actions taken against one employer to put pressure on another employer that does business with the first employer—are banned by NLRA § 8(b)(4). A company that is the victim of a secondary strike or boycott can sue for damages under LMRA § 303.

According to the Seventh Circuit, employees who went out on strike in sympathy when a popular supervisor was fired were overreacting to the firing, so the strike was not protected concerted activity. [*Bob Evans Farms Inc. v. NLRB*, 163 F.3d 1012 (7th Cir. 1998)]

[B] Types of Strike

Employees can lawfully engage in a work stoppage in three situations:

- An economic dispute with the employer;
- A claim that the employer has committed unfair labor practices;
- A claim that workplace conditions are so unreasonably dangerous that they should not be required to continue work.

An "unfair labor practices" strike is caused in whole or part by unfair labor practices. There must be a causal connection between the strike and the employer practices. If the practices are simply cost-related (such as shift changes), then the strike should be characterized as an economic strike. But a strike that begins as an economic strike can be converted to an unfair labor practices strike if the employer acts unfairly or refuses to accept legitimate offers for return to work.

The main difference between an economic strike and an unfair labor practices strike is the extent of employees' reinstatement rights after the strike ends and they want to go back to work. Some issues are areas of managerial prerogative, so employees cannot lawfully strike to challenge management's decisions in these areas.

29 U.S.C. § 143 makes it a protected concerted activity for employees to refuse to work if there is measurable, objective evidence of undue hazards (not just a subjective feeling that something is wrong). The employees must also articulate goals that the employer can respond to: replace a defective machine or install guard rails, for instance, not just "make the workplace safer." [*See* Chapter 31 for information about occupational safety and health]

If the underlying strike is lawful, then a sympathy strike (workers outside the striking bargaining unit refuse to cross the picket line) is probably protected concerted activity as defined by the NLRA.

In contrast to those protected activities, a sitdown strike (an illegal takeover of the employer's premises) is unlawful. A wildcat strike, called by the rank and file without authorization from the union, is not protected activity if the workers want to usurp the union's role as sole bargaining representative for the workers.

A collective bargaining agreement can lawfully be drafted to include a no-strike clause. It is not protected concerted activity to call an economic strike in violation of a no-strike clause. Therefore, the employer can legitimately fire the strikers and deny them reinstatement after the strike ends.

[C] Lockouts and Other Employer Activity

The lockout is the employer's counterpart to the union's strike. In a strike, the employees refuse to come to work. In a lockout, the employer refuses to let them in. An employer that undertakes a lockout for business reasons can hire replacement workers. It can enter into a temporary subcontract for the duration of the lockout. However, the employer is not allowed to use the lockout to permanently contract out work formerly performed by employees. Lockouts are lawful if and only if they have a business motivation, not if they are used to prevent the workers from organizing a union, or to avoid bargaining with an incumbent union. However, a lockout is a justified response to a strike that violates a CBA no-strike clause.

It is an unfair labor practice for an employer to institute a lockout that is inherently destructive of the rights of employees. It is also an unfair labor practice to institute a lockout without having legitimate economic business justification (not just the employer's convenience). The mere possibility of a strike if contract negotiations break down is not a sufficient justification for a lockout during collective bargaining; and it might be treated as an unlawful refusal to bargain. Lockouts are analyzed even more stringently outside the strike context, because the union's power is weaker and there is less need for the employer to counterbalance it.

Employers are allowed to close a business, or shut it down temporarily, with economic motivations. But doing it to harm the union is an unfair labor practice. A "runaway shop" (transferring work between existing locations or opening a new location) is an unfair labor practice if it is based on antiunion motivation rather than a desire to enhance profitability.

During a strike, the employer is not permitted to alter the terms and conditions of employment that affect strikers. However, once a CBA expires, the employer is allowed to change those terms as they affect striker replacements.

[D]   Striker Replacements

During a strike, employers are entitled to keep their operations open by hiring replacements. Employers can always hire replacements for jobs that are described as temporary stopgaps until the strike ends. The question is whether the employer can hire permanent replacements, outsource functions formerly performed by employees, or keep the replacements and deny reinstatement to the strikers post-strike.

It is not an unfair labor practice to discharge strikers who have lost their employee status, and therefore their protection under the NLRA. The NLRA protects only lawful strikes that are conducted in a lawful manner, are called for a protected purpose, and are authorized by the bargaining unit representative (if there is one).

A strike is lawful if it occurs after the expiration of a CBA, if it is either an economic or an unfair labor practices strike, or if it demands concessions from the employer. Wildcat strikes, sitdown strikes, and strikes contrary to a CBA no-strike clause are not protected. Excessive violence removes employee status, although a minor instance of violence would not prevent the perpetrator from being considered an employee.

In an economic strike, the employer can permanently replace the strikers and keep the replacement workers after the end of the strike. However, strikers are entitled to reinstatement after the strike if they have not been replaced. Delay in reinstating them counts as an unfair labor practice. Even after being replaced, an economic striker is still considered an employee. If the former economic striker makes an unconditional application for reinstatement, the employer must reinstate him if the replacement worker quits or is terminated. If no jobs are available at the time of the application, the employer must reinstate the ex-striker when a job becomes available.

However, the former striker does not have to be reinstated if:

- He or she gets regular and substantial employment somewhere else;
- The employer has a legitimate business reason (violence or sabotage during the strike, for instance) for denying reinstatement;
- The job itself has been eliminated (e.g., due to new technology).

The NLRB's position, which has been upheld by the Seventh Circuit, is that the main issue is whether the replacement workers have a reasonable expectation of recall after being laid off. Strikers are entitled to reinstatement if the replacements did not have a reasonable expectation of recall—unless the employer can prove that the job is vacant or there is good cause not to rehire the striker. A "Laidlaw vacancy," otherwise known as a "genuine job vacancy," occurs if the replacement worker cannot reasonably expect recall after layoff.

Unless there is a legitimate and substantial business reason to depart from the rule, a reinstated economic striker must be treated equally with nonstrikers and permanent replacements, with the same benefits, including paid vacations and accrual of seniority. Normally, reinstatement should return the worker to status quo, but he or she can be demoted for a legitimate business reason such as a risk of sabotage.

[E]   Subcontracting

When a strike is imminent, employers who have a pressing business reason, and who are not acting out of anti-union animus, can legitimately subcontract out work that was performed by the bargaining unit, even though employees are displaced. NLRA § 8(a)(3), which penalizes employer actions that are intended to discourage union membership, can be invoked even if there is no direct proof of the employer's motivation—if the employer's action is inherently destructive of important rights of the employees. Subcontracting is a mandatory bargaining subject, so the employer can act unilaterally if a bargaining impasse has been reached.

Contracting out in-house security functions (and therefore firing all the newly unionized employees) violates the NLRA. [*Reno Hilton Resorts v. NLRB*, 196 F.3d 1275 (D.C. Cir. 1999)] The D.C. Circuit reached this conclusion because the employer did not provide enough evidence of the connection between outsourcing and declining revenues (the reason given for the move).

§ 30.10   THE WARN ACT

The Worker Adjustment Retraining and Notice Act ("WARN Act") [29 U.S.C. § 2101] requires employers of 100 or more full-time employees (or a combination of full- and part-timers adding up to at least 100 people and 4000 work hours a week) to provide notice of a plant closing or mass layoff. At least 60 days' notice must be given to employees, unions, and the federal government. The Act defines a plant closing as employment loss (termination, prolonged layoff, serious cutback in work hours) affecting 50 or more workers during a 30-day period.

A mass layoff has a lesser effect on the individual workers (e.g., potential for recall) and affects 500 people or one-third of the workforce. Anyone rehired within six months, or anyone who elected early retirement, should not be counted in determining if a mass layoff has occurred.

WARN Act notice must be given to laid-off employees who have a legitimate expectation of recall. *Kildea v. Electro-Wire Products Inc.* [144 F.3d 400 (6th Cir. 1998)] says that these people are "affected employees" because of the likelihood that plant closing will lead to job loss. Although the WARN Act refers to a "group" of laid-off employees, employers cannot avoid the application of the act by performing layoffs one at a time. All economically motivated layoffs within a 90-day period are aggregated toward the 50-employee figure. [*Hallowell v. Orleans Regional Hospital*, 217 F.3d 379 (5th Cir. 2000)]

If the employer fails to give the required notice, each affected employee is entitled to up to 60 days' back pay (work days, not calendar days) and benefits. A federal civil penalty of up to $500 can also be imposed for every day that the failure to give notice continued. A union can sue for damages on behalf of its members.

A West Virginia state court took the position that back pay and damages awarded under the WARN Act are not covered by a state law mandating timely payment of "wages"—even though the statute describes the damages as back pay. [*Conrad v. Charles Town Races Inc.*, 206 W. Va. 45, 521 S.E.2d 537 (W.Va. 1998)]

WARN Act responsibilities continue after a bankruptcy filing. However, if a company ceases to operate as a going concern and winds up its affairs, it is no longer an "employer" and therefore cannot be held liable if it fails to give WARN Act notice. [*Official Committee of Unsecured Creditors v. United Healthcare Sys. Inc.*, 200 F.3d 170 (3d Cir. 1999)]

§ 30.11   LABOR LAW ISSUES OF SHARED LIABILITY

[A]   Possible Scenarios

There are many situations in which more than one company may be deemed to be a particular person's "employer." Sometimes, both companies will be liable, or the actions of one will be attributed to the other, with respect to unfair labor practices, defining the appropriate bargaining unit, or enforcing a collective bargaining agreement.

Vested benefits under a collective bargaining agreement are transferable when the employer transfers employees to another one of its locations, which is covered by another CBA with another union. [*Anderson v. AT&T Corp.,* 147 F.3d 467 (6th Cir. 1998)]

When one company merges with or takes over another, it is common for many or all of the first company's employees to be retained. Whether the acquiror is now the employer, and whether it is bound by the former employer's CBA and other promises to its workers is a factual question, depending on whether or not real operational changes were made.

In connection with CBAs, a "successor company" is one that continues the same business and hires at least half of the old employees. A successor employer is not bound by the predecessor's contracts, but does have an obligation to recognize and consult with the union. The Supreme Court has ruled that a new company becomes a successor if it is clear that all the former employees will be retained. [*NLRB v. Burns Int'l Security Servs. Inc.*, 406 U.S. 272 (1972)] *Canteen Corp. v. NLRB* [103 F.3d 1355 (7th Cir. 1997)] holds that a company can also be treated as a successor employer if it fails to give employees enough information about the new wages and working conditions to make a meaningful choice about accepting a job offer from the new employer.

After a merger or the purchase of a business, a successor has a duty to bargain collectively and can be liable for unfair labor practices committed by the predecessor if there is "continuity of identity" with the ex-employer, such as using the same facility to produce identical products and services, using the same or substantially the same labor force, without changes in job description, working conditions, supervision, equipment, or production methods.

An alternate test is whether there is a new corporate entity to replace the predecessor, whether there is a hiatus in the enterprise's operations, and whether the employment relationship with the prior workforce was terminated. If it is perfectly clear under the *Burns International* standard that the new owner will hire the entire existing workforce, then the incoming employer has a duty to consult with the union about wage scales. It cannot unilaterally impose cuts. If there is no such consultation, it is presumed that the negotiations would have continued the prior wage scale.

But see Monterey Newspapers Inc. [334 N.L.R.B. 128 (Aug. 9, 2001)], allowing a publishing company that acquired a newspaper to set up a separate "pay band" system for persons hired after the acquisition. The pay band system was adopted unilaterally, without bargaining with the newspaper union. The acquiror recognized the union four days after an acquisition in which most of the existing workforce was rehired. The NLRB interpreted the acquiror's rights under *Burns International* to include setting new initial terms and conditions of employment. But once the new hires joined the work force, any later changes in their compensation would become a mandatory bargaining subject.

Another possibility is that two or more enterprises might be deemed to be "alter egos" (substitutes) for one another, even if they are not formally under common control. Alter egos may be held liable for each other's unfair labor practices. The test is whether transferring business from one alter ego operation to another benefits the transferor by eliminating labor relations obligations. The alter ego theory became part of labor law to prevent "double-breasting": the practice of pairing commonly owned firms, one with a union and one nonunionized. If the double-breasted firms are actually alter egos, a federal district court can require the non-union firm to abide by the union firm's labor agreements, even if there has been no NLRB determination of a single bargaining unit.

Two or more entities organized as legally separate entities might be treated as a "single employer" if there is an integrated enterprise. The factors that determine integration include common ownership, common management, integrated business operations, and centralized control of labor relations.

These tests are similar to the tests to see if companies are alter egos. The difference is that the two alter ego companies are not considered a single enterprise, so all their employees are not necessarily in the same bargaining unit.

A parent company and its subsidiary would probably be treated as a single employer if they were fundamentally in the same industry or business enterprise. This would be manifested by sharing supervisory, technical, and professional personnel; sharing workforce and equipment; having common officers and directors; and operating under the same labor relations policies.

The NLRB might group separate entities together as "joint employers" if they "codetermine" (i.e., make decisions jointly) about essential terms and conditions of employment. Under this theory, the crucial factor is not whether the companies have overlapping ownership, but whether they make joint decisions about hiring and firing, working conditions, compensation, and supervision of employees.

[B] Agents of the Employer

An employer company will be liable for the actions of any "agent" of the company acting in the employer's interest. For example, a labor consultant is considered the employer's agent, but a Chapter 7 bankruptcy trustee is not. The determination uses factors similar to those used in deciding if someone is a common-law employee. The employer's degree of control is crucial: the right to hire and fire the agent; furnishing tools and materials; prescribing what the agent will do and how to do it.

Someone can become an agent of the company either by actual agency (explicitly granted) or apparent agency (where a principal says that the agent can speak for it, or knowingly lets the agent exercise authority). An employer is responsible for the actions performed by a supervisor in the course of actual or apparent authority. Even if a supervisor acts without authority, the employer can become liable by ratifying the supervisor's action (i.e., offering support for it after the fact). In general, however, the employer will not be responsible for actions for someone who is not an employee, or perhaps not a supervisory employee, unless the employer initiates, promotes, or ratifies the conduct. If the agent's improper conduct was an isolated, unpremeditated act, or if the employer repudiates the conduct, it is possible that the employer will be relieved of liability.

In general, the NLRB will blame the employer for an unfair labor practice only if it was committed directly by the employer, or by the employer's agent. But in a representation proceeding, a finding of agency is not required to set aside an election if the election was unfair enough to prevent employees from exercising a rational, unforced choice.

> **Tip:** Unions are also liable for actions taken by their agents, including rank-and-file union members advancing union goals. Unless the union takes preventive or corrective action to stem inappropriate picket-line behavior, the union is likely to be held liable for unfair labor practices. But when several unions engage in joint picketing during an organization drive, *Washington v. HCA Health Services of Texas Inc.* [152 F.3d 464 (5th Cir. 1998)] says that one union is not responsible for the actions of the others just because they share the objective of organizing the workplace.

§ 30.12   EMPLOYER DOMINATION

In Europe, "codetermination," where union representatives collaborate closely with management, and where joint management-labor committees play an important decision-making role, is well accepted. However, under U.S. law, employer domination of a labor organization is an unfair labor practice. [*See* NLRA § 8(a)(2)] Although this provision was originally enacted to bar "sweetheart unions" (formed or taken over by the employer), it has been applied more broadly.

A Sixth Circuit case concerned a plant council that was created just after the employer won a certification election. [*NLRB v. Webcor Packaging Inc.*, 118 F.3d 1115 (6th Cir. 1997)] The plant council met during working hours to discuss work rules, wages, and benefits. The council, made up of five employees and three management representatives, reviewed ideas from the Suggestion Box and made proposals to management, some of which were accepted.

The DOL challenged the council as an employer-dominated labor organization. The NLRB and the Sixth Circuit agreed, because it fit into the statutory definition. It represented employees, dealt with the employer, and was concerned with conditions of employment. Employer domination was present because management created the committee and could disband it; it met during working hours; and management representatives were always present.

In 1992, the NLRB ruled that an "action committee" created by the employer in response to employee dissatisfaction was improperly employer-dominated. [*Electromation, Inc.*, 309 N.L.R.B. 163 (1992)] The NLRB considered it a labor organization, not a way to improve communications, because its purpose was to solve employee grievances and because the employee members acted in a representative capacity. The agency's decision was upheld by the Seventh Circuit in 1994. [35 F.3d 1148 (7th Cir. 1994)]

In 1993, the NLRB found that six joint labor-management safety committees, and a joint committee on fitness, were also labor organizations, because their purpose was to deal with the employer, and because they dealt with important issues such as safety, incentive awards, and exercise facilities for employees. [E.I. DuPont de Nemours, 311 N.L.R.B. 88 (1993)]

To avoid NLRB characterization of a work team or quality circle as an unduly dominated "labor organization," the employer should consider these steps:

- Look for a neutral meeting place away from the workplace, such as a local library, Rotary club, or City Hall;
- Rotate membership of the team, to involve as many people as possible and get new viewpoints;
- Focus the team on productivity and workplace issues, not compensation;
- Don't use the team to avoid contract negotiations;
- Employee representatives, not management, should draft the bylaws under which the team operates. [*Polaroid Corp. & Scivally*, 329 N.L.R.B. 47 (1999); *EFCO Corp.*, 327 N.L.R.B. (1998); *NLRB v. Webcor Packaging Inc.*, 118 F.3d 1115 (6th Cir. 1997); *Electromation, Inc.*, 309 N.L.R.B. 163 (1992)]

§ 30.13   NLRB JURISDICTION

The National Labor Relations Board has the power to get involved in a situation if:

- It is a labor dispute—i.e., there is any controversy about conditions of employment or representation of workers. Strikes, walkouts, picketing, and employer refusals to bargain are labor disputes;
- It affects interstate commerce. The threshold is so low that virtually any business will be deemed to affect interstate commerce;
- Employers and employees, rather than independent contractors and their clients, are involved;
- The dispute involves working conditions.

When it has issued a complaint or filed an unfair labor practices charge, the NLRB can ask a federal District Court to issue a temporary injunction. In fact, the agency has an obligation to seek an injunction if it charges unlawful secondary activity (such as striking one employer to put pressure on another), some forms of improper activity, or certain boycotts. However, permanent injunctions are very rare, because of the Norris-LaGuardia Anti-Injunction Act.

Theoretically, the NLRB has jurisdiction over all unfair labor practice claims that require interpretation of a CBA that is still in effect. In practice, the NLRB often declines to exercise its jurisdiction, allowing the parties to use the contract's grievance arbitration machinery, to proceed with ongoing arbitration, or to enforce an arbitration award. However, it is up to the NLRB to intervene or stay out. The employer and union cannot deprive the NLRB of jurisdiction by agreeing to arbitrate.

The NLRB did not abuse its discretion in extending the certification year by six months, and ordering the employer to reinstate its bargaining proposals, in a case where the employer withdrew all its proposals just before the certification year ended. [*NLRB v. Beverly Health & Rehab Servs.*, 187 F.3d 769 (8th Cir. 1999)]

In 1997, the Court of Appeals for the District of Columbia Circuit overturned a long-held belief that the NLRB has the power to order an employer to reimburse the union for negotiating and litigation effects if the employer has been found to have committed unfair labor practices during collective bargaining. But the D.C. Circuit decided that the National Labor Relations Act is not specific enough on this point to justify a departure from the normal American rule that litigants have to pay their own litigation costs. [*Unbelievable Inc. v. NLRB*, 118 F.3d 795 (D.C. Cir. 1997)]

The Seventh Circuit upheld the NLRB's imposition of a corporate-wide remedial order against a corporation that operates about 900 separate nursing homes. Remedies at the corporate level were proper because violations were found in a number of facilities, not just one, and the company is centrally administered. [*Beverly California Corp. v. NLRB*, 227 F.3d 817 (7th Cir. 2000)]

§ 30.14   LABOR LAW IMPLICATIONS OF BANKRUPTCY FILINGS

The general rule is that the "automatic stay" on litigation as soon as a bankruptcy petition is filed will protect the company that files from being sued. However, because the NLRB is considered a unit of the federal government exercising its regulatory powers, NLRB unfair labor practices hearings are exempt from the automatic stay. However, the bankruptcy court has the power to enjoin the NLRB from doing anything that would prevent the reorganization of the bankrupt company.

Part of the bankruptcy process is a decision about which executory contracts (i.e., contracts to be performed in the future) will be carried out by the reorganized company and which can and should be rejected. The company seeking bankruptcy protection can petition the court to allow it to assume or reject a CBA. The court's standard for granting a rejection request is whether it would be fair to reject the contract, or whether the union unreasonably refused to accept contract modifications proposed by the employer. The employer does not have to prove that the proposed plan of reorganization will fail unless the contract can be rejected.

However, if the collective bargaining agreement expires while bankruptcy proceedings are pending, the whole issue becomes moot, because there is nothing for the employer to either accept or reject.

§ 30.15 PREVENTIVE LABOR RELATIONS

There are many reasons why employees would favor an organizing drive. The more positive the employees' feelings about the company they work for, and the more truthful and candid they believe employer communications to be, the less likely a representation election is to succeed.

Employers can promote positive feelings by making employees feel valued and wanted; listening to their suggestions and implementing the most useful ones; and offering a grievance procedure at least as generous as a union would provide under a CBA. Major compensation increases for top executives, while rank-and-file pay is steady or declining, tend to promote serious dissatisfaction. [*See* J. Derek Braziel's white paper, *Avoid the Union Label: How to Fight Organizers Without Violating the Law*, <http://www.lawnewsnetwork.com> for insights into unions' new, and sometimes successful, push to organize]

CHAPTER 31

OCCUPATIONAL SAFETY AND HEALTH

§ 31.01 INTRODUCTION

The federal Occupational Safety and Health Act and the agency that administers it, the Occupational Safety and Health Administration (both abbreviated OSHA) have as their mission protecting employees against unreasonably hazardous workplaces. All employers must satisfy the "general duty standard" of maintaining a workplace that is reasonably free of recognized dangers. Additional standards are imposed in some circumstances, particularly in the construction industry.

Employers are not held to an impossible standard of a hazard-free workplace, but they must be prepared to deal with known hazards (including disease and chemical toxicity as well as accident). They must use the reasonably available methods and technology to keep the dangers within bounds.

At the end of 2001, the Secretary of Labor announced that the reported rates of injuries and illnesses in the workplace declined in 2000, to the lowest level since the early 1970s. The rate of illness and injury was 6.1 cases for every 100 workers. The number of cases reported in 2000 was about the same as in 1999 (5.7 million), but the rate was lower because the number of hours worked was 2% higher in 2000. [National News Release USDL 01-488 (Dec. 18, 2001) <http://www.osha.gov/media/oshnews/dec01/national-20011218.html>] Workplace violence also declined in 1999; workplace violence decreased 44% between 1993 and 1999. During this time period, about 18% of violent crimes occurred in the workplace. Police officers (261 incidents per 1,000 officers) and correction officers had the highest rates of being attacked at work, followed by cab drivers (128 incidents per 1,000 workers); university professors had the lowest rate (2 incidents per 1,000 workers). [No by-line, *Violent Crime Reported Declining in Workplace*, New York Times, Dec. 21, 2001, at p. A18]

Wood v. Chao [275 F.3d 107 (D.C. Cir. 2001)] involves a discharged worker who alleges that his discharge occurred in retaliation for reporting unsafe conditions at a facility for disposal of military chemical weapons. The employer says he was discharged for insubordination (he refused to work in a toxic area because the employer had not provided him with corrective lenses for his protective mask; he had already received a final reprimand for refusal to work in the past). The Department of Labor refused to file suit on his behalf, on the grounds that the right to refuse to work is very narrow. The DOL's position was that he did not satisfy the necessary criteria, so discharging him did not violate OSHA. The D.C. Circuit said that it is up to OSHA to decide what investigations and lawsuits are appropriate, and employees cannot sue the Department of Labor to force it to bring suits on their behalf.

§ 31.02 OSHA POWERS

Under the OSH Act, OSHA has the authority to inspect workplaces, order correction of violations, and impose penalties if correction does not occur as mandated. It has been held that it is not a violation of the OSH Act, or the Fourth

Amendment's ban on unreasonable searches and seizures, for an OSHA compliance officer to videotape a construction site from across the street before going to the site and presenting his credentials. The theory is that looking at a site (to determine if fall protection techniques were adequate) is not a "search," so no warrant is required. [*L.R. Willson & Sons Inc. v. OSHRC*, 134 F.3d 1235 (4th Cir. 1998)]

The OSH Act also requires employers to keep records of workplace injuries and to use this information to generate annual reports (which must be disclosed to the workforce as well as being submitted to OSHA).

All employers whose operations affect commerce among the states are subject to OSHA. There is no minimum number of employees. However, small-scale or low-risk enterprises are entitled to relaxation of some reporting requirements.

Tip: An employer who would be damaged by full compliance with OSHA requirements can petition the Secretary of Labor for a temporary or permanent "variance" that protects the company against noncompliance penalties. Variances are effective only for the company that applies for them. It is no defense against a charge of noncompliance that a variance was granted to a different company in a similar situation.

The OSH Act interacts with various other statutes. It is probably a violation of public policy to discharge a worker because he or she filed a Worker's Compensation claim after suffering an occupational injury; to retaliate against a whistleblower who reported unsafe conditions to OSHA; or to take steps against someone who cooperated in an OSHA investigation.

Federal labor law says that a walkout premised on unsafe working conditions will not be treated as a strike. Furthermore, it is a protected concerted activity for workers to complain about safety conditions in the workplace, and therefore the employer cannot use this as a premise for employee discipline.

However, state courts will not necessarily consider an OSHA violation relevant evidence of neglect if the employer is sued. A 1997 case says that, under the law of that particular state, OSHA regulations do not have the "compulsory force" under state law that would prove that the employer was negligent. [*Sumrall v. Mississippi Power Co.*, 639 So.2d 359 (Miss. 1997)]

§ 31.03   OSHA REGULATIONS

The main authority for federal regulation of workplace safety comes from the OSH Act itself. OSHA's agency rules appear in the Code of Federal Regulations. In addition to the General Duty Clause, OSHA enforces more specific guidance in the form of the General Industry Standards that cover most industrial workplaces, and the Construction Standards.

The General Industry Standards deal with topics such as:

• Condition of floors (this is called the "walking/working" standard);
• Number and design of entrances and exits;

- Noise control;
- Radiation safety;
- Proper handling of hazardous materials (known as "hazmats")—toxic chemicals and toxic wastes;
- Personal Protective Equipment (PPE) such as respirators, hard hats, steel-toed shoes, work gloves, etc.;
- Fire prevention and safety;
- On-site first aid and medical treatment;
- Requirements for guards on machinery;
- Proper use of tools and other hand-held equipment;
- Welding and cutting;
- Control of electrical hazards;
- Design and maintenance of lifts and powered platforms;
- Access to employees' health records.

The Construction Industry Standards overlap with the General Industry Standards. The two rules sometimes treat the same topics, but the construction rules tend to be more stringent in this case. The construction standards also cover control of asbestos, welding and cutting, scaffolding, steel construction, and the use of masonry and concrete in construction. In 1994, OSHA proposed an "indoor air quality standard" that would have banned smoking in nearly all workplaces. This was a very controversial rule (more than 100,000 comments were received!), and at the end of 2001, OSHA finally withdrew the proposal, stating that it would focus its attention on other safety and health problems. [*See* 66 Fed. Reg. 64,946 (Dec. 17, 2001)]

§ 31.04   CONTROLLING PHYSICAL HAZARDS

[A]   Personal Protective Equipment

An important part of the employer's duty of providing a safe workplace is to furnish protective equipment and to make sure that machinery is guarded and that, where appropriate, moving parts will stop before employees are injured.

The legal system treats PPE (Personal Protective Equipment) as essential to workplace safety. Wherever possible, employers should eliminate hazards directly, by reducing the likelihood of falls, falling objects, burns, chemical exposure, etc. But it is not always possible to remove the hazard, and even when it is physically possible, the cost may be prohibitive.

In such situations, the employer has a duty to provide PPE, and the employee has a complementary duty to use it. The employer must provide suitable equipment, in sizes that fit the workers, and must train them in how to use the equipment. The obligation exists whenever a reasonable person, familiar with workplace conditions and industry practices, would require PPE. The industry standard is not a defense, however, if the employer knew or should have known that dangerous conditions were present—for instance, if injuries had occurred in the past under similar circumstances.

A Proposed Rule [64 Fed. Reg. 15401 (March 31, 1999)] requires the employer not only to require use of PPE where appropriate, but also to pay for all such equipment other than prescription eyewear, safety-toe shoes, and logging boots (i.e., items that have general usefulness outside the workplace).

A respiratory protection rule took effect October 5, 1998. The standard, known as 1910.134, covers respirator use in general industry, shipyards, longshore work, and construction, but not in agriculture. For guidance to employers, OSHA issued compliance directive CPL 2-0.120, explaining how to analyze workplace hazards, select respirators, when to change the chemical cartridges in respirators, and how to make sure respirators fit properly. [*See* <http://www.osha.gov>]

[B]   Lockout/Tagout

OSHA's lockout/tagout rule applies in nonconstruction workplaces where the machinery has potentially dangerous moving parts. The rule imposes obligations on employers to immobilize machinery while it is being serviced, cleaned, repaired, etc. The rule does not apply to normal operation of the machinery, because in those situations the equipment and work routines are supposed to prevent injuries due to moving parts.

To comply with the lockout/tagout rule, machinery could be equipped with a trip control ("panic button") so it can be shut down quickly in an emergency. Blades and other dangerous parts can be protected with guards that protect workers' bodies from contact and prevent scrap materials from becoming projectiles. If guards are impractical, machinery could be equipped with sensing devices that turn off the machine if a body part goes beyond the safe point. Machinery can also be designed to require two hands to operate, so that it will not work when a hand is within reach of moving parts.

[C]   Bathroom Breaks

The OSHA general industry sanitation standard [29 C.F.R. § 1910.141] requires the presence of toilet facilities in the workplace. An April 6, 1998, letter from OSHA forbids employers to impose unreasonable restrictions on bathroom use. OSHA inspectors who receive complaints on this issue are directed to investigate the reasonableness of the employer's policy.

Female workers (especially pregnant women) need more bathroom breaks than male workers, although older male workers may need to use the restroom more often because of prostate enlargement.

If increased need for elimination is due to a health condition, it may be necessary to provide reasonable accommodation under the Americans with Disabilities Act. For instance, the worker might be allowed more breaks during the day—but short breaks, just long enough to visit the restroom. Or the employee might be assigned the workstation closest to the restroom, so he or she can return to work more quickly. [*See* 66 L.W. 2579 (March 31, 1998), and 2636 (April 21, 1998), and Mary Williams Walsh, *Blue-Collar Urgency: Bathroom Rights*, New York Times, Nov. 22, 2000, at p. G1]

§ 31.05 CONTROLLING EXPOSURE TO HAZARDOUS CONDITIONS

[A] Generally

The employer must limit employees' exposure to hazardous materials (e.g., asbestos, lead) and conditions (e.g., potentially damaging noise levels). Hazardous substances must be stored properly. Employees must be warned about their presence and taught how to handle the materials safely.

Other laws, such as environmental laws and laws requiring notification to the community of the presence or accidental release of hazardous substances, are also triggered when dangerous materials are used in a workplace. The company must have an emergency-response plan that involves coordination with fire departments and other community resources.

[B] PELs

A PEL, or Permissible Exposure Limit, is set for certain hazardous substances such as asbestos and lead. A PEL is a level of contact with the substance that employees can encounter without becoming endangered. The employer has an obligation to monitor the plant environment to determine the level of the regulated substance, to provide appropriate safety equipment (e.g., face masks and respirators) and to train employees in safety techniques.

OSHA rules require that employees have access to showers, changing rooms, eye baths, first aid, and other measures for preventing long-term contamination. Where necessary, the employer must provide protective clothing and appropriate containers for collecting contaminated clothing for treatment or disposal. Employees must not be permitted to smoke or eat in any environment where asbestos, lead, etc., are present. Warning signs must be posted in danger areas.

The employer's basic job is to keep employee exposure below the PEL. In some instances, this is impossible. When exposure reaches the "action level" defined by OSHA, the employer must take additional steps, such as periodic medical testing of employees to see if they have suffered environmental injury or illness.

[C] Noise Levels

In workplaces where the noise level routinely exceeds 85 decibels per eight-hour shift, the employer has an obligation to create and maintain a comprehensive program for hearing conservation. The environmental noise level must be monitored; employees' hearing must be tested (with a baseline reading within six months of initial exposure to high occupational noise levels, and an annual checkup after that), and they must be trained to protect themselves against hearing loss. If any audiometric test shows that an employee's hearing has deteriorated, the employer's obligation is to notify that worker within 21 days and then make sure that the worker uses hearing protection devices in the future.

§ 31.06   ERGONOMICS

Ergonomics is the study of the mutual adaptation between tools and the human body. Ergonomically efficient tools will reduce the number, or at least the degree, of injuries associated with tool use.

OSHA has made several attempts to impose ergonomic requirements on industry. This has been an extremely controversial quest. Congress's appropriation bills for OSHA between 1996 and 1998 actually forbade the agency to adopt ergonomics standards.

The Occupational Safety and Health Review Commission (OSHRC) issued an April 1997 decision that was the first declaration that the Secretary of Labor can properly cite ergonomic hazards under the general duty clause. [*Secretary of Labor v. Pepperidge Farm Inc.*, 65 L.W. 2725 (OSHRC April 26, 1997). *See also Reich v. Arcadian Corp.*, 110 F.3d 1192 (5th Cir. 1997)]

In July 1997, NIOSH released a study indicating a strong correlation between job activities and injury to the musculoskeletal system of the back, neck, and upper arms—a subject that was to become highly controversial. [NIOSH, *Musculoskeletal Disorders and Workplace Factors*, July 1997]

OSHA published a draft ergonomics regulation on January 6, 1999. A revised Working Draft of March 12, 1999, was placed on the OSHA Web site but marked "do not cite or quote."

OSHA issued proposed regulations on ergonomics on November 2, 1999, calling for comments by February 1, 2000. Under the proposal, about 1.6 million employers would have to set up a basic ergonomics program of education and reporting. If at least one musculoskeletal disorder (MSD) occurred in the workplace at any time, a full program of prevention would be required.

Informal public hearings were scheduled to begin on February 2, 2000. The proposal said that regulations would become effective 60 days after OSHA's publication of a final standard reflecting the comments received. However, on January 27, 2000, then-Secretary of Labor Alexis Herman extended the comment period to March 2 and re-scheduled the hearings for March 13.

In June 2000, the House of Representatives voted 220–203 to prevent the Department of Labor from implementing new ergonomics standards at least until October 2001. However, OSHA published a very lengthy Final Rule in the November 14, 2000 Federal Register.

The rule, as a general industry standard, was supposed to cover approximately 6.1 million worksites with 102 million workers. The final rule provides a two-page checklist of MSD situations and risk factors, including use of a computer keyboard or mouse for more than four hours a day, kneeling or squatting for over two hours a day, or repeatedly lifting heavy packages during the work shift. The rule requires implementation of a program for managing MSDs within seven days of the occurrence of such an injury. Under this rule, employees suffering work-related MSDs are entitled to receive paid leave and benefits when off work or returned to a light-duty job.

The Final Rule was immediately challenged in court by organizations including the Society for Human Resource Management, U.S. Chamber of Commerce, and the National Association of Manufacturers. [*See* Yochi J. Dreazen, *Ergonomics Rules Are First in a Wave of Late Regulations*, Wall Street Journal, Nov. 14, 2000, at p. A4; Darryl Van Duch, *Ergonomics Rules Draw Attacks*, National Law Journal, Dec. 5, 2000 (law.com); *OSHA's Final Ergonomics Rule Hits Federal Register; Lawsuit Filed*, <http://www.hrnext.com>]

In March 2001, both Houses of Congress used a little-known federal statute called the Congressional Review Act of 1996 (CRA) to repeal the ergonomics regulations. It was the first time the CRA had actually been put into practice. Under the CRA, as long as 30 Senators agree, a vote can be taken directly on the floor of Congress, without committee discussions, to overturn Regulations promulgated during the preceding 60 days. Furthermore, if the CRA is invoked, the agency that issued the regulations struck down by Congress will never be permitted to enact "substantially similar" rules in the future.

Senate Joint Resolution 6, dealing with the ergonomics rules, was introduced on March 1, 2001. The Senate voted 56–44 to overturn the ergonomics rules. The House vote was 223–206 to overturn the regulations. By and large, the Republicans voted against the rules, the Democrats in favor of them. [*See* Steven Greenhouse, *House Joins Senate in Repealing Rules on Workplace Injuries*, New York Times, March 8, 2001 at p. A19]

In April 2002, the Bush administration announced its policy for reducing repetitive stress injuries through the adoption of voluntary industry safety guidelines. The DOL did not get any additional funding to supervise adherence to the guidelines. The plan calls for OSHA to work with industries with unusually high rates of RSIs to develop industry-specific guidelines for reducing injuries, and for OSHA to take action against companies that do not take adequate steps to reduce their injury rates. [Steven Greenhouse, *Bush Plan to Avert Work Injuries Seeks Voluntary Steps by Industry,* New York Times Apr. 6, 2002, at p. A1; Kathy Chen, *Bush Proposal on Repetitive Stress Injuries Relies on Voluntary Industry Guidelines,* Wall Street Journal Apr. 8, 2002, at p. A28.]

At the end of April, OSHA announced the formation of a 15-member National Advisory Committee on Ergonomics to advise on gaps in existing research and how to perform the needed research and communicate research results to industry and the public. The first industry-specific guidelines to be developed were in the nursing home industry, because workers in this industry have a very high injury rate (resulting, e.g., from lifting patients, moving equipment, and assaults by patients). In June 2002, OSHA announced an initiative to develop guidelines in the retail grocery and poultry processing industries. It was expected that the three sets of draft guidelines would be published for public comment late in 2002. [For OSHA actions, *see* OSHA Trade News Releases, *OSHA Announces Formation of National Advisory Committee on Ergonomics,* <http://www.osha.gov/media/ oshnews/apr02/trade-20020430.html> and *OSHA To Develop Ergonomics Guidelines for Retail Grocery Stores, Poultry Processing,* <http://www.osha.gov/media/ oshnews/june02/trade-20020610.html>]

§ 31.07   VARIANCES

The OSH Act permits employers to petition for variances that will excuse them from having to comply with requirements that are particularly onerous. A variance can only be granted if employees will not be exposed to undue risk or danger.

The CFR includes rules for "national security variances" and "experimental variances," but most of the variances granted are classified as either "temporary" or "permanent."

Grounds for a temporary variance are that the company will eventually comply with a new regulation, but cannot do so by its scheduled effective date because of a shortage of staff, materials, or equipment. (Being unable to afford to comply is not considered good cause for a variance.) A temporary variance lasts up to one year. It can be renewed twice, for up to 180 days at a time. The application must demonstrate that the employer is doing everything it can to comply as soon as possible, and that employees are being protected from undue hazards in the meantime.

A permanent variance is granted to an employer whose work methods are unconventional but still provide at least as much protection for employees as the OSHA regulations do. A company asking for a permanent variance can also apply for an interim variance.

The original plus six copies of the variance application and supporting documents must be filed. The documents must be signed by an authorized representative of the company, such as a corporate officer or the corporation's attorney.

Employees are entitled to notice of the variance application. They can ask that a hearing examiner conduct a hearing on the application.

Variance applications are reviewed, and then granted or denied, by the Assistant Secretary of Labor of Occupational Health and Safety in Washington. Anyone affected by a variance after it is granted can petition for modification or revocation of the order granting the variance. After a temporary variance ends, the employer can petition to have it renewed or extended.

§ 31.08   DIVISION OF RESPONSIBILITY

For OSHA purposes, companies are responsible for the safety of their "employees." A company that has all its work done by leased employees or independent contractors will not be subject to OSHA unless the arrangements are only a subterfuge to avoid liability. What counts is the economic reality of the work relationship, including the degree of control over the work, who signs the paycheck, and whether payment is a regular salary or a per-project amount. The power to change working conditions or fire the employee is considered especially significant. If several employers are involved (e.g., a temporary employment agency and its clients), OSHA responsibilities will be allocated based on actual job performance and working conditions. The basic rule is that the general contractor has primary OSHA responsibility for a construction worksite.

OSHA liability of general contractors can derive from several theories:

- A construction contract provision under which the general contractor agrees to provide safety equipment;
- The general contractor's role of controlling conditions because it is in charge of the site;
- The general contractor is the only party involved with the specialized knowledge to abate the hazards;
- The general contractor's actual knowledge of the hazards (by observation or by notice from a subcontractor), creating a duty to cope with the hazards.

In doubtful cases, OSHA cites all possibly responsible parties and then allows them to make arguments why they are not liable. However, both a company that creates a hazard and the actual employer of the employees exposed to the hazard (and who were not protected by their employer) can be found liable.

OSHA's internal directive, CPL 2-0.214 [*see* <http://www.osha.gov>] explains how the agency will issue citations to multi-employer workplaces. If a particular employer is in a position to create, control, or correct hazards, or if it exposes employees to danger, OSHA will check the employer's conduct. If it failed to satisfy all its occupational safety and health obligations, citations can be issued.

OSHA uses a two-step test to see whether the Construction Standard should be applied to nonconstruction companies. The tests are ability to direct or control trade contractors, and a degree of involvement in the multiple activities that are needed to complete a construction project. The Seventh Circuit found that an engineering firm that consulted on a sewer project where a fatal accident occurred, did not become subject to the Construction Standard. [*CH2M Hill Inc. v. Herman*, 192 F.3d 711 (7th Cir. 1999)] The court found that the engineering firm did not exercise substantial supervision over actual construction, and therefore did not have enough control for liability to be imposed.

Under the "peculiar risk" doctrine, someone who hires an independent contractor to perform inherently dangerous work is liable for any torts committed by the independent contractor against others in the course of doing the work. However, in California, this doctrine cannot be used by employees of a subcontractor who are injured by the subcontractor's negligence, to sue the general contractor. [*Toland v. Sunland Hous. Group Inc.*, 18 Cal. 4th 253, 74 Cal. Rptr. 2d 504, 955 P.2d 504 (1998)]

Secretary of Labor v. Yandell [OSHRC No. 94-3080 (March 12, 1999)] permits an individual or corporate employer to be cited for violating OSHA regulations even after it has gone out of business.

§ 31.09   OSHA ENFORCEMENT

[A]   Generally

Unlike ERISA enforcement (where federal jurisdiction preempts the state role), OSHA enforcement is coordinated between the states and the federal government. States have discretion to shape the degree of their occupational safety enforcement involvement. They can draft regulatory plans; if the Department of Labor believes the plan does enough to protect worker safety, it becomes an "approved state plan."

About half the states have approved state plans: Alaska, Arizona, California, Connecticut, Hawaii, Indiana, Iowa, Kentucky Maryland, Michigan, Minnesota, Nevada, New Jersey, New Mexico, New York, North Carolina, Oregon, South Carolina, Tennessee, Utah, Vermont, Virginia, Washington, and Wyoming. However, the Connecticut and New York plans are limited to coverage of state employees, not private-sector workers.

In states that do not have an approved state plan, OSHA has primary responsibility for safety enforcement. State governments, however, are allowed to regulate issues that the OSH Act does not cover (such as boiler and elevator safety) as well as broader safety issues (such as fire protection in buildings that are open to the public).

One important function of state OSH agencies is offering free on-site consultations about how to maintain a safer workplace. The consultation is a simulated inspection, but the inspector is only authorized to point out problem areas and suggest solutions, not to issue citations or penalize the company. The consultation begins with an opening conference with the employer, proceeds to a walk-through and identification of safety problems, and ends with a closing conference about how to solve those problems.

This program has been criticized by the GAO, which says that the consultation program does not collect the right information to actually help reduce workplace injuries. The GAO says that although the number of consultations is going up, the number of workplace hazards identified has been declining. [Jeff Bailey, *GAO Criticizes OSHA's Program for Small Businesses*, Wall Street Journal, Oct. 30, 2001, at p. B2]

In July 2001, the Department of Labor announced that it would relax its OSHA enforcement but would add staff to help companies achieve initial compliance and avoid violating OSHA. DOL said that most of its oversight would go to the 5% of companies with the worst health and safety record (e.g., certain construction companies). [Kathy Chen, *Labor Department to Ease Workplace Enforcement*, Wall Street Journal, July 3, 2001, at p. A2]

[B] Inspections

Inspections are a central part of OSHA's enforcement function, because direct evidence about workplace conditions is necessary. In the OSHA fiscal year ending in September 2000, 2400 federal and state inspectors performed 36,000 inspections.

A "programmed inspection" takes place on a routine basis, when workplaces are chosen at random from a list of sites with above-average injury rates.

Inspections can also be made based on written complaints from employees, former employees, or their representatives, such as attorneys and union staff. Complaints are made to OSHA's area director or Compliance Officer (CO). OSHA investigates the complaint and sends a copy of the complaint to the employer. (The complainant can request that his or her name be suppressed on the employer's copy.) Depending on the nature of the complaint, OSHA will either send the employer a letter describing the hazard that has been charged and giving a date for abatement, or schedule an inspection. The inspection probably will be scheduled if the employer ignores a letter from OSHA or if there is evidence of other safety problems.

OSHA is supposed to respond to a complaint of imminent danger within one day, to an allegation of a serious hazard within five working days, or within 30 working days if the complaint is less serious. A serious hazard is one that creates a reasonable expectation that it could cause death or irreversible bodily injury.

Generally speaking, OSHA inspections are made on an unannounced basis. However, the employer is entitled to notice if an imminently dangerous situation is alleged (because abatement is more important than detecting violations), if special arrangements are needed for the inspection, or if the inspection will be made outside normal business hours.

The CO shows credentials at the workplace and asks for permission to inspect. If permission is refused, the CO cannot perform a search without an administrative search warrant granted by a court, based on OSHA's showing that it has reason to believe that violations of the General Duty Clause or a more specific standard have occurred. However, courts need far less proof to authorize an administrative search than a search in a criminal case.

Most employers grant permission, so the CO explains the procedure in the opening conference with the employer. Next is the "walk-through" (employer and employee representatives are allowed to comment). At this stage, the CO makes notes on any hazardous or noncompliant conditions prevailing in the workplace. At this point, the inspector often points out trivial violations that can be corrected on the spot: mopping up a pool of water that could cause a slip, for instance. At this stage, the CO usually asks to see the business's logs, summary reports, exposure records, training records, and other safety-related paperwork.

If the inspection is based on a complaint, the employer has the right to review the complaint, and can instruct the CO to limit the inspection to the issues raised by the complaint. Employers who take this option should make a written record of the scope of authorization, give a copy to the inspector, and retain a copy for their records.

The last part of the inspection is the "closing conference" when the CO reveals findings about potential OSHA violations.

COs do not have the power to issue citations during an inspection. The CO must return to the OSHA office and confer with the Area Director about the level of citation (if any) that should be issued in response to each perceived deficiency.

The procedure is slightly different in the construction industry. A "targeted inspection" is a short-form inspection that concentrates on the major hazards to construction workers' safety: falls, falling objects, electrical hazards, and vehicle accidents. The CO decides whether to do a focused or a full inspection during the opening conference. At sites where the general or prime contractor has a workable safety plan and designates a representative to work with OSHA, only a focused inspection will be performed. In contrast to a nonconstruction inspection, citations can be issued during a focused inspection if there are serious violations, or nonserious violations that are not abated immediately.

[C]   Tips for Easier Inspections

For advice about how to sail through an inspection with the minimum of trauma, *see* the informative article by Robert J. Grossman [Robert J. Grossman, *Handling Inspections: Tips From Insiders*, HR Magazine, Oct. 1999, at p. 40] including these tips:

- Check the credentials of anyone claiming to be an OSHA inspector. (The OSHA photo IDs have the Department of Labor seal on the back). An environmental activist, labor organizer, or industrial spy could be trying to gain behind-the-scenes access to your operation by impersonating an OSHA inspector;
- Ask if the inspection is programmed; is based on a complaint; or is a follow-up after an accident;
- Find out if the complainant is a current employee. (The inspector will not give you the name, but will tell you if the complainant falls into this category);
- Have your lawyer review all requests for documents and information, and review what you turn over;
- The inspector may quit after a record review, if the records are complete and up to date;
- At the opening conference, get the inspector to agree to protect your trade secrets;
- If the inspector takes photographs or makes a video during the walk-around stage, take your own confirming photos and videos and keep them for comparison;
- Get duplicates of physical samples taken by the inspector, and ask for copies of OSHA's test reports;

- Make sure that someone within the organization has ongoing OSHA responsibility (HR often takes this role). Train employees how to respond to questions from an OSHA inspector;
- Take the inspector to the area he or she wants to see by the shortest, most direct route and not the long way around—in case the inspector sees something else that raises questions;
- Get to know the personnel in the OSHA area office and develop a cooperative working relationship with them.

§ 31.10   OSHA CITATIONS

[A]   Categories of Violations

The CO's comments during an inspection are not official OSHA pronouncements, and the employer cannot be penalized for failing to respond to them. However, penalties can be imposed for failure to respond to a written citation from the OSHA Area Director that is sent within six months after the date of the alleged violation that is cited. The citation form lists the violations, classified by seriousness, imposes penalties, and sets a date for abating each violation. Usually, the citation will be Form OSHA-2, sent by certified mail, although other forms can be used.

OSHA violations are generally divided into four categories: de minimis (trivial), nonserious, serious, and other. Penalties are heavier on willful violations or repeat violations within a three-year period. Criminal penalties might be imposed in the very worst cases, such as the preventable death of an employee.

[B]   Penalties

Penalties are set under OSHA § 17. [For OSHA's Field Inspection Reference Manual, CPL 2.103, Section 8-Chapter IV Post Inspection Procedures, *see* <http://www.osha-slc.gov/Firm_osha_data/100008.html>]

It's hard to predict what penalty will be imposed for any particular OSHA violation. There are many factors involved, primarily the gravity of the violation. However, the size of the business, the employer's past history of violations, and whether or not the employer acted in good faith are all important considerations.

The civil penalty for a violation, including a violation that consists of failure to post the mandatory notice, can go up to $7,000 per violation. If a violation is not serious, and the penalty would be less than $100, then no penalty is assessed; there is a $100 minimum penalty for serious violations. Furthermore, if a violation is willful, the minimum penalty is $5,000 for a nonserious or posting violation—and this minimum amount cannot be reduced by administrative discretion. The minimum penalty for a willful serious violation is $25,000.

The gravity of a violation depends on two factors: the severity of the damage that the violation could cause and how probable it is that the violation will result in occupational injury or illness.

The multifactorial penalty analysis also reflects factors such as the number of workers exposed, how close they were to the danger, how frequently they were exposed, and how long exposure continued, whether appropriate PPE was used to reduce the risk, and other working conditions.

OSHA has the discretion to reduce penalties greatly, to reflect good faith, small business size (no reduction can be made on this basis if the enterprise has more than 250 employees), and previous acceptable history with regard to occupational safety and health violations.

Failure-to-abate penalties are applied when a cited violation becomes a final order, and the employer fails to correct the violation. Normally, the maximum failure-to-abate penalty will be limited to 30 times the daily proposed penalty for that violation.

An employer who repeatedly violates OSHA is subject to much harsher penalties: up to $70,000 per violation. If the employer has fewer than 250 employees, the penalty based on the gravity of the violation (GBP) is doubled for the first repeated violation, and quintupled if a violation was previously cited twice. For employers of over 250, the GBP is multiplied by five for a first repeated violation, by 10 for a second repeated violation. (The overall potential for harm is greater in a larger workplace, which explains the difference.)

The civil penalty for failure to maintain the proper records can be as high as $7,000 per violation: *see* OSHA § 17(c). Failure to post the annual record in February each year, so employees can review it, can be penalized by a $1,000 fine. (Starting in 2003, the annual summary will have to remain posted throughout February, March, and April of each year.)

Failure to post OSHA citations as required by 29 C.F.R. § 1903.16 is punishable by a fine of $3,000. Failure to report a fatal accident is penalized by $5,000 to $7,000. Refusing to provide records to employees or their representatives to examine or copy is subject to a fine of $1,000 per form per year that is denied to employees. A penalty of $2,000 can be imposed if the employer has advance notice of an inspection but fails to inform the employee representative (thus preventing the representative from participating in the inspection).

29 U.S.C. § 666(e) imposes penalties whenever a willful violation of an OSHA standard leads to the death of any employee. This penalty can be assessed against the culpable employer on a multiemployer worksite, even though the deceased worker was employed by one of the other companies at the site. [*United States v. Pitt-Des Moines Inc.*, 168 F.3d 976 (7th Cir. 1999)]

Criminal penalties (imposed by courts, not directly by OSHA) can be imposed, under OSHA § 17(f)-(h), for giving advance notice of an inspection that is supposed to be made unannounced, for giving false information, or assaulting or interfering with the work of a CO.

It does not constitute double jeopardy to impose administrative penalties on an employer after it has been convicted of criminal OSHA violations, because the administrative penalties are clearly civil and cannot result in imprisonment. [*S.A. Healy Co. v. OSHRC*, 138 F.3d 686 (7th Cir. 1998)]

§ 31.11   OSHA APPEALS

Employers don't have to agree with an OSHA citation. There are several administrative steps that can be taken to protest—although these administrative remedies do have to be exhausted before filing suit.

If an employer challenges a citation, OSHA has to prove that the employer failed to live up to some applicable standard. The agency also has to prove that feasible corrective measures existed that could have brought the employer into compliance. If the standard has a time element (for example, the noise exposure standard does), then OSHA also has to prove that the condition existed long enough and intensely enough to constitute a violation.

OSHA has to prove that the employer knew about the condition or could have become aware by exercising due diligence. It is not necessary to prove that the employer was aware of the standard and deliberately chose to violate it. A supervisor's or foreman's knowledge will be attributed to the employer, unless the employer maintained work rules that satisfied the OSHA standard, communicated those rules to employees, and enforced the work rules.

OSHA is entitled to prove the employer's knowledge (and therefore does not have to prove actual knowledge) in some situations:

- Another employee has already been injured by the same hazardous conditions;
- Several written employee complaints have already been made to OSHA;
- The employer knows that employees habitually omit safety equipment, or otherwise allow hazardous conditions to be present in the workplace;
- The employer doesn't provide enough training;
- The employer doesn't enforce its own safety rules;
- The hazards would easily have been discovered if the employer had performed an adequate inspection.

An employer that receives an OSHA citation has 15 days to file a Notice of Contest, disputing that there was a violation, demanding a fair period of time to abate the violation, or challenging the size of the penalty. If the employer is not sure whether or not to contest, it can schedule an informal conference with the OSHA area director to discuss OSHA's position on workplace conditions and how to improve them.

There is no official form for the Notice of Contest; it is simply a letter stating in plain English that the employer disagrees with the citation and wants to contest some or all of the violations, to ask for a smaller penalty, and/or ask for more time to comply. If the Notice of Contest is not filed within the required 15 days, the citation becomes final, and no court has the power to reverse it or even to review it.

Tip: If an employer appeals in bad faith, knowing that the citation is valid, the whole period of time until the challenge is resolved is treated as a period of noncompliance, with additional penalties for each day.

Another factor is whether the citation will affect other cases. For instance, some courts allow an OSHA citation, especially an uncontested one, to be introduced as evidence of dangerous conditions (e.g., in a Worker's Compensation hearing). Contesting the violation can help clear the employer's name.

When a notice is filed, an OSHA Administrative Law Judge (ALJ) will set a date for a hearing. Although the hearing is informal, it is still governed by the Federal Rules of Evidence. The ALJ's decision becomes final 30 days after it is rendered, unless it is contested.

All Notices of Contest, and all ALJ decisions, are automatically passed along to the Occupational Safety and Health Review Commission (OSHRC). OSHRC has the power to order review of part or all of an ALJ decision. The employer, or any other party adversely affected by the decision, can file a Petition for Discretionary Review. Although it has the power to raise the level of a violation, OSHRC usually doesn't do so.

The employer can raise many arguments to OSHRC:

- The CO got the facts wrong;
- The employer did not know, and had no duty to know, that the violation had occurred;
- The inspection itself was improper—for example, the inspection was really a search, requiring a warrant that had not been obtained;
- OSHA applied the wrong standard;
- The standard itself was invalid, because it was not properly promulgated, or was so vague that employers could not reasonably be expected to understand and comply with it;
- The real cause of the violation was misconduct by employees, beyond the employer's control; this misconduct is unlikely to recur;
- Complying with the OSHA requirement actually increased the hazards to employees rather than decreasing them, but the employer was unable to get a variance.

OSHRC issues an order after considering the employer's arguments and defenses. The employer has 60 days from the date of the OSHRC order to file a further appeal. The employer can now go to federal court, because administrative remedies have been appealed. In fact, the employer can bypass the District Court (the lowest tier in the federal court system, where federal cases normally begin) and appeal either to the Court of Appeals for the Circuit where the violation is alleged to have occurred, or to the District of Columbia Circuit.

§ 31.12   ABATEMENT

Abatement—removal of hazardous conditions—is the rationale for the whole OSHA process. An uncontested citation, a citation for which the contest period has expired, and a citation where the employer's challenge was partially or wholly unsuccessful, all give rise to abatement responsibilities.

Employers are required to abate violations within the shortest reasonable interval for correction. The CO orders an abatement date. Ordinarily, this will not be more than 30 days, although the initial abatement date could be more than 30 days from the date of the inspection if structural changes are needed, or if abatement relies on components that take a long time to deliver. [*See* OSHA Field Inspection Reference Manual CPL 2.103, at <http://www.osha-slc.gov/ Firm_osha_data/100008.html>]

Tip: If a citation notes several violations, only some of which are contested, the appropriate action is to correct the uncontested violations, notify the OSHA area director that correction has occurred, and pay the penalties for the uncontested violations. With respect to contested citations, abatement and payment of fines will be suspended until there is an OSHRC final order.

OSHA reinspects the premises. If the same conditions are detected, penalties of up to $1,000 a day can be imposed. The employer, however, can contest penalties in the same way as an original citation.

The employer is entitled to file a Petition for Modification of Abatement (PMA) with the OSHA Area Director, no later than the scheduled abatement date, if factors beyond the employer's control prevent abatement. The PMA explains what the employer has done to cure the problem, how much additional time is required and why, and what the employer will do to protect employees until full abatement is achieved. The PMA must be posted and served on the employer's workforce, because they have the right to contest it.

If the PMA is uncontested, the Secretary of Labor has the power to approve it. OSHRC holds a hearing on contested PMAs, to determine if the employer did in fact act in good faith and was really unable to achieve full compliance. The employer does not have to comply with the underlying citation during the time that the PMA is under consideration.

§ 31.13 OSHA CONSULTATION

State OSH agencies, working under grants from the federal OSHA, offer free on-site consultation services to identify and eliminate potential safety problems before they become real ones. The consultants are also available by telephone for advice and discussion. On-site visits are followed up by a written analysis of workplace hazards and suggestions for correction.

The consultants do not have the authority to impose penalties, but participating employers must agree to take steps to correct whatever problems the program uncovered.

Consultations cannot take place while an OSHA inspection is already underway, but if a consultation is scheduled, there is a good chance that OSHA will cancel a scheduled inspection, unless it is investigating a fatality or serious accident, or it is suspected that employees are in imminent danger.

An employer that has completed a consultation, made corrections based on the recommendations, and who posts a notice of correction where employees can see it, is entitled to request one year's immunity from scheduled OSHA inspections.

OSHA gives priority to scheduling consultation in industries with high hazards. The names of companies engaging in consultation will not be disclosed to state or federal enforcers unless the employer refuses to correct imminent hazards that are discovered during the process. [For OSHA's August 2001 procedure manual for the consultation program, *see* <http://www.osha-slc.gov/OshDoc/toc_directive.html>]

§ 31.14   VOLUNTARY PROGRAMS

Under the title of Voluntary Protection Programs (VPP), OSHA has three incentive programs (Star, Merit, and Demonstration) for employers with good safety records, who are supposed to serve as examples for other companies. Participants qualify for participation by proving that they maintain safe workplace and provide ongoing safety training for workers. OSHA and state authorities do not do programmed inspections at participating companies, although inspections will still be made if a complaint is registered.

Employers can apply to OSHA for VPP certification. They must complete applications that demonstrate their qualifications for participation. OSHA sends an inspector to check the company's safety records and site conditions.

Also see the OSHA Partnership page, <http://www.osha-slc.gov/fso/vpp/partnership/index.html>, explaining the Partnership program, "an extended, voluntary, cooperative relationship with groups of employers, employees, and employee representatives" to improve safety and health.

CHAPTER 32

UNEMPLOYMENT INSURANCE

§ 32.01   INTRODUCTION

In the late 1990s, the subject of unemployment insurance was something of a backwater: a topic of limited interest in a booming, full-employment economy. However, starting in mid-2001, and accelerating after the September 11 attack, unemployment insurance, and especially the employer's experience rating and funding obligations, became far more interesting.

Unemployment compensation (UC) is a state-administered insurance system. Employers make contributions to a fund. The State Employment Security Agencies (SESAs) that administer the system receive federal funding. In exchange, they must perform investigations and other managerial tasks.

Each state creates an Unemployment Insurance Trust Fund from employer contributions. In a few states, employee contributions are also required. However, FICA tax imposes equal (and substantial) burdens on both employer and employee, but unemployment tax is almost exclusively a responsibility of the employer. The theory is that in good times, unemployment will be low, and the fund will accumulate a surplus that can be used in bad times to pay unemployment insurance claims.

The Department of Labor's unadjusted and seasonally adjusted data on the number of unemployment insurance claims can be found at <http://www.dol.gov>. You can order Unemployment Insurance Weekly Claims Reports from (202) 219-6871.

§ 32.02   ELIGIBILITY FOR BENEFITS

[A]   Generally

Two of the most important determinants in entitlement are whether the employee worked long enough before termination to qualify for benefits; and the reason for termination. The "base period" is the period of time used to analyze whether the job continued long enough.

In most states, the base period is the first four of the preceding five completed calendar quarters. Some states allow the four most recent quarters of employment to be counted. The difference is whether the most recent months of employment (which might have higher earnings) will be counted. Theoretically, only persons who earned at least a minimum amount during the base period can collect UI benefits. In practice, these limits are so low that nearly all employees meet them.

The rationale for the UI system is to provide benefits for employees who lose their jobs through "no fault of their own." But in this context, an employee will not be considered to be at fault even if the employer was justified in firing him or her—for instance, if an employee is fired for incompetence but there was no crime or wrongdoing.

In general, benefits will not be available to anyone who quit voluntarily without good cause. However, states vary as to whether employees who quit will be entirely denied UI benefits, or whether benefit eligibility will merely be delayed. If the employer's conduct has been so abusive as to constitute constructive discharge, then the employee will be deemed to have had good cause to resign. However, there are situations where the employee is considered to have acted with good cause, even if the employer was not at fault. Many states interpret quitting a job to follow a spouse who has gotten a job elsewhere to constitute good cause.

Benefits are also denied to persons who are guilty of "misconduct detrimental to the best interests of the employer." This is interpreted in an industrial rather than moral light, so improper activities are likely to rule out UI benefit eligibility even if they are not criminal in nature. Poor job performance would not be treated as "misconduct," unless it demonstrated gross negligence or willful disregard of the employer's best interests.

Depending on the state, disqualifying misconduct might also have to be work-related. Excessive absence or insubordination might be treated as misconduct. Being intoxicated on business premises would almost certainly be considered misconduct.

Continued eligibility requires the claimant to make a serious search for work. Benefits will be terminated if the claimant receives but rejects a legitimate job offer for suitable work. Benefits will not be paid in any week in which the claimant receives a pension, annuity, retirement pay, or any other private or government payment based on past work history. But benefits can be paid in a week in which the claimant receives a distribution from a profit-sharing plan, because that is not treated as compensation for work.

Benefits can be paid based on job loss due to a material change in working conditions imposed by the employer, if the employee has a valid reason for being unable to work under the new conditions. (This is referred to as "voluntary with good cause attributable to the employer.") A published job description can be evidence of the original nature of the job, and therefore whether material change has occurred. If a job is described as a day-shift position, a change to a night or swing shift might well be considered material.

In a Wisconsin case from 2001, for example, benefits were granted because it was not considered unreasonable for the employee to quit instead of accepting a transfer to a plant 25 miles away. Although the offered new job was similar to the old one, and paid the same hourly base rate, the employee would suffer an effective 19% reduction in net pay because of commuting costs, loss of lead worker pay, and lower incentive pay. [*Research Prods. Corp.*, Unempl. Ins. Rep. (CCH) ¶9507 (Wis. Cir. 2001)]

The employer's failure to investigate a claimant's repeated reports of sexual harassment made her resignation a voluntary quit with good cause attributable to the employer, so benefits were available. [*Yaeger*, Unempl. Ins. Rep. (CCH) ¶8915 (Fla. Dist. App. 2001)]

[B] BAA-UC

On December 3, 1999, the DOL published a Notice of Proposed Rulemaking at 64 Fed. Reg. 67972, affecting 20 C.F.R. Part 604, creating a program known as BAA-UC. BAA stands for Birth and Adoption. DOL finalized the rule, with no significant changes from the proposal, on June 13, 2000 [*see* 65 Fed. Reg. 37,209] Under this rule, unemployment benefits can provide partial wage replacement for new parents. The theory is that families and the economy, as a whole, will benefit by a period of time when parents stay at home with newborns and newly adopted children before returning to work. (*See* § 38.03 for a discussion of FMLA birth and adoption leave.)

Under BAA-UC, new parents can be treated as "able and available" for work, for a one-year period beginning with the week of birth or placement for adoption. States can pass laws and start an unemployment program for new parents, starting with the enactment of the Final Rule. States can limit BAA-UC to "approved leave" that has been negotiated between parents and employers, with a specified date for return to work.

Also see *Wilson* [Unempl. Ins. Rep. (CCH) ¶8227 (Del. Super. 2000)], holding that an employee who quits because a shift change conflicts with parental obligations has acted with good cause, and therefore is entitled to benefits.

[C] Disaster Unemployment and the JCWAA

One of the responses to the September 11, 2001, terrorist attack was a Department of Labor Interim Final Rule published in the Federal Register on November 13, 2001. [66 Fed. Reg. 56959–56962, taking effect as of that date]

A federal statute, 42 U.S.C. § 177(a), the Robert T. Stafford Disaster Relief and Emergency Assistance Act, establishes the Disaster Unemployment Assistance (DUA) program. Up to 26 weeks of benefits can be furnished after a major disaster declared by the President, for unemployment caused by that disaster for which no other benefits are available. DUA eligibility ceases when the state agency finds that unemployment is no longer directly traceable to the major disaster.

The DUA benefit is considered a UC benefit. It cannot exceed the maximum benefit payable under the state's UC law.

The November 2001 rule provides a definition of "unemployment as a direct result" of a major disaster [20 C.F.R. § 625.5(c)]—a term that was not previously defined. According to the Interim Final Rule, the DUA benefits are limited to the immediate result of the disaster itself, not more remote consequences of a chain of events that was started or made worse by the disaster. Examples of direct results are unemployment caused by damage to or destruction of the physical worksite, lack of access to the worksite because the government has ordered it closed, or lack of work and lost revenues caused to a business that got the majority of its income from the premises that were damaged, destroyed, or shut down. But "ripple effects" (for instance, if an office building is closed, workers who can't come in to work don't stop at a coffee shop for snacks) are not covered.

The Interim Final Rule gives, as an example of potential DUA beneficiaries, workers at airports (including restaurant and store employees and service personnel) closed by government orders. But workers at other airports would not be entitled, even if a decline in air travel resulted in job loss.

As of March 2002, seven states had extension programs under which laid-off employees could qualify for an additional 13 weeks of benefits, paid for by the federal system, over and above the standard 26 weeks and the 13-week extension that applied in all the states. In Arkansas, Idaho, Massachusetts, Michigan, Nevada, Pennsylvania, and Wisconsin, the extension was granted because the state's unemployment rate exceeded 4%.

In addition to this federal law, some states have state "optional trigger" laws that let them provide a 13-week extended benefit period when the state unemployment rate hits 6.5%. Oregon and Washington were the only states that both had such a statute and had a high enough unemployment rate to kick it into operation. [Russell Gold, *Extending Benefits*, Wall Street Journal, March 13, 2001, at p. B8]

Part of the Job Creation and Worker Assistance Act of 2002 (JWCAA) [Pub. L. No. 107-147] is the Temporary Extended Unemployment Compensation Act. JCWAA § 202 gives the states the power to enter into an agreement with the U.S. Secretary of Labor under which the state provides temporary extended unemployment benefits to people who have used up their other unemployment benefits; for example, if they have received the maximum amount of benefits payable under state law, or their benefit year has expired. (The federal government reimburses the state for the temporary extended benefits that the state pays.)

A beneficiary's eligibility also requires having worked 20 weeks in the base year. The temporary extended unemployment benefit amount is the same as the unemployment benefit payable during the regular benefit year for a week of total unemployment. Temporary benefits can be paid starting in the week the state enters into the agreement with the Secretary of Labor, but must end (unless Congress passes additional legislation) by January 1, 2003.

The agreement between the state and the Secretary of Labor must provide for creation of a temporary extended unemployment compensation account for each eligible individual; the balance of the account is the most that can be paid out in temporary extended benefits. The account, in turn (*see* JCWAA § 203) contains either 13 times the beneficiary's average weekly benefit for the benefit year, or 50% of his or her regular compensation payable during the benefit year—whichever is smaller. The account is replenished with an amount equal to its original balance if the account is exhausted at a time that the state is in an extended benefit period under the Federal-State Extended Unemployment Compensation Act.

[D]   Case Law on Benefit Eligibility

The treasurer of a corporation (of which he was also a 25% shareholder) applied for UI benefits. The New Jersey Superior Court ruled that he was not unemployed at the point when the company stopped operating but had not yet dissolved or applied for bankruptcy protection. In this reading, UI benefits are not available to a 5% or greater stockholder as long as he or she holds corporate ownership or continues to own stock. [*Fernicola*, Unempl. Ins. Rep. (CCH) ¶8637 (N.J. Super. 2000)]

The question of who should be considered an employee arises in many contexts, including unemployment compensation. The UI system is for "employees," not independent contractors, so characterization is important. The Ohio Court of Appeals held that a delivery driver who subleased a truck from a trucking company was an employee and hence potentially entitled to benefits, because the company controlled his work schedule and maintained the truck, which had to be returned to a designated storage location at the end of the work shift. [*Toth*, Unempl. Ins. Rep. (CCH) ¶10,109 (Ohio App. 2001)]

In the view of the Arkansas Court of Appeals, benefits should have been granted to a person who was discharged for pleading "no contest" to a domestic violence felony. The charges did not harm the employer's interests, because they were not work-related. [*Baldor Elec. Co.*, Unempl. Ins. Rep. (CCH) ¶8501 (Ark. App. 2000)] But the Mississippi Court of Appeals denied benefits, on the grounds of disqualifying misconduct, to two claimants who participated in an unauthorized strike that violated the no-strike provision of their Collective Bargaining Agreement (CBA). [*Berry*, Unempl. Ins. Rep. (CCH) ¶8284 (Miss. App. 2001)] They were aware that the strike violated the CBA. They had used grievance procedures in the past; this time, they were too impatient to go through channels.

An individual who has a reasonable expectation of reemployment (absolute certainty is not required) will not be required to make a formal search for other work. [*Thomas*, Unempl. Ins. Rep. (CCH) ¶9510 (Wis. Cir. 2000)] The claimant, #2 on the seniority list of a unionized workplace where the Collective Bargaining Agreement stipulated recall on the basis of seniority, could reasonably expect to be called back to work when the workplace re-opened after it was purchased. So he could collect unemployment benefits in the interim, even if he didn't make a job search.

Benefits were denied to a person who quit to get a higher-paid job, then was laid off from that job: The offer of higher pay elsewhere is not good cause to leave a job, because the first employer is not at fault. [*Total Audio-Visual Systems, Inc.*, Unempl. Ins. Rep. (CCH) ¶8484 (Md. App. 2000)] But ending a relationship with a temporary placement agency in order to accept a full-time permanent job constitutes good cause for quitting temporary work. [*Duby*, Unempl. Ins. Rep. (CCH) ¶8896 (Fla. App. 2000)] Benefits could therefore be granted after the loss of the permanent job.

Ability to work is another important criterion. The claimant in *Daniels* [Unempl. Ins. Rep. (CCH) ¶9022 (Iowa Dist. Ct. 2000)] was seven months pregnant when her doctor told her to find a job she could do sitting down. She worked as a blackjack dealer, required to stand for her entire seven-hour shift. Her employer put her on medical leave; unemployment benefits were denied because of her medically based inability to work.

In contrast, a truck driver was granted benefits in another Iowa case. [*Priority Express Inc.*, Unempl. Ins. Rep. (CCH) ¶9026 (Iowa Dist. Ct. 2000)] Her work-related back injury required her to drive a vehicle with an automatic transmission. The employer transferred her from the only route that had a truck she could drive. The district court treated her leaving the job as justified by the employer's refusal to accommodate her disability-related needs.

As the ADA chapter shows, both parties must participate in the process of accommodation. The Washington Court of Appeals denied benefits to a claimant who developed sensitivity to the chemicals used in his job. The employer moved him to a job in an outside tunnel, but the problems continued. The company's HR director suggested that he seek accommodation under the ADA, but he quit instead. Benefits were denied because he failed to exhaust all reasonable alternatives before leaving the job. [*Woods*, Unempl. Ins. Rep. (CCH) ¶9022 (Wash. App. 2000)]

Even if there is no statutory bar to duplicate benefits, unemployment benefits cannot be paid at the same time as Worker's Compensation benefits—because one is premised on the ability to work, the other on *inability* to work. [*Ballard*, Unempl. Ins. Rep. (CCH) ¶8594 (Ind. App. 2000)]

Benefits were denied for misconduct in the case of an employee who, after three warnings for sleeping on the job, was found asleep in a parked truck. [*DeMaria*, Unempl. Ins. Rep. (CCH) ¶12,279 (N.Y. App. Div. 2001)]

[E] Cases Involving Drugs

In a 1998 Missouri appellate case, a truck driver was fired after failing a drug test. The employer said that benefits should be denied because he was fired for good cause. The truck driver's argument was that the report from the drug testing lab was hearsay and not admissible. The employer's contention was that the law of evidence provides a hearsay exception for documents kept in the course of business. But the trial court agreed with the fired employee, because the record was prepared in the course of the lab's business, not the trucking company's. But when the case was appealed, the employer prevailed: Anybody's business records can be introduced, as long as they were made in the normal course of business, they were made close enough to the event to be reliable, and there are other reasons to consider them reliable. [*Associated Wholesale Grocers v. Moncrief*, 970 S.W.2d 425 (Mo. App. 1998)]

An employer's policy called for termination of any employee found with a detectable level of alcohol or illegal drugs. The plaintiff of *Smith v. Zero Defects*

Inc. [132 Idaho 881 (1999)] tested positive for amphetamines in a random test, although he did not appear to be impaired at that time. Several states (Idaho, Nebraska, Nevada, Oklahoma, and Utah) consider violation of an employer's zero-tolerance policy to be misconduct serious enough to rule out benefits. In these states, off-duty drug use can be serious enough to prevent the user from receiving unemployment benefits. But Arizona, Kansas, Oregon and Washington require evidence of workplace impairment.

The Oregon Court of Appeals said that it was not disqualifying misconduct for an employee to refuse when the employer ordered him to take a drug test on his own time, without compensation, after being written up for insubordination. [*Andrews*, Unempl. Ins. Rep. (CCH) ¶8878 (Ore. App. 2000)] The court held that the employer's policy of requiring a drug test after all reprimands was not reasonable in cases where there was no evidence of drug use.

§ 32.03 CALCULATION OF BENEFITS

[A] Basic Calculation

The actual benefit depends either on the claimant's average weekly wage, or the wage earned in the quarter of the base period when wages were highest. For partial weeks of unemployment, a reduced benefit is available, although the various states use different calculation methods.

Individual claimants are usually assigned a 52-week "benefit year," beginning when the claim is filed, although some states use the same benefit year for all claimants. Usually, a one-week waiting period is imposed before benefits become payable. Most states limit the payment of basic benefits to 26 weeks, although a few states permit 30 weeks of payments. Once claimants use up the basic benefit, they must wait until the next benefit year before starting another base period and therefore qualifying for unemployment benefits all over again. So someone who receives benefits in a particular benefit year will have to be re-employed and work for at least a second base period before qualifying for a second benefit period.

Extensions to the basic benefits are available under appropriate circumstances. The Employment Security Amendments of 1970 created a program of Federal-State Extended Benefits, covering benefits during weeks 27–39 of a spell of unemployment. Some states (Alaska, California, Connecticut, Hawaii, Minnesota, Oregon) have state-funded extended benefits programs that do not receive federal funding.

[B] Benefit Offsets

Benefit offsets may be applied in two situations: if the unemployment benefit is reduced because other income is received, or if the UI benefits offset other amounts that the person would otherwise be entitled to receive.

As noted above, payments (e.g., pension, IRA) reduce entitlement to unemployment compensation if they can be traced to work done by the employee in the past. The offset is applied only to a plan maintained or contributed to by the company that was the employer during the base payment period, or the employer that is chargeable with the unemployment claim. So if the pension was earned at Company A, but the worker became unemployed while working for Company A, pension will not offset the unemployment insurance benefit.

States differ in their treatment of rollovers. Some states (e.g., New York and North Carolina) require a reduction of unemployment benefits because of rollovers; the other states do not. The Department of Labor's interpretation is that rollovers should not reduce unemployment benefits, but each state is permitted to set its own unemployment rules; this is not an exclusively federal area of regulation. [*See* Dori R. Perrucci, *When Pension and Unemployment Checks Don't Mix*, New York Times, Jan. 13, 2001, at p. Bus8] Furthermore, reduction is necessary only for amounts based on the claimant's own past work history, not when a person receiving benefits gets a distribution as a surviving spouse.

A New York case [*Sokolowski*, Unempl. Ins. Rep. (CCH) ¶12,280 (N.Y. App. Div. 2001)] holds that benefits should not have been reduced to zero on account of the pension paid by the employer. The pension was based on years of service and wages in the employee's high-five years, but that period occurred before his unemployment insurance base period. The employee did accrue service credit after being laid off, but that was not employment during the base period either. In contrast, the Florida Court of Appeals treated a back pay award from NLRB proceedings as "earned wages," so the claimant had to repay unemployment benefits that were previously awarded. [*Ching*, Unempl. Ins. Rep. (CCH) ¶8913 (Fla. App. 2001)]

About half the states deny unemployment benefits in weeks in which Worker's Compensation benefits are also received, or consider the Comp benefit income that reduces the benefit. (There is also a question of whether someone whose condition is bad enough to justify Comp benefits is "ready and able" to work even if he or she wants to work.)

Vacation pay also generally offsets unemployment benefits although an exception might be made if the claimant is deemed to be on vacation involuntarily rather than choosing to take time off.

Back pay awarded in a Title VII case generally is not reduced by UI. However, some courts, like the Second Circuit, say that courts that hear Title VII cases have discretion to reduce the award to account for UI received.

§ 32.04   EXPERIENCE RATING

[A]   Determination of Rating

The unemployment insurance rate that employers pay to help fund the system is partially based on their "experience" (the number of claims against them). The more claims, the higher the insurance rate. Seasonal businesses in particular often have a regular pattern of laying off workers who rely on UI until they are rehired.

The standard rate is 5.4%, although many employers qualify for a more favorable experience rate because of their record of few discharges and layoffs. The treatment of new employers varies from state to state. Some states impose a higher initial rate, until the employer can demonstrate its compliance with filing and payment requirements and its low experience of unemployment. On the other hand, some states have a special low rate for new employers until and unless they demonstrate bad claims experience. Some states even allow a zero rate (no tax at all) on employers with especially good claims experience. But all employers may become subject to the standard rate, and perhaps even additional "subsidiary contributions" if the state as a whole has a high unemployment rate and consequently has a low balance in its UI fund.

> **Tip:** Many states allow companies to lower their experience rates by making additional voluntary contributions to the state fund.

There are four basic methods of experience rating:

- Variations in payroll over time (showing whether the workforce has increased or decreased);
- Reserve ratio;
- Benefit ratio;
- Ratio of benefits to wages.

Some states use hybrid methods. States often permit joint filing and risk pooling: joint payment by a group of employers who get a combined experience rate for the group as a whole. A further refinement is a distinction between "charging" and "noncharging" claims. Some claims are not charged against the last employer's experience rating: for instance, claims for very brief periods of unemployment, or cases where the employee spent very little time working for the last employer. In some states, the employer is not charged for benefits paid after a period of disqualification based on voluntary quitting or misconduct, or when benefits are terminated because of the claimant's failure to seek suitable work. The rationale is that employers should not be penalized for circumstances beyond their control.

Another question is whether all employers in the base period, or only the last one in the series, will be charged with the claim. If more than one employer is charged, they might be charged with the most recent employer charged first, or the charge might be divided proportionate to the amount of wages they paid during the base period.

> **Tip:** Faced with the dual blows of a declining stock market and the September 11 attack, several state unemployment systems are running out of funds. The Texas Unemployment Compensation Trust Fund ran out in March 2002; the Missouri fund was expected to be exhausted in 2003. Other states may follow. So be prepared for an increase in the payroll tax rate to improve the financial soundness of your state's fund. [Russell Gold, *State Trust Funds For Unemployment Are Being Depleted*, Wall Street Journal, Jan. 24, 2002, at p. A2]

[B] Collateral Estoppel

Two related legal doctrines, collateral estoppel and res judicata, may come into play in contesting unemployment claims. An employer's unsuccessful contest of one worker's claim could harm the employer in later lawsuits. Legal advice is required as to the comparative risk of letting a claim go through without opposition (which will increase the employer's experience rating and therefore its rates) or contesting the claim but losing and being at a disadvantage when similar claims are made later.

The doctrine of res judicata refers to a matter that has already been tried. If one court has already dealt with a case, a higher court may handle an appeal of the matter, but a different court, which is not in the same line of authority, will not decide a matter that has already been decided. The doctrine of res judicata applies only to the same legal issues and the same or closely related parties. So if one employee sues his or her employer for race discrimination, the defense of res judicata will not be available if a different employee sues another employer for race discrimination. But Employee A's suit against Company B may have "collateral estoppel" effect on Employee C's suit against Company B, because Employee A's suit involves decisions on some basic issues about Company B's policies.

Either side can use collateral estoppel. In a later court case, the employer says that the administrative decision proves that the employee was guilty of misconduct, so terminating the employee was not wrongful. [*See* Chapter 39 for wrongful termination suits] The employee might assert that having received unemployment benefits proves that he or she did not quit and was not guilty of misconduct. Usually, administrative decisions in an unemployment matter will be granted collateral estoppel effect—but some states say that only a court decision can have that effect.

[C] Planning Steps to Reduce Unemployment Tax Liability

The unemployment insurance system is designed to stabilize employment, so it penalizes employers who dislocate workers unnecessarily. Terminated employees often find it much easier to get a new job if their employment record indicates that they quit instead of being fired. Agreeing to treat the termination as a resignation can benefit both employer and employee, if the employer's experience rate stays low. But employees must understand the effect that the characterization of the termination will have on their UI application.

Benefits were not available to an employee who took a severance package that provided substantial compensation in exchange for the employee's agreement to resign. The severance package was the result of extensive negotiations, in which the employee was represented by an attorney, so it was clear that the employee understood the implications of the deal. [*Operadelaware*, Unempl. Ins. Rep. (CCH) ¶8226 (Del. Sup. 2001)]

Companies can take various steps to reduce their experience rating and therefore their liability for unemployment tax:

- Understanding the nature and interaction of the federal and state payroll taxes;
- Reducing FUTA payments appropriately to compensate for state tax payments;
- Making sure taxes are paid when due;
- Reviewing state experience records for correctness;
- Understanding the experience rating system and the claims appeal procedure;
- Transferring employees within the organization instead of terminating them, to reduce unemployment claims;
- Analyzing operations to see if they could be made more consistent, less seasonal (thus avoiding layoffs and terminations);
- Firing unsatisfactory employees quickly, before they become eligible for benefits;
- Holding exit interviews with employees who quit, with a view to resolving problems that lead to resignations;
- Scheduling layoffs for Fridays, not earlier in the week wherever possible, because all the states provide benefits for partial weeks of employment;
- Maintaining adequate documentation of misconduct (which will also be useful if the terminated employee makes discrimination or wrongful termination claims);
- Monitoring all benefit claims and appealing claims that the company believes to be unfounded (e.g., employees who quit asserting involuntary termination).

Employers should also take prompt action, applying their own rules fairly and objectively. The Texas Court of Appeals, for instance, allowed benefits to be paid to an employee who was placed on indefinite suspension without pay 18 months after the first violation of the employer's rules, and 9 months after the last violation, because the employer failed to prove that the delay in discharge was reasonable. [*Morris III*, Unempl. Ins. Rep. (CCH) ¶8457 (Tex. App. 2001)] In a West Virginia case, benefits were barred for a time, but only for the period for simple misconduct. The claimant, who had already received four warnings for various infractions, was fired after leaving the work area without permission of her supervisor. The court said that she was not guilty of gross misconduct, because none of the warnings said she was at risk of being fired. [*Williams*, Unempl. Ins. Rep. (CCH) ¶8774 (W. Va. Cir. Ct. 2001)]

§ 32.05 ADMINISTRATION AND APPEALS

If and when an ex-employee applies for UI benefits, the employer is asked for the reason for the termination. The employer is given a certain number of days to contest the claim. Once this period elapses, the employer can no longer protest the granting of benefits. If the employer objects to the grant of benefits, the state agency that administers unemployment benefits will assess the matter. The decision can be appealed to an Administrative Law Judge, an administrative board, and finally through the state court system (the federal courts are not appropriate for these questions).

If the employer fails to meet its burden of proof about the employee's disqualification at the administrative hearing, the case will not be remanded to give the employer another chance—and a remand will probably not be granted to sub-mit additional evidence [*Holmes*, Unempl. Ins. Rep. (CCH) ¶8664 (La. App. 2001)], so it's important to prepare well for the initial administrative hearing.

§ 32.06   FUTA COMPLIANCE

[A]   Generally

Employers (but not employees) have an obligation to make payments under the Federal Unemployment Tax Act (FUTA) to fund the federal program of unem-ployment insurance. The federal FUTA tax rate is 6.2%, but this tax is imposed only on the first $7,000 of wages. The states set their own taxable wage bases. For 2001, the amount ranged from $7,000 in Arkansas, California, Florida, Indiana, Louisiana, Mississippi, Missouri, Nebraska, South Carolina, South Dakota, and Tennessee to $28,400 in Hawaii. The wage base was $20,000 or more in Alaska, Idaho, Minnesota, Nevada, New Jersey, Oregon, Utah, and Washington.

Most employers actually pay a rate lower than 6.2%, because they qualify for a 5.4% credit for state employment taxes they have already paid. This is some-times referred to as the "normal credit" or "90% credit." Sometimes the company will qualify for an even lower FUTA rate if its experience rating is good. The addi-tional credit equals the difference between the basic state rate of 5.4% and the em-ployer's actual experience rate. However, the full credit can be claimed only in states that the Department of Labor certifies as compliant with federal require-ments. To qualify for the full credit, the employer must make all state contribu-tions by January 31 (the due date for Form 940).

The employer reports its FUTA liability on IRS Forms 940 or 940-EZ. The short form can be used by any employer (no matter how many workers it employs) that makes unemployment tax contributions to only one state, in which all wages subject to FUTA are also subject to the state tax, and the state taxes are paid no later than the due date for the federal form. Rev. Proc. 2001-9, 2001-3 I.R.B. 328 explains how to file Form 940 electronically. However, some states exempt the pay of corporate officers from state unemployment tax—so, in those states, the short form cannot be used.

Calculations and deposits of FUTA tax, plus Form 8109, are due quarterly. Deposits must be made at the local Federal Reserve Bank or other authorized fi-nancial institution on April 30, July 31, October 31, and January 31 of each year. Interest and perhaps penalties will be imposed for underpayment of FUTA tax. I.R.C. § 6321 and state laws impose a lien on the company's real and personal property for taxes (plus interest and penalties) that remain unpaid after the taxing authority files a demand for payment.

The employer is entitled to file Form 843 to apply for a refund of over-payments of FUTA. The employer must file the refund claim with the IRS before bringing suit for a refund.

IRS Final Regulations issued January 29, 1999, affecting I.R.C. § 3121 deal with the status of nonqualified deferred compensation for FUTA (as well as FICA) purposes. Wages are subject to these taxes when they are actually or constructively paid. Welfare plan benefits and severance pay are not considered deferred compensation; neither are early retirement benefits paid after January 1, 2000, but available only during a limited "window" period. FICA and FUTA taxes are due on nonqualified deferred compensation either when the work is performed or when the right to collect the deferred amounts is no longer subject to a substantial risk of forfeiture—whichever comes later.

[B] Other Tax Issues

The Supreme Court decision, *United States v. Cleveland Indians Baseball Co.* [532 U.S. 200 (2001)], holds that for FICA and FUTA purposes, if a case is settled through back pay payments to employees, the funds are taxed in the year the wages are actually paid—and if rates have increased over time, the later payment date means that higher rates apply.

Under a mid-2001 decision of the Eighth Circuit, payments made to tenured faculty members under an early retirement program were not wages, and therefore not subject to FICA withholding, because tenure is a property right, not merely an employment right. Therefore, they were being paid for surrendering this property right, not for their work for the university. [*North Dakota State U. v. United States,* Unempl. Ins. Rep. (CCH) ¶16,568 (8th Cir. 2001)]

Recipients of unemployment benefits can direct the state to withhold federal and/or state income tax from the benefits. [*See* Pub. L. No. 103-463, also known as GATT (General Agreement on Taxes and Tariffs) or the Uruguay Round Agreements Act]

Supplemental Unemployment Benefit funds (SUBs) are private funds maintained by employers to increase the level of income replacement that workers receive when they are discharged or laid off. Alabama, Alaska, California, Connecticut, Georgia, Hawaii, Illinois, Indiana, Maryland, New Hampshire, North Carolina, Ohio, Virginia, and West Virginia all have laws relevant to SUBs.

The question is whether SUB benefits are taxable wages for the people who receive them—and whether people who get SUB benefits are really unemployed or are still getting payments that are the equivalent of wages. Most states take the position that SUB benefits are not compensation, so they will not bar the receipt of UI benefits.

For federal tax purposes, SUB benefits are not considered wages if the employer funds the benefits by making deposits into a fund that has an independent trustee, and if the employee has no right or title in the fund until a layoff occurs. Payments from a collectively bargained SUB arrangement are not considered taxable wages. Only periodic payments, not lump sums, are permitted. Benefits received at a time when the employee has another job, or has turned down work permitted under a union agreement, are taxable.

If a payment merely returns to employees amounts that have already been included in taxable income, the money will not be taxed again, and withholding will not be required. But if employees are temporarily or permanently separated from service under a RIF, or when a plant is closed or an operation is discontinued, withholding may be required. [*See* IRS Publication 525, *Taxable and Nontaxable Income*, for information about SUB withholding]

IRS Private Letter Ruling 9525054 deals with a corporation's contributions to a trust that provided benefits linked to receipt of state UI benefits. The IRS ruled that the payments were not wages for FICA or FUTA purposes. Income tax withholding was not required. The tax treatment was the same even for employees who received benefits from the fund when they were ineligible for state unemployment benefits, e.g., before the waiting period had expired; because they didn't have enough wage credits; or they had exhausted the state benefits. Benefits from the trust became taxable wages if, when they added to all other remuneration including the state UI benefit, the total was greater than the worker's weekly pay earned during employment.

A SESA's claim for reimbursement of a bankrupt company's unemployment compensation liability gets priority as an "excise tax" in the company's Chapter 11 proceeding. Worker's Compensation, in contrast, is not treated as an excise tax, because the Comp system offers opportunities for private insurance that are absent in the UI context.

CHAPTER 33

WORKER'S COMPENSATION

§ 33.01   INTRODUCTION

The states administer the Worker's Compensation (WC) system to provide income to individuals who are unable to work because of employment-related illnesses and injuries. WC benefits, like unemployment insurance benefits, are funded by insurance maintained by the employer.

There were an estimated 11 million work-related injuries in 1997, requiring the Comp system to provide $111 billion for medical expenses and lost wages. The average injured employee was a 34-year-old male who suffered a musculoskeletal injury such as a wrenched back or an injured elbow. [Worker's Comp. Bus. Mgmt. Guide (CCH) Jan. 21, 1997, at 204]

A later estimate, from the National Safety Council, is that workplace injuries cost $125 billion a year, including $62 billion in lost wages and productivity, $19.9 billion in medical costs, and $16.7 billion for other costs to the employer. Furthermore, employers spend $42.4 billion a year for WC insurance. The Council says that 6.2% of employees file for compensation benefits each year, with the cost of a claim averaging $10,488. [Worker's Comp. Bus. Mgmt. Guide (CCH) 189, Aug. 7, 2001, at p. 309]

In 2001, an analysis of WC costs by region showed a pattern of surprisingly high costs in the South. Total WC payments were equal to 2.24% of workers' gross earnings in the South, versus 2.14% in the West, 1.97% in the Midwest, and 1.82% in the Northeast. Hourly cost of WC to the employer was 33 cents an hour in the South, 34 cents an hour in the Northeast, 31 cents in the Midwest, and 37 cents in the West. However, John F. Burton, Jr., author of the study, attributes the regional differences to inadequate wage replacement in the Northeast. Wage replacement is somewhat higher in the South, where wages tend to be low. The nationwide average hourly pay at the time of the study was $16.37, versus only $14.30 in the South, $15.74 in the Midwest, and $17.32 in the West. [Robert Gavin, *Cost of Worker's Comp.*, Wall Street Journal, July 25, 2001, at B12]

The WC system balances the interests of employers and employees: the employees' need for continuing income; the employer's need to have claims resolved quickly, in an administrative system that is not prone to make large sympathy awards the way the jury system is. Employers have a duty to make a prompt report of all accidents to the agency that administers the WC system. If an employee claims job-related injury or illness, the claim is heard by a WC tribunal. Depending on the state, this may be referred to as a board or a commission. The tribunal decides if the claim is valid. If so, benefits are awarded: reimbursement of medical expenses, plus weekly income.

WC benefits do not begin until a waiting period (typically three–seven days) has elapsed. This serves to distinguish genuine temporary disability from minor incidents without lasting consequences. However, most state WC laws also provide that, if a disability continues for a period of time (set by the state at anywhere from five days to over seven weeks), retroactive payments dating back to the original date of the injury will be granted.

The weekly benefit is usually limited to half to two-thirds of the pre-accident wage, subject to fixed minimum and maximum payments (often keyed to the state's average income) and also subject to an overall limitation on payments. In some states, additional payments are available if the worker has dependent children—especially in cases where the work-related incident caused the death of the worker. A burial benefit is also paid in death cases. Depending on the state it ranges between $1,000 and $5,000. In 2000, several states raised their maximum WC benefits. [*See* Glenn Whittington's summary of 2000 legislative changes in the January 2001 issue of the Monthly Labor Review at <http://www.bls.gov/opub/mlr/2001/01/art3exc.htm>]

However, a study by two labor professors concludes that WC benefits in 1998 were not adequate when compared to the recommendations of a 1974 model state Worker's Compensation law. In fact, in some states, the benefits were 25% or less of the benefits recommended in 1974. Louisiana workers got the lowest cash benefits for injuries ($4,395); Washington, D.C. workers got the highest, $30,907. [Robert Gavin, *Unjust Compensation?* Wall Street Journal, Jan. 23, 2002, at p. B12]

In 1999, the Supreme Court decided a Worker's Compensation case, *American Manufacturers Mutual Insurance Co. v. Sullivan.* [526 U.S. 46 (1999)] Under Pennsylvania's WC Act, once liability is no longer contested, the employer (or its insurer) has an obligation to pay for all reasonable or necessary treatment. However, an insurer or a self-insured employer is permitted to withhold payment for disputed treatment pending utilization review by an independent third party. The plaintiffs in this case sued state officials, WC insurers and a self-insured school district for civil rights and Due Process violations charging that their benefits had been withheld without notice, depriving the employees of a property right.

The Supreme Court held for the defendants. In the court's analysis, private insurers carrying out utilization review are not "state actors" subject to the Due Process Clause of the Constitution. Employees only have a property right after the treatment has been found reasonable and necessary. Therefore, the insurer has no obligation to notify employees, or to hold a hearing, if it withholds benefits until review has been completed and a decision made in the employees' favor.

§ 33.02   CLASSIFICATION OF BENEFITS

[A]   Type and Degree of Disability

If the initial tribunal accepts the contention that the worker is genuinely disabled, and the disability is in fact work-related, benefits are awarded based on the type and degree of disability.

There are four categories:

- Permanent total disability;
- Permanent partial disability;
- Temporary total disability;

- Temporary partial disability.

Permanent disability payments can be based on wage loss, earning capacity, physical impairment, or some combination. A "schedule injury" is loss of a finger, toe, arm, eye, or leg. The schedule determines the number of weeks of benefits payable for such an injury. Death benefits are also available to the survivors of persons killed in work-related incidents. For injuries such as back strains related to lifting, the tribunal must make a case-by-case determination of the number of weeks of disability that can be anticipated, and the seriousness of the disability.

Benefits can be granted for either "disability" or "impairment." The difference is that disability is defined to mean loss of wages, whereas impairment is permanent partial disability that does not cause wage loss.

The concept of Maximum Medical Improvement (MMI) comes into play in the case of a temporary disability. MMI is a doctor's opinion that there is no reasonable medical probability of further improvement in function (as determined based on factors such as current and proposed treatment, history of improvement, and preexisting conditions). Most states impose an obligation on the employer to notify the employee that MMI has been reached, and the employee is likely to lose benefits within 90 days unless he or she returns to work or finds other employment. Benefits can be extended past the MMI if the claimant makes an honest effort yet cannot find suitable work.

In addition to making wage-based payments, the employer must provide the employee with reasonable and necessary medical treatment, continued as long as the injured employee's medical condition requires. Most states include chiropractic in the definition of medical care. Many include home health attendants as well.

Tip: Sometimes, entitlement to WC is suspended during any period of time when the tribunal has ordered, or the employer has requested, a medical examination that the employee refuses. But protective state laws require confidentiality of information not related to the case. These laws also permit the employee to bring his or her own doctor to the examination, and permit the employee to see the examination report.

[B] Compensable Injuries

Whether an incident is covered by WC depends on several factors:

- Whether the injured person is a common-law employee rather than an independent contractor. Top managers may be denied benefits on the theory that they are the corporation's alter ego rather than ordinary employees. [*See also Granados v. Windson Development Corp.*, 257 Va. 103, 509 S.E.2d 290 (1999) (an illegal alien who was hired on the basis of forged IRCA documentation did not become an "employee" because no valid employment contract could have been formed. Therefore, when the alien was injured on the job, he was not a lawful employee and therefore was not eligible for WC);

- Whether the injury arises out of employment (illness or damage that could have happened to anyone, employed or not, is not covered under WC);

- Whether the injury arose in the course of employment (not during the commute to work or during horseplay).

In an Illinois case, benefits were denied for an at-work ankle injury suffered by an employee who hitched a ride on a forklift. The injury was not deemed work-related (he was on his way to the break room to pick up his lunch). Furthermore, the employer had an adequately publicized policy against riding double on fork-lifts, because they are not designed to carry passengers safely. [*Saunders v. The Industrial Comm'n*, 189 Ill. 2d 623 (Ill. Sup. 2000)]

Although injuries during commuting are usually not covered, under *Lee v. BSI Temporaries, Inc.* [114 Md. App. 1 (1997)], a temporary services agency was held responsible for injuries occurring on the private bus the agency furnished for its employees, on the theory that providing transportation made it more likely that the employees would arrive at work on time, thus enhancing the agency's reputation.

The Washington Court of Appeals found that a "drive-through lane" between the roadway on the employer's property and the sidewalk next to the workplace was not a "parking area" (injuries occurring in parking areas are excluded by many state WC systems). It was a temporary loading zone, and picking up a paycheck is a work-related activity, so an employee was entitled to WC benefits when she slipped and fell on ice and snow in the loading zone. [*Madera v. J.R. Simplot*, 104 Wash. App. 93 (2001)]

Sometimes injuries occurring outside the workplace will be covered—e.g., if the employer sent the employee to make a delivery or perform an errand, and the injury occurred in that place or en route. Injuries occurring during employer-sponsored athletics, or at a company picnic or holiday party, are probably compensable. Injuries on company premises during scheduled breaks are probably compensable, but employees take unscheduled breaks at their own risk because such injuries are considered to occur outside working hours. If employees are engaged in work-related tasks, injuries occurring at home can be compensable. [*A.E. Clevite, Inc. v. Tjas*, 996 P.2d 1072 (Utah App. 2000) (worker who became a paraplegic when he slipped while salting down his driveway so it would be safe for the expected delivery of a work-related package)]

Whether an incident is covered by WC may also depend on:

- Whether the injury results from an "accident" (an unexpected occurrence that can be linked to a definite time, place and occasion);

- Whether there is any reason that removes the injury from statutory coverage (e.g., the employee's substance abuse was a significant causative factor). The Arkansas Supreme Court reversed the lower court, for instance, finding that testimony that a carpenter smelled of alcohol at the time of his fall from a roof was enough to trigger the statutory presumption that the accident was caused by substance abuse, even though the hospital staff did not perform a blood alcohol test that would yield results that could be introduced into the record. [*Flowers v. Norman Oaks Construction*, 341 Ark. 474 (2000)]

One of the most vital factors is the employer's degree of control over the employee's activities. A Missouri case [*Leslie v. School Servs. & Leasing Inc.*, 947 S.W.2d 97 (Mo. App. 1997)] holds that a job applicant injured during training had not become an "employee," and therefore was not covered by WC. In this case, the potential employer didn't require her to take the training, didn't control her activities during the training process, and in fact didn't even guarantee her a job if she completed the training successfully.

At-work assaults raise difficult questions. The general rule is that injuries caused by assaults are compensable if the job increases the risk of encountering dangerous people (e.g., convenience store clerks are at risk of being robbed). But if the assault occurred for personal reasons, for instance if an abusive spouse commits an assault at the victim's workplace, the fact that the assault occurred at work will not necessarily render the injury a compensable one, if it is not work-related in any way. The WC system is essentially a no-fault system, so it will not be necessary to decide if the employer was at fault in not having a better security system.

Schmidt v. Smith [155 N.J. 44, 713 A.2d 1014 (1998)] says that bodily injury caused by sexual harassment is covered by the employer liability section of the Worker's Compensation insurance policy, because this section of the policy is designed to make funds available to compensate employees for their work-related injuries, even those for which Worker's Compensation payments are not available.

If the incident is covered, the next question is whether WC exclusivity applies. [*See* § 33.03]

[C]   Problems of Co-Employment

There are many reasons for employers to use temporary, contingent, part-time, or leased workers. In some cases, employee leasing results in lower WC costs. For employers who do not self-insure, the insurance rate has a lot to do with past experience. The smaller the workplace, the greater the impact that a few claims—especially a few very large claims—will have on its experience rating. That is one of the motivations for using leased workers to replace some or all of a company's common-law employees. [*See* § 1.09 for more about employee leasing]

Although a large leasing company will not qualify for small business discounted rates, a leasing company can offer the services of a broad range of workers, some in low-risk occupations such as office work.

In its initial years, a leasing company will probably qualify for low rates, because there has not been enough time for many accidents to happen. Abuses of the system are possible, if companies dissolve and re-form to manipulate their experience rates. Just for this reason, some states (e.g., Arizona, California, Colorado,

Florida, Nevada, New Hampshire, New Mexico, Oregon, South Carolina, Texas, and Utah) disregard the presence of leasing companies, and still require the underlying employer to buy WC insurance and maintain its own experience rating.

Furthermore, state courts may decide that the leasing company or temporary agency's client is the actual employer, because it has real control over the worker's activities and therefore is legally responsible for compensation for injuries. Both companies might also be treated as co-employers.

Another possibility is that, if the underlying employer takes the position that the leasing company is the true employer, the underlying employer might be treated as a third party that can be sued for tort claims and cannot assert WC exclusivity. The underlying employer might be sued for negligence or for violating established safety rules, and might be forced to pay damages (including punitive damages). Nor would the employee's WC benefits be used to offset the underlying employer's liability in this situation.

The National Association of Insurance Commissioners (NAIC) has drafted an Employee Leasing Registration Model Act under which leasing firms must register with the state before they purchase WC insurance. At the time of registration, they must disclose their ownership and their past WC history. Registration will not be permitted if the company has had its insurance policies terminated in the past for failure to pay premiums.

A laborer who worked for Southern Personnel died after incurring injuries at Compression Coat, a pipe coating facility. Compression Coat paid weekly invoices to Southern Personnel for staffing costs, including WC insurance. Because another Southern Personnel employee died in a similar accident, Southern's WC insurer refused to provide insurance at the Compression Coat facility. Southern transferred all its employees to C.L. Management, which leased them back to Southern. C.L. got lower WC rates than Southern could have.

After the laborer's death, his family sued Southern and Compression Coat for wrongful death and survivor benefits. Compression Coat said that it was his special employer, Southern said it was immune from tort suit because it was his general employer. The plaintiffs identified C.L. Management as his employer. The Louisiana Court of Appeals dismissed the suit against Southern, because either it was his employer and immune from tort suit or it was not his employer and therefore owed him no duty. Compression Coat was also exempt, as a borrowing employer. [*Pradia v. Southern Personnel of Louisiana Inc.*, 776 So. 2d 474 (La. App. 2000)]

In a less drastic case, a worker was injured when he fell into an uncovered floor drain. He received comp benefits from his employer, the Stanley Jones Corporation, which was a subcontractor of Haskell Co. The injured person sued Haskell for personal injuries, based on a Kansas statute that relieves the principal contractor of responsibility for providing WC when the subcontractor obtains the coverage. The Kansas court said that the contractor is still the statutory employer, and therefore immune from tort suits. [*Robinett v. The Haskell Co.*, 12 P.3d 411

(Kan. 2000). *See Shared Employees—Who Provides Coverage?* Claims Magazine (January 2001) <http://www.claimsmag.com/Issues/Jan01/decisions.asp>]

[D]   How the WC System Handles Disease Claims

WC benefits are also available if an employee develops a work-related disease. However, occupational diseases create some difficult problems of analysis. Disease is covered only if there is a close connection between onset of the disease and the work environment. This is fairly clear for "brown lung" disease and cotton mills, but more difficult if the claim is that nonsmoking employees have been harmed by cigarette smoke exhaled by customers and co-employees who smoke.

Depending on the state, benefits may also be available if workplace conditions aggravate a disease that the individual already had. In California, Florida, Kentucky, Maryland, Mississippi, North Dakota, and South Carolina, WC benefits will be available but will be reduced to compensate for the pre-existing condition. If, for instance, the worker's condition was 25% due to workplace factors, 75% due to the preexisting condition, only 25% of the full benefit will be payable.

Occupational disease creates difficult questions involving "long tail" claims: claims made on the basis that it took years, or even decades, for the symptoms caused by occupational exposure to hazardous substances to manifest themselves. During this long period of time, the employee could have held several jobs (involving exposure to different hazards) and/or engaged in behavior such as smoking that is hazardous or compounds other hazards.

The general rule under the legal system is that claims are timely if they are filed within a reasonable time after the individual first experiences disability or symptoms, and could reasonably be expected to draw a connection between work exposure and illness.

Another question is whether the employee's exposure was extensive enough to trigger the claimed symptoms. The epidemiology (disease pattern) for similar exposures should be studied to see if the employee's alleged experience is typical. Furthermore, one disease claim by an employee could trigger a wave of related claims from other employees who actually are ill, believe themselves to be ill because they have developed psychosomatic symptoms, or who just hope for easy money.

Repetitive stress injuries, such as carpal tunnel syndrome caused by use of computer keyboards, raise difficult issues. In a way, they have aspects of both disease and injury.

The Nebraska Supreme Court granted benefits to a secretary who claimed cumulative trauma injury to her neck and shoulder. The court ruled that three factors are required for compensability: an unexpected or unforeseen event; objective symptoms; and "sudden or violent" onset of the symptoms. The court said that onset can be sudden or violent even if the injury does not occur instantaneously and with force—as long as there is an identifiable point in time when it does occur, requiring cessation of work and medical treatment. The secretary did require medical treatment and did become unable to work, so her RSI claim was sustained. [*Fay v. Dowding, Dowding & Dowding*, 261 Neb. 216 (2001)]

The South Carolina Court of Appeals granted benefits in a carpal tunnel syndrome case, ruling that it was an "injury by accident" (and not, as the employer claimed, an occupational disease) even though it had a gradual rather than a distinct onset. [*Pee v. AVM, Inc.*, 344 S.C. 162 (S.C. App. 2001)]

[E] Psychological Injuries

By and large, the WC system deals with palpable physical injuries and diseases, although in some circumstances mental and emotional illnesses can be compensable. Emotional and mental injuries are analyzed in three categories:

- Mental-physical—physical impact of mental conditions, such as chest pains and high blood pressure;
- Physical-mental—such as suffering a phobia after being involved in an accident or developing "AIDS-phobia" after a needle-stick incident;
- Mental-mental—injuries with no physical component.

In all the states, mental-physical and physical-mental injuries are compensable as long as a causal connection between the two is established. Compensability of mental-mental injuries is less clear-cut. Some states, including Alabama, Florida, Georgia, Kansas, Minnesota, Montana, Nebraska, Ohio, Oklahoma, and South Dakota refuse to compensate cases where there is no demonstrated physical involvement. In the other states, it may be necessary to prove a connection to a severe, unpredictable event, and compensability may depend on whether the onset was gradual or sudden.

A Wyoming case holds that it is not a violation of the constitutional guarantee of equal protection for a WC system to impose a higher standard of proof for mental than for physical injuries. [*Frantz v. Campbell County Mem. Hosp.*, 932 P.2d 750 (Wyo. 1997)]

According to the New York Supreme Court, suicide can be compensable, even if the worker suffered from pre-existing depression, as long as a work-related injury was at least a contributing cause of the suicide. [*Altes v. Petrocelli Elec. Co.*, 270 A.D.2d 767 (N.Y. Sup. 2000)]

In the past few years, Pennsylvania has decided a number of interesting cases relating to mental-mental injuries. In early 1999, a mental injury award was upheld for an employee who was falsely blamed for theft because the employer's records were inaccurate. The plaintiff underwent so much stress that she was unable to work and was institutionalized in a mental hospital. [Danielle N. Rodier, *Mental Injury Wins Rare Comp*, National Law Journal, March 1, 1999, at p. B2]

In May 2000, the Pennsylvania Supreme Court ruled that the burden of proof is the same for mental-mental as for mental-physical claims—the claimant must prove that the injury arose out of abnormal working conditions. Oppressive behavior by a supervisor, if extreme enough, can constitute abnormal working conditions. In one case, the claimant's pre-existing depression was exacerbated; in the other, the supervisor physically touched and pushed the employee who was being accused. [*See* Tracy Blitz Newman, *PA High Court Raises Bar on Workers' Comp. Mental/Physical Claims*, The Legal Intelligencer, (May 22, 2000) (law.com); Danielle N. Rodier, *Run-Ins With Screaming Supervisors Can Be Abnormal Working Conditions*, The Legal Intelligencer (June 2, 2000) (law.com)]

§ 33.03   WC EXCLUSIVITY

The WC system gives employers the protection of "worker's compensation exclusivity": In other words, in the normal work-related injury or illness case, the employee's only remedy against the employer is to collect compensation benefits. Tort lawsuits are not permitted. However, exclusivity applies only against the employer. If the employee is injured by a product manufactured by the employer, the employee can sue the employer in its capacity as manufacturer. Suits against other manufacturers, or non-employer parties responsible for hazardous conditions at the workplace, are also a possibility. The employer itself can sue the third party in order to recover the medical benefits that the employer provided on behalf of the employee.

WC is essentially a no-fault system, so negligence by any party is usually irrelevant. However, in some states, a worker's failure to use safety equipment can reduce (but not eliminate) the benefits that would otherwise be payable after an accident. Sometimes, the employer's wrongdoing will take the case out of WC exclusivity. Some (but not all) courts would allow an ordinary tort suit against an employer that deliberately concealed information about workplace hazards.

Compensation benefits will be granted only if the employee has medical evidence to prove the connection between the job and the disabling condition. See, for example, *Hanten v. Palace Builders, Inc.* [1997 S.D. 3 (1997)], where an employee who underwent surgery for tendonitis returned to work and applied for WC benefits for a syndrome she claimed was related to keyboard use. Her claim was denied: Her medical witness said merely that the syndrome was possibly work-related. For the employee to be awarded benefits, the testimony must at least establish that the symptoms are probably connected to work.

Furthermore, the employee must be incapacitated by the condition, so benefits will not be awarded to a person who stoically continues to work despite pain. Courts have reached different conclusions as to whether a person is permanently and totally disabled only if there is absolutely no job he or she can perform, or whether "human factors" such as job availability within a reasonable commuting distance must be considered.

In a 1999 Pennsylvania case, one worker made a deliberate false claim that another worker threatened "to bring a gun in here and kill somebody." The police took the employee who was supposed to have made the threat to a mental hospital. After an interview with a psychiatrist, she was released. She sued the employer for defamation, claiming severe emotional distress. The employer claimed WC exclusivity because defamation is an intentional tort causing emotional distress. But the employee was permitted to maintain the defamation lawsuit, on the theory that WC deals with physical or mental injuries, whereas defamation deals with damage to reputation. [*Urban v. Dollar Bank*, 725 A.2d 815 (Pa. Super. 1999)]

For WC purposes, rape and robbery committed at a workplace by an unknown assailant are considered "accidental workplace injury." Therefore, according to *Melo v. Jewish Board of Family & Children's Servs. Inc.* [N.Y. L. J., Feb. 8, 2000, at p. 29, col. 3] WC exclusivity applies, and the victim does not have the right to bring tort claims against the employer.

The Northern District of Illinois refused to dismiss a case brought by a waitress who alleged ongoing sexual harassment by a waiter, several cooks, and the restaurant manager. After the manager not merely refused to investigate her complaints, but served drinks to other employees who then increased the harassment, the waitress quit her job and sued the employer and manager for physical pain, lost income, and emotional distress. The District Court required a full trial to resolve issues of WC exclusivity and liability. [*Bartoli v. Applebee's Restaurant*, No. 00-C-5954 (N.D. Ill. Jan. 17, 2001)]

A technician who had to stop working because of respiratory problems lost his WC case for failure to prove compensable injury. He sued his employer for negligence. The Oregon Supreme Court accepted his constitutional argument that he had an injury, so there had to be some forum that could provide him with a remedy. [*Smothers v. Gresham Transfer, Inc.*, 332 Or. 83 (2001)]

In a Florida case [*Turner v. PCR, Inc.*, 754 So. 2d 683 (Fla. Sup. 2000)] one worker died and one was seriously injured in an explosion that occurred while they were mixing chemicals. The plaintiffs asserted the intentional tort exception to WC exclusivity. This requires proof either of the employer's deliberate intent to injure, or conduct that a reasonable fact-finder would consider substantially certain to result in injury or death. The case was allowed to go to trial, because the employer concealed the hazards of the mixing process, did not provide training or safety equipment, and was aware of the risks because there had been three similar explosions in the previous two years.

In contrast, however, WC exclusivity was found in a California case. [*Gunnell v Metrocolor Laboratories Inc.*, 112 Cal. Rptr. 2d 195 (Cal. App. 2001)] Employees were hurt when the employer removed warning labels, told employees that a hazardous chemical was safe and failed to provide safety equipment. A case of criminal battery would not have been WC exclusive, but here the employer did not use physical force or violence against employees.

§ 33.04   ALTERNATIVES FOR INSURING WC

[A]   Types of Available Insurance

Depending on state law and the employer's own financial status and risk category, there are several ways to cope with the obligation to provide benefits for injured employees.

- Buying insurance from a state-run fund that is the sole source of WC coverage within the state;
- Buying insurance from a commercial carrier. Nearly all privately purchased policies will follow the form of the "standard policy"—the Worker's Compensation and Employers' Liability Policy developed by the national Council on Compensation Insurance (NCCI);
- Buying insurance from a state fund that competes with commercial carriers;
- Self-insurance (most employers who take this option combine it with third-party administration, reinsurance, or both);
- Insurance through a captive insurer owned by the employer;
- Participating in an assigned risk pool (depending on circumstances, this can be either mandatory or voluntary).

Although Bankruptcy Code § 507(a)(4) provides that contributions to an employee benefit plan get priority when creditors divide up the assets of a bankrupt company, the Tenth Circuit ruled in 1997 that unpaid WC premiums are not entitled to priority status [*State Ins. Fund v. Mather*, 210 B.R. 838 (10th Cir. 1997)], and the Sixth Circuit echoed this in 2000. [*Travelers Prop. Cas. Corp. v. Birmingham-Nashville Express Inc.*, 224 F.3d 511 (6th Cir. 2000)] The rationale is that priority is given only to wage substitutes that employees traded for other forms of compensation. WC premiums are mandatory, so they really benefit the employer, not the employee.

One of the innumerable effects of the September 11 attack was to focus attention on the possibility of large-scale losses when large groups of employees are hurt or killed at the same time. In fact, about 10% of the estimated economic impact of the attack ($4 billion out of the overall $40 billion) was estimated to be related to WC. Most states allowed insurers to exclude losses due to terrorism from other lines of coverage, but this was not permitted in WC policies. According to Standard & Poor's Ratings Group, many insurers and reinsurers would stop selling WC coverage—and rates could go up as much as 50% for the coverage that was available. [Christopher Oster and Michael Schroeder, *Workers' Comp Insurance Now Harder to Get*, Wall Street Journal, Jan. 9. 2002, at p. A3]

[B] State Funds

The states of North Dakota, Ohio, Washington, West Virginia, and Wyoming have monopolistic state funds: i.e., all covered employers have to buy their coverage from the fund. Until July 1, 1997, Nevada was in this category, but now it maintains a state fund but allows private coverage.

The states that have competitive state funds (i.e., the employer chooses whether to purchase coverage from the state funds or a private insurer) are Arizona, California, Colorado, Idaho, Louisiana, Maine, Maryland, Michigan, Minnesota, Montana, New Mexico, Nevada, New York, Oklahoma, Oregon, Pennsylvania, Rhode Island, Texas, and Utah. State funds set their own rates, which can be low because the fund has very low marketing expenses.

Texas allows employers to self-insure for WC, but they must be careful to provide benefits at least roughly comparable to the benefits that would be available under an insured plan. In *Reyes v. Storage & Processors Inc.* [995 S.W.2d 722 (Tex. App. 1999)], the court said that employers cannot require arbitration of claims for work-related injuries if the benefits they provide are substantially less generous than Comp benefits.

Strawn v. AFC Enterprises Inc. [70 F. Supp. 2d 717 (S.D. Tex. 1999)] builds on this by refusing to enforce an arbitration agreement imposed on all employees. Because the employer's plan offered only "miserly" benefits to injured employees, an employee was allowed to raise tort claims even after accepting an arbitration award of about $50,000 for work-related injuries. In the court's view, the arbitration award was completely void, not just voidable, and therefore was not ratified by the employee's acceptance of benefits.

The employers involved in *Lawrence v. CDB Services, Inc.* [44 S.W.3d 544 (Tex. Sup. 2001)] and *Lambert v. Affiliated Foods* [20 S.W.3d 1 (Tex. Sup. 2001)] were nonsubscribers to the Texas WC Act. Employees were offered a plan of disability, dismemberment, and death benefits, but participants in the plan had to waive the right to bring either common-law or WC suits against the employer. Their only remedy was to pursue their benefits under the plan. The cases came to court when two employees who had signed waivers claimed the waivers were unenforceable because they were against public policy. The Texas Supreme Court said that the WC Act does not rule out pre-injury waivers like these; that the plan did not shift the risk of injury unfairly to workers—in fact, the plan provided immediate and certain benefits in exchange for the waiver of the right to sue in a case which might never arise. The court did not accept the public policy argument, because the WC statute does not explicitly ban such waivers.

[C]   Assigned Risk Pools

In any situation in which people or organizations have a legal obligation to maintain insurance coverage, some of them will not be insurable under normal underwriting standards. Assigned risk pools are created to issue coverage. In the WC context, the NCCI administers the National Worker's Compensation Reassurance Pool. It covers about 25% of all employers, making it the largest single WC insurer in the United States.

This WC assigned risk pool has some unusual features. Commercial insurers have to support it by paying "residual market assessments" of approximately 14 cents on every premium dollar they receive. But because of this heavy assessment, commercial insurers are less willing to grant discounts to their insurable customers, thus driving more employers to see the assigned risk pool as an attractive alternative.

[D]   Self-Insurance and Captive Companies

In all the states except North Dakota and Wyoming, employers who satisfy certain criteria (e.g., being financially capable of paying all WC claims that arise in the course of operations; posting bond or establishing an escrow) can elect to self-insure.

> **Tip:** Self-insurance is considered a privilege. It can be revoked by the state if an employer fails to file the necessary reports, does not maintain the required amount of excess insurance, or otherwise fails to keep up its end of the bargain. A change in corporate ownership might also lead to revocation of the privilege, even if the corporate structure remains the same.

In practice, self-insurance is practical only for very large companies with six- or seven-figure WC premium obligations; about one-third of the WC market is now self-insured because some economic giants have taken this option.

More than half the states impose a requirement that self-insured companies maintain reinsurance (excess coverage). It is prudent for companies to do this even if it is not required. Self-insured employers generally must show that they have arranged for claims administration, employee communications, and safety programs. These functions are usually performed under a Third Party Administration (TPA) arrangement. An effective TPA should have 24-hour-a-day claims service; low turnover (experienced representatives do a much better job than novices); a high proportion of employees who have obtained professional certification in loss control; quick settlement of claims; and a low average final cost per claim.

In a pure self-insurance arrangement, the employer sets up reserves and pays all WC claims from these reserves. In a group arrangement, several companies join forces. Each one is jointly and severally liable for all Comp claims within the group. Most of the states permit group self-insurance; nationwide, there are over 250 group self-insurance pools. In a limited self-insurance arrangement, the employer is responsible for the Self-Insured Retention (SIR), which is roughly equal to a deductible, and excess insurance pays the rest.

Excess coverage can be written on a per-occurrence or per-loss basis, covering an aggregate amount for the year or per accident per payment year. (The payment year is a relevant concept because the consequences of an injury might extend over several years.) Specific excess insurance limits the employer's liability for claims for any occurrence where the exposure exceeds the SIR. Aggregate excess insurance copes with the possibility of a bad year. The employer has to pay the amount in the aggregate retention or loss fund. This is usually expressed as a percentage, such as 125%, of the reinsurance premium for the year. Aggregate excess coverage usually stops at $1 million or $2 million, so the employer will be at risk once again if the exposure is greater. Specific excess insurance is both easier to obtain and less expensive than aggregate insurance.

To self-insure, the company must file an application with the state (this typically costs $100–$1,000). The employer may have to post a letter of credit as security, and the lending bank will impose fees. Excess insurance and TPA fees each costs about 8–13% of the amount that would otherwise be the WC premium.

States also impose taxes on self-insurance arrangements—about 1–4% of the premium that would have been charged by an insurer, incurred losses, or paid losses.

Working through a captive insurance company (one that does business only with a company that is its sole shareholder, or a small group of cooperating companies) is another option. The advantage of this arrangement to the employer is the ability to keep the underwriting income (deposits that are the equivalent of premiums, plus investment income), but the company will also have to pay the expenses of the captive insurer.

[E]   High-Deductible Plans

A high-deductible plan combines features of both insurance and self-insurance. To reduce its premiums, the employer agrees to accept a higher deductible. Usually, it falls between $100,000 and $1 million, but policies are available with deductibles up to $5 million. Any employer can purchase a high-deductible policy. Unlike self-insurance, there are no financial qualifications imposed by the state.

When a claim is made under a high-deductible plan, the insurer pays the full claim, then bills the policyholder for payments made that fell within the deductible. Bills are usually sent on a monthly basis. Employers who buy high-deductible policies are generally required to create an escrow fund equal to about three moths' potential loss payments, and must submit a letter of credit in an amount equal to the deductible. At the end of the first year of high deductible coverage, the letter of credit is adjusted upward or downward to reflect experience. Paid losses are billed until all claims have been closed. The high-deductible insurer may require indemnification or a hold-harmless agreement offering remedies against the employer if, for instance, legislation is passed subjecting the insurer to increased losses that fall within the deductible.

§ 33.05   SETTING THE WC PREMIUM

There are 600 industry classifications, each identified by a four-digit number. An employer's basic WC premium is the "manual rate" for its industry classification. The manual rate is the average cost of WC coverage for the classification, based on the number of claims in the past three years for injuries serious enough to cause lost work time. The rate is sometimes expressed as a percentage of total payroll, but is usually defined as a number of dollars per $100 of payroll. Large employers may qualify for premium discounts, because the administrative expenses are fairly similar for policies of all sizes.

The manual rate is only one factor in setting an individual employer's rate. Experience rating (the employer's actual claims experience for the previous two years) can increase or decrease the base premium that will be imposed in the future. States can also adopt retrospective rating, under which past losses are used to adjust the premium already charged for a particular year, so that either the employer is entitled to a refund or will have to make additional payments.

WC policies have both general inclusions, which recur in many industries (for workers in employee cafeterias, and repair and maintenance crews, for instance) and general exclusions that are written out of ordinary industry classifications (for instance, construction activities performed by employees; running an employer-operated day care center).

§ 33.06   BAN ON RETALIATION

Nearly all the states have passed statutes making it illegal to retaliate against an employee, either specifically for filing a Worker's Compensation claim or for filing any "wage claim" or "wage complaint," a broad category that includes WC. The states are Alabama, Arizona, California, Connecticut, Delaware, Florida, Hawaii, Idaho, Illinois, Indiana, Kansas, Kentucky, Louisiana, Maine, Maryland, Mississippi, Michigan, Minnesota, Missouri, Montana, New Hampshire, New Jersey, New Mexico, New York, North Carolina, North Dakota, Ohio, Oklahoma, Rhode Island, South Carolina, South Dakota, Texas, Vermont, Virginia, Washington, West Virginia, Wisconsin, and Wyoming.

Even in the minority of states that do not have a statue, it is very likely that courts will treat retaliatory discharge as an illegal violation of public policy.

Discharge is not the only employment action that can give rise to retaliation charges: A retaliatory demotion, that results in a pay cut, is also wrongful, and can give rise to a lawsuit. [*Brigham v. Dillon Cos. Inc.,* 935 P.2d 1054 (Kan. Sup. 1997)]

The Washington State case of *Warnek v. ABB Combustion Engineering* [137 Wash. 2d 450 (1999)] permits an employer to refuse to rehire employees who made WC claims against the same employer in another state. In this reading, the antiretaliation statute applies only within a state, not inside it. The court also drew a distinction between refusing to rehire and discrimination during employment or discharge. Only discrimination is unlawful.

However, not all employees can use the state courts to bring claims of retaliatory discharge. According to the First Circuit, if the workplace is unionized, § 301 of the Labor-Management Relations Act preempts a claim that the employee was not rehired after a period of disability because the employer retaliated against her for filing a WC claim. The court deemed the claim preempted because the "management rights" clause in the collective bargaining agreement gave management the sole right to hire and fire. Therefore, assessing the validity of the retaliation claim requires interpretation of the CBA, and therefore § 301 comes into play. [*Martin v. Shaw's Supermarkets Inc.,* 105 F.3d 40 (1st Cir. 1997)]

In contrast, the Eighth Circuit's 1995 decision is that an employee's claim of unlawful retaliatory discharge cannot be removed from state to federal court, because state remedies are not preempted in that situation. The Eighth Circuit did not believe that deciding the case required interpretation of the CBA. [*Humphrey v. Sequentia Inc.,* 58 F.3d 1238 (8th Cir. 1995). *See* § 30.02[D] for further discussion of LMRA § 301]

Also see 28 U.S.C. § 1445(c), which says that civil actions "arising under" state WC laws cannot be removed to federal court. But there is an exception for suits alleging "deliberate injury," which can be removed to federal court. According to the District Court for the District of West Virginia, a retaliatory discharge case arises under WC and therefore belongs in state, not federal, court. [*Thorne v. Wampler Foods*, Civil Action No. 3:00-CV-24 (N.D.W.V. Aug. 29, 2000)]

§ 33.07   ADMINISTRATION OF WC

[A]   Generally

In most states, employers are required to participate in the WC system (although Texas and New Jersey allow private employers to opt out of the system entirely, as long as they notify the Compensation Commission and their employees that they have left the system). The tradeoff is that injured employees have the right to bring tort suits against employers who are outside the WC system, whereas in most cases workers who are injured in a WC-covered workplace will not be allowed to sue the employer.

Some states allow employees to opt out of WC coverage as long as they do so in writing, within a reasonable time after starting a new job, and before any accident or injury has occurred. Corporate officers are often given the option of leaving the WC system.

In about a third of the states, the state itself runs the WC fund. Those states give employers three choices for handling their responsibilities:

- Pay into the state fund;
- Buy insurance from a private carrier;
- Self-insure by maintaining a segregated fund that contains enough money to handle the expected compensation claims.

In states with no state fund, employers can either buy insurance or self-insure.

The insurance premium depends on the level of risk: A coal mine is much more likely to have occupational injury claims than a boutique. The nationwide average premium is about 2.5% of compensation.

The general rule is that employees are obligated to notify the employer within a short time (usually about five days) after an injury or the onset of an illness. Employers should encourage reporting, because such information is needed for WC and other purposes (OSHA reports, improving safety conditions).

In some WC systems, the employer notifies its WC insurer, which then files the report. In other systems, the employer (whether it has insurance or is self-insured) is responsible for notifying the compensation board. If the employer fails to make the necessary report, the employee will probably be given additional time to pursue his or her claim.

If the employer agrees that the injury or disease is work-related and accepts the employee's characterization of its seriousness, the claim is uncontested. Most states follow the "agreement system" under which a settlement is negotiated by the parties, or by the employee and the employer's WC insurer. In some states, the agency that administers WC claims must approve all settlements, even in uncontested cases. Most settlements involve payment of ongoing benefits at a continuing rate: either a percentage of the employee's pre-accident income, or a percentage of the state's average income. However, there is an increasing trend to settle WC cases for a lump sum.

However, some uncontested cases are treated as "direct payment" cases. Either the employer or the insurer initiates the process, by making the statutory initial installment payment to the employee. Under this option, the employee does not have to sign anything or agree to anything—unlike the agreement system, which results in a written agreement.

WC settlements cover only the matters specifically set out in the agreement, so agreements must be drafted carefully. Employers are allowed to settle claims that have already accrued, but not future claims (such as claims for future medical expenses), because employees cannot be required to give up future claims that are hard to quantify in advance.

Generally, any settlement between employer and employee will be final. However, there are grounds for which agreements can be set aside, such as fraud, mutual mistake of fact (both sides believe something about the employee's condition that turns out not to be accurate), or mistake of law (misinterpretation of the legal rules and their consequences). Usually, the mere fact that the employee did not have a lawyer is not enough to invalidate a settlement—unless, perhaps, the employer prevented the employee from seeking legal advice. Just to be on the safe side, employers should inform employees that they have the right to be represented by counsel.

Contested cases are heard and decided by the agency administering the system. However, there are comparatively few contested cases. In most cases, it is quite clear that there has been an injury. Because WC is a no-fault system, it is not necessary to apportion blame.

In some states, mediation is either an option that is available (but only if both sides agree); in other states, it is compulsory. In mediated cases, a neutral mediator has at least one informal meeting with the parties. Sometimes, the meeting is held off the record, so both sides can speak freely, without having to restrict what they say to things that would help their case in formal legal proceedings. If necessary, the mediator arranges more meetings, until the mediator is either able to facilitate a settlement, or it is clear that an impasse has been reached.

In some states, when mediation fails, binding arbitration can be applied; in other states, the case is sent to the Comp board for adjudication.

Appeal rights are granted to dissatisfied employers and employees. Usually, parties get 30 days to file for an appeal, although the requirements of different states range from 10 days to one year. Grounds for appeal include improprieties in the process and changed circumstances (such as unpredictable improvement or deterioration in the employee's condition) that were unknown at the time of the award.

After exhaustion of remedies (the process of going through all the administrative appeals), the case can be taken to court by a dissatisfied party.

Many state laws entitle the employee to an additional payment of 10–20% if the employer is late in making a required payment. Civil fines may also be imposed, and the unpaid amounts could operate as a lien on the employer's assets.

[B] Responding to an Accident

Even before there have been any accidents, your workplace should have an effective procedure in place, and should hold regular drills to make sure everyone can handle the procedure. Make sure that employees learn first aid and CPR. Keep plenty of first aid kits around, with fresh supplies, in convenient locations. It's important to provide first aid for all minor incidents, and immediate medical care in more serious cases.

Somebody must be designated to take charge of taking the injured worker to a doctor's office or hospital emergency room, or to call an ambulance. Someone must be in charge of filing the initial accident report (and an OSHA incident report if necessary). [See § 24.02[A]] Some insurers have 24-hour telephone lines that can be used for WC and OSHA reporting, and to assign a case manager to review utilization of care and the injured person's potential for rehabilitation. There is clear evidence that the earlier and more aggressively rehabilitation can be pursued, the more likely it is that the employee will be able to return to work (or at least to limited duties or a less strenuous job) instead of becoming permanently disabled.

In addition to immediate accident reports, some states require a yearly report of all workplace incidents, similar to the OSHA annual report. [See § 24.02[A]] Follow-up status reports may also be required on individual accidents. Employers who fail to make mandatory reports can be subject to fines; there may even be criminal penalties.

As Chapter 18 shows, managed care dominates the U.S. health care system. It also plays a role in WC cases. Some states such as Connecticut, Florida, and Ohio make managed care involvement in WC cases compulsory. Many other states have laws authorizing managed care as an option in WC cases: Arkansas, California, Georgia, Kentucky, Massachusetts, Minnesota, Missouri, Montana, Nebraska, Nevada, New Hampshire, New Jersey, New York, North Carolina, North Dakota, Oregon, Pennsylvania, Rhode Island, South Dakota, Utah, Washington.

According to the Workers Compensation Research Institute, using a network of providers to treat injured workers saves a great deal of money and offers a quality of care comparable to that offered by individual providers. Based on a sample of claims filed in California, Connecticut and Texas between 1995 and 1997, the average cost of treatment of a back injury by a network provider was $884. Non-network providers charged an average of $1,233—about 50% more. For miscellaneous injuries, the average cost of treatment by network providers was $752; by non-network providers it was $1,012. However, in 1996 and 1997, the cost disparity between the two narrowed. [Alisa Tang, *Bending the Cost Averages for Those Aching Backs*, New York Times, Dec. 29, 1999, at p. G1]

§ 33.08 WC IN RELATION TO OTHER SYSTEMS

[A] Taxation of WC Benefits

Generally speaking, WC insurance premiums paid by employers, or WC benefits received by employees, are not taxable income for the employee. Therefore, the employer does not have to perform tax withholding on these amounts, or withhold or pay FICA or FUTA tax on them. However, in a limited range of situations, WC benefits will be taxable: e.g. if they are paid to a person who has returned to work in a light-duty position; if they reduce Social Security benefits; or if state law calls for payment of non-occupational disability benefits. [*See* Chapter 20 for the related topic of disability benefits provided under a fringe benefit plan]

The amount that the employer pays in WC premiums is tax deductible. So are loss amounts paid by a self-insured employer. However, reserves maintained in order to satisfy the deductible under a WC policy are not tax-deductible.

[B] ERISA

The general tenor of court decisions on this subject is that WC benefits can legitimately be used to offset accrued benefits that derive from the employer's contribution to a pension plan—but only if a statute specifically provides this, or if the plan has been drafted to include this specific provision. ERISA preempts state WC laws to the extent that they "relate" to an ERISA plan.

In 1992, the Supreme Court decided that a state law relates to an ERISA plan if it refers to or has a connection with the plan, even if the effect is indirect, and even if the law was not designed to affect the plan. Therefore, a law requiring employers to provide health insurance to employees who received or were eligible for WC was preempted. [*District of Columbia v. Greater Wash. Bd. of Trade*, 506 U.S. 125 (1992)]

[C] The ADA

A person might claim disability discrimination and also claim eligibility for WC benefits, at the same time or at different times. [*See When Regs Collide: The ADA and Workers' Compensation*, WestGroup Employment Alert, Nov. 25, 1998, at p. 1]

The right to get WC benefits is considered a privilege of employment for ADA purposes [*see, e.g., Harding v. Winn-Dixie Stores*, 907 F. Supp. 386 (M.D. Fla. 1995)], so a case can be brought premised on alleged discrimination in this area. However, the ADA does not have the strong preemptive power that ERISA does to rule out state-law claims. In 1998, for instance, a case was allowed to proceed even though the ADA's standard of proof is higher for employees with pre-existing conditions. [*Baley v. Reynolds Metals*, 153 Ore. App. 498, 959 P.2d 84 (Ore. App. 1998)]

A person injured at work might be entitled to benefits but still able to work with reasonable accommodation. A WC judge's determination that the injured person could not work even on a reduced schedule is proof that the person is not a "qualified individual with a disability." [*Dush v. Appleton Elec. Co.*, 124 F.3d 957 (8th Cir. 1997)] An employee who enters into an agreement stating that he or she needs a stress-free work environment is not qualified for a high-stress job like being a safety police officer. [*Jackson v. County of Los Angeles*, 60 Cal. App. 4th 171, 70 Cal. Rptr. 2d 96 (1998)]

The testimony or findings from an ADA case can have an important evidentiary effect in a WC case. Someone who sued under the ADA because of a past injury cannot deny that the injury was a preexisting disability when it comes to a later injury that becomes the subject of a WC case. [*Cobb v. Coyne Cylinder Co.*, 719 So.2d 219 (Ala. App. 1998)]

Should the value of health insurance premiums paid by the employer be included in calculating the injured person's "weekly wage" for WC purposes? In 2000, the Georgia Court of Appeals said no, but early in 2001 the Washington Supreme Court said yes, on the grounds that wages includes the reasonable value of any "consideration of like nature" paid to a worker. [*Groover v. Johnson Controls World Wide Serv.*, 241 Ga. App. 791 (2000); *Cockle v. Department of Labor & Indus.*, 142 Wash. 2d 801 (2001)]

There are also problems in relating WC to the ADA if an employer interviews a job applicant who seems to have some physical limitations, which might have been caused by an earlier compensable injury.

Job interviews are not appropriate settings for discussing an employee's history of injuries—or health status in general. Inquiries about past WC claims are not allowed, because they are considered to be disability-related.

However, during the interview, it is permissible for the interviewer to discuss the essential duties of the job and tasks that are sometimes necessary. The interviewer can find out whether the applicant can perform the essential duties, with or without reasonable accommodation by the employer.

Once an employer is ready to extend a conditional job offer to an applicant, asking about past WC claims is allowed, but only if the question is posed to everyone who gets a conditional job offer, not just those who seem to have some impairment. Concern that hiring someone with a prior injury will increase the company's WC costs is not a legitimate reason for denying a job to a qualified applicant.

It probably violates the ADA to maintain a policy that injured employees cannot return to work until they are 100% fit to resume all their old duties. When an employee wants to return to work, the ADA requires the employer to offer a light-duty assignment if this would be a reasonable accommodation to disability. But the employer is not required to create new jobs just to help employees get back on their feet. Nor is it necessary to "bump" another employee to accommodate disability.

Referring an injured person to a vocational rehabilitation program is not considered a reasonable accommodation, if the employee could return to work with accommodations that do not constitute a hardship to the employer.

The ADA does not preempt state case law that denies WC to a person whose injuries are causally connected to an underlying physical condition (such as earlier injuries) and who lied about the existing condition before being hired.

The ADA does not preempt the state law because the ADA permits pre-employment inquiries that are related to the applicant's ability to do the job. Even if the employer asks improper questions, lying is not an appropriate response. [*Caldwell v. Aarlin/Holcombe Armature Co.*, 267 Ga. 613, 481 S.E.2d 196 (Ga. Sup. 1997)] So even if the employer should not have asked questions that violated the ADA, the employee's answers can still be legitimate evidence in a WC case. [*See Dureoun v. C&P Production Specialist*, 718 So. 2d 460 (La. App. 1998)]

In *Gutermuth v. Bedford* [43 S.W.3d 270 (Ky. Sup. 2001)], the employee could not collect WC benefits for a neck injury incurred when she drove a cherry-picker over a break in the concrete floor, because her job application concealed her six previous arm operations and medically imposed restrictions on lifting her arms. She also had work-related knee problems, and non-work-related back problems. She would not have been hired for the physically demanding jobs if she had disclosed these limitations, so WC benefits were unavailable.

The Seventh Circuit decided that it is not a violation of the ADA to reject a group of job applicants whose "nerve conduction tests" showed that they had neuropathy, and therefore were vulnerable to future repetitive stress injuries. [*EEOC v. Rockwell Int'l Corp.*, 243 F.3d 1012 (7th Cir. 2001)] In the Seventh Circuit's view, the employees were not currently disabled. The employer did not discriminate against them on the basis of perceived disability, because the employer did not regard them as potentially unable to perform a broad range of jobs.

[D] Second Injury Funds

Although they predate the ADA, in a way "second injury funds" serve the same purpose as the ADA: promoting the employment of people with disabilities. Second injury funds (which exist in, for example, California, Missouri, New Jersey, and Washington State) deal with the situation in which a permanent disability is compounded by a later injury to become either a permanent partial disability that is more serious than before, or a permanent total disability. In states that do not have these funds, an employer who hires someone whose pre-existing condition deteriorates because of occupational factors, would be responsible for all of the employee's WC benefits, even though the occupational factors may be comparatively less important than the pre-existing condition.

When there is a second injury fund in the picture, the employer is responsible only for the economic consequences of the later injury. The second injury fund, which is publicly funded, takes on the rest of the economic burden.

The first injury must have been serious enough to be compensable, but need not actually have come under the WC system. For instance, the second injury fund could get involved if a work-related injury aggravates an existing condition caused by a non-work-related automobile accident or a birth defect.

> **Tip:** To collect from the fund, the employer may have to certify that it knew about the pre-existing condition at the time of hiring. This, in turn, requires asking questions in a way that does not violate the ADA.

[E]   Social Security Disability Income

In many states, the Social Security Disability Income (SSDI) system is considered the primary payer whenever an employee is injured seriously enough to meet the Social Security Administration's stringent definition of total disability. The states in this category are Alaska, Arkansas, California, Colorado, Florida, Louisiana, Maine, Massachusetts, Michigan, Minnesota, Missouri, Montana, Nevada, New Jersey, New York, North Dakota, Ohio, Oregon, Utah, Washington, and Wisconsin.

When SSDI is involved, the payments from the federal agency reduce the WC benefit dollar-for-dollar, until the combination of SSDI and WC reaches the level of 80% of the worker's pre-accident earnings. However, SSDI reduces only the part of the benefit that represents lost income, not the part that goes to medical care or legal fees.

In states that coordinate with SSDI, employers sometimes hire lawyers to represent injured workers in their SSDI cases. That way, the employer's WC experience is charged with a much smaller claim. Self-insured employers, who would otherwise have to pay the whole claim themselves, have an even stronger reason for promoting the employee's claim.

§ 33.09   TECHNIQUES FOR LOWERING COMP COSTS

Employers can reduce their costs via good planning—sorting valid from invalid claims, and finding more economical ways to handle the valid claims. Companies have had some success by educating workers that everyone is responsible for reducing injuries and maintaining a safer workplace. Focusing on getting injured workers back to work as soon as possible also helps cut costs. Departments can be made responsible for their own injury rates, and be made responsible for keeping their rates at least as low as those for comparable operations.

HR policies that are associated with lower WC rates include:

- Increasing employee involvement (e.g., through the use of quality circles). The more employees get involved, the more careful they will be about identifying potentially dangerous conditions, finding ways to correct them—and the more motivation they will have to return to work quickly after an injury;
- Strengthening grievance and conflict resolution procedures if dangerous conditions are alleged, and to resolve claims;
- Reducing turnover: Experienced workers are less likely to get hurt than novices;
- Training workers better—especially in lifting and safe handling of hazardous materials;
- Using health maintenance and wellness programs.

The National Institute of Occupational Safety and Health (NIOSH) defines three areas in which employers can be proactive to cut Comp costs:

- Using engineering controls, such as workstation layout, choice of tools, work methods, to tailor the job to fit employee capabilities and limitations;
- Reducing risk exposure through administrative controls, such as more rest breaks, better training, task rotation;
- Supplying workers with Personal Protective Equipment (PPE), although scientific consensus has not been reached on which devices are effective.

An article in CCH's Worker's Compensation newsletter gives some useful tips for spotting claims that might be fraudulent:

- Delayed reporting of injury;
- Accidents of a type that might be staged;
- The worker claiming injury was on probation or has been identified as having a poor work record;
- The alleged injury is not consistent with the worker's assigned duties;
- The injury is reported just after a weekend or holiday—showing that the injury might have been incurred away from the workplace, or work might have exacerbated a non-work-based injury.

Sometimes, a WC insurance premium quote will be inaccurate, and the premium can be reduced simply by:

- Checking to see if payroll is stated accurately, because the higher the payroll, the higher the premium;
- Making sure that employees are assigned to the lowest risk classification that accurately reflects their duties;
- Having your insurance agent review the calculations.

PART VII

SUBSTANTIVE LAWS AGAINST DISCRIMINATION

CHAPTER 34

TITLE VII

§ 34.01   INTRODUCTION

Title VII, passed as part of the Civil Rights Act of 1964, is the main federal civil rights statute that bans discrimination in employment. It has been enacted at 42 U.S.C. § 2000e *et seq.* (By the time Title VII came around, the United States Code was pretty much "full-up," leading to some very odd section numbers. Title VII starts with just plain § 2000e, which is divided into subsections running from § 2000e(a) to 2000e(n). The next section is § 2000e-1, with additional sections up to § 2000e-17.)

Title VII is supplemented by other civil rights statutes: Sometimes other parts of the United States Code (such as 42 U.S.C. §§ 1981, 1983, and 1985) are invoked in employment discrimination suits. Disability discrimination is barred by the Americans with Disabilities Act. [*See* Chapter 36] Age discrimination is barred by the Age Discrimination in Employment Act. [*See* Chapter 37]

In a sense, the Family and Medical Leave Act [29 U.S.C. § 2601 *et seq.*], discussed in detail in Chapter 38, is also an antidiscrimination statute as well as an employee benefits statute, because it prevents discrimination against individuals who are ill or who must cope with illness as part of their family responsibilities. Note that any federal, state, or local law that creates special rights or preferences for veterans continues in force and is not repealed by Title VII [42 U.S.C. § 2000e-11], a provision that is more prominent in the post-9/11 environment.

The areas of discrimination forbidden by Title VII are race, color, religion, sex, and national origin. These are known as "suspect classifications," because employers are not supposed to discriminate for reasons involving these classifications.

Also see 42 U.S.C. § 2000e-2(h), which says that it is not an unlawful employment practice for an employer to abide by FLSA § 6(d) [29 U.S.C. § 206(d)], which allows certain differences in the minimum wage.

Title VII enforcement has two aspects: public (governmental) and private (suits brought by employees, job applicants, ex-employees, or groups of people in these categories). Section 2000e-5 gives the Equal Employment Opportunities Commission (EEOC) the power "to prevent any person from engaging in any unlawful employment practice" that is banned by 42 U.S.C. §§ 2000e-2 or 2000e-3.

State laws still remain in force, although state laws are not permitted to require or even allow anything that is treated as an unlawful employment practice under Title VII. [42 U.S.C. § 2000e-7]

§ 34.02   TREATMENT/IMPACT

Discrimination claims are divided into two categories, each of which has its own requirements for drafting complaints and proving the case, and its own defenses that the employer can assert to win its case.

The two categories are disparate treatment and disparate impact. A disparate treatment case alleges that persons were singled out for inferior treatment because of the group they belong to. A disparate impact case alleges subtler forms of discrimination.

For instance, an allegation that a police department refused to hire Hispanics would be a disparate treatment claim. A disparate impact claim might challenge the police department's requirement that all newly hired officers be over 5'10" tall, on the grounds that more Hispanics than people from other backgrounds are unable to meet this requirement, and therefore a requirement that seems at first glance to be acceptable actually discriminates against members of a protected group.

Under Title VII, a "mixed motive" case can be maintained. That is, if an employer has several motivations for making an employment decision or adopting an employment practice, Title VII forbids practices that are partially motivated by discrimination against a protected group, not just those where discrimination is the sole motivation. [*See* 42 U.S.C. § 2000e-2(m)]

§ 34.03   TITLE VII COVERAGE

Title VII bans "unlawful employment practices." Unlawful employment practices discriminate against an employee or job applicant on the basis of the individual's race, color, religion, sex, or national origin. [42 U.S.C. § 2000e-2(a)] Note that Title VII does not ban sexual-orientation discrimination, but some applicable state and local statutes do.

Unlawful employment practices on the part of the employer are defined by 42 U.S.C. § 2000e-2(a) as:

- To fail or refuse to hire;
- To discharge;
- To discriminate with respect to compensation, terms, conditions, or privileges of employment;
- To limit, segregate, or classify employees or job applicants in a way that deprives or tends to deprive them of employment opportunities, or otherwise adversely affects their status as employees.

Title VII also bans discriminatory practices by employment agencies and labor unions, but their activities are outside the scope of this book.

In late 1998, the Fourth Circuit joined the Third, Fifth, Seventh, Eighth, Tenth, Eleventh, and D.C. Circuits in ruling that only employer companies, and not individuals, can be held liable under Title VII. [*Lissau v. Southern Food Serv.*, 159 F.3d 177 (4th Cir. 1998)]

An important—and growing—part of the employment discrimination caseload is the "retaliation" case. Section 2000e-3(a) makes it unlawful for an employer to discriminate against anyone who has opposed an unlawful employment practice or who has "made a charge, testified, assisted, or participated in any manner in an investigation, proceeding, or hearing" under Title VII. [*See* § 34.08 for more about retaliation cases]

It is also an unlawful employment practice to indicate "any preference, limitation, specification, or discrimination" based on race, color, religion, sex, or national origin in a help-wanted ad, unless belonging to a particular group is a Bona Fide Occupational Qualification (BFOQ). [*See* 42 U.S.C. § 2000e-3(b)]

It might be a BFOQ to be male or female (e.g., because of authenticity, for an actor or actress; for privacy, for a restroom attendant); to be under 40 (in a job where public safety depends on youthful reactions) or even to belong to a particular religion (e.g., to work in a kosher slaughterhouse). In the disability context, it is a BFOQ not to pose a safety risk to oneself or others. Where safety or efficiency is involved, it may be possible to raise a "business necessity" defense for a discriminatory business practice.

Race is never a BFOQ. [*See Ferrill v. Parker Group, Inc.*, 168 F.3d 468 (11th Cir. 1999)] A black woman was hired to telemarket to black voters and then fired after the election. The employer failed in its claim that race is a BFOQ for telemarketers (on the theory that consumers are more responsive to persons of their own race).

§ 34.04 EXCEPTIONS TO TITLE VII COVERAGE

[A] Definition of Employer

Perhaps the most important exception is found in 42 U.S.C. § 2000e(b), which defines an "employer" as a natural person or business engaged in an industry affecting commerce—and having 15 or more employees for each work day in 20 or more weeks either in the year in question or the preceding calendar year. So a very small business will be exempt from Title VII. Possibly some businesses with even more than 15 employees will escape coverage because their business does not "affect commerce," but most businesses do sell or at least attempt to make interstate sales, so their business will be deemed to "affect commerce."

The 15-employee figure is calculated based on the number of people on the payroll, not the number of full-time employees. [*Walters v. Metropolitan Educ. Enters., Inc.*, 519 U.S. 202 (1997)]

Another exception is allowed under 42 U.S.C. § 2000e-2(e) if religion, sex, or national origin is a bona fide occupational qualification "reasonably necessary to the normal operation" of the business. Educational institutions sponsored by a religious organization, (e.g., Notre Dame or Yeshiva University) or institutions "directed toward the propagation of a particular religion" are permitted to base hiring and other employment decisions on religion—parochial schools can, but do not have to, employ staffers of other religions.

[B] Aliens

Section 2000e-1 provides that Title VII does not apply to the employment of "aliens." In August 1998, the Fourth Circuit reversed its earlier ruling. Now *Egbuna v. Time-Life Libraries, Inc.* [153 F.3d 184 (4th Cir. 1998)] holds that it is necessary to be a U.S. citizen or an alien holding a valid work visa, to be a "qualified" individual. So an alien who does not have legal worker status in the United States cannot make out a Title VII prima facie case.

Furthermore, an employer does not violate Title VII if it (or a corporation it controls) takes an action with respect to an employee in a foreign country that is necessary to avoid violating that country's law—even if the action would be barred by Title VII if it were taken in the United States. The factors in whether an employer controls a corporation include whether there is common management, ownership, or financial control, and whether the two organizations have related operations.

Private social clubs such as country clubs are exempt from Title VII. However, the Eastern District of Virginia allows 42 U.S.C. § 1981 civil rights claims to be brought by employees and ex-employees of private clubs. In this reading, the Title VII exclusion is designed to protect freedom of association, but allowing § 1981 suits does not restrict freedom of association. [*Crawford v. Willow Oaks Country Club*, 66 F.3d 767 (E.D. Va. 1999)]

[C]   National Security

Another exception, that will probably become far more important after September 11, 2001, than before, is the 42 U.S.C. § 2000e-2(g) national security exception. It does not violate Title VII to fire or refuse to hire someone who has not met, or no longer meets, security clearance requirements "in effect pursuant to or administered under any statute of the United States or any Executive order of the President."

[D]   Seniority Systems

Employers are permitted, under 42 U.S.C. § 2000e-2(h), to abide by "bona fide seniority or merit systems," or to base compensation on quantity or quality of production, or to pay different rates at different locations—even if the result is to provide different standards of compensation or different terms, conditions, or privileges of employment. However, employers are not allowed to impose such differences in treatment if they are "the result of an intention to discriminate" on the basis of race, color, religion, sex, or national origin.

Also see 42 U.S.C. § 2000e-5(e)(2), which says that the unlawful unemployment practice occurs, with respect to a seniority system that was adopted "for an intentionally discriminatory purpose," whether or not the purpose can be discerned from the face of the provision, either when the seniority system is adopted, when the potential plaintiff becomes subject to the seniority system, or when the seniority system is applied in a way that injures the potential plaintiff.

Section 2000e-2(h) also allows employers to use validated pre-employment tests of ability, as long as testing is not designed, intended or used to discriminate. The subject of test scores is taken up again in 42 U.S.C. § 2000e-2(l), which states that it is an unlawful employment practice to adjust scores or use different cutoff scores in hiring or promotion tests, based on the race, color, religion, sex or national origin of the test taker.

§ 34.05   RACIAL DISCRIMINATION

[A]   Basic Protections

The first equal opportunity laws were bans on racial discrimination. The Civil Rights Act of 1866, enacted at 42 U.S.C. § 1981, was passed to give former slaves the same rights as "white citizens." There is no requirement of a minimum number of employees for a § 1981 suit, and the EEOC and state antidiscrimination procedures do not have to be invoked before bringing suit under this provision.

The Civil Rights Act of 1991 generally requires plaintiffs to proceed under § 1981 if they have claims of racial discrimination, before using Title VII. Compensatory and punitive damages are not available under Title VII for any plaintiff who can get such damages under § 1981.

There have been some major recent cases about race discrimination. The quest to have a completely race-neutral workplace is a difficult one, and claims have been raised both by majority and minority groups that their rights have been violated.

In January 2002, the Social Security Administration settled a suit by 2,200 black male employees via an agreement to pay $7.75 million in damages and an agreement to take steps to avoid future discrimination. The group of active and former employees charged the agency with denying them promotions and disciplining them more often than other employees in comparable situations. [Laurie Kellman, *Social Security Settles Discrimination Suit for $7.75M*, The Associated Press (Jan. 16, 2002) (law.com)]

In *Johnson v. Zema Systems Corp.* [170 F.3d 734 (7th Cir. 1999)], a black manager said he was fired because he spent much of his time supervising white rather than black employees in a segregated and hostile environment. The employer relied on the "same actor" defense, i.e., if the manager who hired the plaintiff also fired him or her, the manager could not have been motivated by racial bigotry. The Seventh Circuit did not accept this as a valid defense, noting that the firing might occur because the hiree did not conform to the hirer's stereotypes about the group he or she belongs to.

The Seventh Circuit ruled in mid-2001 that it is permissible to use date of birth as a tie-breaker for an eligibility list for promotions, where the candidates have the same test score and the same amount of seniority. (The plaintiff, a black woman, was younger than the white man who was competing for the promotion.) It was not sufficient for the plaintiff to show that there were possible alternative tie-breaking practices that the employer failed to adopt. [*Price v. Chicago*, 251 F.3d 656 (7th Cir. 2001)]

The Tenth Circuit has applied the *Faragher/Burlington* test [*see* § 35.02] to conduct that creates a racially hostile environment. Conduct is deemed to be within the scope of employment if it is motivated by intent to serve the employer. So the employer will be liable for discriminatory conduct by a supervisor reflecting prejudice within the labor force. [*Wright-Simmons v. City of Oklahoma City*, 155 F.3d 1264 (10th Cir. 1998)] Even a single racial slur by a supervisor in the presence of another supervisor can be severe enough to create a hostile work environment. [*Taylor v. Metzger*, 706 A.2d 685 (N.J. 1998)]

Swinton v. Potomac Corp. [270 F.3d 794 (9th Cir. 2001)] does not allow the defendant employer to use the *Faragher/Burlington* affirmative defense. However, the plaintiff must prove that the employer knew or should have known of the harassment, and failed to take appropriate corrective steps. A $1 million dollar punitive damage award was upheld.

[B] Reverse Discrimination

A white male plaintiff claimed that he was denied a promotion because of reverse discrimination, and the woman who got the promotion was less qualified. Because a white male is not a member of a protected class, the Seventh Circuit defined the prima face case as showing "background circumstances" (e.g., a pattern of not promoting white males; the choice of a significantly weaker candidate) evidencing reverse discrimination. The Seventh Circuit held that the plaintiff did produce a prima facie case by showing that most of the promotions went to women. But he did not win at trial: the plaintiff failed to show that the employer's defense, that it believed the woman was better qualified for the promotion—was false or pretextual. [*Mills v. Health Care Serv. Corp.*, 171 F.3d 450 (7th Cir. 1999)]

The Southern District of New York does not require "special circumstances" for a white male to bring a reverse bias claim; he is not required to meet a higher pleading standard for white males than for minorities or women who charge violations of Title VII. [*Tappe v. Alliance Capital Mgmt.*, 198 F. Supp. 2d 368 (S.D.N.Y. 2001). *See* Mark Hamblett, *Special Circumstances Not Required for Reverse Bias Claim*, N.Y.L.J. (Oct. 30, 2001) (law.com)]

A white female plaintiff was allowed to pursue a Title VII reverse discrimination claim when her employer gave her a rating of "excellent" rather than "outstanding," with the result that she received a smaller bonus than a similarly situated black employee. [*Russell v. Principi*, 257 F.3d 815 (D.C. Cir. 2001)]

Eight white female librarians were awarded $25 million in compensatory and punitive damages against members of the library board and the director of the board for racially motivated demotions and transfers to less desirable branch locations. But the jury did not award any damages against the library system itself, finding that discrimination against white employees was not official policy. [*Bogle v. McClure*, No. 1:00-CV-2071 (N.D. Ga. Jan. 7, 2002). *See* R. Robin McDonald, *Georgia Jury Awards Librarians $25M for Race Bias*, Fulton County Daily Report (Jan. 17, 2002) (law.com)]

[C]   Affirmative Action and Quotas

A very important question in employment law is how to balance the rights of current employees and applicants against the desire to have a workplace that is truly representative and does not reflect past discrimination.

According to 42 U.S.C. § 2000e-2(j), Title VII does not require employers to grant preferential treatment to any individual or any group because the workforce is imbalanced in terms of the number or percentage of workers from groups that have been discriminated against in the past. In other words, employers do not have to use quotas in hiring, promotion, etc.

In 1977, the Supreme Court decided that it is unlawful to perpetuate the present effects of past discrimination, although bona fide seniority systems can be left in operation. [*Teamsters v. U.S.*, 431 U.S. 324 (1977)] Under this approach, preferential hiring of women and minorities might be acceptable to correct an imbalance in the workforce that results from past discrimination. It might also be acceptable to set goals to remove past discrimination and to remove the barriers that existed in the past to prevent racially neutral hiring, but the hiring system must not exclude white applicants.

Cases in the late 1990s say that employers should not set up affirmative action programs merely to enhance diversity within the workplace, but an affirmative action program might be an appropriate corrective measure if there is a history of racism in a particular industry. [*Johnson v. Transportation Agency of Santa Clara County*, 480 U.S. 616 (1987); *Eldredge v. Carpenters Joint Apprenticeship and Training Committee*, 94 F.3d 1366 (9th Cir. 1996); *Schurr v. Resorts Int'l Hotel*, 196 F.3d 486 (3rd Cir. 1999)]

The Supreme Court agreed to hear the case of *Piscataway Township Board of Education v. Taxman* [#96-679, *cert. dismissed*, 522 U.S. 1010 (1997)] involving the important issue of whether a well-qualified employee can be laid off to promote the goal of diversity in the workplace. However, the case was settled out of court in late November, 1997, so the Supreme Court did not issue a decision.

On December 14, 1998, the EEOC and the Department of Labor proposed a new work-sharing plan, under which the DOL can sue federal contractors for remedies (including punitive damages) if the contractors are guilty of race, sex, or religious discrimination. Employees of federal contractors have the option of filing discrimination charges with either the EEOC or the DOL.

In the past two decades or so, affirmative action has been most prominent in the context of government contracts. In 1995, the U.S. Supreme Court decided that race-based preferences in government contracting are permissible only if the actual contractor has been the victim of discrimination—not merely that he or she belongs to a group that has historically been economically disadvantaged. [*Adarand Constructors Inc. v. Pena*, 513 U.S. 1108, and 515 U.S. 200 (1995)] The case continued to bounce up and down the court system with various decisions that had more to do with technical legal issues than with the rights and wrongs of affirmative action. The case was supposed to be reheard by the Supreme Court, but in November 2001, the Supreme Court dismissed certiorari as having been improvidently granted. [*Adarand Constructors v. Mineta*, 534 U.S. 103 (2001)]

[D] Executive Order 11246

Executive Order 11246 requires government contractors and contractors on federally assisted construction projects worth over $10,000 to have a policy of furthering equal employment opportunity. If the contractor or subcontractor has more than 50 employees, and the contract is worth over $50,000, the company must have a formal affirmative action program, which must be submitted to the Office of Federal Contract Compliance Programs (OFCCP) within 30 days of the OFCCP's request to see the program.

Contracts over $1 million require a pre-award audit of the affirmative action program. [*See* 41 C.F.R. Part 60] There are separate, slightly different, rules for construction contractors.

A company charged with reverse discrimination because of its affirmative action program can cite as a defense that it followed the EEOC's Guidelines on Affirmative Action. To qualify for this defense, the employer must have a written plan. It must act reasonably, taking actions based on self-analysis that leads to a reasonable conclusion that there are actual problems of job bias that require correction. The plan of action must be tailored to eliminate inequality. It must last only as long as it takes to eliminate the effects of past discrimination.

§ 34.06 SEX DISCRIMINATION

[A] Generally

Discrimination on account of sex is unlawful, except if there is a gender-based BFOQ. In 1983, the Supreme Court decided that it constitutes sex discrimination for a health plan to provide less comprehensive benefits to male employees and their wives than to female employees and their husbands. [*Newport News Shipbuilding v. EEOC*, 462 U.S. 669 (1983)]

A male social worker's sex-discrimination claim, challenging the employer's subjective interview practices, failed in *Scott v. Parkview Memorial Hospital*. [175 F.3d 523 (7th Cir. 1999)] The plaintiff claimed that the interview process unfairly favored women because it privileged traditional feminine qualities such as warmth and empathy. However, the Seventh Circuit viewed subjective interviews as a necessary part of professional recruitment, and furthermore that the qualities useful in the interview were also useful in performing the job, so the interview practice was valid and job-related.

It violates the Fourteenth Amendment's guarantee of Equal Protection to apply a facially neutral state law in a way that reflects sexual stereotyping. Therefore, a male state trooper should have been granted a 30-day parental leave when his child was born. (Leave was denied on the basis that only women can be primary caregivers for infants.) However, *Knussman v. Maryland* [272 F.3d 625 (4th Cir. 2001)] holds that an award of $375,000 in emotional distress damages was disproportionate to the actual damages that the trooper suffered.

A Ninth Circuit decision holds that it is illegal sex discrimination for an airline to set its weight limits for female flight attendants based on tables for persons with a medium frame, while using tables for a large frame to set limits for male flight attendants. The court treated this as disparate impact discrimination not qualifying for a BFOQ defense. The airline called it a grooming standard (which can permissibly differ by sex), but the court said that requiring woman flight attendants to be thinner than males of the same height did not improve their ability to do their jobs. [*Frank v. United Airlines*, 216 F.3d 845 (9th Cir. 2000)] It does not constitute sexual-orientation discrimination to require a transsexual employee to use the rest room on the basis of biological rather than perceived gender. [*Goins v. WestGroup*, 635 N.W.2d 717 (Minn. 2001)]

According to the Sixth Circuit, a company's antinepotism policy (requiring one spouse to resign when two employees marry) was rational. However, firing someone for criticizing the policy could be a violation of the employee's right of freedom of thought. In *Vaughn v. Lawrenceburg Power System* [269 F.3d 703 (6th Cir. 2001)], the bride agreed to resign, then the groom was fired for agreeing with the statement, "I take it you do not fully agree with our policy." The Sixth Circuit said that antinepotism rules get heightened scrutiny under the First Amendment right of freedom of association if, but only if, they place a direct and substantial burden on the right to marry. [*See also Montgomery v. Carr*, 101 F.3d 1124 (6th Cir. 1996)]

The Seventh Circuit did not agree with a female supervisor that she was constructively discharged when she was transferred to an evening schedule. She claimed that these "intolerable" working conditions violated her "wifely instincts" that would force her to quit her job in order to take care of her husband's needs in the evening. The court was not impressed by these arguments. [*Grube v. Lau Indus. Inc.*, 257 F.3d 723 (7th Cir. 2001)]

[B] The Pregnancy Discrimination Act (PDA)

Section 2000e contains vital definitions for understanding federal anti-discrimination law. Sex discrimination includes, but is not limited to, discrimination "because or on the basis of pregnancy, childbirth, or related medical conditions." [42 U.S.C. § 2000e(k)]

This part of Title VII is referred to as the Pregnancy Discrimination Act (PDA). Under the PDA, women "affected by pregnancy, childbirth, or related medical conditions" have to be treated the same way as "other persons" who are not affected by such conditions, but who are comparable in their ability or inability to work. In other words, the PDA does not treat pregnancy itself as a disability, but to the extent that a particular pregnant worker does encounter disability, the employer must treat it the same way as other non-occupationally-related disability.

The PDA requires equal treatment for "all employment-related purposes," including fringe benefits—a category that includes the all-important health benefits. However, employers do not have to provide health coverage if they would not otherwise. Employers have the discretion to provide abortion benefits, and are required to cover medical complications of abortion, but do not have to cover elective abortions, only abortions in situations where the mother's life would be endangered by carrying the fetus to term.

If pregnant employees are covered by the plan, the pregnant wives of employees must be covered (in a plan with dependent coverage), and vice versa. However, it is permissible to exclude the pregnancy-related conditions of dependents other than the spouses of employees, as long as the exclusion is applied equally for male and female employees and their dependents.

29 C.F.R. Part 1604, Question 17 says that if an employer has a policy of continuing benefits for employees who are on leave (e.g., when they are injured; when they are on military leave), then benefits must be continued for pregnancy-related leave to the same extent.

Peralta v. Chromium Plating & Polishing Corp. [2000 U.S. Dist. LEXIS 17416 (E.D.N.Y. Sept. 15, 2000), N.Y.L.J., Oct. 18, 2000, at p. 38 col. 4] makes it clear that it was improper to fire a pregnant employee whose doctor said she should be placed on light duty. The employer said that she was placed on unpaid leave, but in either case she was treated differently from nonpregnant employees. The Eastern District would not allow the employer to treat protecting the unborn baby as a reason to impose a BFOQ of not being pregnant (even though the employee had miscarried an earlier pregnancy while working there).

The Southern District says that the BFOQ exception only comes into play when the employer seeks to protect third parties whose safety is part of the company's central mission. Customers are in that category, but employees' unborn children are not. In this analysis, potential tort liability is not a BFOQ either. The way to handle potential liability risk is to get a waiver from an employee who wants to keep working, rather than to fire her.

Pregnant workers may be unable to perform all the tasks associated with their jobs, but are healthy and fit enough that they are not "disabled." They may need limitations on lifting weights or standing for long periods of time. Each year, close to two million employed women become pregnant; about 640,000 of them have jobs that involve at least some physical exertion. However, employers seldom make an effort to find light-duty assignments for pregnant workers. A lot of companies have only a few light-duty jobs, and prefer to use them for Worker's Compensation recipients who were injured at work and therefore must be kept on the payroll with or without work assignments. [*See* Sue Shellenbarger, *Pregnant Workers Clash with Employers over Job Inflexibility*, Wall Street Journal, Feb. 10, 1999, at p. B1]

The Fifth Circuit upheld an employer's policy of limiting light-duty assignments to workers injured on the job. As long as pregnancy-related disability is treated on a par with other nonoccupational disability, there has been no PDA violation, even if pregnant workers have to stop work earlier than they would have preferred. [*Urbano v. Continental Airlines*, 138 F.3d 204 (5th Cir. 1998)]

In a case where the discharge occurs significantly after pregnancy and delivery, the plaintiff must show that she was affected by pregnancy, childbirth, or a related medical condition at the time of the adverse job action. A case where the plaintiff was fired eight months after her return from maternity leave (eleven months after the baby's birth) was dismissed for lack of evidence. Alleged harassing comments before the baby's birth were not sufficient to demonstrate discrimination nearly a year later. [*Solomen v. Redwood Advisory Co.*, 183 F. Supp. 2d 748 (E.D. Pa. 2002), discussed in Shannon P. Duffy, *Plaintiff Fails to Meet Burden in Pregnancy Bias Case*, The Legal Intelligencer (Feb. 5, 2002) (law.com)]

[C] The Equal Pay Act (EPA)

The Equal Pay Act [29 U.S.C. § 206] is related to the Title VII provisions that forbid sex discrimination, but it is not a part of Title VII. The EPA covers all employers with *two* or more employees. It forbids discrimination in compensation, including all forms of benefits, on the basis of sex—if the two jobs are of equal skill, effort, and responsibility and are performed under similar working conditions. In other words, the statute does not apply to "comparable worth" claims under which women claim that a typically female job is of greater value to society than a higher-paid but different job typically performed by men (e.g., child care workers and parking lot attendants).

Cost-based defenses are not allowed under the EPA [*see* 29 C.F.R. § 216(b)], which says that even if it costs more to provide benefits to women than to men, the employer must either eliminate the benefit or provide it to everyone.

The EPA imposes civil penalties on employers who violate it; even criminal penalties, as prescribed by Fair Labor Standards Act § 216(a), are a possibility. Punitive damages are not allowed, but double back pay is. A winning plaintiff can get costs and attorneys' fees.

According to the Bureau of Labor Statistics, in 2001 the weekly median earnings for woman workers were $511—76% of the median of $672 a week earned by men. But the differences between female and male salaries differed from industry to industry. In technical, sales, and administrative support, women earned a median of $473 a week—only 70.9% of the median salary of $667 for men. But in the administrative support/clerical category, women earned a median of $469 a week, 81.4% of the men's median earnings of $576. In the highest-paid category, executive, administrative, and managerial, women earned a median of $732 a week, 70.5% of the male median of $1,038 a week. [BLS, "Household Data Annual Averages 2001," <ftp://ftp.bls.gov/pub/special.requests/lf/aat39.txt>] NOTE: this is an FTP file and not an HTML one, so the URL does not include http or www.

An EPA suit by female professors against a state university was vacated and remanded by the Supreme Court. On remand, the Seventh Circuit upheld the

EPA as a valid exercise of congressional authority, which meant that it was also legitimate for Congress to take away the state's Eleventh Amendment immunity from being sued. [*Varner v. Illinois State U.*, 226 F.3d 927 (7th Cir. 2000)]

For pay equity resources, see the DOL Women's Bureau, <http://www2.dol.gov/wb/10step71.htm> and the Equal Employment Advisory Council, <http://www.eeac.org>. Federal contractors can access the audit manual for OFCCP compliance at <http://www.dol.gov/esa/regs/compliance/ofccp/compdata.htm>.

§ 34.07   RELIGIOUS DISCRIMINATION AND REASONABLE ACCOMMODATION

[A]   Employer's Duties and Obligations

According to the EEOC, charges of religious discrimination, although few in number, are increasing. In 1997, there were 1709 such charges—43% higher than the level prevailing early in the 1990s. In 2000, about one out of every 40 charges involved religion.

Religion includes belief and all forms of religious observance and practice, but employers do not have an obligation to incur "undue hardship on the conduct" of their business if they can demonstrate that they are unable to make reasonable accommodation to an employee's or applicant's religious observance or practice. [42 U.S.C. § 2000e(j)] In fact, a 1977 Supreme Court case holds that investing more than a minimal amount in accommodation can actually represent an illegal preference in favor of the employee who receives the accommodation. [*TWA v. Hardison*, 432 U.S. 63 (1977)]

Except in very limited cases (being a priest or minister, for example) religious beliefs are irrelevant to employment and cannot be used as a hiring criterion. Employers are not supposed to prefer one religion over another, or even to prefer organized religion over atheism or agnosticism.

The duty of reasonable accommodation requires employers to try to fit in with employees' beliefs and religious duties. Under EEOC guidelines, all sincerely held moral and ethical beliefs are entitled to the same protection as religious beliefs.

In 1986, the Supreme Court held that employers are not obligated to accept the employee's characterization of what would be a reasonable religious accommodation. The employer can make its own reasonable suggestion of how to accommodate the employee's belief. [*Ansonia Bd. of Educ. v. Philbrook*, 479 U.S. 60 (1986)]

The Society for Human Resource Management's 1997 study showed that about two-thirds of managers say that their company offers flexible schedules that can be used for religious holidays. However, only 19% included religious issues in diversity training; 18% trained their managers in accommodating religious preference; 15% provided space or time for prayer, study, or discussion; and only 13% accommodated religious attire.

Employees will probably have to be permitted to wear forms of dress, jewelry, and hairstyles required by their religion. The exception might be a situation in which the employer can show a genuine safety hazard that cannot be accommodated in another way. For example, a "no-beard" policy could not be enforced against an employee whose religion requires him to grow a beard, unless the beard is unsanitary or creates a hazard of getting caught in machinery—and there is no method of securing the beard that would preserve safety and cleanliness.

Probably the most common religious accommodation issue involves work assignments when the employee is supposed to observe a Sabbath, attend religious services, study the scriptures, teach in a religious school, or the like. The consensus is that the employer has to accommodate activities (or non-activities, like avoiding work on the Sabbath) that are mandated by an organized religion, but not employee's personal wishes about religious observance.

The EEOC considers it unlawful discrimination to set overtime rates in a way that disadvantages employees who observe a Sabbath other than Sunday. [*See* Guidelines, 29 C.F.R. Part 1605] The EEOC considers acceptable accommodations to include voluntary substitution of one employee for another, swapping shifts, lateral transfers, changes of job assignment, and flextime (i.e., the employee makes up the time devoted to religious observance).

However, employers are not required to accommodate religious observance by violating the seniority rights of a nonobservant employee. In the view of the EEOC, it would be undue hardship for the employer to have to pay overtime to other employees to cover for the religious employee or to have an untrained or inexperienced person covering for the religious employee.

When it comes to union security, the National Labor Relations Act, at 29 U.S.C. § 169, provides that if an employee belongs to a religion that has traditionally objected to unions, then the employer cannot require the employee to join or support a union, even if the operation is an agency shop or participates in another union security arrangement. However, the employee's religious objection can be accommodated by requiring him or her to contribute an amount equivalent to the union initiation fee and dues to a charitable organization that is neither a union nor religious in nature. That way the employee does not benefit financially from the anti-union belief, but is not required to perform a religiously repugnant act.

States are not allowed to pass laws that give employees an absolute right to get their Sabbath day as a day off—that would be an unconstitutional establishment of religion. [*Estate of Thornton v. Caldor, Inc.*, 472 U.S. 703 (1985)] However, an employee who is fired for refusing to work on the Sabbath is entitled to collect unemployment benefits. [*Hobbie v. Unemployment Appeals Comm'n of Florida*, 480 U.S. 136 (1987)] Some state laws, including New York's Human Rights Law, make it clear that employees who get time off for religious observances must make up the time at another time that is religiously acceptable.

Employers may have to become umpires if an employee claims that his or her own faith requires preaching and seeking converts at work, but co-workers aren't interested or are actively hostile? A 1997 case [*Venters v. City of Delphi*, 123

F.3d 956 (7th Cir. 1997)] involves a police dispatcher who alleged that she was fired because her born-again boss insisted she share his religious views. The decision suggests that unwanted proselytizing could create a "hostile religious environment" in the workplace, similar to a climate of racial hostility or sexual harassment.

It should be noted that employees who are not allowed to preach in the workplace can invite co-workers to a church service, prayer meeting, Bible study group, etc., that meets outside the workplace, so their religious expression can be continued elsewhere.

The plaintiff's claim of a religiously hostile workplace was rejected in *Hernandez-Torres v. Intercontinental Trading Co.* [158 F.3d 43 (1st Cir. 1998)] Although he received a number of e-mails urging greater productivity, he was not singled out: Nonreligious employees received similar messages. He continued to receive favorable assessments, so he did not suffer job detriment because of his religious convictions. When his claim of religious discrimination failed, his retaliation claim also had to be dismissed.

[B] Steps Toward Religious Accommodation

Employers should extend at least the same tolerance to religious garb as to "fashion statements." Where there are actual risks (such as robes getting caught in machinery), document the risk, and work with religious leaders to find out what kinds of safety garments are compatible with religious needs.

Bulletin board postings or the corporate intranets can be used to get volunteers to cover for workers taking prayer time or observing religious holidays. A diverse workforce really helps here—Christian employees can cover the holidays of non-Christian religions, and vice versa. Optional or floating personal days can be used for religious observance.

Because Islam requires five daily prayers, several occurring during the normal work day, it can be difficult to accommodate Muslim employees in a production line environment. Part of the prayer obligation is keyed to sundown, so it does not occur at the same time every day, making it harder to schedule prayers. The need for Muslims to wash their hands and feet before prayer can cause hazardous wet conditions in the washrooms (or hallways, if water is tracked). One simple solution is to install a special self-draining basin, or arrange to have the floors mopped more often.

Although it is often impossible to arrange the menu in the employee cafeteria to conform to all dietary requirements, it is a reasonable gesture to provide some vegetarian alternatives, and to make sure that people whose religion bans the consumption of pork or beef will have other menu choices available.

[C] Case Law on Reasonable Accommodation

According to *Weber v. Roadway Express Inc.* [199 F.3d 270 (5th Cir. 2000)], the employer had no obligation to accommodate a Jehovah's Witness truck driver who wanted to be assigned only male driving partners, because his religion forbade him to take overnight trips with any woman other than his wife. The employer would have encountered a serious burden to reconfigure the schedules. Although the employer had accommodated nonreligious requests in the past, it did so only consistent with business needs and did not have an obligation to encounter undue hardship to accommodate the truck driver.

In *Shelton v. University of Medicine & Dentistry of New Jersey* [223 F.3d 220 (3rd Cir. 2000), discussed in Shannon P. Duffy, *Religious Employee Must Cooperate in Accommodation, 3rd Circuit Rules*, The Legal Intelligencer, (law.com)] a nurse alleged that she was not offered reasonable accommodation to her religious objection to performing tasks that would allow infants to die. The hospital did not perform elective abortions, but sometimes the labor and delivery staff had to assist in abortions performed for reasons of the mother's health. Therefore, the hospital offered her a transfer from the labor ward to the neonatal ICU. She refused to discuss open nursing positions with the hospital's HR department.

In the Third Circuit view, the plaintiff satisfied her prima facie case of religious discrimination, in that she did hold sincere religious views, and she did lose her job. But the court still ruled for the employer, on the theory that the employer's duty is satisfied by offering any reasonable accommodation, even one that is not accepted by the employee. In this case, the employee forfeited her cause of action by refusing to discuss alternatives, so she would have lost even if the proposed accommodation had not been reasonable.

§ 34.08 RETALIATION

Retaliation claims are a large and growing share of the EEOC's caseload. There were fewer than 8,000 retaliation claims in 1991, but more than 18,000 in 1998. [*See* Simon J. Nadel, *Claims of Retaliation Gain Status as Effective Employee Litigation Tool*, 67 L.W. 2259]

Section 8 of the EEOC Compliance Manual (used by EEOC offices), EEOC Directives Transmittal 915.003 (May 20, 1998), covers retaliation. There are three essential elements in a retaliation claim that the EEOC will pursue:

- The charging party engaged in protected activity, such as opposing discrimination or participating in the Title VII complaint process;
- The employer took adverse action against the charging party;
- There was a causal connection between the protected activity and the employer's adverse action.

A retaliation complaint might be proper if the charging party had a reasonable good-faith belief that the employer committed discrimination (even if this belief was incorrect), and the charging party used a reasonable means to protest this to the employer.

It is illegal to retaliate against a charging party if he or she, or someone closely associated with him or her, participated in any statutory enforcement proceeding. This includes any investigation, proceeding, hearing, or suit under any of the statutes enforced by the EEOC. It is unlawful for one employer to retaliate on the basis of a complaint against another employer.

Trivial adverse actions are not covered by the compliance manual, but "more significant retaliatory treatment that is reasonably likely to deter protected activity" is banned. The adverse action need not materially affect the terms, conditions, or privileges of employment. Ex-employees have the right to complain of retaliation (e.g., bad references).

The EEOC might seek temporary or preliminary relief such as injunction if the retaliation places the charging party at risk of irreparable injury and there is a substantial likelihood that the retaliation claim will succeed. The compliance manual notes that all of the statutes enforced by the EEOC make both compensatory and punitive damages available to victims of retaliation.

Although Title VII retaliation damages are subject to the statutory cap, there is no cap on ADEA or EPA damages.

According to the Eleventh Circuit, protection against retaliation for participation in an investigation is limited to the EEOC investigation. An employer is not liable for retaliation on the basis of participation in the employer's own internal investigation. [*Clover v. Total Sys. Servs. Inc.*, 157 F.3d 824 (11th Cir. 1998)] It is not unlawful retaliation to discharge an employee based on the employer's good-faith belief that she lied during such an internal investigation, because the retaliation provision is not triggered until there has been an EEOC filing. [*EEOC v. Total Sys. Servs. Inc.*, 221 F.3d 1171 (11th Cir. 2000)]

An employee who gives a deposition during another person's sex-discrimination case is protected against retaliation for the testimony. The employer is not permitted to impose a requirement that the testimony be "reasonable." [*Glover v. South Carolina Law Enforcement Div.*, 170 F.3d 411 (4th Cir. 1999)]

A lateral transfer requiring the employee to perform tasks that the employer knew the employee would be unable to handle (because of phobia), in retaliation for complaining about harassment by a supervisor, is actionable under Title VII. Although the transfer involved the same pay, benefits, and status, the employer knew that the alleged transfer was really a constructive discharge. [*DiIenno v. Goodwill Indus.*, 162 F.3d 235 (3d Cir. 1998)]

CHAPTER 35
SEXUAL HARASSMENT

§ 35.01   INTRODUCTION

Sexual harassment is the subjection of an employee to unwanted sexual contact, propositions, or innuendoes. Sexual harassment occurs in two forms: either "quid pro quo" harassment, where an employee is threatened with job detriment for not complying with a sexual proposition or offered job benefits for compliance, or "hostile environment" harassment, where the atmosphere in the workplace is offensive.

Although it may be unprofessional, it is not unlawful for a supervisor to date or have sexual relations with a subordinate. The essence of harassment is continued pressing of unwanted sexual attentions. Sexual harassment can also occur if a supervisor penalizes a subordinate who terminates or wishes to terminate a sexual relationship that was consensual at the outset.

Sexual harassment is considered a form of sex discrimination and therefore is forbidden by Title VII. The EEOC has adopted a two-part test. Conduct is unwanted if the employee did not solicit or initiate the conduct, and the employee finds it undesirable or offensive.

However, the Eleventh Circuit did not permit a "reverse-discrimination" sexual harassment suit, brought by a plaintiff who was denied the promotion that went to the employee who had a consensual sexual relationship with the boss. The holding of *Womack v. Runyon* [147 F.3d 1298 (11th Cir. 1998)] is that an isolated instance of favoring a sexual partner cannot constitute sex discrimination, because the plaintiff class would consist of all of the company's employees (male and female), because they were all equally disadvantaged by such favoritism.

Although one or more individuals may commit sexual harassment, it is the employer company that has the legal liability. The only way the employer can avoid liability is by carrying out appropriate investigations of allegations of harassment and by taking appropriate steps to deal with harassment accusations that are well founded.

Under a commercial general liability (CGL) or umbrella liability policy, insurers have no duty to defend against an EEOC suit for intentional sexual harassment. [*American States Insurance Co. v. Natchez Steam Laundry*, 131 F.3d 551 (5th Cir. 1998)] Therefore, the insurance company did not act in bad faith by not providing a defense or insurance benefits. The agency's allegations came under the intentional-acts exception of the policy, and the insurer made an adequate investigation before denying the claim.

§ 35.02   THE EMPLOYER'S BURDEN

In this context, two of the key cases are *Burlington Industries, Inc. v. Ellerth* [524 U.S. 742 (1998)] and *Faragher v. City of Boca Raton.* [524 U.S. 775 (1998)] If the action that the plaintiff complains of had adverse employment effect on the victim, the employer is absolutely liable. The employer is still liable even if no adverse employment effect occurred—unless the employer can assert as a defense that it maintained proper antiharassment and grievance policies.

The *Ellerth* case involved a sales representative who felt threatened by repeated remarks and gestures from a manager (not her immediate supervisor). She was not deprived of job benefits. Although she knew the company had an antiharassment policy, she did not complain about the harassment while it was occurring. She quit her job but did not attribute her resignation to harassment. Three weeks later, she sent a letter to the company explaining why she resigned.

The Supreme Court's decision was that the supervisor's threats of adverse job action created a hostile work environment. In such a situation, the employer becomes vicariously liable for the supervisor's conduct by:

- Failing to stop it after learning about it;
- Giving the supervisor apparent authority over the victim, thus making harassment possible;
- Allowing the supervisor to actually take adverse job action against the victim.

However, the other side of the coin is that the employer can be free of liability by taking reasonable care to maintain a workable complaint procedure, if the plaintiff fails to use the procedure.

In the *Faragher* case, a lifeguard sued her municipal employer and two supervisors for creating a hostile environment (including lewd touching of female employees). The employer did have an antiharassment policy, but it was not publicized to the employees. The employer didn't supervise the conduct of the supervisors themselves, and didn't create a procedure for reporting to someone other than the supervisor who committed the harassment. Therefore, the Supreme Court held that the employer was legally responsible for the hostile environment, because it failed to communicate the antiharassment policy and didn't track the conduct of supervisors.

Although many cases involve the conduct of supervisors (because of their ability to affect working conditions), employers have also been held liable, in appropriate cases, for harassment committed by nonsupervisory, fellow employees, and by customers.

In a quid pro quo case, a series of minor effects that would not be actionable by themselves can be joined together to prove tangible job detriment, and therefore make out the case. [*Reinhold v. Virginia*, 151 F.3d 920 (4th Cir. 1998)]

§ 35.03   APPROPRIATE EMPLOYER RESPONSES

[A]   Statutory and Case Law

Most companies are aware of the potential risk of sexual harassment litigation. When the Society for Human Resource Management (SHRM) did a survey, 97% of respondents said that they have written antiharassment policies. Nearly all (86%) have a formal complaint investigation procedure. Close to two-thirds (62%) provide formal training so employees can recognize, avoid, and prevent harassment. Nevertheless, respondents indicated that the number of sexual harassment complaints made by employers increased in every year between 1995 and 1999. Investigation shows that two-thirds of the complaints can be substantiated.

After the landmark *Ellerth* and *Faragher* cases, the employer must prevent severe, pervasive unwelcome physical and verbal conduct to prevent the development of a hostile, intimidating, or offensive environment. Supervisors and managers must be trained to recognize and report harassment. There must be a chain of command that can bypass an alleged harasser. Employees must believe that their complaints will be taken seriously. Top management must be involved, to prove that the company takes these matters seriously.

If customers commit the harassment, the Tenth Circuit analyzes the situation as if the harassers were co-employees (not supervisors). So the employer will not be strictly liable for the actions of customers, but will be liable if its negligence permitted the harassment to continue. [*Lockard v. Pizza Hut Inc.*, 162 F.3d 1062 (10th Cir. 1998)]

These cases rely on agency law concepts such as the apparent authority of the supervisor. Therefore, the employer should not only limit the extent to which harassers can take action against employees, it should make sure that all disciplinary actions are legitimate. It is important to look behind supervisors' write-ups to make sure that the lateness, poor work habits, etc., actually occurred—and that one subordinate was not singled out for conduct that was not punished in employees who did not become sexual targets.

The rule of California's Fair Employment and Housing Act is that the employer is strictly liable for harassment by a supervisor, even under circumstances where the employer satisfied the *Faragher/Burlington* test and is not liable under Title VII. [*Lai v. Prudential Ins. Co.*, 72 Cal. Rptr. 2d 551 (Cal. App. 1998); *Department of Health Servs. v. Superior Court*, 94 Cal. App. 4th 14 (2001)] Under the FEHA, a law firm was directly, not vicariously, liable for failing to protect an employee against harassment by a partner [*Weeks v. Baker & McKenzie*, 74 Cal. Rptr. 2d 510 (Cal. App. 1998)], on the theory that the firm employed the partner in conscious disregard of the safety and rights of vulnerable employees. Therefore, $3.5 million in punitive damages could be assessed against the firm; its liability was not limited to the $225,000 punitive damage award against the harassing partner. FEHA says that an individual manager, although potentially liable for harassment, is not an "employer" as defined by the statute. [*Reno v. Baird*, 957 P.2d 1333 (Cal. 1998)]

A parent corporation can be directly as well as vicariously liable (as part of an "integrated enterprise") when its wholly owned subsidiary retaliates against an employee who complained of sexual harassment, if the parent company set the policy, employed the person who received the complaint, and issued the layoff notice. [*Ferrell v. Harvard Indus. Inc.*, 70 L.W. 1304 (E.D. Pa. Oct. 23, 2001)]

In *Corcoran v. Shoney's Colonial Inc.* [24 F. Supp. 2d 601 (W.D. Va. 1998)], the employer was held vicariously liable on the plaintiff's hostile environment claim, despite the employer's prompt investigation and separation of harasser from victim. The court read *Faragher/Burlington* to impose vicarious liability, even if prompt remedial action is taken, unless the employee failed to take advantage of the employer's corrective mechanism.

For an example of how an employer met its burden, *see Montero v. AGCO Corp.* [192 F.3d 856 (9th Cir. 1999)] The employee's claim was dismissed because the employer promptly investigated and resolved an allegation of sexual harassment (within 11 days of the complaint). Furthermore, because the employee had taken two years to complain, she was also at fault for failing to make use of the complaint mechanism.

An employer refused to reinstate a worker returning from medical leave. The employer said that she was totally disabled by paranoid schizophrenia, whereas the employee charged that the employer retaliated against her for complaining about on-the-job sexual harassment. During the leave, the employee had applied for, and been granted, Social Security Disability Income (SSDI) benefits. The Seventh Circuit ruled, in *Wilson v. Chrysler Corp.* [172 F.3d 500 (7th Cir. 1999)] that applying for disability benefits rules out a sexual harassment claim, because in a Title VII case (a category that includes sexual harassment), there is no obligation of reasonable accommodation.

The employer's failure to investigate a claimant's repeated reports of sexual harassment made her resignation a voluntary quit with good cause attributable to the employer, so benefits were available. [*Yaeger*, Unempl. Ins. Rep. (CCH) ¶8915 (Fla. Dist. App. 2001)]

[B] EEOC Enforcement Guidance

The EEOC's position about what employers should do is summed up in its 20-page guidance available online. [*Enforcement Guidance: Vicarious Employer Liability for Unlawful Harassment by Supervisors*, Number 915.002, (June 18, 1999) <http://www.eeoc.gov/docs/harassment.html>]

The Guidance makes employers responsible for preventing harassment of all kinds—harassment based on sex (including derogation of women or men because they are women or men, even if the harasser is not seeking sexual gratification); race, color, religion, national origin, age, disability, or protected activity such as enforcing legal rights.

Under this Guidance, the employer will not be liable if harassment does not subject the employee to tangible disadvantages, as long as the employer uses reasonable care to prevent harassment. The employer is also free of liability if it takes reasonable steps to correct harassment that has already occurred, provided that the employee is also at fault by failing to take advantage of the policies and procedures in place.

The actions of "supervisors" can subject the employer to liability—but this term is not defined in Title VII. The key test is whether, based on the real situation in the workplace, the alleged harasser had enough authority over the alleged victim to make it easier to harass and harder for the victim to resist.

The EEOC uses a two-part test. Either a supervisor has authority to direct someone else's daily work activities, or has authority to implement or at least recommend tangible employment decisions such as awarding a raise or bonus, promoting or firing the employee. The employer can also be liable for harassment by someone whom the victim reasonably thought was a supervisor, even if this was not the case.

Merely having a policy isn't enough: It must really be enforced. The EEOC encourages employers to terminate harassment even before it reaches the severe, protracted level that would justify a lawsuit.

Under the EEOC interpretation, the employer is always liable when a harassing supervisor subjects an employee to tangible employment action. A tangible employment action means a significant change in employment status such as firing, denial of a promotion, reassignment, an undesirable work assignment. An unfulfilled threat, a trivial effect, or causing hurt feelings doesn't count.

This is the minimum that the EEOC will accept as a satisfactory corporate antiharassment policy:

- Clear explanations of what constitutes prohibited harassment;
- Assurances that employees who report harassment will not suffer retaliation;
- A clear explanation of a workable procedure for investigating complaints promptly, fairly, and thoroughly (with alternatives so that no one will be expected to report harassment to the person who committed it);
- A confidentiality procedure for complaints;
- Assurance of fast, appropriate response when the investigation shows that harassment has occurred.

Adequate responses to confirmation of a harassment allegation include:

- A warning or an oral or written reprimand to the harasser;
- Training and counseling the harasser about why the conduct violated the employer's policy;
- Transferring, reassigning, demoting, suspending, or, in appropriate cases, firing the harasser;
- Monitoring to make sure harassment has ended;
- Allowing the victim to take leave to get out of the range of harassment;
- Correcting the victim's file to remove unfair evaluations;
- Having the harasser apologize to the victim;
- Checking to make sure that there is no retaliation for reporting the harassment.

[C] Internal Investigations of Harassment Allegations

An article by two Winston & Strawn attorneys [Susan Schenkel-Savitt and Jill H. Turner, <http://www.lawnewsnetwork.com>] gives some insights into appropriate investigation of sexual harassment charges. [For more how-tos for internal investigations, *see* Jonathan A. Segal, *HR as Judge, Jury, Prosecutor, and Defender*, HR Magazine, October 2001, at p. 141]

Employers can't just summarily fire everyone accused of harassment, because some of those charges could be fabricated; the result of honest misunderstanding; or the accused person's misconduct might not have been serious enough to justify termination. Overreaction on the employer's part could constitute wrongful termination. [*See* Chapter 39] A mechanism for unbiased internal investigations is necessary, to strike the proper balance between the rights of accusers and accused persons.

Whoever conducts the investigation may have to testify later on, so an in-house or outside attorney who normally represents the corporation could be a poor choice. Attorneys are not allowed to serve as witnesses in cases where they are also representing a party.

However, choosing an attorney rather than someone else can be a good choice, because communications between attorney and client are privileged (opposing parties in litigation can't get hold of them). An attorney's "work product"—the materials drafted by the attorney while preparing the case—is also protected. Similar privileges are not extended to other professionals. If the company will want to assert confidentiality at the pretrial and trial stages, it will have to be sure to keep the materials confidential. Access must be limited to the people involved in the investigation; there must be no general distribution.

The investigator must determine:

- Who claims to have been the victim of harassment (in many cases, harassment involves a number of people);
- Everyone who is accused of committing harassment, contributing to a hostile work environment, or participating in a cover-up;
- Everyone who is claimed to be a witness—and the extent to which their recollection tallies with the complainant's;
- Detailed information about the alleged acts of harassment or the duration and nature of the hostile environment;
- Whether the acts occurred on company property, at company functions, or elsewhere;
- Did the complainant make a prompt report of the alleged harassment? To whom was it made? If there was no report, was there any justification for failing to report at or close to the time of the incident?

The investigator should follow up by contacting witnesses and checking matters of fact. For instance, if an incident is charged on a particular date, the investigator should verify whether the alleged harasser was out of town at the time.

The interview with the alleged harasser is very important. It is up to the employer whether or not to reveal the name of the person making the allegation. To protect the employer against later claims by the alleged harasser, the investigator should make it clear that an investigation is underway, and no conclusions have yet been reached as to the validity of the accusation. The accused person must be given a full, fair chance to get his or her own story on the record.

Additional rounds of interviews may be needed to follow new lines of investigation or confirm disputed facts. The end product of the investigation should be a confidential written report to the person with corporate-level HR responsibility.

Whenever it is determined that an allegation is well founded, the company has a responsibility to take action. The appropriate action is proportionate to the seriousness of the conduct and serves to deter future harassment. The action should also be proportionate to steps the employer has taken in similar cases in the past. The harasser's employment record may provide either mitigation factors (such as a long history of good performance) or aggravating factors (past instances of discipline, especially prior instances of harassment).

If the employer determines that a sanction short of dismissal is appropriate, steps should be taken to keep the harasser and victim apart, but without retaliating against the victim for having complained! The employer should also follow up (and keep written records) to make sure that the disciplinary action has served to prevent future harassment incidents.

In addition to its arbitration activities, the American Arbitration Association has a program under which it will send a two-person fact-finding team to investigate. The AAA can be reached at (212) 484-4000 or its local regional offices. Bringing in neutral observers from a respected organization can be an efficient and cost-effective way to resolve complaints, especially if widespread harassment is alleged, and the objectivity of corporate management might be questioned.

In April 1999, the Federal Trade Commission took the position that an attorney who is paid by a corporation to investigate sexual harassment charges is acting as a "credit reporting agency" and therefore must conform to the Fair Credit Reporting Act (FCRA) or be penalized by fines, punitive damages, and the obligation to pay the opponents' attorneys' fees. Reports prepared by attorneys in this "credit investigation" role might be denied the protection of the attorney-client privilege. [The letter, from an FTC staffer to an attorney who posed a query, was published at <http://www.ftc.gov/os/statutes/fcra/vail.htm>. *See* § 23.13 for a discussion on the limitations on employers' use of the credit reports of employees and job applicants]

§35.04   HOSTILE WORK ENVIRONMENT HARASSMENT

A hostile work environment is one where actions are taken to make an employee feel unwelcome. Harassment cases have been recognized dealing with race, religion, disability, and age, as well as cases in which women are made uncomfortable by, e.g., unwanted touching, crude propositions, dirty jokes, pin-ups, etc. Hostile work environment sexual harassment cases have been recognized for many years, dating back to the Supreme Court case of *Meritor Savings Bank v. Vinson*. [477 U.S. 57 (1986)]

It can be difficult to predict what conduct will be considered sufficiently outrageous to create a hostile environment, because different courts have reached very different conclusions. There is often disagreement about the seriousness of conduct that constitutes harassment, how severe and prolonged it must be, and the extent of injuries that the complainant must suffer before having a sustainable case.

According to *Howley v. Town of Stratford* [217 F.3d 141 (2d Cir. 2000)], one incident of verbal harassment of a female fire lieutenant by a male subordinate, at a union meeting, can be deemed to constitute an intolerable alteration of the work environment. The theory was that it diminished subordinates' respect for the commanding officer, which in turn impaired the fire department's basic public safety mission.

In contrast, one incident in which a male employee touched a female co-worker's breast and stomach was held not to create a hostile environment. No physical injury occurred, and the employer promptly removed the harasser from the workplace. According to *Brooks v. San Mateo, California* [69 L.W. 1265 (9th Cir. Oct. 23, 2000)], although similar incidents had occurred in the past (but were not reported), the Ninth Circuit did not believe that a reasonable employee would have believed that the terms and conditions of employment were altered for the worse. Ostracism suffered by the female employee from co-workers, because she reported the incident, cannot be considered adverse employment action.

In the case of *Breda v. Wolf Camera* [222 F.3d 890 (11th Cir.); *on remand*, 148 F. Supp. 2d 1371 (S.D. Ga. 2001)], first the defendant succeeded in getting summary judgment. However, the Eleventh Circuit remanded the case for a new trial. The new trial, in July 2001, resulted in another dismissal. The Southern District of Georgia judge held that, given the crudity and vulgarity of modern culture, a certain amount of vulgarity, even boorish behavior, must be tolerated in the workplace. The judge characterized the conduct at the workplace that impelled the plaintiff to resign as "juvenile, offensive, and at times even mean-spirited" but also said that the tally of sexualized comments and gestures did not add up to enough for a Title VII cause of action. [*Id. See* R. Robin McDonald, *Modern "Vulgarism" May Doom Sex Harassment Laws, Says Federal Judge*, Fulton County Daily Report, (July 11, 2001) (law.com)]

Suggestive male nude pictures posted on an office bulletin board by a male co-worker did not create a hostile sexual environment for the female plaintiff because the court did not believe that a rational jury could find that the terms of the plaintiff's employment were altered to create a pervasive atmosphere of intimidation, ridicule, and insult. [*Brennan v. Metropolitan Opera Ass'n Inc.*, 192 F.3d 310 (2d Cir. 1999)]

The Sixth Circuit held that, in an all-male workforce, the employer is not liable for vulgar horseplay by co-workers. Because all the workers were male, there was no element of sex discrimination and therefore no case against the employer. [*EEOC v. Harbert-Yeargin Inc.*, 266 F.3d 498 (6th Cir. 2001)]

§35.05   SAME-SEX HARASSMENT

For several years, courts were divided about whether sexual harassment of a male employee by a male supervisor, or a female employee by a female supervisor, was barred by Title VII. Perhaps this reflects a stereotype of sexual harassment as only something that is perpetrated by males against females. Questions were raised as to whether same-sex harassment could be described as occurring "on account of sex," because the harasser is of the same sex as the victim.

The uncertainty was resolved by the Supreme Court in *Oncale v. Offshore Services Inc.* [523 U.S. 45 (1998)], which brought same-sex harassment into the ambit of Title VII.

Surprisingly, however, the Seventh Circuit ruled that neither male nor female state-government employees could sue for sexual harassment, on the grounds that a supervisor who propositioned both male and female employees could not have been committing discrimination on account of sex. [*Holman v. State of Indiana*, 211 F.3d 399 (7th Cir. 2000)]

§35.06   ORIENTATION AND PERCEIVED ORIENTATION

Although a number of states and cities have their own laws against sexual-orientation discrimination, Title VII itself does not forbid discrimination on the basis of homosexual or bisexual orientation. [*Higgins v. New Balance Athletic Shoes Inc.*, 194 F.3d 252 (1st Cir. 1999); *Bibby v. Philadelphia Coca-Cola Bottling Co.*, 260 F.3d 257 (3d Cir. 2001)] The *Bibby* case says that three kinds of same-sex harassment are illegal: unwanted sexual advances made toward an employee of the same sex; harassment because the harasser believes that women or men do not belong in that type of workplace; or harassment for failure to behave with appropriate masculinity or femininity.

The Eastern District of Pennsylvania granted summary judgment for the employer in *Bianchi v. City of Philadelphia.* [99-CV-2409 (E.D. Pa. Jan. 7, 2002)] The plaintiff claimed that, although he was not homosexual, his co-workers believed he was and harassed him on that account. The opinion says that plaintiffs who bring claims of this type can get past a motion for summary judgment only by proving that the alleged discrimination resulted from failure to satisfy social ideas about appropriate gender behavior: about conformity to ideas about masculinity for men and femininity for women. [*See* Shannon Duffy, *Lack of Evidence Ends Same-Sex Harassment Title VII Claim*, The Legal Intelligencer, (Jan. 10, 2002) (law.com)]

For example, the Seventh Circuit allowed a young man to litigate a sexual harassment claim based on alleged harassment targeting him as effeminate because he wore an earring. [*Doe v. City of Belleville*, 119 F.3d 563 (7th Cir. 2001)] A claim of harassment on the basis of perceived effeminacy was upheld in *Nichols v. Azteca Restaurant Enterprises Inc.* [256 F.3d 864 (9th Cir. 2001)] In contrast, in deciding *Bibby* the Third Circuit treated the *Bianchi* case as an allegation of harassment on the basis of a false perception of homosexuality—a ground that is not covered by Title VII.

Hamner v. St. Vincent Hospital and Health Care Center Inc. [224 F.3d 701 (7th Cir. 2000)] holds that sexual-orientation discrimination and harassment by a supervisor premised on the plaintiff's perceived effeminacy is not covered by Title VII, because it is not "specifically intimidating to men and their manhood" or premised on "general hostility to men."

In July 2001, a New Jersey state court allowed a transsexual doctor to sue the ex-employer who discharged her from the job once held (as a man) as a medical director, because the state antidiscrimination law deals with transsexualism as a disability. However, the court dismissed the doctor's claim of sexual-orientation discrimination, on the grounds that the plaintiff was not, and was not perceived as, homosexual or bisexual. [*Enriquez v. West Jersey Health Sys.*, 342 N.J. Super. 501 (2001), discussed in Mary P. Gallagher, *Transsexuals Held to be Protected Class Under New Jersey Law*, N.J.L.J. (July 11, 2001) (law.com)]

§ 35.07   WRONGFUL DISCHARGE CLAIMS

Employers often fear that they may be caught between two fires. If they do not respond to allegations, they face EEOC charges and/or lawsuits. But if they fire an alleged harasser, he or she may sue for wrongful termination. It is a delicate balance, but the employer can avoid liability by carrying out a thorough investigation in each case and taking proportionate steps against anyone found to have committed harassment. A complete "paper trail" is very important here (as in many other contexts).

A company with a no-tolerance policy fired an employee after investigation showed that he had sexually harassed another worker. The discharged employee went to arbitration. The arbitrator held that discharge was too severe a punishment. Reinstatement (although without back pay) was ordered. The practical effect was a nine-month unpaid suspension.

The employer sued the harasser's union under Labor-Management Relations Act § 301 claiming that reinstating the harasser would violate public policy. The Fourth Circuit disagreed, agreeing with the arbitrator that the loss of nine months' pay was adequate punishment. [*Westvaco Corp. v. United Paperworkers Int'l Union*, 171 F.3d 971 (4th Cir. 1999)]

In *Ribando v. United Airlines Inc.* [200 F.3d 507 (7th Cir. 1999)], a male worker accused a female co-worker of making harassing or derogatory remarks about him. The employer went through union-managed mediation, questioned several people, put a letter of concern in the female worker's file, but took no other action. The Seventh Circuit held that the woman could not maintain that the employer had engaged in severe or pervasive gender-based harassment against her: In fact, it had fulfilled its obligation to investigate the harassment charge.

Another implication of wrongful termination law is that in Maryland, an employee discharged for refusing to have sexual intercourse with a harasser can pursue a tort claim for abusive discharge in addition to the sexual harassment charges. The additional tort claim can be pursued because the state has a public policy against prostitution—and having sex to keep a job is, in effect, prostitution. [*Insignia Residential Corp. v. Ashton, Maryland*, 755 A.2d 1080 (Md. 2000)]

§ 35.08 DAMAGE ISSUES

The Seventh Circuit allows a sexual harassment plaintiff to get punitive damages in cases in which there were no compensatory damages. [*See Timm v. Progressive Steel Treating Inc.*, 137 F.3d 1008 (7th Cir. 1998)] This might occur, for instance, where a company fails to establish a complaint procedure and then blames the plaintiff for failure to go through channels. In this case, the plaintiff mitigated her damages so effectively that she got a higher-paying job, and therefore could not collect a back pay award.

Using the California state antidiscrimination law rather than federal law, the California Court of Appeals ruled that a law firm is directly, not just vicariously, liable for failing to protect a staff member against harassment by a partner. The ruling of *Weeks v. Baker & McKenzie* [74 Cal. Rptr. 2d 510 (Cal. App. 1998)] is that the firm employed the partner in conscious disregard of the safety and rights of vulnerable employees. Therefore, the firm's liability was not limited to the $225,000 punitive damage award against the harassing partner—$3.5 million in punitive damages could be awarded against the firm.

§ 35.09 LIABILITY OF INDIVIDUALS

Sexual harassment charges are not really very similar to charges of, say, environmental pollution, commercial fraud, or tax evasion. Although a corporation is only an artificial person, so individuals must commit its wrongful acts, in some cases individuals who commit a tort or a crime are doing so on behalf of the corporation. People who commit sexual harassment may be echoing a corporate culture that tolerates such things, but they are not benefiting the corporation!

Nevertheless, the language of Title VII, like most antidiscrimination statutes, refers only to "employers," and with few exceptions, courts have ruled that only the employer corporation, and not the individual, is liable for harassment. [No individual liability: *Carrisales v. Department of Corrections*, 90 Cal. Rptr. 2d 804 (Cal. 1999). *But see Speight v. Albano Cleaners*, 21 F. Supp. 2d 560 (E.D. Va. 1998), where the individual supervisor was held liable, but the corporation was not held liable]

Reno v. Baird [957 P.2d 1333 (Cal. 1998)] holds that an individual manager, although potentially liable for harassment, is not an "employer" under California's antidiscrimination statute. Although the state's Fair Employment and Housing Act defines "employer" to include "any person acting as an agent of an employer, directly or indirectly" the *Baird* court interpreted this language to make employers liable for the action of their agents, not to make agents personally liable.

§ 35.10   INTERACTION WITH OTHER STATUTES

It is a familiar theme throughout this book that legal concepts do not exist in isolation, and a single case may trigger many statutes and regulations.

In *Wilson v. Chrysler Corp.* [172 F.3d 500 (7th Cir. 1999)], the employer refused to reinstate a worker returning from medical leave. The employer's position was that she was totally disabled by paranoid schizophrenia, whereas the employee charged that the employer was retaliating against her for complaining about on-the-job sexual harassment. During the leave, the employee had applied for, and was granted, Social Security Disability Income (SSDI) benefits.

The Seventh Circuit ruled that applying for disability benefits rules out a sexual harassment claim. This is not necessarily true of an ADA claim: The Seventh Circuit view is that in ADA cases, a qualified disabled person may be able to work if reasonable accommodation is provided, but reasonable accommodation is not an issue in sexual harassment and other Title VII cases.

CHAPTER 36

AMERICANS WITH DISABILITIES ACT (ADA)

§ 36.01   INTRODUCTION

Since its passage in 1990, the Americans With Disabilities Act (ADA) has been contentious and controversial. In recent years, the Supreme Court and the lower courts have greatly limited the scope of this Act, especially in the employment arena.

The ADA starts at 42 U.S.C. § 12101 (regulations at 29 C.F.R. § 1630.1). Title I is the employment title; Title II deals with public services (i.e., provided by government agencies), Title III with public accommodations, and Title IV with miscellaneous issues, some of which relate to employment.

Although the ADA aims (among other things) at promoting employment of the disabled, the National Council on Disability (an independent federal agency) estimates that more than 70% of the 54 million people with disabilities are unemployed. Only about one-third of disabled adults under age 65 work full-time or even part-time (versus 81% of the non-disabled working-age population). Yet more than two-thirds of unemployed people with disabilities say they would prefer to work.

EEOC figures show that, since 1994, more than one-fifth of all the charges filed with the agency have been brought under the ADA. Half of those claims result in findings of "no reasonable cause." Between July 1992 and September 1999, 126,946 charges of all types were filed; 67,717 got no-cause findings. And, in 1999, the ABA reported that employers won 95.7% of the ADA Title I cases litigated in that year. [Susan J. Wells, *Is the ADA Working?* HR Magazine, April 2001, at p. 38]

For the fiscal year ending in September 2001, the EEOC received harassment (rather than discrimination) charges in 9353 sex cases, 6620 race cases, 2405 national origin cases, 2357 disability cases, 2127 age cases, and 688 religion cases. Employees with disabilities say that they often face harassment from supervisors and co-workers who accuse them of malingering or who try to force them to resign. [Reed Abelson, *Employers Increasingly Face Disability-Based Bias Cases*, New York Times, Nov. 20, 2001, at p. G1]

Earlier, the ABA found that the employer won 92% of 1200 reported and unreported cases that went to a final decision between 1992 and 1998. [*See* 67 L.W. 2005] But the vast majority of cases did not get litigated to a conclusion. According to the EEOC's own statistics, between FY 1992 and FY 1997 93,133 ADA charges were filed. About half the charges were deemed by the EEOC not to have reasonable cause, and about one-third (36.9%) were closed administratively. Conciliation succeeded in about one-third of the good-cause cases. About half of all charges alleged discriminatory firing, and 28.9% alleged failure to make reasonable accommodation; about one-eighth alleged harassment of disabled persons. [This information comes from *Employment Alert*, Sept. 3, 1998, at p. 4]

§ 36.02   REACH AND RANGE OF ADA TITLE I

According to 42 U.S.C. § 12101, Congress went on record that the over 43 million employees with disabilities (a number that is increasing as the population ages) have a history of social alienation and discrimination in important areas such as work, housing, public accommodations, health services, and education. Congress declared that people with disabilities are a minority group that has suffered discrimination—and that our national goal in dealing with people with disabilities should be "to assure equality of opportunity, full participation, independent living, and economic self-sufficiency." The legislative purpose is given as providing "clear, strong, consistent, enforceable standards addressing discrimination against individuals with disabilities."

A "covered entity," as defined by 42 U.S.C. § 12111(2), means an employer, an employment agency, a union, or a joint labor-management committee.

Only employers who have at least 15 employees in each working day in each of 20 or more weeks in the current or preceding year are subject to the ADA. [42 U.S.C. § 12111(5)]

Tip: In an ADA case (or an ADEA case), several closely related small affiliates of a larger corporation can have their workforces aggregated to determine if the 15-worker test has been met. Aggregation is proper if the corporate veil can be pierced (i.e., if practical realities justify disregarding the formal organization) and the parent company is liable for the debts, torts, and breaches of contract of its subsidiaries; if the business was divided up to avoid having to comply with employment laws; or if the parent company directed the discriminatory act or policy. [*Papa v. Katy Indus. Inc.*, 166 F.3d 937 (7th Cir. 1999)]

Individuals are nearly always exempt from being sued under antidiscrimination suits (only the employer company is liable). *Alberte v. Anew Health Care Services* [588 N.W.2d 298 (Wis. App. 1998)] permits an ADA suit against an individual who was president, administrator, and 47.5% shareholder in a company accused of disability discrimination. In this reading, the president was the company's agent and personally liable for both compensatory and punitive damages.

A U.S. citizen who works outside the United States can count as an employee entitled to protection under the ADA. [42 U.S.C. § 12111(4)] However, it is not unlawful for a workplace outside the United States to comply with local law, even if the result is discrimination. Foreign operations of a foreign company that is not controlled by an American employer are exempt from the ADA. [42 U.S.C. § 12112(c)]

Section 12115 requires employers to post notices of ADA rights "in an accessible format" in the workplace.

The ADA does not invalidate or limit the remedies, rights, and procedures of any state or federal law that provides additional protection of the rights of individuals with disabilities. [42 U.S.C. § 12201]

"Mixed-motive" cases (where disability discrimination is alleged to be only one factor in the employer's decision) can be brought; it is not necessary for the plaintiff to allege that the employer was solely motivated by disability discrimination. [*McNely v. Ocala Star-Banner Corp.*, 99 F.3d 1068 (11th Cir. 1996)] ADA suits can be brought for disability-based harassment and hostile work environment. [*Hendler v. Intelecom USA Inc.,* 963 F. Supp. 200 (E.D.N.Y. 1997); *Fox v. General Motors*, 94 F. Supp. 2d 723 (N.D. Wash. 2000)]

Although Congress specifically stated in 42 U.S.C. § 12202 that states are NOT immune from ADA suits, the Supreme Court held in 2001 that Congress had no right to abrogate the states' "sovereign immunity" (freedom from being sued) with respect to ADA Title I cases that seek money damages rather than injunctions, because there was no documentation of a past history of disability discrimination perpetrated by the states themselves. [*See Board of Trustees of the Univ. of Ala. v. Garrett*, 531 U.S. 356 (2001)] In 2002, the Supreme Court held that punitive damages are not available in a suit for discrimination against disability discrimination committed by a public body, or by an agency that receives federal funding. [*Barnes v. Gorman,* #01-682 (Sup. Ct. June 17, 2002] Although this is not directly relevant to private employment, it is another indication of the Supreme Court's attitude toward the ADA.

The Fifth Circuit later ruled that Congress did not properly abrogate the states' sovereign immunity with respect to ADA Title II either [*Reickenbacker v. Foster*, 274 F.3d 974 (5th Cir. 2001)], and the Second Circuit agrees. [*Garcia v. SUNY Health Sciences Ctr.*, 280 F.3d 98 (2d Cir. 2001)] *Gibson v. Arkansas Dep't of Corrections* [265 F.3d 718 (8th Cir. 2001)] says that although the states themselves are immune from suits for damages under the ADA, state officials can be sued to get prospective injunctive relief. It has also been held that states can be held liable for retaliation against employees who exercise ADA rights. [*Roberts v. Pennsylvania Dep't of Pub. Welfare*, Civ. No. 99-3836 (E.D. Pa. Feb. 20, 2002). *See* Shannon P. Duffy, *States Not Immune From ADA Retaliation Suits*, The Legal Intelligencer (Feb. 27, 2002) (law.com)]

The Eleventh Circuit allowed a former employee to sue under Title I to challenge the different caps in the employer's long-term disability plan for physical and mental disabilities—Title I suits are not restricted to current employees. [*Johnson v. KMart Corp.*, 281 F.3d 1368 (11th Cir. 2001)]

§ 36.03   FORBIDDEN DISCRIMINATION

It is unlawful to discriminate against a qualified individual with a disability (QIWD) because of that person's disability, with respect to the terms, conditions, and privileges of employment: e.g., job application, hiring, promotion, discharge, compensation, and training. [*See* 42 U.S.C. § 12112]

Section 12112 goes on to enumerate seven types of action that constitute disability discrimination:

- Limiting, segregating, or classifying applicants or employees in ways that affect their opportunities, because of disability;
- Entering into a relationship (for instance, with an employment agency) that results in disability discrimination;
- Using standards, criteria, or methods of administration that either discriminate or perpetuate discrimination by another party under the same administrative control (e.g., another division in the same company);
- Denying jobs or benefits to a qualified person who has a relationship or association with someone else who has a disability (e.g., refusing to hire someone merely because he or she is married to a person with a disability who has high medical bills that might result in higher EGHP premiums);
- Failing to make a reasonable accommodation to known physical or mental limitations of an employee or applicant who is a QIWD—unless the accommodation would work undue hardship on the employer; or denying employment opportunities to QIWDs if the denial is based on the need to accommodate;
- Using employment tests or other standards or criteria that screen out people with disabilities—but a defense is available for job-related measures that are consistent with business necessity;
- Using tests that are biased by an applicant's or employee's impairment (speech difficulties, for instance) and therefore fail to reflect the job aptitudes that the test is supposed to assess.

It is also unlawful to retaliate against anyone who opposed any act of disability discrimination, or who made a charge, testified, assisted, or participated in an investigation, administrative proceeding, or court case. It is unlawful to interfere with the ADA investigation process, or to "coerce, intimidate, threaten, or interfere with" anyone because of enforcement of ADA rights. [42 U.S.C. § 12203]

Although it is not an employment case (it deals with discrimination by a dentist against an HIV-positive patient), *Bragdon v. Abbott* [524 U.S. 624 (1998)] has some interesting things to say about the ADA. *Bragdon* sets up a three-step test for ADA cases:

- Does the plaintiff have an impairment?
- Is the major life activity that is impaired covered by the ADA?
- Does the plaintiff's impairment substantially limit that major life activity?

A plaintiff who can show directly that the employer refused to train her to use a specific piece of machinery (in this case, a high-speed scanner) because of her disability (she had only one hand) can pursue a disparate treatment ADA claim without having to prove that the refusal was an adverse job action. Unlike other antidiscrimination statutes, the ADA specifically refers to denial of training. In the case of *Hoffman v. Caterpillar Inc.* [256 F.3d 568 (7th Cir. 2001)], the plaintiff said that knowing how to use the high-speed scanner was essential to eligibility for promotion. However, the Seventh Circuit ruled that, to get damages, she would have to prove that she was physically capable of running the scanner. Because using the scanner was not an essential function of her job, the employer did not have a duty to reasonably accommodate her in this regard.

§ 36.04   DEFINING "DISABILITY"

[A]   Generally

According to 42 U.S.C. § 12102, there are three forms of disability:

- A physical or mental impairment that substantially limits one or more of the major life activities of such individual;
- A record of such an impairment;
- Being regarded as having such an impairment (even if the impairment is only perceived and does not exist).

According to the statute, transvestism is not a disability [42 U.S.C. § 12209], nor are homosexuality, bisexuality, transsexualism, pedophilia, exhibitionism, gender identity disorders, compulsive gambling, kleptomania, pyromania, or current use of illegal drugs. [42 U.S.C. § 12211]

However, state laws may impose different requirements. For instance, a 2001 New Jersey case says that transsexuals are protected against gender and disability discrimination under the state Law Against Discrimination. The plaintiff's sexual orientation discrimination claim was dismissed on the grounds that the male-to-female transsexual plaintiff neither was nor was perceived to be homosexual or bisexual. [*Enriquez v. West Jersey Health Sys.*, 342 N.J. Super. 501 (2001), discussed in Mary P. Gallagher, *Transsexuals Held to Be Protected Class Under New Jersey Law*, N.J. Law (July 11, 2001) (law.com)]

A QIWD is defined by 42 U.S.C. § 12111(8) as one who can perform the essential functions of the job (with or without accommodation). The employer's determination about which functions of a job are essential is entitled to consideration. Written job descriptions used in advertising or job interviews are considered evidence of the essential functions of the job. In other words, these descriptions must be drafted with care!

The EEOC's position is that determining which functions are essential to a job is a complex process involving several factors, e.g.:

- Expertise or skill needed to do that task;
- Other employees available to perform that function (as individuals or as a team);
- If that function is the entire rationale of the job;
- Time spent on that particular function;

- Qualifications of people who held the same job in the past;
- What would happen if the individual did not perform the function in question;
- What the Collective Bargaining Agreement (if there is one) says about the function as it relates to the job.

[B] Attendance

The question is often raised whether predictable, regular attendance is a fundamental job qualification. If it is, then it does not violate the ADA to fire, refuse to hire, etc., a person who cannot satisfy attendance requirements because of disability. [*See. e.g., EEOC v. Yellow Freight Sys., Inc.*, 253 F.3d 943 (7th Cir. 2001) (granting an unlimited number of sick days is not a reasonable accommodation); *Carlson v. Inacom Corp.*, 885 F. Supp. 1314 (E.D. Mich. 1996); *Fritz v. Mascotech Automotive Sys. Group. Inc.*, 914 F. Supp. 1481 (E.D. Mich. 1996); *Vorhies v. Pioneer Mfg.*, 906 F. Supp. 578 (D. Colo. 1995)] *Cehrs v. Northeast Ohio Alzheimer's Research Center* [155 F.3d 775 (6th Cir. 1998)] does not permit employers to rely on a presumption that regular attendance is an essential job function: They must provide evidence about the need for predictability in that particular job as distinct from employment in general.

A person whose physical or mental condition precludes working more than 40 hours a week has been held not to be ADA disabled [*Tardie v. Rehabilitation Hosp. of R.I.*, 168 F.3d 538 (1st Cir. 1999)], given that there are many jobs available that do not require a commitment of over 40 hours a week. *Also see Davis v. Florida Power & Light* [205 F.3d 1301 (11th Cir. 2000)], finding that mandatory overtime was an essential function of the job, and it would violate the collective bargaining agreement to provide a no-overtime or selective-overtime arrangement for a disabled worker.

However, in *Alifano v. Merck & Co. Inc.* [175 F. Supp. 2d 792 (E.D. Pa. 2001)], the Eastern District of Pennsylvania held that fibromyalgia/chronic fatigue syndrome could result in substantial impairment of major life activities, including working, even though the plaintiff claimed only that she could not travel on business or work more than an eight-hour day. [Shannon P. Duffy, *Federal Judge Rejects Worker's Claim "Interference" With FMLA Rights*, The Legal Intelligencer (Dec. 17, 2001) (law.com)]

In June 1999, the Supreme Court decided three major employment-related cases, concluding that an individual is not disabled if the condition has been corrected, e.g., through medication or an assistive device. [*Murphy v. United Parcel Serv.*, 527 U.S. 516 (1999); *Sutton v United Air Lines*, 527 U.S. 471 (1999); *Albertsons v. Kirkingburg*, 527 U.S. 555 (1999). *See* 65 Fed. Reg. 36327 (June 8, 2000) for the EEOC's Final Rule drafted to conform to these rulings]

On January 8, 2002, the Supreme Court rendered a unanimous decision in *Toyota Motor Manufacturing, Kentucky, Inc. v. Williams* [534 U.S. 184 (2002)] that a woman with carpal tunnel syndrome was not disabled for ADA purposes because she was able to care for herself and perform ordinary daily tasks. In this view, merely having an impairment does not make a person disabled, nor does being unable to perform the tasks associated with his or her specific job, as long as other tasks can be managed. But the *Williams* case doesn't necessarily mean that employers are out of the woods on carpal tunnel syndrome cases. A post-*Williams* case from the Northern District of Illinois refuses to dismiss an ADA complaint that alleged only carpal tunnel syndrome, without facts indicating substantial limitation in daily activities, on the grounds that the employee might be able to produce proof at trial on the impact of the condition on daily life. [*Carroll v. Chicago Transit Auth.,* 70 L.W. 1560 (N.D. Ill. Feb. 8, 2002)]

A late 2001 decision by the Tenth Circuit says that a truck driver who took medication to control seizures was not a QIWD even though his doctor certified him as fit to drive, because the need for medication made him unable to meet job-related Department of Transportation standards. [*Tate v. Farmland Indus. Inc.,* 268 F.3d 989 (10th Cir. 2001)]

The Seventh Circuit held that "liver function" is not a major life activity under the ADA, so firing someone for having cirrhosis does not violate the ADA, a statute that focuses on the activities that are limited by an impairment, not on the characterization of the impairment. [*Furnish v. SVI Sys. Inc.,* 270 F.3d 445 (7th Cir. 2001)]

Although the trend in most recent cases is to find that the plaintiff was not disabled for ADA purposes, the Second Circuit ruled early in 2002 that the ability to interact harmoniously with others is a major life activity. Therefore, a person whose problems with other employees could be traced to bipolar syndrome could be ADA-disabled or considered disabled by her employer. [*Jacques v. DiMarzio Inc.,* No. 97-CV-2884 (2d Cir. 2002). *See* Mark Hamblett, *Plaintiff With Bipolar Disorder Protected Under ADA,* N.Y.L.J. (March 4, 2002) (law.com)] The fact that the company told the plaintiff to see a psychiatrist, and a letter to the NLRB saying "we had to deal with her as if she was emotionally disturbed" because of her tendency to "blow up on us" furnished evidence that the employer regarded the plaintiff as disabled.

The court also raised the question of whether the $500,000 counterclaim that the employer filed against the plaintiff, charging her with harassment, interference with business operations, and damage to morale and business reputation, should be subjected to sanctions as retaliation against the ex-employee for exercising her legal rights. Early in 2002, the Eighth Circuit took the view that an engineer who suffered brain damage was disabled for ADA purposes. He had long-term impairments that prevented him from working full-time, and his condition affected more than a single aspect of a single job; he was severely restricted in the kinds of work he could do. [*Moysis v. DTG Datanet,* 70 L.W. 1528 (8th Cir. Jan. 29, 2002)]

[C] Infertility

An EEOC Administrative Decision says that denying a female employee coverage for infertility treatments and related medical expenses violates Title VII and the ADA, because the plan covered medically necessary treatments of other ailments that had a comparable effect on body function. [*See* 64 Fed. Reg. 22769 (April 27, 1999)]

A 1996 case says that reproduction is not a major life activity, but in 1997, the Northern District of Illinois disagreed, even though reproduction does not directly affect employment. [*Compare Krauel v. Iowa Methodist Med. Ctr.*, 95 F.3d 674 (8th Cir. 1996), *with Erickson v. Board of Governors, Northeastern Ill. Univ.*, 911 F. Supp. 316 (N.D. Ill. 1997, *later proceedings*, 207 F.3d 945 (7th Cir. 2000)]

The plaintiff in *Saks v. Franklin Covey Co.* [117 F. Supp. 2d 318 (S.D.N.Y. 2000)] was covered by a self-insured health plan that excluded "surgical impregnation procedures." She sued under Title VII, the ADA, and the Pregnancy Discrimination Act. The court ruled that infertility might be a disability, because it interferes with the major life activity of procreation.

However, the ADA claim was dismissed because all employees got the same coverage; infertile employees were not singled out for inferior coverage of reproductive services. The plan also qualified for the safe harbor for bona fide employee benefit plans. The Title VII claim failed because both male and female infertility were excluded. Surgical procedures were excluded for both female employees and wives of male employees. The PDA claim failed because infertility treatments were equally unavailable to pregnant and nonpregnant employees and beneficiaries.

According to the Northern District of Illinois, it did not violate the ADA to refuse to pay for infertility treatment for an employee's spouse, because the law does not extend to dependents of an employee if the dependents do not perform services for the employer. [*Niemeier v. Tri-State Fire Protection Dist.*, 2000 U.S. Dist. LEXIS 12621 (N.D. Ill. Aug. 24, 2000). Furthermore, non-employees can't sue the employer under Title VII or the PDA. The employee had standing (the legal right to pursue the PDA claim), but the claim itself was invalid, because the plan did not cover fertility treatment for either sex.

[D] Psychiatric Disability

For the period between July 1992 and September 1996, about one-eighth of the ADA charges filed related to psychiatric disability, so this is a significant area in which guidance is needed.

ADA regulations [29 C.F.R. § 1630.2(h)(2)] define mental impairment to include developmental disability, learning disabilities, organic brain syndrome, and neurological disease, as well as mental or psychological disorders. The examples given by the EEOC are major depression, bipolar disorder, panic disorder, obsessive-compulsive disorder, post-traumatic stress disorder, schizophrenia, and personality disorders.

The psychiatric profession's official compendium, the Diagnostic and Statistical Manual of Mental Disorders (DSM), is the first step in identifying mental disorders. However, certain disorders are included in the DSM but excluded from

ADA coverage—for instance, current drug and alcohol abuse, compulsive gambling, certain sexual disorders, and kleptomania.

Furthermore, persons who are troubled but not classically mentally ill may seek treatment such as family therapy. Such individuals are not impaired for ADA purposes. A mental illness impairment may be present yet not covered by the ADA, if it is mild enough not to substantially limit the impaired person's ability to work and carry out other major life activities.

The EEOC Guidance on mental disability deals with impairment of the major life activity of interacting with others. The test is whether, compared to an average person in the general population, the employee is significantly restricted in human interactions because of severe problems such as "consistently high levels of hostility, social withdrawal, or failure to communicate where necessary," with a long-term or potential long-term duration. Similar considerations are used to assess alleged limitations in the ability to concentrate, or the ability to get adequate sleep or care for one's self.

The EEOC Guidance on mental disability [EEOC Guidance No. 915.002 (March 25, 1997)] says that an individual poses a direct risk if an individualized assessment is made based on reasonable medical judgment, the most current medical knowledge, and/or the best objective evidence available. More specifically, the fact that a person has a history of psychiatric disability, or is currently under psychiatric treatment, is not enough to render that person a direct risk.

Does providing a lower level of disability benefits for mental illnesses than for physical ailments violate the ADA? *Kimber v. Thiokol Corp.* [196 F.3d 1092 (10th Cir. 1999)] says no. *Rogers v. Department of Health and Environmental Control* [174 F.3d 431 (4th Cir. 1999)] says that neither the ADA nor Title VII requires plans for state employees to furnish the same benefit levels for physical and mental ailments. *Morrill v. Lorillard Tobacco Co.* [2000 U.S. Dist. LEXIS 18810 (D.N.H. Dec. 7, 2000)] finds that ADA Title I was not violated by imposing a 50% copayment and 20-visit limit on mental health benefits, versus a 15–20% copayment for an unlimited number of visits for other claims.

Although ADA Title IV [42 U.S.C. § 12201(c) *et seq.*] provides a safe harbor for insurers and employee benefit plans that underwrite, classify, and administer risk in a way that is not a subterfuge to avoid the ADA, *Lewis v. Aetna Life Ins. Co.* [7 F. Supp. 2d 743 (E.D. Va. 1998)] says that the plan's distinction between physical and mental disabilities violated the ADA because the insurer was unable to furnish actuarial support for the distinction.

§ 36.05 REASONABLE ACCOMMODATION

[A] Employer's Obligation

Employers have an obligation to engage in an interactive process of reasonable accommodation, to permit employment or continued employment of qualified individuals with disabilities. However, it is not required that employers undergo undue hardship in making such accommodations.

Section 12111(9) says that the category of reasonable accommodation may include making existing facilities readily accessible and usable by QIWDs. It can also include job restructuring, part-time or other altered work schedules, reassignment to a *vacant* position (in April 2002, the Supreme Court ruled that it is not in general "reasonable" to reassign an employee if the reassignment violated an established seniority system—but the employee can demonstrate that an exception should be made in his or her individual case: *U.S. Airways v. Barnett,* 70 LW 4285 (Sup. Ct. April 29, 2002)). Other possible reasonable accommodations include acquiring or modifying equipment, providing training, making readers or interpreters available, etc.

According to the First Circuit, ability to lift more than 50 pounds is an essential function of nursing. Therefore, the employer does not have to accommodate a nurse with a back injury, either by assigning other employees to help her lift, or by reinstating the position of "medicine nurse" (which did not involve lifting) after the position had been abolished. [*Phelps v. Optima Health Inc.*, 251 F.3d 21 (1st Cir. 2001)]

"Auxiliary aids and services" is defined by § 12102 to mean interpreters or other effective methods of communicating with hearing-impaired people, readers, taped texts, and other ways to deliver texts to the visually impaired, acquiring or modifying adaptive equipment or devices, or "other similar services and actions."

An undue hardship is an action that requires significant difficulty or expense. [42 U.S.C. § 12111(10)] This determination is made based on factors such as the cost of the accommodation and how it compares to the employer's budget.

The employer must retain records about requests for accommodation for one year after the request or personnel action, whichever is later. [29 C.F.R. § 1602.14]

The Ticket To Work and Work Incentives Improvement Act of 1999 [Pub. L. No. 106-170] allows disabled persons to retain Medicare and/or Medicaid coverage for their health needs after they return to the workforce. It has been proposed that the federal government budget up to $2 billion over a five-year period for research on development of assistive technologies.

[B] EEOC Enforcement Guidance

On March 2, 1999, the EEOC released a major enforcement guidance. [*Enforcement Guidance: Reasonable Accommodation and Undue Hardship Under the Americans With Disabilities Act*, <http://www.eeoc.gov/docs/accommodation.html>] Compliance with these guidelines will assure that the corporation will not become the target of EEOC enforcement activities—although it is quite likely that courts will not require employers to satisfy all of the EEOC's concerns.

Under the Guidelines, employers need not eliminate essential job functions. Employers do not have to provide items used for both work and nonwork tasks; employees are responsible for furnishing their own prostheses, eyeglasses, and hearing aids.

Employees who want accommodation must make a clear request but need not use the term "reasonable accommodation," as long as it is clear what they mean. Employers must act on reasonable verbal requests but can ask to have them confirmed by a written memorandum.

The employer can demand reasonable documentation of, for instance, the nature, severity, and duration of the impairment, which activities are impaired, and the extent to which the employee's functional ability is limited. But documentation cannot be required if the disability and accommodation are obvious, or if the employee has already furnished adequate information. The employer can choose its preferred (usually the most cost-effective) reasonable accommodation, and need not follow the employee's suggestion.

Using accrued paid leave, or unpaid leave, is a reasonable accommodation, but employers do not have to offer additional paid leave to employees with a disability. Employees should be allowed to exhaust paid leave before taking unpaid leave. Unless it is an undue hardship, the employer must keep the job open during leave. A leave request need not be granted if the employer can keep the employee at work via a reasonable alternative accommodation.

The EEOC position is that employers should consider ADA and FMLA entitlement separately and then determine whether the two statutes overlap. The EEOC's example is an ADA-disabled person who needs 13 weeks of leave. The FMLA requires only 12 weeks of leave, but the EEOC says the ADA requires the employer to provide the 13th week unless that would be an undue hardship.

If there is a vacant position available for transfer, the employer does not have to train the person with a disability as an accommodation, unless training would be offered to a nondisabled employee. The EEOC position is that a transfer is a reasonable accommodation, so it must be offered even if the employer does not normally provide transfers. It is not enough to allow the disabled employee to compete for a vacant position; it should be offered to any QIWD who wants the transfer as an accommodation.

Even the EEOC sometimes concedes that affirmative action is inappropriate. A January 31, 2000, Opinion Letter says that if there is only one vacant position, it should be used to provide reasonable accommodation to a disabled current employee rather than hiring a black female applicant or promoting a black female employee to take the position—in fact, reasonable accommodation might justify assigning an employee with a disability rather than a more qualified candidate. [*EEOC Says Accommodation Takes Priority Over Affirmative Action*, <http://www.lawnewsnetwork.com]

[C]   Case Law

Some courts say that the employee must take the first step by requesting accommodation. [*Gaston v. Bellingrath Gardens & Home Inc.*, 167 F.3d 1361 (11th Cir. 1999); *Mole v. Buckhorn Rubber Prods. Inc.*, 165 F.3d 1212 (8th Cir. 1999)]

Taylor v. Phoenixville School District [174 F.3d 142 (3rd Cir. 1999)] adopts the EEOC position that, as soon as an employee asks for reasonable accommodation, the employer has a duty to engage in an interactive process with the employee and must cooperate with the employee to find out if the employee really is ADA-disabled, finding out what accommodations the employee wants, and determining if they are practical.

The employer can decide which reasonable accommodation to offer; it is not obligated to accept the employee's suggestions. [*Keever v. City of Middletown*, 145 F.3d 809 (6th Cir. 1998); *Rehling v. City of Chicago*, 207 F.3d 1009 (7th Cir. 2000)] Finding a job free of stress caused by fellow-employees is not a reasonable accommodation to which a clinically depressed employee is entitled. [*Gaul v. Lucent Techs., Inc.*, 134 F.3d 576 (3rd Cir. 1998)]

The Third Circuit obligates the employer to think creatively to create accommodation. In *Skerski v. Time Warner Cable Co.* [257 F.3d 273 (3d Cir. 2001) discussed in Shannon P. Duffy, *Employers Must be Creative on ADA Accommodations, Says 3rd Circuit*, The Legal Intelligencer (July 10, 2001) (law.com)], the plaintiff was a cable installer who couldn't climb as a result of panic attacks. The employee wanted the employer to provide him with a bucket truck, which he could use to perform his job even if he did have an attack. The employer had a bucket truck available, but demoted him to a lower-paying job. The Western District of Pennsylvania dismissed the case, calling climbing an essential function of the installer's job. The Third Circuit reversed and remanded the case to see if climbing really was essential; inconvenience to the employer is not undue hardship. Courts usually do not require as much of employers as the EEOC Regulations; this is an unusual case in which the court ordered even more than the EEOC would have demanded.

According to *Donahue v. Consolidated Rail Corp.* [224 F.3d 226 (3d Cir. 2000), discussed in Shannon P. Duffy, *When No Jobs Available, Employer's Duty Eliminated*, The Legal Intelligencer (Aug. 22, 2000) (law.com)], the employer need not engage in the interactive process if the employee failed to show that there were any available jobs he or she could have done with reasonable accommodation.

Furthermore, a person who claims that his or her injury prevents full-time work, and therefore is allowed to work a part-time schedule, is estopped from claiming that the employer refused accommodation, because the person is unable to work full-time even with accommodation. [*DeVito v. Chicago Park Dist.*, 270 F.3d 532 (7th Cir. 2001)]

The EEOC position [29 C.F.R. § 1630.2(o)], echoed by several appellate cases, is that reassignment to a job that the employee can handle constitutes a reasonable accommodation. [*Dalton v. Subaru-Isuzu Automotive, Inc.*, 141 F.3d 667 (7th Cir. 1998); *Cravens v. Blue Cross/Blue Shield*, 214 F.3d 1011 (8th Cir. 2000); *Aka v. Washington Hosp. Ctr.*, 156 F.3d 1284 (D.C. Cir. 1998)] The disabled person in search of accommodation must be able to prove his or her ability to handle the new job. [*DePaoli v. Abbott Labs.*, 140 F.3d 668 (7th Cir. 1998)] The Second

Circuit said that as long as a comparable job is available, it is not a reasonable accommodation to offer an ADA plaintiff reassignment to a part-time job (with much lower compensation and benefits) or to another location (resulting in loss of seniority). [*Norville v. Staten Island Univ. Hosp.*, 196 F.3d 89 (2d Cir. 1999)]

Yet other courts say that if the employee is not able to perform the tasks of the current job, he or she is not qualified, and therefore the employer is not obligated to offer another job assignment. [*Smith v. Midland Brake Inc.*, 138 F.3d 1304 (10th Cir. 1998); *Malabarba v. Chicago Tribune Co.*, 149 F.3d 690 (7th Cir. 1998)]

Employers can legitimately stipulate that light-duty assignments are temporary. However, if no end date is given for the assignment, a court might treat the light-duty job as a permanent accommodation that cannot be withdrawn without violating the ADA. [*Hendricks-Robinson v. Excel Corp.*, 154 F.3d 685 (7th Cir. 1998)]

The Tenth Circuit says that the employer has the burden of persuasion as to whether a proposed accommodation would be an undue hardship, but other courts have disagreed. [*Colorado Cross Disability Coalition v. Hermanson Family Ltd. Partnership*, 264 F.3d 999 (10th Cir. 2001)]

The employee as well as the employer must participate in the process. A $1.5 million verdict for the plaintiff was vacated because the plaintiff rejected the proposed accommodation without discussion or counter-offer, and applied for long-term disability instead. [*Davis v. Guardian Life Ins. Co. of Am.*, discussed in Shannon P. Duffy, *Judge Vacates $1.5 Million Verdict in ADA Case*, The Legal Intelligencer (Dec. 20, 2000) (law.com)]

§ 36.06   DEFENSES

[A]   Primary Defense

The primary defense, under 42 U.S.C. § 12113, is that the employer's criterion, standards, or tests may screen out individuals with a disability, but are nevertheless appropriate because they are job-related and consistent with business necessity, and the employer cannot achieve the same goals via reasonable accommodation. Qualification standards can lawfully rule out employment of anyone who poses a direct threat to the health or safety of others. According to 42 U.S.C. § 12111(3), a "direct threat" is a significant risk to the health or safety of others that cannot be eliminated by reasonable accommodation.

Furthermore, the Secretary of Health and Human Services publishes a list of infectious and communicable diseases that can be transmitted by food handling. If the risk cannot be eliminated by reasonable accommodation, then an employer can legitimately refuse to assign or continue to assign someone who suffers from such a disease to a food handling position. This provision does not preempt state public health laws about food safety. The Supreme court greatly increased the applicability of this exception in a June 2002 decision [*Chevron USA Inc. v. Echazabal*, #00-1406 (Sup. Ct. June 10, 2002)] by allowing employers to use it in the context of danger to a job applicant or employee whose own physical condition would be endangered by workplace conditions.

The Eleventh Circuit held in late 2001 that an HIV positive dental technician poses a direct threat to others and therefore is not a QIWD. [*Waddell v. Valley Forge Dental Assoc.*, 276 F.3d 1275 (11th Cir. 2001)]

A Wyoming state case says that it was not a violation of the ADA for the state medical board to revoke the license of a doctor suffering from bipolar disorder, even without granting him the treatment options offered to substance-abusing doctors. He was not a "qualified individual" because of the severe health and safety risk he posed to others. He had performed unnecessary and inappropriate surgery, and at least one patient had died. [*Kirbens v. Wyoming State Bd. of Medicine*, 992 P.2d 1056 (Wyo. 1999)]

[B] Drug and Alcohol Exception

Congress must have been concerned about the potential for claims of disability on the basis of substance abuse, because there are several statutory references. According to 42 U.S.C. § 12111(6), a "drug" is a controlled substance as defined by federal law, and "illegal use of drugs" means using controlled substances, but does not include drugs taken under the supervision of a licensed health professional.

Section 12114 says that an employee or job applicant who is currently engaging in the illegal use of drugs is not a qualified individual with a disability. However, a person who is in rehab, has completed a rehab program, or otherwise stopped using drugs can be considered a qualified individual with a disability. So can a person who is not in fact using illegal drugs, but who is incorrectly perceived to be.

Employers are allowed to forbid the use of alcohol or illegal drugs at the workplace, can enforce the requirements of the Drug-Free Workplace Act, can make a rule that employees not be under the influence of alcohol or drugs when they are at work (even if they used the substances outside the workplace), and can adopt reasonable procedures (including drug testing) to make sure employees are not currently abusing substances. Drug testing is not considered a "medical examination" for ADA purposes. Many of these provisions are repeated in 42 U.S.C. § 12210.

According to the Fifth Circuit, a hospital did not violate the ADA by firing a hospital pharmacist who voluntarily reported his cocaine addiction and entered a rehab program. [*Zenor v. El Paso Healthcare Sys. Ltd.*, 176 F.3d 847 (5th Cir. 1999)] He was considered to be a "current user" because of the risk of relapse, so the "rehab program" safe harbor did not apply in his case. Furthermore, his job gave him access to pharmaceutical cocaine, greatly increasing the risk of future drug abuse. Although he might have been qualified for many other jobs, the contact with controlled substances meant that, as a substance abuser, he was not a QIWD for the specific job of hospital pharmacist.

Some cases take the view that, once an employee goes through rehab, it constitutes discrimination against the disability of alcoholism to fire or otherwise discipline the employee for absenteeism before he or she entered treatment. [*See, e.g., McEniry v. Landi*, 84 N.Y.2d 554 (1994)] But even this case points out that employees who do not complete rehab successfully, or who are likely to relapse, are not protected against the consequences of a lapse. *Myszcenko v. City of Poughkeepsie* [239 A.D.2d 584 (N.Y. App. Div. 1997)] says that an employee can lawfully be fired for misconduct that occurred after a post-rehab relapse. *Brennan v. N.Y.C. Police Dep't* [1997 U.S. Dist. LEXIS 23193 (S.D.N.Y. May 27, 1997)] is similar, Several courts have concluded that employers can apply the same standards of conduct to all employees—whether or not they have a substance abuse problem. [*Mercado v. N.Y.C. Hous. Auth.*, 1998 WL 151039 (S.D.N.Y. March 31, 1998); *Williams v. Widnall*, 79 F.3d 1003 (10th Cir. 1996); *Rollison v. Gwinnett County*, 865 F. Supp. 1564 (N.D. Ga. 1994)]

A "last chance" agreement, where reinstatement after rehab is conditional on continued good performance (and perhaps on passing periodic drug tests) has been upheld as a reasonable accommodation to the disability of alcoholism. [*See, e.g., Marrari v. WCI Steel Inc.*, 130 F.3d 1180 (6th Cir. 1997)]

Tip: A typical agreement of this type is signed by an employee who has completed a rehab program. The employee agrees to get clearance from the Employee Assistance Program before returning to work. The employee agrees to stay clean and sober and abide by the program requirements of Alcoholics Anonymous, Narcotics Anonymous, or other program. In a drug rehab situation, the employee agrees to periodic unannounced drug tests for a period of a year and agrees to automatic termination for failing a test—or refusing to take a test. The employee agrees that this is a last chance, and that he or she must comply with all of the employer's normal disciplinary rules (e.g., attendance and promptness) despite the substance problem.

The Fifth Circuit allowed Exxon to defend its policy of permanently refusing employees who have been treated for substance abuse from safety-sensitive positions with little supervision. [*EEOC v. Exxon*, 203 F.3d 871 (5th Cir. 2000)] As long as the standard is applied equally to all employees within a class, the employer can assert business necessity without proving that former substance abusers constitute a direct threat to safety.

Tip: A substance abuser entering a rehab program (at least if it is an inpatient program) may be entitled to FMLA leave. Reasonable ADA accommodation may require providing additional leave after the 12 weeks of FMLA leave have been used up.

---

§ 36.07   "REGARDED AS" LIABILITY

The ADA covers qualified individuals who actually do not have a disability, but who are discriminated against because of the perception that they do. According to *EEOC v. R.J. Gallagher Co.* [181 F.3d 645 (5th Cir. 1999)], the relevant evidence is what the employer believed—not medical testimony about the true state of the employee's health and abilities.

An employer can be liable on a "regarded as disabled" claim based on an innocent misunderstanding (or stereotypes) about the employee's capacity. But if the employee is responsible for the error, or unreasonably fails to correct the employer's misconceptions, then the employer cannot be held liable. [*Taylor v. Pathmark*, 177 F.3d 180 (3d Cir. 1999)]

In *Hilburn v. Murata Electronics* [181 F.3d 1220 (11th Cir. 1999)], the employee had two problems: her own heart disease, and the serious illness of family members, requiring substantial time off. After she had a heart attack, she had some limitations in lifting, but could walk, run, and carry out all other normal activities. Her "regarded-as" claim failed, because the Eleventh Circuit ruled that the major life activity of working was substantially unimpaired.

The "regarded-as" claim was also unsuccessful in *Shipley v. City of University City* [195 F.3d 1020 (8th Cir. 1999)], because the refusal to reinstate him after an injury-related absence was caused by the employer's belief that he could no longer perform that particular job, not that he was incapable of working at all.

The duty of reasonable accommodation applies only to actual, not perceived, disability. [*Weber v. Strippit, Inc.*, 186 F.3d 907 (8th Cir. 1999)]

§ 36.08   DISABILITY AND THE BENEFIT PLAN

[A]   Employer's Obligations and Challenges

Under the ADA, employers are permitted to make benefit plan decisions that are consistent with underwriting, reasonable risk classifications, or actual or reasonably anticipated experience. If the employer does not normally provide health benefits, it has no obligation to provide special insurance coverage for the disabled or to adopt a plan that covers both disabled and nondisabled employees.

EEOC Interpretive Guidelines No. 1630.2(m) say that employers are not permitted to fire or refuse to hire a QIWD because of the benefit plan's exclusions or limitations. Nor may adverse employment decisions be based on anticipated cost increases in the benefit plan because of the health care needs of an applicant, an employee, or their dependents.

In several cases, employees have been unsuccessful in using ERISA to challenge a "cap" (maximum amount that will be paid, e.g., $100,000 or $1 million) imposed on health benefits payable for treatment of AIDS-related illnesses. Courts have found that there was no ERISA violation in imposing a cap only on HIV-related health care, or on capping HIV-related treatment at a lower level than treatment of other expensive illnesses. [*McGann v. H&H Music Co.*, 946 F.2d 401 (5th Cir. 1991); *Owens v. Storehouse Inc.*, 948 F.2d 394 (11th Cir. 1993)]

The Western District of Michigan dismissed an ADA case brought by a plan participant who had hearing and mobility limitations and who asserted that the plan's lifetime plan cap for employees with hearing problems was discriminatory because benefits for other disabilities were not capped. But, to the court, the ADA only mandates equality between the disabled and the nondisabled, not among all forms of disability. If all employees have access to the plan, it is permissible to provide lower benefits for a specific type of disability. [*Schultz v. Alticor/Amway Corp.*, 177 F. Supp. 2d 674 (W.D. Mich. 2001)]

The Supreme Court's denial of rehearing had the effect of affirming the Seventh Circuit (although without opinion) in *Doe v. Mutual of Omaha* [528 U.S. 1106 (2000)]: Title II of the ADA (the title dealing with public programs) is not violated by a health insurance policy or self-funded health plan that puts a much lower limitation on AIDS-related health care than other illnesses. The Seventh Circuit's rationale is that the insurer did not refuse to sell insurance to persons with AIDS, although the policy was less valuable to them than to people with other health problems.

Three Circuit Courts (the Sixth, Seventh, and Eleventh) have ruled that a totally disabled retiree or ex-employee is not "qualified" (because he or she is unable to perform job functions) and therefore cannot sue for fringe-benefit discrimination. [*Morgan v. Joint Admin. Bd. Retirement Plan*, 268 F.3d 456 (7th Cir. 2001); *EEOC v. CAN Ins. Cos.*, 96 F.3d 1038 (7th Cir. 1997); *Parker v. Metropolitan Life Ins. Co.*, 99 F.3d 181, *aff'd*, 121 F.3d 1006 (6th Cir. 1997); *Gonzalez v. Garner Food Servs., Inc.*, 89 F.3d 1523 (11th Cir. 1996)]

Those cases were brought under Title I, the employment discrimination part of the statute. Employers may also be sued under Title III, the public accommodations title. If an employee benefits plan is considered a public accommodation (this is not settled law), then excluding a disabled person from it could violate the ADA, even if the person with a disability is no longer a qualified employee. Most courts limit "place of public accommodations" to a physical place like an office or shopping mall—e.g., *Ford v. Schering-Plough Corp.* [145 F.3d 601 (3d Cir. 1998)]

[B] EEOC Compliance Manual

In 2000, the EEOC redrafted its Compliance Manual Section 3, which can be found at <http://www.eeoc.gov/docs/benefits.html>. (However, the viability of the EEOC's position may be questionable in light of later Supreme Court decisions.) The employer must provide "equal" benefits for all employees, irrespective of disability. However, benefits can be "equal" even if there are certain distinctions drawn on the basis of disability. The employer is entitled to employ practices that reflect sound actuarial principles or are related to actual or reasonably anticipated experience.

The first question is whether benefits for the employee who has a disability are the same (same types of benefits, same payment options, same coverage for the same costs). If the benefits are unequal, the question is whether the difference is based on the disability. If benefits are unequal because of disability, the employer has violated the ADA unless it can show that the difference is not a subterfuge to avoid the purposes of the ADA. (A practice can be a subterfuge even if it was adopted before the ADA became effective—and even if the employer does not have intent to discriminate.)

The "same coverage" for all employees means the same as to premiums, deductibles, waiting periods, and coverage caps. A distinction is based on disability if it singles out a particular disability, a discrete group of disabilities, or disability in general. Therefore, a distinction is not disability-based if it applies to many dissimilar conditions, and imposes limitations on individuals with and without disabilities.

The employer can rebut charges of disability discrimination by proving that disparate treatment is necessary to maintain the solvency of the plan, because covering the disabilities at issue would cost enough to threaten the fiscal soundness of the plan, and there is no way to change the plan without affecting disabilities.

The EEOC position is that, because employers are not required to maintain plans at all, the ADA is not violated by offering service retirement benefits (based on length of service for the employer) but not disability retirement benefits. But if the employer offers both types of retirement plan, disability discrimination is forbidden.

In the EEOC view, it violates the ADA to:

- Exclude an employee from participation in a service or disability retirement plan because of disabilities;
- Have a different length of participation requirement in the same plan because of disability;
- Provide different levels of types of coverage within a plan (although coverage levels can be lower in disability than in service retirement plans).

Service retirement benefits can legitimately be denied to any employee who voluntarily took disability retirement.

§ 36.09   QUESTIONS AND MEDICAL TESTS

The general ADA rule is that employers are not permitted to ask job applicants or do medical exams to find out if the applicant has a disability or to discover the nature and severity of the disability. However, it is permissible to tell the applicant what the job entails and ask about ability to perform these tasks. So "have you ever had any back problems?" is not a legitimate question, but "This job involves lifting 25-pound weights several times an hour, and sometimes involves lifting up to 100 pounds—can you handle that?" is acceptable.

Once the company decides to extend a job offer, then it is permissible to require a medical examination, as long as all employees (whether or not they have a disability) are subject to this requirement, and the results of the examination are kept in separate medical files and kept confidential, disclosed only to persons with a genuine work-related need to know.

Furthermore, any medical examination or inquiries must be job-related and consistent with business necessity. Voluntary medical examinations (including taking medical histories) are allowable if they are part of a program available to all employees at a work site, and an employer can ask about an employee's ability to perform job-related functions. [42 U.S.C. § 12112(d)]

If the employer wants to impose a requirement of HIV testing, it must be applied uniformly to everyone who applies within a particular job category. It is not permissible to identify some applicants as appearing to be at risk of AIDS, and single them out for HIV testing. Even if an applicant tests positive, the employer is not allowed to withdraw its conditional job offer on this basis, unless being HIV positive renders the applicant unable to perform the central functions of the job.

Section 12112 also requires employers to maintain the confidentiality of HIV test results, which must be kept separate from other employee records and even from other medical records. Access must be restricted to individuals with a real need to know, such as supervisors who may have to offer reasonable accommodation, first aid personnel, and government officials who are assessing the employer's ADA compliance.

An employer's requirement that a worker who claims to be disabled must have an independent medical exam is not enough to prove that the employer regarded that employee as disabled. The employer can demand an independent examination as long as it is job-related and there is a business necessity for it. [*Tice v. Centre Area Transp. Auth.*, 247 F.3d 506 (3d Cir. 2001). *See* Shannon P. Duffy, *3rd Circuit Looks at Use of Medical Exams Under ADA*, The Legal Intelligencer (April 25, 2001) (law.com)]

The Sixth Circuit agreed that a grocery store was justified in firing a produce clerk who said he was HIV positive but neither verified his condition nor took the medical examination requested by the employer. The examination was job-related and consistent with business necessity, because minor injuries at work could endanger an HIV positive employee or other people. [*EEOC v. Prevo's Family Market Inc.*, 135 F.3d 1089 (6th Cir. 1998)]

For more about workplace HIV issues, including a sample business case and sample workplace policies and training manuals, *see* HIV/AIDS Workplace Toolkit available at <http://www.shrm.org/diversity/aidsguide/brta.htm>, explaining Business Response to AIDS, a joint venture between business groups and the Centers for Disease Control.

> **Tip:** After the September 11 attack, the EEOC announced that it is not a violation of the ADA for an employer to ask employees about their medical condition in case they need help in an emergency evacuation, Nor is it a violation of employee privacy to share such information with safety and first aid workers. The Fact Sheet on obtaining and using emergency evacuation information was published at <http://www.eeoc.gov/facts/evacuation.html>.

It has been held that it does not violate the ADA for a factory to reject job applicants if pre-employment testing shows that they are prone to develop carpal tunnel syndrome. [*EEOC v. Woodbridge Co.*, 263 F.3d 812 (8th Cir. 2000); *EEOC v. Rockwell Int'l Corp.*, 243 F.3d 1012 (7th Cir. 2001)] The courts held that these were not sustainable "regarded-as" cases, because the employer did not view the applicants as limited in their ability to hold a broad variety of jobs—only as unsuitable for the particular job.

A job applicant is not entitled to damages when an employer makes inappropriate prehiring inquiries if there were other reasons not to hire that person (here, lack of experience and availability of a laid-off employee to fill the job). [*Griffin v. Steeltek Inc.*, 261 F.3d 1026 (10th Cir. 2001)]

§ 36.10   INTERACTION WITH OTHER STATUTES

[A]   The Rehabilitation Act

The ADA is a successor statute to the Rehabilitation Act. There are many circumstances in which the HR department will have to apply the ADA in conjunction with other laws—typically, the FMLA and ERISA.

The ADA was preceded by the Rehabilitation Act of 1973 (Rehab Act). [29 U.S.C. § 793 *et seq.*] The Rehab Act applies to federal contractors and subcontractors whose government contract involves more than $2,500, and to federal programs and federal grantees. It does not apply to businesses that are not involved in government contracting.

Rehab Act § 503 protects qualified handicapped applicants against discrimination in employment practices. However, one reason that the ADA was passed is that the Rehab Act does not contain a private right of action. In other words, handicapped persons who charge that they were victims of discrimination cannot sue the alleged discriminators. Another section, § 504, does carry a private right of action, but only for discrimination solely on account of handicap in a federally financed program or activity.

Rehab Act § 503 imposes an affirmative action requirement. Federal contractors must have goals for hiring and promotion of qualified handicapped individuals. However, the Department of Labor does not have the power to enforce this requirement by bringing administrative prosecutions against companies that violate it.

In the case of *Hiler v. Brown* [177 F.3d 542 (6th Cir. 1999)], a brain-injured

Vietnam veteran claimed that he was denied a promotion because of war-related inability to communicate quickly in writing. He sued his supervisors as individual defendants under the Rehab Act. The Sixth Circuit held that the Rehab Act's language tracks the Title VII language, and only the employer company, not individuals, can be sued under Title VII.

[B] The ADA and Disability Benefits

A February 12, 1997, EEOC Notice No. 915.002, sets out the EEOC's position that employees can legitimately make ADA claims (based on the assertion that they are qualified to perform essential job functions) at the same time that they apply for disability benefits (which are premised on inability to do gainful work). The EEOC's view is that the two positions are not necessarily contradictory. The ADA assumes that people with disabilities can work; disability programs assume that they can't. Worker's Compensation, Social Security Disability, and other disability programs concentrate on classes of disabled people (e.g., by drafting schedules of impairments). The concept of accommodation is not involved. Nor do the disability-related programs distinguish between essential and marginal job tasks.

The EEOC's position is that even representations of disability made in a Worker's Compensation or disability hearing will not necessarily prevent the person from filing an ADA claim, because the questions posed at the hearing may be imprecise or may focus on disability rather than employability. The EEOC wants to prevent situations in which someone is in effect driven out of the workforce by outright discrimination or by the employer's refusal to make the reasonable accommodations that would have made the person employable. Another possibility is that the person might have been unable to work when he or she applied for disability benefits, but at the earlier or later time referenced in the ADA claim, he or she could have worked if he or she had not been subjected to disability-based discrimination.

This position was adopted by the Supreme Court. [*Cleveland v. Policy Mgmt. Sys. Corp.*, 526 U.S. 795 (1999)] According to *King v. Herbert J. Thomas Memorial Hospital* [159 F.3d 192 (4th Cir. 1998)], actually receiving disability benefits (as distinct from just applying for them) prevents an age-discrimination plaintiff from claiming she was able to perform the job at the time of her discharge.

According to *EEOC v. Stowe-Pharr Mills Inc.* [216 F.3d 373 (4th Cir. 2000)], the employer is not entitled to summary judgment just because the plaintiff applied for Social Security Disability Income benefits—the employee must be given a chance at trial to explain the apparent contradictions. However, information provided in the benefits application is admissible as evidence in the ADA case, because it proves whether or not the plaintiff previously requested accommodation. [*Whitbeck v. Vital Signs Inc.*, 159 F.3d 1369 (D.C. Cir. 1998)] A Social Security Disability determination can affect the plaintiff's damages, by proving the periods of time during which the plaintiff would not have been able to perform the essential job functions even with accommodation. [*Flowers v. Komatsu Mining Sys.*, 165 F.3d 554 (7th Cir. 1999)]

[C] The FMLA

A person with a "serious health condition" (as defined by the FMLA) may also be a QIWD. FMLA leave, although unpaid, is easier to obtain than medical leave as a reasonable ADA accommodation, because employers with 50 or more employees have to grant FMLA leave to eligible employees. Reinstatement after FMLA leave is automatic, but ADA reinstatement requires showing of ability to perform essential work tasks (with or without reasonable accommodation). [*See Employee Leave and the Law*, WestGroup Employment Alert, Sept. 17, 1998, at p. 4]

§ 36.11   ADA ENFORCEMENT

The EEOC has enforcement power over the ADA. [42 U.S.C. § 12111(1)] The remedies available for disability discrimination are also available in retaliation cases. [42 U.S.C. § 12203(c)] ADA charges must be filed with the EEOC or the state agency. [*See* § 41.03 for an explanation of the process] The charge must be filed within 180 days of the last discriminatory act (in nondeferral states) or within 300 days of the last act (in deferral states). The Title VII investigation and conciliation procedures will be followed, and the ADA remedies are equivalent to Title VII remedies, with the distinction that reasonable accommodation can be ordered as an ADA remedy.

The EEOC and the federal courts have discretion to make an attorneys' fee award to the prevailing party. If the United States loses a case, it can be required to pay attorneys' fees—but if the United States wins, the other party cannot be required to compensate the government for the costs of the case. [*See* 42 U.S.C. § 12205]

§ 36.12   THE ADA PRIMA FACIE CASE

Once a disabled employee makes out a prima facie case, the burden then shifts to the employer to prove, by a preponderance of the evidence, that it either offered the plaintiff reasonable accommodation or was unable to do so because of undue hardship. [*Community Hospital v. Fail*, 969 P.2d 667 (Colo. Sup. 1998)] The court's theory is that the employer has more information about the availability of accommodation, so it is up to the employer to prove this issue.

§ 36.13   DAMAGES

Under *EEOC v. Wal-Mart Stores* [187 F.3d 1241 (10th Cir. 1999)], a written antidiscrimination policy, taken by itself, is not the equivalent of a good-faith effort to comply with the ADA. That made the employer vicariously liable and subject to punitive damages when a supervisor discriminated against a hearing-impaired employee. Failure to provide ADA training for supervisors meant that the policy was not really implemented. The Eighth Circuit upheld the jury's $75,000 punitive damage award, finding that it was not high enough to shock the conscience.

§36.14 ARBITRATION OF ADA CLAIMS

Wright v. Universal Maritime Service Corp. [525 U.S. 70 (1998)] involves an injured stevedore who was denied employment because potential employers deemed him to be permanently disabled. The plaintiff sued under the ADA without first filing a grievance or going through arbitration under the collective bargaining agreement.

The lower federal courts dismissed his case because of his failure to exhaust grievance remedies, but the Supreme Court unanimously reversed. Although ADA claims are subject to compulsory arbitration under the U-4 (securities industry employment agreement), the Supreme Court treated this case differently because Wright's claims arose under a statute, not a contract. Contract claims are presumed to be subject to arbitration, but statutory claims are not.

For a CBA to rule out litigation of a claim under an antidiscrimination statute, *Wright* says that the CBA must be very clear on that point. A generalized arbitration clause that fails to specify the antidiscrimination statutes that it covers will not be enough to keep disgruntled employees out of the court system.

Carson v. Giant Food Inc. [175 F.3d 325 (4th Cir. 1999)] says that there has been a clear and unmistakable waiver of the right to litigate if a CBA clause either specifically says that statutory discrimination claims are arbitrable, or fully incorporates the antidiscrimination statutes into the contract. *But see Brown v. ABF Freight Sys. Inc.* [183 F.3d 319 (4th Cir. 1999)], which found that although the CBA referred to the ADA it did not fully incorporate it. Therefore, the employee could bring an ADA suit.

According to *EEOC v. Waffle House Inc.* [534 U.S. 279 (2002)], the EEOC can pursue an ADA case, including victim-specific relief, even though the employee him- or herself was covered by a mandatory predispute arbitration requirement and would not have been able to sue the employer because of this requirement. [*See* Chapter 40 for fuller discussion of arbitration and ADR]

CHAPTER 37

AGE DISCRIMINATION IN EMPLOYMENT ACT

§ 37.01   INTRODUCTION

The Age Discrimination in Employment Act (ADEA), unlike Title VII and the ADA, is found in Title 29 of the United States Code starting at Section 621. (Title VII and the ADEA are in Title 42). In other words, Congress considered the ADEA to be labor law instead of civil rights law. [*See* § 41.06[A] for a discussion of EEOC procedure for filing discrimination charges, and § 42.11 for a discussion of procedural issues arising in private ADEA lawsuits filed by an employee or class of employees]

Congress defined its purpose in passing the ADEA as protecting older people who want to stay in the workforce and are still capable of working from discrimination involving "arbitrary age limits." The ADEA's aim is to "promote employment of older persons based on their ability rather than age; to prohibit arbitrary age discrimination in employment; to help employers and workers find ways of meeting problems arising from the impact of age on employment." [29 U.S.C. § 621]

The basic rule is that anyone over age 40 is protected by the ADEA [29 U.S.C. § 631], so the protected group is not restricted to senior citizens. In a limited range of situations, being under 40 is a bona fide occupational qualification (BFOQ). In other cases, adverse employment action against an older person could be legally justified by a Reasonable Factor Other than Age (RFOA). State age discrimination suits have been upheld when young people are deprived of employment opportunities because of their youth because this, too, is discrimination "on account of age." [*Bergen Commercial Bank v. Sisler*, 157 N.J. 188 (N.J. 1999); *Zanni v. Medaphis Physician Servs. Corp.*, 240 Mich. App. 472 (2000)]

According to the EEOC's data about its 2001 fiscal year (ending September 30, 2001), although discrimination complaints in most categories were more or less level in fiscal 2000 and 2001, age discrimination complaints went up 1½%. EEOC Chair Cari M. Dominguez said that age discrimination (and disability discrimination) seem to be increasing even as demographic changes lead to "the graying of America." [*See EEOC Issues Fiscal 2001 Enforcement Data*, <http://eeoc.gov/press/2-22-02.html> (no www.)] In fiscal 2001, there were 17,405 age discrimination charges filed with the EEOC: 21.5% of the total of 80,840 charges of all types.

Tip: The Supreme Court granted certiorari and heard arguments in the case of *Adams v. Florida Power*, #01-584, dealing with the issue of whether disparate impact cases are even appropriate in the ADEA context (as distinct from disparate-treatment cases that claim that workplace conduct actually treats older workers differently from younger ones). However, the issue remains open, because in April 2002, the Supreme Court dismissed the case, holding that it should not have granted certiorari in the first place. [122 S. Ct. 1290 (2002)]

---

§ 37.02   ADEA EXCEPTIONS

The ADEA bars job discrimination, so a discharge for good cause will not violate the ADEA. As is true of many other labor and anti-discrimination laws, the ADEA exempts very small businesses. The definition of "employer" is limited to industries affecting commerce and having 20 or more employees for each workday in each of 20 or more weeks in the current or previous year. [29 U.S.C. § 630(b)]

The ADEA applies to employees of the United States branch of a foreign corporation that has 20 or more employees worldwide; there need not be 20 employees at the U.S. branch. [*Morelli v. Cedel*, 141 F.3d 39 (2d Cir. 1998)] The number of employees at several small affiliates of a larger corporation can be aggregated for the 20-employee test if the parent company directed the discriminatory act or policy; the original larger enterprise was split up to avoid liability; and the corporate veil can be pierced (i.e., the parent can be held liable for the subsidiaries' debts, torts, and breaches of contract). [*Papa v. Katy Industries Inc.*, 166 F.3d 937 (7th Cir. 1999)]

Although the general rule under the ADEA is that no one can be compelled to retire simply because of that person's age, there is an important exception. Under 29 U.S.C. § 631, a person who has been a "bona fide executive or high policy maker" for two years just before retirement, can lawfully be compelled to retire at 65, as long as he or she is entitled to aggregate retirement benefits that are the equivalent of an annuity of $44,000 a year or more.

The Higher Education Amendments of 1998 [H.R. 6 (Oct. 7, 1998)], reinstate a traditional ADEA exception. Under the Amendments, it is lawful to require tenured faculty members to retire solely on the basis of age. Although this act affects a small group of individuals, it is significant in showing a possible trend toward restricting the scope of the ADEA and other civil rights legislation.

The Supreme Court has also ruled that Congress had no right to remove sovereign immunity from states with respect to ADEA claims brought by state employees. [*Kimel v. Florida Bd. of Regents*, 528 U.S. 62 (1999)]

EEOC Guidelines [29 C.F.R. § 1625.12(d)] define a bona fide policymaker as the manager of an entire enterprise, or at least a customarily recognized department or subdivision. He or she must direct the work of at least two employees, and must hold a job that regularly involves the exercise of discretionary power. At least 80% of work time (or at least 60% in a retail or service business) must be spent on managing the business rather than on routine tasks.

§ 37.03   FORBIDDEN PRACTICES

[A]   Statutory Prohibitions

Under 29 U.S.C. § 623, employers are forbidden to:

- Discriminate because of age (by firing or failing or refusing to hire, or in any other way) against anyone in connection with "compensation, terms, conditions, or privileges of employment";
- Use age to "limit, segregate, or classify" employees that reduce employment opportunities or "otherwise adversely affect" status as an employee;
- Reduce any employee's wage rate to comply with the ADEA;
- Discriminate against an employee or job applicant because of that person's protests about age discrimination, or in retaliation for that person's bringing an ADEA charge or involvement in someone else's ADEA charge;
- Publish Help Wanted ads that indicate "any preference, limitation, specification, or discrimination, based on age".

Section 623 also forbids age discrimination perpetrated by employment agencies and unions, but those provisions are outside the scope of this book.

However, in late 1998, the Eighth Circuit joined the Fifth, Sixth, and Seventh Circuits in ruling that it does not constitute age discrimination for an employer to make reasonable inquiries about an older person's retirement plans. [*Watkins v. J&S Oil Co.*, 164 F.3d 55 (8th Cir. 1998)]

[B] Supreme Court Precedents

A Supreme Court case, *Public Employees Retirement System of Ohio v. Betts* [492 U.S. 158 (1989)] held that the ADEA did not apply to employee benefits. In 1990, Congress amended the statute, adding a new § 630(l), extending the ADEA ban on age discrimination in "compensation, terms, conditions, or privileges of employment" to cover "benefits provided pursuant to a bona fide employee benefit plan."

To win, the ADEA plaintiff does not have to show that he or she was replaced by someone under 40; it may even be possible to win by showing age-motivated replacement by another person over 40 (for instance, choosing someone who will retire soon, thus removing two older workers from the workplace). [*O'Connor v. Consolidated Coin Caterers Corp.*, 517 U.S. 308 (1997)]

Furthermore, ADEA cases can turn on "age-related factors" rather than the mere fact of age. A 30-year-old can't have 30 years of employment experience. However, an employee with 20 years' seniority might be only 38, and could have more seniority than an older person who joined the company later. *Hazen Paper Co. v. Biggins* [507 U.S. 604 (1993)] requires ADEA plaintiffs to prove that age, and not just age-related factors, influenced the employer's decision.

In mixed-motive cases, *Price Waterhouse v. Hopkins* [490 U.S. 228 (1989)] says that the plaintiff must show that age is a substantial factor in the employment decision—it doesn't have to be the only factor or even the most important one. But if the employer can offer a defense (by a preponderance of the evidence, not proof beyond a reasonable doubt) that it would have made the same decision even if age had not been used as a criterion, the defendant will win the case. The Civil Rights Act of 1991 overruled this decision for Title VII cases—but not for ADEA cases.

St. Mary's Honor Center v. Hicks [509 U.S. 502 (1993)] says that the plaintiff always has the "ultimate burden of persuasion." So if the judge or jury (whichever is responsible for determining the facts of the case) does not believe the employer's explanation of the reasons behind its conduct, the plaintiff could still lose—if he or she fails to provide adequate evidence. The *Hicks* standard is sometimes called "pretext-plus": The plaintiff has to do more than show the defendant's excuses are a mere pretext for discrimination.

Late in 2000, the Second Circuit found that if there is enough evidence of the plaintiff's poor work performance, then the jury cannot accept the plaintiff's pretextuality argument. Therefore, summary judgment can validly be granted for the employer. [*Schnabel v. Abramson*, 232 F.3d 83 (2d Cir. 2000)]

The Supreme Court's June 2000 decision in *Reeves v. Sanderson Plumbing Products Inc.* [530 U.S. 133 (2000)] is a narrow procedural one. It holds that an ADEA plaintiff can defeat a motion for judgment as a matter of law (a procedural technique for terminating a lawsuit without a full trial) by establishing a prima facie case plus enough evidence for a reasonable court or jury to find that the employer's defense is merely pretextual. It is not required that the plaintiff introduce any further evidence at this stage, unless a rational finder of fact would not be able to find the defendant's conduct discriminatory. However, *Reeves* had little practical impact on the litigation climate [*see* 69 L.W. 2185 (Oct. 3, 2000)]; it certainly didn't issue in a new pro-plaintiff era.

[C] Employee Status

ADEA cases are limited to the employment context, not all aspects of economic life. Therefore, it could not be an ADEA violation to use age to refuse an automobile dealership to an applicant; dealers are contractors, not employees. [*Mangram v. GM Corp.*, 108 F.3d 61 (4th Cir. 1997)]

Salespersons who are independent contractors are not covered by the ADEA. [*Oestman v. Nat'l Farmers Unions Inc.*, 958 F.2d 303 (10th Cir. 1992)] However, the Second Circuit has ruled that members of a corporation's Board of Directors are entitled to the protections of the ADEA if they work full time as corporate managers or officers, and report to senior board members. [*Caruso v. Peat, Marwick Mitchell & Co.*, 664 F. Supp. 144 (S.D.N.Y. 1987)]

Although the ADEA statute refers to "employees," coverage is not limited to current active employees. Retirees have standing to sue their union for ADEA violations in connection with health plan amendments that excluded Medicare-eligible retirees. [*McKeever v. Ironworkers' Dist. Council*, 65 L.W. 2608 (E.D. Pa. March 7, 1997)] The D.C. Circuit also allowed federal employees to bring ADEA retaliation suits after their discharge or resignation. [*Forman v. Small*, 271 F.3d 285 (D.C. Cir. 2001)]

[D]   Occupational Qualifications and RFOAs

Being under 40 can be a bona fide occupational qualification (BFOQ) for a narrow range of jobs, usually involving public safety (e.g., the strength, agility, and quick reaction time required of police officers and firefighters). [*See* 29 U.S.C. § 623(f)(1)], but most ordinary private sector jobs will not give rise to a BFOQ defense.

Reasonable factors other than age (RFOA) can offer a defense, as long as the employer used objective, job-related criteria to make the employment decision, and applied those criteria uniformly. Courts have often accepted arguments that the employer's decision was not really age-based, but was inspired by factors that merely tend to go along with age: for instance, the tendency of salaries to rise with experience. Employers in search of cost cutting might discharge higher-paid older workers in order to replace them with lower-paid workers. The EEOC Regulations say that, if the RFOA has a disparate impact on over-40 workers, the employer must prove that it has a business necessity for the action.

It is a defense to an age discrimination charge if an employer follows the provisions of "a bona fide seniority system that is not intended to evade" the ADEA's purposes. [29 U.S.C. § 623(f); 29 C.F.R. § 1625.8] However, even a valid seniority system cannot be used to impose involuntary retirement on an employee who is capable of working and wants to continue. Furthermore, older seniority systems (and retirement plans) are not "grandfathered in." Section 623(k) requires all seniority systems and benefit plans to comply with the ADEA, no matter when they were adopted.

§ 37.04   IMPLICATIONS FOR BENEFIT PLANS

[A]   Generally

At one time, it would have been accurate to say that the ADEA covered only hiring, firing, and salary, but not employee benefits, based on a Supreme Court decision, *Public Employees Retirement System of Ohio v. Betts* [492 U.S. 158 (1989)] In 1990, however, Congress passed a statute, the Older Workers Benefit Protection Act (OWBPA) to make it clear that the ADEA covers all of the terms and conditions of employment, including the full compensation package. Therefore, in the current legal environment, it is important to discover how the ADEA interacts with ERISA, insurance laws, and other laws affecting compensation and benefits.

Section 623(i) takes up the question of how the ADEA interacts with employee benefit plans. Employers are forbidden to "establish or maintain" a pension plan that requires or even permits age-based termination or reduction of pension credits. In a defined benefit plan, benefits must continue to accrue at the same rate. In a defined contribution plan, the employer's allocations must be made to all employees' accounts on the same basis, irrespective of their ages. [29 U.S.C. § 623(i)(1)] People who count as "highly compensated employees" for tax purposes are not entitled to this protection. [*See* 29 U.S.C. § 623(i)(5)]

The ADEA provides various defenses and safe harbors for employers. Voluntary early retirement plans are allowable as long as they are consistent with the ADEA's purpose of protecting employment rights for older workers. [29 U.S.C. § 623(f)(B)(2)]

It is permissible for a plan to put an upper limit on the amount of benefits a plan can provide to anyone, or to limit the number of years of employment that can be taken into account, as long as these provisions are imposed without regard to age. [29 U.S.C. § 623(i)(2)] For instance, if the plan does not permit crediting of more than 30 years of service, this is an allowable age-neutral provision because it applies to employees with more than 30 years' tenure whether they started working for the company at age 18 or age 40.

Once an employee has reached the plan's Normal Retirement Age (NRA) and has started to receive a pension, then the employer's obligation to continue accruing benefits is satisfied by the actuarial equivalent of the pension benefits themselves. [29 U.S.C. § 623(i)(3)(A)]

Section 623(i)(3)(B) says that, for employees who have reached NRA but have not started to draw a pension (typically, employees who defer their retirement and are still working), and whose benefits have not been suspended pursuant to ERISA § 203(a)(3)(B) or I.R.C. § 411(a)(3)(B), the employer's obligation to keep accruing benefits is satisfied by making an actuarial adjustment to the pension that the employee eventually receives, so that he or she gets a larger pension because of deferred retirement.

Because the ADEA covers persons over age 40, the protected group includes many people who will voluntarily elect early retirement. Section 623(l) says that it does not constitute age discrimination for a pension plan to set a minimum retirement age as a condition for being eligible for either early or normal retirement.

A defined benefit plan can lawfully provide early retirement subsidies, or supplement the Social Security benefits of retirees who get a reduced benefit because they retire before the plan's NRA. [29 U.S.C. § 623(l)(1)(B). With respect to retiree health benefits, also see 29 U.S.C. § 623(l)(2)(D)]

There is no ADEA violation if a departing employee's severance pay is reduced to account for the value of retiree health benefits, and/or the value of additional pension benefits that are made available because of a contingency that is not based on age to a person who is already eligible for a full retirement benefit. [29 U.S.C. § 623(l)(2)] For this purpose, severance pay is defined to include certain supplemental unemployment insurance benefits. [*See* 29 U.S.C. § 613(l)(2)(C) and I.R.C. § 501(c)(17)]

Tip: If the employer says that retiree health benefits will be provided, and reduces severance pay accordingly, but fails to provide retiree health benefits, 29 U.S.C. § 623(l)(2)(F) lets employees sue for "specific performance" (i.e., to make the employer provide the benefits). This is an additional right, over and above any other remedies the individual has.

However, according to the Eleventh Circuit, Social Security benefits should not be used to reduce back pay under the ADEA; neither should unemployment compensation. However, if the employee applies for Social Security benefits, that could be evidence that the employee didn't try hard enough to get another job—which could be grounds for reducing the back pay award. [*Dominguez v. Tom James Co.*, 113 F.3d 1188 (11th Cir. 1997); *Brown v. A.J. Gerrard Mfg. Co.*, 715 F.2d 1549 (11th Cir. 1983)]

[B] Case Law on Pension and Benefit Issues

The Ninth Circuit decided in 1999 that it violates the ADEA to calculate disability retirement benefits based on the age at the time of hiring. [*Arnett v. California Pub. Employees Retirement Sys.*, 207 F.3d 565 (9th Cir. 1999)] Under *Hazen*, calculations based on actual years of service are acceptable, because a younger person might have more years of service than an older person who was hired at a later age. However, age at hire raises different issues because it had a strong effect on the potential disability benefit. The Ninth Circuit remanded the case to the District Court for disposition.

Unlike the ADA, the ADEA does not contain a concept of reasonable accommodation. Receiving disability benefits therefore prevents an ADEA plaintiff from claiming she was able to perform the job from which she was discharged. [*King v. Herbert J. Thomas Mem. Hosp.*, 159 F.3d 192 (4th Cir. 1998)]

§ 37.05 HEALTH BENEFITS

[A] Bona Fide Plans

If the employer maintains a group health plan, the plan must cover over-65 employees on equal terms with younger employees. Either the cost per employee must be the same, irrespective of age, or the employer must offer equal benefits.

Under ADEA § 3(f)(2), an employer can abide by the terms of a bona fide employee benefit plan without violating the ADEA or the OWBPA. A bona fide plan is one which:

- Existed before the challenged employment action occurred;
- The terms of the plan are observed;
- The plan is not used to force anyone into involuntary retirement;
- (Except for voluntary early retirement plans) the costs incurred, or the benefits paid, are equivalent for older and younger employees.

For EEOC regulations on this subject, see 29 C.F.R. § 1625.10.

Under ADEA § 4(f)(2), the employer is allowed to compare costs quoted on the basis of five-year age brackets (e.g., employees aged 30–35). Comparisons must be made using adjacent age brackets: not the costs of employees 65–70 versus those of employees aged 20–25, for instance.

ADEA § 4(l)(3)(B) allows long-term disability benefits to be reduced by pension benefits for which the individual is eligible at age 62 or normal retirement age. Also see Regulations at 29 C.F.R. § 1625.10(f)(1)(ii). The EEOC says it will not pursue an ADEA claim in situations where disability benefits stop at 65 for disabilities occurring before 60, or stop five years after a disability that occurred after age 60.

[B]   October 2000 EEOC Transmittal

On October 3, 2000, the EEOC published Transmittal Number 915.003 accessible at <http://www.eeoc.gov/docs/benefits.html>. The Transmittal explains the EEOC's view of the employer's duties to avoid age and disability discrimination in the pension context. The EEOC's view is that ERISA compliance is no defense to a charge of age discrimination.

If the employer provides the same benefits for older and younger workers, there is no ADEA issue. Even certain differentials are acceptable under the ADEA, including legitimate early retirement incentives and differences in benefits justified by the employer spending the same amount, or incurring the same cost, for all employees irrespective of age. Offsets are allowed under the ADEA to make sure that the older employee's benefits from all sources are no less favorable than the total benefit their younger counterparts receive.

An "equal" benefit means that workers of all ages, who are similarly situated and have equal seniority, must have access to the same payment options (e.g., lump sum or annuity for both). They must have access to the same types of benefits, in the same amount. It is acceptable to provide the same monthly benefit, even though it is likely that the older workers will die sooner and collect fewer benefits. But benefits are not equal if an age-based cutoff is imposed, or where benefits are eliminated or reduced on the basis of a criterion that is partially or wholly defined by age.

> **Tip:** The EEOC allows comparisons based on hypothetical employees; its investigators do not have to find a specific younger employee who has better benefits than an older employee.

The EEOC allows employers to provide *better* benefits for older than younger employees, if this is done to redress past age discrimiination. If unequal benefits favor younger rather than older employees, there has been an ADEA violation unless a justification such as the "equal cost" rule is available.

The equal cost rule can be applied only to life insurance, health insurance, and disability benefits, because the cost of providing such benefits increases with the age of the employee. It cannot be used to justify refusal to hire or involuntary retirement. Benefits may be reduced only enough to provide equivalency. However, the defense can be based on the entire package of benefits whose cost rises with age, making it permissible to reduce one benefit even more than cost justifies if other benefits are increased to compensate.

In plans funded in whole or in part by employee contributions, the employer may not force the older employee to pay more for the benefit as a condition of employment. When older employees are faced with a premium increase, they must be given the option of withdrawing from the plan or paying the original premium in return for a reduced level of coverage.

The EEOC manual interprets the ADEA to permit certain offsets to prevent duplication of benefits. Certain pension benefits can be offset by long-term disability (LTD) payments. Some retiree health benefits and extra pension benefits can be deducted from severance pay.

The EEOC position is that all similarly situated employees must be given parity in severance benefits, regardless of age, and that severance benefits cannot be denied on the grounds that the employee is eligible for a pension, although under some circumstances retiree health benefits can be used to offset severance pay. It constitutes illegal forced retirement to deny recall rights to older workers.

The EEOC accepts the legitimacy of setting a normal and/or early retirement age for receiving pension benefits. Employers can lawfully require a certain number of years of service or a time period before an employee will be eligible for retirement. Employers can even limit the total amount of benefits that will be provided to an individual under a plan, or limit the number of years of service that will be credited toward benefits from a defined benefit plan—just as long as those limits are not linked to age.

The EEOC view is that, with the three exceptions noted below, it is an ADEA violation to exclude an employee from participation in a plan because he or she was close to the plan's Normal Retirement Age at the time of hiring. Nor may employers stop or reduce the rate of accruals or contributions because of the employee's age. No equal cost defense is available.

However, if the employer actuarially increases the value of the pension to represent work after the NRA, this extra amount can be offset from pension accruals. If the employee continues to work after beginning to receive pension benefits, the actuarial value of payments actually made can offset further pension accruals. Social Security integration (i.e., the Social Security benefits offset the pension) is also permitted. [*See* § 9.04 for a discussion of the EEOC Compliance Manual's treatment of the ADEA implications of early retirement incentive programs]

In August 2001, the EEOC revoked its earlier position that ending or reducing a benefit plan when an employee or retiree becomes eligible for Medicare violates the ADEA. The EEOC agreed not to litigate any more of these "Medicare bridge" cases until it reached a final policy decision. [*See EEOC Reverses Position on Curtailing Retiree Benefits Upon Medicare Eligibility* (no by-line)]

§ 37.06   PROVING THE ADEA CASE

In an October 2000 case, summary judgment was granted for the employer. The plaintiff failed to rebut testimony that he was not hired because of his poor interview performance. He didn't ask any questions about the position; he didn't give a good explanation for having held so many jobs in the past; and he rambled instead of giving concise answers to the interviewer's questions. [*Chapman v. AI Transport Inc.,* 229 F.3d 1012 (11th Cir. 2000)]

A 60-year-old employee was terminated when his employer lost government contracts. At his exit interview, he asked if he was being fired for poor performance. He was told "absolutely not." When he filed suit under the ADEA, the employer claimed that he was terminated because he was impossible to get along with. The jury (as upheld by the Seventh Circuit) didn't believe this, particularly since there was no documentation of the alleged personality problems in his generally good evaluations. [*Wilson v. AMGen Corp.,* 167 F.3d 1114 (7th Cir. 1999)]

According to the Fourth Circuit, disparaging comments about age are weaker evidence of discrimination than similar comments about race or sex. Racist or sexist remarks can be made by "outsiders," whereas everyone ages. [*Dockins v. Benchmark Communications*, 176 F.3d 745 (4th Cir. 1999). *See* § 42.08 for a discussion of technical rules of proof]

§ 37.07   WAIVERS OF ADEA RIGHTS

[A]   Requirements for Valid Waiver

It makes sense for employers to make it part of the severance process to request that terminating employees sign a waiver of their rights to bring suit for discrimination allegedly occurring in the course of the employment relationship. However, in order to be valid and enforceable, a waiver of ADEA rights must be strictly tailored to satisfy the requirements of the Older Workers Benefits Protection Act, a 1990 statute that has been enacted as 29 U.S.C. § 626(f)(1). Furthermore, waivers do not prevent the EEOC from carrying out an age discrimination investigation or bringing suit against the employer. It is unlawful for ADEA waivers to prohibit employees from filing charges with the EEOC or participating in EEOC investigations.

A waiver is not valid if it is not "knowing and voluntary" on the part of the employee. No one can surrender legal rights without receiving full disclosure of the implications of the document he or she signs. The ADEA provides a definition of what is required before a waiver will be considered knowing and voluntary:

- The agreement that contains the waiver must be written in understandable terms;
- The waiver specifically mentions ADEA rights or claims;
- Only claims that have already arisen are waived—not claims that might arise in the future;

- The employee receives something in return for the waiver; it is not enough that the employee receives severance or other benefits that would be provided even if there had been no waiver;
- The document includes a written warning that the employee should consult a lawyer before signing the agreement;
- The employee gets at least 21 days to think over the employer's severance offer. If the agreement is offered to an entire group (e.g., in connection with a layoff or incentives for voluntary departure) then the offer must remain open for at least 45 days;
- When incentives are offered to a group, everyone in the group must get an understandable notification of the features of the program: who can participate; eligibility factors; time limits; and the ages and job titles of everyone eligible or chosen for the program, vis a vis the ages of workers in the organizational unit or job classification who were not eligible or selected. (This was included in the law to make it easier for potential plaintiffs to decide if age was an improper factor in selecting employees for the program.)

Waivers are also used when charges have been filed, and then the employer and employee agree on a settlement. In this case, the waiver is only considered knowing and voluntary if all the rules noted above have been observed, and the employee has been given a reasonable time to consider the offer.

Getting a waiver does not provide complete protection for the employer. Sometimes the employee will go to court and sue anyway, claiming that the lawsuit is permissible because the waiver was defective in some way. Section 626(f)(3) provides that it is up to the employer to prove that the waiver satisfied the various requirements and therefore was knowing and voluntary. The employee is not required to prove that the waiver was invalid.

The EEOC's response to widespread layoffs in 2001 was that waivers from laid-off employees can offer an affirmative defense—but that the employer must be ready to prove the validity of the waivers. [Darryl Van Duch, *New EEOC Rule Targets 'Won't Sue' Severance Pledges*, National Law Journal, (March 5, 2001) (law.com)] A little later, Ida L. Castro (who was then the Chair of the EEOC) said "unlawful waivers that strip older workers of their rights under the ADEA will be pursued by the EEOC to the fullest extent of the law." [*See EEOC Scores Victory in Age Bias Suit Against Major Information Technology Company*, <http://eeoc.gov/press/6-12-01.html>]

[B] EEOC Rules

The EEOC's rule on waivers, effective July 6, 1998, can be found at 29 C.F.R. § 1625.22. A valid ADEA waiver must:

- Be embodied in a written document that contains the entire agreement (the agreement cannot be written but supplemented by oral discussion);
- Be written in plain English, appropriate to the signer's educational level;

- Information about exit incentives must also be understandable;
- Be honest and accurate, not misleading;
- Specify that it relates to ADEA claims;
- Advise the employee to consult an attorney before signing.

In general, waivers can release existing claims but not those that might arise in the future. However, the Final Rule allows an otherwise valid waiver to include the signer's agreement to retire, or otherwise terminate employment at a specified future date.

For the waiver to be valid, the signer must receive consideration specific to the waiver, which he or she would not receive otherwise. Therefore, normal severance pay is not adequate to support a waiver. Nor does it constitute valuable consideration if the employer restores a benefit that was wrongfully terminated in the past. However, the Final Rule says that it is not necessary to give greater consideration to over-40 employees who sign waivers than to under-40 employees, even though the older employees waive an additional range of claims (those arising under the ADEA).

Despite the existence of waivers, a certain number of employees will nevertheless bring age discrimination claims against the employer, claiming that the waivers were invalid and therefore did not constitute a knowing and voluntary waiver of the right to sue.

The Supreme Court's decision in *Oubre v. Entergy Operations Inc.* [522 U.S. 422 (1988)] says that such a person can bring suit under the ADEA even without tendering back (returning) the severance pay received under the agreement that included the allegedly invalid waiver. The rationale is that the defective waiver does not qualify for ratification by the ex-employee, so it is not necessary to return the consideration to avoid ratification.

The EEOC published Final Regulations to implement *Oubre.* [*See* 29 C.F.R. Part 1625 as amended by 65 Fed. Reg. 77438 (Dec. 11, 2000), effective January 1, 2001] The EEOC's position is that the existence of a valid waiver is an affirmative defense for the employer. That means that the employer has the burden of proving the validity, but the employee can produce evidence that the waiver was not knowing and voluntary. The EEOC analyzes covenants not to sue in the same way as waivers, and in fact believes they may be even more damaging to employee rights because employees might be deterred from bringing suit with respect to wrongdoing occurring after the covenant was signed.

According to the agency, ordinary contract principles about ratification and tender-back do not apply to employment waivers, because ex-employees might not be able to afford to give back the consideration even if they have a valid claim against the former employer.

Tender-back is not required even if the waiver seems to be lawful, and even if the employee does not allege fraud or duress. Once the case is resolved, the trial court may have to determine the employer's entitlement to restitution, recoupment or sell-off. However, the employer can only recover the amount of consideration paid for the waiver, or the amount the plaintiff is awarded for winning the case—whichever is lower. Employees who file suit in bad faith can also be required to pay the employers' attorneys' fees.

[C] Case Law on ADEA Waivers

Note that, although the OWBPA requires employers to give employees 21 days to consider an early retirement offer, the employer retains the power to withdraw the offer; it does not become irrevocable for the 21-day period. [*Ellison v. Premier Salons Int'l Inc.*, 164 F.3d 111 (8th Cir. 1999)]

As a result of *Wright v. Universal Maritime Service Corp.* [525 U.S. 70 (1998)], a general arbitration clause in a collective bargaining agreement will not preclude litigation of claims under the ADEA or other federal antidiscrimination statutes. Only a detailed clause that specifically refers to a particular antidiscrimination statute can prevent employees from litigating such claims if they prefer not to arbitrate them.

The most important issue is OWBPA compliance, which in turn depends on the terms of the waiver and the circumstances of its signing. The Seventh Circuit enforced a clear, unambiguous waiver signed by a lawyer (of all people!) who worked for a corporation. Presumably, he was able to understand the document. Even though he believed he was forced into a choice between resigning and being terminated on account of age, he was still bound by the waiver he signed. [*Lloyd v. Brunswick Corp.*, 180 F.3d 893 (7th Cir. 1999)] In another case, however, given the possibility that the company used fraud to induce employees to sign waivers, the Tenth Circuit refused to give effect to the waivers. [*Bennett v. Coors Brewing Co.*, 189 F.3d 1221 (10th Cir. 1999)]

CHAPTER 38

THE FAMILY AND MEDICAL LEAVE ACT (FMLA)

§ 38.01   INTRODUCTION

The Family and Medical Leave Act (FMLA) was enacted on February 3, 1993, as 29 U.S.C. § 2601–2654. Congress stated an intention to aid families in which both parents, or the single parent, work outside the home, and to minimize sex discrimination by making leave available in a gender-neutral manner.

The FMLA focuses on two subjects: health care (whether for the employee's own serious health condition or for a family member for whom the employee is a caregiver) and parenting a newborn or newly adopted child. 29 U.S.C. § 2601(a)(2) says that "it is important for the development of children and the family unit that fathers and mothers be able to participate in early childrearing and the care of family members who have serious health conditions."

Under appropriate circumstances, qualifying employees can take up to 12 weeks of leave a year, whether the leave is taken all at once, in several blocks, or intermittently in small units. FMLA leave can be important for preserving the job (and benefits) of someone who has used up all of his or her sick days and is too sick to maintain a normal work schedule, but not sick enough to obtain disability benefits or file for disability retirement.

Employers have the option of providing paid leave under these circumstances, but it does not violate the statute for the employer to provide only unpaid FMLA leave.

> **Tip:** Providing unpaid leave to an employee who is exempt from the Fair Labor Standards overtime requirements does not convert the employee from exempt to nonexempt. [29 U.S.C. § 2612(c)]

Leave can be taken, under 29 U.S.C. § 2612, for a total of 12 weeks in any 12-month period (not necessarily a calendar year), when the employee has or adopts or fosters a child (but this leave can only be taken during the first year after the child's birth or after the adoption or foster care placement) or for a serious health condition suffered by the employee or his or her spouse, parent, or child. If the employee is the sick person, the serious health condition must prevent the employee from performing the functions of the job.

The employer must give employees at least 60 days' notice of changes in the method of calculating the leave year. [29 C.F.R. § 825.200(d)] The 12-week limit applies per year, not per illness. Therefore, an employee who uses up the allowance is not entitled to additional leave based on events later in the same leave year.

As defined by 29 U.S.C. § 2611(9), a reduced leave schedule is a partial leave under which the employee does work, but for less than the usual number of hours per workday or workweek.

It is unlawful for employers to interfere with employees' exercise of FMLA right or to discriminate or retaliate against them for exercising such rights, charging the employer with FMLA violations, or participating in an investigation. [29 U.S.C. § 2615]

The FMLA does not modify federal or state antidiscrimination laws. [*See* 29 U.S.C. § 2651(a)] Employers always have a legal right to set up their own policies that are *more* generous than the FMLA: § 2653, and the federal statute does not preempt state and local laws that require employees to offer even more leave than the FMLA does. [29 U.S.C. § 2651(b)]

Employers do not have the power to draft their benefit plans or programs to limit FMLA rights, nor can a Collective Bargaining Agreement be used to cut back FMLA rights. [*See* 29 U.S.C. § 2652(b)]

The DOL's interpretation is that it violates the FMLA to deny awards or bonuses for perfect attendance to employees who take FMLA leave but have no other absences. However, the DOL permits productivity awards, and presumably workers who do not take FMLA leave are present on more days and therefore more productive. [*See* Kathryn Tyler, *All Present and Accounted For?* HR Magazine, Oct. 2001, at p. 101]

According to the Department of Labor's 2000 Family and Medical Leave Survey, available at <http://www.dol.gov/asp/fmla/factsheet.htm>, more than 35 million workers have taken FMLA leave since the statute was enacted. According to most of the survey respondents, the FMLA did not have adverse effects on their productivity, profitability, or growth. The 2001 survey showed that over 80% of employers did not think the FMLA had any effect (positive or negative) on productivity, profitability, or growth. However, private surveys found that employers were not confident that they were tracking FMLA leave correctly. Most employees who use the FMLA do not schedule their leaves in advance, creating inconvenience for other employees who have to cover for them. [*See* Kevin Sweeney, *Studies Question Success of Family and Medical Leave Act*, WSJ.com CareerJournal, April 19, 2001]

FMLA Title I covers private employment. The statute also has a Title II, covering federal employees. However, there is no private right of action under FMLA Title II, and the federal government never expressly waived sovereign immunity. [*Russell v. Department of the Army*, 191 F.3d 1016 (9th Cir. 1999)] According to *Garrett v. University of Alabama* [193 F.3d 1214 (11th Cir. 1999)], the states have sovereign immunity that prevents FMLA suits by state employees.

§ 38.02   FMLA ELIGIBILITY ISSUES

Like most federal employment discrimination laws, the FMLA exempts very small employers. The FMLA applies only to employers engaged in interstate commerce or activities affecting commerce (but most employers fit into this category)—and only if, in the current year or the previous calendar year, there were at least 50 employees on each workday of 20 or more work weeks. Furthermore, the FMLA does not apply when there are fewer than 50 people at that worksite and the total number of employees at all of the employer's sites within a 75-mile radius is less than 50. Anyone who acts on behalf of the employer, whether directly or indirectly, also counts as an employer. So does the successor in interest of a past employer. [29 U.S.C. § 2611(4)]

A group of automobile service companies that shared a majority shareholder lacked common management and therefore could not be treated as a single integrated employer, even though they had some interrelated operations. Therefore, an FMLA claim had to be dismissed because the particular unit where the plaintiff worked had fewer than 50 employees and aggregation with the other units was denied. [*Hukill v. Auto Care Inc.*, 192 F.3d 437 (4th Cir. 1999)]

Even after it is established that an employer is covered, not all employees are entitled to take FMLA leave. Comparatively veteran employees have FMLA rights, but new hires do not. Eligibility is limited to an employee who not only has worked for the employer for at least 12 months, but put in at least 1,250 hours for that employer in the preceding year. [*See* 29 U.S.C. § 2611(2)(A)]

Vacation days, personal days, sick days, suspensions, and holidays do not count toward the required 1,250 hours. [*Clark v. Allegheny Univ. Hosp.*, 1998 WL 94803 (E.D. Pa. 1998)] The 1250 hours are counted back from the time the employee went on FMLA leave, not from the time the employer fired the employee or took other adverse action. Therefore, a plaintiff who took three leaves that she claimed satisfied FMLA requirements, and therefore did not work 1250 hours during the year before her discharge, was still entitled to bring an FMLA suit. [*Butler v. Owens-Brockway Plastic Prods. Inc.*, 199 F.3d 314 (6th Cir. 1999)]

Even if an employer's own policies are more generous than the FMLA, FMLA leave is not available to persons who have worked for the employer for less than 12 months. DOL regulations require employers to live up to their own policies—but only with respect to extended periods of leave, not basic eligibility. [*Dolese v. Office Depot Inc.*, 231 F.3d 202 (5th Cir. 2000)]

In the *Ragsdale v. Wolverine Worldwide* [#00-6029, — U.S. — (2002), discussed in Gina Holland, *High Court Rules for Business in Medical Leave Dispute*, The Associated Press (March 20, 2002) (law.com)], the Supreme Court ruled that the DOL regulation [29 C.F.R. § 825.700(a)] is invalid to the extent that it requires employers to disclose the relationship between FMLA leave and the employer's own leave policies. [For a background on *Ragsdale* and related issues, see *Focus on the FMLA: Integrating FMLA Leave With Other Leave Demands* (Dec. 2001) <http://www.ebia.com>]

The plaintiff in *Kosakow v. New Rochelle Radiology Associates* [274 F.3d 706 (2d Cir. 2001)] alleged that her employer knew that she was taking medical leave, but failed to inform her that she had failed to satisfy the 1,250 requirement, but only by about fifty hours. She had nonemergency surgery that could have been rescheduled a few weeks later, after she met the 1,250 hour requirement. The Second Circuit ruled that the employer had a legal duty to inform her of the requirements for taking FMLA leave. Failure to post the required notice, and to discuss the matter in the employee handbook, was tantamount to failure to disclose. Therefore, the employer was estopped (prevented) from raising her failure to meet the 1250 hour test.

Although seven of the thirteen federal Circuit Courts have decided that state government employees do not have the right to bring FMLA suits against the state agencies that employ them, in December 2001, the Ninth Circuit held that state employees are entitled to bring FMLA suits. [*Hibbs v. Department of Human Resources*, 273 F.3d 844 (9th Cir. 2001)]

§ 38.03   WHEN LEAVE IS AVAILABLE

An eligible employee can take FMLA leave for his or her own serious health condition or the serious health condition of an eligible family member.

The statute itself defines "serious health condition" as an "illness, injury, impairment, or physical or mental condition" that requires either inpatient care (in a hospital, nursing home or hospice) or at least continuing treatment by a health care provider. [29 U.S.C. §§ 2611(6) and (11)]

According to 29 C.F.R. § 825.114(c), the flu is ordinarily not a serious illness unless complications ensue. According to the Fourth Circuit, the flu was a serious health condition where the employee was incapacitated for a period of time, and needed three visits to the doctor. [*Miller v. AT&T Corp.*, 250 F.3d 820 (4th Cir. 2001)]

The Eighth Circuit found that a serious health condition justifying FMLA leave was present where the employee was off work for a week with what a nurse practitioner diagnosed as a viral infection, and there was continuing treatment (two visits). [*Rankin v. Seagate Techs. Inc.*, 246 F.3d 1145 (8th Cir. 2001)]

A UPS driver fired for poor attendance did not prevail on his FMLA claim. [*Haefling v. UPS*, 169 F.3d 494 (7th Cir. 1999)] Although he saw a doctor and got physical therapy for a neck injury, he did not prove that he had a period of incapacity lasting at least three days, or even that medical treatment was really necessary. Therefore, he did not prove that he had suffered a serious medical condition.

Qualifying family members are spouse (husband or wife only—not cohabitant), child (including adopted or foster child) who is either under 18 years old or mentally or physically disabled, or parent (biological parent or someone who played a parental role—but NOT a mother- or father-in-law, even though many individuals become caregivers for their in-laws). [*See* 29 U.S.C. §§ 2611(7) and (12)]

The EEOC's Interpretive Guidelines on defining ADA disability cannot be used to decide whether an employee's adult child is disabled in the context of deciding whether the employee is entitled to FMLA leave to care for the son or daughter. [*Navarro v. Pfizer Corp.*, 261 F.3d 90 (1st Cir. 2001)]

> **Tip:** If both spouses work for different employers, each one is entitled to 12 weeks of leave when a child is born or adopted, but if they work for the same employer, the employer can legally require them to split a single 12-week leave period, or to share the 12 weeks when they are caring for the same sick parent. [*See* 29 U.S.C. § 2612(f)]

FMLA leave can be taken for adoption or foster care hearings, but not for custody hearings. [*Kelley v. Crossfield Catalysts*, 1997 WL 80960 (N.D. Ill. Feb. 21, 1997)]

§ 38.04   THE EMPLOYER'S OBLIGATION

[A]   Benefits

The employer must reinstate the employee after leave, and must maintain all employee benefits during leave. [*See* 29 U.S.C. § 2615(c) for health coverage requirements] However, the employee does not accrue seniority or additional benefits. FMLA leave is not considered a break in service when pension eligibility is determined.

"Benefits" means all of the employer's benefits (not just those offered under ERISA plans)—e.g., "group life insurance, health insurance, disability insurance, sick leave, annual leave, educational benefits, and pensions." [29 U.S.C. § 2611(5)]

When employees are on FMLA leave, the EGHP must maintain their coverage at the original level. If employees are required to pay part of the EGHP premium under normal circumstances, the plan can require them to continue contributing during FMLA leave. Furthermore, if the employee is more than 30 days late paying the premium, health insurance coverage can legitimately be terminated. If coverage is terminated in this manner, but the employee returns to work and is reinstated, then he or she is entitled to immediate reinstatement in the EGHP, with no need to satisfy plan requirements a second time.

If the employee quits instead of returning from leave, the employer is entitled to recover the health premiums expended on the employee's behalf during the leave period. But if the employee files a health claim for treatment during the leave period, a claim that would otherwise be allowable cannot be denied because the employee later terminates employment.

[B]   Reinstatement

Section 2614 takes up the subject of reinstatement in more detail. It provides that an employee who returns from leave not only must not lose any benefits because of taking leave, but must be reinstated either in the old job or an equivalent new one. The second job is equivalent to the first if it provides equivalent terms and conditions of employment (benefits, pay, etc.)

The FMLA creates an exception for employees earning in the top 10% of the employer's workforce. It is not necessary to reinstate them after leave if reinstatement would cause "substantial and grievous economic injury" to the employer, and the employer promptly notifies the employee that reinstatement will be denied.

However, taking FMLA leave does not entitle any employee to anything he or she would not have been entitled to by remaining at work without taking leave, and seniority and employment benefits do not have to accrue during the leave.

If the employee never does return from leave (for instance, the mother of a newborn decides to stay at home with the baby), the employer is entitled to recoup health insurance premiums paid during the leave, as long as the failure to return is not caused by ill health or other factors beyond the control of the employee.

When an employee has been pronounced fit for work by his or her doctor and returns to work, the employer can require another medical examination only if the employee's behavior justifies an inference of ongoing limitations that interfere with the ability to work. [*Albert v. Runyon*, 6 F. Supp. 2d 57 (D. Mass. 1998)]. According to *Underhill v. Willamina Lumber Co.* [1999 WL 421596 (D. Ore. 1999)], the employer's duty is to reinstate the worker; if there is a reasonable doubt about ability to return to work, the employer can then ask for an independent examination of fitness for duty. It is not acceptable to delay reinstatement until the examination has been completed to the satisfaction of the employer.

In the First Circuit view, there is no duty of reasonable accommodation under the FMLA—so it is not unlawful to fire an employee who is on medical leave. Anyone who is on FMLA leave can be laid off during a RIF, if he or she would have been laid off anyway. [*O'Connor v. PLA Family Health Plan Inc.*, 200 F.3d 1349 (11th Cir. 2000)]

If a person's work performance is bad enough to justify termination anyway, it does not violate the FMLA to terminate that person while he or she is on FMLA leave. [*Hubbard v. Blue Cross/Blue Shield Ass'n*, 1 F. Supp. 2d 867 (N.D. Ill. 1998)]

When there is no reason to believe that the individual will be able to return to work and perform the essential functions of the job within the 12-week leave period, the individual is not protected by the FMLA. [*Reynolds v. Phillips & Temro Indus. Inc.*, 195 F.3d 411 (8th Cir. 1999)] Here, the plaintiff applied for no-fault insurance economic loss benefits, which included a doctor's certification of continuing disability that would preclude his return to his normal occupation.

After returning from leave, an employee suffering from multiple sclerosis was able to work only a four-day week. Instead of reinstating her to her old job as purchasing agent, the employer placed her as a payroll clerk until her intermittent leave allowance was used up. She was told she would be placed on unpaid leave until a suitable job opened up. The plaintiff quit and sued, claiming that the FMLA entitled her to reinstatement in her former position. But the court in *Covey v. Methodist Hospital of Dyersburg* [56 F. Supp. 2d 965 (W.D. Tenn. 1999)] disagreed. The court read 29 C.F.R. § 825.204(a) to mean that reinstatement is required if—but only if—the employee is able to work a full normal schedule. Employees on intermittent leave can be transferred to any available position that satisfies the employee's need for time off.

There was another issue in this case. The plaintiff said that, while the FMLA permitted the employer to put her on unpaid leave, the employer's own policy was more generous. The employer prevailed on this issue too. The court said that employees cannot sue under the FMLA to enforce the employer's own policies. The remedy, if any, is a suit for breach of contract.

There were two major issues in *Hunt v. Rapides Healthcare System Inc.* [277 F.3d 757 (5th Cir. 2001)] The first was whether the plaintiff made a reinstatement request before or after her FMLA leave expired. The second was whether the job she received (part-time, as-needed shifts in the unit she preferred, at lower pay and without health, retirement, or leave benefits) was equivalent to her preleave position, or whether it was adverse job action taken in retaliation against her use of FMLA leave. The plaintiff, a critical care nurse, turned down the offer of a full-time night shift job because she was a single mother who needed to be home at night; her day-shift job had been assigned to another worker, so it was not vacant or available for her to return to.

The FMLA Regulations say, at 29 C.F.R. § 825.216(a)(2), that the basic rule is that an employee returning from FMLA leave is entitled to return to the same shift on an equivalent work schedule. The exception is if the worker's job has been eliminated, but this exception is not available if the job has simply been assigned to another employee.

The issue in this case was whether summary judgment should have been granted for the employer. The plaintiff was allowed to continue her case with respect to whether she was entitled to reinstatement and, if so, whether the employer satisfied its duty to reinstate her. But her claims of retaliation and constructive discharge were dismissed. The Fifth Circuit's position is that a shift change by itself is not an adverse employment action that will support a retaliation claim. [*Serna v. City of San Antonio*, 244 F.3d 479 (5th Cir. 2001); *Benningfield v. City of Houston*, 157 F.3d 369 (5th Cir. 1998)] Therefore, the plaintiff did not have a viable retaliation claim, because she could have accepted the night shift job without losing pay or benefits.

She lost her claim that she was constructively discharged when she took the part-time job with lower pay and fewer benefits because she could not take the full-time night shift position. In the Fifth Circuit, the test of constructive discharge is not whether the plaintiff felt compelled to resign, but whether a reasonable employee would have felt that way in the same situation.

§ 38.05   INTERMITTENT LEAVE

Section 2612(b) governs intermittent leave and leave that produces a reduced work schedule. The FMLA provides the equivalent of 12 weeks of work: up to 480 hours a year for full-time workers, and an equivalent prorated amount for part-time workers, such as 240 hours a year for someone who works a half-time schedule. The FMLA regulations [*see* 29 C.F.R. § 825.205(b)] refer to the actual number of hours the employee usually works in a week; or in an average week, if the schedule varies. Therefore, a person who is exempt from receiving overtime benefits but who typically works longer than 40 hours a week can get additional intermittent leave because of this work history.

Employers are not obligated to grant intermittent leave for cosmetic procedures. The general rule is that leave to care for a newly born or adopted child must be taken in a block of time off, and not on an intermittent or reduced schedule—unless the employer agrees to the special schedule. Intermittent leave for parents can be denied unless the child has a serious health condition, or unless a pregnant employee has severe morning sickness or needs time off for prenatal care. Leave premised on a serious health condition can be taken intermittently or on a reduced schedule when it is medically necessary.

It is permitted for the employer to use health-related intermittent/reduced leave to offset birth or adoption leave taken by the employee in the same year, but only to the actual extent of intermittent or reduced leave that was taken.

When a health-related intermittent leave can be predicted, based on scheduled medical treatment, the employer can lawfully transfer the employee to an available alternative position—as long as:

- The employee is qualified for the position;
- The two jobs are equivalent in pay and benefits;
- The second job provides a better accommodation to the changed work schedule than the first job did. [See 29 C.F.R. § 825.205]

Once the need for intermittent leave ends, the transferred employee must be offered reinstatement in the former job or a comparable job. It violates the FMLA for employers to use transfers deliberately to discourage the use of FMLA leave or to retaliate against employees who take or request leave.

Tip: The employer is allowed to set the minimum span of intermittent leave as the shortest period that the payroll system can accommodate. If the payroll system can only handle full days, then intermittent leave periods can be added up until they total a full day, at which point a day's pay can be deducted from the worker's paycheck. The employees should be given advance written notice if this is the policy, and they should be asked to sign the notice showing that they are aware of the policy.

---

§ 38.06   RELATING FMLA LEAVE TO PAID LEAVE

[A]   Generally

Because the employer can legally provide all FMLA leave on an unpaid basis, it is logical to allow the employer to provide paid leave for only part of the required FMLA leave period. Under § 2612(d), if the employer provides paid leave for part of the time, the balance of the 12 weeks can be unpaid. The employer can also require the employee (and the employee can elect) to receive payment for any part of the 12 FMLA weeks for which the employee has accrued vacation, personal, or family leave.

The same is true of substituting accrued paid vacation, personal, medical, or sick leave for unpaid FMLA leave based on a serious health condition. However, the FMLA does not require employers to adopt a policy of offering paid medical or sick leave if they did not already have such a policy.

The Eleventh Circuit says that employees are not required to use up their paid sick leave before taking FMLA leave. [*Strickland v. Water Works*, 239 F.3d 1199 (11th Cir. 2001)] The FMLA does not preempt a Wisconsin law that allows an employee to substitute any type of paid or unpaid leave for FMLA leave, on the grounds that Congress did not intend to preempt this type of additional protection. [*Aurora Med. Group v. Department of Workforce Development*, 612 N.W.2d 646 (Wis. 2000)]

The Ninth Circuit case of *Rowe v. Laidlaw Transit, Inc.* [244 F.3d 1115 (9th Cir. 2001)] explains that qualifying unpaid leave is protected under the FMLA, even if it is not specifically designated as such by the employee. The plaintiff in this case suffered a serious ankle injury. She used up her sick leave and vacation days. Her doctor said she could only work five hours a day, subject to restrictions. She asked for a part-time schedule. The employer agreed to a reduced schedule, and paid her on an hourly basis. The plaintiff did not ask for FMLA leave; the employer did not discuss the matter with her. When she could resume full-time work, the employer resumed paying her based on her salary before the injury. The employee quit the year after the injury and sued the employer for failure to pay overtime. The employer said that she was a supervisor, exempt from overtime payment.

The Ninth Circuit upheld the District Court, which said that the employee was entitled to FMLA leave because of the nature of her serious health condition, and under 29 C.F.R. § 825.208(c), employees are entitled to FMLA protection if the employer fails to notify an employee that his or her paid leave satisfies FMLA conditions after the employee has provided a reason for the leave that qualifies under the FMLA. Unpaid leave must be treated like paid leave for this purpose.

State law may require employers to provide intermittent leave on more generous terms than the FMLA does. If the employee is also a qualified person with a disability as defined by the ADA, then it may be necessary to grant even more than the equivalent of 12 weeks' intermittent leave as a reasonable accommodation.

Sometimes it is hard to distinguish between leave taken because of complications of pregnancy and leave taken to prepare for parenting. Under Wage and Hour Division regulations, FMLA leave is not available after the employee has taken a disability leave for pregnancy-related complications. However, if there is a post-delivery period when the mother is physically unable to work, that period can be counted as a leave for serious illness, even though it also represents parenting leave. This is especially significant if both parents work for the same employer and would otherwise have to split a single 12-week leave period.

If the state has a law obligating employers to provide paid or partially paid maternity leave, employees are entitled to unpaid FMLA law in addition to the paid leave required by state law. Furthermore, if the state has an FMLA-type law that extends coverage in circumstances that the federal law does not provide for (e.g., taking care of a friend or parent-in-law), the state-required leave is treated as if it were taken for non-FMLA purposes and therefore does not reduce the 12-week FMLA allowance.

[B]   ADA Interface

See 29 C.F.R. §§ 825.701 and .702 for a discussion of the relationship between the FMLA and the ADA. An employer can satisfy both statutes by offering a reduced work schedule to a disabled employee until he or she has used the 12 weeks of FMLA leave. After FMLA leave, employees are entitled to reinstatement in a job equivalent to the original job. The FMLA permits the employer to demand a physical exam to determine if a worker can be reinstated after a health-related FMLA leave. To satisfy the ADA as well, the examination must be job-related, not a comprehensive inventory of all physical conditions.

Although the two statutes were designed to accomplish different goals, workers sometimes find that FMLA leave is more accessible than taking time off as an ADA reasonable accommodation. Remember, FMLA leave is available when the employee is the sick person—not just when the employee is a caregiver.

Furthermore, if the company employs at least 50 people and the employee has put in the necessary 1,250 hours in the previous 12 months, entitlement to FMLA leave is automatic. The employer's discretion as to what constitutes a reasonable accommodation is not a factor. The right to reinstatement is also automatic. Employers can raise a defense of unreasonable hardship in ADA cases—but not in FMLA cases.

The Western District of Pennsylvania granted summary judgment for a clinically depressed nurse, finding that firing her violated the FMLA and the ADA. [*Wilson v. Leamington Home for the Aged*, Civil Action No. 99-1893 (W.D. Pa. June 25, 2001)] The employer said that FMLA leave was not provided because she did not ask for it specifically and did not disclose her doctor's diagnosis when she said she needed a month off (although she did say that she had suffered diarrhea, vomiting, and chest pains). But the District Court held that, when an employer knows that an employee has requested leave, it has an obligation to provide written notice of FMLA rights and responsibilities. The employer asked the employee for certification on December 19 and December 26. The employee responded that her doctor was out of the office until December 30. She was fired on December 19, and the employer treated her December 13 visit to the office to pick up personal items as a voluntary quit.

The Western District of Pennsylvania found direct evidence that the plaintiff was fired for exercising her FMLA rights. She was not properly notified of the certification requirements, so she could not legitimately be punished for not offering certification. It was improper to treat retrieval of personal items as resignation; in fact, the employer continued to ask for certification after the alleged resignation.

A disabled person's claims based on denial of a handicapped parking spot at work cannot be brought under both ADA Title I (employment) and Title III (public accommodations). According to *DeWyer v. Temple University* [*See* Shannon P. Duffy, *Federal Judge Throws Out Double ADA Claim*, The Legal Intelligencer (Feb. 8, 2001) (law.com)], the ADA was drafted to require all employment-related claims to be brought under Title I. Title III claims are available only to non-employees who have been denied their right to accessible public spaces.

A December 2001 case dismisses claims that the plaintiff's FMLA rights were "interfered with," because there was no actual violation of her FMLA rights. The plaintiff, who suffered from fibromyalgia and chronic fatigue syndrome, was allowed to pursue ADA claims (because her symptoms could substantially impair major life activities, in that she could not work overtime hours or travel on business). However, although she charged that the employer fired her because she was disabled and because she tried to exercise her FMLA rights (despite the employer's failure to provide required disclosure about the FMLA), the court did not accept this argument. The Eastern District of Pennsylvania's decision in *Alifano v. Merck & Co.* says that the FMLA (unlike the ADA) does not impose a duty on employers to offer reasonable accommodation to employees who return from leave. It does not violate the FMLA to terminate an employee who has taken FMLA leave—if the reason for the termination is that the employee is no longer capable of performing the essential functions of the job. [*See* Shannon P. Duffy, *Federal Judge Rejects Worker's Claim of "Interference" With FMLA Rights*, The Legal Intelligencer (Dec. 17, 2001) (law.com)]

[C] COBRA

An IRS Final Rule, published starting at 64 Fed. Reg. 5160 (Feb. 3, 1999), provides that merely taking FMLA leave is not a COBRA qualifying event. However, a qualifying event does occur with respect to an employee (and any dependents of the employee who are at risk of losing health coverage) who fails to return to work at the end of the FMLA leave. The typical example is a new mother who does not return to work after the end of maternity leave.

Under the Final Rule, the COBRA qualifying event occurs on the last day of the FMLA leave. The employer is not allowed to condition the COBRA election on the employee paying the EGHP back for premiums paid on his or her behalf during the leave. However, if the employer has actually terminated coverage under the group plan for the whole class of employees that the employee belonged to before the FMLA leave, continuation coverage does not have to be offered to employees who do not return from leave.

[D] Cafeteria Plans

The IRS published Final Regulations, effective October 17, 2001, applicable for cafeteria plan years beginning on or after January 1, 2002, explicating the FMLA obligations of cafeteria plans. [*See* T.D. 8966, RIN 1545-AT47, 66 Fed. Reg. 52676]

> **Tip:** The law firm of Ballard Spahr Andrews & Ingersoll, LLP has a good Web-based explanation of these Regulations. [*See FMLA and Cafeteria Plan Elections* (Dec. 2001) <http://www.ballardspahr.com/press/article.asp?ID=299>]

The Final Regulations are based, with some significant changes, on a set of 1995 Proposed Regulations. The Final Rule states that the basic FMLA obligation is to offer coverage under any group health plan as long as the employee is on paid or unpaid leave, on the same conditions as coverage would have been provided if the employee had continued to work during the leave period.

When the employee is on unpaid FMLA leave, the employer must either allow the employee to revoke the coverage or continue coverage but stop contributing premiums to the plan. The employer can then maintain the coverage by taking over both the employer and the employee share of the premium. The employer can recover the employee share of contributions when the employee returns from the leave. If the employee does not return, 29 C.F.R. § 825.213(a) permits the employer to recover both the employer and the employee shares of the premium from the employee. However, an employee who directed that premium payments be discontinued cannot be required to make contributions until after the end of unpaid leave.

One difference between the Final Rule and the Proposed Regulations is that, under the Final Rule, employers can require employees who return from unpaid FMLA leave to resume participation in the plan, if the employer imposes the same requirement on employees returning from non-FMLA leave.

When an employee is not covered under an FSA (Flexible Spending Account) during leave either because the employee revoked coverage or because he or she failed to pay premiums, the employer must provide a choice between resuming the original level of coverage by making up for the missed premium payments, or resuming coverage at a prorated reduced level and resuming the original level of premium payments.

On the other hand, if FSA coverage continued during the FMLA leave, there is no proration. Employees on FMLA leave have the same rights during the leave period as cafeteria plan participants who are not on leave—including the same rights to enroll or change elections as any active employee. [*See* Treas. Reg. § 1.125-4(g)] This Final Rule supplements T.D. 8878 [65 Fed. Reg. 15548 (March 2000)] and T.D. 8921 [66 Fed. Reg. 1837 (Jan. 2001)] with respect to changes in cafeteria plan elections made during a plan year.

[E] Fair Labor Standards Act

A 1998 Opinion Letter from the Department of Labor [Opinion Letter #89 (1998)] says that salaried workers who are exempt from the FLSA (and therefore are not entitled to overtime pay) are not entitled to FLSA protection merely because their employer docks their paychecks to reflect unpaid FMLA leave, even though pay deductions for absence are more characteristic of FLSA-covered wage workers than of "exempts."

§ 38.07 NOTIFYING THE EMPLOYER

No one schedules an emergency, of course. However, treatment for some serious health conditions is scheduled in advance (e.g., elective surgery). Section 2612(e) requires the employee to give at least 30 days' notice before leave based on the expected due date of a baby, or the expected placement date for adoption or foster care. If the date of birth or placement is less than 30 days from the time the employee decides to apply for FMLA leave, the employee must give as much notice as is practicable.

The FMLA imposes a duty on employees taking leave based on planned medical treatment to make reasonable efforts to schedule the treatment in the way that causes the least disruption to the employer (as long as this does not endanger the sick person's health). The employee should provide at least 30 days' notice before the leave is scheduled to begin—but if the need for the treatment becomes known less than 30 days in advance, the employee must provide as much notice as is practicable.

The case of *Satterfield v. Wal-Mart Stores Inc.* [135 F.3d 973 (5th Cir. 1998)] involved an employee who did not have a telephone. She sent a note telling the employer she could not come in to work because of a pain in her side. She did not communicate with the employer at all for 12 days, after she had been operated on. This was her fourth unexcused absence in three weeks, so she was fired. The Fifth Circuit ruled that she did not even give the employer enough notice to trigger a duty to investigate her need for FMLA leave. Her prior unexcused absences made it reasonable for the employer to conclude that she was merely being irresponsible, not in need of medical leave.

Although depression is a "serious illness" that can trigger FMLA rights, the employee in *Collins v. NTN-Bower Corp.* [272 F.3d 1006 (7th Cir. 2001)] merely called in "sick" and did not cite depression as an explanation for her poor attendance record. The employer had no way of knowing that FMLA leave might have been appropriate, and therefore did not violate the FMLA for firing the employee for poor attendance.

§ 38.08 CERTIFICATION OF HEALTH CARE LEAVE

Employers have the right, under 29 U.S.C. § 2613, to require employees to prove that their request for medical leave is supported by a health care provider. This process is called certification. Employees have a duty to furnish the employer with a copy of the certification document, in a timely manner. (The best time for the employer to ask for certification is the time when the employee requests the leave, but the employer can defer the request for up to two days; the employee has 15 days to produce the certification.)

Appendix B to 29 C.F.R. Part 825 is an official form that can be used for certification. Employers and doctors can draft their own forms, but employers do not have the right to demand more information than the official form requires. An adequate certification provides at least this much information:

- The date when the serious health condition started;
- How long the health care provider predicts it will continue;
- The medical facts the health care provider has about the condition;
- Either a statement that the employee is too sick to carry out the functions of the job or that the employee is needed as a caregiver for an eligible family member (and how long the need for care is expected to continue);
- (If the employee wants intermittent leave or a reduced schedule for medical treatment such as cancer chemotherapy) how long the treatment is expected to last; the dates of the scheduled treatment;
- (For intermittent leave/reduced schedules in general) why the leave is medically necessary; how long it is expected to continue necessary.

If the employer has reason to doubt that the certification is valid, the employer has the right to demand (but will then have to pay for) a second opinion from a health care provider selected by the employer. The health care provider must be independent—not an employee of the employer company (i.e., the company physician is not allowed to take on this role). If the certification and the second opinion disagree about the need for the leave, then the employer can demand a third opinion from a health care provider agreed on by both the employer and the employee. The third opinion is final and binding on both employer and employee.

The employer can require further recertifications on a reasonable basis. Under 29 U.S.C. § 2613(a) and 29 C.F.R. § 825.308, demanding certification more often than once every 30 days will be considered unreasonable unless:

- The employee requested an extension of the leave;
- Circumstances have changed, making the original certification inaccurate;
- The employer has learned something that casts doubt on the original certification.

At the other end of the process, the employer is entitled to impose a policy (as long as it is uniformly applied) requiring employees returning from FMLA leave based on their own serious medical conditions to present written certification from their health care provider that they are fit to return to work. [29 U.S.C. § 2614(a)(4)]

If the employee's doctor reports that there is no need for leave, the employer is entitled to rely on that and deny the leave request. The plaintiff cannot claim that circumstances changed since the medical consultation. *Stoops v. One Call Com-*

munications, Inc. [141 F.3d 309 (7th Cir. 1997)] says that the employee should have gotten an undated medical certificate instead.

It is improper for the employer to fire the employee for failure to provide adequate certification if the employer has not given the employee the amount of time provided by the FMLA (15 days for initial certification; recertification no more than every 30 days). As *LeGrand v. Village of McCook* [1998 WL 182462 (N.D. Ill. 1998)] points out, reducing the time frame makes it impossible to determine if the employee could have assembled the necessary proof in time.

An employer who doubts the accuracy of a medical certification (or questions whether the need for leave continues as long as the employee says it does) should be sure to ask for a second opinion right away. Failure to do so might prevent a courtroom challenge to the medical findings, although *Rhoads v. FDIC* [257 F.3d 373 (4th Cir. 2001)] says that it will not.

§ 38.09   DISCLOSURE TO EMPLOYEES

Employers have an obligation to post the standard EEOC notice to inform employees of their rights under the FMLA. Failure to do so can result in a civil penalty of up to $100 per offense. [29 U.S.C. § 2619] The notice, which must be at least 8½ × 11″, can be obtained from the local office of the DOL Wage and Hour Division, or can be enlarged and copied from 29 C.F.R. Part 825, Appendix C. Employers who employ a significant number of people who are literate in a language other than English must also post a translation of the notice into that language.

Companies that have employee handbooks must include FMLA information in the handbook. Even if there is no handbook, employees who actually request leave are entitled to a written explanation of their rights. Employers who have not satisfied the posting requirement can make up for this deficiency by providing adequate written notice at the time of a request for leave. [*Fry v. First Fidelity Bancorp.*, 67 EPD ¶43,943]

According to 29 C.F.R. § 825.301(b)(1), the employer's FMLA notice to employees must provide at least this much information:

- That the requested leave reduces the employee's "bank" of FMLA leave for the year;
- Whether the employer requires medical certification of the serious health condition; consequences if the certification is not provided;
- The fact that employees who are entitled to paid leave have a right to substitute paid leave for FMLA leave; the conditions under which the employer will substitute paid leave on its own initiative;
- The employee's right to be reinstated in a comparable job after returning from leave;
- The method for the employee to pay health premiums while he or she is on FMLA leave;

- Disclosure of the employee's obligation to reimburse the employer for premiums if the employee does not return to work after the leave;
- Any requirements for proving fitness for duty before returning to work;
- (For key employees) limitations on the right to reinstatement.

Tip: It is not a substitute for the required notice, but employees can be referred to the DOL's toll-free FMLA hotline, (800) 959-FMLA, for more information. FMLA information intended for employees can also be found at <http://www.dol.gov>.

A statement in the employee handbook that employees can take up to 12 weeks of FMLA leave in any 12-month period is inadequate because it fails to explain how the employer calculates the 12-month period. Therefore, the Ninth Circuit did not permit the employer to fire the plaintiff for taking too much sick leave. [*Bachelder v. America West Airlines, Inc.*, 259 F.3d 1112 (9th Cir. 2001)]

As noted above, in March 2002, the Supreme Court's decision in *Ragsdale v. Wolverine Worldwide, Inc.* struck down the DOL's regulation at 29 C.F.R. § 825.208 (saying that, where the employer fails to notify employees that FMLA leave will run concurrently with other leave—for example, paid sick leave—the two leave periods must be permitted to run consecutively, thereby increasing the amount of leave the employee can take.) The Supreme Court adopted the position of the Eighth and Eleventh Circuits, disagreeing with the Sixth Circuit, which found the rule to be valid. [*See Ragsdale v. Wolverine Worldwide Inc.*, 218 F.3d 933 (8th Cir. 2000); *McGregor v. AutoZone Inc.*, 180 F.3d 1305 (11th Cir. 1999); *Plant v. Morton International Inc.*, 212 F.3d 929 (6th Cir. 2000)]

Another regulation, 29 C.F.R. § 815.1100(d) says that employers that fail to respond promptly to FMLA leave requests may be compelled to provide leave that would otherwise be unavailable. Two Circuits—the Seventh and Eleventh—found this regulation invalid and unenforceable and are discussed below.

Dormeyer v. Comerica Bank-Illinois [223 F.3d 579 (7th Cir. 2000)] holds that the DOL did not have the authority to promulgate this regulation, which is unreasonable because it forces employers to provide benefits to which employees would not otherwise be entitled. The Eleventh Circuit held that the regulation is invalid because it alters the terms of the statute as passed by Congress. [*Brungart v. Bell South Telecommunications Inc.*, 231 F.3d 791 (11th Cir. 2000)]

Yet the District Court for the District of New Hampshire upheld another DOL regulation, 29 C.F.R. § 825.219(a), which requires the employer to reinstate a highly paid employee returning from FMLA leave, even if the job has been eliminated and the company undergoes substantial and grievous economic injury—if the employer failed to inform the employee of his key-employee status and discuss the implications of this status when he requested FMLA leave. [*Panza v. Grappone Co.*, 69 L.W. 1272 (D.N.H. Oct. 20, 2000)]

29 C.F.R. § 110(d) says that the employer is not allowed to challenge eligi-

bility for leave once it has confirmed that the employee is entitled to it. But the court in *Seaman v. Downtown Partnership of Baltimore Inc.* [991 F. Supp. 751 (D. Md. 1998)] ruled that this regulation is invalid—it goes too far, because it usurps Congress' authority to set policy. [*See* Deborah Billings, *DOL Rule on Employer Notification Duty to Employees on FMLA Leave Under Attack*, 67 L.W. 2419 (Jan. 26, 1999)]

§ 38.10 ADMINISTRATIVE REQUIREMENTS

The Department of Labor's investigative authority under the FMLA is the same as its authority under FLSA § 11(a), including subpoena power. Employers have a duty to make and retain records showing FMLA compliance. The general rule is that the DOL can only require employers and employee plans to submit books and records once a year, unless the DOL is investigating a charge made by an employee, or has reason to believe that there has been an FMLA violation. [29 U.S.C. § 2616]

§ 38.11 FMLA ENFORCEMENT

Employees are allowed to sue employers for FMLA violations. Employees can sue on their own behalf or on behalf of other similarly situated employees. FMLA suits (like Title VII, FLSA, ADEA, and NLRA suits) can be brought by ex-employees charging retaliation for exercising their FMLA rights; the cause of action is not limited to current employees. [*Smith v. Bellsouth Telecommunications, Inc.*, 273 F.3d 1303 (11th Cir. 2001)] *Duckworth v. Pratt & Whitney* [152 F.3d 1 (1st Cir. 1998)] also allows ex-employees to bring FMLA suits.

If the employees win, 29 U.S.C. § 2617(a) provides that the court can order damages equal to the wages and benefits that the employee lost as a result of the violation. Even employees who have not lost compensation can receive damages to compensate them for financial losses (such as costs of hiring someone to care for sick relatives), but damages of this type are limited to 12 weeks' salary for the employee-plaintiff.

According to *Barrilleaux v. Thayer Lodging Groups Inc.* [1998 WL 61481 (E.D. La. 1998)], someone who sues for lost wages is not entitled to be compensated for care costs too.

Furthermore, winning FMLA plaintiffs can receive double damages: their damages (plus interest) and also an equal amount of liquidated damages. However, if the employer can prove that it acted in good faith and reasonably believed that it was in compliance with the FMLA, the court has discretion not to order double damages.

There is no statutory definition of "good faith," so the Western District of Missouri adopted the FLSA standard: whether the defendant made a good-faith effort to determine and observe the rights of the plaintiff. [*Morris v. VCW Inc.*, 1996 WL 740544 (W.D. Mo. 1996)]

Although most of the remedies are equitable ones, the Southern District of Georgia allows jury trials in FMLA cases, because they are allowed in Fair Labor Standards Act cases, and the two statutes contain many similar provisions. [*Helmly v. Stone Container Corp.*, 957 F. Supp. 1274 (S.D. Ga. 1997)] So does the Sixth Circuit. [*Frizzell v. Southwester Motor Freight*, 154 F.3d 641 (6th Cir. 1998)]

According to *Petsche v. Home Federal Savings Bank* [952 F. Supp. 536 (N.D. Ohio 1997)], the burden-shifting analysis used in Title VII cases also applies to the FMLA. Once the employee makes a prima facie case that the employer has violated the FMLA, the employer has to introduce evidence that the action taken against the employee did not constitute retaliation for exercising FMLA rights. However, *Diaz v. Fort Wayne Foundry Corp.* [131 F.3d 711 (7th Cir. 1997)] reaches precisely the opposite conclusion: that burden-shifting analysis doesn't apply. Instead, the FMLA plaintiff's obligation is to prove, by preponderance of the evidence, that his or her discharge violated FMLA rights.

Working conditions, not just demotions or pay cuts, can support an FMLA retaliation claim. [*Hite v. Biomet Inc.*, 38 F. Supp. 2d 720 (N.D. Ind. 1999)]

In one case, *McDonnell v. Miller Oil Co.* [110 F.3d 60 (4th Cir. 1997)], the jury believed the plaintiff's claim that she was fired for exercising FMLA rights in connection with maternity leave. However, the jury did not award any damages, because the plaintiff failed to make a reasonable effort to get another job.

In addition to money damages, courts in FMLA cases can award the appropriate equitable relief for the case, including hiring, reinstatement, and promotion. FMLA winners are entitled to receive reasonable costs, defined to include attorneys' fees and expert witness fees. Section 2617(a)(3) makes this automatic for plaintiffs who win, not a matter of discretion for the court.

This is not true of all federal statutes. Some of them do not allow attorneys' fee awards at all, others allow a fee award to any prevailing party (plaintiff or defendant) or leave it up to the court whether an award should be made, or limit fee awards to cases in which the losing party's conduct has been outrageous.

Not only do employers face FMLA suits from employees or groups of employees; they can also be sued by the Department of Labor, which can sue on behalf of employees to recover the same kind of damages employees would get. If the DOL wins an FMLA case, the damages got to the employee, not to the government agency (unless it is impossible to locate the employees within three years). [*See* 29 U.S.C. § 2617(b)] The Secretary of Labor has the power to investigate and try to resolve complaints of FMLA violations, to the same degree as investigations and resolutions of violations of FLSA §§ 6 and 7. But employees are no longer allowed to bring FMLA suits once the DOL starts a suit. [29 U.S.C. § 2617(a)(4)]

The Southern District of New York held that a state human rights agency's determination that an employer had a valid business reason for eliminating the employee's job while she was out on FMLA leave would preclude the employee from suing under the FMLA, claiming that eliminating the job discriminated against her for exercising FMLA rights. (The legal concept in question is called "collateral estoppel.") But when the case was appealed, the Second Circuit held that the state agency case did not involve a formal hearing, an attorney for the claimant, or full discovery. The issue of business justification was not fully explored, much less settled, so the issue was properly brought before the federal court. [*Kosakow v. New Rochelle Radiology Assocs.*, 88 F. Supp. 2d 199 (S.D.N.Y. 2000), *vacated and remanded*, 274 F.3d 706 (2d Cir. 2001)]

PART VIII

PROCEDURE FOR HANDLING DISCRIMINATION CHARGES

CHAPTER 39
WRONGFUL TERMINATION AND AT-WILL EMPLOYMENT

§ 39.01   INTRODUCTION

Employees always have the right to quit their jobs, no matter how inconvenient their departure may be for the employer (although employment contracts can require a certain amount of notice, can obligate the employee to compensate the employer for economic loss caused by a resignation, and can impose reasonable restrictions on re-employment and use of the employer's proprietary information).

The employer's right to fire an employee is not so simple and clear-cut. Some employees have written contracts that specify the conditions under which they can be terminated. Unionized employees are covered by collective bargaining agreements (CBAs). In CBAs or individual employment contracts, if the agreement sets out a termination procedure (such as a warning, then a chance for the employee to respond to charges, a suspension, and then termination), then it is a breach of contract to terminate the employee without following the procedure.

Employers may also find that they are subject to responsibilities under implied contracts. The employer's written documents that it issues such as the employee handbook or even its oral statements are deemed to constitute a legally enforceable contract, then the employer will have to abide by that contract.

Tip: Severance pay will probably not have to be given to an employee who is discharged for good cause—unless there is an implied contract to provide severance.

A supervisor is a representative of the employer when he or she is acting in the scope of his or her job, in a situation in which he or she is authorized to act. The supervisor's conduct will then have legal implications for the employer. A supervisor's negligence or outrageous conduct (such as abusive treatment of an employee that results in emotional distress) can be imputed to the employer. In many instances, the supervisor will *not* be personally liable, e.g., under federal and state antidiscrimination statutes or for inducing a breach of contract.

Even if termination is justifiable, however, it must be carried out in a reasonable manner, avoiding intentional infliction of emotional distress. The employer must also avoid both actionable defamation (destructive false statements) and depriving another employer of the accurate information needed to make a rational hiring decision.

"Constructive discharge" is the legal concept that an employee who responds to intolerable conditions by quitting is entitled to be treated as if he or she had been fired, because the employer's conduct was the equivalent of a discharge. To prove constructive discharge, the employee does not have to prove that the employer intended to force a resignation, only that it was reasonably foreseeable that a reasonable employee would quit under the same circumstances.

The vast majority of employees do not have a written contract. They are legally defined as "at-will" employees who work "at the will of the employer." However, at-will employers are not permitted to discharge employees for reasons that violate an antidiscrimination statute, or for reasons contrary to public policy.

Employees who want to bring suit under federal antidiscrimination laws (Title VII, the ADA, the ADEA, and the FMLA) have to satisfy elaborate procedural requirements. [*See* Chapters 40 and 41] Employees who charge the employer with wrongful termination merely have to go to state court and file a complaint. This is much easier to do, so employers may find themselves fighting on two fronts, or may be able to raise the argument that a wrongful termination case should be dismissed because the employee was required—but failed—to use the procedure for a discrimination suit.

§ 39.02   EMPLOYEE TENURE

The courts of some states (e.g., California) may treat the fact that an employee has worked for an employer for a long time as an implied promise of continuing employment. Especially if tenure has been very long (for instance, a decade or more), the state may impose an implied covenant of good faith and fair dealing. This has been done in Alabama, Alaska, Arizona, California, Connecticut, Delaware, Idaho, Massachusetts, Montana, Nevada, New Hampshire, New Jersey, New Mexico, South Carolina, Utah, and Wyoming.

This line of cases deems the employer to have implied a promise to treat the employee fairly and to avoid bad faith. This implied covenant has been held to invalidate the firing of some long-term workers, at least without the corporate equivalent of due process of law.

However, courts in other states, including Florida, Kansas, Michigan, Minnesota, Missouri, Nebraska, New York, Oklahoma, Texas, and Washington have rejected the implied covenant theory.

Nearly all of the states recognize a public policy exception (i.e., that it is illegal to fire even an at-will employee if the rationale for the firing violates public policy). The minority states that do not recognize this theory are Alabama, Florida, Georgia, Louisiana, Maine, Nebraska, New York, and Rhode Island. [*See* Charles J. Muhl, *The Employment-at-Will Doctrine: Three Major Exceptions*, Monthly Labor Review (Jan. 2001) <http://www.bls.gov/opub/mlr/2001/01/art1full.pdf>]

In a 1998 case, a church employee was fired when the priest observed him receiving illegal anabolic steroids at the church. The employee brought suit, alleging breach of his written contract, which called for 30 days' notice of termination. Naturally, he lost his case. The New Jersey court required both employer and employee to operate in good faith. The employee's serious violation of his obligation relieved the church of its obligation to give notice. [*McGarry v. St. Anthony of Padua Roman Catholic Church*, 307 N.J. Super. 525, 704 A.3d 1353 (1998)]

§ 39.03   PROMISSORY ESTOPPEL

The theory of "promissory estoppel" is sometimes decisive in employment cases. The theory is that the employer's promise to the employee estops (precludes) the employer from disavowing that promise, often because the employee has "undergone detrimental reliance" (suffered in some way after relying on a statement or implication from the employer).

The classic example is a top executive recruited from another company, who gives up a high salary and stock options, has expenses of relocation, and then is fired shortly after taking up the new job.

In a 1994 Alabama case, the plaintiff won a claim for fraud in the inducement of contract because the employer lied about the facts she relied on in quitting her old job and going to work for the defendant company. A year later, another Alabama case imposed another requirement that plaintiffs must meet to prevail: the employer's promises must have been made with the intent to deceive. [*Kidder v. American South Bank,* 639 So. 2d 1361 (Ala. 1994); *National Security Ins. Co. v. Donaldson,* 664 So. 2d 871 (Ala. 1995)]

In a Colorado case, a company recruited one of its competitor's employees to open a new office. She was hesitant about leaving an established firm for a start-up, so they promised her that her new job would be much better in the long run than the old one. The new office closed in two months, and she was fired. The court decided that she was promised a "reasonable" term of employment, which the court interpreted to mean one year. [*Pickell v. Arizona Components Co.,* 931 P.2d 1184 (Colo. 1997)]

A Wisconsin case says that there is no breach of contract if an oral offer of at-will employment for an indefinite period is made and then withdrawn before the potential employee starts work [*Heinritz v. Lawrence Univ.,* 194 Wis. 2d 607, 535 N.W.2d 81 (Wis. App. 1995)]—a situation faced by many 2001 and 2002 graduates.

When an oral promise of continued employment was made to induce an employee to remain at her job during a merger so she could assist the transition team, her continued service with the company and surrender of the opportunity to look for another job were found to create an implied contract. [*Rinck v. Association of Reserve City Bankers,* 676 A.2d 12 (D.C. App. 1996)]

In contrast, Illinois says that an oral "contract" cannot be enforced because of a legal concept called the Statute of Frauds that requires all contracts lasting a year or more to be in writing in order to be enforceable. [*McInerney v. Chater Golf Inc.,* 176 Ill. 2d 482, 680 N.E.2d 1347 (1997)]

An employee may claim to have provided consideration for a promise of lifetime employment, by staying on the job and not pursuing other opportunities. But some courts say that a person can only hold one job at a time anyway, and therefore does not surrender any rights that would support a promise of lifetime employment. [*Bynum v. Boeing Co.,* 85 Wash. App. 1065 (1997)]

§ 39.04   PUBLIC POLICY

[A]   Generally

A whole line of cases permits employees to sue when they are fired for a reason contrary to the public policy of the state. In other words, it is unlawful to fire an employee for doing something that is acceptable or even admirable. For instance, no matter how inconvenient the timing is for the employer, it is not permitted to fire an employee for serving jury duty.

It violates ERISA § 510 to fire an employee merely to prevent access to pension or welfare benefits. [*See* Chapter 15]

It has often been argued that states have a policy of promoting equal employment opportunity, so any discriminatory discharge would have to violate state policy. However, this argument usually is not successful. For instance, a 1996 Oklahoma case says that state laws against age discrimination prevent a discharged employee from suing for wrongful termination on this basis. [*List v. Anchor Paint Mfg.* Co., 910 P.2d 1011 (Okla. Sup. Jan. 9, 1996)]

The First Amendment free speech rights of a welfare department investigator were not violated when she was fired for making a racist joke at an off-duty political dinner. According to the Massachusetts court, she was not making a speech on a matter of public concern (which would have been protected), and racism can undermine the agency's mission. [*Pereira v. Commissioner of Social Servs.*, 733 N.E.2d 112 (Mass. 2000)]

In Maryland, an employee fired for refusing to have sex with a harasser can add a tort claim for abusive discharge to the sexual harassment suit, because the harasser's action violates the public policy against prostitution. (In effect, an employee who has sexual relations to keep a job is unlawfully engaging in sex for pay). [*Insignia Residential Corp. v. Ashton, Maryland*, 755 A.2d 1080 (Md. 2000)]

The plaintiff in *Lagatree v. Luce, Forward, Hamilton & Scripps* [88 Cal. Rptr. 2d 664 (Cal. App. Sept. 13, 1999)] was fired for refusing to sign a mandatory predispute arbitration agreement covering all job-related claims. He alleged that imposing an arbitration requirement on unwilling employees violates public policy. The California Court of Appeals did not accept this argument, holding that, in fact, public policy favors arbitration.

The employer claimed that the plaintiff in *Daley v. Aetna Life & Casualty* [249 Conn. 766 (1999)] was fired for incompetence. But even if her contention (that she was fired for asking for a family-friendly work schedule) was correct, she would not be able to assert a wrongful termination claim. Although it is meritorious of employers to offer a flexible work schedule, they are not obligated to do so, and not doing so is not a violation of public policy.

[B]   Whistleblower Employees

The case of the "whistleblower" employee is more complex. Employees (often those who are dissatisfied for other reasons) go to the press, or file complaints with enforcement agencies, about some aspect of corporate conduct they find unsatisfactory. In some instances, firing (or taking other adverse employment action) against whistleblowers violates public policy, because in appropriate cases, whistleblowers are exposing violations of law or other improprieties.

At the end of 1998, the Supreme Court held that an action under 42 U.S.C. § 1985 (damage to person or property) can be maintained by an at-will employee who alleges that he was fired for assisting a federal criminal investigation of the employer company [*Haddle v. Garrison*, 525 U.S. 121 (1998)]

Some states have statutes extending specific protection to whistle-blower employees. However, some of these statutes apply only to government workers, not employees of private-sector companies. The trend in the courts is to limit the number of situations in which employees will be considered protected whistleblowers.

For instance, the FDA regulations require reporting of research results that demonstrate a serious risk. A drug company director of research was fired for insisting that some test results be reported, when company officials did not think that the results were poor enough to be reported. The research director lost his wrongful discharge case. In the court's view, there had simply been a difference of opinion, and it is legitimate to fire someone for exercising poor judgment. [*Chelly v. Knoll Pharmaceuticals*, 295 N.J. Super. 478, 685 A.2d 498 (1996)]

A Colorado employee was fired for sending a letter to a newspaper criticizing the employer's business practices. A Colorado statute makes it unlawful to fire anyone for lawful activity carried on outside the workplace, but that statute has an exception for bona fide occupational qualifications. The District Court for the District of Colorado read this to mean that employers are entitled to an implied right of loyalty in public communications. The employee wasn't entitled to whistle-blower protection. He failed to use the internal grievance procedure (which he probably would have done if he had a good-faith objective of solving the problem) and what was at issue was customer service quality, not public safety. [*Marsh v. Delta Air Lines Inc.*, 952 F. Supp. 1458 (D. Colo. Feb. 7, 1997)]

A Texas nurse reported a co-employee's apparent drug use at work and mishandling of prescription drugs. But it was not the alleged drug user who got fired—it was the reporting nurse. The nurse lost a whistleblower action in state court. Although the Texas Supreme Court agreed that protection of the safety of hospital patients is part of public policy, it also held that Texas legislators have limited whistleblower protection to specific context, but there is no general protection for employees discharged for reporting wrongdoing in the workplace. [*Austin v. Healthtrust, Inc.*, 967 S.W.2d 400 (Tex. 1998)]

In general, Wisconsin is not hospitable to whistleblower claims. Employees can be fired for complying with a law (but not for refusing to break one). Most whistleblower claims involve reporting of wrongdoing. However, in 1997, the state's Supreme Court created a special exemption, allowing wrongful discharge suits only by nursing home whistleblowers. [*Hausman v. St. Croix Care Ctr.*, 571 N.W.2d 393 (Wis. 1997)]

A quality control inspector said that she informed management about tainted meat, but was ignored. She contacted government inspectors, who found deficiencies in the plant. She was ordered not to contact the inspectors again. She was fired when the employer suspected her of "leaking" information to the inspectors. Her wrongful termination/whistleblower suit was unsuccessful. The court said that it was legitimate to fire her for disobeying an order to avoid further contact with inspectors. [*Dray v. New Market Poultry Prods. Inc.*, 518 S.E.2d 312 (Va. 1999)]

A fired whistleblower brought, and settled, a False Claims Act qui tam action against the ex-employer. (A qui tam action is brought to challenge alleged wrongdoing.) The Eleventh Circuit ruled that he could bring a later False Claims Act retaliation action. The qui tam and retaliation claims are based on the same facts, and the firing had already occurred, so both claims should have been resolved at the same time. The legal doctrine of res judicata ("matter already decided") prevented him from pursuing the retaliation claim.

Peggy Farrior, a one-time secretary for a Connecticut school board, brought a 42 U.S.C. § 1983 case against her ex-employer, charging harassment and retaliation for blowing the whistle on irregularities in purchasing and accounting. The ex-employer said that it had legitimate reasons to fire her for being rude and disruptive. In 1998, a federal jury awarded her $42,534 for lost wages and $118,940 for emotional harm. However, in 1999, District Judge Alvin W. Thompson, considering evidence about the plaintiff's angry and rude behavior, including taking two weeks off after an argument, threw out the jury verdict on the grounds that it was against the weight of the evidence. He granted a new trial, which resulted in a verdict for the employer in December 2000. Therefore, no conclusions should be drawn about the outcome of a case until it has been carried through to a complete resolution. [*See* Thomas Sheffey, *561,000 Whistleblower Verdict Cut to $0*, Connecticut Law Tribune (Jan. 8, 2001) (law.com)]

Courts have said that "wrongful discharge" means just that: There is no cause of action for wrongful transfer if there is no loss of salary or benefits. In the case of *White v. State of Washington* [131 Wash. 2d 1 (Wash. 1997)], the plaintiff reported what she perceived to be patient abuse to the state nursing home regulators. In this analysis, she did not lose any money, so no legally enforceable rights had been violated.

[C] WC Claimants

The Pennsylvania Worker's Compensation statute doesn't say in so many words that it is illegal for employers to retaliate against employees who file Worker's Compensation claims. Nevertheless, employees in this situation are allowed to bring wrongful discharge claims, on the grounds that the legislature did not rule out retaliation actions—it just failed to make explicit provisions for them. [*Shick v. Shirey*, 716 A.2d 1231 (Pa. 1998)]

Worker's Compensation was also involved in the case of *Lins v. Children's Discovery Center of America, Inc.* [95 Wash. App. 486 (1999)] The plaintiff was a manager with responsibility for six day care centers. She and five other employees were hurt in a work-related automobile accident. All six filed Worker's Compensation claims. The plaintiff's supervisor ordered her to fire the other five employees because the supervisor expected them to sue the employer.

The plaintiff refused to do this because she knew that the Washington State statute (unlike its Pennsylvania counterpart) explicitly bans retaliation for filing a WC claim. The plaintiff, who previously had received good performance ratings, got a bad performance rating and was put on probation, then was fired for neglect of duty and poor performance.

She sued for wrongful discharge in violation of public policy, claiming that she was fired for refusing to perform an act of illegal retaliation. The employer's contention was that it is not illegal to fire an employee for insubordination, even if the employee refused to obey an illegal order. The Washington Court of Appeals favored the plaintiff's argument, extending the public policy cause of action to protect employees who refuse to violate the law. The public interest favors law enforcement, and employees who are not afraid of losing their jobs will be more likely to refuse illegal orders.

§ 39.05   PREEMPTION ARGUMENTS

Preemption is the legal doctrine under which passage of a federal law limits or eliminates the state's power to regulate that subject. ERISA preempts state wrongful termination claims based on alleged termination to avoid paying pension benefits. All such claims must be brought in federal court, under ERISA § 510, and not in state court.

According to the plaintiff in *Group Dekko Services LLC v. Miller* [717 N.E.2d 967 (Ind. App. 1999)], she was fired for protesting the mishandling of an employee's benefit claim. (The plaintiff was a benefits administrator, afraid that she would be held liable as a fiduciary for the way the claim was handled.) The court held that state wrongful discharge claims were preempted by ERISA, because determining whether she was a fiduciary would require interpretation of the plan.

The Family and Medical Leave Act preempts common-law claims of retaliatory discharge when an employee says he or she was fired as punishment for taking FMLA leave. [*Hamros v. Bethany Homes*, 894 F. Supp. 1176 (N.D. Ill. 1995)]

According to the Massachusetts Superior Court, because OSHA has no private right of action, it does not preempt state claims that an employee was wrongfully discharged for reporting safety violations. [*Antlitz v. CMJ Mgmt. Co.*, 1997 WL 42396 (Mass. Super. Jan. 30, 1997)] Kansas took a similar position in 1998. [*Flenker v. Willamette Indus. Inc.*, 1998 WL 271624 (Kan. 1998)]

Preemption arguments can also be used in state court. If the employee is covered by a state antidiscrimination law that is not preempted by federal law, the employer may be able to get a wrongful termination suit dismissed, because the employee should have sued for discrimination. From the employer's viewpoint, the best-case scenario is that the employee waited too long, so the discrimination charges must be dismissed.

ARBITRATION AND ADR

§ 40.01   INTRODUCTION

Taking a case to the court system is time-consuming, expensive, and often frustrating. Therefore, companies encounter nonlitigation means of dispute resolution in many contexts. In addition to commercial arbitration, which is beyond the scope of this book, unionized companies will often wind up arbitrating labor disputes.

Alternative Dispute Resolution (ADR) methods are supposed to be informal, governed more by justice and fairness than by strict rules of legal procedure. Depending on the ADR method, either one person or a panel of people will either assist the parties to work out their own solution (mediation) or will make a decision (arbitration). It has been estimated that an employment lawsuit takes an average of a year and a half from the date the case is filed to resolve, versus only one year for arbitration. Once the case gets to the arbitrator, 90% of arbitration hearings are completed in two days or less.

Furthermore, it has been pointed out that although employees may finally pursue a case to a large jury verdict, the verdict could be overturned on appeal, but far more employees prevail in arbitration than prevail in court. So, according to a prominent ACLU attorney, it is not fair to describe employment arbitration as "second class justice." [*See* Lewis Maltby, *Employment Arbitration*, Dispute Resolution Magazine 23 (Fall 1999)]

Both unionized and nonunionized companies often find mediation or arbitration a superior alternative to litigation when employees make claims that they have suffered employment discrimination. In fact, employers often use various methods to make sure that all claims will have to go through arbitration. The question is when and how it is legitimate to impose an arbitration requirement on employees. If the employees freely choose arbitration over litigation, this problem does not arise, but nevertheless, the employer will still have to find a way to present its case effectively to the arbitrator.

The "first principles" of arbitration are that arbitration should be independent of the court system and should provide flexibility and respect the rights of the parties.

§ 40.02   GRIEVANCES AND DISCIPLINE

[A]   "Progressive Discipline"

The typical Collective Bargaining Agreement for a unionized company spells out a system of "progressive discipline" under which employees whose work performance is unsatisfactory will be warned, offered guidance and training, and given a series of escalating penalties before being fired. Progressive discipline is sometimes used in nonunionized environment, although less frequently.

The system must make it clear to employees what the employer's expectations are and what the employer intends to do if the rules are violated. Once employees have been told what they are doing wrong, they should be given a

691

reasonable amount of time to correct it. There should be a monitoring process to sort out the employees who have made adequate progress from those who have not. The time period should probably be between 30 and 90 days: Too long a period may make the arbitrator believe that the employer is stringing together isolated, unrelated incidents to make a case.

Employees who have been subject to discipline are likely to feel that they were unfairly singled out—and in some cases, this will result in discrimination or wrongful termination charges. An important HR function is creating a legally sustainable system of progressive discipline, and making sure that supervisors understand the system and apply it objectively.

A legally sustainable disciplinary system should be:

- Consistent—not only must discrimination be avoided but employees should not be subjected to supervisors' whims or penalized when the supervisor has a bad day;
- Well documented—an arbitrator or court should be able to see that each step reflects the employer's own rules;
- Clear—employees should know that if they fail to meet X goals in Y days, they will be put on probation, lose wages, or be terminated;
- Appropriate—the degree of the sanction should reflect the severity of the error or misconduct;
- Reciprocal—employees should get a chance to give their side of the story to an objective decision maker who isn't already committed to management's viewpoint.

Arbitrators will examine the "step formula" under the system and see if it was followed. For example, if the first step results in a determination that the employee was at fault, then he or she might be verbally admonished, whereas by the fourth step, dismissal could be appropriate. If the step formula is not followed, the arbitrator is likely to reverse the decision or substitute a lesser penalty, and there's a good chance that the courts will uphold the arbitrator.

Presenting grievances to the employer is one of the clearest cases of concerted activity protected by the NLRA, whether or not the employees are unionized. However, they must in fact act in concert, or one employee must present a shared grievance. One person pressing his or her own agenda is not protected under the NLRA. For NLRA purposes, a grievance must be something that relates directly to the terms and conditions of employment.

Once they have made a complaint, employees are required to return to work within a reasonable time. In fact, one of the bywords of labor arbitration is "obey now, grieve later."

Sometimes, the employer will want to investigate a situation or will give the employee a chance to put his or her interpretation of contested facts on the record. If there is a reasonable likelihood that the "investigatory interview" will lead to dismissal or lesser forms of employee discipline, the employee has the right to bring a representative to the meeting.

Traditionally, this was known as the Weingarten right (named after an NLRB case) and was limited to unionized employees; in fact, it was a major recruitment tool for unions that joining a union would imply this right of representation. However, the NLRB, affirmed by the D.C. Circuit, extended the right to nonunion employees. [*Epilepsy Foundation of Northeast Ohio v. NLRB*, 268 F.3d 1095 (D.C. Cir. 2001)]

There is no right of representation (for unionized or nonunionized employees) if the meeting is simply a review of work rules, or is used to provide training—in other words, if the employee can't get into any trouble.

[B]   Grievance Records

It makes sense to buy or design standard forms for keeping track of employee grievances, although there is no specific federal requirement for making such records or keeping them for a particular length of time. The grievance form should contain:

- Identification of the CBA that creates the grievance procedure and the specific clause of that contract that has to be interpreted;
- Date the grievance was submitted;
- Grievance case number;
- Name, department, shift, and job title of the employee who submits the grievance;
- What the employee says is wrong;
- Records of statements by witnesses;
- Documentary evidence relevant to the grievance;
- Whether the employee was represented (e.g., by the shop steward or a fellow employee);
- Written decisions by the first-level supervisor or others involved in processing the grievance;
- A signed statement by the union representative as to whether the union considers the grievance to be adequately resolved;
- Signatures of the employee and all decision makers.

It can be very helpful to analyze past grievances to see how patterns change over time.

> **Tip:** If the grievance could be construed as alleging a hostile work environment (e.g., pervasive sexual harassment or harassment on the basis of race, nationality, or diversity), be sure to investigate thoroughly; failure to do so can subject the employer to liability.

[C] NLRB Deference

Although the NLRB has the power, under the NLRA § 10(a), to prevent unfair labor practices, the NLRB will defer to grievance arbitration (i.e., will not interfere) if several criteria are satisfied:

- Understanding the meaning of the CBA is central to resolving the dispute;
- The dispute came up during an ongoing collective bargaining relationship;
- The employees do not claim that the employer prevented them from exercising all their rights under labor law;
- The employer has agreed to a broad-based arbitration clause—in fact, one broad enough to cover the existing dispute.

§ 40.03   MEDIATION

A mediator is a neutral third party who listens to both sides and helps the parties themselves work out a solution that is acceptable to both of them. The American Arbitration Association has a set of uniform Employment Mediation Rules. Parties can trigger this procedure by writing a request to the AAA for mediation, or by filing a Submission to Mediation form, also with the AAA.

One reason that the procedure for filing discrimination charges is so elaborate is that part of the EEOC's job is to attempt mediation of the charge. [*See* Chapter 41]

§ 40.04   ARBITRATION VS. LITIGATION

Many studies have been done comparing the experience of resolving discrimination charges by arbitration versus litigation. In 1997, the federal General Accounting Office (GAO) found that 19% of employers they surveyed were using arbitration to resolve employment disputes. By 1996, over 3 million employees were subject to arbitration using the rules of the American Arbitration Association (AAA). [This information comes from *Arbitration Now*, a book published by the American Bar Association Section of Dispute Resolution in 1999, edited by Paul H. Haagen.]

Concerns have been expressed that arbitration is pro-employer. The average discrimination court case costs the employer $124,000 in defense costs, so reducing costs is a boon for the employer. The risk is that arbitrators will, consciously or unconsciously, favor employers, because an employer is much more likely to need to pick arbitrators in the future than is an individual employee.

Statistics showing the number of times employees win when they go to trial in the federal courts show only the tip of the iceberg. Sixty percent of cases brought in federal court become the subject of motions to dismiss the case before a full trial is held—and employers win 98% of those motions. [This information comes from *Arbitration Now*, a book published by the American Bar Association

Section of Dispute Resolution in 1999, edited by Paul H. Haagen.] Therefore, a tremendous number of employment cases wash out before they ever get to the jury stage.

Another important difference is that, although employees are much more likely to win at arbitration, the awards average much smaller than amounts awarded by judges or juries. In litigation, employers are always at risk of a head-line-making, multimillion dollar damage award (although really high awards are often reduced by an appellate court or the plaintiff settles for less than the full amount).

A 1995 study showed that the mean damages awarded by arbitrators to winning employees were $49,030—and the mean damages in District Court for the small number of employees who managed to prevail were $530,611! Not only did arbitrators make smaller awards, they also provided employees with a smaller percentage of what they asked for: 25% in arbitration, versus 70% in court cases. [This information comes from *Arbitration Now*, a book published by the American Bar Association Section of Dispute Resolution in 1999, edited by Paul H. Haagen]

§ 40.05   LABOR ARBITRATION

[A]   Grievance Arbitration and Contract or Interest Arbitration

Arbitration and mediation have a long history as means to settle disputes between labor and management without a strike and without litigation. By agreeing to arbitrate an issue, in effect the union agrees not to strike over that issue. The employer agrees not to take unilateral action.

The two main types of labor arbitration are grievance arbitration (also known as rights arbitration), used when there is a disagreement about interpretation of an existing contract, and contract or interest arbitration, invoked when the parties are not sure which provisions should be included in a new, renewed, or reopened CBA. However, this promotes a somewhat different mind-set from the type of arbitration discussed later in this chapter, where the focus is not on avoiding a strike dealing with an entire bargaining unit, but a court case involving one person's discrimination charge.

Nearly all collective bargaining agreements allow for an in-house grievance procedure, but if that does not resolve the problem, then final, binding arbitration, resulting in a decree that can be enforced by the court system, is the last part of the procedure.

Organizations such as the American Arbitration Association and the Federal Mediation and Conciliation Service maintain lists of qualified arbitrators, who are familiar both with the conditions in a particular industry and with arbitration rules and practices. If there will be only one arbitrator, then both sides will have to agree on an acceptable arbitrator. If there are three arbitrators, usually each side selects one arbitrator, and the two arbitrators select the third.

As a preliminary step, the employer and union try to agree on a statement of the issues involved in the grievance. If they cannot even agree on that, the arbitrator may have to draft the statement.

Tip: If the employer wants to discharge or discipline an employee, it will proceed first in arbitration; in other matters, the union usually proceeds first.

[B] Arbitrability

If it is not clear whether a company has agreed to submit a particular issue to arbitration, then the issue is arbitrable. This principle comes from "The Steelworkers' Trilogy," three cases decided by the Supreme Court in 1960. [*Steelworkers v. American Mfg. Co.*, 363 U.S. 564 (1960); *United Steelworkers of Am. v. Warrior Gulf Navigation Co.*, 363 U.S. 574 (1960); *United Steelworkers of Am. v. Enterprise Wheel and Car Corp.*, 363 U.S. 593 (1960)] If a CBA contains both an arbitration clause and a no-strike clause, any dispute that involves the application and interpretation of the CBA is arbitrable unless arbitration is specifically ruled out by the terms of the contract.

Under the Steelworkers' Trilogy, the language of the CBA is the first thing the arbitrators consult, but this is not the only factor in the analysis. The "law of the shop" (practices that have evolved in that particular operation) can be considered. Factors such as the effect of the arbitrator's decision on productivity, morale, and workplace tensions are also legitimate considerations. Courts can't review the merits of an arbitration decision or whether a different resolution would have been more sensible. All the court can do is decide whether the arbitration award "draws its essence" from the arbitration agreement.

However, because of a later Supreme Court case [*First Options of Chicago, Inc. v. Kaplan*, 514 U.S. 938 (1995)], the court system rather than the arbitrator decides whether a party agreed to arbitrate a particular type of dispute, if there is no clear, unmistakable evidence of the parties' intentions. There is no right to re-arbitrate an issue already considered by the NLRB in an unfair labor practice proceeding.

[C] Potentially Arbitrable Issues

Many issues have been found potentially arbitrable. In fact, because collective bargaining and arbitration are complementary processes, the list is similar to the list of issues that are mandatory bargaining subjects:

• Sale of a business;
• Relocation of operations;
• Contracting out bargaining unit work;
• Temporary shutdowns;

- Discharge of an individual employee;
- Layoffs;
- Recalls after a layoff;
- Disputes about work assignments (including assigning supervisors to bargaining unit work);
- Work schedules;
- Classification of work;
- Compensation, including bonuses, overtime pay, incentive pay, and severance;
- Vacation, sick leave, and holidays;
- Seniority systems;
- Safety disputes;
- No-strike clauses.

[D] The Process of Labor Arbitration

In most instances, when management and union hit a deadlock over a grievance or dispute, resort to arbitration will be automatic. However, depending on needs and comparative bargaining power, the arbitration clause might be drafted to allow only the union to invoke arbitration. Employees might also be given the right to invoke arbitration in situations where the union declines to press an employee grievance.

> **Tip:** Even if the CBA does not include a formal arbitration clause, management and union can sign a "submission agreement" agreeing to be bound by the arbitration decision on a one-time basis.

Arbitration clauses usually call for the involvement of either the Federal Mediation and Conciliation Service (FMCS) or the American Arbitration Association (AAA). However, the parties can agree on other ways to resolve disputes if they so choose.

Arbitration begins with a "demand": Either side invokes the CBA arbitration clause and notifies the appropriate agency. The FMCS can be called in by either management or union to assist in the negotiating process. The FMCS can also offer its services, but cannot demand to be made part of the process. FMCS will not mediate a dispute that has only minor effect on interstate commerce if there are other conciliation services (e.g., state agencies) available. The FMCS can also refuse to intervene on behalf of parties who have a record of noncooperation with arbitration, including failure to pay arbitration fees.

Once an arbitration award is rendered, it is usually final, binding, and not subject to judicial review by any court. In other words, agreeing to submit to arbitration is a very significant decision that cannot be undertaken casually. It will probably be impossible to get any kind of review or have the decision set aside.

However, a serious irregularity in the process, such as proof that the arbitrator was not impartial, may justify setting aside the award.

In June 1997, the FMCS published long-awaited rules for a streamlined, expedited process for simple cases. [*See* 62 Fed. Reg. 34175 (June 25, 1997)] Parties to a labor dispute submit FMCS Form R-43 to get an arbitration panel. If both parties agree, they can use the new expedited procedure, which shortens the deadlines, so that the arbitrator must draft a simple award within seven days (rather than the 60 days allowed for a full award). The expedited procedure is not suitable for cases that require a great deal of research, and where the request is unsuitable for arbitration because it is "overly burdensome or otherwise impractical," FMCS can refer the parties to an FMCS mediator to help them work out a compromise. Arbitrators who are consistently late in preparing awards can be removed from the panel.

[E]   Case Law on Labor Arbitration

In late 2000, the Supreme Court decided that, in a unionized workplace, an arbitrator's decision is enforceable by the court system as long as the arbitration award draws its essence from the Collective Bargaining Agreement (CBA). So, unless the arbitrator's decision actually violates a statute or regulation, it must be enforced—even if it violates public policy. [*Eastern Associated Coal Corp. v. UMW*, 531 U.S. 57 (2000)]

According to the Seventh Circuit, an employer is only permitted to make unilateral alterations in the terms and conditions of employment when an overall impasse in negotiations has been reached. In this view, inability to resolve a particular issue is not sufficient. [*Duffy Tool & Stamping LLC v. NLRB*, 233 F.3d 995 (7th Cir. 2000)] The Fifth Circuit does allow unilateral changes after a single-issue impasse, but the First, Sixth, and D.C. Circuits had already adopted the NLRB position (that impasse must be total to justify unilateral alterations) before the *Duffy* case.

Ohmite Manufacturing Co. [290 N.L.R.B. 1036 (1988)] says that it is unlawful to restrict permission to attend another employee's NLRB hearing to employees who have a real need to attend. It is also unlawful for the employer to base a denial on an improper motivation. In the case of *Cadbury Beverages Inc. v. NLRB* [160 F.3d 24 (D.C. Cir. 1998)], the employer fired an employee who disobeyed an order forbidding him to change his lunch hour to attend a co-worker's arbitration hearing. The discharged employee helped his co-worker prepare for the arbitration hearing, and therefore had a legitimate reason to attend, even though the case did not fall under *Ohmite*. The D.C. Circuit decided that Cadbury Beverages acted out of improper anti-union animus.

LMRA § 301 permits a federal District Court to enforce a subpoena *duces tecum* (for production of documents) issued by a labor arbitrator to a person or entity that is not a party to the collective bargaining agreement. [*AFTRA v. WJBK-TV*,

164 F.3d 1004 (6th Cir. 1999)] However, the labor arbitrator cannot order nonparties to appear and testify, only to produce documents.

[F]   Just Cause

One of the distinctive features of a collective bargaining agreement is that it means that employees no longer work at the will of the employer. Therefore, they cannot be discharged, or even subjected to lesser forms of discipline, without just cause. So the arbitrator's task becomes to determine whether the employer did, indeed, act with just cause. The arbitrator must determine if the employee really did whatever the employer claims he or she did; whether the employer offered the employee due process before imposing discipline; and whether the discipline was reasonable and not out of proportion to the offense. Usually, arbitrators divide offenses into very serious offenses such as assaulting someone at work, stealing, or creating a safety hazard (which will justify dismissal) and less serious rules, which are appropriate for progressive discipline such as admonition, notations in the permanent record, or suspension with or without pay.

[G]   Contract Interpretation

When arbitrators interpret a contract, their job is to find out what the parties meant. If the language of the contract is plain, clear, and unambiguous, the arbitrator has to follow it—even if the arbitrator doesn't think that the contract as written is very sensible or fair. In fact, if the arbitrator doesn't follow this "plain meaning rule," a court is likely to decide that the arbitrator's award is invalid and not entitled to be enforced by the court system.

In fact, if a contract (any kind of contract, not just a CBA) is supposed to represent the whole agreement between the parties, a legal principle called the "parol evidence rule" says that evidence of anything said or written before or during the negotiations cannot be introduced to contradict the written contract or vary its terms. ("Parol" is an archaic term for "word" or "speech.") However, parol evidence can be used to explain terms that are unclear or ambiguous.

§ 40.06   ARBITRATION OF EMPLOYMENT DISCRIMINATION CLAIMS

[A]   Employer-Imposed Clauses

The reputation of arbitration has had its ups and downs. A Supreme Court case, *Alexander v. Gardner-Denver* [415 U.S. 36 (1974)], allowed an employee to litigate after pursuing arbitration remedies, on the grounds that the arbitration provision in the plaintiff's CBA did not offer enough protection for statutory claims—i.e., claims that arise under Title VII, the Americans With Disabilities Act, or other antidiscrimination law.

In 1991, however, the Supreme Court took a different tack. The important case of *Gilmer v. Interstate/Johnson Lane Corp.* [500 U.S. 20 (1991)], allowed an employer to impose mandatory arbitration (under the U-4 securities industry employment agreement) for ADEA claims. The Supreme Court said that it wasn't really contradicting the earlier *Gardner-Denver* decision, because that involved a union contract that the plaintiff was subject to along with all the other union members, whereas Gilmer signed the U-4 agreement as an individual.

Under *Gilmer,* an arbitration clause can be valid as long as the process provides a written award rendered by a neutral arbitrator, and as long as discovery and adequate remedies are available under the arbitration process.

The *Gilmer* case was the "opening bell" for recognition of employers' right to impose predispute arbitration requirements: That is, employees would be covered by employment agreements, job handbooks, or other means of ensuring that they would have to arbitrate discrimination claims instead of litigating them. *Welles v. DeanWitter Reynolds Inc.* [948 F.2d 305 (6th Cir. 1991)] allows enforcement of a predispute mandatory arbitration requirement in Title VII cases. *Solomon v. Duke University* [850 F. Supp. 372 (M.D.N.C. 1993)] does the same for the ADA.

The Civil Rights Act of 1991 and the Americans with Disabilities Act (ADA) both include language favoring arbitration and other forms of Alternative Dispute Resolution (ADR) as means of handling discrimination charges. For the ADA provision, *see* 42 U.S.C. § 12212: Wherever it is lawful and appropriate, ADR (including settlement negotiations, conciliation, facilitation, mediation, factfinding, minitrials, and arbitration) is "encouraged" when ADA charges are asserted.

The two main ADR methods are arbitration (a trusted person or panel renders a decision) and mediation (a trusted person helps the parties reach a mutually acceptable decision).

Tip: If an employer offers to arbitrate, and the employee refuses, this could be treated as evidence of the employer's good faith—preventing the employee from collecting damages for breach of the covenant of good faith and fair dealing.

Then, in the early 1990s, the courts retrenched somewhat from their support of predispute arbitration requirements under at least some circumstances. For example, in *Prudential Insurance Co. v. Lai* [42 F.3d 1299 (9th Cir. 1995)], the court refused to compel arbitration under the U-4 agreement, because the plaintiff had not been warned about, and did not understand, that she had surrendered her statutory rights under Title VII. *Ramirez v. Circuit City Stores Inc.* [90 Cal. Rptr. 2d 916 (Cal. App. 1999)] says that the ADR policy in an employer's standard contract was unenforceable because it was a contract of adhesion (a one-sided contract imposed with no opportunity for negotiation), was oppressive to employees, and imposed obligations on employees but not the employer.

Rogers v. New York University [220 F.3d 73 (2d Cir. 2000)] permits a university employee to sue the university for ADA, FMLA, state and city human rights law violations despite a broad, general arbitration provision that was deemed not to be clear and unmistakeable enough to mandate arbitration in every situation.

In a unionized workplace, *ALPA v. Northwest Airlines Inc.* [199 F.3d 477 (D.C. Cir. 1999)] holds that unions cannot agree to substitute litigation for arbitration for all statutory discrimination claims asserted by union members. That takes arbitration out of the category of mandatory bargaining subjects. And that, in turn, frees employers to require arbitration agreements as a condition of employment, without negotiating with the union first.

The Fourth Circuit says that it is a material breach of the collective bargaining agreement for an employer to adopt arbitration rules that are grossly in its own favor and too strict on the employee. The FAA will not require enforcement of arbitration rules that are unfair. Therefore, even though there is an arbitration agreement already in place, the employee will be able to bring suit. [*Hooters of America Inc. v. Phillips*, 173 F.3d 933 (4th Cir. 1999); *Gonzalez v. Hughes Aircraft Employees Federal Credit Union*, 70 Cal App. 4th 468 (Cal. App. 1999)]

A mandatory arbitration provision was held to include provisions that violate public policy, and therefore the provision would not be enforced: *Armendariz v. Foundation Health Psycare Services Inc.* [99 Cal. Rptr. 2d 745 (Cal. 2000)] The agreement was unfairly one-sided. It allowed the employer (but not the employees) to use the court system. It also deprived employees of remedies, such as injunctions and compensatory and punitive damages, which would otherwise be available under state law. The California court found so many defects in the agreement that it required the entire agreement to be discarded, instead of merely removing the invalid sections.

However, in 1999, the California Court of Appeals ruled that it is not wrongful discharge to fire an employee for refusing to sign a broad predispute arbitration agreement as a condition of employment. According to *Lagatree v. Luce, Forward, Hamilton & Scripps* [88 Cal. Rptr. 2d 664 (Cal. App. 1999)], California law allows people to waive the right to a jury trial (or any trial at all) by contract. Current California law requires the employer to pay the full cost of arbitration.

Issues of cost have arisen in several cases, as part of the determination of fairness. The Florida Court of Appeals did not require arbitration of a pregnancy-discrimination claim, on the grounds that requiring the employee to pay half the arbitration costs violates the successful Title VII plaintiff's statutory right to recover all attorneys' fees and costs. [*Flyer Printing Co. v. Hill*, 805 So. 2d 829 (Fla. App. 2001)] But *Bond v. Twin City Carpenters & Joiners Pension Fund* [70 L.W. 1240 (D. Minn. Aug. 23, 2001)] says that it is permissible to give the arbitrator discretion to divide the costs between employer and employee, because this does not impose an undue burden on employees who want to pursue workplace grievances.

A 2002 case from the Seventh Circuit [*McCaskill v. SCI Management Corp.*, 70 L.W. 1615 (7th Cir. April 4, 2002)] holds that an arbitration agreement that made each party responsible for its own costs (no matter who won) was invalid and unenforceable, and therefore could not prevent an employee from bringing a Title VII suit against the employer. The Seventh Circuit's view was that Title VII enforcement calls for making the losing party pay the winning party's fees in appropriate situations. Therefore, if an arbitration agreement makes it too expensive for employees to enforce their rights, the arbitration agreement is invalid.

It can be tough to enforce provisions contained in an employee handbook. [*See* Chapter 24] After all, it is typical for the handbook to say that its provisions do not create an enforceable employment contract.

According to the Ninth Circuit, the arbitration clause was put in unilaterally by the employer, so it does not mean that the employee made a "knowing" waiver of the right to litigate. [*Nelson v. Cyprus Bagdad Copper Corp.*, 119 F.3d 756 (9th Cir. 1997)] The Eleventh Circuit refused to enforce a handbook's mandatory arbitration provision because it did not specify that Title VII claims were covered. [*Paladino v. Avnet Computer Techs. Inc.*, 134 F.3d 1054 (11th Cir. 1998)] The District of Columbia Circuit similarly refused enforcement of a handbook provision because the employee did not sign a document indicating that the handbook had been received and understood. [*Phox v. Allied Capital Advisers*, 74 FEP Cases 809 (D.D.C. 1997)]

In fact, arbitration wasn't even compelled in *Trumbull v. Century Marketing Corp.* [12 F. Supp. 2d 683 (N.D. Ohio 1998)], a case in which the employee signed an acknowledgment of receiving the handbook. The court's rationale was that the handbook did not refer to the application of the arbitration policy, so it could not provide a valid waiver of the right to sue.

What about situations in which the employee is covered by a written employment contract, and that contract imposes a predispute requirement of arbitration? The California Court of Appeals has decided that it is unconscionable (and therefore, the clause is unenforceable) to allow the employer to litigate certain types of cases while the employee was required to arbitrate all claims, to limit the size of the award the employee can receive, imposing an absolute one-year statute of limitations, and allowing the employee to be terminated before the employer's claims could be resolved. [*Stirlen v. Supercuts, Inc.*, 51 Cal. App. 4th 1519, 60 Cal. Rptr. 2d 138 (1997)]

Although it is certainly less complex and formal than litigation, arbitration is still a formal system with defined rules and an objective decision maker. An employer's internal grievance procedure is not equivalent to arbitration. Therefore, an employee can sue for wrongful termination based on race and sex discrimination, because an agreement to use the internal grievance procedure is not an agreement to arbitrate. [*Cheng-Canindin v. Renaissance Hotel Assocs.*, 50 Cal. App. 4th 676, 57 Cal. Rptr. 2d 867 (1996)]

An arbitration clause imposed by one employer can operate for the benefit of its successors. [*Jones v. Tenet Health Network Inc.*, 65 L.W. 1815 (E.D. La. April 7, 1997] In this case, an employee's agreement with the owner of a hospital barred an ADA suit against a later purchaser of the hospital, on the grounds that the new employer inherited the old employer's arbitration clauses as well as liability for its actions toward its employees.

In 1996, the Second Circuit ruled that a company was not guilty of retaliation merely because it had a policy of terminating its internal grievance procedures and sending the file to the corporate legal department as soon as an employee claim became the subject of an agency charge or litigation. [*United States v. New York Transit Auth.*, 97 F.3d 672 (2d Cir. 1996)] There was no unlawful retaliation, because referring the file to the legal department did not harm the complaining employee.

[B] AAA Arbitration

The American Arbitration Association (AAA) has long been respected for its work in dispute resolution. The AAA's National Rules for the Resolution of Employment Disputes (promulgated in 1993; amended in 1995 to increase due process protection for employees) cover about three million workers.

The due process standards for fair arbitration require that:

- The employee's role in selecting the arbitrator(s) is equal to the employer's role;
- Each side has a right to counsel;
- The arbitrator can order whatever discovery he or she thinks is necessary;
- The parties are entitled to the same remedies in arbitration that they could get from the court system;
- The arbitrator will provide a written opinion explaining the reasons behind his or her decision;
- Attorneys' fees will be awarded in the interests of justice, so the employee does not have to be successful enough to be considered the "prevailing party" to get a fee award.

Tip: The employer can indicate in employment applications, the employee handbook, and/or employment contracts that employment disputes will be resolved under AAA rules.

Since 1996, AAA arbitrators have had the power to order discovery. Either employers or employees can be ordered to produce documents, answer written lists of questions, or appear and answer questions posed by an attorney. Under the 1996 rules, any party can be represented by an attorney. The arbitrator has a duty to make a decision and render a written award within 30 days of the end of the hearing. The arbitrator has the power to render whatever award he or she thinks is just, including ordering one side to pay the attorneys' fees and costs of the other side.

The arbitrator gets paid a fee for working on the case, and the AAA itself is entitled to an administration fee. The AAA fee depends on the size of the claim or counterclaim, determined at the time it is filed, not by any later amendments.

The AAA's general policy is that it will administer arbitration even if the employer unilaterally imposed the arbitration requirement as a condition of employment. However, the organization reserves the right to refuse to enforce unfair arbitration policies—policies that fail to provide basic due process protection to employees.

[C] Securities Industry Arbitration

Workers in the securities industry have to sign a standard employment agreement called the U-4 as a condition of working in the industry. It was the only industry to have a uniform mandatory arbitration requirement, so it served as a kind of "test bed" for studying legal issues about arbitration.

As of August 7, 1997, the National Association of Securities Dealers (NASD) voted to eliminate mandatory arbitration of employment discrimination claims brought by registered brokers under federal and state antidiscrimination statutes.

[D] Getting Ready for Arbitration

To be prepared for arbitration, you should:

- Review how the dispute arose, and what has already been done to resolve it;
- Check all relevant work rules and policies and how they were applied, both to the grievant and the other employees;
- Makes copies of all relevant documents for your own file, for the employee, and for the arbitrator;
- Inform the employee of documents in the employee's possession that you want copies of, and that you want copies sent to the arbitrator;
- If necessary, ask the arbitrator to subpoena necessary documents that you have not been able to get by informal means;
- Make sure all the witnesses sound accurate and articulate, but not mechanical or coached;
- Anticipate questions that will be asked during cross-examination, and prepare the witnesses to answer them;
- Make a list of points that you want each witness's testimony to put into the record;
- Review collections of published arbitration decisions, because even though arbitrators don't absolutely have to follow past precedents, they will often be swayed by interpretations that other arbitrators have reached in similar cases.

The first stage in an arbitration hearing is the opening statement. Usually, in a case where the employer's termination or discipline is being challenged, the employer will present its case first, because the employer has to prove the justification for its actions. In other types of cases, the employee usually gives the first opening statement. Next comes the other opening statement, and then the side that goes first introduces the testimony of its witnesses; the other side has the right to cross-examine. Then, the parties sum up their cases, and it is up to the arbitrator to decide.

§ 40.07 MANDATORY PREDISPUTE ARBITRATION CLAUSES

[A] "Predispute" v. "Postdispute" Clauses

There are many ways to draft an arbitration provision. Predispute arbitration clauses specify in advance that future disputes, if they occur, will be arbitrable. Such a provision can be either voluntary or mandatory. If voluntary, arbitration is just one option available for resolving disputes. If mandatory, the employee is blocked from suing the employer. Postdispute arbitration clauses are an agreement between employer and employee after a claim has been raised, and the best way to handle it is via arbitration.

In 1998, the Supreme Court resolved some difficult issues in *Wright v. Universal Maritime Service Corp.* [525 U.S. 70 (1998)] In this case, an injured stevedore was denied employment because companies that might have employed him considered him permanently disabled. He sued under the ADA without filing a grievance or going through arbitration under the CBA. The district court dismissed his case because he did not exhaust his grievance remedies. The Fourth Circuit upheld the district court.

However, the Supreme Court reversed the Fourth Circuit. The *Gilmer* case permits compulsory arbitration of an ADA claim, but the Supreme Court ruled that a contract claim must be treated differently from a statutory claim. Contract claims are presumed arbitrable, but statutory claims are not. A CBA must be very explicit to prevent litigation of a claim under a civil rights statute. A general arbitration clause that does not list the civil rights statutes that are covered will not prevent litigation under those statutes.

According to the Eighth Circuit, the employer's adoption of a mandatory arbitration requirement shifts the operation away from strict at-will employment. Therefore, the employer must show "discernable cause" for discharging any employees. [*PaineWebber Inc. v. Agron*, 49 F.3d 347 (8th Cir. 1995)]

A 2001 case, *Circuit City v. Adams* [532 U.S. 105 (2002)] allowed a company to enforce its predispute arbitration requirement to prevent an employee from suing in state court. The employee's argument was that the FAA excludes "contracts of employment of seamen, railroad employees, or any other class of workers engaged in foreign or interstate commerce," and that he, like nearly all workers, was engaged in interstate commerce so the FAA should not apply. The Supreme

Court, however, said that the exclusion was limited to transportation workers, not everyone whose work affects interstate commerce. Otherwise, the FAA would hardly ever be applicable, and would serve no purpose—whereas Congress clearly intended to promote arbitration as a means of settling disputes.

However, the case was sent back to the lower courts, and the Ninth Circuit decided that the agreement itself is unenforceable, because even though the Supreme Court decided that it satisfied the requirements of the FAA, it was too unfair and one-sided to survive California law. [Alexei Oreskovic, *9th Circuit Tosses Circuit City's Arbitration Pact*, The Recorder (Feb. 5, 2002) (law.com)]

Early in 2002, the Supreme Court returned to the subject of predispute arbitration mandates. The ruling in *EEOC v. Waffle House Inc.* [534 U.S. 279 (2002)] is that the EEOC can pursue employment discrimination litigation (in this case, involving the Americans with Disabilities Act) even if the employees themselves would be required to submit their disputes to arbitration. The decision is very important as an indicator of legal thinking about arbitration, but it will not have much practical effect, because the EEOC doesn't take on many cases a year, and not all of them involve companies with mandatory arbitration requirements.

[B] Claims Other than Discrimination

Mandatory predispute arbitration clauses are not limited to use in connection with discrimination claims. Five of the federal Circuit Courts have ruled that arbitration can be a proper way to handle ERISA claims. [*Bird v. Shearson Lehman/ American Express*, 926 F.2d 116 (2d Cir. 1991); *Pritzer v. Merrill Lynch*, 7 F.3d 1110 (3d Cir. 1993); *Kramer v. Smith Barney*, 80 F.3d 1080 (5th Cir. 1996); *Amulfo P. Sulit, Inc. v. Dean Witter Reynolds, Inc.*, 847 F.2d 475 (8th Cir. 1988); *Williams v. Imhoff*, 203 F.3d 758 (10th Cir. 2000)]

In *Strawn v. AFC Enterprises Inc.* [70 F. Supp. 2d 717 (S.D. Tex. 1999)], all employees had to sign a "Value Deal Agreement" mandating arbitration of all injury claims. Texas allows employers to opt out of the Worker's Compensation system, as this employer did. It had its own benefit plan, providing much less for injured workers than the Compensation system. The case arose when an injured worker received about $50,000 in benefits in arbitration, but then sued for additional tort damages.

The employer moved to compel arbitration. The employee countered that the arbitration agreement was unenforceable, relying on *Reyes v. Storage & Processors Inc.* [995 S.W.2d 722 (Tex. App. 1999)] *Reyes* says that a waiver of common-law causes of action is void as against public policy if the employer provides benefits substantially less generous than the Worker's Comp system does. The court agreed with the employee that AFC Enterprises' "miserly" benefits were not good enough. However, the arbitration agreement was merely voidable, and not void—and the employee did not ratify the agreement by accepting benefits under the arbitration award.

The Fifth Circuit separated collective bargaining act claims from claims involving the Fair Labor Standards Act, ruling that arbitration is inadequate for the latter because it does not give workers access to FLSA remedies such as liquidated damages and attorneys' fees. [*Bernard v. IPB, Inc. of Nebraska*, 154 F.3d 259 (5th Cir. 1998)]

In *Montes v. Shearson Lehman Brothers* [128 F.3d 1456 (11th Cir. 1997)], the plaintiff sought arbitration to get overtime pay. The employer characterized her as an exempt executive or administrator. The arbitration award was vacated, and the case sent back for a new arbitration panel. The employer's lawyer urged the arbitrators to ignore the Fair Labor Standards Act. Apparently they gave in to this argument. Arbitration should not deprive participants of legal principles or protections available through the court system. Arbitration awards cannot be reversed based on misinterpretation of the law. But if the applicable law is actually disregarded, then the award can be thrown out.

§ 40.08   FACTORS THAT PROMOTE ADR SUCCESS

Most successful ADR systems embody several steps, including in-house procedures for resolving grievances before outside parties get involved. In-house resolutions can be quick and inexpensive. Using a mediator or arbitrator always involves some degree of delay and expense, even if it is far less than the ruinous effort of litigation.

Any ADR system should specify whether the matter will be heard by one mediator or arbitrator or by a panel. Panels usually have three members; it's definitely better to have an odd number to prevent 2–2 or 3–3 splits.

The ADR policy should specify not only the number but the qualifications of the decision makers. It should be clear which employees will be allowed to use ADR to settle disputes—and which ones will be compelled to use it. The policy should clarify which disputes are involved: All employment-related disputes? All federal statutory discrimination claims? Only certain federal claims? Only claims that would otherwise go to state court?

An appropriate policy is fair to employees, providing them with as much due process protection as litigation would offer. They should have an adequate opportunity to assert claims, get evidence about what the employer did, and receive adequate remedies if the mediator or arbitrator decides in their favor.

The American Bar Association's "Due Process Protocol" sets out these standards for fairness in mandatory arbitration matters:

- The employee is aware of the arbitration requirement and accepts it voluntarily;
- The employee can be represented at arbitration (e.g., by a lawyer or union representative);
- The employee has access to a full range of remedies;
- The arbitrator has the power to make the employer pay the employee's arbitration-related costs. Some cases about arbitration take the position that, since the

employer wanted arbitration in the first place, it should pay the full cost. The system could also be set up so that the employee never has to pay more than 50% of the cost of arbitration, or never has to pay more than one day's fee for the arbitrators.

An agreement to arbitrate employment disputes capped punitive damages at $5,000. The Eighth Circuit ruled [*Gannon v. Circuit City Stores Inc.*, 262 F.3d 677 (8th Cir. 2001)] that even if this provision was invalid, it did not render the entire agreement unenforceable; it could have been severed and the rest of the agreement left in place. The Eighth Circuit did not hold that the provision was necessarily invalid even though the punitive damage limitation was much lower than what would have been permitted under CRA '91.

CHAPTER 41

EEOC AND STATE ENFORCEMENT OF ANTIDISCRIMINATION LAWS

§ 41.01   INTRODUCTION

The Equal Employment Opportunity Commission (EEOC) is in charge of enforcing Title VII and the Americans with Disabilities Act (ADA). It also enforces the Equal Pay Act (EPA) and Age Discrimination in Employment Act (ADEA), although the enforcement provisions for these acts are slightly different because they reflect their derivation from the Fair Labor Standards Act. EPA complainants do not have to file an EEOC charge; the rules for ADEA charges are found in 29 C.F.R. § 1626.4.

The basic enforcement scheme is that people who believe they have been discriminated against file charges with the EEOC. The EEOC works with state antidiscrimination agencies, using methods ranging from informal persuasion to litigation to get employers to comply with the law and eliminate any discriminatory practices occurring in the workplace.

The EEOC can intervene in a suit brought by an employee or can bring its own lawsuits against employers. The EEOC has the power to collect data, investigate allegations of discrimination, view conditions in the workplace, and inspect records. It can also advise employers about how to comply with the law. The EEOC has the power to subpoena witnesses and documents, bring suits, and supervise the collection of damages that courts have ordered or that employers have agreed to pay under a settlement.

Therefore, the EEOC has a dual role. It investigates charges brought by employees, but it can also litigate as a plaintiff. The theory is that the EEOC acts as plaintiff to preserve the rights of all the employees within the workplace. The EEOC always has a right to investigate and, where it believes a cause of action exists, to litigate. So employees' waivers and releases, or their settlement of claims against the employer, can prevent those employees from suing their employers, but will not prevent a suit by the EEOC. Furthermore, waivers and releases are void as against public policy if they try to prevent employees from assisting in an EEOC investigation.

Similarly, the EEOC can pursue an ADA case (including seeking specific relief for an individual) even if the individual employee was covered by a mandatory predispute arbitration agreement [*see* § 40.07] and therefore could not sue the employer. [*EEOC v. Waffle House*, 534 U.S. 279 (2002)]

As Jathan W. Janove explains [Jathan W. Janove, *Soothing the EEOC Dragon*, HR Magazine, May 2001, at p. 137], the worst-case scenario for a company is for the EEOC to expand a complaint into a class action, because then not only will the agency examine the company's conduct in past years, it may start a media campaign to recruit new plaintiffs, creating significant bad publicity.

To head off this very negative possibility, it often helps to volunteer significant nonmonetary relief measures; to offer to donate part of the amount that might otherwise be assessed as damages to worthy causes; or permit the EEOC to issue a press release describing the remedial measures (rather than the alleged discrimination).

EEOC investigators assign cases to classifications of A (the most serious), B, and C. In an A-1 case, the EEOC itself may pursue the case as plaintiff. An A-2 case is likely to result in a finding of good cause, but no litigation by the EEOC itself. It's a bad sign if the EEOC sends out a questionnaire to potential plaintiffs; asks the defendant for a statement of its position; if the EEOC does not ask the employer to mediate; or if it's a deferral state (see below) but the first contact comes from the federal EEOC.

It is often helpful to demonstrate good faith by offering unconditional reinstatement to a charging party. There are many cases indicating that if the charging party rejects such an offer, he or she will not be eligible for various kinds of relief (back pay, front pay, possibly even court-ordered reinstatement).

The Department of Labor also has the right to sue federal contractors for remedies, including punitive damages, if the contractors are guilty of race, sex, or religious discrimination. Employees of federal contractors get a choice of filing their complaints with the EEOC or the DOL. The EEOC and DOL entered into a new work-sharing plan on December 14, 1998. [*See* Glenn Burkins, *EEOC Gives Labor Department Power to Seek Damages in Worker Bias Cases*, Wall Street Journal, April 9, 1999, at p. A20]

§ 41.02   EEOC ADR

At times, the EEOC itself will engage in ADR with employers and employees as an alternative to normal charge processing methods. The EEOC issued two policy statements on these subjects in 1997, although formal regulations were not issued at that time.

Under these policy statements, the EEOC said ADR was not appropriate in some cases. The agency did not treat ADR as fair or appropriate in important test cases where the EEOC wishes to establish policy or set a precedent; where the EEOC would have to maintain an ongoing presence to monitor compliance; or where the case has significant implications for people besides the parties to the individual charge—for instance, other employees and other companies in the same or different industries.

The EEOC took the position that ADR was fair and appropriate if:

- It is voluntarily elected, not compelled;
- The EEOC provides help to employees who are confused about the process;
- The decision maker (mediator or arbitrator) is truly neutral;
- The proceedings are confidential;
- The outcome of the process is an enforceable written agreement.

EEOC ADR began in 1997. In that year, 780 cases were settled for a total of $10.8 million. In 1998, there were 1,500 settlements for an aggregate of $17 million. [Steven A. Holmes, *Jobs Discrimination Agency Lightening Its Load*, New York Times, Feb. 22, 1999, at p. A1. *See also* 67 L.W. 2342 and Bill Leonard, *HR Update*, HR Magazine, Nov. 1999, at p. 32] Between February 1999 and the end of that year, almost 4,000 successful mediations had been conducted, and the EEOC considered mediation an integral part of its enforcement efforts. In fiscal 1999, about 30% of the overall $188 million discrimination settlements came about through mediation.

The Janove article discussed above quotes EEOC staffer David Grinberg, saying that in fiscal 2000, 81% of charging parties who were offered mediation accepted it (but only 31% of employers agreed). About two-thirds of claims that went to mediation were resolved, in an average of 96 days.

As for using mediation later in the process, mediator Hunter R. Hughes said at a September 2000 seminar that mediating class actions before the suit is filed, or just afterwards, reduces defense costs and gives plaintiffs the chance to make their employers implement systemic changes in their employment practices. Hughes said that the earlier mediation begins, the better—because litigating positions have not hardened yet, and there will be less unfavorable publicity and bad feeling. Plaintiff attorneys are less supportive of this option. They believe that it gives class representatives more than their fair share of the settlement, because the class has not really come together by the time the settlement is obtained. [No by-line, *Early Mediation of Class Actions Provides Advantages for Defendants and Plaintiffs*, 69 L.W. 2207 (Oct. 10, 2000)]

§ 41.03   TITLE VII ENFORCEMENT

Both the EEOC and state antidiscrimination agencies have a role in investigating an employee's allegations of discrimination. Initial charges can be filed with either the EEOC or the state or local agency.

However, if the employee goes to the EEOC first, it generally "defers" to the state or local agency. That is, it sends the paperwork to the state or local agency, and gives it a 60-day deferral period to resolve the complaint. [*See* 29 C.F.R. § 1601.74 for a list of state and local agencies that are deemed to have enough enforcement power to handle a discrimination charge] Furthermore, some agencies (listed in 29 C.F.R. § 1601.80) are "certified" by the EEOC, based on a track record of at least four years as a deferral agency, during which time the EEOC found its work product to be acceptable.

Title VII and ADA charges must be filed within the EEOC within 180 days of the time of the alleged discrimination (if there is no deferral agency in the picture) or within 300 days of the alleged discrimination, or 30 days of the time the deferral agency terminates processing of the charge (if a deferral agency is involved).

However, these timing requirements are tricky and provide many opportunities for the employer to get cases dismissed. In a case involving a deferral agency, the filing period is really only 240 days, because of the 60-day period when the EEOC steps aside and lets the deferral agency handle the matter. However, most deferral agencies have what is called "work sharing" agreements with the EEOC. In the jurisdiction of those agencies, an employee's complaint is timely if it is made more than 240, but less than 300, days after the alleged discrimination occurred.

Once the EEOC gets a charge, it is required to notify the subject of the charge. Because nearly all discrimination charges are brought against the employer corporation, and not against individuals, this will nearly always be the corporation. The EEOC's job is to attempt conciliation—to get the parties to agree on a view of what happened in the past and how discrimination is to be avoided or remedied in the future.

It can be hard to determine when alleged violations of the law occurred. The problem gets even harder if the employee charges that there was more than a single discriminatory act. If there was a continuing violation (one that lasts a long time), or a series of related violations, then the timing requirements probably run from the latest action in the series. There could also be two separate violations, each with its own timing requirements: for example, discriminatory refusal to promote, followed by retaliation against the employee for filing discrimination charges.

Where the employer is accused of adopting a seniority system for intentionally discriminatory reasons (e.g., a desire to limit opportunities for women or minorities entering the workforce), the time to file the EEOC charge is the time at which the employee is injured by application of the seniority system to his or her particular case. That sounds innocent enough, but it had to be added to Title VII by the Civil Rights Act of 1991, to reverse a 1989 Supreme Court case [*Lorance v. AT&T Techs. Inc.*, 109 S. Ct. 2261 (1989)] that said that the time ran from the date the seniority system was adopted. In many cases, the system was adopted long before the would-be plaintiff was hired by the company—and possibly long before he or she was born.

According to the Fifth Circuit, procedural failures required that a judgment in favor of an employee had to be vacated and his age discrimination case had to be dismissed. He filed a complaint with the EEOC and failed to check the box on the form indicating that he wanted the charge filed with both the EEOC and the Texas Commission on Human Rights. Therefore, he failed to go through the mandatory step of filing a state charge—so his federal lawsuit was invalid.

Texas has a work-sharing arrangement with the EEOC, but that only means that a single filing can apply to both state and federal procedures—not that the state procedure can be ignored, even in a case like this one where only federal claims are asserted against the employer. [*Jones v. Grinnell Corp.*, 235 F.3d 972 (5th Cir. Jan. 4, 2001). *See* Stephanie Hoops, *5th Circuit Tosses Case Because "X" Didn't Mark the Spot*, Texas Lawyer (Jan. 19, 2001) (law.com)]

Another Fifth Circuit case, *Villma v. Eureka Co.* [218 F.3d 458 (5th Cir. 2001)] says that because Texas is a deferral state, the EEOC has to hold off on its charge processing for at least 60 days to permit the state investigation to proceed. Although the only way to trigger the 90-day period for bringing a federal suit is to get an EEOC right-to-sue letter, the EEOC letter does not start the 60-day period for a suit in state court under the Texas Human Rights Act. Only a civil action letter from the Texas Commission on Human Rights will trigger the state time period.

§ 41.04   EEOC INVESTIGATION

If the EEOC can't settle a charge informally, its next step is to investigate the facts and determine if there is reasonable cause to believe that the employee's complaint is well-founded. If it makes such a "reasonable cause" determination, it has an obligation to attempt to conciliate: to get the employer to improve its equal opportunity policies, sign a compliance agreement, and compensate the employee for past discrimination. The EEOC can't close its case file until it has evidence of the employer's actual compliance with the conciliation agreement.

If the EEOC believes that the employer is blocking the process, it sends a written notice demanding compliance. Title VII § 706(c) gives the EEOC discretion to sue the employer if an acceptable conciliation agreement cannot be reached within 30 days after the end of the period when the EEOC defers to state agency jurisdiction, or 30 days of the date a charge is filed with the EEOC. There is no statute of limitations for suits brought directly by the EEOC: They can sue even for events in the distant past.

The Fifth Circuit ruled in late 2001 that the district court was right to refuse to enforce the EEOC's subpoena seeking evidence of sex discrimination at a point 19 months into a race-discrimination investigation; the EEOC should have filed its own charge if it wanted to pursue potential sex discrimination. [*EEOC v. Southern Farm Bureau Cas. Ins. Co.*, 70 L.W. 1352 (5th Cir. Nov. 5, 2001)]

If and when the EEOC concludes that there is no reasonable cause to believe that the facts are as charged by the employee, the EEOC will inform the charging party of this determination. In Title VII and ADA cases (but not Equal Pay Act or ADEA cases), the charging party can still sue the employer in federal court, but must get a "right to sue" letter from the EEOC indicating that the case has been closed. Usually, the EEOC gets 180 days to attempt conciliation, but the employee can ask for earlier termination of the EEOC's involvement, and earlier issuance of the right-to-sue letter. However, the employee can't bypass the conciliation process entirely.

Once the right-to-sue letter is issued, the employee has only 90 days to file the federal suit. If the 90 days pass without commencement of a suit, the EEOC can still bring suit, on the theory that the potential private plaintiff's inaction has reinstated the agency's own powers.

Although the EEOC has reduced its backlog, it is still clear that the heavily burdened agency is not going to complete its investigation of every charge within 180 days. Courts differ on whether the EEOC can issue right-to-sue letters based on simple inability to resolve the charge on time. [*See* Helen D. Irvin, *Courts Differ on "Early" Right-to-Sue Letters*, 69 L.W. 2259 (Nov. 7, 2000)]

The EEOC's own regulations [29 C.F.R. § 1601.28(a)(2)] say that an early letter can be issued if the EEOC determines that it probably will not be able to complete the investigation on time. Various District Courts have agreed. However, some courts say that the EEOC must wait to issue the letter until the 180 days have elapsed, because issuing an early letter would permit the agency to avoid its obligation to investigate. *Martini v. FNMA* [179 F.3d 1336 (D.C. Cir. 1999)] says that Title VII requires complainants to wait the full 180 days, to encourage informal resolution of as many charges as possible.

The EEOC's investigative powers generally end as soon as a right-to-sue letter has been issued. [*EEOC v. Federal Home Loan Mortgage Co.*, 37 F. Supp. 2d 769 (E.D. Va. 1999)] The exception is the case in which the EEOC thinks its investigation goes beyond the litigation, in which case it can intervene in the employee's private suit or file its own charges. However, the EEOC will not intervene in a suit, or bring a suit, if it makes a "no reasonable cause" determination.

Suits with the EEOC as plaintiff are limited to matters investigated as a result of a charge, not matters outside the scope of the matter for which the EEOC attempted to conciliate. In other words, the EEOC's efforts to conciliate one charge won't make the employer vulnerable to a host of other charges. Furthermore, because of the burden of its workload, the EEOC files only a few hundred suits a year.

§ 41.05   ADEA ENFORCEMENT

The rules for ADEA cases are quite similar, but not identical, to those for Title VII cases, so you should check to see if ADEA plaintiffs have violated any of the requirements for that type of suit.

In addition to suits brought by employees who charge that they have been subjected to age discrimination, the ADEA statute provides for enforcement by the Secretary of Labor; 29 U.S.C. § 26 gives the Secretary the power to investigate ADEA charges, including subpoenaeing witnesses and inspecting employers' business records. (The DOL has delegated this power to the EEOC.)

Even criminal penalties can be imposed against anyone who "shall forcibly resist, oppose, impede, intimidate or interfere with" a DOL representative engaged in enforcing the ADEA. [*See* 29 U.S.C. § 629] The criminal penalty is a fine of up to $500 and/or up to one year's imprisonment, although imprisonment will be ordered only in the case of someone who has already been convicted of the same offense in the past.

Although the EEOC can become an ADEA plaintiff, it seldom does so. The cases it selects are usually large-scale, involving egregious practices, many employees, or a pattern or practice of discrimination. The EEOC can bring a suit even if no employee of the company has filed timely charges of age discrimination.

If the EEOC files suit after an employee has already sued based on the same conduct on the employer's part, the earlier individual suit can proceed. However, an individual who wants back pay or other monetary relief cannot file suit after the EEOC starts its own suit, because the EEOC litigates on behalf of all affected employees.

However, if the EEOC complaint covers a pattern or practice of discrimination lasting "up to the present time," this means the date when the EEOC filed its complaint, so an individual can file a private suit charging the employer with committing discrimination after the filing of the EEOC complaint.

The EEOC doesn't need written consent from employees to file a suit on their behalf. The EEOC can seek relief for all employees on the basis of a charge filed by one employee who only reported discrimination against him- or herself. The EEOC can also undertake a single conciliation effort for multiple charges, as long as the employer is notified that the charge involves more than one complainant.

No employee who has already sued the employer can get back pay or other individual relief as part of an EEOC suit involving the same facts. However, if an employee tried to sue, but the case was dismissed on the basis of untimely filing, then the EEOC can bring a suit to get an injunction against the employer, even if the EEOC's case is based on the same facts as the suit that was dismissed.

Tip: The general rule is that a company that files for bankruptcy protection is entitled to an automatic stay—a period of time during which suits against the company cannot proceed. However, a suit by the EEOC is considered an exercise of the government's regulatory, policing function, and therefore can proceed even while the automatic stay is in place.

---

§ 41.06 THE FEDERAL-STATE RELATIONSHIP

[A] ADEA Interaction

Unlike ERISA, which preempts whole classes of state laws dealing with certain retirement and employee benefit issues, the ADEA specifically provides for a joint working relationship between the federal government and state antidiscrimination agencies; 29 U.S.C. § 625(b) gives the Secretary of Labor the power to cooperate with state and local agencies to carry out the purposes of ADEA.

Section 633(a) provides that state agencies retain their jurisdiction over age-discrimination claims. However, federal ADEA suits supersede state age-discrimination enforcement efforts. A potential age-discrimination plaintiff has to go through enforcement procedures at both the state and the federal level. However, if the federal charge is filed on time, the complainant doesn't have to complete the state enforcement process—only to file a charge within the state system.

The federal ADEA provides that, if a state has a statute against age discrimination and has an enforcement agency, then potential plaintiffs have to file charges within both systems. The federal-state enforcement relationship revolves around the concepts of "referral" and "deferral."

Referral means that a state has a work-sharing arrangement with the EEOC, as provided by 29 C.F.R. § 1616.9. When an age-discrimination complaint is made to the state agency, the state agency refers it to the EEOC. If the state charge is dismissed, the EEOC has the power to conduct an independent investigation. Originally, the EEOC Regulations listed states that were identified as "referral" states because they had age discrimination laws. However, in August 2002, the EEOC proposed a set of regulations for ADEA litigation procedures: *see* 67 Fed. Reg. 52431 (August 12, 2002). In the proposal, the EEOC says that because most of the states now have laws to forbid age discrimination, it is no longer necessary to maintain these lists. The EEOC will simply make referrals to the state agencies as appropriate.

An additional group of states (Arizona, Colorado, Kansas, Maine, Ohio, Rhode Island, South Dakota, and Washington) are "conditional referral" states. They do have antidiscrimination statutes, but the terms of these state laws are quite different from the federal ADEA. This situation creates the possibility that employees will bring claims that are covered by the state law, but not by the federal law. In such instances, the state-only claims will not be referred to the EEOC. Claims that are covered only by federal law must be filed directly with the EEOC, within 180 days of the discriminatory act.

The deferral concept means that the EEOC defers to the state and does not process the charge for a period of 60 days after the referral, so that the state agency can take action.

Except in a deferral state, the charge must be filed no later than 180 days after the discriminatory act, or the latest act that forms part of a pattern. In a deferral state, the last permissible filing date is either 300 days after the discriminatory act (or last discriminatory act in a series) or 30 days after the state agency dismisses its charge and notifies the complainant of the dismissal—whichever comes earlier. Unlike Title VII plaintiffs, ADEA plaintiffs do not have to get a right-to-sue letter.

If a state has a law against age discrimination, 29 U.S.C. § 633(b) provides that employees may not bring ADEA suits in that state until they have waited 60 days for the state to resolve the charges. If state charges have been dismissed in less than 60 days, the employee doesn't have to wait for the full 60-day period to end. The 60-day period is imposed to allow for conciliation of the charge. [*See* 29 U.S.C. § 626(d)]

During this period, the EEOC's task is to decide if it has a "reasonable basis to conclude that a violation of the Act has occurred or will occur." If the answer is "yes," the EEOC makes a "good cause" or "reasonable cause" finding—i.e., that the employee had good cause to complain. Then the EEOC will probably issue a Letter of Violation. However, the mere fact that no letter is issued does not prove that the EEOC did not detect any violations.

Courts have reached different conclusions about what to do if the plaintiff does not wait 60 days as required. The Sixth Circuit says that the case should be dismissed (but without prejudice, so it can be refiled later). On the other hand, the Eighth Circuit says that the case should not be dismissed, only suspended pending the administrative disposition of the complaint. [*Compare Chapman v. City of De-*

troit, 808 F.2d 459 (6th Cir. 1986), *with Wilson v. Westinghouse Elec. Co.*, 838 F.2d 286 (8th Cir. 1988)] The August 2002 EEOC Proposed Regulations call for the EEOC to issue a Notice of Dismissal or Termination when the agency finishes processing a charge. A complainant can file suit in federal or state court at any time after 60 days have passed since the filing of the age discrimination charge—whether or not the EEOC has issued its Notice of Dismissal or Termination. But once the Notice is issued, the complainant has only 90 days from the date of the notice to bring suit; otherwise, the suit will be dismissed as untimely.

Next, the EEOC tries to get the company into compliance by informal persuasion. If the company and the EEOC reach an agreement that the agency believes will eliminate the discrimination, then the agreement will be written down and signed by the EEOC representative, a company representative, and the employee who charged the discrimination. If the charging party is not satisfied, he or she can withdraw the charge. The EEOC still has independent authority to settle on behalf of other employees affecting the discrimination.

On the other hand, if conciliation fails and no agreement is reached (possibly because there has been no discrimination, and therefore the employer is unwilling to admit culpability and "admit" discrimination that never occurred in the first place), the EEOC and/or the charging party can sue. The charging party's suit must be brought no later than 90 days after receipt of notice from the EEOC that conciliation has failed, but it is not necessary to get a right-to-sue letter.

[B] State Laws Against Age Discrimination

Most of the states have some kind of law prohibiting age discrimination in employment. However, Alabama does not. Missouri, Oklahoma, and Wyoming have general antidiscrimination laws that do not go into detail about age claims. In Arkansas, Mississippi, and South Dakota, state employees, but not private-sector employees, are covered by the state ADEA. North Carolina provides that age discrimination violates public policy, but there is no comprehensive anti-discrimination law.

Some of the state laws cover all employers, whereas others cover only companies that employ at least a certain number of workers (which can be anywhere from 4 to 25, depending on the state). In other words, some small companies are subject to state ADEAs but not to the federal law. The Indiana statute, however, applies only in circumstances outside the federal law.

> **Tip:** In Georgia, Nebraska, New Hampshire, and South Dakota, violation of state antidiscrimination law can be a criminal offense.

Although the procedure varies from state to state, usually a person who claims to be a victim of age discrimination begins the state enforcement process by filing a charge with the state human rights/equal employment opportunity agency, within the time frame set out by the statute. Depending on the statute, this could be anywhere from 30 days after the alleged discriminatory practice to one year plus 90 days of the time the complainant discovered the employer acted illegally.

Most of the states, like the federal government, have a dual system of agency enforcement and private litigation. The agency investigates the charge and issues either a finding of good cause or a no-cause finding. If the agency deems that the charge is well-founded, then it tries to conciliate or sues the employer. On the other hand, if it makes a no-cause finding, or cannot resolve the matter promptly, the employee has the right to bring suit in state court, under the state antidiscrimination law. However, in some states, there is no agency enforcement, so employers are only at risk of private suit.

Another group of states (Massachusetts, Michigan, New York, Ohio, Pennsylvania) have a different dual system. Complaining employees get a choice: either to file a state-court suit right away, without going to the antidiscrimination agency, or to file an administrative complaint. However, election of remedies is usually required. So once an employee files in state court, he or she cannot go back and initiate the administrative process. Complainants in these states are entitled to use the 300-day filing period available in deferral states.

CHAPTER 42

DISCRIMINATION SUITS BY EMPLOYEES: PROCEDURAL ISSUES

§ 42.01 INTRODUCTION

When it comes to litigating discrimination claims, it's understandable that both employers and employees feel vulnerable. Employers often feel that, no matter how little substance there is to a charge of discrimination, the employer will still have to fight the charge (which can be time-consuming and expensive) and might be ordered to pay immense damages. Employees feel that they are at the mercy of employers—that the only means of redress is complex and takes many years, by which time memories will have faded.

§ 42.02 CAUSES OF ACTION

In legal parlance, a cause of action is something for which someone can be sued. Employees can charge employers with various kinds of wrongdoing, and the same suit can combine discrimination charges with other causes of action, such as:

- Violation of Title VII of the Civil Rights Act of 1964 (discrimination on the grounds of race, sex, nationality, or color—sexual harassment is considered a type of sex discrimination);
- Violation of the Pregnancy Discrimination Act (PDA), an addition to Title VII, which forbids treating a qualified pregnant employee on less favorable terms than a comparably-situated, nonpregnant employee;
- Violation of the Age Discrimination Act (discriminating against an individual who is age 40 or over, in any term or condition of employment, including hiring, firing, promotion, and benefits);
- Violation of 42 U.S.C. § 1981, the Civil War-era statute that gives all citizens the same right to make contracts as "white citizens." Four Circuits allow § 1981 suits by at-will employees who claim they were discharged on the basis of racial prejudice—even though they had no written employment contracts. [*Lauture v. IBM*, 216 F.3d 238 (2d Cir. 2000); *Perry v. Woodward*, 199 F.3d 1126 (10th Cir. 1999); *Spriggs v. Diamond Auto Glass*, 165 F.3d 1015 (4th Cir. 1999); *Fadeyi v. Planned Parenthood*, 160 F.3d 1048 (5th Cir. 1998)];
- Wrongful refusal to re-employ a military veteran;
- Violation of the Equal Pay Act: paying women less than men for the same job. This law does not permit "comparable worth" claims that allege that a typically female job is more valuable than a different and higher-paid job that is typically performed by men;
- Retaliation against an employee who filed a discrimination claim (or exercised other legal rights, e.g., in connection with unemployment benefits or Worker's Compensation) or cooperated in an investigation;
- Any act of wrongful termination for other reasons (e.g., discharging someone who "blew the whistle" on corporate wrongdoing);
- Violation of labor law (e.g., retaliating against someone for protected activity such as supporting the union or asserting a grievance against the employer). Nearly all labor law claims must be brought in federal, not state, court, because

the federal statute the Labor Management Relations Act (LMRA) preempts
state regulation—in other words, this is considered purely a federal matter;
- Breach of contract (either an explicit, written contract such as an employment
  contract or a collective bargaining agreement, or an implied contract);
- Defamation (in the context of an unfavorable reference or unfavorable statements in the press, and if the employer cannot assert a defense of truth);
- Interference with contractual relations, e.g, the employer prevents an ex-
  employee from getting a new job or establishing a business;
- Infliction of emotional distress (either negligent or intentional).

Frequently, employees will engage in several different proceedings, involving different statutes. Then, it becomes important to determine if the results of one
proceeding will affect other proceedings (or prevent potential claims from being
pursued). Denial of a person's FMLA claim for being fired while on maternity
leave is res judicata to Title VII, ADEA, and the Florida Civil Rights Act claims.
That is, the negative FMLA ruling is considered to have determined the other
claims, because all the claims involve the same facts, which have already been litigated. [*O'Connor v. PCA Family Health Plan*, 81 FEP Cases 1112 (11th Cir. Jan.
18, 2000)]

"Testers" are often used in housing discrimination litigation: Minority group
members apply to rent or buy a property. If the property is offered to white people
after the testers are told that the property is off the market, this is potent evidence
of discrimination. The Seventh Circuit decided that employment testers play a
valuable role in combating employment discrimination. Therefore, they have
standing to sue under Title VII, even though they don't really want the job. But
they don't have standing under 42 U.S.C. § 1981, which would require actual intent to form a contract. [*Kyles v. J.K. Guardian Security Servs. Inc.*, 69 L.W. 1038,
2170 (7th Cir. 2000)]

§ 42.03   STATISTICS ABOUT CHARGES AND RESULTS

The EEOC gets about 80,000 charges a year. About one-third of the charges
allege race discrimination, and a slightly lower percentage allege sex discrimination. Disability and age discrimination each represent about 20% of charges, and
national origin discrimination accounted for about 10%. A quarter of all charges
allege retaliation in addition to the initial act of discrimination. (The numbers
add up to more than 100% because of the potential for allegations of more than
one type of discrimination.) [No by-line, *Charge Backlog, Processing Time
Dropped; EEOC Litigation Increased During FY 2001*, 70 L.W. 2355 (Dec. 11,
2001); Leigh Strope, *Job Discrimination Complaints Rise* (Feb. 22, 2002) <http://
www.lexisone.com/news/ap/ap_b02202a.html> (posted on Feb. 22, 2002)]

It is easy to predict that, in a recession (and officially, a recession began in
March 2001) discrimination complaints will increase—and this is in fact what
happened in 2001, when 80,840 discrimination charges were filed—the highest
level since 1995.

In fiscal 2001, the EEOC speeded up its processing (to an average of six months per charge) and reduced its backlog to the lowest level in two decades: 32,500, as compared with 34,300 in 2000 and approximately 40,000 in 1999.

In fiscal 2001, the EEOC process required employers to pay $285 million in response to discrimination charges. Nearly all of that ($248 million) came from settlements before suit was filed; the other $37 million came through litigation. In fiscal 2001, the EEOC brought or intervened in 384 suits (more than the 327 in FY 2000). Of these suits, 271 were Title VII cases, versus 61 ADA cases, 31 ADEA cases, three Equal Pay Act cases, and eighteen cases involving two or more statutes. Of these suits, 130 were class actions.

In mid-2001, the results of research by two Cornell law professors were released. They studied nine years of data from the Administrative Office of the United States Courts. There were 7,378 civil cases of all kinds that were tried and appealed between 1988 and 1997.

During that time period, there were about 58,000 civil trials in the District Courts. Overall, plaintiffs won 43% of the cases—but of the 7,575 employment discrimination cases that went to trial (don't forget that the vast majority of claims wash out long before there is a trial), the plaintiffs won only about 30%.

When a plaintiff appealed a victory by the defendant, 12% of District Court verdicts of all types were overturned by the Court of Appeals—but plaintiffs only succeeded in upsetting a defense victory in an employment discrimination case 5.8% of the time. Overall, defendants were able to overturn plaintiffs' verdicts 32.5% of the time, but they were able to do this 43.6% of the time when employment-discrimination plaintiffs won at the trial court level.

The professors concluded that, although there were some regional variations, employers had a "huge advantage" in all 12 of the federal Courts of Appeals, especially the Fifth Circuit (which covers Louisiana, Mississippi, and Texas), where 14 of the 23 wins by employees were reversed, and 95.7% of the verdicts for employers were affirmed. [*See* Jess Bravin, *U.S. Courts Are Tough on Job-Bias Suits*, Wall Street Journal, July 16, 2001 at p. A2]

The consulting firm Jury Verdict Research compared compensatory damages awarded by juries during the period 1994–2000 with settlements for the same time period. Settlements were much lower in each category, showing the advantage of being able to resolve a case before it gets to a jury. The median award (i.e., the number at which half the awards were higher, half lower) for all employment practices cases was $151,000 in 1999, rising to $218,000 in 2000. For all discrimination cases, the median jury verdict for the 1994–2000 period was $150,000, versus a median settlement of $60,000. For hostile work environment cases, the median verdict was $155,000, the median settlement was $60,000. For retaliation claims, the median verdict was $139,800; the median settlement was a comparatively modest $32,500. In wrongful termination cases not involving discrimination, the median jury award was $157,000; the median settlement was $44,000. [Michael Barrier, *EPLI Providers Turn Up the Heat,* HR Magazine May 2002, at 46.

§ 42.04   TITLE VII PROCEDURE

[A]   Complaining Party

Federal antidiscrimination laws include extremely complicated procedures for bringing a complaint, and one of the employer's main lines of defense is that the potential plaintiff has failed to satisfy the procedural requirements.

42 U.S.C. § 2000e(l) defines "complaining party" in a Title VII case as either the private person who brings a case or the EEOC or the U.S. Attorney General.

[B]   The Charging Process

Nearly every phrase or term in this section has already been extensively litigated. Individuals who think they have experienced an unlawful employment practice cannot simply go to the relevant federal court and file a complaint. Instead, they must file a written, sworn document called a "charge" with an administrative agency. Would-be plaintiffs cannot go to court until there has been an administrative investigation and attempts to settle the matter without getting the court system involved.

The EEOC notifies the employer of the charge within ten days, disclosing the date, place, and circumstances of the allegedly unlawful practices, and then starts an investigation to see if there is reasonable cause for the charge. The EEOC's duty is to complete the investigation as soon as possible—and within 120 days of the filing of the charge (or the referral date) "so far as practicable." (The EEOC has a big backlog and often misses the 120-day deadline.)

Grievance procedures under a CBA, or company-sponsored grievance procedures in a nonunion company, have no effect on Title VII suits. So the employee doesn't have to use those procedures before filing a charge with an antidiscrimination agency. On the other hand, ongoing grievances under the CBA won't prevent or delay a Title VII suit.

If the EEOC does not believe that the charge is supported by reasonable cause, it dismisses the charge, and the employee then has the right to sue. In fact, it is not even held against the employee that the EEOC made a "no-cause" finding. A no-cause determination does not prevent the employee from suing. It does not limit the suit, what the employee can try to prove, or even the remedies he or she can receive. The judge or jury makes its own independent inquiry into the facts and is not influenced by the EEOC investigation.

But if the EEOC does believe that the charge is supported, then the EEOC's job is to try to use "informal methods of conference, conciliation, and persuasion" to get the employer to change the employment practice. The conciliation process is confidential, and statements made during the process can only be publicized or used as evidence in litigation based on the written consent of the person making the statement. Violating this confidentiality can be punished by as much as $1,000 fine and/or a year in prison.

The EEOC's powers to investigate a charge include having access "at all reasonable times" to all evidence that is relevant to the charges, and the EEOC also is entitled to make copies. [42 U.S.C. § 2000e-8(a)]

[C]   State Agencies

In a Fifth Circuit case, procedural failures required dismissal of an age-discrimination judgment in favor of the plaintiff. He filed a complaint with the EEOC and did not check the box on the form indicating that he wanted the charge filed with both the EEOC and the Texas Commission on Human Rights. Therefore, he failed to go through the mandatory step of filing a state charge—and his federal lawsuit was invalid. [*Jones v. Grinnell Corp.*, 235 F.3d 972 (5th Cir. 2001), discussed in Stephanie Hoops, *5th Circuit Tosses Case Because "X" Didn't Mark the Spot,* Texas Lawyer (Jan. 19, 2001) (law.com)] Although Texas has a work-sharing agreement, this merely means that a single filing can cover both state and federal requirements—not that the state procedure can be ignored, even in a case where the charging party asserts only federal claims.

§ 42.05   TIMING REQUIREMENTS

[A]   Generally

Section 2000e-5(c) says that if the state where the alleged unlawful employment practice occurred has a state antidiscrimination law, then EEOC charges may not be filed until 60 days have passed since commencement of state antidiscrimination charges. If the EEOC itself files a charge, it has an obligation to notify the appropriate state authority and give it sixty days to enforce the local law and eliminate the unlawful employment practice.

The basic rule is that, to avoid being dismissed as untimely, EEOC charges must be filed within 180 days of the date of the wrongful action. Then papers must be served on the employer within ten days. However, if the state has an antidiscrimination agency, the employee has 300 days from the date of the wrongful action to file with the EEOC. There is an additional requirement that the employee not wait more than 30 days after the state or local agency has dismissed a state charge to file with the EEOC. [42 U.S.C. § 2000e-5(e)(1)]

The charge has to be verified (the charging party has to state under penalty of perjury that the statements in the charge are true). [42 U.S.C. § 2000e5(b)] In March, 2002, the U.S. Supreme Court upheld an EEOC regulation, 29 C.F.R. § 1601.12(b), that allows "relation back." That is, if a charge is made within the 300-day period but verified later, it will still be timely because the verification "relates back" to the timely charge. The Supreme Court ruled in *Edelman v. Lynchburg College* [122 S. Ct. 1145 (2002)] that Title VII requires both filing within 300 days and verification, but the two need not occur at the same time.

Another case from the same term deals with another timing issue. If the plaintiff's claim is for only one act of discrimination or retaliation, or for several separate acts, then the claim must meet the 180-day or 300-day requirement to be timely. However, if the plaintiff charges a number of acts that he or she claims made up part of the same practice creating a hostile work environment, then the claim is timely as long as there was at least one act in the series that occurred during the 180-day or 300-day period. [*National Railroad Passenger Corp. v. Morgan,* #00-1614, 70 L.W. 4524 (Sup. Ct. June 10, 2002)]

For charges claiming that a seniority system was intentionally adopted to be discriminatory (whether or not the system is facially discriminatory), the date from which the time to file runs is either the date of adoption of the seniority system, when the claimant becomes subject to the system, or when the claimant suffers injury as a result of the application of the system. [42 U.S.C. § 2000e-5(e)(2)]

The EEOC has 30 days after filing of a charge, or 30 days after the expiration of the period for referring charges from state agencies, to negotiate with the employer to produce a conciliation agreement that ends the unlawful employment practice. If the 30-day period expires without a conciliation agreement, the EEOC has the power to sue the employer in federal court.

On the other hand, if the EEOC makes a "no-cause" finding about the charge, or 180 days have passed since the charge was filed with the EEOC or referred from the state agency, and the EEOC has not filed suit and there has been no conciliation agreement, then the EEOC will notify the charging party. This is known as a "right-to-sue letter," because it enables the charging party to bring a federal suit.

In nearly all cases, the appropriate defendant is the employer company—there are virtually no situations in which Title VII suits can appropriately be brought against an individual person who is alleged to have performed discriminatory acts. The charging party must file suit within 90 days of the date of the right-to-sue letter—otherwise, the case can be dismissed for being untimely. [*See* 42 U.S.C. § 2000e-5(f)(1)]

Section 2000e-5(f)(3) provides that the suit can be filed in any federal District Court in the state where the alleged unlawful employment practice occurred. (The number of federal judicial districts in a state ranges from one to four.) The suit can also be brought in the judicial district where the relevant employment records are kept, or in the district where the plaintiff would have worked if there had been no unlawful employment practice. Finally, if the defendant company can't be found in any of those districts, the plaintiff can sue the defendant company in the judicial district where the company's principal office is located.

Although the general statute of limitations for civil actions brought under CRA '91 and other statutes passed since 1990 is four years, *Zubi v. AT&T Corp.* [219 F.3d 220 (3d Cir. 2000)] says that the correct statute of limitations for a § 1981 wrongful discharge case is whatever the statute of limitations would be for a state-court wrongful discharge suit in the state in which the federal court is located.

[B] Tolling

In a limited group of circumstances, the statute of limitations can be tolled (suspended) when it would be unjust to insist on strict compliance. Tolling may be permitted if:

- The employer was guilty of deception or some other wrongdoing that prevented the employee from asserting Title VII rights;
- The employee tried to file a timely lawsuit, but the pleading was rejected as defective;
- The employee filed in time, but in the wrong court.

Tolling is usually considered a defense, which means that it is up to the plaintiff to prove that it was available, and not up to the defendant to prove that it was not.

The term "tolling" is sometimes used to cover two different but related concepts. "Equitable tolling" allows a delayed case to continue because, even though the plaintiff's excusable ignorance or oversight caused the delay, the defendant is not prejudiced (harmed) by the delay. "Equitable estoppel" prevents the defendant from complaining about a delay that was caused in whole or part by the defendant's deceit or other conduct prejudicial to the plaintiff's interests—e.g., if the employee is afraid to approach the EEOC and endanger the internal investigation and grievance procedure that being carried out. [*Currier v. Radio Free Europe*, 159 F.3d 1363 (D.C. Cir. 1998)]

If a Title VII suit is dismissed for being untimely, but the employee can assert another charge based on other facts, he or she can file a suit based on the second charge—as long as that one is timely! [*Criales v. American Airlines Inc.*, 65 L.W. 2551 (2d Cir. Jan. 21, 1997)]

Two sexual harassment cases a few months apart reach different conclusions as to whether the 90-day filing period should have been tolled. The D.C. Circuit refused to grant equitable tolling to an employee who claimed that severe, continuing harassment rendered her *non compos mentis* and unable to protect her own interests by filing in time. To the court in *Smith-Haynie v. District of Columbia* [155 F.3d 575 (D.C. Cir. 1998)], the only evidence of the plaintiff's distraction was her own statement. But the Ninth Circuit did permit equitable tolling in *Stoll v. Runyon* [165 F.3d 1238 (9th Cir. 1999)], where the plaintiff suffered psychiatric disability after repeated sexual abuse, assault, and rape.

§ 42.06   CLASS ACTIONS

Class actions are governed by Rule 23 of the Federal Rules of Civil Procedure, especially Rule 23(b). The various subsections of Rule 23 create several alternative methods of litigating a class action, but each method has its own procedural requirements that must be satisfied. The requirements relate to what the plaintiffs want (money damages, or just an injunction?) and how people become members of the class (are they automatically included unless they opt out, or do they have to opt in?). It can also be difficult and expensive for the potential plaintiffs to give the required notice to everyone who might want to join the class. [*See, e.g., Jefferson v. Ingersoll Int'l Inc.*, 195 F.3d 994 (7th Cir. 1999)]

Discrimination cases focusing on monetary damages can be hard to certify as class actions. Rule 23(b)(2) requires not only a common injury but uniform remedies for the whole class. Would-be plaintiffs who can't use Rule 23(b)(2) may have to fall back on Rule 23(b)(3), which requires them to prove that class-wide issues are more important in the case than individual issues. They must also prove that a class action is better than other methods of resolving the dispute. In some cases, a "hybrid" class action will be allowed. First a class is certified under Rule 23(b)(2) to decide if the employer is liable. If it is, damages are determined under Rule 23(b)(2). [*See Defense Attorneys Describe Strategies for Blocking Class Action Certification*, 69 L.W. 2206 (Oct. 10, 2000)]

In 1998, the Fourth Circuit decertified the employee class in a case alleging a pattern or practice of racial discrimination. [*Lowery v. Circuit City Stores Inc.*, 158 F.3d 742 (4th Cir. 1998)] Individual employees who were once members of the class were not allowed to maintain the pattern or practice case. Each must satisfy the *McDonnell-Douglas* burden-shifting analysis individually. The Fourth Circuit vacated most of the District Court's $4.2 million judgment ($3.9 million of that was attorneys' fees). Most of the injunctive relief, such as establishment of a department of diversity management (career paths for black employees), was held to be excessively broad and therefore was struck down.

Late in 2001, nationwide class certification was denied to a group of black hotel workers suing the Adams Mark hotel chain who charged racially-motivated unfair discipline and discrimination in promotions. The judge ruled that the would-be class members were not all affected by a centralized decision-making process (as distinct from decisions made by the management of a particular hotel).

Therefore, they could not show that their own claims were typical of the claims of the class or that common interests outweighed individual ones. Under current litigation practice, it is not enough for would-be class action plaintiffs just to allege discrimination against an entire group. The potential plaintiffs have to show that the discriminatory practice was pervasive or reflected in other employment activities. They must also provide detailed allegations, affidavits, and other evidence that the claims raised by individuals on their own behalf share questions of law or fact with the class claim. They must show that the individual claims are typical of the class as a whole. [*Vinson v. Seven Seventeen HB Philadelphia Corp.*, discussed in Shannon P. Duffy, *Class Action Claims Fail in Race Bias Suit Against Hotel Chain*, The Legal Intelligencer (Nov. 7, 2001) (law.com)]

§ 42.07 THE DISCRIMINATION COMPLAINT

Once the case is cleared for litigation in federal court, the plaintiff must draft a complaint to inform the defendant and the court system of the nature of the allegations against the defendant. However, because the complaint is the first stage in litigation, the plaintiff may not have all the information that he or she will need to prove the case at the trial level. Early in 2002, the Supreme Court held that a valid discrimination complaint merely has to include a "short and plain statement" of the plaintiff's claim. Although once the trial occurs, the plaintiff will have to prove a prima facie case (see below), it is not necessary to set out a complete prima facie case at the complaint stage. [*Swierkiewicz v. Sorema N.A.*, 534 U.S. 506 (2002)]

Late in 2001, the Eleventh Circuit adopted a position already held by the Third, Seventh, and Eighth Circuits: An EEOC intake questionnaire constitutes a "charge" if it is verified and has the information a charge would contain, and a reasonable person would consider the questionnaire to manifest an intent to seek Title VII remedies. [*Wilkerson v. Grinnell Corp.*, 270 F.3d 1314 (11th Cir. Oct. 22, 2001)]

§ 42.08   MEETING BURDENS

In legal parlance, "the burden of production" means having to provide evidence to prove a particular point, and "the burden of proof" is the standard used to determine if adequate evidence has been supplied.

Section 2000e(m) says that "demonstrates" means "meets the burdens of production and persuasion." This covers the extremely important legal issue of who has to provide evidence of what. It is always easier to wait for the other party to produce evidence and then show that this evidence is incorrect, incomplete, not technically satisfactory, or inadequate to prove the case, than to have to submit independent evidence of one's own viewpoint.

Section 2000e-2(k) explains what the plaintiff has to prove in order to win a disparate-impact case. The complaining party must show that the employer's challenged employment practice has a disparate impact on a protected group. At this stage, the employer has a chance to prove that the employment practice is valid because it is job-related and consistent with the needs of the employer's business. However, if the employer demonstrates that the employment practice does not cause disparate impact, it is not necessary to prove business necessity for that practice. On the other hand, business necessity is only a defense against disparate impact claims, not against claims of intentional discrimination.

Another route for proving disparate impact is for the complaining party to demonstrate disparate impact and also show that the employer refused to adopt an alternative employment practice that would eliminate the disparate impact.

The EEOC, like other administrative agencies, has the right to issue regulations. These regulations do not have the force of law, and some of them have been struck down by various courts (although some regulations—sometimes the same ones—have been upheld by other courts).

The EEOC also issues official guidance and opinions. According to § 2000e-12, it is a valid defense for an employer to assert that it acted, or failed to act, based on a written EEOC interpretation or opinion—even if the EEOC later rescinds the document.

§ 42.09   RETALIATION CHARGES

The limitation of remedies in mixed-motive cases does not apply to Title VII retaliation claims, because the statute does not specifically refer to retaliation. To win, the retaliation plaintiff must prove that the employer's improper motive had a "determinative effect" on its action. If the employer defends itself by asserting a legitimate reason for the discharge, it has to prove not only that it would have fired the plaintiff even if there had been no discriminatory motive—and that the firing would have occurred then, and not later. [*Sagendorf-Teal v. Rensselaer County*, 100 F.3d 270 (2d Cir. 1996)]

§ 42.10   TITLE VII LITIGATION

[A]   Three-Step Process

A Title VII case is very different from other civil cases, because so much revolves around questions of intentions and statistics, not just the proof of simple facts.

The basic Title VII case is a three-step process. The plaintiff establishes a prima facie case: the basic facts that are suggestive of discrimination. This is sometimes referred to as "*McDonnell-Douglas* burden-shifting analysis" after the Supreme Court case that established this technique.

After the plaintiff submits a prima facie case, the defendant can ask the court to dismiss the case at that stage (summary judgment), if the prima facie case would not be good enough for the plaintiff to win if the defendant did not submit a case of its own.

On the other hand, if the prima facie case is strong enough to keep the case going, the defendant employer gets a chance to rebut the plaintiff's charge of discrimination. The employer can do this by proving a legitimate, nondiscriminatory reason for the job action against the plaintiff. The employer can also prevail by proving that its action was impelled by business necessity. If summary judgment is not granted, then there will have to be a full trial. The jury (or the judge, if there is no jury in the case) will have to decide the facts.

The third step is the plaintiff's again. At this stage, the plaintiff gets to show "pretextuality": that the employer's allegedly nondiscriminatory reasons are fabricated to hide its discriminatory motive.

[B]   Elements of the Prima Facie Case

The kind and amount of evidence that the plaintiff has to introduce to make a prima facie case depends on the kind of case (sex discrimination, sexual harassment, age discrimination, racial discrimination, etc.) and whether the plaintiff charges disparate treatment or disparate impact. Disparate treatment is a practice of intentional discrimination against an individual or group, whereas disparate impact is a practice that seems to be neutral and nondiscriminatory, but that has a heavier negative impact on some groups than others.

Furthermore, if the plaintiff charges that an employment practice has a disparate impact, and the employer responds by showing business necessity for that practice, the plaintiff can nevertheless win by proving that there was an alternative practice that would also have satisfied business necessity, but the employer refused to adopt that practice.

If a workplace decision involves many factors (for instance, promotion could be based on educational attainment, objective measures such as sales performance or departmental productivity, written tests, interviews, and assessments from supervisors), and the plaintiff challenges more than one of those criteria, the plaintiff has to be able to prove that each of those factors had harmful disparate impact on the plaintiff. If the various elements can't be separated and analyzed individually, then the whole decision-making practice can be treated as a single employment practice.

The "mixed motive" case works somewhat differently. It arises out of the situation in which several motivations influence the employer's decision. Some of them are lawful, others are discriminatory. The plaintiff can win a mixed motive case by showing that the discriminatory motive was influential. It is not necessary to prove that there were no legitimate motives involved. However, if the employer would have done the same thing even without a discriminatory motive being present, then the remedies available to the plaintiff will be reduced.

To establish the prima facie case, the plaintiff must show the following:

- That he or she belonged to a protected group;
- He or she had the necessary qualifications for the job (allegation of discriminatory failure to hire);
- He or she was doing an adequate job (if the allegation is improper discharge or failure to promote).

While disparate treatment cases usually depend on direct or indirect evidence of explicit discrimination, disparate impact cases usually turn on statistics about matters such as job applications and the composition of the workforce.

A white male plaintiff said he was denied a promotion because he was the victim of reverse discrimination, and the woman who was promoted was less qualified than he was. Because a white male is not a member of a protected class, the Seventh Circuit defined the prima facie case as showing "background circumstances" evidencing reverse discrimination. For instance, a pattern of not promoting white males, or the choice of a significantly weaker candidate, would suffice. It was held that the plaintiff did present a prima facie case by showing that most of the promotions were given to women. However, he did not win the case, when the issue was the employer's intent to discriminate. The plaintiff failed to prove that the employer's contention (that it believed the woman was actually better qualified for promotion) was pretextual. [*Mills v. Health Care Serv. Corp.*, 171 F.3d 450 (7th Cir. 1999)]

The plaintiff's prima facie case in a Title VII failure-to-promote case requires the employee to identify specific positions that he or she applied for but was denied. Saying that he or she was qualified for numerous promotions is not sufficient. [*Brown v. Coach Stores Inc.*, 163 F.3d 706 (2d Cir. 1998)]

[C] Evidence

Not only can each side introduce evidence about the course of the plaintiff's employment with the defendant company; in appropriate cases, the employer can introduce evidence about the plaintiff that the employer did not have at the time of the employment action.

The basic case on the use of after-acquired evidence is *McKennon v. Nashville Banner Pub. Co.* [513 U.S. 352 (1995)] In this case, the employer was allowed to introduce, at the trial, negative evidence about the plaintiff that the defendant learned after the employment action. Although the after-acquired evidence couldn't have motivated the employer, it was still relevant to the plaintiff's qualifications and credibility, so it can be introduced at trial.

O'Day v. McDonnell-Douglas Helicopter Co. [959 P.2d 792 (Ariz. 1998)] explains how to apply *McKennon* in state courts. If an employee sues for breach of contract, seeking lost wages and benefits, the after-acquired evidence can provide a complete defense for the employer as long as the employer can prove that the after-acquired evidence was serious enough to justify firing the employee if the employer had known about it earlier. In a tort suit for wrongful termination, the after-acquired evidence is not a complete defense, but does have the effect of limiting the remedies available to the plaintiff.

The Michigan Court of Appeals applied the after-acquired-evidence doctrine to a case in which the plaintiff was not hired (as opposed to a case where someone was hired, fired, and sued for discrimination—at which point the defendant employer discovered misconduct such as resume fabrication). *Smith v. Charter Township of Union* [1998 WL 17798 (Mich. App. 1998)] holds that, in failure-to-hire cases, the damage period can extend only from the date of the wrongful denial of hiring until the inevitable point at which the employer would have fired the employee based on the lack of minimum qualifications that were falsely stated on the fabricated resume.

[D] Admissible and Inadmissible Evidence

A defense expert witness should not have been allowed to testify about the plaintiff's psychiatric credibility. This was not a proper subject for testimony under Federal Rules of Evidence 702, in that it invaded the jury's role of deciding whether testimony is credible. Nor should the defendant have been allowed to introduce evidence of the plaintiff's abortion (a decade earlier), because such evidence is prejudicial and not probative. A new trial was ordered in *Nichols v. American National Insurance Co.* [154 F.3d 875 (8th Cir. 1998)] because of the improperly introduced evidence.

The Second Circuit ruled that racist comments by a white employee can be used to show that the work environment was hostile to black people, even if the remarks were made after the black plaintiff resigned. [*Whidbee v. Garzarelli Food Specialties,* 223 F.3d 62 (2d Cir. 2000)] But testimony by four of the plaintiff's coworkers (that a supervisor's treatment of the demoted black employee was racially motivated) should not have been admitted. [*Hester v. BIC Corp.,* 225 F.3d 178 (2d Cir. 2000)] The witnesses could testify about their observations, but because they didn't know how good or bad the plaintiff's work performance actually was, they couldn't testify about the supervisor's motivation.

[E] Other Litigation Issues

If the plaintiff files suit in state court, the employer often tries to get the case removed to federal court. State courts usually have less crowded calendars, so cases can be decided faster. Sometimes, state law permits the employee to assert additional causes of action, or to get remedies that would not be available in federal court. Sometimes, too, a particular action is subject to state but not federal law. For example, some states ban discrimination in workplaces that are too small to be covered by the federal law. Sexual-orientation discrimination is not covered by Title VII, but is covered by certain state or local laws.

In many cases, federal law preempts state law. In other words, certain matters, such as most of labor law and benefit law, is covered by federal law, and the states cannot interfere. Therefore, if a plaintiff's state-court claims operate in one of these preempted areas, the employer has a strong argument for getting the case removed to federal court, or even dismissed.

A 2001 article [Dan Corditz, *Forum Shopping*, Miami Daily Business Review (Dec. 5, 2000) (law.com)] says that, although plaintiffs' attorneys expect to handle many suits charging employers with performing layoffs in a discriminatory manner, the national mood places a lower value on individual rights. State judges are not always sympathetic to frivolous suits, or even suits that are technically defective.

[F] Avoiding Litigation Mistakes

Trial lawyer Gilmore E. Diekmann, Jr., tackles the mistakes that employer defendants make. [*See The Top Three Mistakes Employers Make at Trial,* <http://www.lawnewsnetwork.com>] Although the vast majority of claims of employment discrimination wash out long before trial, and employers can get summary judgment (i.e., dismissal of poorly supported claims without a full trial), the fact remains that of the cases that actually go to a jury, the employee-plaintiff wins about two out of three.

Some of these are cases in which the employer got caught doing something obviously wrong and has to take its medicine. But others are cases that the employer could have won with better trial tactics and a better job of showing its side of the story to the jury.

Diekmann suggests that some cases go to trial because the employer's lawyer got involved too late and failed to identify a losing case that should have been settled. Sometimes, the wrong lawyer handles the case: a business lawyer rather than an experienced employment law litigator, for instance.

It is especially important for the trial lawyer to be completely familiar with all the depositions in the case. Depositions not only reflect testimony that was given at a particular time (and can be used to challenge inconsistent trial testimony) but give insight into the witness's character and thought processes (and thus the best way to challenge the testimony).

Juries are predisposed to like and sympathize with employee plaintiffs. It is usually counterproductive for the defense lawyer to seem arrogant, hostile, or bullying. In Diekmann's analysis, the defense lawyer's job is to present a simple story that the jury can understand and accept. Juries have to learn to look at the facts and the legal strategies rather than maintaining their initial sympathy for the plaintiff in situations where, in fact, the employer has the stronger legal arguments and the facts on its side.

§ 42.11   ADEA SUITS

[A]   Generally

It is clear that the ADEA creates a private right of action—i.e., individuals can bring suit if they claim to have been subjected to age discrimination in employment. [*See* 29 U.S.C. § 626(c)] The statute is not very detailed. It says only that individuals can sue for "such legal or equitable relief as will effectuate the purposes" of the ADEA. However, a suit brought by the Secretary will terminate the rights of individuals to bring their own lawsuits involving their ADEA claims.

Under 29 U.S.C. § 626(d), would-be ADEA plaintiffs have to file their charges within 180 days of the alleged unlawful practice. In a "referral" state (a state whose antidiscrimination agency has a work-sharing agreement) the charge has to be filed within 300 days of the alleged unlawful practice. If the state-law proceedings are terminated, the potential plaintiff must file the charge within 30 days of the termination of the state proceeding.

When a charge is filed, all potential defendants are notified. In both the Title VII and ADEA contexts, the Secretary's duty is to "promptly seek to eliminate any alleged unlawful practice by informal methods of conciliation, conference, and persuasion."

In the federal system, whether a case can be heard by a jury (instead of just a judge) depends on several factors, including the preferences of the litigants and the nature of the suit itself. The basic rule is that juries are more appropriate for cases seeking money damages than those asking for purely equitable remedies such as injunctions or reinstatement. However, ADEA plaintiffs can demand a jury trial whenever they seek money damages, even if there are also equitable claims in the same suit.

[B]   Timing Issues for ADEA Suits

If the EEOC dismisses an age discrimination charge as unfounded, it will issue a "right to sue letter" to the complainant. The complainant will then be able to file a suit in the appropriate federal District Court, and in fact the EEOC's negative determination will not be held against the complainant. However, the complaint must be filed no later than 90 days after the notification of the EEOC dismissal. The statute of limitations for ADEA cases derives from the Portal to Portal Act [29 U.S.C. § 2591]

The 90-day requirement was added by the Civil Rights Act of 1991. Earlier, the ADEA statute of limitations was two years from the last discriminatory act, or three years from the last willful discriminatory act. But given the EEOC's large workload and small staff, in many cases the statute of limitations has actually gotten longer rather than shorter, because many charges take far more than two years for resolution.

It is in the employer's best interest for the court to rule that the cause of action "accrued" earlier—i.e., that the clock started ticking when the employee had to file suit. The earlier the cause of action accrues, the more likely it is that a claim can be dismissed as untimely.

If the alleged discriminatory act is firing the employee, there is a single act of discrimination. Most cases hold that the discriminatory act occurs on the date the plaintiff is unambiguously informed that he or she will be fired. The important date is the date of this notice, and not the first warning the plaintiff receives of impending termination, and not the last day the employee works for the employer or the last date he or she is on the payroll. The notice does not have to be formal, or even written, but it must be a definite statement that a final decision has been made to terminate the employee.

It is harder to place other discriminatory acts on a time continuum. It has been held that a claim of failure to promote accrues when the employees know or should have known about the facts that support the claim—probably, that a younger individual received the promotion that the plaintiff wanted.

If there is only a single employment decision, there is only a single act that might be discriminatory. However, some courts allow a plaintiff to argue that there was a continuing violation lasting over a period of time—for example, that the plaintiff kept his or her job, but was denied promotions he or she deserved because of age discrimination. In a case where the court accepts the continuing violation theory, the cause of action accrues with the last discriminatory act in the series. A filing that is timely for one act of discrimination will be timely for all acts of discrimination in the same series.

A bad performance appraisal that makes an employee more vulnerable to being laid off or RIFed (but that is not an actual threat of dismissal unless performance improves) is not considered an employment action that could give rise to an ADEA claim.

For discriminatory layoff charges, courts reach different conclusions as to when the cause of action accrues. One theory is that accrual occurs on the actual date of layoff. The other is that the cause of action accrues later, when the possibility of reinstatement ends because the employer has filled the last job for which the plaintiff might have been recalled.

In Title VII cases, the Civil Rights Act of 1991 clearly provides that the statute of limitations for a seniority system accrues on the latest of three dates: when the system is adopted; when an employee becomes subject to it; or when the plaintiff is injured by it. But Congress did not enact a similar provision relating to the ADEA. Some courts continue to foreclose employee claims, on the grounds that the claim accrued when the plan was adopted, often many years before the employee became subject to the plan.

[C] Tolling the ADEA Statute of Limitations

The statute of limitations can be tolled (suspended), giving employees additional time to litigate, in various circumstances—usually as a result of deception or other misconduct on the part of the employer. However, certain circumstances have been held not to be wrongful conduct, and will not toll the statute of limitations:

- Putting an employee on "special assignment" until termination takes effect;
- Offering a severance benefits package. However, offering a lavish severance package, but preventing employees from discussing it, was held to discourage employees from vindicating their legal rights, and therefore to toll the statute of limitations.

> **Tip:** The statute of limitations is not tolled during the employer's in-house grievance procedure. However, a collective bargaining agreement provision is invalid if it terminates the employee's right to pursue a grievance once he or she files age discrimination charges with the EEOC or the local antidiscrimination agency. The clause is void because it punishes employees for exercising their legal rights.

Even if tolling occurs, it probably cannot last beyond the point at which an employee who took reasonable steps to investigate would have been aware of discrimination.

Do not forget that 29 U.S.C. § 627 requires the employer to post a notice of ADEA rights. The EEOC and Department of Labor distribute free copies of the mandatory notice; posters can also be purchased from many publishers. If the notice is duly posted, then the court will presume that the employee could have read the poster and become aware of at least basic ADEA rights.

However, if the information is not posted, the court may conclude that the employer deprived the employee of access to information about ADEA rights, thus tolling the statute of limitations. Yet some courts say that the real test is whether the employee actually was aware of what the ADEA says. Given actual knowledge, the court may decide that the absence of a poster in the workplace does not justify extending the time to bring suit.

[D] The ADEA Plaintiff's Burden of Proof

The *McDonnell-Douglas* pattern applies in ADEA cases. That is, first the plaintiff introduces evidence of a prima facie case of discrimination. If the evidence (taken at face value) is inadequate, the defendant employer can get summary judgment—that is, can have the case dismissed because of this inadequacy.

If, however, the case is good enough to survive a motion for summary judgment, it is the employer's turn at bat. By and large, proof is up to the plaintiff, but a BFOQ is an affirmative defense, which means that the employer has the burden of proving it. [*Western Air Lines Inc. v. Criswell*, 472 U.S. 400 (1985)] In non-BFOQ cases, the employer can rebut the prima facie case by showing a legitimate, non-discriminatory reason for the conduct challenged by the employee. Then the employee gets another chance, to demonstrate that the employer's justification is actually a pretext for discrimination.

It is not necessary in all cases for the plaintiff to prove that he or she was replaced by someone under 40 (i.e., outside the protected group). [*O'Connor v. Consolidated Coin Caterers Corp.*, 517 U.S. 308 (1997)] It is possible, although difficult, for the plaintiff to win a case in which he or she was replaced by another person over 40, as long as improper age-related motives are shown.

In 1993, the Supreme Court set a new standard for proving ADEA cases based on age-related factors rather than on age itself. For instance, a 30-year-old cannot have 30 years' employment experience, but a 38-year-old employee might have worked for the company for 20 years, and therefore have more seniority than a 50-year-old hired only 10 years earlier. In that example, the allegedly age-related factors of higher salary and benefits would actually make the 38-year-old the more expensive employee.

The key case on this issue is *Hazen Paper Co. v. Biggins* [507 U.S. 604 (1993)], which requires the plaintiff to prove that the employer's decision was influenced by age, not merely by age-related factors.

According to the Eleventh Circuit, laid-off older workers don't always have to be rehired or offered a transfer to a new job, but they must at least be considered for rehiring; the possibility must not be rejected on the basis of age. Therefore, a prima facie case is made out when a younger employee is hired or transferred to replace an older employee who was RIFed. [*Jameson v. Arrow Co.*, 75 F.3d 1528 (11th Cir. 1996)]

In a disparate-treatment age-discrimination case, the plaintiff can prevail by having an adequate amount of either direct or indirect evidence. However, the burden of proof, and the way it shifts, is applied differently for direct versus indirect evidence. Evidence is direct if its introduction does not require the judge or jury to use any presumptions or make any inferences. Indirect evidence requires interpretation of the employer's actions and statements. [*See Torrey v. Casio Inc.*, 42 F.3d 825 (3rd Cir. 1994)]

Price Waterhouse v. Hopkins [490 U.S. 228 (1989)] says that plaintiffs who have direct evidence of discrimination can require employers to prove that they would have fired or otherwise acted against the plaintiff even without discrimination. But without direct evidence, the ordinary three-step *McDonnell-Douglas* pretextuality analysis applies. *Hopkins* also covers mixed-motive cases, those in which the employer had several motivations. (The text of the ADEA has been amended to make it clear that mixed-motivate cases are covered.)

Hopkins requires the plaintiff to show that age is a substantial factor in the decision, but not necessarily the only one or even the most salient one. The employer can offer a defense that it would have taken the same employment decision even if age had not been used as a criterion. The employer merely has to prove this by a preponderance of the evidence, not beyond a reasonable doubt. The Civil Rights Act of 1991 overrules *Hopkins* in Title VII cases, but it remains in effect for ADEA cases.

Direct evidence of age discrimination is hard to find—especially since even employers who do practice discrimination usually have enough sophistication to conceal it. As a practical matter, then, most ADEA cases will be based on statistical evidence in support of the allegation, with or without evidence about statements made by executives and supervisors. Statistics are especially prominent in disparate impact cases.

However, the legal trend has been to reduce the credence given to statistics. In *St. Mary's Honor Center v. Hicks* [509 U.S. 502 (1993)], the court held that the plaintiff always has the "ultimate burden of persuasion." So if the fact-finder (which will be the jury or the judge in a nonjury case) doesn't believe the employer's explanation of why its conduct was legitimate, the plaintiff can still lose—if the plaintiff simply fails to offer enough evidence. The *Hicks* standard is sometimes called "pretext-plus": The plaintiff has to do more than just show that the defendant's excuses are a mere pretext for discrimination.

Late in 2001, an ADEA suit was dismissed. The defendant claimed economic justification for eliminating a job. The plaintiff said that it would be cost-effective to retrain him for a newly created job. But the judge said that there was no evidence presented to rebut the reason asserted for the layoff. Nor did the plaintiff provide solid evidence of his qualification to handle the additional responsibilities of the proposed new job. Furthermore, another employee, who was even older than the plaintiff, was retained, and two people over 40 were hired for new jobs. The plaintiff also charged that, because one of the new hires earned more than he did, the employer must be lying about the economic reasons for the changes, but the court found that the reorganization saved money overall. According to the Eastern District of Pennsylvania, plaintiffs "cannot rely on unsupported assertions, conclusory allegations, or mere suspicion" to get a case past the summary judgment stage. [*Merriweather v. Philadelphia Federation of Teachers Health & Welfare Fund,* (E.D. Pa. 2001). *See* Shannon P. Duffy, *Lack of Evidence Dooms Age Discrimination Case, Federal Judge Rules,* The Legal Intelligencer (Nov. 13, 2001) (law.com)]

The District Court, upheld by the Ninth Circuit, granted summary judgment for the employer in a suit brought by a group of over-40 Quaker Oats workers who alleged that a skill test (used to choose employees to be RIFed during a corporate reorganization) had a disparate impact on older workers. [*Coleman v. Quaker Oats,* 232 F.3d 1271 (9th Cir. 2000)] The Ninth Circuit did not find their statistical evidence (showing twice as many over-40 as under-40 employees were selected for RIF) persuasive.

The Ninth Circuit accepted the employer's argument that the test results were not random, but reflected legitimate nondiscriminatory factors affecting job performance: educational levels, for example. Furthermore, the plaintiffs did not plead their disparate impact theory correctly. It should have been raised in the original complaint, but they did not make the claim until they responded to the defense motion for summary judgment.

[E] The ADEA Prima Facie Case

The basic prima facie (initial) case for an ADEA lawsuit is:

- The plaintiff belongs to the protected group—that is, is over 40;
- The plaintiff was qualified for the position he or she held or applied for;
- The plaintiff was not hired, discharged, demoted, deprived of a raise, or otherwise disfavored because of age;
- (In appropriate cases) The plaintiff was replaced—especially by someone under 40, although it is not absolutely required that the replacement come from outside the protected age group. If the charge is a discriminatory RIF, plaintiffs must show that age was **a** factor (although not necessarily the only factor) in targeting them for termination, or at least that the employer was not age-neutral in implementing the RIF program. Employers can defend against an accusation of a discriminatory RIF by showing good economic reason for cutting back; it isn't necessary to show that the company would be at the brink of bankruptcy without the reductions.

Depending on the type of case, the court where it is heard and the individual facts, the plaintiff may have to prove that his or her own qualifications and/or job performance were satisfactory, or may have to prove that they were superior to those of the person who replaced him or her.

[F] ADEA Class Actions

Sometimes, an employee contends that he or she is the only person to suffer discrimination. Sometimes, however, it is alleged that the company engages in a pattern or practice of discrimination, affecting many people, and it becomes necessary to determine whether it is appropriate to certify a class action (i.e., to allow employees to combine their claims and present a single body of evidence).

The theory of "virtual representation" is sometimes used to prevent a second class action covering issues that have already been raised in another class action. However, *Tice v. American Airlines* [162 F.3d 966 (7th Cir. 1998)] rejects application of this theory to a challenge by a group of airline pilots to an airline's policies about over-60 pilots. The Seventh Circuit said that the litigants in that case were not adequately represented by the earlier class action dealing with pilots and copilots, who are subject to a Federal Aviation Administration (FAA) policy mandating retirement at 60.

The *Tice* case dealt with the job for first officer. FAA rules allow people over 60 to hold the position of first officer, but the airline refused to employ any first officer who could not be promoted to captain. The indirect effect of this policy was to deny the job opportunity to persons over 60.

In the Seventh Circuit view, the earlier class action did not resolve the current case. ADEA class actions are "opt-in" rather than "opt-out" (i.e., no one is covered without electing to be included). The earlier case dealt with potential employees denied employment because of age; *Tice* dealt with current employees seeking to remain employed by accepting a demotion. Therefore, the *Tice* case was allowed to proceed.

In April 2002, however, the Seventh Circuit took a new tack, finding that the dispute should not be in the courts at all, because it was subject to mandatory arbitration under the Federal Arbitration Act (61 Stat. 669). However, the Seventh Circuit did not dismiss the case—it stayed (suspended) the case until the arbitration was resolved—because of the possibility that plaintiffs might be entitled to additional remedies by combining arbitration and litigation. [*Tice v. American Airlines Inc.*, 70 L.W. 1694 (7th Cir. April 30, 2002)]

The question of timing in class actions was also addressed in *Armstrong v. Martin Marietta Corp.* [138 F.3d 1374 (11th Cir. 1998)] Certain employees were dismissed as plaintiffs from a pending ADEA class action. They brought their own suits. The Eleventh Circuit held that the statute of limitations is tolled (suspended) while a class action is pending, but starts all over again as soon as the District Court issues an order denying class certification.

Would-be plaintiffs who are thrown out of a class action because they are not similarly situated to the proper plaintiffs must file their own suits within 90 days of being removed from the class. Equitable tolling (i.e., permitting an action that would otherwise be too late to continue, on the grounds of fairness) can be granted only if the EEOC actually misinformed the plaintiffs about the statute of limitations, not if the plaintiffs simply failed to consider this issue or made an incorrect determination of how long they had to bring suit.

§ 42.12   TITLE VII REMEDIES

[A]   Fundamental Remedies

Once the case gets to court and is tried to a conclusion (many cases are either settled along the way, or are dismissed before a full trial has occurred), and if the plaintiff wins (most employment discrimination cases are won by the employer), then the question becomes what remedies the court will order. Remedies are governed by 42 U.S.C. § 2000e-5(g).

The fundamental remedies under this section are equitable: hiring or reinstatement (plus up to two years' back pay for the time the plaintiff would have been working absent discrimination). Furthermore, the amount that the plaintiff earned in the meantime—or could have earned by making reasonable efforts—is offset against the back pay. In other words, plaintiffs have a duty to mitigate their damages. They have an obligation to use their best efforts to earn a living, instead of relying on the hope the defendant employer will eventually be ordered to pay up.

If the plaintiff further succeeds in proving disparate treatment (as distinct from facially neutral practices that have a disparate impact on the group the plaintiff belongs to), then compensatory damages can be awarded to the plaintiff as reimbursement for costs (such as job hunting or therapy) incurred directly as a result of the discrimination.

However, in cases of racial discrimination, the plaintiff must look to the Civil Rights Act of 1866 [42 U.S.C. § 1981], and not to Title VII, for compensatory and punitive damages. If the alleged discrimination consists of failing to accommodate a disability, the employer will not have to pay compensatory damages if it made a good-faith effort at reasonable accommodation, even if the offer of accommodation was later deemed inadequate.

If the court finds that the employer engaged in the unlawful employment practice that the plaintiff charged, it can enjoin the respondent from continuing that abusive practice. The court can order the defendant to take remedial steps, including but not limited to hiring an applicant or reinstating an ex-employee.

Employers cannot be ordered to hire, reinstate, or promote anyone, or pay back pay to him or her, if the employment action was taken "for any reason other than discrimination on account of race, color, religion, sex, or national origin" or unlawful retaliation. [42 U.S.C. § 2000e-5(g)(2)(A)]

In a mixed-motive case where the defendant demonstrates that, although a discriminatory motive was present, it would have taken the same action (e.g., fired or refused to promote the plaintiff) purely on the basis of the other motivations even if there had been no discrimination, then the court can grant a declaratory judgment (a declaration that the employment practice was unlawful), enjoin its continued use, or award attorneys' fees that can be traced directly to the mixed-motive claim. But, because the employer would have taken the same action even without discrimination, the court cannot award damages to the plaintiff or order the defendant to hire, rehire or promote the plaintiff. [42 U.S.C. § 2000e-5(g)(2)(B)]

The court has discretion, under 42 U.S.C. § 2000e-5(k), to order the loser—whether plaintiff or defendant—to pay the winner's attorneys' fees (including fees for expert witnesses, which can be very high) and court costs. However, losing defendants can't be ordered to pay fees to the EEOC. If the EEOC sues a company and loses, it can be ordered to reimburse the defendant for its fees and costs for the suit.

Also note that 42 U.S.C. § 2000e-2(n) provides that employees usually cannot challenge employment practices that were adopted based on a court order or to carry out a consent decree in an employment discrimination case, if the employees knew about the case and either had their interests represented or had a chance to voice their objections. However, employees who actually were parties in the case can enforce their rights under the order or settlement, and judgments and orders can be challenged on the grounds of fraud or the court's lack of jurisdiction over the case.

One important factor in analyzing employment cases is what claim(s) the employee raises. Some employment discrimination claims fit into the "breach of contract" category, but most of them are more like "tort" claims. The importance of the tort/contract distinction is that the remedies are different for the two categories. If a plaintiff proves breach of contract, the court's job is to put the plaintiff back in the position he, she, or it would have been in if the contract had been carried out. In the context of an employment contract, or implied employment contract, that probably means earnings and fringe benefits that were lost because of the breach, possibly plus out-of-pocket expenses for finding a new job. (The doctrine of mitigation of damages requires plaintiffs to do whatever they can to limit the amount of damages they suffer—which definitely includes finding a new job if at all possible, pending resolution of the claims against the former employer.)

Back pay is not limited to simple salary. It includes benefits, overtime, shift differentials, merit raises, and the like. However, if the employer can prove that the employee would have been laid off, or was unavailable for work, back pay will not be available for the time the employee would not have been working anyway.

Fringe benefits are valued at the cost the employee would have to pay to replace them, not the (probably lower) cost the employer incurred to offer them.

Amounts earned in the new job reduce what the ex-employer will have to pay in damages. On the other hand, to the extent that the plaintiff proves that the employer committed one or more torts, the successful plaintiff can be awarded back pay, front pay (moving from the end of the trial forward), lost earnings, medical expenses, and value of pain and anguish, and emotional distress. The plaintiff's spouse might be granted an award for loss of consortium (marital services that were not rendered because of the employer's wrongdoing). In most states, interest on the judgment, running from the time the case is decided, can also be ordered—which mounts up quickly if the award is in six or seven figures.

Sometimes, front pay and reinstatement can be combined, i.e., if the remedies don't overlap, chronologically or economically. Front pay can be awarded to get the plaintiff to the "point of employability," at which point he or she can be reinstated.

The general rule is that unemployment benefits received will not reduce the amount of back pay available to a successful Title VII plaintiff. However, in the Second Circuit, courts have the discretion to offset unemployment compensation against the back pay award.

[B] CRA '91 Cap on Damages

The Civil Rights Act of 1991 (CRA '91) [Pub. L. No. 102-166] imposes a cap on total damages that can be awarded to a successful Title VII plaintiff: The amount depends on the size of the corporate defendant, not the number or seriousness of the charges. The cap applies to punitive damages and most compensatory damages (but not to medical bills or other monetary losses that the plaintiff incurred before the trial).

Companies with fewer than 15 employees are exempt from Title VII, so the cap calculation begins at the 15-employee level. The damage cap is $50,000 for a company with 15–100 employees. The cap is set at $100,000 for companies with 101–200 employees, $200,000 for 201–500 employees, and $300,000 for companies with over 500 workers.

Pollard v. DuPont [532 U.S. 843 (2001)], a sex-discrimination and harassment case (not sexual harassment—the harassment was directed at the plaintiff because she was a woman, not because the co-workers who sabotaged her work were trying to obtain sexual gratification), did not apply the $300,000 damage cap to the plaintiff's front pay claim. This case treats front pay as "such affirmative action as may be appropriate" as relief, rather than as compensatory damages. Therefore, front pay is not capped and can be awarded in whatever amount is equitable.

In the Seventh Circuit, a Title VII plaintiff can get both front pay and lost future earnings. [*Williams v. Pharmacia Inc.*, 137 F.3d 944 (7th Cir. 1998)] The court found that the two remedies are not duplicative, because front pay substitutes for reinstatement and is ordered for a limited period. It is an equitable remedy, and the judge sets its amount. In contrast, lost future earnings, as authorized by CRA '91, represent the future pecuniary loss that can be traced to the effects of discrimination.

In mid-1999, the Supreme Court decided that compensatory damages, as defined by CRA '91, can be awarded against a federal agency defendant. [*West v. Gibson*, 527 U.S. 212 (1999)]

The cap on foreign employers who violate Title VII is based on their total number of employees throughout the world, not just those in the United States. [*Morelli v. Cedel*, 141 F.3d 39 (2d Cir. 1998); *Greenbaum v. Svenska*

Handelsbanken, 26 F. Supp. 2d 649 (S.D.N.Y. 1998)] More employees means a higher damage cap, so these decisions increase the damage exposure of foreign corporations.

The Eleventh Circuit says that every employee who is represented by the EEOC in a Title VII action is entitled to recover the full cap amount without filing a separate action or even intervening in the EEOC's action. They are not required to divide a single cap amount among them. [*EEOC v. W&O Inc.*, 213 F.3d 600 (11th Cir. 2000)]

[C] Punitive Damages

One of the most controversial questions is the matter of punitive damages. In a few cases, judges or juries have awarded a small or fairly small sum in compensatory damages, to compensate the plaintiff for actual losses chargeable to the fault of the defendant, but accompanied the small compensatory damages with enormous punitive damage awards. [*See, e.g., Cush-Crawford v. Adchem Corp.*, 271 F.3d 352 (2d Cir. 2001)], where punitive damages were granted, at the cap amount of $100,000, even though there were no compensatory damages, on the theory that compensatory and punitive damages serve very different purposes, and therefore punitive damages might be appropriate in a case where there were no compensatory damages.

Theoretically, punitive damages are supposed to be quite rare, ordered only in those cases where the defendant's conduct has been worse than merely negligent or improper.

A defendant that has acted maliciously, or at least with reckless indifference to the plaintiff's rights, can be ordered to pay punitive damages. The employer's conduct need not be "egregious" for punitive damages to be available. [*Kolstad v. American Dental Ass'n*, 527 U.S. 526 (1999)]

Zimmerman v. Associates First Capital Corp. [70 L.W. 1016 (2d Cir. May 31, 2001)] says that it was proper to impose punitive damages against a company on the basis of the vice president's acknowledgment that he had received EEO training, showing that he acted with reckless indifference toward federally protected rights.

The New Jersey Law Against Discrimination makes employers liable for punitive damages based on actions of their "upper management." In *Cavuotti v. New Jersey Transit Corp.* [735 A.2d 548 (N.J. 1999)], a case about an alleged age-based refusal to promote, the court held that the category "upper management" is not limited to major corporate officers. Instead, it includes all managers with broad supervisory powers over the plaintiff-employee, as well as all managers to whom the employer company has delegated the responsibility for maintaining a nondiscriminatory workplace.

There are not many instances in which very large punitive damages have actually been paid. Such awards are vulnerable to being reduced on appeal. Or the plaintiff may feel both emotionally vindicated and sick of litigating the case, and may settle the case post-trial for much less than the theoretical award. Nevertheless, even if the order is never carried out, it can be a real public relations disaster for a company to be ordered to pay millions of dollars as a punishment.

The EEOC's Compliance Manual lists appropriate factors for deciding whether the employer acted with malice or reckless indifference:

- Degree of unacceptability of the conduct;
- The nature, severity, and extent of the harm suffered by the complaining employee;
- The duration of the conduct: A practice that persists for years is more serious than one that is terminated after a short period of time;
- Whether there was an extensive pattern of past discrimination, or only a few isolated incidents;
- Whether the employer tried to remedy the situation, or exacerbated it by covering up or retaliating against complainants.

The Tenth Circuit's test for awarding Title VII punitive damages is the preponderance of the evidence, not proof beyond a reasonable doubt, of the employer's willful conduct. [*Karnes v. SCI Colorado Funeral Servs.*, 162 F.3d 1077 (10th Cir. 1998)]

The First Circuit imposed punitive damages on both a parent company and a subsidiary company in a sex-discrimination case. [*Romano v. U-Haul Int'l*, 233 F.3d 655 (1st Cir. 2000)]

[D] Attorneys' Fees and Costs

An attorney who wins a mixed-motive Title VII case, proving the role of discrimination in the adverse job action against the plaintiff, performs the important public function of discouraging employment discrimination. In the view of the Tenth Circuit, this function justifies a fee award under 42 U.S.C. § 2000e-5(g)(2)(B), even if the actual damages awarded to the plaintiff are limited or even nonexistent. [*Gudenkauf v. Stauffer Communications Inc.*, 158 F.3d 1074 (10th Cir. 1998); *Rodriguez v. McLoughlin*, 20 F. Supp. 2d 597 (S.D.N.Y. 1998); *Brandau v. Kansas*, 168 F.3d 1179 (10th Cir. 1999)]

An employer-defendant that won its sexual harassment case was awarded costs (transcription, copying, and videotaping) when the plaintiff's case was weak enough for summary judgment to be granted to the employer. [*Cherry v. Champion Int'l Inc.*, 186 F.3d 442 (4th Cir. 1999)] In fact, the Fourth Circuit said that the district court, which did not award the costs, abused its discretion, and the lower court should not have considered factors such as the plaintiff's good faith, lack of economic power as compared with the defendant, or the public interest in the courts being used to bring Title VII claims.

A Florida court went even further, requiring a plaintiff whose frivolous suit was dismissed at the summary judgment stage to pay $160,000 of the employer's fees and costs. [*Bernard v. Air Express Int'l USA Inc.*, discussed in Susan R.

Miller, *Judges Reversing Tide, Making Some Plaintiffs Pay Attorney Fees, Costs,* Miami Daily Business Review (Dec. 7, 2000) (law.com)]

District court jurisdiction to hear suits "brought under" Title VII doesn't extend to a suit in federal court brought purely to recover attorneys' fees after winning an administrative claim, because no substantive rights under the statute are involved. [*Chris v. Tenet*, 221 F.3d 648 (4th Cir. 2000)]

§ 42.13   SETTLEMENT OF A DISCRIMINATION SUIT

[A]   Generally

Suits can be settled at any time before a verdict or judicial decision is rendered. In fact, they can even be settled after the judge and jury have spoken. As long as there are appeal rights that could be exercised, the case is still open for negotiation. The objective of any settlement is to provide something for both parties: for the defendant employer, the chance to dispose of the case expeditiously and to eliminate the risk of a huge jury verdict; for the plaintiff, the chance to get at least some money quickly instead of many years later.

At a very early stage, the matter might be resolved by an agreement to let the employee resign instead of being fired and receive severance pay, and perhaps some other benefits, in exchange for releasing the employer from all liability. Both sides must agree on how the matter will be treated for unemployment insurance purposes (based on counsel from a lawyer).

In a situation where the employer acknowledges that the plaintiff has a valid case, or at least that the claims have some validity, the employer may want to settle early to limit its possible liability exposure and bad publicity.

Even if the employer thinks the plaintiff's claims are fabricated, exaggerated, or legally invalid, it still might be prudent to settle the case because of the sheer cost and effort involved in litigating a major suit, even if the final result is victory for the employer.

Usually, cases are settled somewhere around halfway between the plaintiff's demand and the defendant's counter-offer. Of course, both sides know this, and it influences the amounts they suggest at the negotiating table. No one should ever engage in negotiations without authority actually to settle the case, and without a range of acceptable settlement figures.

Tip: Cases that are settled quickly are also often settled within the policy limits of the employer's liability insurance policy. Therefore, the insurer will assume the entire cost of settlement. Moreover, if the employer does a prompt investigation of the allegations, negotiates in good faith, and does not unduly delay the settlement, the employer has not acted outrageously and has not violated the norms of public policy. Therefore, there will probably be no grounds for assessing punitive damages against the employer.

There are statutes, such as California's Civil Procedure Code § 998, that penalize plaintiffs who reject fair settlement offers. If the judge or jury awards less than a settlement offer previously made, then the statute may require the plaintiff to pay the defendant's lawsuit costs, on the grounds that the suit could have been avoided by the plaintiff's acceptance of a reasonable settlement.

When a settlement is reached, there are two major legal documents to be prepared. The first is a court order dismissing the case with prejudice (i.e., in a way that prevents it from being refiled later) and a release containing the terms of the settlement. It is usually prudent to try to provide the text of the release, in order to control the basic form of its terms.

A settlement can be offered without admitting culpability. Also, under 29 C.F.R. § 1601.20(a), the EEOC has the power to dismiss an employee's discrimination charge if the employee rejects a written settlement offer from the employer that is a legitimate offer of "full relief" (i.e., adequate compensation for the discrimination suffered by the employee). The EEOC sends the employee a strongly worded form letter that gives him or her only two choices: to accept the settlement offer promptly, or have the EEOC charge dismissed. (This only means that the EEOC will not be involved in the case, not that the employee is prevented from suing.)

Full relief means that the employee gets full back pay, plus any out-of-pocket expenses related to discrimination (such as moving expenses after a wrongful termination, or psychological counseling for a stressed-out employee). Compensation must also be included for nonmonetary losses such as loss of sleep, anxiety, and indigestion.

However, the employer must be aware that settling with one employee is not necessarily the end of the problem. It is against public policy (and a court might issue an injunction forbidding this) to include a provision in a settlement agreement that forbids a current or former employee to cooperate with an EEOC investigation. A settlement can prevent a person from pursuing his or her own claims against the employer, but the EEOC's right to investigate workplace conditions, and pursue claims on its own behalf (and on behalf of other employees) continues.

In early 1998, Astra USA agreed to pay close to $10 million to settle EEOC claims of widespread sexual harassment. In 1999, a special master determined how the funds should be allocated among the 120 employees whose harassment claims were deemed to be valid. The special master created a hierarchy of harassment injuries, awarding anywhere from $12,000 to $300,000, depending on the seriousness of the conduct. Seriousness was assessed along two axes: the nature of the conduct, and whether it was committed by a co-employee, a low-level manager, or a high-level manager.

For instance, isolated verbal harassment by low-ranking perpetrators gave rise to a $25,000 award. Persistent verbal harassment was penalized by a $75,000 award, and repeated sexual solicitation or actual unwanted sexual touching by high-level managers was evaluated at $250,000. [Mark Maremont, *A Case Puts a Value on Touching and Fondling*, Wall Street Journal, May 25, 1999, p. B1]

[B] Tax Factors in Settling Discrimination Cases

The plaintiff's objective is to wind up with the best after-tax result from pursuing or settling a case. In some instances, appropriate structuring of the settlement can produce a better after-tax result for the plaintiff while reducing the cash-flow impact on the defendant.

Damages for breach of contract are taxable income for the plaintiff, because they are treated as delayed payment of compensation that the employee would have received earlier if there had been no breach of contract.

The treatment of tort damages is more complex. Damages are not taxable if they are payable because of the plaintiff's "personal injury." The Supreme Court has ruled that Title VII damages and ADEA damages are not received for personal injury, because they are not similar enough to the damages received in traditional tort cases (car crashes, for instance). [*United States v. Burke*, 504 U.S. 229 (1992); *Commissioner of Internal Revenue v. Schleier*, 115 S. Ct. 2159 (1995)]

The Small Business Job Protection Act of 1996 clarified the application of I.R.C. § 104(a)(2), the provision on taxation of damages. Starting August 21, 1996, damages received for "personal physical injuries" and physical illness are received free of tax—for instance, if the employer's wrongful conduct makes the employee physically ill. Damages for emotional distress are taxable except to the extent of medical expenses for their treatment.

Taxable damages that are wage replacements (under the FLSA, NLRA, Title VII, and ADEA, for example) may be FICA wages and may be subject to withholding. *But see Newhouse v. McCormack & Co.* [157 F.3d 582 (8th Cir. 1998)], where front and back pay awarded under the ADEA to a job applicant who was not hired was not considered "wages" subject to tax withholding.

CHAPTER 43

INSURANCE COVERAGE FOR CLAIMS AGAINST THE EMPLOYER

§ 43.01   INTRODUCTION

It is only prudent for a company to maintain insurance against significant risks. However, although the potential risk exposure in a discrimination, harassment, or wrongful termination suit is quite large, it can be difficult to buy insurance that will fully cover these claims—or even cover them at all.

Between 1994 and 2000, for example, the number of comparatively small judgments in employment-related suits decreased. In 1994, 52% of plaintiff's judgments were under $100,000, versus 30% in 2000. (Of course, some of the difference was due to inflation as well as changes in the law and jury attitudes.) In 1994, a mere 7% of plaintiff's verdicts were $1 million or more, whereas this was true of 20% of the plaintiff's verdicts in 2000. In 1999, the median award was $151,000; only a year later, it was $218,000. [Reed Abelson, *Surge in Bias Cases Punishes Insurers and Premiums Rise,* New York Times, Jan. 9, 2002, at C1; the same data is also quoted in Michael Barrier, *EPCI Providers Turn Up the Heat,* HR Magazine, May 2002, at p. 46]

Liability insurers expected a heavy increase in the volume of litigation as a result of recession and lay-offs. Some insurers responded by doubling or even tripling the premiums for employment practices liability insurance (EPLI), whereas some stopped selling the coverage altogether. EPLI insureds, like health insureds, also faced higher deductibles and lower coverage limits.

There was also concern that they under-priced their policies in the 1990s to build business; one unanticipated side effect was that companies, reassured by the presence of coverage, did not correct their discriminatory practices and are now embroiled in lawsuits or at risk of being sued. [Reed Abelson, *Surge in Bias Cases Punishes Insurers, and Premiums Rise*, New York Times, Jan. 9, 2002, at p. C1]

§ 43.02   COMMERCIAL GENERAL LIABILITY

[A]   Use of the CGL Policy

Most businesses get their basic liability coverage under the Commercial General Liability (CGL) policy. In fact, for most companies, this is the only liability insurance.

The CGL has two basic aims. The first is to provide a defense (i.e., supply a lawyer who will investigate, negotiate, and settle or try the case). The second is to pay whatever settlement or judgment the defendant company would otherwise have to pay to a successful plaintiff. The insurer's obligation is subject to the insured's obligation to pay a deductible. The insurer is not required to pay more than the limits of the policy. CGL policies are not really uniform. The Insurance Standards Organization (ISO) has published a very influential model policy, but insurers have the option of tailoring the model as they see fit.

Furthermore, the insurer must only pay for covered claims, not excluded ones. ISO has drafted an "employment-related practices exclusion," and the trend is for recent policies to follow this and simply exclude all claims related to a plaintiff's employment by a defendant. Even this is not as simple as it seems. For instance, a court might rule that the real injury to the plaintiff occurred after he or she was fired and therefore ceased to be an employee.

Even if the policy doesn't exclude all employment-related claims, there may be other factors that prevent the employer from collecting benefits under the policy.

[B] Bodily Injury and Personal Injury

Coverage A of the CGL provides liability insurance when the insured becomes liable to someone who has suffered "bodily injury." It's rare for employment plaintiffs to claim that they suffered physically. Usually, they assert that they lost economic benefits (such as salary and pension) because of the employer's wrongful conduct. CGL Coverage A will *not* apply to charges of breach of contract or other economic consequences.

For this and other reasons, plaintiffs often ask for damages based on their emotional suffering. Their complaints allege pain and suffering, intentional infliction of emotional distress, or negligent infliction of emotional distress. (The availability of these causes of action varies between the federal and state systems, and from state to state.)

Most courts that have dealt with this question say that there is no "bodily injury" in an emotional suffering case unless the plaintiff can prove that there was at least some physical consequence of the emotional injury: an ulcer or high blood pressure, for instance. Even if there are physical consequences, they could be considered basically economic and therefore outside the scope of Coverage A.

The CGL's Coverage B deals with liability that the insured encounters for "personal injury" (such as libel or slander) or advertising injury (such as defaming another company's products in your ads). Coverage B might get involved in an employment-related case if, for instance, the plaintiff claims that the employer not only fired him or her, but blacklisted him or her and used a campaign of lies to prevent the ex-employee from getting another job or establishing business relationships.

[C] CGL Case Law

A church music director claimed that the pastor defamed her by spreading negative and untruthful explanations of why the music director was fired. The church had an insurance policy that covered defamation, but that included a separate exclusion of all kinds of employment-related liability. There was no coverage under the policy, because whatever the pastor said related to the rationale for the discharge, and therefore fell under the employment exclusion. [*Parish of Christ Church v. Church Ins. Co.*, 166 F.3d 419 (1st Cir. 1999)]

The CGL exclusion for "employment-related practices" does exclude direct coverage for sexual harassment liability, but not a claim against the employer for negligent retention of the supervisor who committed the harassment, on the theory that negligent retention is a negligence claim, not a claim of intentional injury. [*Mactown Inc. v. Continental Ins. Co.*, 1998 WL 390612 (Fla. App. 1998)]

According to *SCI Liquidating Corp. v. Hartford Fire Insurance Co.* [181 F.3d 1210 (11th Cir. 1999)], the CGL doesn't have to cover claims made by an employee who alleged sexual harassment (including assault and battery), retaliation, intentional infliction of emotional distress, and negligent hiring and retention of the perpetrator. In this reading, there was no CGL occurrence, because intentional harassment is not an accident. Because of the close relationship with the harassment, injury arising out of negligent hiring and retention didn't fit the definition of occurrence either. Although the CGL included discrimination in its category of covered personal injury, it excluded employment-related claims.

The employer also had an umbrella policy covering personal injury, specifically including injury related to discrimination. The Eleventh Circuit sent the case back to the Georgia Supreme Court to determine whether sexual harassment by a fellow employee "arises out of and in the course of employment." At least in the Worker's Compensation context, the Georgia law is that co-employee harassment does not arise out of employment. If this is so, the employer would be covered under the umbrella policy because the exclusion of employment-related claims would not come into play.

§ 43.03   OCCURRENCES AND THE PROBLEM OF INTENTION

[A]   Nature of Employment Claims

Coverage under Coverage A depends on there being an "occurrence," which is defined as an accident that was neither intended nor expected by the insured. Coverage B does not have an occurrence requirement, but it does exclude coverage of personal injuries that stem from a willful violation of the law, committed by or with the consent of the insured company.

At first glance, it would seem that employment cases could never be covered under the CGL, because the plaintiff accuses someone of deliberately injuring him or her. There is no form of corporate Alzheimer's that makes companies fire or underpay their employees in a fit of absent-mindedness.

The picture is far more complex. Some discrimination charges allege "disparate treatment" (roughly speaking, intentional discrimination), while others claim "disparate impact," (subtle negative effects on a protected group of employees). An employer's actions in adopting a policy or publishing an employee manual could have unintended consequences, which could possibly be treated as CGL "occurrences."

However, intentional discrimination would not be. Courts often treat some conduct (e.g., sexual harassment) as being so likely to have bad consequences for their victims that the consequences are presumed to have been intended, or at least expected, by the insured company.

Employment discrimination plaintiffs usually want the insurance company to be involved, because they know that liability insurance is another potential source of payment if they settle or win the case. In this instance, they are on the same side as the employer. They both want the CGL to cover the employee's claim. One simple strategy is for plaintiffs to add claims of negligent supervision by the employer, or negligent infliction of emotional distress, in the hope that these charges of negligence will be classified as covered "occurrences." The CGL exclusion of "intentional" conduct does not apply to conduct that is negligent, or even grossly negligent. However, this tactic usually fails because the negligence charges are treated as purely incidental to more important charges of intentional conduct.

In most instances, termination of an employee, even wrongful termination, does not involve the intention or expectation of harm, so the insurer will probably have a duty to defend. CGL personal injury coverage often excludes damage resulting from the willful violations of a penal statute or ordinance, committed by the insured or with the knowledge of the insured. Civil rights laws are not considered "penal statutes" for this purpose. Even if actions are "willful" for Title VII purposes, the criminal law exclusion will not be triggered.

Some CGL policies offer an endorsement or rider (at additional cost over the basic premium) that covers discrimination and harassment claims, often by broadening the underlying policy's definition of personal injury.

CGL policies typically exclude bodily injury to employees, arising out of and in the course of employment, whether the employer is liable as an employer or in other capacities. But that provision is probably included in the policy simply for coordination with Worker's Compensation. The employee could succeed in arguing that the tort claims they make do not arise out of or in the course of the employment relationship, because supervisors are not employed to commit discrimination or harassment. The insurer may have at least a duty to defend. Furthermore, occupational injuries could be treated as a known risk that employees are aware of, whereas discrimination and harassment are not risks of the same category.

[B]   Public Policy Issues

A basic principle of insurance law is that you can't buy insurance to protect yourself against the consequences of your own intentional wrongdoing.

The current interpretation of this rule is that it does not violate public policy for companies to buy insurance covering employment-related liability, because this enhances winning plaintiffs' chances to collect. This benefit is deemed to outweigh the risk that companies will be more willing to engage in improper employment practices if they know they are protected by insurance.

A related policy question is whether insurance can cover punitive damages. About two-thirds of the states that have decided cases about this say yes. However, punitive damages for intentional wrongdoing cannot be covered, and most punitive damages are imposed precisely because of the intentionality of the defendant's wrongful conduct.

§ 43.04   EMPLOYMENT PRACTICES LIABILITY INSURANCE

Because of the gaps in CGL coverage of employment matters, a separate form of policy, Employment Practices Liability Insurance (EPLI) evolved as of about 1990. The EPLI is designed to cover damages, judgments, settlements, defense costs, and attorneys' fee awards in the employment liability context (suits, proceedings, or written demands seeking to hold the employer civilly liable). Events included under the EPLI are discrimination, sexual harassment, and wrongful termination, but not "golden parachutes" (payments to top managers who lose their jobs because of corporate transitions) or contractual obligations to make payments to terminated employees. The EPLI policy generally excludes criminal charges, fines, punitive damages, retaliation, and any amounts that are uninsurable because of a relevant state law.

In 1994, only 10 carriers issued such coverage, but by 1999, there were over 100 insurers in the EPLI market, and the Insurance Services Organization (ISO) had published a standard EPLI form. [*See* Daniel C. Skinner, William T. Edwards, and Gregory L. Gravlee, *Selecting Employment Practices Liability Insurance*, HR Magazine, Sept. 1998, at p. 146; Simon J. Nadel, *Employment Practices Liability Insurance Makes Some Headway With Employers*, 66 L.W. 2275]

The usual coverage limit is $1 million–$5 million, but some insurers offer "jumbo" policies of up to $100 million in coverage.

EPLI owners can benefit even if they are never sued, because insurers require insured parties to audit their HR functions, improve their procedures, and add new procedures to minimize the risk of suit. The policy may offer access to valuable low-cost consulting services, and compliance advice that would otherwise carry a high price tag.

A claims-made policy is one that provides coverage when claims are made while the insured still has coverage, but not for claims made after coverage expires, even if the allegedly wrongful conduct occurred while the policy was still in force. The ISO EPLI form modifies this by covering claims made during the 30 days after policy expiration, unless another insurer is already in the picture. If the same employee makes multiple claims, they are all considered to have arisen on the date of the first claim, so coverage will be continuous, and it will not be necessary to figure out whether the initial or the later insurer is responsible. Sometimes, it is a false economy to replace a liability insurance policy if the new policy has a waiting period, creating a gap in coverage.

Two commentators suggest the following questions for evaluating an EPLI policy:

- Does it cover all employees? What about the liability consequences of actions of leased employees and independent contractors?
- Are former employees covered?
- Are claims for breach of explicit or implied employment contract covered by or excluded from the policy?

- Is any coverage available for employment-related claims such as defamation or infliction of emotional distress?
- Can you choose the lawyer or law firm that will defend you, or are you required to accept the insurer's choice of counsel? How much control can you exercise over the defense strategy for your case?
- Does the insurer have to provide you with a defense in administrative (e.g., EEOC and local antidiscrimination agencies) proceedings, or only at trial? (Only a small percentage of discrimination charges make it to the trial stage, but the investigative stage can be very unpleasant for the employer.)
- Are retaliation claims (including retaliation for filing Worker's Compensation claims) covered? (This is a large and growing part of the discrimination caseload.)
- Are injunctive and declaratory relief covered, or only money damages?
- Is the deductible imposed on a per-year or per-claimant basis? (If the latter is true, an insured employer might end up having to pay several deductibles a year.)
- Are punitive damages covered? (Some states do not allow insurance coverage of such damages.) [Stephanie E. Trudeau and William Edwards, Employment Law Letter, <http://www.ulmer.com>]

According to a late-2001 issue of The Betterley Report (an insurance industry newsletter), EPLI insurers for small and mid-sized companies planned rate increases of 15–30%. Insurers often investigate insureds' and applicants' loss prevention and loss management practices. Loss prevention means averting claims; loss management keeps the claims of manageable size. Applicants with poor loss practices are likely to get charged higher rates or even turned down for coverage.

Companies should make sure that they assign properly trained persons to do a thorough investigation of discrimination and harassment claims; that they are careful to avoid wrongful termination; that employees who make discrimination claims or participate in an investigation do not suffer harassment; and that all these measures are properly documented and records are retained long enough. Michael Barrier, *EPLI Providers Turn Up the Heat,* May 2002, at 46.]

§ 43.05   OTHER INSURANCE

[A]   Excess Liability and Umbrella Coverage

Every CGL policy has limits: maximum amounts of coverage obtainable under particular circumstances. If your company already has maximum CGL coverage, but feels that more is necessary, there are two ways to supplement it.

The first is "follow-form" excess liability insurance, which increases the dollar amount of coverage available under your CGL, Worker's Compensation, and Business Automobile Liability coverage, but subject to the same terms and exclusions. For many companies, an "umbrella" policy is a better choice, because it is more broadly defined and may cover situations that were excluded by the underlying policy. This kind of "gap" coverage is generally subject to a "retained limit," another term for "deductible."

Umbrella policies offer coverage in more situations because their definition of "personal injury" is broader than Coverage A or Coverage B of the standard CGL. A typical provision includes both bodily injury and mental injury, mental anguish, shock, sickness, disease, discrimination, humiliation, libel, slander, defamation of character, and invasion of property. Therefore, many employment-related claims would be covered.

[B] Worker's Compensation

Specialized Worker's Compensation coverage is available to deal with the employer's obligation to pay benefits to employees who are injured in job-related situations. Of course, because of WC exclusivity, the employer does not have to worry about ordinary liability suits from injured workers, although there may be special situations in which suit can be brought (against the employer or another party, such as the manufacturer of unsafe factory machinery) even though Worker's Compensation is involved. In a WC employment liability policy, Worker's Compensation is Coverage A; the employment liability (e.g., bodily injury that is not subject to WC exclusivity) is Coverage B.

Schmidt v. Smith [155 N.J. 44, 713 A.2d 1014 (1998)] says that bodily injury that results from sexual harassment is covered by the employer liability section of the Worker's Compensation insurance policy, which is a "gap-filler" designed to come into play when a person suffers job-related injuries, even if that person is not covered by Worker's Compensation. The Insurance Standards Organization (ISO) has not drafted a form for these policies, so they vary widely from insurer to insurer.

> **Tip:** If the charges you face involve an injured worker (for instance, one who alleges disability discrimination after an injury), your Worker's Compensation insurer may have a duty to defend you because of the possibility that you could dispose of the case by claiming WC exclusivity.

[C] Directors' and Officers' Liability (D&O)

D&O insurance covers the situation in which a corporation's directors and officers get not only themselves but the corporation into trouble. Frequently, executives will not agree to serve as directors or officers unless the corporation first promises them indemnification, i.e., that the corporation will pay the executive whatever amount he or she has to pay because of liability incurred while acting as a director or officer.

D&O insurance, in turn, reimburses the corporation for whatever it spends on indemnification, subject to a deductible and up to the limit of the policy.

[D]   Errors & Omissions (E&O)

Errors and Omissions insurance pays, on behalf of the insured, all loss for which the insured person is not indemnified by the insured organization if the person is liable because of any wrongful act he or she committed or attempted. In general, committing disparate treatment discrimination will be considered a wrongful act that can be covered under the policy, unless the policy definition covers only negligent, and not intentional, acts and omissions.

In many companies, E&O insurance is complemented by D&O insurance that covers the company for losses it incurs when it indemnifies directors and officers acting in that capacity.

An important issue is whether or not administrative actions (such as state agency and EEOC proceedings) are considered "claims or suits" for insurance purposes. The insurer is likely to make the argument that back pay awarded to a prevailing plaintiff is equitable relief and not "damages" that could be covered under the policy.

However, many courts have rejected this argument and required liability insurers to handle back-pay awards against their policyholders. E&O insurers may also resist paying back pay if the policy excludes amounts owed under a "contractual obligation," but here again, the insured will probably prevail if a back pay award is made.

Another insurance form covers plans, administrators, and trustees against allegations of impropriety. Many employment-related claims involve ERISA allegations, so the employer should at least consider adding this coverage to its insurance portfolio.

§ 43.06   DUTY OF THE INSURANCE CONTRACT

[A]   Duty to Defend

A lesser-known, but perhaps more important, part of the liability insurance policy is the insurer's duty to defend. That is, whenever a claim is made against the employer, the insurer has to provide a lawyer and take care of the case. However, usually the insurer is in control of the litigation, and decides how vigorously to defend the case and when to settle (although some policies return control of litigation to the insured). Most policies are drafted so that, if the insured company settles the case without consent and participation of the insurer, the insured company will not be able to recover any part of the settlement costs from the insurer.

The insurer's duty to indemnify is the duty to pay on the insured's behalf when the insured settles or loses a lawsuit. The duty to defend is much broader. If the allegations against an insured company are invalid, or can't be proved, then the liability insurer's role is to get the charge dismissed, even though there is no liability to indemnify. In general, if the charges combine claims that are covered by liability insurance with others that are not, the insurer has a duty to defend against all the charges, not just the covered ones.

Usually, the insurer's duty to defend is triggered by a "claim" made against the insured employer. This is usually interpreted as filing a complaint with a court. EEOC or local agency proceedings are not generally considered "claims," so an insured company is on its own for a significant part of the process before the duty to defend begins.

[B] Duties of the Insured

Insurance companies are relieved of their obligation to pay claims if the insured company fails to satisfy its obligations. The most obvious duty is paying premiums. Liability policies also require the insured to notify the insurer as soon as possible whenever a "claim" is made. Therefore, legal advice is necessary to determine which allegations have the legal status of a claim.

§ 43.07 QUESTIONS OF TIMING

Liability policies are divided into "occurrence" and "claims-made" policies. If there is an "occurrence" covered by the policy (see above), all the occurrence policies in force at that time must make payments. But the insured doesn't get five times the amount of the liability. Coverage is coordinated (divided among them) to prevent windfalls.

A claims-made policy works differently. It covers only claims that are made during the policy term with respect to events that happened during the policy term. Because this can be a difficult standard to meet, claims-made policies are often extended to cover events after the policy's "retroactive date." There may also be an "extended reporting period" after the policy expires, where events are covered if they occurred while the policy was still in force, but were reported later.

An employer covered by a claims-made EPLI policy faced an ADEA suit. The policy covered claims first made while the policy was in force, reported to the company not later than 60 days after expiration of the policy. On November 7, the EEOC notified the employer of an ADEA charge. The employee filed suit on December 22, and the employer notified the insurer on January 21. The Eastern District of Louisiana found that timely notice was not given. [*Specialty Food Sys. Inc. v. Reliance Ins. Co.*, 45 F. Supp. 2d 541 (E.D. La. 1999), *aff'd without opinion*, 200 F.3d 816 (5th Cir. 1999)] The EEOC charge was a "written demand or notice" received by the insured from "any person or administrative agency," so notice was due within 60 days of November 7.

§ 43.08 FIDUCIARY LIABILITY INSURANCE

Where the policy covers the plan itself, the insurer can sue the fiduciary to recover the amount it had to pay out because of the fiduciary's conduct. Fiduciary liability insurance is usually available only in limited amounts, on a claims-made basis.

Fiduciary liability insurance is an asset of the plan, but also protects trustees' personal assets. Furthermore, a fiduciary who breaches his or her duty may not be able to afford to reimburse the plan for its full losses.

For the policy to be truly useful, the definition of the "insured" should include the plan and/or trust, all past, present and future trustees and employees, and their successors. Coverage for the spouse of an insured if named as an additional defendant should also be included. The general rule is that most fiduciary liability policies don't cover third-party administrators or service providers who act as fiduciaries, although it may be possible to add them to the policy under an endorsement.

The definition of "loss" should include defense costs (including costs for investigators and expert witnesses) settlements, judgments, and pre- and post-judgment interest. Although liability insurance typically excludes coverage of fines and penalties, IRS Employee Plans Compliance Resolution System (EPCRS) penalties and amounts paid to the DOL when it wins or settles an ERISA § 502(l) case are usually either included in the basic coverage or added by endorsement.

> **Tip:** The entire policy has to be examined to see if there are additional limitations—for instance, the definition of "loss" may exclude fines and penalties.

Most fiduciary liability policies are claims-made policies. At each anniversary date, the insured can evaluate and adjust the policy limits and scope of coverage, bearing affordability in mind. Once a policy is purchased, it is hard to change carriers, because the application requires a warranty that there are no known claims or circumstances that would be excluded by the new insurer if they were fully disclosed—and it's very common for companies to face claims of this type!

If the policy is purchased with assets of a pension or benefit plan, the insurer will have the right to recover any losses it pays out from the fiduciary whose fault caused the liability in the first place. Therefore, the plan will be protected, but the fiduciary will not be. Fiduciaries can buy nonrecourse riders to cover them too. The cost is low (only about $25 per fiduciary per year) but knowing wrongful acts like dishonesty and self-dealing are excluded. [*Fiduciary Liability Insurance: A Valuable But Often Overlooked Asset* (Nov. 2001) (segalco.com)]

INDEX

References are to sections.

A

AAA, 40.06[B]
Abatement, OSHA, 31.12
"ABC" test of employee status, 1.12[C]
Ability to work requirement in unemploy-
    ment insurance, 32.02[D]
Access to managed care, 18.13[F]
Access to records, 24.01
Accidental workplace injuries, 33.03
Accounting
    PBGC, 5.08[C]
    retiree health benefits, 9.11
Accrual of benefits in defined benefit plans,
    5.06, 5.07
Actions
    arbitration and ADR compared, 40.04
    class actions, 42.06, 42.11[F]
    COBRA, 19.04[B]
    discrimination actions by employees. *See*
        Discrimination actions by employees
    enforcement and compliance for qualified
        plans, 15.10, 15.11, 15.18
    ERISA, 15.10, 15.18
    FMLA, 38.11
    pay planning, 1.06
Active employees for life insurance, 21.02[F]
"Actively at work" clauses in EGHPs, 18.08
ADA, 36.01
    alcohol exception, 36.06[B]
    arbitration of claims, 36.14
    attendance, 36.04[B]
    auxiliary aids and services, 36.05[A]
    breast-feeding, 28.03
    case law, 36.05[C]
    covered entities, 36.02
    damages, 36.13
    defenses, 36.06
        alcohol exception, 36.06[B]
        drug exception, 36.06[B]

primary defense, 36.06[A]
disability benefits and, 20.04[C], 36.10[B]
"disability" defined, 36.04[A]
    attendance, 36.04[B]
    infertility, 36.04[C]
    psychiatric disability, 36.04[D]
discrimination, 36.03
drug testing, 26.03[B]
EEOC and, 36.05[B], 36.08[B], 41.03,
    41.04
employer's obligations, 36.05[A], 36.08[A]
enforcement, 36.05[B], 36.08[B], 36.11
evidence, 36.12
FMLA and, 36.10[C], 38.06[B]
foreign-based workers, 36.02
goals, 36.01
hiring, 23.12, 36.09
individual liability, 36.02
infertility, 36.04[C]
medical examinations, 36.09
mixed-motive cases, 36.02
notices, 36.02
pre-employment medical examinations,
    36.09
prima facie case, 36.12
psychiatric disability, 36.04[D]
reasonable accommodation, 36.05
    auxiliary aids and services, 36.05[A]
    case law, 36.05[C]
    EEOC enforcement, 36.05[B]
    employer's obligations, 36.05[A]
"regarded as" liability, 36.07
Rehabilitation Act and, 36.10[A]
retaliation, 36.03
sexual harassment and, 35.10
sovereign immunity, 36.02
Title I of Act, 36.02
unemployment insurance and, 32.02[D]
worker's compensation and, 33.08[C]

Constructive discharge, 39.01
Consumer Credit Protection Act (CCPA), 1.17[A], 1.17[C]
Contingency search firms, 23.05
Contingent worker pay planning, 1.10, 1.13
Contraceptives, 18.03[D]
Contracts and agreements
  collective bargaining. *See* Collective bargaining
  employment contracts. *See* Employment contracts
  federal contracts
    drug testing, 26.03
    immigration issues in hiring, 23.11[C]
    racial discrimination, 34.05[D]
  noncompete agreements, 25.02[C]
  releases, 21.02[F], 25.13
  resignations, 25.12
Contract worker pay planning, 1.09
Control test of employee status, 1.12[C]
Conversion in cash balance plans, 7.04, 7.05
Corporate communications. *See* Communications
Corporate opportunity doctrine, 25.02[C]
Corporate transitions, 16.01
  alter egos, 16.01
  amendments to plans. *See* Amending a plan
  anticutback rule, 16.03
  bonuses, 16.07[B]
  choice of form, 16.02
  Collective Bargaining Agreements (CBA), 16.02[C]
  culture issues, 16.10
  defined benefit plans, 16.03, 16.05
  defined contribution plans, 16.03, 16.05
  distributions, 16.06
  early retirement benefits, 16.03
  early warning program, 16.08
  ERISA, 16.01
  FICA, 16.02[D]
  401 (k) plans, 16.06
  FUTA tax, 16.02[D]
  golden parachutes, 16.07[B]
  in-service distributions, 16.06
  labor laws and, 16.02[C]
  minimum participation rule, 16.05
  notice of reduction of benefits, 16.04
  parachute payments, 16.07[B]
  PBGC Early Warning Program, 16.08
  reduction of benefits, 16.04
  rehiring, 16.06

  stock options, 16.09
  tax issues, 16.07
  T.D. 8928, 16.02[B]
  termination of plan. *See* Termination of plan
  unemployment insurance, 16.02[D]
Correction programs for qualified plans, 15.19
Costs
  managed care, 18.13[E], 18.13[F]
  pay planning, 1.06
  pension plans, 4.28
  workers' compensation, 33.01, 33.09
Creditable coverage, HIPAA, 19.05[A]
Credit checks, 23.13, 26.04
Criminal penalties
  enforcement and compliance for qualified plans, 15.11
  OSHA, 31.10[B]
Criminal-record checks, 23.08
Culture issues in corporate transitions, 16.10
Custodial services in health plan claims, 13.05[C]

D

Damages
  ADA, 36.13
  COBRA, 19.04[B]
  discrimination actions by employees, 42.12[A], 42.12[B], 42.12[C]
  enforcement and compliance for qualified plans, 15.18[A]
  FMLA, 38.11
  mitigation of damages, 21.02[F]
  pay planning, 1.06
  searches and surveillance, 26.06[B]
  sexual harassment, 35.08
Dating records, 24.01
Day care, 28.01, 28.02
Death benefits, 4.08
Deauthorization of union, 30.08
Decertification of union, 30.08
Deduction limit in defined benefit plans, 5.05[B]
Deemed IRAs, 4.07
Defamation
  corporate communications, 25.08, 25.09, 25.11
  discrimination actions by employees, 42.02

INDEX

Defenses
ADA, 36.06
  alcohol exception, 36.06[B]
  drug exception, 36.06[B]
  primary defense, 36.06[A]
ADEA, 37.03[D]
Deferral limits in 401 (k) plans, 6.04[B]
Deferred benefits notice, 11.06[A]
Deferred compensation and severance pay,
  3.03[C]
Defined benefit plans, 4.05, 5.01
accrual of benefits, 5.06, 5.07
adoption and administration. *See* Adoption
  and administration of plans
amendments. *See* Amending a plan
appeals. *See* Claims and appeals
cash balance plans. *See* Cash balance plans
claims and appeals. *See* Claims and
  appeals
contribution calculations, 5.05[C]
corporate transitions, 16.03, 16.05
coverage, 4.13
deduction limit, 5.05[B]
distributions. *See* Distributions
enforcement and compliance. *See* Enforcement and compliance for qualified
  plans
ERISA, 4.05
form of benefits, 5.03
full funding limitation (FFL), 5.05[E]
funding, 5.05
funding changes, 5.05[J]
interest rates, 5.05[I]
liens based on funding failures, 5.05[G]
limitations, 4.16, 5.02
minimum funding standard, 5.05[A]
minimum funding standard account,
  5.05[D]
minimum funding waivers, 5.05[K]
mortality tables, 5.04
notices of reduction of benefit accruals,
  5.07
participation, 4.13
PBGC compliance. *See* PBGC
plan form factors, 4.27
procedures for funding, 5.05[F]
reduction of benefit accruals, 5.07
reportable events, 5.09
termination of plan. *See* Termination of
  plan
valuation issues, 5.05[H]

Defined contribution plans, 4.05, 6.01, 6.02
adoption and administration. *See* Adoption
  and administration of plans
amendments. *See* Amending a plan
claims and appeals. *See* Claims and
  appeals
corporate transitions, 16.03, 16.05
coverage, 4.13
distributions. *See* Distributions
enforcement and compliance. *See* Enforcement and compliance for qualified
  plans
ERISA, 4.05
limitations, 4.16
managed care, 18.13[I]
new comparability plans, 4.06[E], 6.03
participation, 4.13
plan form factors, 4.27
termination of plan. *See* Termination of
  plan
Degree of disability in workers' compensation, 33.02[A]
De minimis fringe benefits, 22.06
Demographics and pension plans, 4.03
Dental plans, 18.04
Dependent care assistance plans, 28.07
Deposits
FICA, 2.07
FUTA tax, 32.06[A]
income tax withholding, 2.07
Desk searches, 26.06[A]
Destruction of records, 24.01, 24.08
Determination letters, 10.02
Directors' and officers' (D&O) liability insurance, 43.05[C]
Disability plans, 20.01
ADA, 20.04[C], 36.04[A], 36.10[B]
  attendance, 36.04[B]
  infertility, 36.04[C]
  psychiatric disability, 36.04[D]
ADEA, 20.04[E], 37.04[B], 37.05[A]
amending a plan, 20.06
"any occupation," 20.02
arbitrary and capricious standard of review,
  20.07
cafeteria plans, 22.03[A]
claims and appeals, 20.07, 20.08
COBRA coverage, 20.04[E]
EEOC Compliance Manual, 20.04[D]
employment-based plans, 20.02

G

Pre-employment testing, 23.10, 23.12, 24.03, 26.03[B]
Preemption
  discrimination actions by employees, 42.10[E]
  early retirement, 9.05[B]
  enforcement and compliance for qualified plans, 15.18[B]
  FMLA, 39.05
  labor law, 30.02[D]
  termination of employment, 39.05
Pre-existing conditions, 19.05[A]
Pregnancy Discrimination Act (PDA)
  breast-feeding, 28.03
  discrimination actions by employees, 42.02
  sex discrimination, 34.06[B]
Premiums
  PBGC, 5.08[B]
  workers' compensation, 33.05
Prescription drug coverage, 18.05
Preventive labor relations, 30.15
Privacy, 26.01
  credit checks, 26.04
  drug testing, 26.03
  enforcement and compliance for qualified plans, 15.11
  genetic testing, 26.05
  HIPAA rules, 26.07
  hiring, 23.12
  notice, 26.07
  polygraphs, 26.02
  protected health information (PHI), 26.07
  searches and surveillance. See Searches and surveillance
Privileges and immunities, 25.09[A]
  attorney-client privilege
    enforcement and compliance for qualified plans, 15.11
    privileged communications, 25.09[B]
    self-critical analysis privilege, 25.09[C]
  sovereign immunity
    ADA, 36.02
    ADEA, 37.02
Productive hiring, 23.02
Profit sharing plans, 4.06[B]
Progressive discipline, 25.05, 40.02
Promissory estoppel
  retiree health benefits, 9.08
  termination of employment, 39.03
Promoting diversity, 29.06
Protected health information (PHI), 26.07

Psychiatric/psychological disability
  ADA, 36.04[D]
  workers' compensation, 33.02[E]
PTO bank, 1.16
Public policy
  insurance for claims against employers, 43.03[B]
  termination of employment, 39.04

Q

QDROs, 12.08[A]
  administrator's response, 12.08[C]
  cafeteria plans, 22.03[B]
  case law, 12.08[D]
  life insurance, 21.02[F]
  methodology, 12.08[B]
  pension plans, 11.06[D]
  termination of plan, 17.03[D]
QJSA/QPSA
  distributions, 12.05, 12.06
  pension plans, 11.06[C]
QSERP, 8.01[B][2]
Qualified Domestic Relations Orders. See QDROs
Qualified Medical Child Support Orders (QMCSOs)
  cafeteria plans, 22.03[B]
  distributions, 12.08[A]
  EGHPs, 18.16
Qualified plans
  defined, 4.01
  enforcement and compliance. See Enforcement and compliance for qualified plans
  integration, 4.05
  required provisions, 4.10
Qualifying events, COBRA, 19.02[A], 19.04
Quotas and racial discrimination, 34.05[C]

R

Rabbi trusts, 8.01[B][3]
Racial discrimination, 34.03, 34.05[A]
  affirmative action, 34.05[C]
  federal contracts, 34.05[D]
  quotas, 34.05[C]
  reverse discrimination, 34.05[B]
RBD. See Required beginning date (RBD)

Maximum Medical Improvement
(MMI), 33.02[A]
mental-mental injuries, 33.02[E]
mental-physical injuries, 33.02[E]
permanent partial disability, 33.02[A]
permanent total disability, 33.02[A]
physical-mental injuries, 33.02[E]
psychological injuries, 33.02[E]
temporary partial disability, 33.02[A]
temporary total disability, 33.02[A]
type of disability, 33.02[A]
co-employment, 33.02[C]
compensable injuries, 33.02[B]
costs, 33.01, 33.09
degree of disability, 33.02[A]
discrimination actions by employees, 42.02
disease claims, 33.02[D]
ERISA, 33.08[B]
evidence, 33.03
exclusivity, 33.03
health plan claims, 13.05[C]
immigration issues in hiring, 23.11[F]
incapacitation requirement, 33.03
insurance for claims against employers,
43.05[B]
long tail claims, 33.02[D]
manual rate, 33.05
Maximum Medical Improvement (MMI),
33.02[A]
mental-mental injuries, 33.02[E]
mental-physical injuries, 33.02[E]
permanent partial disability, 33.02[A]
permanent total disability, 33.02[A]
physical-mental injuries, 33.02[E]
premium setting, 33.05
psychological injuries, 33.02[E]

responding to accidents, 33.07[B]
retaliation, 33.06
second injury funds, 33.08[D]
self-insurance, 33.04[D]
SSDI, 33.08[E]
tax aspects of pay planning, 2.01
taxation of benefits, 33.08[A]
temporary partial disability, 33.02[A]
temporary total disability, 33.02[A]
termination of employment, 39.04[C]
terrorism, 33.04[A]
type of disability, 33.02[A]
unemployment insurance, 32.02[D]
Work-family issues, 28.01
adoption assistance, 28.04
breast feeding, 28.03
day care, 28.01, 28.02
dependent care assistance plans, 28.07
elder care, 28.05, 28.06
lactation programs, 28.03
Working condition fringe benefits, 22.06
Work rules, 25.04
Work scheduling, 1.14
"Workweek," 1.15[C]
"Wrap" documents, 10.05
Wrap plans, 8.01[B][9]
Wrongful termination, 39.01
life insurance, 21.02[F]
sexual harassment, 35.07
whistleblower protection, 39.04[B]

Y

Year of FUTA tax, 32.06[B]